More Praise for *The Exile*

"Where did Osama bin Laden, his family, and Al Qaeda disappear to for a decade after 9/11 and Tora Bora? In *The Exile*, Cathy Scott-Clark and Adrian Levy reveal a staggering amount of fresh information as to how Osama bin Laden survived and give us a picture of the 'missing years.' This is a remarkable book that readers will not be able to put down."

—Ahmed Rashid, author of *Taliban, Descent into Chaos,*
and *Pakistan on the Brink*

"The West spends far too little time trying to understand those who attacked on 9/11, and if we do not understand them, we will never combat their ideology. *The Exile* fills the gap in a very thorough and readable way."

—Clive Stafford Smith, director of Reprieve and legal
representative of more than one hundred Guantánamo detainees

"*The Exile* combines a reporter's meticulous research with the skill of a thriller writer. This is a must-read for those interested in understanding the dynamics of global jihad."

—Husain Haqqani, former Pakistan ambassador to the United States
and author of *Magnificent Delusions: Pakistan, the United States,*
and an Epic History of Misunderstanding

"A fascinating, dynamic, and detailed account—based on considerable research—of how the ideas and people of Al Qaeda survived and revived after 9/11. Informative and highly readable."

—Richard Barrett, former head of counterterrorism for MI5 and MI6

The Exile

The Stone of Heaven: Unearthing the Secret History of Imperial Green Jade

Nuclear Deception: The Dangerous Relationship between the United States and Pakistan

The Meadow: Kashmir 1995—Where the Terror Began

The Amber Room: The Fate of the World's Greatest Lost Treasure

The Siege: 68 Hours inside the Taj Hotel

THE EXILE

*The Stunning
Inside Story of
Osama bin Laden
and Al Qaeda
in Flight*

CATHY SCOTT-CLARK AND ADRIAN LEVY

B L O O M S B U R Y

NEW YORK · LONDON · OXFORD · NEW DELHI · SYDNEY

Bloomsbury USA
An imprint of Bloomsbury Publishing Plc

1385 Broadway	50 Bedford Square
New York	London
NY 10018	WC1B 3DP
USA	UK

www.bloomsbury.com

BLOOMSBURY and the Diana logo are trademarks of Bloomsbury Publishing Plc

First published 2017

ISBN: HB: 978-1-62040-984-8
       ePub: 978-1-62040-985-5

LIBRARY OF CONGRESS CATALOGING-IN-PUBLICATION DATA

Names: Levy, Adrian, 1965–, author. | Scott-Clark, Cathy, 1965– author.
Title: The exile: the stunning inside story of Osama bin Laden and Al Qaeda
in flight / Cathy Scott-Clark and Adrian Levy.
Description: New York: Bloomsbury USA, 2017.
Identifiers: LCCN 2017008379 | ISBN 9781620409848 (hardback) |
ISBN 9781620409855 (ePub)
Subjects: LCSH: Bin Laden, Osama, 1957–2011. | Terrorists—Biography. |
Terrorism. | Bin Laden, Osama, 1957–2011—Family. | BISAC: HISTORY /
United States / 21st Century.
Classification: LCC HV6430.B55 L48 2017 | DDC 958.104/6092 [B]—dc23 LC record
available at https://lccn.loc.gov/2017008379

2 4 6 8 10 9 7 5 3 1

Typeset by Westchester Publishing Services
Printed and bound in the U.S.A. by Berryville Graphics Inc., Berryville, Virginia

For GG

Contents

The Exile

BULGARIA

Black Sea

RUSSIA 45°E

Istanbul

GEORGIA
Tbilisi ★

ARMENIA AZ
Yerevan ★

Ankara ★

GREECE

TURKEY

Athens ★

Gaziantep ●

Urmia ●

Mosul ●

Aleppo ● Raqqa ● Khurmal ●

Nicosia ●

SYRIA

Tigris

Mediterranean Sea

CYPRUS
Beirut ●
Damascus ★ Tikrit ★

LEBANON
Baghdad ★

PALESTINE/ISRAEL

Zarqa ● **IRAQ**

Jerusalem ★ ★ Amman

Euphrate

LIBYA

Cairo

JORDAN

KUW

EGYPT 30°

30°

Riyadh

SWAT DISTRICT

AFGHANISTAN

Indus

SAUDI ARABIA

BAGRAM AIR BASE ■

KUNAR PROVINCE
Damadola ●

SHANGLA DISTRICT

Mingora ● Kutkey ●
Martung Tehsil ●

SALT PIT
★ **Kabul**

Jalalabad ●

Mansehra ●

Mecca ●

Mehwa Valley

Mardan ●

Abbottabad ●
Nawan Shehr ●

Jeddah ●

TORA BORA
Parachinar ●

Peshawar ●

Haripur ●

Red Sea

Islamabad ★

Rawalpindi ●

Khost ●

Kohat Tunnel
Suleman
Talaab Kohat

ERITREA
Asmara ★

CAMP CHAPMAN

PAKISTAN

Sana'a ●

15°

Miram Shah ●

Garyom ● Mir Ali ●

YEM

Ibb ●

NORTH WAZIRISTAN

Barmal ●

SOUTH WAZIRISTAN

DJIBOUTI
★ Djibouti

Wana ● *Shakai Valley*

PAKISTAN TRIBAL AREAS

Dera Ismail Khan ●

SOM

Addis Ababa ★

Indus

0 Miles   50

ETHIOPIA

45°

0 Kilometers   100

© 2017 Jeffrey L. Ward

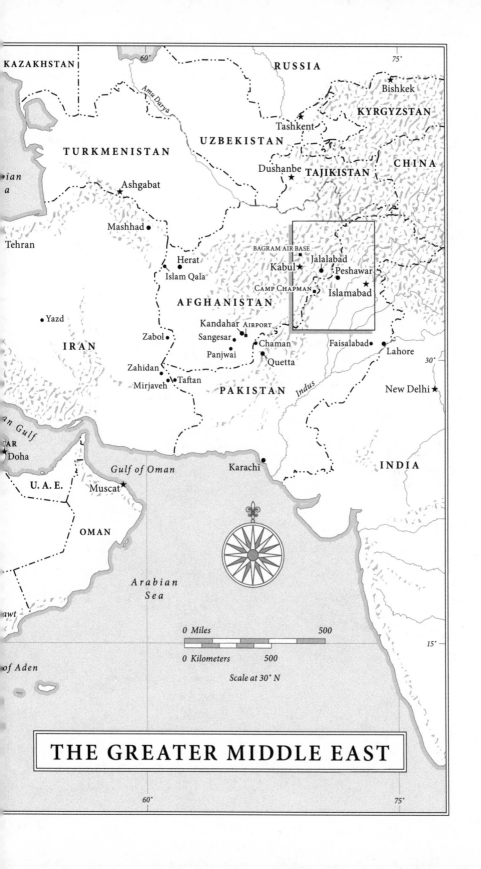

KAZAKHSTAN

RUSSIA

Bishkek ★

KYRGYZSTAN

Amu Darya

TURKMENISTAN

UZBEKISTAN

Tashkent ★

CHINA

Dushanbe ★ TAJIKISTAN

Ashgabat ★

Mashhad ●

Tehran

BAGRAM AIR BASE

Herat ■ Kabul ★ Jalalabad ●

Islam Qala ● Peshawar ●

CAMP CHAPMAN ● Islamabad ●

AFGHANISTAN

● Yazd

IRAN

Zabol ● Kandahar AIRPORT ●

Sangesar ● Chaman ● Faisalabad ● ● Lahore

Panjwai ● Quetta ●

Zahidan ● 30°

Mirjaveh ● ● Taftan PAKISTAN

Indus

New Delhi ★

an Gulf

AR

● Doha

Gulf of Oman Karachi ●

U.A.E. Muscat ★

INDIA

OMAN

Arabian
Sea

0 Miles 500

awt

0 Kilometers 500 15°

of Aden

Scale at 30° N

THE GREATER MIDDLE EAST

60° 75°

Preface

EIGHTEEN YEARS INTO AN EPOCH of Islamist terror that began with horrific attacks on U.S. embassies in East Africa in 1998, few books have told the story of Al Qaeda from the inside.

Part of this is due to difficulty. Getting into any volatile, paranoiac outfit, one that executes outsiders as spies or lures reporters to meetings that become kidnappings—is hair-raising. Instead, we have had gripping tales of those in the West and the Gulf states who have hunted Al Qaeda. The prism through which we see this bloody era has become a police procedural—pathological killers triangulated by deep-in-the-weeds analysts using sources procured by intelligence officers out in the field, parrying with American special agents for interrogation rights.

However, there is another reason why apart from the great volumes that chart the road to 9/11 there has been no history of these times told by the other side, and that is an extraordinary act of control by Western governments. To find an equivalent, one would have to go all the way back to the 1980s and the actions of the British government in its dealings with the Irish Republican Army, when jury trials were suspended, Catholics were interned, and the voice of Sinn Féin leader Gerry Adams was banned on TV and replaced with that of an actor (while secretly Prime Minister Margaret Thatcher's emissary negotiated with the IRA).

After 9/11, the Bush administration incarcerated, en masse, as many as 779 suspected enemy combatants in Guantánamo military prison in Cuba. Even now that the number has been whittled down to 41 at the time of press, the prison still costs half a billion dollars a year to run. Only five men accused of being directly involved in the planning or execution of 9/11 have been put on trial, and their hearings drag on at a snail's pace.

In August 2016, Abu Zubaydah, who the Bush administration claimed was Number Three in Al Qaeda but who the Obama administration concluded had never been a formal member of the outfit, appeared before a Guantánamo review board, the first time he had been seen publicly in almost fifteen years. He had been rendered to Thailand in 2002; waterboarded eighty-three times; confined in a coffin-shaped box and a smaller one resembling a dog kennel; kept awake for days, frozen, naked, shackled, and beaten; and spirited away to several more CIA black sites before landing in Guantánamo in 2006. Even now, observers of the review board hearing were not allowed to listen to his voice. Instead, a Pentagon-appointed "personal representative"—Gitmo-speak for a uniformed U.S. soldier—read out his words.

Of the other prisoners who remain in Cuba, we have heard little or nothing. Meanwhile, on the outside, Al Qaeda leaders are mostly dead, in hiding, or compelled to be silent by the Arab, Asian, and African governments that took them in.

What we do have, courtesy of the U.S. government, is a cherry-picked history. In 2012, a sample of Al Qaeda's letters and communiqués was released to academics from the Combating Terrorism Center at the U.S. Military Academy at West Point. They were previewed in a powerful *Washington Post* opinion piece by David Ignatius, "Osama bin Laden, a Lion in Winter," and suggested that fractious Al Qaeda was as finished as its newly dead emir. Also put into the public domain were well-chosen images showing Osama, graying and diminished, watching his TV set or fudging his words in outtakes from videoed speeches. Unnamed Defense officials claimed that he had become delusional and impotent, and that his organization was defunct. To further undercut Al Qaeda's well-crafted image of a pious Sheikh who saw himself as a *ghazi*, or holy warrior, rumors were started about his alleged pornography collection.

The same year, the Obama administration backed *Zero Dark Thirty*—an overt wedding of the White House to Hollywood, where the CIA, Pentagon, and West Wing facilitated a thrilling cinematic account of the sleuthing that led to the raid on Abbottabad. The impact of the photographs, documents, and this film was to suggest that a president, Obama, canvassing for his second term in the White House, had beaten an old enemy, Al Qaeda, that was so pathological that U.S. interrogators had been required to deploy pitiless means to crack it. The killing of Osama bin Laden was a major factor in Obama's reelection.

But *Zero Dark Thirty*, nominated for five Academy Awards, was materially wrong in many ways, perhaps none more important than its claim that torture unearthed vital knowledge leading to Osama's capture. In truth, the real trail had been pieced together through dogged detective work, good luck, and well-crafted interrogations conducted well before the beatings and mock executions.

While falsehoods were advanced, behind the scenes the Pentagon and White House aggressively pursued those who broke real stories. In August 2016, as Abu Zubaydah rose in silence from his cell in Guantánamo, former U.S. Navy SEAL Matthew Bissonnette, who wrote a no-holds-barred account of the real Abbottabad raid called *No Easy Day*, was compelled by a Federal Court to pay back $6.8 million in royalties and speaking fees. He was also made to apologize for failing to clear his disclosures with the Pentagon, even as the Senate Intelligence Committee lashed out at *Zero Dark Thirty* for being "grossly inaccurate and misleading."

There were three more selective releases of documents by the Defense Department, in 2015, 2016, and 2017, as well as a list of books that Osama was reading. The declassified paperwork represented about 1 percent of the million-plus-document trove recovered from Abbottabad, but its appearance came as another large cache of enemy documents, including records of Saddam Hussein's high command in Iraq and Al Qaeda material from Afghanistan, vanished. The Conflict Records Research Center at the National Defense University in Washington, D.C.—that was, according to the *New York Times*, a resource like no other to "provide insights about inner workings of United States foes"—was being shuttered. The Pentagon, whose budget request for 2016 was $600 billion, could not afford the $1 million needed to keep it open.

All of which made it more essential than ever to get behind the history that was being told. We need more detail and not less. We require more nuance and understanding if we are to ever tamp down a bloody conflict that threatens the globe. And it is from this place—a desire for a contemporary, complex, untidy, knotted, verbal history, where no one is regular or consistent, and where allies are murderously betraying their friends, in which good men make poor choices, and switch sides, and wives become double agents—that this book begins.

The idea began to coalesce after a last-minute meeting on a dark Islamabad night in February 2012 with Zakariya al-Sadeh, a Yemeni student, pro-democracy campaigner, and brother of Amal bin Laden, Osama's youngest wife. At the time Zakariya was trying to free his sister from the legal limbo that Pakistan's intelligence service, the ISI, had slung her into, having captured her at Abbottabad after U.S. SEAL Team Six flew off with her dead husband's body and his letters.

At that meeting, everyone was nervous. Zakariya was frightened of worsening his sister's predicament by being caught with Western journalists, and we were worried about being glimpsed with him, as we were in the middle of complex negotiations with the Pakistan Army on another delicate project. The memory of the Abbottabad raid was still raw and remained incredibly sensitive in-country. But that tense discussion with Zakariya led to nervy conversations with many others that resulted eventually (after trust being won) in meetings with Osama's family, friends, mentors, companions, factotums, security chiefs, and religious and media advisers.

We traveled to wherever a meeting could be brokered—from Mauritania to Yemen, Jordan, Saudi Arabia, the Emirates, Kuwait, the United States, Pakistan, Afghanistan, and back home to London. Gradually, something unique came into focus—a story told about Al Qaeda by Al Qaeda men and women with nothing more to lose but lots to prove. They, too, had letters, e-mails, text messages and chat transcripts, videos and photo albums that corroborated their claims.

Al Qaeda *shura* (leadership council) members revealed the schism that opened up when 9/11 was first plotted, describing how they rejected the plan while Osama and Khalid Shaikh Mohammad (who was not in Al Qaeda) pressed on in secret. They described how they had all been astonished on the day the Twin Towers fell, excited at Al Qaeda having achieved something so staggeringly shocking, as well as being a little panicked by the knowledge that they had no choice but to back the operation.

These fighters, religious thinkers, friends, and family members recalled how as war came to Afghanistan, they rumbled along the desert plains of Jalalabad with Osama's terrified family, and watched tracer fire light up the night sky from a redoubt they called the Star Wars camp. As the United States struck back, they feared capture and were daunted by the way in which they had been condemned to a life on the run, their lives subordinated into a mission most of them had never chosen. But there was no way back.

Some sources took us along the rat runs to the Afghanistan-Pakistan border as Osama's family, friends, and advisers fled and Kandahar and Kabul fell, eviscerating the Taliban dream of an Islamic homeland. Talking to homecoming British forces stationed in Helmand Province, we heard firsthand the impact of a close-quarter campaign: veterans shattered and broken, mentally and physically. The same happened with Al Qaeda's force, bombed into the dust while those who did escape told how and why they were guided and nourished by Pakistan-based jihad fronts. Gradually they coalesced again in new locations—Pakistan and Iran—and began plotting new attacks.

Daniel Pearl's killing and the Bali bombings of 2002, the Riyadh compound bombings of 2003, the Madrid train bombings of 2004, the London public transport attacks of July 2005, and the Amman hotel bombing in 2005, the list goes on—exploding tankers, suicide bombers in mosques, nightclubs, and universities in Pakistan, Syria, Turkey, and Iraq, schools strafed with automatic fire—individual acts of cruelty have become all-too familiar. But here they were described from the other side, the plotter and bomber who fueled a war that could not be stopped, as well as the victims—men and women who also saw the aerial war from the ground up, the sound of drones swarming like wasps.

They detailed the secret cease-fire deals fielded by the masters of espionage in Pakistan, spies who shielded Al Qaeda leaders as they became greedy for U.S. reward money. And all the while, Osama's closest family was battered by the ebb and flow of war. Here came news of one son's death, Saad bin Laden, a boy groomed by Osama and killed accidentally. Then the revelation of a parallel world in distant Iran known as the Tourist Complex, where many bin Laden family members, much of Al Qaeda's original military leadership and most of its *shura* had become caught up in a nerve-jangling real-life game of Risk. But in Washington, where politics required wars to be endless, the Bush administration stepped away from making a deal that might have lanced the boil.

One of Osama's long-lost wives would materialize, even as those keeping watch in Abbottabad succumbed to chronic depression and battled cancer. The bin Laden family could not stop growing, and eventually eroded the generosity of its guardians, who slapped the world's most wanted man with an eviction notice. Requiring a new hideout, fearing betrayal by his most beloved spouse—who might be a double agent or a dupe, with her dental fillings swapped out for Iranian tracking devices—and only weeks away from SEAL Team Six storming Abbottabad, Osama cut what he regarded as a great deal. He renegotiated an agreement to stay put in Abbottabad, rather than having to seek a new bolt-hole elsewhere.

Outside, the Black Hawks were coming and another of Osama's sons, Hamzah, the real heir apparent to Al Qaeda, arrived, only to be shooed away by his fearful father. Inside, Osama fired off letters and paced, directing family and friends, frantically plotting, exhorting his outfit to work until it burst, like the chief mechanic in the engine room of the *Titanic*.

The Exile dives deep inside this world, recounting for the first time the stories of Al Qaeda's leaders, gunmen, planners, and their spiritual guides, fighters made outlaws by their brutal acts. Through them, we meet their wives and children, who as a result of their affiliations and blood—marriages and births—also became fugitives.

The piecing together of their stories begins high in the peaks above Khost, inside a cave where Osama bin Laden, swaddled in blankets, sits impatiently, confronted by the galling news that his mobile satellite TV set is malfunctioning, while thousands of miles away the long-awaited Planes Operation is about to commence.

CHAPTER ONE

"Shit. I think we bit off more than we could chew."

—Mokhtar to his deputies on
September 11, 2001[1]

September 11, 2001, noon, Khost, Afghanistan

Settling down into a nest of shawls and bolsters, fortified by sweetened tea, Osama bin Laden was anxious and excited, watching as a scrawny Yemeni bodyguard, who also covered duties in Al Qaeda's media office, ranged around the mouth of the cave balancing a large satellite dish, humming to himself.

"It is *very* important we are able to watch the news today," Osama insisted, directing the guard this way and that.[2]

Installed up in the Sulaiman mountain range, high above the city of Khost, and accompanied by his teenage sons Othman and Mohammed, Osama had driven across the plains from Kandahar in his improvised media truck, loaded down with a satellite dish, a receiver, a small television set, laptops, and an old generator.[3] In the last few minutes, a message had come through on the radio that Mohamed Atta, the lead hijacker, had passed security and was boarding his flight, American Airlines 11.[4] Osama now intended to observe the "Planes Operation" unfolding from a position of complete safety.

But wherever the bodyguard moved the dish, finding new ledges and handholds in the rock face, the mountains got in the way of the signal. Osama clicked his tongue in annoyance. Was it the heavy cloud cover? Or was his man just incompetent? It might have been the cabling, which he could see was poorly spliced. Whatever it was, there was no picture and it became obvious to everyone that they were going to have to listen to the radio, while the rest of the world watched.

Osama's military chief, Abu Hafs the Commander, had given a hint of the plan to a trusted Al Jazeera journalist in Kandahar a few months earlier during the wedding of his daughter, Khadija, to Osama's son Mohammed.[5] "The United States is going to be forced to invade Afghanistan soon," the reporter was warned as the Commander chewed on a knuckle of roasted goat. "And we are preparing for *that*. We *want* them to come."

The marriage had taken place at Tarnak Qila, an ancient fort in the desert southwest of Kandahar airport that Al Qaeda had made its field headquarters, the outfit's second most important base after Osama's cherished Tora Bora cave complex in the far northeast of the country.

The celebrations had been the most lavish of several weddings that Osama had fixed over the past year to ensure that all his children of marriageable age were wed to soldiers, thinkers, and funders before the Planes Operation unfolded. Al Qaeda needed all the support it could get in the months ahead, he supposed, and matchmaking with his children gave the outfit an economic and strategic depth. There was another reason for the rush. For a Gulf Arab, a father facing possible death was compelled to ensure his offspring's future. If Osama were martyred in the coming war, leaving his children without betrothals, he would forfeit his reward in the afterlife.

By lunchtime, his blood sugar level was dropping. This was supposed to be his greatest moment and yet he was unsettled. There had been weeks of upheavals within Al Qaeda, a grueling falling-out with Taliban leader Mullah Mohammed Omar, which was ongoing, and profound family discord.

Until recently Osama had lived with four wives and more than a dozen children and grandchildren at Tarnak Qila. The family was a font of pride that spoke of his virility, and demonstrated his power. But his fourth son, Omar, and his senior wife, Najwa, had both walked out on him—unexpected acts of desertion that had sent him into a spiral of rage.

Many Al Qaeda brothers had witnessed the screaming rows he had had with Omar, a teenager who Osama had been training as his heir, and who bore a striking resemblance to his father. But Omar had never shared his father's obsession with war. "I want to leave this place, I must leave this place," the teen had sobbed, after he learned of the coming Planes Operation. *Please* could his father stop?

Osama, who could not tolerate being challenged, had shouted back: "Omar, I will fight until my dying day! . . . I will never stop this jihad!"

Realizing that his father was beyond reach, Omar went to his mother, Najwa, pleading for her to leave with him. "Please leave mother and come back to real life with me." But timid, downtrodden Najwa, who had never disobeyed her husband, refused and so Omar had slipped away alone.[6] "[My father's] violent path had separated us forever," he later recalled.[7]

The remaining bin Laden boys were more robust. Othman, who Omar had regarded as brutish, stepped into the breach, attempting to impress his father with a public pledge: "Jihad is in my mind, heart and blood veins. No fear, nor intimidation can ever take that feeling out of my mind and body."[8]

At the end of August 2001, Najwa had had a change of heart, and with Omar's words playing on her mind, she had asked to leave, an unexpected act of rebellion from a woman who had loyally stuck by her husband's side for twenty-six years and given him eleven children.

Najwa had never intended to be a jihad bride. Glamorous and beautiful, she was a Ghanem, one of the oldest families in Syria, and she had grown up in the cosmopolitan seaside resort of Latakia, where women wore bikinis. Arriving as Osama's young wife in Jeddah in 1974 she had reluctantly donned a *chador* and *niqab*. She consented when he also insisted that she wear black socks and gloves, but underneath the black folds she still wore lipstick and designer clothes. Nevertheless, over the years, his exacting demands dragged her down. His brothers' wives recalled her being downcast, drab, and permanently pregnant. "Najwah [sic] seemed almost completely invisible," recalled Carmen bin Laden, who was once married to Osama's brother Yeslam.[9]

Even so, Najwa could never have predicted that she would end up in a shack in Kandahar, wearing an Afghan *burqa*, cooking on a "one-eyed camping burner" and plugging the bullet holes in her hut with raw wool to keep out snakes, scorpions, and the bitter wind. "I never stopped praying that everything in the world would be peaceful," she said later, "and that our lives might return to normal."[10]

The Planes Operation and her husband's recent decision to marry yet again, this time to a Yemeni teenager, was what had made up Najwa's mind to leave. "Osama, can I go to Syria?" she asked in the last week of August 2001. She knew whatever was coming was imminent and felt a duty to save those children not yet pledged to Al Qaeda.

Osama's face fell. "Are you sure, Najwa?" he asked, incredulous.

"Yes," she said falteringly. "I *need* to go."

They had made their final farewells on the morning of September 9. "I will *never* divorce you, Najwa," he told her earnestly. "Even if you hear I have divorced you, know that it cannot be true."

Najwa slid a ring from her finger and pressed it into his hand.

Osama took it. "But these," he said, his voice changing register, and pointing to their eleven-year-old daughter Iman and nine-year-old son Ladin, "belong with their father. You can only take the babies."

Najwa's eyes filled with tears as Osama pushed the older children away. She knew that under Saudi law she had no rights to keep them and that in Afghanistan there was virtually no law protecting women at all.

She was helped into a pickup with her youngest two daughters—Rukaiya, three, and Nour, one. Her disabled adult son, Abdul Rahman, who could not function without her and so was also leaving, sat up front next to moody Othman, the family bully. He would escort his mother to the Pakistan border and then return to his father's side.

As they drove away, Najwa turned to see her family enveloped in the dust. "My mother's heart broke into little pieces watching the silhouettes of my little children fade into the distance," she said later.[11] She did not expect to ever see them again.

Back in the cave above Khost, Osama picked up a VHF walkie-talkie and sent a brief message. Someone had to find his spiritual adviser, a Mauritanian scholar called Mahfouz Ibn El Waleed. He should have been here, supporting Osama and sitting beside him sipping tea. But the Mauritanian had chosen to remain in Kandahar.

He and Osama were no longer talking after he had voted against the Planes Operation, leading a revolt and taking more than half of Al Qaeda's ruling *shura* with him. A few weeks back, the Mauritanian had gone further and quit Al Qaeda altogether—a move that Osama had not seen coming and subsequently had tried to hush up as it threatened to split the outfit irreconcilably.

Today, September 11, 2001, and with the countdown to the attacks ticking, Osama knew what he wanted to do. Najwa and Omar might have been beyond his control, but he could still rub the Mauritanian's nose in the dust.

September 11, 2001, 3 P.M., Kandahar, Afghanistan

Down on the plains, the Mauritanian was working in the Taliban media center, assembling the latest edition of *Islamic Emirate* magazine, when

Osama's messenger poked his head around the door. The cleric looked up. "Yes?" he asked, frustrated, knowing who the man served.

"The Sheikh says you should listen out for some joyous news," the messenger said, scuttling away.[12]

Disturbed and fully understanding what this meant, the Mauritanian packed up his papers, made an excuse to the Taliban brothers, and returned home to dig out his old Sony radio. Had it already started? He could not bear to be with the Talibs when the Planes Operation—which none of them had been consulted about and which he had been unable to stop—was reported around the world.

For ten years the Mauritanian had been at Osama's side, becoming a pivotal, highly respected figure on Al Qaeda's *shura* and chairman of the outfit's influential *sharia* (legal) committee. Osama relied on him to construct the religious justification for Al Qaeda operations and anchor them in Koranic values. The Mauritanian would be asked whether a particular broadside could be defended. And if so, how? His was not a crowded field. Even though Al Qaeda was seen in the West through an Islamist prism and was commonly portrayed as a ferocious clerical turbine, the Mauritanian was the sole member of the leadership to have had any genuine religious training. And for that reason he commanded Osama's utmost respect.

For years, he had successfully finessed his Sheikh's wilder plans, acting as his censor, confessor, counselor, voice, and, on more than one occasion, his accountant cum investment consultant. He understood Osama's weaknesses: vanity, single-mindedness, a fierce anger quick to spark, and a quixotic vision that was virtually impossible to temper with facts.

When he wasn't at his Sheikh's side, he was in Kandahar city, acting as liaison to the Taliban's Mullah Omar or running the House of the Pomegranates, a finishing school where Al Qaeda and Taliban recruits delved deeper into the cultural and religious foundations of jihad.[13] Here, war-weary veterans came to relearn Koranic teachings. Everyone was encouraged to write poetry. This was as much about betterment, instilling discipline, and learning as it was about indoctrination.

The Mauritanian had always been culturally minded. He had won prizes for his odes when growing up in the low-rise dustbowl of Nouakchott, the Mauritanian capital.[14] Over the years, he had ghost-written most of Osama's speeches, religious judgments, and press releases, even authoring a lengthy and controversial tirade excoriating King Fahd of Saudi Arabia for allowing

U.S. troops into the holy land—a correspondence that had cost Osama his Saudi citizenship.

The Mauritanian's duties also reached beyond the Sheikh to his sons, helping them memorize the Koran and understand Islamic jurisprudence, acting as their mentor and counselor. His wife and daughters did the same for Osama's wives and girls.

The Mauritanian could, on occasion, play a strategic hand, as he did after Osama's first great international broadside—the August 1998 attacks on U.S. embassies in Nairobi and Dar-es-Salaam, which killed 224 and catapulted Al Qaeda into the spotlight. Afterward, he had helped log and direct the money and recruits that poured in, particularly from donors in the Gulf states.

Toward the end of 1998, while investigating the atrocities, the CIA identified the Mauritanian while hunting down Osama's assets. Suspecting that he had arranged finances for the embassy operations, they tracked him to a hotel in Khartoum, Sudan, but missed him by minutes as he fled out of a kitchen door. Subsequently, he vocally criticized the East Africa attacks for having cost the lives of so many civilians.

When the Mauritanian first picked up rumors about the Planes Operation in 1999, he was infuriated. From what he could discern, many innocent people would be killed, and he sought out the Sheikh to warn him that it was against Islam. Al Qaeda should concentrate its energies on attacking Israel. This operation would also drive a coach and horses through the Taliban's wishes. Mullah Omar had offered Al Qaeda sanctuary when it had none, asking only that Osama refrain from plotting any attacks against America while on Afghan soil. "Our donkey is in the mud," the Taliban's emir had explained, using a Kandahari expression to suggest that his movement was far from full strength. They needed time to achieve legitimacy, to raise funds, recruit, and win international backing.[15] Osama had responded disrespectfully, telling Mullah Omar that "jihad against America is an individual duty and it cannot be given up." If the Islamic Emirate of Afghanistan was unable to protect him, then he would leave with the women and children and "go for jihad in God's name."

A second Al Qaeda spectacular against the United States in October 2000—a bomb-laden skiff that had rammed into the side of the USS *Cole*, an American warship refueling in Aden harbor, Yemen, killing seventeen American sailors—had only made the situation worse.

From that moment on, the two leaders had been on a collision course: Osama, who encouraged his men to see him as a modern incarnation of the

Prophet, railing against Mullah Omar, the self-styled Commander of the Faithful, who was frequently talked of as the Caliph of All True Islam.

September 11, 2001, 5:30 P.M., Kandahar

All afternoon, the Mauritanian remained stooped over the radio, skipping channels while his wife and children watched him nervously.

After sunset, the first report came in. A plane had hit a skyscraper in New York City. Then another.

Outside, in darkened Kandahar, a crescendoing cry traveled up and down the street, like a New Year's countdown in Times Square. Then jabbering, laughing, and whooping as people began spilling out of their homes.

September 11, 2001, 6 P.M., Islamabad, Pakistan

Pakistani journalist Hamid Mir was at his office contemplating dinner when an agitated Pashtun visitor arrived at the gate.[16] "I am here with a message from the Sheikh," he whispered over the internal phone.

"Which sheikh?" Mir replied coolly. He knew plenty.

"The Sheikh with the plastic wristwatch," the man replied.

"What are you talking about?" countered Mir, who was in no mood for riddles. Then, he recalled windswept Tarnak Qila and a meeting with Osama bin Laden. He had complimented *that* sheikh on his wristwatch that sang out prayer times, half-hoping to receive it as a gift.

Mir told the man to come inside.

"Put on the TV," the visitor urged as he entered. "Look, look," he said excitedly, pointing to footage of flames and black smoke pouring from the North Tower of the World Trade Center in New York City.

They both watched as a plane hit the South Tower, a fireball flaring. Stunned TV anchors tried to make sense of what they were witnessing, "Oh my goodness, there's another one," said one. "Now it's obvious. This may not be an accident."

The visitor put his hand in his pocket and pulled out a watch.

"A present from the Sheikh," he said, handing it over.[17]

*   *   *

September 11, 2001, 7 P.M., Rawalpindi, Pakistan

General Javed Alam Khan, a barrel-chested spook in charge of analysis and foreign liaison at Pakistan's Inter-Services Intelligence directorate (ISI), was at home following reports of a plane crashing into the Pentagon. He rang the Pakistani embassy in Washington, D.C., even though the line was not secure. "What the hell's going on?" he asked the ISI station chief. "Where's the DG?"[18]

The Washington station chief sounded harried. The ISI director general was in the United States on an official visit, which was good or bad news—depending on whose office he was now in. It would fall to General Khan to brief him on how to handle the Americans.

Khan pulled out a Dunhill cigarette and pushed away his dinner. A pit bull with a locking jaw, he smoked more than he ate. His phone rang. "Sir." The station chief's tone said it all: "The DG's attending a breakfast meeting on Capitol Hill discussing *terrorism generated in Afghanistan!*" Khan choked on a lungful of smoke.

Someone had to exfiltrate the phlegmatic chief before he did a disservice to the republic. General Mahmud Ahmed hated Americans and had a tendency to lash out when cornered.[19] "Get him to a *phone*," Khan rasped. "And can someone trace my brother-in-law?" He lived in Manhattan and was not answering his cell phone.

Khan crushed his cigarette, lit another, and reflected on how he was in a job he loathed, facing a shit-storm not of his making. He suspected that soon everyone who mattered would focus on trying to prove his agency's complicity in the unfolding chaos.

A former tank commander, Khan had never sought out this plainclothes desk job, but he had been seconded to the ISI in 1999, and as a patriot, he lived to serve. Most of his family had worn uniforms: a father who served with the British Army in India, one brother in the navy, three in the air force, and five in the army—one of whom had been martyred in the bloodletting of 1971 in which East Pakistan had been torn away and become Bangladesh. The only fillip with this job was the intrigue that went with it and his cordial but combative relationship with his opposite number in the CIA, the forensically minded Islamabad station chief, Robert Grenier.

Short and lean, Grenier had been squeezing Khan for months about the Taliban and Al Qaeda, asking for capillary-level details about religious factions, warlords, and jihad leaders, demonstrating a level of knowledge about Pakistan that he doubted existed about America in the ISI station in D.C.[20]

Khan called for his staff car. He needed to get ahead of Grenier, and the good news was that his side had languages and deep, unctuous connections. They sped along the highway linking army-dominated Rawalpindi to its twin city, the Pakistani capital, Islamabad. "Aabpara," he hissed at the driver, naming the hulking gray spy complex that dominated the G-7/4 district.

As the car pulled up at ISI headquarters, Khan was greeted by a phalanx of senior officials "standing with their mouths open" like Venus flytraps waiting for a feeding.

"Shut those," he shouted, "and use *these*." He raised a dialing finger. Taking a long drag on his cigarette, he stomped inside.[21]

September 11, 2001, 7 P.M., Diplomatic Zone, Islamabad

Three and a half miles northeast, beyond the civic runway of Constitution Avenue, Robert Grenier was sitting in his fortress within a fortress watching footage of people jumping from the burning World Trade Center towers. At the U.S. embassy, a nest of buildings encircled with razor wire and surveillance cameras, the CIA station occupied its own warren, accessed through doors with coded locks.

Grenier was already focused on one man, the same one he had been tracking for the past two years, flooding bazaars and villages on the Afghan border with matchbooks printed with his picture and advertising a $5 million reward.

Although Grenier did not trust the ISI's General Khan, he now desperately needed Pakistan's help as all previous attempts to interdict Osama had been disastrous. One intervention attempted with the CIA's blessing and that had gone disastrously wrong was to send Saudi Arabia's intelligence chief to visit Mullah Omar shortly after Osama had issued his first fatwa against the West, announcing that "the killing of Americans and their allies, both civilians and military, is a duty for every Muslim."

Arriving on a Boeing 747 belonging to the Saudi Arabian royal family, an extraordinary sight in Kandahar, where all international flights had long since stopped, Prince Turki al-Faisal had confronted the Taliban emir, Muslim to Muslim, demanding he hand over Osama and his family. Mullah Omar had reacted badly, sickened to see a prince of an Islamic state doing what he considered to be the bidding of the West.

"Where is your zeal to religion and the sanctity of Islam?" Omar asked the prince quietly. "Are you sent by your country or by the Americans?"

As a generous benefactor of Islamic causes the world over and a well-practiced interlocutor, the prince was not used to being called out, and according to the Mauritanian, who witnessed the scene, he exploded. The Mauritanian recalled how Turki stamped all over the feast that had been laid out in his honor on the floor, knocking over teacups. "Do you want *me* to deliver a *believer* to an *unbeliever*?" asked Mullah Omar quietly.[22]

In 1999, Grenier had tried again after the ISI chief before General Ahmed clawed a potential jewel out of the Kandahari mud by securing the tentative blessing of Mullah Omar to abduct Osama from Afghanistan.[23] Many Afghanis had died when U.S cruise missiles had rained down on his country as a result of the U.S. embassy attacks and he made it clear that he would not stand in the way if the ISI deployed ninety retired Pakistani commandos to seize Osama at Tarnak Qila.

However, in October 1999, shortly before the plan could be actioned, the malleable civilian government of Pakistan was toppled by army chief General Pervez Musharraf, a putsch that saw the Western-leaning ISI chief (who was running the Osama kidnapping operation) slung in jail and replaced by zealot General Mahmud Ahmed. A portcullis dropped on ISI–CIA relations. Overnight, Grenier's "in" ran out, as Peshawar-born Ahmed, who distrusted the Americans for their "on-off" support of Pakistan during and after the Soviet war of the 1980s, shuttered Aabpara against foreigners. It would be three months before Grenier was even allowed back inside the building, and when he did get an invitation, his recommendation to revive the plan deploying former commandos to nab Osama was mocked by Ahmed, who told him: "In my experience those who are *retired* are *tired*."[24]

Ahmed was strong-armed by pragmatist Musharraf into visiting Washington soon after, but irreparable damage had been done. After U.S officials ruffled his feathers by accusing him of supporting Al Qaeda and being "in bed with those who threaten us," the affronted ISI chief, who despised what he considered to be America's lack of a fingertip-feel for Pakistan, had returned home telling friends that he was "born again as a Muslim." An exasperated Grenier wrote strongly worded cables back to CIA headquarters, asking them to back off: "The new guy's not pro *Al Qaeda*. He's pro-*Taliban*." One was a terrorist outfit, while the other, the Pakistan

Army chiefs based in Rawalpindi liked to believe, offered them strategic depth.

Langley ignored Grenier's advice and set out to track Osama without Pakistan's help. In September 2000, the first unarmed Predator drone flew over Afghanistan and within days it had captured real-time footage of the Al Qaeda leader walking around Tarnak Qila, encircled by guards.[25]

Pictures seduced generals at the Pentagon, Grenier thought. They seemed to offer the prospect of risk-free rapid victories. But overheard conversations and fuzzy photographs were useless unless they guided some kind of physical force, deniable or otherwise, able to target Osama on the ground.

In an attempt to restore relations with the ISI, in August 2001 Grenier had helped to bring a U.S. congressional delegation to Islamabad to meet General Musharraf and spy chief General Ahmed. The meetings had gone badly.

Now that 9/11 was under way and Ahmed was trapped in Washington as all flights in and out of the country were grounded, Grenier hoped U.S officials were making best use of his enforced presence.

Sitting in the dark watching news reports of the attacks in the United States on his TV, he called ISI analysis chief General Javed Alam Khan, one vulture circling another.

"It's going to be a long night," Grenier said.

Khan grunted. His brother-in-law and family were still missing in New York. "How could one chap sitting in an Afghan cave be commanding things all over the world?" he muttered disingenuously.

Grenier resisted the bait.

September 11, 2001, 7:15 P.M., Karachi, Pakistan

General Pervez Musharraf was inspecting the well-tended gardens of Mazar-e-Quaid, the Moorish-style mausoleum for Pakistan's founding father, Mohammed Ali Jinnah, when his military secretary informed him of the news from the United States. His thoughts turned immediately to the World Trade Center attack of 1993. He grimaced as he recalled how that plot had led back to Islamabad, where mastermind Ramzi Yousef was run to ground, the arrest implying a link between Pakistan and the first World Trade Center attack.[26]

Having recently appointed himself Pakistan's president and head of state, Musharraf could not afford a repeat of the 1993 debacle. But rather than deal with the situation immediately, he zoned out the news and barreled into a scheduled meeting at his fortified bungalow in the exclusive Zamzama district of Karachi.

His staff officers, who were watching TV in a side room, tried to interrupt. But Musharraf made it clear that he should not be disturbed, so they loitered outside until both towers collapsed in New York, at which point his military secretary entered the room and started fiddling with the general's TV set. "What's the urgency?" Musharraf bridled.

"Please! Watch, sir," the officer said.

Musharraf felt queasy. "America is going to react *violently*," he muttered. If the perpetrator of these attacks turned out to be Al Qaeda, which had been allowed to traverse Pakistan for more than a decade, the United States would come straight down the middle lane looking for a strike.

But that was only a first impression. He made a quick back-of-the-cigarette-packet calculation.[27] This appalling tragedy could be an opportunity for a cool strategist who two years earlier had brought his country to the brink of nuclear war with India, when it suited, only to let tensions die back again.

In a region that was always underpinned by uncertainty, Pakistan could once again become a staging post, as it had been in the 1980s, for the funds, munitions, and matériel imported by the West, Musharraf reasoned. Throughout the 1990s, the United States had snubbed the Islamic Republic of Pakistan in favor of trade deals with India, shuttering defense spending and throttling diplomatic ties. There had been times when Islamabad had felt like Pyongyang, he told himself. But now that America had been attacked on its own soil, the possibilities were legion. He could also use this momentous day to choke thorny elements within his own military and intelligence apparatus—especially the radicals and career Islamists who ran the secret beehive of jihad from the ISI's strategic S-Wing.[28]

Musharraf considered his vulnerabilities.[29] There were so many; but among his inner circle of advisers the weakest link was his ISI chief, General Mahmud Ahmed, whose religious conservatism the army had once actively encouraged but given what was unfolding in the United States now seemed out of step.

"Get Mahmud on the phone," Musharraf shouted.

"Everyone is already looking for him," came the reply.

When the general finally called in, Musharraf asked him to listen, and say nothing. There was no such thing as a secure line in Pakistan. "Don't *argue* with them," he instructed. "Offer *condolences*. They need to hear that they have our *unqualified* support."

Replacing the handset, Musharraf ordered a stiff whiskey. He saw his staff eyeing each other. He was happy to appear blasé. He had learned the trick from the man he had deposed as prime minister—Nawaz Sharif—who dealt with every crisis by ordering a large bowl of *nihari* (beef stew) to chow down on, using the time to think through his options. Musharraf quaffed as he calculated: a staging post, more F16s, billions of dollars in assistance, a purge inside the army's general headquarters (GHQ) in Rawalpindi and at Aabpara. Out of a heinous and unimaginable act of terror would come pure gold.[30]

September 11, 2001, 7:45 P.M., Tariq Road, Karachi

Three miles away as the crow flies, in a popular Karachi shopping district where traders arranged their carts of *chappels* (slippers) into peacock plumes and Anil's and Miss Fashion vied with the Shalimar Centre arcade for customers, "Mokhtar" glowed like a well-fanned fire. He just could not stop smiling as he soaked up praise from the throng gathered around him.[31]

Mokhtar—a *kunya* (nom de guerre) that he had selected as it meant "the chosen one"—had first turned up in Osama's Tora Bora in 1996 with what seemed at the time to be a crazy plan: turning commercial passenger jets into flying bombs. But while Al Qaeda old hands scoffed, Osama was entranced: Mokhtar was a breath of fresh air for a visionary but disorganized jihad leader who spent his days surrounded by blunt-knuckled and illiterate Yemenis armed with sickle-shaped Hadrami daggers, their waists cinched by explosives belts. Mokhtar talked of how the plot would finish what his nephew Ramzi Yousef had attempted in 1993 and how the atrocities would play out on TV for weeks after and make Osama famous. Combining spectacular violence with modern communications was potentially the most powerful weapon of all.

But Mokhtar's scheme was unworkable, as he wanted $500,000 to get it started and Osama did not have any cash.

Then, in October 1999, after an EgyptAir plane was downed over the Atlantic Ocean by the first officer, who had put the plane into a deliberate spin when the captain left the cockpit to use the toilet, Osama began thinking about Mokhtar's plot again. Media reports reveled in how the last sounds recorded by the black box voice recorder of the doomed EgyptAir plane were of the first officer repeating, "I rely on Allah," making this potentially mass murder by Koranic diktat. It was that simple, Mokhtar had told Osama.

Al Qaeda would become the most notorious jihad outfit in the world if it could pull off something similar.

Osama was hooked and over the next eighteen months spent increasing amounts of time with Mokhtar, planning a secret off-the-books operation in meetings from which the Al Qaeda *shura* was excluded—an extraordinary departure for an organization that was otherwise run with the fastidious inclusiveness of an S corp. The old guard, who mostly doubted the plan, mistrusted Mokhtar, who refused to swear *bayat* (allegiance) to Osama or pay them any respect. Only Abu Hafs al-Masri, Osama's deputy, and Dr. Ayman al-Zawahiri, of Egyptian Islamic Jihad, were brought into the operational planning.

To keep things tight, Mokhtar moved the operational base down to Karachi, hiring the Tariq Road apartment and putting it in the hands of two ethnic Burmese brothers, both reformed alcoholics brought up in Saudi Arabia. So many people passed through the safe house that neighbors suspected it was a brothel, or perhaps just another *hawala* center, where foreign laborers could deposit cash for gold to be sent invisibly to family members overseas.

Now as he watched the fruits of his labors, Mokhtar called for takeout from the local branch of Dunkin' Donuts and toasted Ramzi bin al-Shibh, a bucktoothed Yemeni who had been earmarked as a potential hijacker but had to settle for plot coordinator after failing to gain entry to the United States. He had collected bin al-Shibh off a bus from Quetta that morning. Later, they had driven to the airport to fetch Mustafa Ahmad al-Hawsawi, a mobile phone salesman from Jeddah, who had supervised the hijackers' finances. Ammar al-Balochi, Mokhtar's nephew, who had hosted some of the hijackers in Dubai, also dropped by, accompanied by a one-legged Yemeni thug they all called Silver, who had sent Western Union funds to pay flight school bills in small college towns.

Crowded around the TV set, watching reruns of United 175 hurtling toward the World Trade Center, they chanted: "God . . . aim . . . aim . . . aim."

Only after the Twin Towers actually collapsed did Mokhtar momentarily look panicked.

"Shit," he said, whistling. "I think we bit off more than we could chew."[32]

September 11, 2001, 9 P.M., Kandahar

Mahfouz the Mauritanian was conflicted. He felt remorse, but the giddy jubilation coursing through Kandahar's crowded lanes was infectious. Even though he had voted it down, his ruling running to a dozen pages, the scale of the attack was dazzling, something none of them had believed could ever happen. Like many others who had been on the scene for years, he knew that everyone would have to rally around Osama now.[33]

Growing up as a naïve, religious student in Nouakchott, Mauritania, he had been drawn to Afghanistan after reading a copy of *Al Jihad*, a magazine published by Osama bin Laden and his mentor, a radical Palestinian cleric called Abdullah Azzam.[34] In 1988 they had cofounded Al Qaeda and, electrified by talk of a fight that could unite all Muslims and make them proud, Mahfouz had siphoned off his college fees and bought a plane ticket to Pakistan. Eventually, he had found his way to Al Qaeda's secretive Al Farouk training camp, located in Afghanistan near Khost. But he had learned pretty quickly that he was not cut out for war.

Al Farouk was, according to Osama's dour Egyptian adviser Dr. Ayman al-Zawahiri, a "den of garrisoned lions." Mahfouz, a slight, bookish figure, struggled to complete the basic training. He had been thinking of leaving until the morning Osama arrived to address them. Mesmerized by this handsome, tall, and soldierly Saudi heir, he also had been entranced by Osama's story of having abandoned a life of plenty to defend persecuted brothers and sisters who had nothing.[35]

Now, the Mauritanian was brought back to the present by the chants of "Allahu Akhbar!" filling the air. Some in Kandahar were in tears and kissing the ground. Others seemed struck dumb.

"Happiness was not [the right word for it]," wrote the Mauritanian's friend Abu Zubaydah, who also witnessed the scenes and wrote about them later in his diary. An ethnic Palestinian, Zubaydah had been born in Saudi Arabia, so he was technically stateless. After rejecting his conservative middle-class parents, who wanted him to train as a doctor, he had ended up in Afghanistan, training with Al Qaeda recruits around the same time Mahfouz arrived. After being injured in battle in 1991, he had struck out on his own as a freelance logistics man for the jihad. Operating out of Peshawar, he organized identity and travel documents for new recruits and collected donations. He had shifted to Kandahar in June 2001.

Zubaydah would later claim (and many supported him) that he had not known in advance about the Planes Operation. But like everyone else, he was overcome by the enormity of the event and scale of an old enemy's defeat. "Lambs were slaughtered, juice and sweets were distributed . . ." he reported. "We were in a state of elation that God only knows."[36]

By ten P.M., hundreds had converged on Al Qaeda's media center—a ramshackle building where the city's only legal television set was located. Faces pressed up against windows. The Mauritanian, who was among them, saw several Taliban ministers, in their black turbans, furtively darting in to snatch glimpses of the scenes broadcasting from New York until a team of technically minded brothers was given permission to splice into the feed so another screen could be erected in a street where previously all privately owned sets had been smashed.

It was not long before conspiracy theories started to circulate. The Jews had done it, or the CIA. When someone recognized the Mauritanian, they asked for his opinion. "Israel is behind this, right?"

He shrugged, not sure of how to react.

"The U.S. will take extreme revenge," predicted an Afghan brother.

"They will pound Afghanistan into the dust," worried another, glancing to the sky.

The Mauritanian interrupted them. "Let's worry about that tomorrow," he said.[37]

September 11, 2001, 11:30 P.M., Kabul, Afghanistan

Kuwaiti preacher Sulaiman Abu Ghaith sat alone in his lodgings, listening to the radio and fiddling with his gold wedding ring, the only conspicuous thing about him. Stout, soft-spoken, and not prone to the declamatory style of sermonizing loved by many jihad-espousing scholars, he was young, serious, and devout, and he had ended up in Afghanistan almost by mistake.

Listening to the gunfire and shrieks outside his window, he wished he were back home in Kuwait City, where his wife, Fatima, and six daughters would soon be arriving. He had spent the last three days getting them out of Afghanistan, using as an excuse the fact that Fatima was suffering complications with her seventh pregnancy. Anyone who had an inkling of humanity would have done the same, he reasoned. If he thought he could have got away with it, he would not have returned.

Normally at this hour he would have been writing or reading. But right now, Abu Ghaith listened to news of the spewing chaos in America with a sense of mounting dread.

Glancing at his watch, he saw it was midnight. He wondered if his wife had made it to the hospital.

Bam, bam, bam.

A knocking at the door. In Kabul, callers this late could be assassins hired by warlords. He pulled the door open an inch, jamming his foot against it, and saw a bearded figure. Pushing on the door, the man introduced himself as Sheikh Osama's courier.[38]

Abu Ghaith felt his blood drain. He had come to Afghanistan in June, invited by the Mauritanian to lecture at the House of the Pomegranates. Both men believed deeply in the idea of jihad as a force of awakening for the Muslim *ummah* (community). But it was not the physical fight they invested in, rather an embracing of the struggle, an energetic yearning for knowledge and a recommitment to replicating the holy life of the Prophet. Abu Ghaith's association with the Mauritanian had put him, sporadically, in the company of Osama, who was casting around for new religious advisers. Osama persuaded Abu Ghaith to swear "a small *bayat*," which committed him to "do anything he could within his capabilities to help Al Qaeda's emir"—but only as a religious scholar and orator.

Abu Ghaith had been compelled to give a few speeches at Tarnak Qila, and he had lectured on jurisprudence in a training camp.[39] Like everyone else in Afghanistan, he had picked up rumors that a big operation was coming, but he had no idea what it was. Now that his oath was being called in at a critical moment for Al Qaeda he could not believe how stupid he had been.

Trembling, he dressed in a smart, chocolate brown *shalwar kameez*. What plans did the Sheikh have for him, he wondered as he was driven through the night, in silence, and toward Khost. When they reached the Sulaiman foothills, their vehicle began climbing into the high mountains. Finally, they reached the mouth of a cave, where he recognized a silhouette.

Osama bin Laden, dressed in a military jacket, motioned him over. "Have you seen the news?" he asked, patting the cushion beside him. "How did it look?"

Abu Ghaith nervously described the scenes streaming in from New York.

A broad smile spread across Osama's face. "*We* did the Planes Operation," he boasted, eyes blazing, as the courier murmured a congratulatory prayer and Abu Ghaith, overawed to be with this commanding figure at such an auspicious hour, dropped his gaze.

Unseen figures chanted: "Thanks to God." Abu Ghaith squinted and made out a phalanx of heavily armed Yemenis lurking in the shadows. "By Allah, it is great work," they muttered.

Osama silenced them and turned to the Kuwaiti. "What do *you* think America will do?"

He stuttered and frowned, before settling on a turn of phrase. "If it were proven," he said cautiously, as if he were in the *sharia* court adjudicating a marriage dispute, "that *you* were the one that did this . . ." He found a tone that to him sounded juridical. "America will not settle until it accomplishes two things: to kill you and topple the state of the Taliban." Should he have sugarcoated the prognosis?

Osama sighed. "You're being *too* pessimistic," he said. "Lie back and rest a little."[40]

Abu Ghaith woke at dawn. Adjusting to the soft light, he saw figures sitting around a kerosene lamp. He recognized some of the faces—important, forbidding men of the movement he had only ever seen from a distance, most of them notorious.

Osama was sitting with Abu Hafs the Commander and Dr. al-Zawahiri. Breakfast was being served on a green plastic tablecloth laid out on the ground. This tableau, the figures hunched over food in the mouth of a cave, reminded him of nativity scenes he had seen in books.

Noticing that he was awake, Osama called him over: "Come eat."

Sitting beside them, he picked nervously at flatbread, cheese, and dates. For once in his life he was not hungry. Awkwardly, he asked a burning question. "Sheikh, what is it you want me to do?"

Osama smiled. "Deliver a message to the world."

"Me?" Abu Ghaith was aghast. He was an interpreter of scriptures and an emerging adjudicator in religious disputes, not an orator for Al Qaeda. Everyone who knew him thought of him as diligent, harried, and henpecked. He cast around for a way out. "What about the Mauritanian?"

Osama shook his head. "I want *you* to deliver the message."

Someone stepped forward and pressed a sheet of paper into Abu Ghaith's hand.

"Build and deliver a speech around these bullet points," said Osama. "You've got an hour." He was readying to address the world.

Since returning to Afghanistan in 1996, Osama had come to realize that his ambition to be the leader of global jihad went beyond the battlefield and depended upon building a cogent, powerful image. While the Prophet of old had stood on high to address the people, these days the message was best sold on TV, with his favorite outlet being the Qatar-based Arab network Al Jazeera. Normally he fronted these reports himself, wearing a brilliant, billowing Saudi *thobe* (robe) of dazzling whiteness. He often sported an outer cape that encased him in what looked like spun gold. Around his head, a freshly starched white headscarf completed his look of *ghazi* (holy warrior), a wise, just, and brave leader. But today he needed a genuine religious scholar to make the first public response to what was happening thousands of miles away lest it horrify as many people as it delighted. Once the religious justification was out there, and the *ummah* had chewed over it, he would gauge their response and then he could crow.

Abu Ghaith strained to read the bullet points. What would the Mauritanian have written? he asked himself, chewing the end of his pen. In the background he heard a VHF handset hissing. Had war already started down on the plains?

"Are you ready?"

Abu Ghaith looked up and saw Osama observing him carefully. He scribbled into a notepad, and scribbled some more, and then he stood, following him over to the plastic cloth where two cameramen composed the scene: Osama flanked by Dr. al-Zawahiri and Sulaiman Abu Ghaith.

A bodyguard dressed the set, propping a rifle up against the rock wall behind them and placing a black briefcase stuffed with U.S. dollars beside Osama. A voice called out for Abu Ghaith to enter and put on a military jacket.

A microphone was thrust into his hands as he saw Osama lowering his head as if in prayer, or contemplation. The Sheikh was feigning modesty, the position of the listener, hearing news from the battlefront delivered by a renowned priest. Abu Ghaith had never felt more uncomfortable in his life.[41]

He did not *know* these people, and had no deep affiliation, and yet he was being asked to front an extraordinary act of terror that had eclipsed in visceral scope all previous bombings of American citizens abroad. Scanning the roof of the cavern, he recalled a recent conversation about how a U.S. Tomahawk missile took only twenty minutes to reach its target.[42]

When he heard instructions for the cameras to roll he began reading, his voice buffeted by the wind whipping up from Khost. "There are thousands of Muslim youths who are willing to die."

The cameraman interrupted. *Could the respected brother please speak more forcefully?*

"The hijacking of planes is not going to stop." Abu Ghaith's black turban flapped, but he managed to stop it. "[Colin] Powell and others in the American government know that if Al Qaeda promises or threatens to do something they will do it by the will of Allah."

"Cut." Osama held up his hand.

He wanted Abu Ghaith to put on an Arab *keffiyah* (headscarf) so as to look more the part.

Dressed up, Abu Ghaith rattled off some more words.

"Cut."

Osama was still unhappy. He wanted a new location. Everyone followed him along a path to a meadow flanked by rugged hills before another costume change. This time Abu Ghaith was given an Afghan *pakul* (felt cap) to wear.

"Finally," he was directed to say, "we advise . . . the Muslims in the United States and Britain . . . not to travel by plane and we advise them not to live in tower blocks."

Osama beamed and took the microphone. Now it was his turn. "God Almighty hit the United States at its most vulnerable spot." The Lord had decreed it. "Here is the United States . . . filled with terror from its north to its south and from its east to its west. Praise be to God." Osama looked directly into the camera. "What the United States tastes today is a very small thing compared to what we have tasted for tens of years."

The attacks in New York had divided the world into "one of faith where there is no hypocrisy and another of infidelity, from which we hope God will protect us."

Cut.

Osama's courier set off down the mountain with the tape.

September 10, 2001, Wives' Compound Six, Kandahar

Just twenty-four hours earlier, Osama's remaining three wives, Khairiah, Seham, and Amal, had been ordered to pack one suitcase each. No one would say why, only that the Sheikh wanted to move them and the youngest children to a safer location. But not his older sons, Saad, Khalid, and Hamzah, who were to join their father and other brothers.

Osama's sons, most of whom were barely old enough to grow a mustache, were dwarfed by him physically and emotionally. Almost all those he had fathered with Najwa had been born with developmental problems—possibly caused by the fact that their parents were first cousins. The two oldest had been born with hydrocephalus, and the younger ones suffered from varying degrees of autism, especially Saad.[43]

The exceptions were Khalid, aged thirteen, born to Seham, and Hamzah, also thirteen, his only child with Khairiah. Since early childhood Hamzah had had a natural bond with his father, and he was happy to dress up in camouflage uniforms, bandoliers, and mirrored sunglasses, looking every bit the mini-dictator. When Osama once asked if any of them were willing to become suicide bombers, only Hamzah had volunteered.[44] For Osama, all of his children, despite their disabilities, were actors in the pageant of jihad, and he never missed an opportunity to use them to promote his mission. Rather than celebrating birthdays or going on vacations, the boys were filmed on front lines holding firearms, while daughters were married off at the onset of puberty to mujahideen twice their age.

Khairiah and Seham had gone along with Osama's wishes gladly, but Najwa had hated the fact that he beat his vulnerable sons in front of his commanders for ludicrous lapses like telling a joke or "showing their teeth."[45] He forced them to dig pits in the desert with their bare hands and sleep outside in the freezing cold. Most of the boys did their best to avoid him, instead seeking out the Mauritanian or Osama's cheerful Yemeni driver, Salim Hamdan, who taught them to drive in the desert. Until she left, Najwa had struggled to soften this world, and the children had gathered around her gratefully, eager for the treats she procured—a homemade toy, a hand-stitched dress, a tin of tomato puree, a packet of Maggi noodles. Such acts had always infuriated Khairiah and Seham, who were almost as ideological as their husband.[46]

Now, the only boy left out of the role-playing was Najwa's nine-year-old son, Ladin. A timid child who flinched at the sound of gunfire, he and his sister Iman remained panic-stricken at being separated from their mother, who was on the way back to her parents in Latakia, Syria.

The women and children filed onto a corroding Soviet-era bus smeared with mud, setting off on a dirt track parallel to the Silk Road.

"When the engine stops, you get off," Osama told them.

Three uncomfortable days later they lurched to a halt at another *qila* on the outskirts of Jalalabad, a city in the northeast of Afghanistan. The dun-colored fort was surrounded by four-meter-high mud walls and crowned with guard towers.

Khairiah and Seham recognized it immediately. They had stayed here once before, in 1996, having fled Sudan on a military transporter.[47] Younis Khalis, an Afghan warlord sometimes allied to Al Qaeda, had lent them this compound while Osama furnished Tora Bora, his base in the White Mountains, a jagged line of peaks to the south of Jalalabad that merged with the Sulaiman range and was the location of a cave complex to which he had been introduced in 1986.

Osama had grandiosely named this borrowed Jalalabad fort Najm al-Jihad, the Star of the Holy War, but as it was surrounded by adobe huts set into a lunar landscape, Saad bin Laden, his third son and the most profoundly autistic, had dubbed it "Star Wars."[48]

In more recent times the camp had become a barracks for the Al Qaeda training camp located at the nearby village of Daruntah. Discarded ammunition boxes, food packaging, and empty bottles of chemicals lay everywhere. Wife number two, Khairiah, the most ideological, organized a cleanup.

They made it homelike by pinning up woolen rugs to absorb some of the winter chill and plumping up thin foam mattresses with old clothes, inspecting the bedding for scorpions and snakes. Najwa's daughter Iman shared with Seham's younger daughters, Miriam, eleven, and Sumaiya, nine, while Ladin was taken in by Khairiah, who was lost without her beloved Hamzah. Only wife number four, the silent Yemeni teenager, Amal al-Sadeh, sat it out, exhausted and feeding her baby.

Narrow alleys connected the apartments to a tin toilet outhouse that was swilled out, and in the rudimentary kitchen area someone fixed the water pump and got an old generator running. They would cook on a traditional Afghan *bukhar* (open stove), and the three nursing mothers were to have the best pickings.

Seham's fourteen-year-old daughter, Khadija, had recently given birth. She had been married off at the age of thirteen in a double wedding with her twelve-year-old half sister, Fatima (Najwa's daughter). Their husbands, two Saudi brothers in their thirties, both had wives and children already. Saad's wife, Wafa, the daughter of a Yemeni mujahid based in Sudan, also had a baby. They had named him Osama.

While the women worked, one of Khalis's deputies had his men excavate a bomb shelter, filling it with dried food and water.[49] He held drills, all the women racing into it when he banged together some cooking pans. Even Ladin had a role. He was told to lie on his back, staring up into the sky, scouting for enemy jets.

Khairiah and Seham, whose religious conservatism meant they could not speak to the male guards, dissected every scrap of news they overheard.

They wondered what would befall those left behind in the cities. Dr. Ayman al-Zawahiri's wife and five children remained in Kabul, along with Abu Hafs the Commander, whose teenage daughter Khadija was here with them and fretted constantly.

Suffering from a herniated disk, Abu Hafs would go down from the mountains the day after 9/11 and seek treatment in the city, where he would try to keep up his routine, going daily to the Al Qaeda office with his laptop in a briefcase. The rest of the *shura* and their families were scattered about the country.

Until a few days back, Osama's four wives had lived in adjoining concrete huts at Tarnak Qila, sharing a cordoned-off yard that they tilled to make a small allotment and where they reared rabbits and chickens. Sometimes, when the compound emptied of men, they gathered here to uncover their faces, while the children fought over a battered Nintendo or scanned their father's transistor for snatches of Madonna.[50]

But lately there had been dissonance.

When wife one, Najwa, married Osama in 1974, she had just turned sixteen and he was still forging a reputation as a demon soccer player at his university and for driving fast cars recklessly. Her father and Osama's mother, Allia, were brother and sister, and she had been charmed by the doe-eyed shyness of her cousin, who was the seventeenth son of Saudi Arabia's richest man, although he had grown up as a single child after his father divorced his mother when he was still small.

Eventually finding herself in Kandahar, Najwa had clung to the vestiges of her old life, filling her shelves with foreign cosmetics, curling and coloring her long black hair, and donning a jogging suit after dark to run around the inner courtyard, singing to herself.

Wife number two, Khairiah, Osama's favorite, had married him in 1985 when he was already well along the path to jihad, a vision she shared. Seven years older than Osama and a child psychologist by profession, she had been introduced by Najwa, who had met her after seeking out help for her disabled sons at a medical clinic in Jeddah. Plain, dour, and humorless, Khairiah had presumed she would spend her life as a spinster until Najwa suggested she join the family. Osama had already taken a second wife, Khadija, who Najwa did not get along with and who he would later divorce. He now wanted another, telling Najwa he needed to have as many children as possible "for Islam." Determined to have a say in who shared her house and husband, Najwa suggested that ironclad Khairiah could help with their sons' education. Osama judged that she was doubly perfect as the Prophet had decreed that men should wed "unmarriable" women to enable them to share the joy of motherhood.

Although it took her many years to conceive, Khairiah eventually bore him one child, Hamzah, who inherited his parents' fervor. Although Khairiah's physical relationship with her husband had long since ceased, a clean *shalwar kameez* still hung for him on the back of her bedroom door and a bottle of his favorite *aoud* oil perfume sat in the bathroom. A force of nature who Najwa had come to rely on to care for her disabled sons and otherwise deal with their husband, Khairiah had evolved into the extended family's *emira* (matriarch)—and it was in her room in Kandahar that everyone had gathered to resolve disputes and discuss impending changes, or to lobby for an extra sack of rice, basic medicine, or schoolbooks.

Khairiah was unflappable when it came to births or childhood illnesses, giving way occasionally to Dr. Aisha Siam, the only female doctor in Kandahar, or to Dr. al-Zawahiri, who was a trained doctor and liked to dispense advice from behind a thick curtain. Osama's attitude toward his family's medical needs was more negligent. He advanced a spoonful of honey as a desert wonder cure for everything, but honey had not worked for Najwa's oldest two sons. Her oldest, Abdullah, born in 1977, had become ill and dehydrated after Osama banned his wife from using a baby bottle. The next baby, Abdul Rahman, had suffered serious developmental problems when his hydrocephaly went untreated on his father's orders. The wives of Osama's brothers had tried to intervene to no avail.[51]

Wife number three had arrived two years after Khairiah, in 1987. Another uber-religious Saudi woman, Seham claimed to be directly descended from the Prophet Mohammed and her brother was one of Osama's Saudi fighters in Afghanistan. She held a Ph.D. from Medina University and had worked as a teacher before marriage, at which point she dedicated herself to Islam and Osama, in equal measures, setting herself the task of having as many children for the jihad as she could. After a daughter, Khadija, was born in 1987 she had a son, Khalid. The boy was quiet and withdrawn, unlike his older sister or his younger siblings, feisty Miriam and Sumaiya.

After four children, Seham had shut the bedroom door and gone back to her role as a teacher, turning her hut in Kandahar into a classroom, complete with slates, chalk, and a few secondhand matriculation papers purchased at the bazaar. Osama sometimes interrupted, conducting impromptu math and English tests, with his children lined up in order of size as his own father had done with him. The only other time they spent together was on infrequent day trips into the desert, when he and his bodyguard would drive ahead in a pickup, and they would trail in his dusty wake in a rickety bus. For a few hours they would sit together in the hot sand to listen to his stories about great battles against the Soviets, before he took off in the Hilux and they made the lurching journey home.

But the arrival of wife number four, eighteen-year-old Amal, had upended this unconventional but otherwise calm domestic scene.

June 2000, Ibb, Yemen

Osama bin Laden's decision to marry a Yemeni teenager was as much an attempt to deal with an existential question as it was about his libido. By 1999, when he had first come up with the idea of taking another wife, Taliban leader Mullah Omar had made it clear that he was running out of patience. Yemen, the land of Osama's forefathers, a skeletal state and the poorest country in the Arab world, was an obvious choice as a potential sanctuary, should he ever need to escape. Unstable, sparsely populated, and bordering his native Saudi Arabia, it was the kind of holed tapestry where Al Qaeda could prosper in the moth-light.

Marrying into the right tribe would provide a ready-made constituency to absorb the move and provide protection. But since Osama could not travel, he needed an emissary to find the right girl. In early 2000, he dispatched a Yemeni cleric working in the Kabul office, a holy man who started looking in his own hometown, the historic Yemeni city of Ibb. His instructions were to say that he acted for a wealthy Saudi businessman, whose family originated from Hadraumat, in eastern Yemen, where Osama's father had been born.[52]

In a land of few opportunities, many families were initially hooked by this tale. However, as they interrogated the intermediary and he refused to divulge Osama's identity, several backed off. Dejected, he called Kandahar, which came up with a new suggestion. A brother at Tarnak Qila had married the daughter of an unemployed Yemeni civil servant who supposedly had many more daughters still unwed.[53] The family was by no means ideal, the cleric was told. The girls were estranged from their father and living with their mother and uncle in Ibb. They were poor, staying in a home with no television, and were likely to agree if a decent dowry was put on the table.

When he visited, the cleric decided to get the identity of the groom out in the open. No one balked, and he was shown a photo of the teenager: Amal. "The choice is yours," said her uncle, who said later that he was not aware Osama "was wanted by the Americans" for the 1998 bombings of U.S. embassies in Kenya and Tanzania.[54] The bad news was that the girl was only seventeen, had dropped out of school, and sported a mop of short, unveiled black hair that made her look like an ingénue and not a minor wife. But Osama was in a hurry.

Coming from such reduced circumstances, the uncle told the cleric, it would be an honor for her to marry Osama. When Amal, who apparently knew more about Osama than her uncle did, told her mother that she "wanted to go down in history" by marrying such an important figure in the world of jihad, her photograph was dispatched to Kandahar.

While they waited for Osama's reply, some of Amal's better-read siblings tried to talk her out of it. Her younger brother Zakariya, a student activist, said she was "crazy." Osama had been married at least five times already, including to one woman whose name had been erased from the bin Laden family history and who had lasted only three days. What would it be like joining such a harem as wife number four, a position that was akin to being the family servant?

Amal spent several days deliberating with her older sister Farah, who was married to an Al Qaeda commander. "This is destiny from God," she said, playing the odds but needing something to believe in. Osama's offer was better than any other she was likely to receive, and his high-risk lifestyle meant that the marriage was likely to be a short one. "I accept," she decided. Now, all there was left to do was to fix a dowry.

June 2000, Kandahar

Osama called in his Yemeni security chief, Nasser al-Bahri, a pockmarked opportunist from Sana'a. His *kunya*, Abu Jandal, meant "Father of Death" and amused the Sheikh to no end. Since the time of the 1998 embassy attacks,

Abu Jandal had proudly carried around two bullets. "With one," he pledged to Osama, "I will kill you if we are captured." There was no need to ask about the second. The Father of Death could be seen around the camp polishing the rounds daily, like a chauffeur cleaning his ride.

That summer he braced himself, half expecting to be sent on a suicide mission as Osama opened a cashbox and counted out $5,000. It amazed Abu Jandal that so few notes could create mayhem somewhere in the world. Where was he being sent? And would he have time to say his good-byes?

Ignoring his questions, Osama instructed his bodyguard to travel to Sana'a with his wife, Tayez, and check into the Al Jazeera Hotel.[55]

A few mornings later, Abu Jandal was sitting in the lobby waiting nervously for his connect. When the man arrived and took Abu Jandal for juice in a crowded café, asking, "Have you brought the *dowry*?" the visitor's face fell.

Was this really the mission he had been entrusted with? Domestic tomfoolery. He shook his head in amazement. He was not going to die today.

For the next week, he paid the bills as Amal's family enthusiastically shopped for bridal gowns and gold wedding jewelry. Even her father turned up to claim a share of the sudden windfall. After a modest engagement party at the Al Jazeera, Abu Jandal arranged for the bride to be flown to Karachi on a three-month Pakistani visa that stated she was traveling for medical treatment.[56] She would be chaperoned by her sister Farah and by Abu Jandal's wife, Tayez.

Was the teenager apprehensive, Tayez wondered? If it had been her, knowing what lay in wait in Osama's compound, she would have been terrified.[57]

During the last parched sixty-mile push through the Kandahar desert, Amal, now covered with the requisite black *abaya* (robe) and *niqab* (face veil), reached out for Farah as the cab swayed. At her first sight of Tarnak Qila, tears pricked her eyes. For a girl accustomed to the cooled stone cloisters of ancient Ibb, the fort seemed to be little more than a ruin.

She was shown into a drab hut with bolsters and bedrolls lining the walls. A group of Arab women joined her and they silently ate plates of rice and cold mutton. Afterward, she was left alone to wash and wait.

She heard men muttering and then gunfire, and she realized that she was now married. After dark, a tall, lean figure entered, dressed in a white robe. He was far more handsome than she had imagined.

The next morning, when she woke, he was gone, but staring down at her from the window were two glowering female faces.

Khairiah and Seham could not believe what Osama had done: insulting them by marrying a girl who was younger than many of his children. Bringing a teenage bride into the fold broke with the pattern of austerity and moderation, they argued. Khairiah said Osama was suffering from a midlife crisis. A man who had once railed against the sleaziness of President Bill Clinton's indiscretions with Monica Lewinsky, and who described polygamy as like "riding a bicycle, fast but a little unstable," was having sex with a child.[58]

After the wedding, Amal's sister Farah returned to Yemen and Osama left the compound for a round of meetings in Kandahar and Kabul. The wives turned their backs on the new bride.[59] It hit Najwa hardest, but she was too exhausted to complain. The previous year she had given birth to her eleventh child, a girl called Nour, and she was still weak, her body unable to recover after so many births.

Amal, who had no children to fill her time, felt the snub keenly. She longed for her siblings and the political ramblings of her lazy, khat-chewing uncle. Her stomach, filled with gritty rice, ached for grilled fish, salad, and honeycomb bread. She missed the aromatic smell of the southern mountains, and her friends. In the quiet hours before dawn prayer, she traced with her finger lines of the Koran given by her mother.[60]

Abu Jandal's wife, Tayez, was subjected to the wrath of the harem. But unlike Amal, who had no way out of Kandahar, Tayez decided not to take it. She was accused by Khairiah and Seham of having failed to warn them about Osama's intention to marry a teenager; they harangued Tayez until she told her husband she was leaving.

Astounded, he ran to the Sheikh, who, embarrassed by the cattiness of his family, gave his security chief permission to relocate to Sana'a, dressing it up as a "mission." Abu Jandal was to shore up support among Yemeni tribal leaders, sheikhs, and imams in preparation for Al Qaeda's relocation there. There could be no scandal and so the Father of Death was to take his entire family—including his brother-in-law, who worked for Osama as a mechanic and driver.[61]

Unaccustomed to a sensitive political task, Abu Jandal took to it like he did to war. Over the following months, he dragged his brother-in-law across Yemen, armed with videos of their Sheikh, holding public meetings to describe Al Qaeda's training camps, while Tayez quietly set up home in Sana'a. Eventually, Yemeni intelligence came for Abu Jandal, arresting him at his home on suspicion that he had helped facilitate the USS *Cole* attack.[62] His brother-in-law, who was on *hajj* (pilgrimage to Mecca) with his wife at the time, received a tip-off and hotfooted it back to Afghanistan.

August 2001, Kandahar

Just a few weeks before 9/11, Osama celebrated the birth of his first child with Amal, a daughter called Safiyah.

When Amal's unemployed father learned the news through his ex-wife, he sensed an opportunity to cash in and flew to Pakistan. "I want to make sure Amal is happy in her new life," he told relatives, who, knowing him better, wondered how much he intended to ask for.[63]

After waiting in Islamabad for twenty days, he crossed the border and was driven for seven hours until he reached a large tent guarded by the mujahideen. Inside was an opening to an underground passage, which led to a clearing and another vehicle that drove him to a cave where Osama greeted him with a twenty-one-gun salute. Over plates of meat cooked on preheated stones in the Yemeni style, Osama bragged about how many attempts Arab and U.S. intelligence had made on his life since becoming a jihadist. "I was injured . . . and a lot of people were killed," he said. "But I was spared from death because God *wished* it."

Amal's father, a canny operator, nodded appreciatively, but what he saw was a disillusioned man, deserted by many of his advisers.[64] When Osama began to talk of "a big event that will occur in the world," and described a "future strike" that would herald chaos, Amal's father found himself worrying. What would happen to his daughter and granddaughter? Making his excuses, he found Amal. Come home, he pleaded. Osama was unhinged. "I will be your father once again."

Amal shook her head. "It's true that my life is now moving between caves in Afghanistan, but I'm comfortable with Osama," she told him. Her husband was a "noble man" who treated her well.

Another member of the family party overheard Osama talking to Amal later that night. He had picked up the panic in his wife's family. She had a choice: "Stay with me or flee to Yemen, I will not keep you."

Amal stared up at him. "I want to be martyred with you, and I won't leave as long as you're alive," she said.

Her father departed the same evening, worried that he had consigned his daughter and granddaughter to a squalid life or even an early death. But more riling, all he had to show for the trip were bags of Saudi dates and olives from Osama's farms near Tora Bora. He discarded them en route to the Pakistan border.

September 14, 2001, Star Wars Camp, Jalalabad, Afghanistan

A cold, clear night crept over them, and Khairiah and Seham huddled together under a blanket, with a Kalashnikov and a stash of grenades.

Amal remained on her own with her baby daughter, Safiyah, staring up at stars.

Without any adult male relatives to protect them, only Al Qaeda guards who could not enter the same room as them, they had been instructed to blow themselves up if the situation became critical. Death was preferable to Americans, said Khairiah. As always, Seham went along with her.

Amal shuddered. She had no intention of dying.

September 14, 2001, Washington, D.C.

General Mahmud Ahmed shifted nervously in his seat as he willed the plane to take off. After three long days trapped in Washington and New York, the ISI director was at last on his way home to Pakistan: the sole passenger on a CIA-requisitioned flight. His ordeal had begun on the morning of September 12 when he had gone to offer condolences to U.S. deputy secretary of state Richard Armitage, only to be greeted by a furious fifteen-minute fusillade. "You are either with us or against us," Armitage had hectored. War in Afghanistan was coming and if Pakistan did not offer "unqualified support," it would "be bombed back to the Stone Age."[65]

In Karachi, Pervez Musharraf was pulled out of a meeting to take a call from Secretary of State Colin Powell. "You are either with us or against us," Powell said, aping Armitage's words although using a more conciliatory tone. Over the next forty-eight hours, as 5,600 people were listed as dead or missing on the East Coast, the details of what America wanted were reinforced by Wendy Chamberlin, the U.S. ambassador to Pakistan.

The demands made Musharraf's head spin. Selective Pakistani border posts and even some frontier bases had to be opened up to U.S. forces. Islamabad had to cut diplomatic ties with the Taliban. There could be no "no-go" areas.

These are just words, Musharraf reasoned, and language is ambiguous.[66] There were ways through every bottleneck. American units and intelligence operatives could be allowed to embed at key locations. The United States would deny it and so would he. Musharraf could agree to clamp down on anti-U.S. demonstrations, knowing that this promise would be impossible to enforce, since raising a mob was a national pastime. He would allow the United States greater landing rights and overflights. That was something he could get away with as hardly anyone would see.

What Musharraf did need was to find out what the Taliban knew and what they might say when confronted by the United States.

Spy chief General Mahmud Ahmed landed on the afternoon of September 15 and was ordered to debrief Mullah Omar at once. But, as he headed for the Aabpara ISI headquarters, he received some alarming reports. American Predator drones were already in the skies over the Pakistan–Afghan border and Kandahar. Hiding anything now would require more skill and the use of deniable, remote proxies, he thought.

Since 1979, Pakistan had devolved sensitive domestic operations and those that targeted India to ISI-trained but independent jihad outfits, such as Lashkar-e-Taiba (the Army of the Pure), that recruited in dusty towns across the Punjab underpinned by poverty and hereditary malice. Another was Jaish-e-Mohammed, run by a plump Punjabi cleric named Masood Azhar, whose fighters were sporadically called on to unleash well-appointed violence in complex operations in Indian Kashmir.

There were so many splinter groups and there was so much politicking among them that General Ahmed found it hard to keep tabs on them all, and he usually left it to the retired ISI generals who controlled the ISI's S-Wing to discreetly maintain the network on his behalf.[67]

Foremost among these generals was Hamid Gul, a notorious attack dog who had headed the ISI during the Afghan jihad and encouraged a description of himself as Father of the Taliban. Gul's secret work, Ahmed noted, had to continue.

The second message the spy chief received was more worrying: Robert Grenier was already conducting talks with the Taliban. The CIA station chief had beaten the ISI to a meeting.

The general made some calls. As soon as Grenier left, his men would find out what had been said. He then rang Musharraf. "I've been thinking about it, sir. Let the U.S. do its own dirty work. Its enemies are our friends," he said, advising his chief to concede nothing, as America was weaker now than it had been at any point since Pearl Harbor.

Musharraf was incensed by his spymaster's shortsightedness. "The *Taliban* is not worth committing suicide over," he snapped, disconnecting the call, hoping that this one was not being listened to.[68]

On the morning of September 16, General Ahmed reluctantly received the CIA station chief at Aabpara. According to protocol, they should have met one-on-one in his first-floor office, but Grenier was taken to a conference room where a phalanx of Pakistani spooks awaited him.

Ahmed said he had analyzed the available evidence: there wasn't enough to pin 9/11 on Al Qaeda.

Grenier frowned.

Ahmed called forward the director general for analysis, General Javed Alam Khan, presenting him as his newly appointed "counterterrorism tsar." Grenier's old sparring partner leaned over and whispered: "More like a *Rasputin.*"[69] He would have full authority to do whatever was required to demonstrate Pakistan's solidarity with the United States, Ahmed said with a forced smile.

The Taliban, he continued, would require sensitive handling. "After all, they are the legitimate government over there." But it was a mistake to think that Pakistan could *control* them, he continued. Everyone knew the story about a recent cross-border football match for which the Pakistani team had turned up in Kandahar wearing shorts. The Taliban had blackened the players' faces with charcoal, shaved their heads, and lashed them to donkeys, facing the men backward and parading them through the streets like charred mummers. "Afghanistan is a place where you had to barter every step of the way."

Grenier's turn came. He stood and gave "an arm-waving, blow-by-blow account" of his meeting with the Taliban, who, he felt, were reasonably confident they would be able to persuade Mullah Omar to find a solution to "the Osama bin Laden problem."

General Ahmed claimed to be "amazed." The station chief had made "a huge breakthrough," he said. He shook his head in admiration. "These are exploitable concessions," he concluded, announcing that he was due to meet Mullah Omar personally, knowing that even Grenier could not get an audience with a man who declined to share a room with non-Muslims.

As soon as he left the meeting, Ahmed accelerated his schedule. The next day he set off for Kandahar, where he was welcomed at Mullah Omar's office by Mahfouz Ibn El Waleed, Osama's former spiritual guide who was now a senior Taliban adviser. The Mauritanian took notes as the ISI chief dispensed advice. According to Mahfouz, spy chief Ahmed told Mullah Omar he should "never hand over Sheikh Osama," and to protect him "at any cost."[70]

Mullah Omar said nothing.

"Even if the Sheikh is handed over," continued Ahmed, according to Mahfouz, "the Americans will still invade, just as the British did more than a hundred years before."

Mullah Omar spoke his response so quietly that everyone else in the room found themselves staring at his lips trying to unlock the words. The Islamic emirate was dealing with things in a transparent way, he whispered. He had entrusted "the case of Sheikh Osama" to a team of scholars who would arbitrate. But in fact, the matter had already been decided—thanks to a preemptive strike by Osama.

Two days before 9/11, the Al Qaeda leader had sent two Tunisians, posing as journalists, to see Ahmad Shah Massoud, the charismatic and popular leader of the Northern Alliance, a rival warlord faction that was supported by the United States and was therefore Mullah Omar's nemesis. They had detonated a bomb hidden in their camera, killing Massoud in an act that required a quid pro quo. Now, Osama would never be forced out of Afghanistan at any price.

According to Mahfouz, the Pakistani spymaster nodded and offered some tactical advice. "If the United States does attack, they will rely on aerial bombardment rather than putting soldiers on the ground." Given his access to high-ranking U.S. officials, and shared intelligence, he would brief Mullah Omar what those likely targets would be. The ISI was entering into an intelligence sharing agreement with the Taliban.

Eleven days later, Ahmed returned to Kandahar, telling Grenier he was delivering a final ultimatum to Mullah Omar. Instead, according to Mahfouz, he took with him two Pakistani brigadier generals, who would spend several hours talking through simple strategies to commence a "mountain guerrilla war." Outside in a pickup sat a team of ISI specialists, who were to be left behind to rig Kandahar with booby traps, protect Mullah Omar, and train his praetorian guard.

Once back in Islamabad, Ahmed assembled his final gift, dispatching so many Pakistani fuel tankers and supply trucks toward the Taliban that they choked the border crossing into Afghanistan at Chaman.[71]

September 15, 2001, Geneva, Switzerland

Post 9/11, old friends had to stand fast, and new deals had to be made.

As soon as his colleagues cleared out of Foggy Bottom for the weekend, senior State Department official Ryan Crocker caught a taxi to the airport and flew to Geneva, knowing he had a critical twenty-four hours of secret meetings ahead. He would have to be back at his desk by Monday morning, so that his trip went unnoticed.

Crocker, the son of a U.S. Air Force officer, was fresh from a kinetic posting as ambassador to Syria, one in which his embassy had been stormed by protesters, making him a steady pair of hands in a tight spot. A man who could be firm but also informal, he was "never your typical diplomat," as President George W. Bush would joke, finishing off the story by saying, "for social engagements Crocker likes to tell guests: 'no socks required.'"[72]

The cloak-and-dagger of the Geneva mission was proportional, Crocker thought, not only to insulate it from ideologically senior Bush appointees who would try to stop it, especially Richard Armitage, but also because of the risks being taken by those he was about to meet on the other side of the table.

Using the United Nations as cover, Crocker was sitting down with a high-level delegation of Iranian diplomats led by Mohammad Javad Zarif, a deputy minister of foreign affairs who was conversant in all things American, as his affluent family had paid for him to be educated there—in San Francisco and Denver. After graduation, he had taken a post in New York as part of Iran's delegation to the United Nations. Engaging and confident, he spoke English with an American twang, his children had been educated in American schools, and he made it clear to Crocker from the start that he represented the inner sanctum of Iran's Reformist president, Mohammad Khatami.[73]

What was on offer was "extraordinary and extraordinarily sensitive," Crocker thought. Given Iran's shared border with Afghanistan, and a history of vicious anti-Shia pogroms and massacres undertaken by Sunni zealots from there, as well as the more recent instability kicked up by Mullah Omar's regime and its kinship with Osama bin Laden, Tehran's Reformists wanted to be rid of the Taliban and Al Qaeda altogether. This put Iran in the unusual position of seeing—for the first time in many years—its foreign policy goals coalesce with those of the United States, which had blackballed everything Iranian since the fall of the shah and the storming of the U.S. embassy in 1979.

Crocker and his Iranian counterpart stayed up through the night talking. They found they had much in common, and the Iranian delegation was keen to crack on. Khatami, who had been voted into office in 1997, saw the 9/11 tragedy as a chance to usher in a new era of détente with Washington, and Zarif offered introductions to Afghan warlords who might assist the United States in purging the Taliban and their Arab guests, enabling the formation of a new pro-Western government in Kabul.

Several more clandestine meetings were scheduled. As a result of Crocker's trips and over the course of several weeks, the pace picked up and he soon recognized that while Iran was keen to forge ahead, the United States was the tardy partner, always deferring and playing for time.

At one weekend session, an Iranian official slammed a sheaf of papers on the table. The Twin Towers had fallen weeks earlier but the United States had still not responded, he railed. "If you guys don't stop building these fairy-tale governments in the sky, and actually start doing some shooting on the ground, nothing is ever going to happen! When you're ready to talk about serious fighting, you know where to find me."[74]

All Crocker could do was laugh.

The next time they met, Zarif handed him a map of Afghanistan with Taliban positions marked on it. "These are the most sensitive spots," he explained. "You want to strike these first, especially the ones in Kandahar."[75]

Could he write all of this down? Crocker asked.

"Keep the map," Zarif replied, turning on his heel.

October 7, 2001, Kandahar

The U.S. Army was coming. Everyone knew it. The euphoria that the Taliban had felt at seeing America forced to "drink from the bitterness cup" of 9/11 was fading fast.[76]

Inside Mullah Omar's compound, he and his advisers grew more furious by the day at having been blindsided by the Planes Operation. Since Osama had not even bothered to tell them the date for the attack, they had sent their forces to fight the Northern Alliance days beforehand, leaving Kandahar and its half-million citizens undefended.

What should the Commander of the Faithful do? he asked the Mauritanian.

Ready yourself and the city, the cleric advised him.

The Taliban mobilized its citizens, rousing them door-to-door, ordering them to excavate their own air-raid shelters.

Using farm tools, they dug large holes in the ground and covered them with tarpaulins. Their wives dubbed them "mass graves."

CHAPTER TWO

"Terrorism is a duty and assassination is a
Sunnah."
                    —ABU MUSAB AL-SURI, *THE CALL FOR*
                    GLOBAL ISLAMIC RESISTANCE[1]

May 1996, Tora Bora, White Mountains, Afghanistan

WHEN OSAMA MOVED BACK TO AFGHANISTAN in 1996 he returned to a place whose Pashto name "Tora Bora" meant Black Cave. He had first got to know it at the height of the Afghan jihad.

Panicked by the Soviet invasion of 1980, the ISI and its paymasters in the CIA and Saudi intelligence had by 1986 turned this South Asian fault line into a major front in the Cold War. That year, the ISI spotted the potential for Tora Bora, an impenetrable honeycombed aerie, to become a staging post from which to arm the Afghan-bound mujahideen; and it employed Osama to build a route up from the Jalalabad side to fifteen thousand feet—using equipment, engineers, and know-how borrowed from his father's construction empire in Saudi Arabia.[2] When the Soviet war ended, Osama had gone home to Saudi Arabia, but after falling out with the royal family, in 1991 he had shifted his family and supporters to Sudan.

After five arid years in Khartoum, a period in which he had talked of jihad but spent his time building roads and factories, he was thrilled to be back in the jaws of the White Mountains accompanied by his trusted deputy Abu Hafs the Commander, a handful of bodyguards, and his teenage son Omar. Almost immediately, he began to reminisce about the old fighting days, particularly his initiation into real battle in 1987, when he had gone from being a rich facilitator of jihad to a real soldier, establishing a military redoubt he called the Lion's Den a couple of valleys away from Tora Bora, and within sight of a large Soviet base at Jaji.

Sleeping in foxholes with a band of seventy ill-trained Arab fighters, he had expelled from the camp those who had mocked his ability or questioned the strategy of eyeballing the Russian special forces. "This is jihad!" the inexperienced Osama had insisted. "This is the way we go to heaven."[3]

When the Soviets attacked, it had seemed implausible that the Arabs could win. But at the peak of battle, and with nine of Osama's men facing down seventy Spetsnaz troops, the Red Army unexpectedly pulled back, handing Osama an unlikely genesis story that helped him launch Al Qaeda the following year. A snub-nosed Kalashnikov recovered from a dead Russian officer became Osama's totem and he brandished it, saying "men without weapons are incomplete."[4] He was no longer just the rejected seventeenth son of Saudi billionaire Mohammed bin Laden but a warrior fighting a noble cause, a hero of his own making.

Now in 1996, according to Omar, who was at his side, Osama quickly built himself up into a fury about Saudi Arabia and the West. He spent his evenings ranting on a Dictaphone about the wars he intended to launch.[5]

Separated from his family and his closest advisers, who remained in Sudan, vanity hardened into unrelenting solipsism as he began to dream about a new battle for the heart of Islam. Believing that dreams were messages from God, he became transfixed by the idea of inciting war against another superpower: America. He tried to lure Omar into the discussion, but all the boy could think of was how his cousins in Jeddah lived in beautiful houses and drove luxury cars, while his home was a dank cave. "My father did not mind the trying conditions but seemed exhilarated by them as if his previous risky exploits as a warrior in Afghanistan had created a lifelong need for stimulation," Omar recalled.[6]

Omar was shocked when, four months into their stay, his father called for the rest of their family to join them on the mountain, flown over in a chartered plane with hundreds of loyal mujahideen fighters (who had followed him to Africa after finding themselves unable to return to their homes at the end of the Afghan jihad). Najwa, who was pregnant for the tenth time, Khairiah, and Seham arrived with thirteen children among them, to find themselves expected to billet in windowless shepherds' huts on the edge of a precipice, without running water or electricity.

As mujahideen veterans converged on Tora Bora, Omar comparing them to "worker bees looking for their king," Osama ignored his wives' concerns that the nearest doctor was "a long fall away," four hours over in Jalalabad.[7]

They would have to get used to their new home, he said, a place from which he intended to launch a global revolution. If their mothers fretted, the children loved the freedom of Tora Bora, calling it "bin Laden mountain." After being cooped up in a parched Khartoum compound for four years, the caves and cliffs were exhilarating.

Into this febrile atmosphere stepped "the Syrian," whose real name was Mustafa Setmariam Nasar, a confident, red-haired Islamist from middle-class Aleppo who had first been introduced to Osama in Peshawar in 1988 at the height of the Soviet war. The Syrian, whose *kunya* was Abu Musab al-Suri, a man who was considered an extremist within the Syrian Muslim Brotherhood, had a black belt in judo and had been a mujahideen trainer during the 1980s, teaching explosives engineering, urban warfare, and "special operations"—leading some recruits to joke that he was the *ummah*'s Carlos the Jackal.[8]

Preparing a memoir, which he hoped would be instructional, the Syrian recounted how he had received training in 1980 at the age of 22 in a camp in Iraq that set the tone for all that he would accomplish.

> "Are you Muslim brotherhood members." We all said "yes." Then the trainer said while pointing at his neck "you will all get slaughtered, do you approve of that?" Then we happily and joyfully said, "we approve, sir." He then turned to the chalkboard and wrote the title of his very first lecture: "Terrorism is a duty and assassination is a *Sunnah* [an action ordained by the Prophet Mohammed]."[9]

After three years in Afghanistan, the Syrian had left for Europe, as Al Qaeda headed for Sudan. For several years he had had no more contact with Al Qaeda but now he returned armed with a master plan for global jihad that he predicted would culminate in the declaration of a caliphate, God's kingdom on earth, a precursor to the Muslim day of judgment. The thesis was spelled out in a lengthy book that was half-written and that the Syrian wanted Osama to endorse. Much of it was drawn from the writings of Abdullah Azzam.[10]

Al Qaeda could be the beacon on the mountain, the Syrian argued. The Taliban's recent declaration of an Islamic emirate—the precursor to a caliphate—in Afghanistan was a "golden opportunity" to get things started."[11]

After four years of conflict between opposing warlords, the Taliban had seized control of Kabul after ejecting their main rivals, the Northern Alliance—who had retreated to the north. Taliban leader Mullah Omar had

given Al Qaeda tacit permission to stay as long as it vowed loyalty and maintained a low profile. Osama had accepted this deal but had no intention of
keeping quiet.

The Sheikh spent the winter of 1996 feverishly debating the Syrian, both
men wrapped up in shawls and sheltering inside a cave stacked with ammunition boxes and religious texts, plotting the "downfall of the greatest power,
America." Fight the United States and Al Qaeda would become a fountainhead, the Syrian declared.[12] In nearby huts Osama's wives and children
struggled in the sub-zero weather and had barely anything to eat.[13]

When Mahfouz, Osama's Mauritanian spiritual chief, joined the pair in
March 1997, he was delighted to see the Syrian—who he greatly admired—
but he was unnerved by his ambition to attack the West. A charismatic man
of action had captured Osama's attention and both men were plotting global
war, despite Al Qaeda having only a ragtag army of followers and a few thousand dollars to its name.[14]

The Mauritanian had stayed behind in Sudan to tidy up the mess the
outfit had left there after four years in residence, including a broken-down
747 passenger jet bought by Osama in a moment of messianic madness that
was now rusting in the Sudanese desert. He had been charged by Osama
with liberating Al Qaeda's cash, around $29 million, some of it sitting in
various banks in Khartoum, the rest sunk into Sudanese businesses that
needed to be sold. The task was so vital that Osama had promised to pay the
Mauritanian a $300,000 finder's fee, and the current plotting was predi-
cated on this money arriving.[15]

The Mauritanian had to admit that he had failed. The Sheikh's Sudanese
accounts had been frozen on the request of the Saudis and the Americans.
His companies there were either bankrupt or had also had their assets
seized. Many things had been stolen. Touring the Tora Bora cave complex,
the Mauritanian saw the disappointment written on everyone's faces, from
Osama's hungry family to the Afghani villagers who had been dragooned into
expanding the caves and were waiting for payday. Embarrassed, he offered
his resignation.

Osama would not accept it, insisting that the Mauritanian had a vital role
to play alongside the Syrian and a second new member of the inner circle, to
whom he was now introduced.

"Mokhtar the Pakistani," a burly Sufi whose family came from Balochistan
but who had grown up in Kuwait, was touting a plan for an ambitious broadside to force the deployment of U.S. troops in Afghanistan. Osama had typed

up the outlines on his old laptop powered by a portable generator that was off-limits to his wife and children, who lived by candlelight and cooked on gas burners.

The Sheikh's spiritual adviser studied the document. The ramifications of this apocalyptic plan—to set a near-defunct movement against a super-power—struck the Mauritanian as absurd and possibly deranged. Given his failure in Khartoum, Al Qaeda did not have the financial muscle to launch a war or repel one, he warned. The brothers recently arrived from Sudan—many of whom were struggling to adapt from the desert to the mountain cave and were bedridden with malaria and typhoid—did not constitute an army.

He knew how to handle his Sheikh and reasoned with him.

But Osama was not listening. "I have missed you," he said, smiling at the Mauritanian. "Stay, edit and write, help shape our *future*."[16]

The Mauritanian felt torn. Quit now and have no influence over anything, or remain and mold the plan.

He thought hard. The Syrian was a tactician. Mokhtar was—no one knew what Mokhtar was. But the Mauritanian, with his superior religious knowledge, was the only one in Al Qaeda who might be able to moderate the Sheikh's thinking. But where to start? According to the Islamic spirit of learning etiquette, if one's teacher or elder was wrong, there could be no public correction, only praise; even in private, criticism could only ever be implied or inferred—following which it was customary to say, "God knows best; maybe both of us are wrong." The only sensible suggestion Mahfouz could instantly arrive at was to gently ease his way back into Osama's affections by helping to rebuild the outfit's reserves, human and financial. Could they import a machine to counterfeit U.S. dollars? he suggested.

Osama asked him to look into it.[17] For better or worse, the Mauritanian was back, and he would bide his time before trying again to influence Osama.

Over the next few months as the Taliban consolidated its hold over Afghanistan, the Mauritanian stuck to Osama's side, the two of them touring Afghanistan in a battered Hilux, collecting funds, meeting veteran Afghan warlords, making new alliances and shoring up old ones. Sharing oranges and swapping seats at toilet breaks, he tried to steer Osama away from the Syrian's dark imaginings of the day of judgment and calling a caliphate. Mokhtar's apocalyptic plan, which now had the working name of the "Planes Operation," was held at arm's length, too. "We do not need to attack to win,"

Mahfouz repeatedly told Osama. "We are already an idea, a powerful one, and to sustain our influence we need to survive—and grow." These men whose counsel Osama was taking had usurped Al Qaeda's *shura* and, adding insult to injury, Mokhtar was not even in Al Qaeda.

Most disturbing for the Mauritanian was the threat that Osama's plotting posed for the Taliban's embryonic Islamic emirate. Although they had yet to meet Mullah Omar, Osama seemed not to care one jot about the Taliban leader's demands that Al Qaeda remain invisible.

When they returned to Tora Bora, the Mauritanian realized how little progress he had made when Osama immediately sent word to the Syrian, who was in London, asking him to dispatch foreign news crews up to the lair in the Afghan mountains so that he could brief them about a coming war.

"Around now Sheikh Osama fell in love with the media and was quite enchanted by it," the Mauritanian recalled bitterly.[18] He was going to war against the West and would shout it from the mountaintops of Afghanistan irrespective of what the *shura* or the Taliban wanted.

Abu Hafs the Commander, who had been with Osama since the very start, was also suspicious of men he saw as outsiders. He held the Syrian in high regard, although he did not understand most of what he said. Mokhtar, however, he detested.

What galled the Commander was the fact that he had unleashed this man's monstrous ego by sponsoring him when he first emerged in Peshawar in 1985. Back then Abu Hafs had been drawn by Mokhtar's glad-handing confidence. From what he knew, this salesman and fund-raiser had arrived in Peshawar directly from the United States, where he had been sent from Kuwait to study at great cost to his Pakistani-born parents. Riled by the petty racism he had encountered on campus in a small American town, where he had felt smothered by its Christianity, Mokhtar had endured taunts and name-calling from his fellow freshmen who referred to him as the "Abbie Dhabbie."[19]

When he saw on the news that an Islamist insurgent force, the mujahideen, was receiving funding to take on the Red Army in Afghanistan, he was enthralled by the David-and-Goliath narrative and saw it as an odyssey to restore his sense of self. It might even turn a profit.

In Peshawar, Mokhtar had rapidly gained a reputation as a useful hustler who could shake down donors, channeling cash to Afghan warlords.[20] He seldom prayed, preferring to hold court at long discussions over sweetened black tea about the most effective methods of killing, surrounded by an ever-growing gang of admirers.

After the Soviets and CIA withdrew in 1989, Mokhtar began thinking about settling his score with America. Over the next couple of years he absorbed new skills while his nephew, Ramzi Yousef, who had studied electrical engineering in Wales, emerged as a proactive mujahid with a plan. In 1993, Yousef bombed the World Trade Center in New York, killing six and injuring more than one thousand, an operation that aimed to shatter the aura of American invincibility. Mokhtar, who had no role in the attack, was overjoyed. Osama, who was in Sudan lecturing the government on agriculture productivity and the pitiful state of its roads, barely noticed.

However, by the time Mokhtar turned up in Tora Bora, everyone close to Osama had come to appreciate the audacity of the World Trade Center attack and how close it had come to causing mayhem. Being introduced as an uncle of Ramzi Yousef—who a year after his World Trade Center attack had successfully placed a small bomb on a Philippine Airlines flight, killing one passenger—to test out a much larger plan, was enough to gain an audience.

Osama listened as the squat visitor, speaking Kuwaiti Arabic in his squeaky high-pitched voice, flattered him before laying out a plan so ambitious it silenced everyone in the room. Adopting his nephew's idea of turning planes into flying bombs, Mokhtar suggested they hijack a dozen U.S. airliners and crash them into the Pentagon, the U.S. Capitol, the White House, CIA headquarters, the FBI, and the World Trade Center, killing thousands in the air and on the ground. He and Ramzi, whose mother was Mokhtar's sister, had until recently been working on another iteration of this—setting timed devices to explode simultaneously on multiple U.S.-bound transatlantic flights. The plot had been code-named "Bojinka," a word that meant explosion in Serbo-Croat. Ramzi's capture in Islamabad had put paid to those plans and so Mokhtar was now searching for a new partner.

The plot seemed nonsensical to the Mauritanian. Abu Hafs the Commander dismissed it outright. One of those present at the meeting warned Osama that Mokhtar was "a madman from a mental hospital."[21]

But Osama disagreed. He liked his visitor's ambition and scale. Unlike any other Pakistani that he had met during his long association with the country, Mokhtar was self-starting, resourceful, and a details man. For once here was someone who had thought everything through. All that stopped Osama from proceeding was the scale of Mokhtar's demands: $500,000 in cash, a team of suicide bombers, and logistical support—none of which Al Qaeda could presently provide. As a sop, he invited Mokhtar to join Al Qaeda and move his family to Afghanistan, requisite demonstrations of supplication for a new recruit. Mokhtar returned to Karachi. He would do it on his terms only.

After Osama, encouraged by Dr. Ayman al-Zawahiri, issued a fatwa in 1998 against "the Americans and their allies," ruling that it was "an individual duty for every Muslim" to kill them, Mokhtar returned to Afghanistan.[22] This time, he was welcomed by al-Zawahiri, who had recently returned from a spell in Russian detention, where some alleged he had been recruited by the Russian security services to plot attacks against America.[23] Mokhtar ingratiated himself with Osama's circle, replacing Al Qaeda's outdated computers and upgrading its media operation by teaching the brothers how to use a camcorder. He transformed Al Qaeda's embryonic press center, bringing in a new computer-literate team that included a fellow expat Pakistani from Kuwait. Ibrahim Saeed Ahmad had grown up with Mokhtar and had several older brothers who had fought in the Soviet jihad. In Al Qaeda circles he was known by the *kunya* Abu Ahmad al-Kuwaiti and for his noticeable speech impediment.[24]

Mokhtar presented a slimmed-down version of his earlier plan—using just four hijacked jets to destroy four targets. Since funds had started to flow in as a result of the fatwa, Osama gave him some seed money. However, as he was now in open conflict with his *shura* over his refusal to abide by Mullah Omar's request that he maintain a low profile, Osama put Mokhtar's plan in motion without telling them. Only Abu Hafs the Commander was informed as Osama and Dr. al-Zawahiri secretly reached out to potential sponsors in the Gulf.

By 1999, several would-be hijackers had been recruited, mostly Saudi nationals who could obtain U.S. visas more easily than Yemenis or Pakistanis. Mokhtar asked his friend, the freelancing jihad logistician Abu Zubaydah, to supervise their transit, organize passports, and send them for secret training at the Abu Obaida camp that lay just beyond the perimeter wall of Tarnak Qila, although he did not tell Zubaydah what the men were training for.[25]

Mokhtar and Zubaydah had known each other since 1991. After suffering a shrapnel injury to his head in Gardez, where Afghan warlords were fighting one another, Zubaydah had retreated to Peshawar, where he set up a mujahid facilitation network behind the façade of a honey stall in Board Bazaar, a busy shopping district in University Town. He soon came across

Mokhtar, who used a honey-processing factory in Karachi as a front for moving recruits and material up to Peshawar.[26]

Now, Zubaydah was asked to tap into links he had with Islamists all over Europe, including his main contact in the United Kingdom, the Palestinian preacher Abu Qatada, who advocated jihad from the pulpit at Finsbury Park Mosque in London and collected donations for the mujahideen.[27]

When George W. Bush was elected U.S. president in November 2000, Mokhtar and Osama were delighted. "My father was so happy," recalled son Omar, who was still with him at that time. "This is the kind of a president he needs—one who will attack and spend money and break the country."[28]

Soon after, Mokhtar's first would-be pilots graduated from Al Qaeda's Abu Obaida camp, and, without informing the *shura*, Mokhtar escorted them down to Karachi, putting them up at his safe house in the busy shopping district of Tariq Road.

Here, and at several other locations across the city, the men were tutored using flight simulation programs by Mokhtar's childhood friend Abu Ahmad al-Kuwaiti. He also taught them English, how to use the Internet, and the layouts of passenger aircraft—highlighting the weak points in cabin security. They developed a simple code. Mokhtar was answerable to "the Professor," aka Osama. Civilian targets were "schools" and military targets "universities."

June 2001, Tarnak Qila, Kandahar, Afghanistan

By the summer of 2001, everyone in Al Qaeda was aware that *something* was in the offing. New faces appeared, others went off, people talked of the "big plan" or the "Planes Operation," and the ones in the know were frantic.

One night, the Mauritanian received an unexpected visitor: Dr. Ayman al-Zawahiri. The two men were rivals for Osama's attention and yet the Egyptian doctor came asking for "guidance."[29]

Dr. al-Zawahiri revealed that Osama had requested that his organization—Egyptian Islamic Jihad—formally merge with Al Qaeda ahead of the coming operation. He said he was concerned about the implications for the ongoing standoff between Osama and Mullah Omar. Siding with the Sheikh over the Commander of the Faithful might weaken the Islamic Emirate of Afghanistan and the Muslim *ummah*. Was this permissible under *sharia* law?

The Mauritanian saw through Dr. al-Zawahiri's maneuvering. He had no genuine interest in maintaining cordial relations with the Taliban, who he clearly regarded as country cousins, but he was not yet sure he could get away with causing a religious rupture by opposing a man who some regarded as a caliph in waiting.

The Mauritanian could also see that Osama was so determined to get Mokhtar's Planes Operation approved by the Al Qaeda leadership committee that he intended to stack it with new members from Egyptian Islamic Jihad who were blindly loyal to him. When the Mauritanian refused to adjudicate, Dr. al-Zawahiri went home frustrated.

A few days later, Osama announced that Al Qaeda's formal merger with Egyptian Islamic Jihad had gone ahead, giving Dr. al-Zawahiri's group six of the nine seats on the *shura*.[30] Its next meeting would take place on the last Wednesday of June and cover all future operations, he said.

When they gathered, Osama was in a bullish mood, looking expectantly at the new supportive faces on the council.[31] After clearing his throat to silence the room, he revealed what everyone suspected, that Al Qaeda was preparing to strike the United States—again.

The room filled with muttering. Osama was asked to give more details. He shook his head. For security reasons he could not reveal precise plans. Several *shura* members said they could not back what they did not know. The Syrian, who had returned from London, where he had been helping Abu Qatada run his magazine and publicize the Algerian jihad front, was one of them.

"Whatever is being planned," he warned, "will undermine Al Qaeda and alienate the Muslim community."[32] The movement was veering dangerously off track. "Al Qaeda is not an organization, it is not a group, nor do we want it to be," he said. "It is a call, a reference, a methodology."[33] Al Qaeda had to stand above the bloodshed and appear to be the "best of the best." Its goal was to stimulate other groups to commit acts in the name of jihad, not perform these acts itself.

Osama looked stunned.

Someone else demanded to know why Al Qaeda was not targeting Israel, something that Mullah Omar had recently given his blessing for.

Abu Hafs the Commander, who was committed to the operation, spoke: "Attacking America, a sponsor of Jerusalem, is tantamount to a strike on Israel." Any attack on America came with the implicit support of Mullah

Omar. America and Israel were like "one bicycle with two wheels," he argued, echoing a favorite phrase of Osama's.[34]

His logic got the room talking. The Mauritanian asked to speak. "You are following a path that contradicts *sharia*, reason, and logic." Osama looked up. The room hushed. Mahfouz had just broken the etiquette of no public correction or criticism. He tried to temper his words, mumbling, "God knows best—maybe both of us are wrong."

Osama eyed him furiously as Mahfouz continued. The *sharia* committee had met and debated the idea of an attack on America and unanimously opposed it. Not only would it be illegal without Mullah Omar's blessing, but also thousands of innocent people might die. Heads nodded in agreement, even among the new Egyptian inductees.

Emboldened and with his heart beating fast, the Mauritanian stepped up his attack. "In political affairs you do not obey the Taliban's emir even though you believe him to be legitimate. In regulatory matters you do not accept the opinion of the *shura*. And in religious affairs you do not comply with the legal committee's writ." Al Qaeda was no longer a democratic organization but the court of a king.

Everyone dropped their gaze to the floor as Osama shot the Mauritanian a threatening look. "It is not the prerogative of Mullah Omar to prevent me from embarking on jihad," he snapped. "These operations will be our gateway to a solid future, one that is of benefit to all."

Several *shura* members, including those who had backed the embassy bombings of 1998, weighed in and, to Osama's amazement, sided with the Mauritanian. "Put it to the vote," they urged.[35]

Osama held up his hand. There would be no more debating, he said. He could see he was losing the room by raising a plan that he would not explain but that could trigger mass casualties and alienate the Taliban. There would be no vote, he said, as the matter had already been decided. He called the meeting to a close.

The Mauritanian left, too upset to talk. Osama had chosen Mokhtar over men of honor who had stood by him for more than a decade.[36]

At the beginning of July 2001, Dr. al-Zawahiri came to see the Mauritanian again. He sat fiddling with his beads before speaking. "Don't resign," he said at last. "Stay the course."

The Mauritanian shook his head. He did not want to be part of an outfit that "threw Afghanistan into the abyss." He had had enough of his Sheikh's grandstanding. Al Qaeda was not *his* property.

One week later, the Mauritanian was summoned to see Osama. When he walked in with his resignation letter, Osama embraced him, glancing down at the paper.

"I hope *this*," he nodded at the note, "isn't your final decision."

The Mauritanian felt his eyes brim and excused himself to wash his face. When he returned, Osama sat stone-faced. "If you are certain about resigning," he said bitterly, "hand it to Dr. Ayman on the way out." As he left, Osama asked him to keep quiet about his decision. The last thing he needed right now was for the *shura*'s already depleted morale to be hit by the news of the Mauritanian's exit.

By mid-August 2001, Kandahar hummed, as crudely coded messages pinged back and forth from Europe and the United States. On August 21, Mokhtar's buck-toothed Yemeni sidekick Ramzi bin al-Shibh, who was in Hamburg, received a message from his "online boyfriend" Saeed al-Ghamdi, a twenty-one-year-old "muscle" hijacker, who was living in Florida.

Al-Ghamdi spelled out the timeline for the operation and confirmed that two military and two civilian targets had been fixed: "The first semester commences in three weeks. Two high schools and two universities . . . This summer will surely be hot . . . 19 certificates for private education and four exams. Regards to the Professor. Goodbye."[37]

On August 30, al-Shibh was woken in the early hours by a call from Boston. "A friend of mine gave me a puzzle and I want you to help me out," said a voice he immediately recognized as Mohamed Atta, his former flat-mate in Hamburg and the lead hijacker.

"Is this a time for puzzles, Mohamed?" he asked sleepily.

Atta persisted: "Two sticks, a dash and cake with a stick down. What is it?"[38]

Al-Shibh feigned indifference in case someone else was listening: "Did you wake me up just to tell me this?"

But he now knew that the date of the operation had been fixed: 11-9, or, in American styling of dates, 9/11.

From then it also had a new code name: Holy Tuesday.

Al-Shibh packed up the Hamburg flat and flew back to Pakistan. Over the border, Osama upped the ante by giving an interview to Saudi MBC TV in which he threatened to launch a bloody operation against the United States: "Islam's victory is coming."

In Washington, President Bush received a highly classified FBI memo warning that it had information Al Qaeda was preparing for "hijackings or other types of attack" on several targets inside the United States, including "federal buildings in New York." He took little action.

In Kandahar, Abu Walid al-Masri, a former Al Jazeera journalist who had been assigned to report on Al Qaeda and then joined the movement as a media adviser, sought out Mullah Omar's closest aides. Osama had signed their death warrants, he feared. "It should be no surprise if we see missiles falling from the skies over our heads at any time," al-Masri warned the Taliban.[39]

October 7, 2001, Kandahar

Osama had an appointment with Mullah Omar, their first face-to-face meeting since 1998 and their first post-9/11 discussion. Everyone expected it to be a heated affair.

The rendezvous was set for after *al-Isha* prayer—the fifth of the five daily prayers—at the Taliban leader's fortified compound to the west of the city. With its watchtowers, twelve-foot-thick walls, and a mural of paradise, it had replaced Mullah Omar's old home, which had been devastated by a suicide bomber in 1999—an attack that had killed several members of Mullah Omar's family, with many believing that Osama had been behind it.[40]

Al-Isha came, and Mullah Omar filed into a small mosque at the northern corner of his compound as Osama's convoy rumbled across the plains toward Kandahar, one hour late but trying to make up time. By the time Omar had finished praying, Osama's vehicles were stuck in the traffic choking the lanes inside the Old City, and he was still several minutes away from the compound.

In Islamabad, Robert Grenier, the CIA's station chief, was watching too, via a live video feed from a drone. At a height of fifty thousand feet, an armed Predator 3034 hovered, the images it relayed showing Omar's guards coming and going. The drone had been there for two hours already, sending feed to U.S. Central Command (CENTCOM) in Florida and to the Combined Air Operations Centre at Prince Sultan Air Base in Saudi Arabia. Bush officials, the CIA, and military officers could not agree on what to do. Civilians were everywhere, and dropping ordnance on a mosque was taboo. Then someone spotted Mullah Omar. He was unmistakable. Leaving the mosque to return to his private quarters, he was accompanied by several male relatives and an armed guard.

"Go."

Two Hellfire missiles streaked down, the bright blossom of the explosion seen by Osama, who was blocked in by traffic, bumper to bumper. As clouds of dust and dirt rained down on the car's windshield, a Yemeni security guard leaped out and, waving his AK-47 around, cleared some space, while Osama's driver booted the vehicle into reverse and took off.

When the smoke cleared, and the picture over the compound regained focus, figures could be seen running in all directions. The shrieks and cries on the radios down below were vacuumed up by U.S. eavesdroppers, who reported that Mullah Omar's son was dead, as well as an uncle, several bodyguards, and "a prized cow."

But Omar was no longer there.

The drone found him again in a Toyota Land Cruiser that was hurtling west toward the Arghandab Mountains. The U.S. military called in F18 Hornets but by the time they had locked on, the Taliban emir was deep inside a cave complex. He sheltered there for an hour while his men commandeered a new vehicle, and in a pause between woof and bark of heavy strikes all around, he headed out again, telling the driver to make for his home district of Sangesar.

President Bush went on live television to announce that war in Afghanistan had begun. "In this conflict," he told the American people, "there is no neutral ground . . . there can be no peace in a world of terror." He predicted that the Islamic emirate would fall within five days.

Hundreds of miles to the northwest, seven covert CIA operatives were already on the ground with orders from Cofer Black, the head of the CIA's Counterterrorism Center, which in the days after 9/11 had geared up to take the lead on the hunt for Al Qaeda. Armed with tracking equipment, and carrying cardboard boxes filled with $3 million in used notes, they had blunt instructions from Black: "I want bin Laden's head shipped back in a box filled with dry ice. I want to be able to show bin Laden's head to the President."[41]

*   *   *

Night One: October 7, 2001

Tomahawk missiles struck targets all over Afghanistan, with long-range bombers flying more than seven thousand miles from Whiteman Air Force Base in Missouri.

Robert Grenier in Islamabad had drawn up the basic war plan two weeks earlier, at CIA chief George Tenet's request. The intelligence components were beefed up with detailed maps gifted by the Iranians and data derived from the French security services that had warned that Pakistani specialist units, commanded by the ISI, were assisting Taliban out in the field.[42] Striking Mullah Omar's bases with overwhelming force was of huge psychological importance, Grenier said. The more pain America could inflict quickly, the more likely it was that the Al Qaeda leader would be cut loose.

8:25 P.M.: Reuters reported three large flashes in the sky twenty-five miles north of Kabul.

Three minutes later, several loud explosions were heard in the city.

In northern Afghanistan, CNN reported "bright flashes of light, one after another."

8:45 P.M.: Eyewitnesses in Kabul reported at least four large explosions, and a black plume of smoke rising.

Ten minutes later, bombs hit Kandahar, close to the House of the Pomegranates. The Mauritanian, who was at work, scrabbled around in the dark to find his sandals. Running home through deserted streets, wondering if he was in the crosshairs of an unseen drone, he rapped on his door, flying into the room. Corralling his family, he listened with them in the dark to the *whump* of American ordnance pounding the Taliban's communications towers, cutting off Radio Shariat.

Bombs fell on Tarnak Qila, destroying the Abu Obaida camp where the 9/11 team had trained.

Far to the north, in the Star Wars camp, Osama's son Ladin lay on his back, watching wide-eyed as antiaircraft rounds arced through a bruised sky. His aunties Khairiah and Seham had retreated into the bomb shelter, where they listened to the chilling whine of something circling above them. At seven thousand feet, bloated gray Spectre gunships flew like a pod of whales, hunting for targets. In a corner of the shelter, Amal sat on her own, breastfeeding her baby.

In a darkened house in Kabul to where Osama had bolted, he was euphoric and supervising an edit. It had taken three "spectaculars," as he described Al Qaeda's attacks, but he had finally drawn the Americans into war. "I want to tell the United States and its people, I swear by God that he who has praised the sky, the United States will not have peace," he said in one clip, sending the completed video off with a courier, who would try to dodge the bombs and reach the Al Jazeera office.

Dr. Ayman al-Zawahiri called the man back. He wanted to add his own sound bite: "A new Islamic epic is under way."

A couple of days later, Osama commissioned another video, calling back into service his accidental spokesman, Sulaiman Abu Ghaith. Wearing a pure white turban and with a Kalashnikov peeping over his left shoulder, a man who had never fired a gun told viewers: "I send this message to America's foreign minister who was sarcastic about what we said, that there are thousands of Muslim youths who are willing to die. Powell and others in the American government know that if Al Qaeda promises to do something, they will do it by the will of Allah."

Behind the bluster, Abu Ghaith was frantic. He had picked up news that Fatima, his wife, had just given birth to their first son in a Kuwaiti hospital.

"This is the last time," he beseeched the Sheikh. He needed to go home.

"Yes," said the Sheikh. "Go whenever you like."[43]

Outside, ordnance thundered.

October 14, 2001, Kandahar

As he cautiously pushed open the front door, dawn percolated into the Mauritanian's home, and he headed out for the Taliban media center. Inside, he found volunteers frantically clearing up papers and files. He had made a decision: to publish his own version of the war and seek permission from Mullah Omar to buy a television. He called his first bulletin Nevir, or "Mobilization." As he contemplated the destruction raining down on Afghanistan, he wondered, bitterly, what Osama was feeling.

The rest of the Al Qaeda leadership was emerging from the rubble. Abu Hafs the Commander, crippled by back pain, had arrived in the city overnight, deputed to assume control of Kandahar's defenses.

The Mauritanian could see he was overwhelmed. What would happen to the Arab families who had followed the Al Qaeda caravan here from Sudan, Pakistan, and the Gulf? Osama had promised to protect them but he was nowhere to be seen.

He spotted some other figures he knew. Media chief Abu Walid al-Masri was on his way to Kandahar's Al Jazeera office. "The number of dead is huge," he told his friend. "Bodies are on the streets, a number of mosques are destroyed." Asked if he had seen Osama, he replied: "I can't sit face to face with him. I am so angry. These idiots have brought about the destruction of the Islamic State."[44]

Only Mokhtar, who flitted about, seemed energized by the chaos.

Giving him a wide berth, the Mauritanian instead sought out Abu Zubaydah, the master of human traffic. Given how many men, women, and children needed to be evacuated, the logistics chief, with his wealth of Pakistani connections, was the most useful man in town right now.

At the bus station, women in burqas wrangled screaming children and gargantuan bags. Everyone had heard how Mullah Omar's family had been whisked out of the city after the strike on his compound. The local branch of the Al Wafa Foundation stepped in. An Islamic welfare nongovernmental organization (NGO), it supplied Al Qaeda families with medicines and treated wounded fighters. Now it began ferrying families to the villages surrounding Kandahar.

Kandahar's resolve was broken on the night of October 17, when the House of the Pomegranates and the offices of the Taliban's Committee for the Propagation of Virtue and the Prevention of Vice both took direct hits, as did several markets, mosques, and hospitals. The Mauritanian and his family narrowly survived a missile strike. He looked out and saw bodies strewn about. He swore to bury them at Kandahar's martyrs' cemetery. Looking up, he watched a U.S. warplane draw a huge white cross in the sky with its contrails. "The Americans are sending a message. Everyone will die unless we give up the Sheikh," he muttered to his wife.[45]

October 20, 2001, Ghazni, Afghanistan

Nursing his snub-nosed Kalashnikov in one hand and a thimble of tea in the other, Osama was busy planning the next stage of battle from the safety of an Al Qaeda guesthouse one hundred miles south of Kabul in Ghazni.[46] Telling everyone that he would lure and then defeat the Americans on the White Mountains just as he had defeated the Soviets at Jaji, he deliberately communicated the same to brothers digging new trenches up in the heights of Tora Bora, knowing the United States would be listening in too.

While he waited for the refortification works to be completed, he recorded another video: one for his private archive and not to be shared. As the camera rolled, he grew irritated by the framing. "Mokhtar!" he shouted out, and the camera jerked to the right. The 9/11 mastermind had also left bloodied Kandahar to fend for itself.

Osama performed a freewheeling monologue, with none of his usual caution. This was a video diary. "We calculated in advance the number of casualties from the enemy, and who would be killed, based on the position of the tower," he said, as his companions, Khaled al-Harbi and Sulaiman Abu Ghaith, giggled.[47] "We calculated that we would hit at least three or four floors at once," he swaggered, while Mokhtar filmed. "I was the most optimistic of them all."

Within days, the war reached Ghazni and the tape was discovered by U.S. Special Forces operatives. British prime minister Tony Blair, who had already committed British aerial support to the U.S. offensive in Afghanistan and would soon send in ground troops too, referred to it in a speech before the House of Commons. "The intelligence material now leaves no doubt whatever of the guilt of bin Laden and his associates," he said.

Everyone who appeared in the video was now damned.

October 23, 2001, Star Wars Camp, Jalalabad, Afghanistan

The camp had filled up with Al Qaeda fighters, everyone readying to move up to Tora Bora. Seventy people had died in Jalalabad on October 10 when a bomb fell on the Sultanpur mosque. Another 120 were blown to pieces when the U.S. bomber returned to drop a second payload on those massing to rescue the casualties. It was time to retreat to the hills.

Children's toys and boxes of pasta fought for space with land mines, grenades, and a cache of biological weapons, which included three hundred vials of sarin gas hidden in an outhouse. Ladin, lying on his back, spotted the planes circling just in time, and everyone retreated to the shelter. In nearby Daruntah training camp at least one hundred people were killed.

At dawn on October 24, Khairiah, Seham, and Amal bin Laden emerged, picking their way between unexploded cluster bomblets as news arrived from their husband, the first they had heard in weeks. The courier was Mokhtar, but instead of passing on news, he came with an order: Sheikh Osama wanted his nine-year-old son at his side.

"He's too young for the battlefield," Khairiah protested.

A tug-of-war began, with Mokhtar wrestling the boy into his custody.

Days later, Ladin was filmed inspecting a downed U.S. helicopter and wielding a handgun. Beside him was older brother Mohammed, aged sixteen, shouldering a rocket launcher, while Hamzah, thirteen, who did not need encouragement, kneeled amid the wreckage reciting a poem praising Mullah Omar as a "symbol of manhood and pride."

Al Qaeda bodyguards were filmed lecturing the boys in broken English that American soldiers were only strong in Hollywood movies. "Their heroes are only mythical—like Rambo," one said. If they came to Afghanistan, they would "end up in pieces like this," he added, pointing to mangled helicopter parts.

Another brandished an automatic rifle inscribed in Arabic, "Death to Bush," while someone off-camera shouted: "Hey, Mokhtar, come see this."

The footage would end up on Al Jazeera and in Syria, where Ladin's mother, Najwa, watched, horrified at the depths to which her husband had sunk. She called Osama's mother, Allia, in Jeddah. She sympathized. Ladin was being indoctrinated into a world of hatred and violence just like his older siblings had been, said Allia. They had to do something.

A brutal scene came into Najwa's head. She recalled the time when Abdul Rahman, her mentally disturbed son, had been caught trying to strangle their pet cats, and how Othman had mercilessly beaten the boy until he had been pulled off. Just a little longer and Othman would have killed him. It wasn't bad genes but her husband's inhumanity—if that was what you called his pathological lack of interest in society. It had rubbed off on all of their children, Najwa believed.

She had to rescue Ladin before it was too late. She longed to wipe the cruel smirk from his face. She had no idea how to do it or how long it might take, but she was determined that one day she would rescue her children. The question she dared not ask herself was what state would they be in by the time she got them back?[48]

In a cave above Khost, Osama was treating Pakistani journalist Hamid Mir to an exclusive interview. He was tense, snapping that they didn't have long. Mir was surprised at his demeanor. He looked gaunt. Using Dr. Ayman al-Zawahiri as a translator, Osama delivered a stark message. "The U.S. loves life. We love death," he said.[49]

*   *   *

November 10, 2001, New York City

General Musharraf put on his best suit and promised the United Nations General Assembly that Pakistan was *against terror*. He took along his new ISI chief, General Ehsan ul-Haq. Formerly the commander of the Peshawar Corps, ul-Haq had spent the first night of the Afghan war staring up at the contrails from the roof of his villa beside Peshawar golf course. With his hooded eyes and aquiline nose, the general was a smooth glider who slipped by silently and gave nothing away. But he thanked God in a quiet way that he was not in Kandahar or Kabul.[50]

On the night of his appointment, October 7, Musharraf had called him at home.

"General Ahmed's gone."

It took him a second or two to realize that Musharraf was announcing another coup: the ISI chief Mahmud Ahmed had been sacked.

"And," Musharraf continued, "I want *you* to replace him."

General ul-Haq feigned surprise, but he had been expecting the call. Rumors about Ahmed's tenure had been roaring around the Pakistan Army's General Headquarters (GHQ) in Rawalpindi for a week after Indian newspapers had published false reports that the spy chief was linked to a $100,000 transfer that had been made into a bank account connected to the lead 9/11 hijacker, Mohamed Atta.[51]

Ul-Haq knew how this game worked. He had played it many times himself. How likely was it that a spy like Ahmed, with a career in counterintelligence and countersurveillance, would have made a mistake so basic? Instead, GHQ had deliberately spun the allegation in the knowledge that it was made up and leaked it to a stooge in India who had then broken the story.

Pakistan and its intelligence service were at a critical juncture, Musharraf noted, and ul-Haq did not disagree. "The U.S. will try to size you up," Musharraf advised, "and I want you to make sure they conclude that a *moderate* has come."

It was as if General ul-Haq could actually hear the dollar bills whirring through his chief's mind.

Musharraf's first substantial meeting with President Bush took place in a private suite in the Waldorf Astoria. Before 9/11, Bush had not even been able to name the Pakistani leader.[52] Now, the dapper, English-speaking general impressed him, and Musharraf was gleeful when he learned that Pakistan would be offered $1 billion in an assortment of aid for supporting

America. As they clinked glasses before an open fire, Bush summed up: "Pakistan is a strong ally and President Musharraf is a strong leader."[53]

Musharraf savored the moment and his foresight.

General ul-Haq spent his first evening in Washington with CIA director George Tenet, Deputy Secretary of State Richard Armitage, and a small retinue of "denominational" analysts and briefers, by which he meant partisan people half his age with one third of his experience who delivered binary lectures on "the links between Al Qaeda, Pakistan, and the Taliban."

Having listened politely, General ul-Haq, a career soldier, interjected with a dose of reality. Pakistan's influence over the Taliban was limited, he said, and "the Taliban and Al Qaeda are not one and the same."

He felt Armitage sizing him up and went for disarming honesty. "Until 9/11, Al Qaeda wasn't a challenge for us," he explained.[54] There was no point concealing that Pakistan had other priorities. "Yes, they'd transited through Pakistan, with everyone coming and going. But they'd not raised a specific threat—*to us.*"

Armitage looked unimpressed, so ul-Haq turned to Tenet, who, he knew, had been charged with restoring confidence in the CIA—just as Musharraf expected ul-Haq to do with the ISI.

"You know," he said, "the [ISI] has lost more in combat than all the stars you have on the wall at Langley. You have to believe us when we say something is not doable."

Tenet nodded.

The following day, ul-Haq was back at CIA headquarters, watching old drone footage of Osama walking across the parade ground at Tarnak Qila.

"Let's take him out," a cocky analyst quipped. "There's nowhere for him to hide."

Ul-Haq doubted that anyone had been listening to him.

November 11, 2001, Jalalabad

Bombs were falling all over the city when Osama unexpectedly arrived with his sons. Seham and Khairiah were ecstatic, murmuring prayers and thanks to the Prophet. But this was not a lingering reunion. Osama urged them to pack immediately. The Northern Alliance was advancing and so everyone was heading for his olive farm in Melawa Valley, the gateway to Tora Bora.

The next day, Osama sent messages to Mokhtar and Abu Zubaydah, who were both in Kandahar. Militants and jihad-minded religious scholars would need to help conceal his family if Al Qaeda was forced to withdraw into Pakistan.[55]

Late that night Osama's convoy snaked through ancient battlefields and war-scarred villages, arriving at Garikhil, to which Ghilzai tribesmen, whose villages straddled the border, had been called to a last-minute *jirga* (meeting). They ate mutton and rice while envelopes filled with U.S. dollars were thrown into their laps and Osama repeated his Jaji speech. If they stood united, they could teach the Americans a lesson, "the same one we taught the Russians."

Four hundred Kalashnikovs were unloaded. The local *malik* (chief) said his men would do what they could, but he found Osama a mixed bag. "Scornful and in a hurry," was his conclusion.[56]

Midnight. Osama's convoy looped back toward the White Mountains, finally reaching the compound in the foothills where his family was waiting. They would be heading in different directions, he revealed. Only sons Othman and Mohammed would remain with him.

Hamzah, who had grown accustomed to being with his father's group, shook his head. "I want to be beside you, Father," he said, tears of anger forming. "I wish to fight the infidels with you." Osama refused. The situation was deteriorating by the hour, so they should leave right away. Hamzah, Khalid, and Ladin would have to take care of the women and children, although as the oldest male family member, older brother Saad would nominally lead the convoy, which also consisted of in-laws and grandchildren.

But Saad's autism made that role a burdensome one and so Osama gifted the convoy his most trusted driver, Salim Hamdan, and a Saudi fighter who was also his son-in-law—married to daughter Fatima. This man, who Osama trusted, would negotiate with smugglers to take the family across into Pakistan.[57]

Osama sought out his soul mate Khairiah, confiding in her the news of a Taliban collapse in Kabul. "Only a few remain steadfast," he complained. "The rest surrendered or fled like ducklings before they even encountered the enemy." He apologized for making her follow a path fraught with dangers. "I want you to know that I will remain in the land of jihad until God will bring us together in this world or the hereafter, and that will suffice," he said, rehearsing his last will and testament.

He approached Amal and kissed baby Safiyah, before turning to Seham. Please discourage the children from joining this jihad, he said. "And don't re-marry."

He removed Najwa's ring from his finger and gave it to their daughter Iman. "In case we don't meet again in this world," he said.

Back outside, he drew three strings of prayer beads from his pocket, handing one each to Khalid, Hamzah, and Ladin. "Stay strong and true to Islam," he said.

Then, getting into a pickup, he set off, following a narrow streambed that entered a deep gorge leading to Tora Bora. Although the watching children willed him to look back and wave, he did not turn around.[58]

Behind he had left suitcases containing clothes and gold coins. Dressed as Afghan nomads, they would travel through the night and attempt to cross into Pakistan at a remote checkpoint using documents provided by the Sudanese authorities during the time they lived there. Their old Saudi passports were sealed in brown envelopes and hidden away.

As their bus pulled away from the olive grove, Hamzah turned and, looking out of the back window, whispered to his mother: "It is as if we have pulled out our livers and left them there."[59]

November 15, 2001, Kandahar

Leaflets rained down on Ramadan Eve, dropped by U.S. planes and promising substantial rewards for information about Al Qaeda or Taliban leaders. Arabs were being turned over willy-nilly to the Americans and news was spreading fast of the fall of Kabul. Inside Al Qaeda's billet in the city center, Abu Hafs the Commander was laid up in bed being attended to by Osama's personal physician, Dr. Amir Aziz, who had traveled all the way from Lahore to treat him.

The Mauritanian ran in, imploring the Commander to shift locations. "Too many brothers surround you," he warned, as they picked over a poor man's dinner of stale bread and cheese. The noisy comings and goings would have already attracted the attention of the watchers above.

The Commander laughed. His old friend was *not* a fighter and tended to be overly paranoid. He would be fine. They bade farewell after *al-Isha* prayer.[60]

At dawn, two Hellfire missiles struck the building. American analysts studying the feed saw "bodies cartwheeling into the air." When they heard the chatter from Arab rescuers, they called Robert Grenier in Islamabad. One name stood out from the tangle of eavesdropped communications. Abu Hafs the Commander, a man who had stood at Osama bin Laden's side for more than a decade, plotting the 1998 Africa embassy attacks, the USS *Cole* attack, and 9/11, was dead. A note was dispatched to George Tenet and President Bush. America had just claimed a real Al Qaeda scalp.[61]

The first Al Qaeda leader to reach the scene was Abu Hafs's deputy, Saif al-Adel, a sinewy Egyptian "lifer" whose boyish good looks disguised a dangerous cold streak.

Saif had been with Abu Hafs and Osama since the Soviet war, working as chief of security in Sudan and returning with them to Tora Bora in 1996. In Kandahar, he had run the House of the Martyrs, where suicide bombers were bullied into submission using psychology, isolation, and brute force. He had also headed up the Al Qaeda "special operations committee" that conducted chemical and biological warfare experiments, a post no one volunteered for as the self-taught technicians were often maimed by accidental explosions or fell sick in the laboratory, where safety measures for working with toxic poisons were barely understood.[62]

Saif had always lived a martial existence, serving first as a colonel in Egyptian Special Forces before joining those who had plotted the assassination of President Anwar Sadat in 1981. Afterward, he had transferred his loyalties to Dr. al-Zawahiri's Egyptian Islamic Jihad.

Once ensconced in Al Qaeda, he chose a *kunya* that meant Sword of Islam.[63] A central role in planning the East Africa embassies operation followed, ensuring his high standing inside the organization. "I have never liked reading, writing, or rhetoric," he taunted his friend Mahfouz the Mauritanian, who had presided over his wedding inside a cave in Tora Bora in 1997. Back then, there had been no bride because her father had ordered that she remain in the relative safety of Peshawar and so in common with most jihad weddings, a fellow mujahid had stood in as a proxy.[64] But Saif had been blessed with the presence of one special guest personally invited by the Mauritanian: Afghanistan's most feared warlord and an ISI stooge, Jalaluddin Haqqani.

Now, Saif picked through the rubble as American planes buzzed the sky above the house. He found Abu Hafs's body quickly and sat down beside it. When the Mauritanian came by a few minutes later, he hauled Saif up. "I have come to bury the dead," he told his friend. "You rest now."

Seventeen bodies were ferried to the martyrs' cemetery, including three from the Mauritanian's hometown. He returned to see Saif later that afternoon. "We did not bathe them," he told him, following the custom with martyrs, "we did not pray on their bodies, and we buried them with their clothes on." Abu Hafs had gone to his grave "smiling as if he was praising God for his martyrdom."

That night the two caught up over the breaking-the-fast *iftar* meal, which took place after sundown. The meal was tempered by the Mauritanian's irritation that Saif had brought along a guest, someone Mahfouz disrespected and thought of as a blunt blade.

Abu Musab al-Zarqawi, Saif's "loathsome" Jordanian protégé, had arrived in Afghanistan in 1999 and had been trying to inveigle his way into Al Qaeda's inner circle ever since. Before the U.S. war started, he had rubbed everyone in Afghanistan the wrong way, delivering unasked-for critiques lambasting Al Qaeda for being "insufficiently fierce."[65] Everything about him was wrong as far as the Mauritanian was concerned, such as the fact that he had just come out of jail in Amman, having served five years of a fifteen-year sentence, let out ten years early on a royal amnesty that could also have been a cover story disguising the fact that the prisoner had been turned and was now working for Jordanian intelligence.

In truth, Zarqawi was a former street fighter and a drying-out drunk, a thug who had once been known in his native town of Zarqa, outside Amman, as the "green man" in reference to ugly self-inflicted tattoos. Scars on his hands and forearms showed where he had carved them off after discovering religion under the guidance of a former carpet salesman turned influential Salafi cleric, Abu Muhammad al-Maqdisi. Zarqawi and the Palestinian-born scholar had shared a cellblock in prison.

Under Maqdisi's guidance, Zarqawi had chosen as his *kunya*, Abu Musab, a name taken from one of the Prophet's warriors, Musab bin Umayer, who was honored as the patron saint of suicide bombers.[66] A silent man in his youth, according to those who remembered him in Zarqa, he began to spout half-baked, bar-stool jurisprudence, bandying about shoddy interpretations of the Koran, suggesting decapitation was to be encouraged and that "terror" in the name of Islam was a prerequisite of jihad.[67] The deadliest enemies of all were Shias, who he regarded as "servants of the Antichrist." "End of days" predictions contained in one esoteric and hotly debated text, Naeem bin Hammad's *Book of Tribulations*, particularly fascinated him as he dwelled on everything apocalyptic. Setting himself up as a modern day Islamic crusader, Zarqawi wanted to foment revolution across the Fertile Crescent of the Middle East, where many such prophecies located the final battle. The collection of hadiths on which he based his vision had been written down in the ninth century and were popular with the masses, although the Muslim elite scorned them.

"Ignorant, inarticulate, and rank." That was the Mauritanian's verdict on Zarqawi.

The hatred was mutual. Zarqawi liked to describe religious scholars as being "breastfed [on] the milk of defeat." People like the Mauritanian disguised their cowardice with "the cloak of jurisprudence and embroidered it with the clothes of wisdom," he said.

Before 9/11, the Mauritanian had tried to distance Al Qaeda from sleazy Zarqawi—taking up the matter with Osama, who, while mistrusting Zarqawi's lack of education, thought his ferocity and access to Middle Eastern mujahideen might prove useful. Saif felt the same, recommending they support Zarqawi as he would come good in time. He should be given a test somewhere far enough away for it not to impact Al Qaeda Central or Osama should he turn out to be a Jordanian intelligence asset after all.

In 2000 and with Osama's blessing, Saif had packed Zarqawi off to Herat in western Afghanistan with $5,000 to "set up a training camp."[68] "An Al Qaeda offshoot," as Zarqawi boasted the camp attracted Salafists from Jordan, Palestine, Turkey, Syria, Iraq, and Lebanon. Once established in Herat, he also shipped in his own family from Zarqa, including his beautiful Palestinian wife, who had stunning green eyes and had married him when she was just thirteen. His second wife, a Jordanian woman, and several children came too.

Zarqawi had been delighted when Abu Muhammad al-Maqdisi's brother Salahuddin agreed to join the Herat group. Now Zarqawi had scholarship to back him as well as brute force. "Osama gave me five thousand dollars and told me to do what I will," he bragged. "And I am creating something deadly."

The rumor that returned from Herat was that Zarqawi had taken to his task with gusto, and the only criticisms were related not to loyalty or security but to decency. He recruited brutal men in his own image, many of them from his hometown of Zarqa, the Jordanian preferring killers and brawlers who like him had dropped out of school early and were eager to persecute Shias and defend the Palestinian cause. His sidekick was a semiliterate young Jordanian thug who went by the name of Iyad al-Toubasi, and who had once been a ladies' hairdresser. His deputy, Khalid al-Aruri, was a childhood friend and was married to one of Zarqawi's three sisters, a woman called Alia.

Now, in the wake of Abu Hafs the Commander's death on November 16, the Mauritanian tried once again to convince Saif that Zarqawi was a liability. But Saif would not have it.[69] "His fighters from Herat will defend Kandahar," he said. Zarqawi had brought a convoy of several hundred vehicles from Herat, filled with fighters ready to take on American forces.[70] Hairdresser Iyad al-Toubasi, deputy Khalid al-Aruri, and Maqdisi's brother Salahuddin were among them.

Depleted Al Qaeda could not afford to turn them away.

Osama was in the White Mountains when he heard the news of Abu Hafs's death. He sent a courier down with a taped eulogy but no orders as to what to do with the Al Qaeda women and children still pooling in Kandahar.

Sensing that the situation was critical, the rest of the *shura* converged on the Taliban media office. To the Mauritanian's annoyance, Mokhtar and Zarqawi came along, too. At the start of their discussion, Al-Tayyib Agha, personal secretary to Mullah Omar, let rip, furious that hundreds of Arab families had become sitting ducks. "We don't want to spill more blood, and we should help the families leave," he said.

Mokhtar, who was in mourning for his nephew Moaz bin Attash, who had been killed alongside Abu Hafs, disagreed. The Taliban had fled Kabul, but Al Qaeda was not running away.

When the Mauritanian pointed out that Mokhtar was not in Al Qaeda, Zarqawi, who was also not on the outfit's *shura*, piped up in support of him. His forces had not come all this way just to capitulate. They were staying to fight.

Abu Zubaydah, the planning chief, felt the same. "I swear to God I wish for martyrdom, even though I don't want to see the Americans rejoice, having killed one of the Mujahidin," he wrote in his diary, which he still somehow found time to update almost daily. "I wish to see America's fall and destruction . . . I wish to torture and kill them myself with a knife."

They needed to organize. Zarqawi's forces would relocate to Tora Bora, where Osama needed reinforcements, while Saif was appointed as interim military commander of Al Qaeda operations down on the plains. He and the Mauritanian left to search for sensitive documents in the ruins of Abu Hafs's home.

Out in the street, they heard a rending and screeching sound. Looking up, they saw a missile race over their heads and smash into the Taliban building they had just exited. One of Zarqawi's fighters fiddling with his Thuraya satellite phone during the meeting had enabled the Americans to lock on.

They charged back. Was everyone inside dead? As the dust settled, ghostlike bloodied faces began to emerge.

"I came to and the dirt was all over me," wrote Zubaydah. "I stood up and felt like I was dying."

"I am here, I am alive, help me!" Saif's protégé Zarqawi screamed out from under the rubble. He was trapped under a beam and had broken several ribs, which would have to be strapped before he set out for Tora Bora.

When all of the fighters were finally accounted for, having been hauled out of the rubble, it was, Zubaydah wrote, as if they "had come out of the grave."[71]

November 18, 2001, Logar Province, Afghanistan

Dr. Ayman al-Zawahiri's wife, Azza, banged on the door of an abandoned orphanage with five children in tow. She was filthy and delirious, according to the Arab families who were hiding there and took her in. She had been walking for days since becoming caught up in the Taliban retreat from Kabul. Despite sub-zero temperatures, she was barefoot and carried her youngest daughter, Aisha, aged four, who had Down syndrome and wore little more than a dirty diaper.

When she came to her senses, Azza brought worrying news. The Northern Alliance was advancing south of Kabul, and fleeing Taliban fighters she had met along the way had advised against staying in Logar, suggesting she head down to the Haqqani stronghold of Khost.

After cleaning up, Azza joined more refugees, who boarded pickups that clung to the path of dry riverbeds and dirt tracks through a night criss-crossed by laser-like tracers.

By the time they reached the halfway point at Gardez, Aisha was vomiting and suffering from diarrhea. Telling the others to go on without her, Azza sought sanctuary in a house, where she discovered Arab families she recognized from the old days in Peshawar. They stayed up late to break the Ramadan fast.

Azza's eldest daughter, Fatima, first heard the sound of aircraft. "Mother!" she called out, as explosive claps broke over them, their building suddenly imploding, with chunks of masonry and beams falling on top of them.

Fatima came to and, freeing her legs and hands, scrambled outside into the freezing dark. Unable to shine a light, lest the planes return, she was joined by other children who frantically dug through the rubble with their hands. They could hear pitiful cries from beneath the mound. It was Fatima's mother, brother, and sister. She dug until dawn, when the sounds stopped. Finally, she found her sister Aisha, who was fatally wounded. Her mother and her brother, Mohammed—Dr. al-Zawahiri's only son— remained entombed.[72]

November 19, 2001, Kandahar

The rumble of bombs woke Saif al-Adel. He had fallen asleep after sharing a frugal *iftar* meal with five companions, and now the first thing that came to him was the image of his wife and children, who were trapped in occupied Kabul.

Saif roused his fellow sleepers. "We should gather our things and leave immediately," he whispered, just as he heard another *whump*.[73]

Calling around on his old landline, which miraculously still worked, he learned that the Al Wafa charity compound, in the northeastern suburbs, had suffered a direct hit. In the past week, Al Qaeda fighters had moved in, hiding among the refugee families, and the U.S. eavesdroppers had picked up on their chatter.

Saif offered to help but was told to stay put. "It's not *safe*," a man screamed. "We are evacuating."

Saif suggested a plan. "Send the women and children to Panjwai," he said, referring to a village twelve miles west of Kandahar. Dozens of Arab families had already gone there. "I will ring ahead and tell them you are coming."

A missile screamed overhead and exploded at the end of the street. Perhaps they had another five minutes before the next one landed, with greater accuracy, Saif calculated. "Run!" he urged. They reached a sandbagged position just as his house took a direct hit. He waited for the dust to settle, and then, poking his head out, spotted an abandoned taxi. After sparking the ignition, they drove through deserted streets to Mirwais Hospital. He toured the brimming corridors and wards, surveying the hundreds of injured women and children, accounting for the dead and dying, trying to retain numbers in his head so he could report later to Dr. al-Zawahiri, who was keeping the official tally.

When Saif was finished, he drove back to the sandbagged position with a heavy heart, only for the radio to screech out a message. "The dogs machine gunned us and killed the women," a male voice shrieked over the unmistakable whine of helicopter rotors.

"Where are you?" Saif asked.

"On the Panjwai Road," the man said, explaining that he had led survivors out of the Al Wafa compound, as Saif had instructed, trailed by a U.S. helicopter.

"I am on my way to you," Saif said, calling the men around him to get back into the taxi.

As they drove out of the city, he radioed ahead to the safe house in Panjwai. Had anyone made it through? "No one has come," he was told. The village was also under attack. Several families had fled in four Toyota Corolla station wagons back toward the city, as the Northern Alliance was almost upon them.

Saif reached the bridge over the Arghandab River, three miles east of Panjwai, within the hour. The first thing he saw was the abandoned Corollas. They had met vehicles exiting the city and the drivers had got out to discuss where else they could go. As Saif got nearer, he spotted a bloody trail of human remains, mostly women and children. Some had died hiding behind rocks. One vehicle had toppled into a canyon. Under the collapsed bridge was an unidentifiable mound of bodies: a missile had struck women and children who had sheltered there.

Without caring who might be listening in, Saif called Abu Zubaydah and the Mauritanian to help him bury the victims: "Please come. *Now.*"

The Mauritanian was stunned by what he saw. "It was a massacre," he told his wife.[74] The thought of Arab terror had driven him to warn Osama there could be no justification in Islam for 9/11. Now all he could see were the Arab victims of American terror and he felt a terrible fury. "We need the world to hear the truth."

On the journey back from the Panjwai Bridge slaughter, the Mauritanian decided to end his self-imposed silence and seek out any journalists left in Kandahar. His wife insisted on cleaning him up first. "Your turban is covered in blood." She used the last teapot of water in the house to damp it down and wring it out as he fretted over how to dry it. They had an iron but no power to heat it. "Hurry, I can't miss them," he urged.

Prowling the streets, he caught hold of an Al Jazeera correspondent and let rip as soon as the camera began to roll.

"You have to broadcast these horrible pictures . . . of the children killed in their mothers' arms; you broadcast pictures of the ruined mosques and the charred Korans inside them; you broadcast pictures of the villages destroyed along with all their residents. These are the results of the American indiscriminate bombing so far."[75]

But Al Qaeda was far from finished, he raged, and "the ranks are still united." The U.S. bombs had done nothing but harden Al Qaeda's resolve. "I cannot conceal the fact that we here in Afghanistan . . . could not contain our joy when we saw America taste, for one day, what the Islamic people have been swallowing every day—for decades," he fumed. The 9/11 attacks "shoved America's nose into the earth and struck it with lightning."

When the Al Jazeera reporter informed him that his name was on a list of the twenty-two most wanted in connection with those attacks, the Mauritanian smiled. To be classified as America's enemy was "a medal of honor." As images of the incinerated and strafed bodies came back to him, careless, angry words tumbled out: "One of the acts of grace of this generation is to kill Americans; to incite to the killing; to fight jihad— full force." He stared darkly into the camera: "I and my brothers in the Al-Qaeda organization . . . swore an oath to carry out the mission. We obey Allah and one of the most binding commandments for our generation is jihad. And fighting Americans . . . We are lying in wait for them, Allah willing . . ."[76]

He was only the second Al Qaeda leader to give a public interview since 9/11, and his words reverberated around the world.

* * *

November 25, 2001, Tora Bora

Abu Musab al-Zarqawi and his fighters reached Osama high up in the White Mountains, exhausted from the climb and carrying the extra baggage of distressing news. The bin Laden family convoy had been ambushed at the border. Like so many other Arabs, their driver had been hog-tied with electrical wire and turned over to the Americans for a $5,000 bounty, while their chaperone, Osama's autistic son Saad, and his brother-in-law, the Saudi husband of Osama's daughter Fatima, were "missing, presumed dead."

Horrified, Osama sent a courier back down to Kandahar as he set Zarqawi and his men to work fortifying bunkers. The Jordanian hardman was still far from full strength. Now, he lay on his side in a cot inside the lip of a cave, directing his deputies, Iyad al-Toubasi and Khalid al-Aruri, and corralling the fighters, who took up position high in the cliff faces, hefted sandbags, shored up cave walls, and stockpiled munitions and weapons for the coming showdown.

In Kandahar, everyone had pitched in to find Osama's three wives, ten children, three daughters-in-law, and three grandchildren, whose whereabouts following the ambush were unknown. But chaos was overwhelming the alleys and lanes, heightened by the CIA's hacking of Radio Shariat's frequencies so that the airways were filled with Pashtun-speaking turncoats exhorting Afghan citizens to give up Arabs in exchange for thousand-dollar rewards.

Inside one of the last Al Qaeda safe houses, 9/11 architect Mokhtar, planner Abu Zubaydah, military commander Saif al-Adel, and the Mauritanian cleric made a decision to try and send all remaining Arab families to Pakistan.

However, the disheartening news about Sheikh Osama's family complicated everything. Which route was safest? They, too, would have no choice but to rely on tribal smugglers who plied arms and drugs across the border—criminals and thugs whom nobody trusted and who were as likely to betray their charges as assist them.

Saif asked Mokhtar to commandeer taxis, motorbikes, minivans, vegetable trucks, pickups, and even some vintage VW campers left over from Afghanistan's distant days on the hashish trail. Abu Zubaydah began doing what he did best: organizing reception committees on the other side of the border.

Those who made it across would be guided by Lashkar-e-Taiba, the ISI-backed Army of the Pure, deep inside Pakistan. This group and many others like it represented one of Pakistan's most enduring contradictions—a state-sponsored Islamist terror network that shared a public platform with senior generals and intelligence chiefs who made vociferous denials of any connections between them.

Lashkar-e-Taiba had come into being in 1990, when out-of-work mujahideen fighters who had previously fought on behalf of the CIA and ISI in Afghanistan were redirected to lead Pakistan's unofficial military efforts to separate Kashmir from India. Over the years, proxy armies such as Lashkar-e-Taiba had been trained, armed, and financially supported by the ISI, which managed these sensitive relations through S-Wing, its semiautonomous department. It was filled with agents who were inseparable from their clients in outlook and appearance, some of whom claimed to be retired from government service, all of them difficult to keep accountable (enabling plausible deniability on the part of the ISI director general).

In contrast, Lashkar-e-Taiba openly fund-raised and paraded, maintaining a huge training complex and headquarters—at Muridke outside the cosmopolitan city of Lahore—that was run with great discipline and at some cost. The group was led by Hafiz Saeed, an overbearing red-bearded mullah who underlined his outfit's proximity to Pakistan's military elite by giving fiery speeches alongside his close friend General Hamid Gul, the former director general of the ISI.

The ISI's patronage ensured Lashkar-e-Taiba's tendrils were spread all over the Islamic Republic of Pakistan, its training camps pockmarking the Tribal Areas on the Pakistan side of the Sulaiman mountain range. And Lashkar-e-Taiba was not alone. Among the myriad other groups funded and coached by ISI agents was Jaish-e-Mohammed, the Army of Mohammed, which was based in the Pakistan-administered portion of Kashmir and now offered to help too.

Jaish-e-Mohammed had risen to notoriety after kidnapping Western backpackers in India in 1994 and 1995 (one of whom it beheaded). It mainly concentrated its resources on fighting Indian troops in the Indian sector of divided Kashmir, but it also struck at targets all over the subcontinent, brutally targeting Muslims from other sects inside Pakistan, including Shias and Ahmadis. Its founder, cleric Masood Azhar, a fat Punjabi with a reedy voice from Bahawalpur, had pledged assistance to Osama in December 1999 after being released from an Indian jail in exchange for passengers on a hijacked Indian Airlines jet that had been forced down at Kandahar airport, within sight of Tarnak Qila.

Both Lashkar-e-Taiba and Jaish-e-Mohammed had networks of safe houses and agents across Pakistan's seven tribal agencies. In these autonomous areas established by the British during the nineteenth century, the laws of Pakistan did not apply. They were perfect places for Al Qaeda fighters to go to ground.

As Abu Zubaydah worked the phones, convoys of vehicles rumbled out of Kandahar like ragged bunting, heading two hours north to a village where the smugglers were waiting. Three weeks earlier, they had been charging $250 per person, but now they asked four times as much.

At the village, the Mauritanian helped his wife and children into the back of a truck that would eventually head back down Highway 4 to Spin Boldak and the border crossing at Chaman.[77] Osama's family had vanished, Saif's was trapped in occupied Kabul, and Dr. al-Zawahiri, who had lost touch with his wife, Azza, was telling everyone that they had made it over to Pakistan—when he only *hoped* that this was true.

Returning alone to Kandahar, with images of his frightened children's faces etched on his mind, the Mauritanian suspected he might never see them again. For four agonizing days he heard nothing more. He took shelter alongside Saif al-Adel at Kandahar airport, enduring an aerial bombardment so furious that it felt as if the earth was broken.

A courier finally found them, between strikes. He was shaken and carried terrible news. Tribal gangs had switched sides, blocked the Spin Boldak road, and kidnapped several Arab families. Their identities were not yet known. The Mauritanian hoped his wife had followed his suggestion. *Cross at the official border point using your fake Sudanese passports. If that fails, cut on foot through the mountains toward Balochistan.*[78]

But even if they had survived the border kidnappers, how would they cope in the heights that were now bursting with snow?

November 29, 2001, Jalalabad

Muscle-heavy U.S. Navy SEALs crowded around a TV set in the Spin Ghar Hotel to hear U.S. vice president Dick Cheney tell an interviewer that he believed the Al Qaeda leader was trapped in Tora Bora. "He's got a large number of fighters with him probably, a fairly secure personal security force that he has some degree of confidence in, and he'll have to try to leave, that is, he may depart for other territory, but that's not quite as easy as it would have been a few months ago." A *hoo-rah* went up.

In recent days, as it became obvious to everyone in the Bush White House that Tora Bora was to be the scene of the final showdown, Jalalabad had filled up with reporters, CIA operatives, hulking Army Rangers, and Delta Force operatives, their commanders bedding in and seeking alliances with Afghan warlords still loyal to the Taliban's main enemy, the Northern Alliance. When the time came to attack, the plan was for the Afghans to lead the way so as to have as few American boots on the ground as possible.

On a map, it was little more than a mile from the foothills of the White Mountains to the first tier of Al Qaeda caves, but the snow was thick, the slopes were steep, and, for even the fittest Afghan fighters, it was an icy three-hour climb. Despite these disadvantages, Bush and his military commander, General Tommy Franks, were confident that spending $70 million on ground support backed up by U.S. airpower would win them one of the biggest "bargains in history."

From his vantage point in Islamabad, the CIA station chief Robert Grenier hoped they were right, but all of his years in a greasy business that—like rally driving—saw traction come and go told him not to bank on it.

Overheads, radio intercepts, and interrogations all pointed to a significant number of jihadis dug in on ragged peaks that topped fifteen thousand feet and ran along an east-west axis, defining a portion of the Durand Line that the British had demarcated in 1893.

Grenier knew this area incorporated some of the most inhospitable terrain in the world, especially around Tora Bora where Osama, presumably, had superior knowledge. The CIA maps showed that over the years the area had been modified by tunnel rats who had hacked into the quartz and feldspar. Some caverns were supposedly 350 feet deep and fitted with ventilation exhausts, secret exits, and booby-trapped entrances—and even a hydroelectric power plant.[79]

Locked inside the CIA station, Grenier studied large-scale American flight charts that had been drawn up at the height of the Cold War. He had given some to ISI analytic chief General Javed Alam Khan in the days when they had been living in each other's laps, as the ISI's own maps predated the 1947 partition of India and Pakistan. Without consistent satellite time, other than what was secretly lent them by the Chinese, the ISI, the Pakistan

Army, and the Frontier Corps, a paramilitary force staffed by tribal recruits, were reliant on Pashtun guides and Colonial-era gazetteers to hunt and kill along the border. "The blind leading the blind."

Studying the maps now, Grenier could see something disturbing. As U.S. forces converged on Jalalabad, if Osama's fighters were pressed they were likely to spill across the snow line and vanish into Pakistan's Tribal Areas.

He knew that this deeply conservative region was not governed by Islamabad but through tribal customs that demanded residents lend protection to any guests irrespective of the situation. Here an entire army could arrive and vanish under the silk handkerchief called Pashtunwali, an ancient system of laws and ethical codes that bound villagers together.

They had to act. He called on General Khan.

Officially, homegrown paramilitary units raised from Pashtun villages maintained security in the tribal belt, Khan explained. They were led on and off by regular officers from the army and the Frontier Corps. They were well disciplined and could be counted on to stand and fight, unless "a fortuitous war with India" forced the command to reassign all of the armed forces, he joked.[80]

But when Grenier asked to see the snow line for himself, Khan balked. Taking a senior CIA officer on Pakistan's sensitive western frontier was unthinkable.

Or was it? After Grenier reminded the counterterrorism tsar of Musharraf's pledge to assist America unconditionally, Khan sought permissions from his superiors. "Okay. Let's make an inspection," he finally said, wondering how much the top brass would extract from the United States in return.[81]

November 29, 2001, Parachinar, Pakistan

A small stone garrison established by the British on a flat, tree-lined expanse at the northwestern end of the Kurram Valley was fading into shadow when they entered at sunset, the glowering jagged peaks of the White Mountains turning bloodred. The Pakistani commanding officer ushered them into a mess replete with dusty memorabilia and gilt-rimmed honors boards, where he gave them a huge dinner before leaving them to play a frame of billiards in a dark, wood-paneled games room that took the station chief "back to a time of Kipling."

The following morning a briefing reminded Grenier of how the United States might still lose. He could now see that only the thinnest of uniformed lines stretched the length of the White Mountains, given that this sector was patrolled by the Kurram Militia, an anemic unit of the Frontier Corps.

From Peiwar Kotal—a mountain pass at the western end, where Major General Sir Frederick Roberts's rampant forces had struck in 1878, seizing a gateway to Kabul during the Second Afghan War—to Tirah Valley in Khyber Agency to the east, underpaid, poorly armed levies were holding the line. It was impossible to seal off the area, let alone patrol it.

Grenier asked Khan what was needed to bolster security. The general, who had previously joked he was like Rasputin, made a bid: air and ground mobility for one Pakistani brigade of several thousand soldiers kitted out with night-vision equipment and secure communications. "That might work," he said.

Grenier nodded.

As always when it came to dealing with the Pakistanis, hard cash won the day.

December 3, 2001, Tora Bora

Caves meant many things to Osama. Key among them, aside from thick, bomb-resistant walls and their cool shade in scorching summer, was their symbolic value. The Prophet had first encountered the Angel Gabriel in a cave in Mecca, and Osama once astonished the Mauritanian by telling him that his—Osama's—presence in Tora Bora gave credence to the oft-repeated story that he was the Mahdi (Islam's messiah). "A cave is the last pure place on this earth," Osama had said to the Mauritanian, somewhere to retreat from society.

When he and his sons had lived at Tora Bora in 1996, he had taken them on exhausting treks to the Pakistan border, telling them to memorize every rock, natural stream, and fork in the path, drilling into them the notion that one day their lives might depend upon it.

Now, as mujahideen scrambled up the slopes and into grave-like trenches, Osama took out his Yaesu VHF radio set, reminding anyone listening of the great victory at Jaji. "The trench is your gateway to heaven," he declared, ordering fighters to observe the Ramadan fast even in the heat of battle. At his side were sons Othman and Mohammed; his deputy Dr. al-Zawahiri; and his accidental spokesman, Sulaiman Abu Ghaith, who had still not managed to break away. Zarqawi's men were bedded in all around the peaks. Tough it out, the Jordanian ordered. The Americans were too weak and feckless to ever reach the summit.

Prowling the snow line, the gathered Al Qaeda forces were led by Afghan strongman Dr. Amin al-Haq, who was the former Taliban commander of Jalalabad, and Ibn Sheikh al-Libi, a Libyan commander who had been with Osama from the start, opening Khaldan, one of the first mujahideen training camps set up with CIA cash during the 1980s and running it in the early 1990s with the assistance of Abu Zubaydah.[82] In contrast to Zarqawi, whose bravado was obvious, both al-Haq and Ibn Sheikh were deeply worried about the setup. Despite the envelopes stuffed with U.S. dollars, a hasty feast hosted for tribal leaders in Jalalabad shortly before Kabul had fallen, and Kalashnikovs handed out to local tribal militias, Al Qaeda was still incapable of fighting a long campaign. Supply lines could be cut easily and they would never survive a siege, they warned Osama. But he did not listen.

Over the border in Pakistan, Grenier, who was by now back in his office at the U.S. embassy, heard that the U.S. side had caught a break. Local men Osama had employed to build up the mountain complex had been bought up by the CIA to act as guides, leading targeting and reconnaissance specialists toward a ridgeline from which they could look directly into the Melawa Valley and Al Qaeda's forward operating base.

Astonished, Grenier listened to field reports that described Osama's command posts, vehicles, and stone outbuildings. Dozens of Al Qaeda fighters were spotted in machine-gun nests and antiaircraft positions that had been built into the vertiginous cliffs.

The reconnaissance and targeting mission flashed coordinates back to CENTCOM, and the first missiles screeched in. Grenier followed cables about the buildup anxiously, and by the afternoon he could see from the reports that bombers and jets crisscrossed the cloudless sky above Tora Bora, filling the valley with vapors and smoke. Above them, inside his subterranean operations center, Osama called on his men to be patient, while he sipped tea and ate dates.[83]

On the Pakistan side, six Pakistan Army battalions, freshly kitted out with U.S. matériel, were climbing into position high above Parachinar under the command of Lieutenant General Ali Jan Aurakzai, the recalcitrant commander of Pakistan's IX Corps. A Pashtun from the Orakzai tribal agency, the general had overall responsibility for the entire northwest of

Pakistan. His six thousand men ascended, hand over fist, toward Al Qaeda positions.[84]

December 4, 2001, Melawa Valley, Afghanistan

A U.S. Delta Force squadron, bolstered by Afghan irregulars, had overrun Al Qaeda's Melawa garrison at the foot of the climb up to Tora Bora. Backed up by airpower, the squadron had overcome the base more quickly than anyone had expected. The operators radioed back details of olive groves strewn with dismembered bodies. "Even the trees have been upended." Nothing could have survived the firestorm that hit this place. Afghan scavengers scurried about offering to sell videotapes, notebooks, and even cadavers—for $300 apiece.

Combing for pocket litter, the Delta specialists recovered a still-working Yaesu handset. Cupping it to his ear, one Arab-speaking operative wondered if the soft male voice he could hear giving instructions was that of Osama bin Laden. "Bring the food!" he urged. "Kill the Americans!"

Two more days of round-the-clock bombing followed as U.S. forces tried to climb higher and break open Al Qaeda's positions with laser-guided bunker busters and earth-penetrating Joint Direct Attack Munitions (JDAMs), which were bombs made smarter by being strapped into GPS cradles. Although CIA specialists and Delta operatives could see nothing, radio intercepts suggested they were having an impact up above.

"Call the doctor!" a mujahid screamed in Arabic. "Doctor. Doctor. Call the doctor as soon as possible."[85]

"Danger. More planes!" another shouted. "Watch out! Back to the caves!"

The bombs continued to fall. "Trapped inside," a voice announced. "Falling rock. Beware."

On December 7, Northern Alliance fighters allied to the United States broke into one passage blocked by a landslide and found dozens of bodies trapped beneath huge jagged boulders—Afghanis, Pakistanis, Yemenis, Jordanians, and Palestinians.

Believing that a retreat into Pakistan was now imminent, the CIA's Robert Grenier, who was watching events unfold from Islamabad, consulted his charts and sent a formal request for a battalion of U.S. Army Rangers to be dropped into position behind the Al Qaeda lines, just to make sure the blocking job was done right.[86]

General Tommy Franks refused. They were not going to make the same mistake as the Soviets, he said, deploying huge numbers of U.S. forces that could be drawn into a mountaintop trap. The Pakistanis would do the job for them, acting as the catcher on the high slopes and a beater down in the valley of Parachinar. Lieutenant General Aurakzai had their back. His forward units had reached thirteen thousand feet. Osama was surrounded.

Grenier doubted anyone could secure the passes out of the White Mountains and was frustrated that the U.S. military and Bush officials did not press home their distinct advantage. After he recommended that the CIA team on the ground advance, Afghan villagers were dispatched up toward Al Qaeda's position with GPS devices concealed inside food parcels. One excited man returned, adamant that he had seen Osama bin Laden, a teenage boy who could be one of his sons, and Dr. al-Zawahiri in a cave at fourteen thousand feet. The coordinates were passed back to CENTCOM with a request to send in a BLU-82 Daisy Cutter. The fifteen-thousand-pound bomb was designed to explode with intimidating power above the ground, scything a landing strip inside a forest in a split second.

Unused since Vietnam and Laos, the Daisy Cutter was so huge it had to be rolled out of the plane. When it detonated in the air on December 9, it shook the mountains for miles around and the radio once more provided insight: an Al Qaeda fighter hollering for assistance and for the "red truck to move wounded." Another reported: "Cave too hot, can't reach others." Everything was melting and burning or crumbling.

One plaintive voice caught a signals operator's attention: "Father is trying to break through the siege line." Was this code, or had one of Osama's sons radioed through sensitive information on an open line? Working to lock down the signal, the CIA believed it had pinpointed Osama's location to within thirty feet—the closest American forces had ever come to the Al Qaeda leader. But as Delta operatives crawled forward, a firefight exploded with Al Qaeda fighters and a Yemeni rear guard pouring in rounds. Three Delta squadron members were stuck as their Afghan support team retreated down the mountain to break their Ramadan fast.

Even though the battle rested on a knife edge, the specialists were ordered to withdraw. Up above, Dr. Ayman Batarfi, a Yemeni doctor from the Al Wafa charity, was amputating limbs without anesthetic inside the lip of a cave as plumes of smoke drifted in. "I was out of medicine and I had a lot of casualties. I did a hand amputation by a knife, and I did a finger amputation with scissors," he recalled. "There comes a point when you are a butcher carving meat and praying that you are doing good and not just doing *something*. In fact, prayer," the doctor added, "was practically my only instrument."[87]

The only reason he had any medical supplies at all was because he had recently made a dangerous round-trip to Lahore to collect them from Dr. Amir Aziz, Osama's personal physician. Now running out, he sought permission to quit the mountain.

Osama demanded to speak to Dr. Batarfi personally. Appearing suddenly from behind a tree, which Batarfi presumed hid the entrance to a cave, the Al Qaeda leader warned the doctor he was making a mistake. "Where will you go?" he asked accusatorily. Tora Bora was unraveling into a free-for-all, and if the doctor left they would all die.

Batarfi estimated that there were only two hundred mujahideen left. He overheard one of them say that they had just sixteen working Kalashnikovs among them. He walked across the mountain strewn with corpses curled like ferns. "Injured brothers cowered in trenches, praying for a swift and painless martyrdom."[88]

On the night of December 10, Osama reached for his radio set. "What should we do?" he asked the airwaves plaintively.

On the morning of December 12, Ibn Sheikh made radio contact with a U.S.-allied Afghan warlord and offered a cease-fire so that bin Laden could negotiate his surrender. They agreed to talk again at four P.M.[89]

Shortly before the cease-fire was due to expire, Ibn Sheikh called through, asking for an extension until eight A.M. the next morning, explaining: "We need to have a meeting with our guys."

The U.S. side was not sold on the idea but General Franks agreed, overruling the doubters, even though Delta operatives were straining to enter the Tora Bora caves to flush out Al Qaeda's leadership.

"Why take your foot off?" an incandescent Grenier fumed in Islamabad.

On the morning of December 13, the eight A.M. deadline passed without any further communication. Later that afternoon in Islamabad, unscheduled troop activities on the Pakistan side suddenly grabbed the CIA station chief's attention.

Without any explanation, Lieutenant General Aurakzai appeared to be moving his soldiers off the White Mountains.

Grenier radioed to check. It was absolutely happening. The troops had been reassigned to Pakistan's eastern borders, with instructions, intercepted by the CIA, to complete the maneuver "within three hours." When he tried to get through to Aurakzai and to General Khan, there was no response.

December 13, 2001, 11:45 A.M., New Delhi, India

Shortly before noon India Standard Time, militants from Jaish-e-Mohammed, the Pakistani jihad outfit run by Masood Azhar and nurtured by the ISI, attacked the main parliament building in New Delhi, a brazen assault that left twelve men dead and both nations eyeballing each other.[90] Almost immediately, India started deploying soldiers on its border with Pakistan, prompting Major General Musharraf to issue orders to meet them head-on, rerouting Lieutenant General Aurakzai's forces to face them down. "Two active borders are something one would never wish," said major General Rashid Qureshi, Musharraf's spokesman.[91]

Only a war could come between Aurakzai and the White Mountains, General Khan had warned. And now Masood Azhar's mujahideen had launched a humiliating assault that brought India and Pakistan closer to fighting—with nuclear weapons—than at any other time since 1999.

Could Jaish have attacked the Indian parliament without their sponsors in the ISI knowing about it? Grenier fumed. Was the timing some kind of terrible coincidence? It was difficult not to see this as a deliberate ruse to allow Osama bin Laden to escape from Tora Bora into Pakistan.[92]

When Wendy Chamberlin, the U.S. ambassador to Pakistan, finally got to speak to Musharraf about the issue, all he would say was that intelligence was a "dirty business."[93] The military combine in Pakistan was like magma, a molten cauldron of minerals and impurities that occasionally formed a crust and was liable to leak out of unseen vents when the pressure became irresistible.

December 14, 2001, Tora Bora

A radio operator caught a snatch of an all-too-familiar voice speaking Arabic. "The time is now!" Osama declared. "Arm your women and children."

The messages that followed threw light on the unfolding scene on the mountaintop. Al Qaeda was rallying, sending out small scouting teams to test the trails to their rear. Quickly, they returned and reported "no resistance."

Next came an apology "to all of his fighters," Osama sending admiration and regrets "for getting them trapped and pounded by American airstrikes."

Afterward, the thrum of collective prayer filled the airwaves.

In his mind's eye, Grenier imagined the rugged hills above Parachinar. Now instead of a trip wire of forces paid for by the United States, the back door out of Tora Bora was flapping wide open, and through it would stride an exile.

CHAPTER THREE

"These Arabs . . . they have killed Afghans.
They have trained their guns on Afghan
lives . . . We want them out."
—HAMID KARZAI, NOVEMBER 2001[1]

December 5, 2001, Hotel Petersberg, Bonn, Germany

THE IRANIAN DELEGATION'S MOHAMMAD JAVAD ZARIF was busy in every corner of the room, charming and scolding, cajoling and listening. Zarif was the juice that fueled the United Nations–brokered conference on Afghanistan's future. More than anyone else present, he had helped bring together an unwieldy collection of polarized factions: warlords, chieftains, and power brokers, men who were divided by perennial ethnic and territorial rivalries. They had mistrusted each other for generations, and even those that did not fall into this category had concealed agendas.

After days of argument that had unfolded as Tora Bora heated up and then fizzled, agreement had been reached among the four main groups present—the Northern Alliance, which now controlled Kabul; the Peshawar Group of Pashtun exiles; the Cyprus Group that was close to Iran and represented Afghan exiles and former mujahideen fighters; and the Royalists, who were calling for the reinstatement of the former king of Afghanistan, who lived in Rome. Against the odds, all four groups now supported the appointment of Northern Alliance–backed Hamid Karzai, the head of Afghanistan's Popalzai tribe, as chairman of a new interim administration. Karzai, a controversial figure who in 1999 and 2000 had traveled to Europe and the United States to warn that the Taliban and Al Qaeda were in league and plotting atrocities, had been America's preferred candidate from the start.

Now that the final vote had been taken, Zarif—satisfied, exhausted, and slightly dismayed that Washington's candidate had won the day—sought out U.S. State Department official James Dobbins to gloat about what he saw as his pivotal role. Iran, he said, had "done it all."[2] Dobbins had to agree. As a practiced diplomat who was also a realist, he admitted to being amazed at his counterpart's proficiency. After more than twenty years of animosity, the United States and Iran had finally found something they could agree on: routing Al Qaeda and the Taliban from Afghanistan.

Like Ryan Crocker before him, Dobbins had deduced that behind the Iranian negotiations sat a genuine desire to normalize relations with the United States. After handing over maps of Taliban and Al Qaeda military positions and chivying Washington into launching Operation Enduring Freedom, Iranian diplomats had now gifted the United States a peace plan that just might save a country that currently resembled "a shattered dinner service." If there was another game going on in town, Dobbins could not see it. Tehran was realigning itself fortuitously and pragmatically with the United States.

Soon there would be a U.S.-sponsored interim authority in Kabul that might create a transitory authority that could elect a government that was not antagonistic to the West—or Tehran. As things stood, an amenable Karzai would be inaugurated in ten days in Kabul.

"Soon," Zarif prophesized cryptically as he and Dobbins parted, "Iran will reveal that it holds other pieces of this puzzle."[3]

On the flight back to Washington, Dobbins pondered this comment and hoped that the White House would respond to this Iranian endeavor by seizing the chance to dismantle the roadblocks erected after 1979. Using diplomats like Zarif, Iran's President Khatami was repositioning his country, and glancing toward the West—if only President Bush would take notice.

December 7, 2001, Kandahar, Afghanistan

Al Qaeda forces, holed up at the city's shattered airport, were caught between eardrum-popping aerial bombing runs and the rush of mortar shells, fired by fast-advancing Northern Alliance fighters. The U.S. military was close behind, readying to roll right over the bones of the Taliban's rule.

After *maghrib* prayer, just after sunset, the Mauritanian was called away from the Al Qaeda foxholes to Mullah Omar's office in the city, where he witnessed a decisive show of hands. Like its forces had done in Kabul, the Taliban was giving up Kandahar without seeing through the final battle, leaving Al Qaeda to fend for itself.

The Mauritanian scurried back to the airport with the terrible news. Unable to reach Osama, the *shura* took a snap decision. They would never survive alone. While the Taliban could melt away into the civilian population, the predominantly Arab members of Al Qaeda, much paler and taller, and without the local languages, could not. Abu Zubaydah took volunteers to scout for buses, returning with three corroded vehicles, two of which were immediately loaded with boxes of ammunition, kit bags, wounded fighters, food, water, maps, and sacks of U.S. dollars. Next, the Mauritanian watched, astonished, as twenty-four senior Al Qaeda leaders scrambled onto the third bus, the bond of comradeship forged in the pandemonium of the carpet-bombing clouding their common sense that they should split up.

Here they sat, row by row, as rounds pinged off the mud and brick: military commander Saif al-Adel, Planes Operation architect Mokhtar, planner Abu Zubaydah, Al Qaeda strategist Abu Musab al-Suri (aka the Syrian), and many more.

"One strike and the entire world of jihad is gone," the Mauritanian muttered. "Spread out. Spread out. *Please!*"

As the leaders came to their senses and were dispersed, with one unit volunteering to remain behind at the airport, the Afghan drivers asked for directions. Where were they going? The options were limited: running west to the Iranian border, heading east into Pakistan, or following Mullah Omar's forces northeast toward Gardez. After a brief discussion, they chose the last option.

The convoy rumbled out of the city on a track shadowing the main Kabul-bound highway. Zubaydah, who had spent the best part of a decade ferrying mujahideen into Afghanistan, worked the radio, checking that his contacts in Pakistan's jihad fronts were ready to receive the Al Qaeda refugees.

The journey out of Kandahar Province was perilous. Every bridge was down. American jets roared overhead. Scouts hared off to probe silent villages, knowing as they inched forward, there was no way back.

The unit of brothers who had remained at the airport was pinned down and taking on heavy fire; the Mauritanian listened with a heavy heart as the names of the dead were read out over the radio. Who was left to offer funeral rites? he wondered.[4]

At daybreak, they reached Zabul, the last bubble of Taliban control, where they decided to split. "The mere presence of Arabs means that the Americans would bomb the people's houses, kill women and children, and say, 'Sorry,

sorry, we thought that bin Laden was there,'" Zubaydah raged in his diary. Desperate Afghans could no longer protect them.

Noncombatants led by the Mauritanian, including his friend Abu Yahya al-Libi, a scholar from Tripoli who had studied under him in Nouakchott, and Osama's finance chief Sheikh Saeed al-Masri, made a beeline for the Chagai Hills, from where they hoped to cross into Balochistan.

The military faction, led by Saif al-Adel, continued northward, intending to regroup with Al Qaeda units coming from the west and north. They would gather near the town of Zurmat in a remote valley under the protection of Afghan warlord Jalaluddin Haqqani.

They would not be running for long, Saif predicted. He already had a head full of plans and would share them with everyone shortly. "We *will* take revenge—around the world—for the Panjwai massacre," he pledged. "Even if it is only one American life, brutally taken, that will be sufficient."[5]

December 10, 2001, Toba Kakar Mountains, Eastern Zabul Province, Afghanistan

The headlamps of a half dozen vehicles flickered across the darkened hillsides. They were following an old drug-smuggling track that was seeded with hair-trigger land mines sewn in previous conflicts. From the drivers, the Mauritanian overheard stories of Arabs fleeing ahead of them flipping their rides on boulders, or mistaking the shadows for bends and driving off the edge in the dark. His hands shook and he called for the convoy to stop. They had to rest.

The driver knew of a house belonging to an Afghan smuggler, he said. He went off to talk to the man, returning a half hour later to say they could stay the night and in the morning this man would guide them over the border.

As soon as they arrived, the smuggler's mother, who had lived through the Soviet war and was delighted to have Arab guests, began cooking. The Mauritanian watched as the damp wood she fed into the stove bled sooty, pungent smoke. In a place where fuel and food were in short supply, a puffing chimney was sure to attract attention. Neighbors soon began to gather. But their host remained nonchalant, addressing everyone with the grandiloquence that the ignorant do best: "If Afghanistan falls into the hands of the Americans today, we will recover it tomorrow, as we did with the English and the Soviets."

What of Al Qaeda? the Mauritanian thought. His movement—virtually all of it—was here in this room, and in a villager's hands. It was so fractured that it might not survive even a single roundup. For the next twenty-four hours he listened to his old radio set, his paranoia growing as he heard reports that in Kabul a new pro-American power led by Hamid Karzai was rising.

After dark on December 11, the smuggler produced a sack of tribal robes: "Get dressed." It was time to leave, on foot.

The Mauritanian, his former student Abu Yahya, and moneyman Sheikh Saeed set out, winding their way up steep passes and across the forlorn desert. Tracers from ancient Soviet DShK heavy machine guns lit up the sky to the north. They rested a few hours in a shepherd's hut but voices woke them at dawn. Country people were arguing loudly in some gnarly language, and the only things the Mauritanian could understand were the names: "Al Qaeda," "Osama," and "the Arabs."

The bounty was now so high no one could be trusted. He rousted everyone and they got on their way without even a cup of tea. Over the next four days they barely stopped at all, sliding down rocky gorges, notching up as many miles as they could until dawn prayer, when, exhausted, they sheltered through the daylight hours in caves or clefts. By the fifth morning, with everyone starving and sore, the smuggler pointed to the distant horizon: "Pakistan."

A junior brother was chosen as the guinea pig and he set off downhill to join a road, while the others hung back, waiting to see what would happen. A day and a half later, a panting courier arrived with a message: "Success!" Incredibly, the brother had made it to Quetta, the capital of Pakistan's Balochistan Province.[6]

Now it was the Mauritanian's turn, and he, Sheikh Saeed, and Abu Yahya squeezed into a rickety car with a disheveled driver who claimed to be a practiced guide but looked like a ravenous shepherd who would eat his own flock. It was pouring rain, the track was slicked with mud, and the Mauritanian felt his legs shaking. The greater his dread, the hotter he got in his borrowed robes and the more the windows steamed up. But when they reached the border post, the young Pakistani soldiers manning it waved them on. Assuming the misted-up car was crammed with sweaty Afghan nomads, they did not even come out of their hut.

Eight days after leaving Kandahar, they had made it out of the cauldron. The Mauritanian's sense of relief was tinged with guilt for those they had left behind at the airport, where the radio sets were all now silent.

December 17, 2001, Balochistan, Pakistan

They spent their first night of freedom at an old British hill fort. The Eid al-Fitr feast marking the end of Ramadan was upon them and they were about to scout around for something to eat when someone's mobile phone sprang to life. Stifling the ringing, surprised that anyone could get a signal in this wilderness, the Mauritanian answered. A male voice spoke somberly: "Tora Bora has fallen." And Sheikh Osama had vanished.

The Mauritanian gasped. "Kabul, Kandahar, and now this."[7] Desperate and scared, he wrote a letter to his family. "My Dear Wife and Children." He wished them a happy Eid and conjured a day, quite soon, when he hoped they would be reunited. "Under the desert lights I am thinking of you all." Then he crammed it into the pocket of his robe, wondering where to send it.

The next afternoon, they entered Quetta to find it overcome with Afghan refugees and transformed into a jittery roundabout of rumors. The bus station spilled over with veiled travelers. Makeshift camps rose up on every bend with the doors to every improvised dwelling pulled shut, heightening the air of clandestine furtiveness. The city's private Imdad Hospital was filled with injured Al Qaeda fighters, with the Taliban guarding the doors. As they drove through the streets with their faces obscured, the Mauritanian recalled Mullah Omar's warning to Osama in 1998: "Never trust the Pakistanis."

"Do not be deceived by the banners bearing your photograph and the people filling the streets shouting your name," Omar had said. Pakistanis were only ever good at "screaming and holding demonstrations," and they had a history of doing Washington's bidding.

That night, they bedded down among the whitewashed terraces of Pashtunabad, a network of narrow alleys and mud-brick *masjids*, glued together with prayers.

*   *   *

December 18, 2001, Barmal, Paktika Province, Afghanistan

Two hundred miles north in Paktika Province, Afghanistan, Abu Zubaydah reached the frontier district and breathed deeply. This was his kind of place: a border zone filled with brigands, where only religion was cherished more highly than money. To the east lay the forested Pakistani tribal region of Waziristan, and in every spare cot it seemed a wounded Al Qaeda fighter was laid up, awaiting transit to hospitals in Pakistan.

Abu Zubaydah had discovered Barmal in 1991, while he was hiking over from the Pakistani side to bring arms and cash for Ibn Sheikh at Khaldan. "And today, I wangle to bring them out of Afghanistan, all of Afghanistan, and by any means. Praise God," he wrote in his diary.[8]

Doing things in reverse would be touch and go. Disguising these Arabs before they tested the border was a challenge. In skin tone, hair color, beard length, and voice they stood out. He found a local *maulvi* (Islamic scholar) and paid for an edict permitting imperiled (religious) men to shave off their beards, dress as women, and pay bribes. *Burqas* were distributed. Small groups were ferried into the foothills, from where they would climb up to the snow-filled passes. On the Pakistani side, smugglers' trails led down into the deeply forested ravines of Shawal, a dank valley dotted with ancient redbrick fortresses, and on to Shakai, a lush expanse of apple and apricot orchards where Pashtunwali was the only law that mattered. If they got that far they would be safe.

This was the land of Nek Muhammad Wazir, a hardhead from Wana, the bustling hub of South Waziristan. Handsome, cocky, and sporting a lavish, piratical beard, he had been born into the jihad of the 1980s, and while only in his early teens he had been recruited by the ISI, and paid by the CIA, to run guns and dollars into Afghanistan.

The son of a *khasadar* (tribal constable), a birthright that gave him high status, Nek was schooled in the Jamia Darul Uloom Waziristan madrassa, where teachers recounted how he had once flounced out of class having been beaten with a cane, only to return with a rifle.[9]

Nek had squandered the early 1990s carjacking and dealing guns and drugs until an old warlord introduced him to the Afghan Taliban, for whom he became a raging gun, rising to be a midlevel commander known as "the stubborn one," always the last to quit the battle. He had been one of the last to leave the field during the battle for Bagram airport in November 2001, remaining steadfast in his foxhole, eyeballing U.S. and British special forces even as they engulfed the airstrip and his fellow Talibs fled.

Now back in Wana, Nek agreed to Abu Zubaydah's request to host Al Qaeda refugees. He had plenty of accommodations for them, as many locals migrated to the low plains during winter, leaving their compounds empty. Sensing there was good money to be made, and possibly lean times ahead, Nek offered attractive rental terms and onward travel arrangements for fighters searching for new battlegrounds or for a sanctuary in which to shelter their families deeper inside Pakistan.

Those heading down to the plains were concealed on commercial mini-buses and sent first to Dera Ismail Khan, a city on the edge of the Tribal Areas. From there, journeys were coordinated by Abu Zubaydah's "loyal Pakistani brothers" in Lashkar-e-Taiba or Jaish-e-Mohammed.[10]

Over the border in Afghanistan, Saif al-Adel's group had reached Shahikot, a craggy valley south of Gardez. Protected on all sides by snow-clad mountains, its name meant Place of the King and for centuries it had been used as a redoubt for Afghan guerrillas.

On Saif's orders and erring on the side of caution, they split again. One hundred veterans dug in with heavy weapons at an altitude of ten thousand feet to wait for the Americans, while tribal militias loyal to Jalaluddin Haqqani took a second contingent farther northeast, toward Khost, from which point they could be smuggled into Waziristan. Their orders were to regroup in Pakistan, ready, Saif said, "for the next round of attacks." He had one last piece of advice: "Keep listening to the news and you will know when we are on the rise once more."[11]

December 19, 2001, Quetta, Pakistan

On his second day in the city, the Mauritanian received a hand-delivered message from Mokhtar saying that Osama's family had reached Pakistan safely, having escaped the border ambush of November 25 in which their Yemeni driver had been captured. Jubilant that Saad bin Laden and the other family members were still alive, he told his companions: "If Osama's sons are alive, so is the movement." They were currently hiding at a secret location but could not stay permanently. What could the *shura* do to help?

The Mauritanian, Sheikh Saeed, and Abu Yahya discussed how best to safeguard the bin Laden caravan. Feeling slightly overwhelmed by this new responsibility, over the course of several hours they kept returning to the same brazen idea: send Osama's family to Iran.

For the epicenter of Shia power and faith to help an outlawed Sunni militia like Al Qaeda might have seemed to be an unusual concept for them to dwell on, but the situation there was fluid, with sufficient ambiguity in its foreign policy for Al Qaeda to exploit it.

Then there was geography. Iran shared a common border with Balochistan and so was realistically within reach. It also offered a protective bubble that U.S. forces dared not penetrate. Tehran was, the Mauritanian argued, no nearer to restoring diplomatic relations with Washington than in 1979.

From personal experience he also knew that strategic Iran sometimes backed causes it did not personally endorse if only to antagonize its sworn enemies, America and Israel. While living in Sudan in 1995, he and Saif al-Adel had been sent to Tehran by Osama to negotiate a mutually benefi-cial arrangement. As a result, Al Qaeda fighters had been invited to train in a camp run by (Shia) Hezbollah and the Quds Force (a clandestine special division of Iran's Revolutionary Guard) in the Beqaa Valley in Lebanon, where they learned how to manufacture shaped charges that transformed roadside bombs into far more lethal armor-piercing death traps.[12] In the run-up to the embassy bombings of 1998, Osama's phone records showed that 10 percent of the calls he and his deputies made were to Iran.[13] And before 9/11, Tehran publicly railed against the persecution of Shias in Afghanistan while secretly assisting some of the hijackers to transit through Iran to the West.

The downside was obvious. They all suspected that Iran had played a role in the fall of the Taliban, which had by now completely melted away, and they were equally worried about entrusting Osama's family to "rejection-ists," as they described Shias, whose "mannerisms resembled those of Jews and the hypocrites," the Mauritanian said.

Sheikh Saeed, too, advised caution. The world had changed significantly as a result of 9/11. Everyone was scared of Washington's retribution. Iran was unpredictable and capable of shifting in any direction to save itself from regime change by dint of the U.S. military. Who could vouch for it remaining anti-American for long?

Unable to reach an agreement, the Mauritanian sent a message to Saif al-Adel through Abu Zubaydah in Barmal. Saif had the most recent knowledge of Al Qaeda's Iranian network, as he had been Osama's main liaison with Tehran and had coordinated previous meetings with Revolutionary Guard officials.

Saif came back with news that the Iranians seemed receptive. "Create a point in Iran and meet the Islamic Revolutionary Guard Corps (IRGC) that works [against the Jews] in Palestine, but [do it] without the knowledge of the Iranian government," Saif advised. Zubaydah recorded the advice in his diary.

Al Qaeda's best hope was to reach General Qassem Suleimani, the commander of the Quds Force. Qassem, who supposedly described himself as "the smallest soldier" in reference to his short stature and his low profile, was the officer who handled Iran's covert foreign policy interests, and if Al Qaeda was of any use to him, he would find a way to help.

Born in Rabor, an impoverished mountain village in eastern Iran, Qassem had little formal education but joined the Revolutionary Guard at age twenty-two in 1979. Since 1998, when he took command of the Quds Force, he had become close to Iran's supreme leader.[14] "Hajji Qassem," as most Iranians deferentially referred to the reclusive silver-haired military official, pursued a hard-line agenda to create an anti-American archipelago of resistance across the Middle East. The Quds Force—which was conspicuously headquartered in the former U.S. embassy compound in Tehran—stood accused of orchestrating the bombing of the Israeli embassy and of a Jewish center in Buenos Aires, in 1992 and 1994, respectively, killing 114 people.

Because Saif was still on military duties in Afghanistan, everyone agreed that the Mauritanian should go alone to Iran. He was a respected scholar and had been there once before. But with the letter to his family still crumpled in his pocket, he panicked. Compared to General Suleimani, the thirty-three-year-old felt like a minnow. Military chief Saif knew how to speak to high-ranking Iranian soldiers like Qassem. But how would Mahfouz cope alone?

While he was still deliberating, the Taliban got in touch and forced his hand. Mullah Omar, who was now in Quetta, also wanted to explore the Iranian route. Would the Mauritanian represent his interests, too?[15]

Field craft was not his forte, but the Mauritanian was tutored on taking some crude security measures. He would travel under an assumed identity and claim to represent the innocent families of martyrs fleeing the American war in Afghanistan. No one could know of his real position in the outfits he represented or his real name.

The journey to Iran would be hard, warned Abu Zubaydah, who was now putting in the miles and shuttling between Barmal, Miram Shah, and Bannu. Afghanistan had "become a strange jungle" and was descending back into the chaotic days that had preceded the Taliban. "Bandits are widespread, and kidnapping, kidnapping of girls, rather, even boys (the disease of sodomy is widespread here). And stealing cars, and the ropes that stop the cars [on] the roads to collect taxes and levies from all." He should find another way to go.

The Mauritanian sought out relatives of Mokhtar who ran a Quetta-based bus company servicing the Iranian border. An uncle rustled up some fake ID papers and put together an itinerary. He should take the regular passenger service southwest from Quetta along the N40 highway, passing through the arid Chagai Hills, and on to the border town of Taftan, a famous drug-smuggling route that was also used by those fleeing to Europe and was known locally as "the road to London."

He would need plenty of hard cash, as along the 450-mile, twelve-hour journey the bus passed through several Pakistani army and intelligence checkpoints. If he got as far as Taftan, Pakistan's only legal gateway into Iran, he would have to find a backdoor across. Hopefully agents of Hajji Qassem would be waiting for him in Mirjaveh, the town on the other side.

His phone rang. Another of Mokhtar's relatives called from Karachi. "Brace yourself." The Mauritanian could take no more bad news.

"Your wife and children are *alive* and in a safe house here."

The Mauritanian cried. He was delighted and conflicted. Desperate to see them, he was now committed to seeking protection for the bin Laden caravan in Iran. He wavered. Could he get out of the trip? How would he? His panicked mind flicked through a litany of excuses until he stopped it. There was no way out. Warned that phones were being tapped all over Pakistan, he dared not even call his wife.

After *al-Isha* prayer on December 19, cursing these chaotic times, the Mauritanian wrapped himself in tribal robes, took a suitcase of U.S. dollars from Sheikh Saeed, and rehearsed his cover story. "I am Dr. Abdullah, a Mauritanian religious scholar who taught in Kandahar."

The poor bookworm had inadvertently become caught up in the stampede to leave the country and, as a literate man, he carried a message on behalf of two *shuras*.

The first thing that he noticed, stuck to the bus windshield, was the flier bearing Sheikh Osama's face. Was it celebratory or a wanted poster? He dared not study it. He decided to take it as a good omen as he headed for the backseat. Soon, Quetta's grimy streets gave way to a desert that ran beige and lumpy like poor pancake batter. As the dead hours washed over him, so did searing images from Panjwai and the siege of Kandahar airport. He found himself wondering why Osama had brought down so much destruction.

When they lurched to a halt at the first Pakistani checkpoint, he came to his senses, reaching into his pocket to isolate a small bundle of notes from the roll as a soldier boarded to vet everyone's papers. Fear prickled down his spine as he pressed the notes into his passport and offered it up. Without hesitation the soldier pocketed the money and moved on to the next passenger.

The bus set off again, heading into a dark meadow of stars toward where Pakistan had first tested its nuclear bomb in 1998.

A face came into his thoughts. It was his father back in Nouakchott, probably sitting at home in his hand-stitched Mauritanian *boubou* (robe). He doubted they would ever see each other again.

When the bus reached Taftan at dawn, men in uniforms and civilian clothes studied everyone stepping down. The Mauritanian noticed tired Arabs sitting in small huddles in the shadows. Everyone was hoping for a ride across, but many had already been turned away.

Clutching his suitcase of dollars, the Mauritanian followed the fence toward the edge of town until he spotted a small gate guarded by a private militia. Not having done anything like this before, he walked up to the guard and nervously produced the wad of money. It had worked on the bus.

The guard looked at him suspiciously. "Wait!" he hissed, pushing the Mauritanian with some force into a small hut. After a half hour, worried that he would be betrayed and sold to a kidnap gang or an intelligence agency, he opened the door and, looking around, hared off in the direction of the border fence, eventually spotting a group of official-looking men waiting on the other side. On seeing him, they waved.

As he studied the sixty-foot kill zone ahead of him, an area sewn with cameras, razor wire, and mines, the Iranians pointed to a gap in the chain-link fence. He ran for it. Behind him the Pakistani guards screamed for him to stop, warning they would fire. But he kept going, eyes fixed on the gap. Before he knew it, he was across and bundled into the backseat of a car that drove off through Mirjaveh at high speed.

"Welcome to Iran, Dr. Abdullah," a young man said, talking over his shoulder. "My name is Ali."

Within an hour they were in Zahidan, the capital of Iranian Balochistan, where smiling officers who did not give their names told him they were part of the Ansar ul-Mahdi Corps. The Mauritanian had no idea what this meant, that they were with an elite unit within the Quds Force responsible for counterintelligence and the protection of senior officials.

He was shown into a house where an elderly Shia cleric sat waiting. "I am to be your translator," the man said. How different he looked from a Sunni *maulvi*. The Shia with his neatly trimmed beard and gray robe resembled a bank manager.

The Ansar ul-Mahdi agents had many queries about the war in Afghanistan. Could Dr. Abdullah explain the mysterious disappearances of Mullah Omar and Osama bin Laden? Did he know where they were? The Mauritanian squirmed. One of the agents chipped in. "Look, don't worry so much," he said. "We have much in common, you and us, since we all believe in one God, one Prophet, one book, and pray in the same direction. Am I right?"

Mahfouz nodded, but it would take more than this empty patter to open him up.

The Iranian cleric spoke: "We all face the common enemies of the USA and Israel. Is this not the case, *doctor*?"

He agreed. He felt like a village fakir thrown into the role of global inter-locutor. How much should he say? Mullah Omar's message, a plea for assis-tance and sanctuary, was something he could offer up. He started with that, but then he could not stop and so he also explained Al Qaeda's needs: the hundreds of brothers and their families stuck inside Pakistan. He did not mention Osama's family caravan. Above everything he had to protect the outfit's legacy.

Al Qaeda had the financial means to provide for their fighters, he said, pointing at his suitcase. In return Al Qaeda would guarantee a pass card: immunity for Iran from future actions, he continued, unsure about the power of his words. With Osama missing and presumed dead, Tora Bora occupied by Western forces, and Kabul fallen, would these Iranian agencies still perceive Al Qaeda as a threat capable of striking inside their country? What would be useful right now, he could not help but think, was a new broadside against their common enemies in the West. And he hoped Saif al-Adel was thinking the same—if he was even alive. He needed something: a sign that Al Qaeda was a deadly foe but also a formidable friend.

Agent Ali rose. He told the Mauritanian to rest, showing him to a clean, simple room.

"For the first time in several months I slept safely," he recalled.

December 22, 2001, Kabul, Afghanistan

After Hamid Karzai was sworn in as interim president, the International Security Assistance Force (ISAF), a NATO-led security mission established during the Bonn conference of December 2001, began to take shape. An intelligence-collation exercise also began the daunting job of piecing together the Tetris puzzle that was Al Qaeda. There were thousands of names and *kunyas* of unidentified Al Qaeda fighters and functionaries. Albums were filled with CVs, photographs, and letters taken from abandoned safe houses, alongside more than a thousand audiocassettes that had been found in one of Osama's bolt-holes in Kandahar.[16]

The CIA and FBI tried to grapple with the information overload by interrogating captured Al Qaeda fighters. When Osama's Yemeni driver, Salim Hamdan, was turned over to the CIA with a booklet found inside his car's glove compartment containing numerical codes used internally to refer to key figures in the movement, agents learned that Osama bin Laden was 4, Dr. Ayman al-Zawahiri was 22, Saif al-Adel was 11, and someone who used the alias Mokhtar was 10.

Among the early discoveries was a letter written by Mokhtar to a department in Al Qaeda described as "external operations," in which he asked its emir to send all available operatives to the United States or the United Kingdom.[17]

The threat levels across Europe and the United States were raised, while at Kandahar airport, in an outdoor detention pen surrounded by dense coils of razor wire and policed by female U.S. Army guards and barking dogs, a seminaked Salim Hamdan was pressed further to reveal the identity of Mokhtar. Osama's former mechanic refused to talk; but others were more forthcoming, especially those who felt that they had been betrayed by him at Tora Bora.

On the night of December 15, the day after Osama disappeared, Ibn Sheikh al-Libi, the former commander of Khaldan camp, had tried to evacuate his remaining men, strapping the most severely injured to mules that lurched down the mountain to Parachinar—the old British fort previously visited by the CIA's Robert Grenier. But on December 17, Ibn Sheikh and thirty of Osama's Yemeni and Saudi bodyguards were caught by Pashtun villagers and handed over to Pakistan's Frontier Corps. Dubbed the Dirty Thirty by U.S. forces, who hooded and cuffed them, they arrived in Kandahar on December 26.

Dr. Ayman Batarfi, the Al Wafa doctor who had run the first-aid post on the mountaintop and operated without anesthetic, was caught in another group. "Osama didn't care about anyone but himself," he complained, explaining how he had tried to escape down the mountain in a large group of fleeing fighters but had been attacked from the air, with more than forty in his party killed. Forced to return to Tora Bora with the injured, the doctor had discovered that Osama, who had insisted everyone remain, had himself disappeared.

Khalid al-Hubayshi, a young Saudi recruit, complained: "We were ready to lay down our lives for him. What did he care when he sent us over the horizon to die?"[18] For those who had known Osama the longest, it was a disturbingly familiar story of personal cowardice.

Although his well-aired public history had him pitching up in Afghanistan in 1979 with a Kalashnikov in hand, born to be the leader of men, in reality, there had been many years of indecision before Osama had joined the jihad and during which he had lived off others' deeds.

Osama was tied to his mother's real estate and his father's inheritance and had found it hard to break away. "The jihad . . . what is it like?" he would ask visitors to his opulent family home in Jeddah. Among those who came was the son-in-law of Abdullah Azzam, the Palestinian preacher who had lectured at Osama's university mosque and had first fired his imagination with the punchy slogan "Jihad and the rifle alone."[19]

Fresh off the front lines in Mazar-e-Sharif, where he had been battling the Soviets, Azzam's son-in-law had arrived exhausted in Jeddah in 1983, hoping to catch up on his sleep. Osama had demanded that the visitor accompany him to a camp pitched in the Saudi desert. "When we got there, Osama revealed that he had made arrangements for us to enact a sort of pretend jihad," he recalled.[20] "He wanted to imagine what it would be like, so he had dreamed up some scenarios. It was play-acting. I grew tired just listening."

Osama's first genuine trip to Afghanistan had not come until 1984, halfway through the war, when he had inadvertently found himself caught up in battle on a mountaintop. He had cowered in a trench while Afghan mujahideen on a lucky streak shot down four Soviet planes. Afterward, he had snapped a picture of a dead Russian pilot, describing the corpse as resembling a "slaughtered sheep," before returning home with his war story. "I asked forgiveness from God Almighty, feeling that I had sinned because I listened to those who advised me not to go," he admitted later. "I felt this four-year delay could not be pardoned unless I became a martyr."[21]

That same instinct for self-preservation had saved him at Tora Bora in December 2001.

But not his fighters. On January 11, 2002, six were transferred from the Kandahar detention pens to Cuba, becoming the first prisoners at a new offshore U.S. military facility at Guantánamo Bay, a U.S. naval base located on land that had been leased from Cuba since 1903. Ill-judged photographs were distributed of these earliest inmates: cowed men in orange jumpsuits kneeling in the gravel of an open-air pen with their hands and feet shackled, blackout goggles on their eyes, noise-canceling earmuffs, and masks over their mouths and noses.[22]

December 2001, Political Security Organization (PSO) Prison Facility, Sana'a, Yemen

Salim Hamdan's brother-in-law Abu Jandal, the bull-like security man who in 2000 had escorted Osama's new bride Amal from Sana'a to Kandahar, was also talking to the FBI.

Special Agent Ali Soufan, a Lebanese-American who had been tracking Al Qaeda since 1998, had first got to see Jandal on the night of September 17, six days after 9/11. After Soufan had brought some biscuits and they chatted about movies, Jandal opened up.[23]

His favorite film was *Braveheart*, which he had watched with his wife when they had quit Afghanistan as a result of Osama's bickering wives. "Amal was very young, and the others resented me for bringing her, and in turn they were mean to my wife," he complained to Soufan. "And so we ended up leaving."

Over successive sessions, Jandal was cajoled into areas that were more sensitive, including characterizing the personal habits of military chief Saif al-Adel, Osama's deputy Dr. al-Zawahiri, and moneyman Sheikh Saeed.

Soufan already had these men well drawn in his file, but he listened to see if Jandal lied or added rich details.

The Yemeni explained how whenever the *shura* met the younger brothers would joke, "God help us," knowing the older men were plotting a new attack that would inevitably involve a call out for suicide operatives.

The interviews had stepped up a notch when Soufan asked Jandal about Mokhtar. The prisoner said he had no idea who Mokhtar was, although he knew the name from a key Al Qaeda lieutenant based in Karachi, a one-legged heavy, also from Yemen, who he called Silver.[24]

For Soufan the operative called Mokhtar remained the biggest mystery. There were traces of him everywhere, including at the bomb site where Abu Hafs the Commander had been found dead. A letter recovered from the rubble implied that Mokhtar was the 9/11 linchpin. His name had also cropped up in the candid monologue delivered by Osama about the 9/11 operation. Again he was mentioned in the film of Osama's sons inspecting the wreckage of a downed U.S. helicopter, with someone calling to him off-camera. All of these splinters indicated that Mokhtar was significant and close to Osama. But it did not help bring investigators any nearer to unmasking his real identity.

December 11, 2001, Tora Bora, Afghanistan

It would take years to piece together how Osama had slipped away, but the Al Qaeda prisoners in Kandahar's detention pens had been telling the truth. Heeding Mullah Omar's advice and suspecting that Musharraf was looking hard at the $25 million bounty placed on his head by Washington, the Al Qaeda leader had abandoned his Yemeni cohort on the summit of the White Mountains during the night of Ibn Sheikh's cease-fire.

Accompanied by sons Othman and Mohammed, Dr. al-Zawahiri, and his captive adviser Sulaiman Abu Ghaith, he had scrambled down the mountain, heading for Jalalabad in a procession led by Abu Ahmad al-Kuwaiti, Mokhtar's deputy in the media office at Tarnak Qila, who was by now a trusted aide. Guarding the column was strongman Dr. Amin al-Haq, the Tora Bora commander. Working in tandem was a prominent Taliban leader, Awal Gul, who several weeks earlier had secured the Star Wars camp for Osama's wives and children. Now he hid Osama's party at his house on the outskirts of the city, where, "hiding in plain sight," Osama sat with his VHF set. Praying with the mujahideen still out on the mountain slopes, exhorting them to fight to the death and encouraging them to embrace martyrdom, his broadcasts gave the impression to everyone listening that he remained up there, too.[25]

Three days later, Osama had written his will. It was the twenty-seventh day of Ramadan, the so-called Night of Power—an auspicious moment to die for Muslims who believe that on this day only the gates of heaven are open. The next morning, he switched on the VHF set again and declared: "O youth of the nation. Crave death and life will be given to you."

Above the city in the White Mountains, Al Qaeda fighters were consumed by a blitzkrieg: the dead included Abu Ahmad al-Kuwaiti's older brother Habib. On the plains of Jalalabad, Osama's messengers contacted Gulbuddin Hekmatyar, a veteran Afghan warlord, looking for protection. Hekmatyar's murderous fight to control Kabul in the 1990s was often credited with enabling the rise of the Taliban, as Afghanis fell behind the black-robed students who offered protection from the cold-blooded raids carried out by the warlord's cutthroats. These days, Hekmatyar was exiled in Iran, where General Qassem Suleimani's Quds Force protected him: an arrangement that at times more resembled house arrest, as each side pondered how best to use the other.

Steered from Tehran, Hekmatyar's network in Afghanistan remained active, and it responded to Osama's cry for help, instructing commander Gul and strongman Dr. Amin al-Haq to deliver the beleaguered Al Qaeda leader to a veteran Afghan mujahid known as Kashmir Khan. He ruled Kunar, a rugged and isolated Afghan province north of Jalalabad. Its difficult terrain, cave networks, and porous border with Pakistan's North-West Frontier Province, had long been a haven for insurgents, militias, and smugglers. It was, Hekmatyar recalled many years later, "a safe place" for Osama to go to ground.[26]

Dr. al-Haq was instructed to take the party north on horseback, following the upper courses of the Kunar River, staying high up in the tree line and sleeping rough in the forest. Meanwhile in Tora Bora, Zarqawi's party was told to head for Iran, where they would rendezvous with Hekmatyar and shore up new alliances. Abdullah Tabarak, Osama's chief bodyguard, was sent eastward toward Parachinar, carrying his boss's satellite phone. He was instructed to switch it on at regular intervals like a homing beacon for U.S. forces to track.

Tabarak and his group were duly captured as Osama's unseen party reached Shigal after a grueling eighty-mile horse ride bypassing Asadabad, the provincial capital of Kunar. Kashmir Khan had arranged for the Al Qaeda leader and his son Mohammed to stay in a mud-walled fort between two snow-covered summits. Overlooking a river and surrounded by terraced fields, the fort had no neighbors, nor were there roads or passing traffic.

Dr. Ayman al-Zawahiri had split off and gone south, taking Othman bin Laden, a handful of guards, and Sulaiman Abu Ghaith. They would attempt to cross into Pakistan wherever they could and establish an Al Qaeda base in the Tribal Areas.

Abu Ahmad al-Kuwaiti, the erstwhile media man, was told to try to get over the border on his own and rendezvous with his mentor Mokhtar in Karachi.

On December 29, a videotape of Osama was aired on Al Jazeera, showing him dressed in military fatigues and looking physically exhausted. "I am just a poor slave of God," he declared to the camera, his left side immobile during the recording, suggesting some injury had been sustained. "If I live or die, the war will continue."

It was sufficient for his followers to know that he was still alive and committed to global jihad.

Abu Zubaydah, who was still at Barmal, recorded the news in his diary.[27] "Let me dip my pen or quill in my eyes and fill it with tears, not ink, to write you a thing to remember today," he wrote. "Today no one is left around [Osama bin Laden] except for a few individuals in the mountains, even if millions are around him in the outside . . ." Of the Sheikh's exact circumstances, he added: "The group that remains with [the Sheikh] does not exceed six, and they are all well in a very safe location, thank God."

*   *   *

January 2002, Karachi, Pakistan

Mokhtar was busy spinning plates. The dumpy, hirsute Kuwaiti-Pakistani rushed purposefully about the city as if he, not Osama, was the emir, authorizing compensation payments for Al Qaeda widows, rehousing Arab families arriving from Afghanistan, paying off medical bills for injured fighters, as well as distributing stipends to brothers heading out on new projects abroad.

He owned at least three mobile phones on which he texted furiously day and night. Important messages were sent in code by e-mail or downloaded onto encrypted USB drives and hand-delivered by couriers. The most active of them was Hassan Ghul, a large, overweight Pakistani who kept open the communication channels between Mokhtar; financier Sheikh Saeed, who was still holed up in Quetta; and Abu Zubaydah in Barmal.

With Al Qaeda's *shura* split, Mokhtar had formed a new one of his own. A man who had rejected Al Qaeda, and who the outfit had sidelined for being too pathological, was now running the show.

Mokhtar's *shura* consisted of his nephew Ammar al-Balochi, his Yemeni assistant Silver, and another hood from Yemen who the CIA, when they picked up on his trail, would nickname "Riyadh the Facilitator." Riyadh was an Al Qaeda stalwart and had proven himself to Osama by recruiting the Sheikh's bodyguards in Sana'a, Yemen, before becoming Mokhtar's bagman, often carrying around hundreds of thousands of dollars in a brown plastic briefcase. Mustafa Ahmad al-Hawsawi, who had managed finances for the Planes Operation, was deputed to make a record of Al Qaeda's depleted infrastructure on his laptop, one file entitled "Asra" listing dead or injured fighters, while "Caravan 1" and "Caravan 2" detailed those still in flight and capable of being posted to new operations.

The most time-consuming duty was maintaining a pool of apartments for the ever-growing number of Arabs arriving in Karachi. Thanks to 9/11, money was flowing into Al Qaeda from supporters based all over the Gulf and beyond, and Mokhtar now controlled the cash. Most of the safe houses were rented out in the names of Mokhtar's uncles, cousins, and nephews. Although he had grown up in Kuwait, Mokhtar's family was deeply embedded in Karachi as both his parents had been born there. A circle of relatives was used to vet potential safe houses in some of the most desirable districts. Besides the Tariq Road lodging, where the hijackers had gathered, and where

Mokhtar had watched the 9/11 attacks take place, there were bolt-holes dotted around Gulshan-e-Iqbal, a large middle-class district; one close to Karachi University; and another along the road from the city's old drive-in cinema. There were also places in upmarket Clifton, where Pakistan's leaders past and present had residences, and yet farther east, at Malir Town, where Mokhtar's wife and children lived.

All of these comings and goings required oversight, so Mokhtar also employed a network of informers, small-time pickup artists, lowly paid police constables, security guards, and shopkeepers. The one thing these factotums had in common was membership in the Pakistani militant groups—Jaish-e-Mohammed and Lashkar-e-Taiba—which meant they were disciplined and also known to the Pakistani intelligence establishment.

Saudi-Burmese brothers Abdul and Ahmed Rabbani, two former alcoholics who ran Tariq Road, managed this army. Mokhtar had inherited the short-statured Rabbanis from Abu Hafs the Commander in the early days of the Planes Operation. Paying them a paltry two hundred rupees a day to drive him around Karachi, he had bought their loyalty by arranging for one of their sisters to marry his burly Pakistani courier Hassan Ghul. By the time the Planes Operation came together, Mokhtar had felt confident enough about the brothers (and their sobriety) to assign the hijackers to their care.

Indebted, the brothers vetted cooks, gardeners, cleaners, sweepers, and guards. At Mokhtar's request, they rented a house at the end of Faisal Street near the Karachi airport. No families stayed here. All there was inside was a phone line hooked up to the Internet and a workroom used for research, counterfeiting documents, and collating news for the rest of the Karachi *shura*.

The most important of Mokhtar's Karachi guests were Saad bin Laden and his young family, who had arrived with former media man Abu Ahmad al-Kuwaiti and were awaiting news about possible sanctuary in Iran.

Mokhtar was delighted to have Osama's family entrusted to him, a precious cargo requiring special treatment—especially autistic Saad, who could not be left alone for fear he would blab something compromising about his father. Mokhtar had called on the Rabbani brothers to put them up.[28]

Saad and his young family were initially placed in one of the smarter guesthouses in Gulshan-e-Iqbal, where Mokhtar visited almost daily, coaching Osama's third son on what he would need to say when he was taken to meet important guests coming from the Gulf. Always smiling and joking, Saad, who Mokhtar dressed in a Sindhi skullcap and baggy *shalwar kameez*, was an unlikely emissary for a global jihad movement but somehow Mokhtar had to transform him into a simulacrum of his father. He was a bona fide bin Laden, which was what Mokhtar needed to persuade new donors to release money to him.

Within days of Saad's arrival, several potential funders were flown into Karachi and put up at the high-end Hotel Mehran close to the exclusive Sind Club. They included two Saudis who between them were promising to donate $1 million if Mokhtar could prove he had access to Osama's inner circle.

The first meetings went badly. While Mokhtar glad-handed his guests, Saad told rude stories about his wife. Only now did the 9/11 mastermind begin to appreciate how difficult it was going to be to wield the bin Ladens. He assigned his nephew Ammar and Riyadh the Facilitator to assist. Their first job was to take charge of the bin Laden family passports, which Saad had left scattered about the apartment for the servants to see; Ammar locked them away in a cash box and handed the key to Mokhtar.[29]

While Saad was squeezed into his new role, Mokhtar asked his female relatives to keep an eye on Saad's wife, Wafa, and her young son, Osama. An ethnic Yemeni who had been born in Sudan, where her mujahid father had served Al Qaeda, Wafa had been promised to Saad at the age of sixteen in 1998, having already spent most of her childhood as part of the extended Al Qaeda family. Now she was locked up with her son in a small apartment, hidden away from Karachi's nosy residents, and she was deeply unhappy.

Mokhtar's wife and sisters were loud, overbearing women who brought along hordes of screaming children and slopped bowls of homemade biryani over the carpet. Wafa, who only spoke Arabic, could not even communicate her displeasure.

What she wanted was Saad and news about her father, who had disappeared during the battle for Tora Bora. The more depressed Wafa became, the more it upset Saad. Childlike, he did everything he could to get out of Mokhtar's meetings and run home, rolling about on the floor with his gurgling son, guffawing to Jim Carrey movies, eating Domino's pizza, and petulantly refusing to leave again.

Next to arrive in Karachi was another difficult case: Osama's teenage bride, Amal, who came with her baby daughter. Mokhtar put them with Wafa for a week, but Saad quickly grew jealous of Amal, and the women began to make demands, and so Amal and the baby were moved out to Mokhtar's apartment in Malir Town. Close to a park, and within walking distance of a well-loved bakery, Amal realized the apartment was the same one where she had stayed in June 2000 during her first few days in Pakistan.[30] Fresh from Yemen, she had been handed over to a large, gruff Balochi woman whose job had been to prepare her for marriage to Osama.

This minder was still there, and Amal now realized she was Mokhtar's wife. The woman told of how she had grown up in a refugee camp in Peshawar, where her head had been filled with stories of jihad. Mokhtar, a man Amal knew only as "Hafeez," was her cousin, she said, and since marrying him, she had traveled the world.

There was another new companion for Amal: a Pashtun teenager, Maryam, who also lived in the apartment, having recently married Mokhtar's friend, courier Abu Ahmad al-Kuwaiti—although Maryam always referred to him by his real name, Ibrahim Saeed Ahmad.[31] With nothing to do but perform housework and watch Urdu television channels that neither girl understood, Amal and Maryam began teaching each other their languages, with Maryam explaining that she came from Shangla, a beautiful valley in Pakistan's North-West Frontier, a place she had not seen since her marriage.

Maryam had just turned fourteen and was already pregnant. Amal noticed that she appeared to know very little about her husband other than that he had been born in Kuwait, where his father had prayed in a mosque where Mokhtar's father was the imam. Her father, a laborer, had also traveled to Kuwait to find work and first got talking to Mokhtar's father one day after Friday prayers. Mokhtar's father had eventually put the two families together, but in the few months she had been married to Ibrahim, Maryam had barely seen him. She complained to Amal that he spent most of his time away on "business trips" or holed up with Mokhtar, who she knew as "Hafeez."

They sat on the floor in the living room, surrounded by flunkies, laptops, and mobile phones. Amal and Maryam overheard talk about Ibrahim's eight brothers, two of whom had died fighting in Afghanistan. They were perplexed by the steady stream of visitors to the house who addressed Hafeez as Mokhtar and Ibrahim as Abu Ahmad. But Maryam dared not ask her husband any questions: he was twice her age and carried a gun, and he had beaten her on several occasions already.

Amal wanted to guide her friend but thought better of it. She had been repeatedly told not to speak about her own marriage or any of the things she observed about operational security. Instead, she talked about missing her family in Yemen. When the subject of her husband came up, she would say: "He has gone abroad. I have no idea when we will see each other again."[32] When Osama's picture appeared on the television she tried not to react.

The arrivals continued. Osama's overtly religious Saudi wives Khairiah and Seham and their children were next. The Iran plan was progressing more slowly than expected and Mokhtar was happy to ingratiate himself by stepping into the breach. Each family unit was kept separate, Khairiah and her son Hamzah staying together in an apartment in Clifton, while Seham, her unmarried children (Khalid, Miriam, and Sumaiya), and Najwa's children (Iman and Ladin) were sent to addresses in Gulshan-e-Iqbal.

Najwa's married daughter Fatima and Seham's married daughter Khadija remained in Quetta, lodging with the families of Dr. Ayman al-Zawahiri and the deceased Abu Hafs the Commander as Khadija's mujahid husband was on active Al Qaeda duties near the border, while Fatima's husband was still missing.

Out of all of Osama's children, Hamzah found it hardest to settle in Karachi, and he agitated for news of his father whenever he got together with his half brother Saad. Although he was only thirteen, Hamzah was savvy and knew that Saad was incapable of keeping anything secret. Sometimes snippets of information he had overheard from Mokhtar slipped out—of how a cleverly thought-out plan had sent America off in the wrong direction and how their father was now holed up in a remote Afghan valley. What no one told Saad was that Mokhtar was in direct contact with Osama, through Abu Ahmad al-Kuwaiti, who was shuttling weekly between Karachi and Kunar Province in Afghanistan, carrying secret letters—and that Osama was contemplating coming to Karachi himself.

Occasionally, courier al-Kuwaiti brought welcome news about others, too. Saif al-Adel was in Afghanistan preparing to face off against the recently formed International Security Assistance Force (ISAF). Another group of brothers was thriving in Shakai under the protection of the wayward Pashtun mujahid Nek Muhammad Wazir.[33]

Mokhtar and al-Kuwaiti talked about these updates in whispers while Amal and Maryam listened in from next door.

* * *

January 2002, Tehran, Iran

After a night in Zahidan, Agent Ali from the Ansar ul-Mahdi Corps had informed the Mauritanian that he had been invited to present his case in the Iranian capital. As they took their seats on an internal flight, the Arab visitor felt embarrassed. He was still wearing the creased *shalwar kameez* he had put on before leaving Quetta and other passengers in their suit jackets and buttoned-up shirts eyed him suspiciously.

At Mehrabad International Airport, Ali whisked him through an official channel and into a waiting Mercedes. As they were driven through the city's wide avenues, Ali pointed out tourist attractions and famous Shia mosques. The Mauritanian nodded respectfully as he silently contemplated how far he had come in a few short weeks from the carcass of Kandahar airport.

They arrived at a smart apartment with a gas fire, a servant, and a kitchen stacked with Arab, Turkish, and French tea (with a different teapot for each preparation). The Mauritanian felt guilty, thinking of those he had left behind, especially his own family.[34]

That afternoon, senior officials informed him that the highest authority—meaning General Qassem Suleimani—had approved Al Qaeda's safe haven. The Mauritanian wasn't sure whether it was appropriate, but he handed over a suitcase full of money, which was accepted without comment as Ali announced they were going shopping.[35] "If you're going to live here, you will need some Iranian clothes," he said, insisting on paying from his own pocket.

That night, as they shared dinner, the Mauritanian decided to test their new relationship by asking for a favor. He needed to update "the brothers in Pakistan" about General Qassem Suleimani's momentous decision, he said. If this were some kind of charade, Ali would surely dismiss the request.

Ali agreed and escorted his guest to the Central Post Office, arranging for him to call Quetta. "All individuals and families who wish to travel to Iran will be welcomed," the Mauritanian reported in a short conversation with Sheikh Saeed, who informed him in code that Zarqawi and Ramzi bin al-Shibh had also reached Iran. Things were going more smoothly than he could ever have imagined.[36]

By the time he and Ali returned to Zahidan to supervise arrangements, something was preying on the Mauritanian's mind. What would happen when the Iranians found out that other Al Qaeda brothers had entered the country without having sought permission? To protect himself, he told Ali that several had slipped in, helped by Al Qaeda supporters in Zahidan.

The agent shrugged it off. "This method may serve us well," Ali said, remarking that it distanced Tehran from Al Qaeda's actions.

A short while later, when Ali casually asked for names of those wishing to come next, the Mauritanian felt a twinge of anxiety. "Some brothers did not fully trust Iran, and I was not able to inform about their arrival until I had consulted them," he recalled. When Ali left, the Mauritanian secretly purchased a mobile phone to call Sheikh Saeed.

Ali returned later. He was grinning. He had news. "You," he said, laughing, "are *dead.*"

The Mauritanian looked dumbfounded. Ali showed him a newspaper report listing Al Qaeda leaders the Pentagon claimed to have either captured or killed. Near the top was Mahfouz Ibn El Waleed, supposedly killed in an airstrike on January 7.

As Ali's laughter subsided, the Mauritanian realized that the Iranians knew who he was. The Dr. Abdullah story had fooled no one and was simply being used as a fig leaf by the Iranians to cover up the secret Quds Force deal with Al Qaeda. He thought of his family, who would read these stories about his death and believe them. Ali saw his concern. "You cannot tell *them.* Everyone must think you are dead. Believe me, this will work in our favor," he said.[37]

As soon as Ali left, the Mauritanian fetched his secret phone to call Sheikh Saeed again. The financier told him not to fret but to play the news for what it was worth. They would get a message to his wife and children in Karachi. But the rest of the family back in Mauritania—a country that enjoyed full diplomatic relations with the United States—could not know.

Days later, Ali arrived in a darker mood. "Give me the addresses where the senior Al Qaeda brothers are staying," he demanded. "Someone has been making unauthorized phone calls to Pakistan from this city and from other places in Iran," Ali barked. "The intelligence ministry in Tehran is fuming."

The Mauritanian swallowed hard. Everyone was afraid of the Ministry of Intelligence and Security (MOIS), the most powerful ministry in Iran, whose shadowy agents were known as "the Unknown Soldiers of the Imam." On a par with the Quds Force in terms of influence and power, the security ministry was supposed to supervise all covert operations, and the Quds Force was supposed to share all information it collected with them. But General Suleimani had a habit of going his own way, which angered the security minister, Ali Younsei, enormously.[38] The Mauritanian was now stuck in the middle of their row.

Security agents had either overheard his conversations with Sheikh Saeed, or Ramzi bin al-Shibh, Zarqawi, or Zarqawi's fighters holed up in Sunni enclaves along the eastern border had been careless. "Whoever has done this, I am sorry," he replied, unable to look Ali in the eye.

Thinking on his feet, he continued: "I cannot take you to these locations, where other brothers are hiding, as this will jeopardize their hosts."

Ali's face soured. Because of Al Qaeda's duplicity, the Quds Force was now under pressure from the security ministry to hand over everyone, he said. "I can find your people without you. All it will take is a matter of hours," he snapped.

The Mauritanian took this as a threat. "Everyone who entered did so in the way I described earlier," he replied, reminding Ali of his suggestion that Al Qaeda take advantage of the Zahidan smuggling ring, as it gave the Quds Force plausible deniability. "If you want to look for people then go ahead, but I'm not going to help you."

Ali stormed out to confer with a superior. He returned within the hour, angrier still, shouting and demanding answers, names, and numbers.

"*Your* behavior is unacceptable," the Mauritanian said, trying to embarrass him. "We left our countries in the first place because we did not want to accept humiliation and insults."

Ali stormed out of the room again. "Stay here," he shouted over his shoulder.

Despite the risks of being overheard, the Mauritanian activated his secret phone again. Where was Abu Zubaydah when he needed help? No answer. He called Quetta, desperate for advice. Getting a local cell phone number for Ramzi bin al-Shibh from one of Sheikh Saeed's assistants, he took a significant risk by calling him directly. "Look, Iran is *not* safe."

Al-Shibh took a taxi to the border, where he boarded a bus back to Quetta. In the city he spread the news. Iran was a trap. General Qassem Suleimani had agreed to assist Al Qaeda without informing the Reformist government of President Mohammad Khatami. Now that government officials had found out, the Al Qaeda refugees were caught in the middle of a dangerous political tussle. The message was carried to Peshawar, while al-Shibh traveled on to Karachi to meet his boss.

*   *   *

January 2002, Karachi

Mokhtar was crabby and distracted. Despite the risks, Osama bin Laden had turned up in Karachi demanding to spend time with Amal and be updated about future projects. It had taken Herculean efforts to get him in and out of the Malir Town apartment for a brief conjugal visit and he was now holed up in another part of the city. Mokhtar had been embarrassed to inform him about the failure of his most recent projects. Several operations that new donors had funded in the wake of 9/11 had already fizzled. Most centered on the world's tallest buildings, which were featured in an almanac Mokhtar kept at his home and in which he grandiosely crossed out those he had already targeted (the Twin Towers) and circled those he intended to destroy, including Canary Wharf in London.[39] Fighters who witnessed him doing this said he treated the almanac as a to-do list. Ideas there were aplenty, but what was proving far harder was finding reliable operatives.

British recruit Richard Reid was one hopeful who Mokhtar had put into play with catastrophic results.

A loner, dropout, and Muslim convert from southeast London, Reid had come Al Qaeda's way in 1999, redirected through Abu Zubaydah's Peshawar portal, from which point he had been directed to Afghanistan. He had found no mission with Al Qaeda, as Saif al-Adel had judged him "not very bright." Mokhtar saw it differently. He could see the potential of a bomb strapped to a British passport, and he summoned the Londoner to Karachi in early December 2001. Even though Reid, a six-foot-four, two-hundred-pound raddled-looking petty criminal with a ponytail, was an oddity, he was not what immigration officials were looking out for, Mokhtar argued. Neither was the other recruit for Plan A, as he code-named the operation. Saajid Badat, born to a Muslim British Indian family and educated at a Church of England primary and then a grammar school in Gloucester, was a high-scoring student—the least likely suspect in an irregular Al Qaeda plan.

Mokhtar asked his bombmaking team working in Karachi's commercial district to make suitable devices. Al Qaeda's chemist and chief explosives expert, an Egyptian jihadi called Abu Khabab al-Masri, did most of the work. Craft and experimentation went into scaling down the bombs so they could fit in the sole of a shoe without losing too much explosive power. Forensic analysis later confirmed that the detonator cord used in both bombs had come from the same batch: the cut mark on Badat's cord exactly matched that on Reid's.

Before they set out, and to underscore the importance of this Al Qaeda comeback attack, they were taken to a secret meeting with Osama bin Laden in Karachi. He hugged them both and wished them good luck.

The two stunned recruits had gone home to the United Kingdom with the bombs glued into their shoes and carrying instructions to book flights to the United States.[40] At the last minute Badat, who faced a grilling from his parents about where he had been, confessed all and sent an e-mail to his handler pulling out. "You will have to tell Van Damme that he could be on his own," he wrote, referring to Reid by his code name.

Just hours later, Reid contacted his handler from Paris to say that he had been prevented from boarding his connecting flight to the United States. Other passengers in the transit lounge had complained at his disheveled appearance. After being screened by French police, he finally boarded an American Airlines jet bound for Miami on December 22. Midair he had tried to ignite his device, only for passengers and flight attendants, who smelled smoke as he lit matches, to jump on him.

Now this botched operation was all over U.S. newspapers, cited as evidence that as a result of the American war, Al Qaeda was a spent force.

Saif sent urgent, angry messages. Why had Mokhtar trusted a man like Reid—a car thief of limited intellect—when Al Qaeda was already on a knife-edge? Why had he allowed Osama—currently the most wanted man in the world—to come to a city that was teeming with police and undercover intelligence operatives?

Mokhtar carried on regardless. During the few days he had spent with Osama, they had talked about another Planes Operation. This time Mokhtar suggested they enroll a team of British-Pakistani brothers into a flight school outside Karachi. On graduating, they would return to the United Kingdom with the intention of hijacking a British Airways jet departing from Heathrow, turning it around, and crashing it back into the airport.

Osama had given his approval. Fresh back from Iran, Ramzi bin al-Shibh was put in charge of recruiting the suicide team. Mokhtar gave him a bag of money and keys to a safe house in Gulshan-e-Iqbal and told him to wait for further instructions.

*　*　*

January 2002, Islamabad, Pakistan

Daniel Pearl, a reporter for the *Wall Street Journal*, had been working on a story in India when 9/11 happened, but he had flown to Pakistan the following day, accompanied by his pregnant wife, Mariane. Four months later he was on the trail of Sheikh Mubarak Ali Shah Gilani, a radical Karachi-based cleric who was rumored to have been seen with shoe-bomber Richard Reid when he visited Pakistan in December 2001. It was an allegation Pearl's competitors had already tackled but to date no one had got an interview with the elusive Gilani.[41]

Through Pakistani contacts, Pearl met Khalid Khawaja, a veteran ISI officer who had never really retired, had worked with Osama during the 1980s, and knew Gilani. Khawaja was a key figure in the tangled network of ex-spooks who floated around the ISI, a khaki ball of wool of officers who had resigned their commission but could always be recalled to serve their nation. "I got hooked up with one of OBL's buddies, who has been taking me around to see the people who are secretly pro-OBL," Pearl explained in an e-mail to a friend.[42] "I'm writing a story about how everybody here thinks the Jews did it [9/11]. Bound to piss everybody off, but I think people should know what people in other parts of the world REALLY think, and why. Right?"

Pearl asked Khawaja to help him get an interview with Sheikh Gilani, but Khawaja declined.[43] He was worried by Pearl's lack of experience working in the Pakistani jihad labyrinth. Besides, Pearl was an American and a Jew, and Gilani and his group were on a U.S. list of terrorist organizations.

As word about the reporter's interest in Gilani spread through Islamist circles, others stepped forward to help, including freelance jihadi Omar Sheikh, a British-Pakistani with militant views and connections who had been educated at a private school in northeast London and attended the London School of Economics, during which time, on an aid trip to Bosnia, he had been radicalized.

Sheikh invited Pearl to a meeting at the Akbar International Hotel in Rawalpindi and offered to set him up with Gilani in Karachi. "I am sure you will gain a lot from the meeting. Do tell me all the details," he wrote in a follow-up e-mail, using the address nobadmashi@yahoo.com (*badmashi* meaning "troublemaking" in Urdu). In truth, Sheikh had not contacted Gilani but had asked contacts in Karachi to lure Pearl into a trap.

Although Pearl had no reason to suspect Omar Sheikh, who used a pseudonym throughout their correspondence, his record as a dangerous fraudster and kidnapper was well documented. He had been arrested in Delhi in 1994 for luring Western backpackers into an abduction attempt by Jaish-e-Mohammed and was released, alongside Masood Azhar, the fire-brand leader of Jaish, in 1999, in exchange for passengers on an Indian Airlines jet that was hijacked and brought down in Kandahar.

On January 21, Daniel and Mariane Pearl visited a sonogram clinic in Islamabad and discovered that their unborn child was a boy. They chose a name, Adam, and flew the same day to Karachi, a place Pearl had previously described to a friend as a "great city if we weren't scared to go out of the hotel."

On January 23, he went to the meet set up by Omar Sheikh—outside the Village Restaurant in downtown Karachi. Just before seven P.M., a red Suzuki Alto pulled up and the driver beckoned. Pearl got in, and they drove off at speed along Shah-e-Faisal Road toward the airport.

Pearl's phone record showed that he took a call from someone at seven eleven P.M. that lasted four minutes, but when his local fixer rang him thirty minutes later, he did not answer.

The *Wall Street Journal* reporter had been kidnapped and was on his way to a remote compound in Ahsanabad, far from the city center. "The guest is coming. Get ready," was the message texted at eight P.M. to the welcoming party at the other end.

Stepping out of the car at the compound, Pearl was greeted by a man brandishing a pistol who marched him into a cinder-block outhouse. The only other buildings in the vicinity were a mosque and madrassa belonging to Sipah-e-Sahaba, a violent sectarian front raised by the ISI that was respon-sible for brutal attacks on Shias and adherents of other Islamic sects it regarded as heretical.

Inside, more men with guns confronted Pearl. They ordered him to change into a cheap tracksuit and hand over his possessions. "What's going on?" he asked nervously, according to witness statements taken later by the police. "Is this security?" When one of the guards replied that Sheikh Gilani had made the arrangements, Pearl calmed down and complied. Sheikh Gilani later denied any role in the kidnapping of Daniel Pearl.[44]

By the following morning, still with no sign of Gilani turning up, Pearl was getting jittery again. "Let me call someone or let me go," he told his captors. "I don't want to talk to [Gilani] anymore."[45]

One of the guards slapped him. "You are in our custody. Shut up and sit there. If you talk, we will kill you." Photos of Pearl were taken and sent from an e-mail address, kidnapperguy@hotmail.com, with a message that he would be released only if "all Pakistanis being illegally detained by the FBI" were also released or given access to lawyers.

Pearl tried to run for it. He clambered up a six-foot boundary wall, shouting, "Help me!" But he was pulled back down and beaten.

However, Omar Sheikh, who was controlling proceedings on the phone from Islamabad, now began to lose control of his own conspiracy. On January 28, a remorseful member of the kidnappers' circle drafted an e-mail saying that Pearl was a journalist, not a CIA spy, and would be released.

Just before it was dispatched, Omar Sheikh had the kidnappers send another note to say that they had just learned that Pearl was in fact a Mossad agent. "We will execute him within 24 hours unless amreeka [fulfills] our demands," the e-mail declared.

Omar Sheikh was getting cold feet. The chances of winning in a climate of heightened security post 9/11 were minimal, he would later say. He did not want to go back to jail. But rather than release Pearl, he put the word out that he was willing to hand him over to another gang.

The message eventually reached Shahikot, the rugged Afghan valley south of Gardez, where Saif al-Adel and his Al Qaeda fighters were holed up. Delighted that an American hostage was up for grabs, Saif broke with security protocol to call Mokhtar in Karachi. "Listen, *he's* been kidnapped," he told Mokhtar, not using Pearl's name. "*Those* people don't know what to do with *him*. They want to know if *we* want him." Pearl's capture was a "gift from God."

Citing the slaughter at Panjwai Bridge, Al Qaeda's military chief told Mokhtar to take the prisoner and "do something." This was the chance Saif had been looking for to put the catastrophe of the shoe-bomb plot behind them. "We should make sure it's an Al Qaeda thing," Saif stressed.[46]

Mokhtar agreed. "It's good propaganda and the guy is Jewish. Anyhow, if I get caught I want to make sure I get the death penalty."[47] Worried Mokhtar was planning something brutal, Saif made him promise not to do anything too terrible with the hostage.

Next, Mokhtar called Omar Sheikh, who passed on the address where Daniel Pearl was being held. Accompanied by two nephews, Mokhtar reached the Ahsanabad compound in the last days of January, carrying plastic shopping bags containing a video camera, two knives, and a meat cleaver. There, cadres from a local branch of Lashkar-e-Jhangvi (Army of Jhangvi), another violent Islamist sectarian faction often used by the ISI, were waiting. Lashkar-e-Jhangvi had no compunction about killing people it saw as heretics. The guards should allow "the Arabs" to do whatever they wanted, the leader told them.

Mokhtar's younger nephew set up the camera, and Pearl was given a script to read.[48] Afterward, Mokhtar tied Pearl's hands behind his back, wrapped a blindfold around his eyes, and forced him down and onto his side. Two Pakistani guards sat on Pearl's legs and hips as Mokhtar produced the knives, grabbing Pearl by the hair and slashing at his neck. When one of the Pakistanis began to wretch, Mokhtar bellowed at him to "leave the room," as he continued to cut.

However, there was a problem. "*Stop!*" Mokhtar's nephew had forgotten to load a tape into the camera.

Mokhtar looked up in disbelief and screamed at him to get it working, as he tore Pearl's head clean off the body, going against Saif al-Adel's request that he should not behead Pearl.

Once the camera was running properly, Mokhtar pressed down on the corpse so that blood pumped out of the throat, showing the kill was recent. He held the severed head in the air and recited a Koranic prayer, before dismembering the body. They buried the pieces in a corner of the compound, washed the floor of the hut, and then prayed, prostrating themselves on the ground where Pearl had just been butchered.

Mokhtar then returned to his apartment, where Amal and his wife had left out his dinner on the table.

In a city of twenty-three million people, through which organized-crime bosses channeled an estimated $2 billion every year to the religious mafia and their political masters, police chief Mir Zubair Mahmood was a rare bird in that he was widely regarded as incorruptible. And that was why he was going nowhere. So the story went in Karachi.[49]

However, while Mir Zubair despised dishonesty of every kind, and was suspicious of the machinations of Pakistan's deep state, he was not above inflicting physical pain. On recidivists and the intransigent, Mir used a bamboo cane on the soles of the feet, which left fewer marks and adhered to Koranic instruction on permitted punishments. With Pearl reported missing, and Osama still sheltering in a Mokhtar safe house, Mir's search teams fanned out across the city.

They traced the e-mailed ransom notes to a bungling computer programmer who had forgotten to erase photos of Pearl as hostage from his hard drive. Under interrogation, and now accused of a kidnapping, he named Omar Sheikh as the instigator, saying he had been told: "This is a big job and you are going to be part of it." Within hours, police raided addresses all over Karachi, arresting Omar Sheikh's relatives and rounding up low-level militants. However, even in a city this vast, the seventh largest in the world, networks intermingled, and on February 7, in a joint ISI–CIA operation, Mokhtar's hood Riyadh the Facilitator was caught up in the web, along with seventeen others.

Recovered from Riyadh's house were two life jackets containing traces of explosives. Riyadh was so keen to distance himself from the Pearl disappearance that he told the truth about what he really did.

He explained how he had helped more than one hundred Arab fighters escape from Pakistan. He said it had cost him $500,000 and the man who provided the cash was a Pakistani-Balochi brother called Mokhtar. This Mokhtar was dependent on several couriers, the most important of all being a man known as Abu Ahmad al-Kuwaiti, who had once worked in Al Qaeda's media office and was now married to a young girl from Swat. The CIA had stumbled across treasure on Al Qaeda, even if it could not find Daniel Pearl.

Robert Grenier, the CIA station chief, reviewed Riyadh's file. His information linked Mokhtar to Osama bin Laden via a courier, al-Kuwaiti. Did it also put Mokhtar in the frame for Pearl's kidnapping? he wondered.[50]

When the news of Riyadh's capture reached the logistics chief Abu Zubaydah, who had left the border and was now ensconced in a Lashkar-e-Taiba guesthouse in Lahore, he was fearful. "I need to be more cautious," he told his diary. "This news made our situation shakey."[51] With huge rewards being offered, he was anxious about being betrayed by "the Pakistani brothers" on whom he relied. Osama, who as far as he knew had been to Karachi more than once, was at risk and so was he. "Some of them know me, I mean some Pakistanis whom I deal with in the smuggling of the brothers, and exchanging money in order to free the brothers from their captors."[52]

*   *   *

February 2002, Islamabad

Although the mystery of Daniel Pearl's whereabouts persisted, Robert Grenier felt as if the tide was turning on Al Qaeda. The business end of the CIA operation inside Pakistan was revving up, too. With the help of General Javed Alam Khan, his opposite number in the ISI, he had opened up "the Clubhouse," an off-the-grid holding facility in the middle of Islamabad, located on Nizamuddin Road in G-6, a smart sector close to the ISI headquarters at Aabpara and thronged with ISI safe houses. As a result of intelligence recovered in the Pearl raids, they were now inundated with prisoners.

Hidden behind high walls and tall, dense shrubbery, the Clubhouse was surrounded by the homes of expats and diplomats and staffed by plain-clothes interrogators who worked around the clock. Several small rooms on the ground floor had been converted into interrogation suites, with security cameras and secret recording devices, while upstairs were bedrooms where the interrogators could rest.[53]

Grenier and his deputy, a case officer known as Dave, watched as suspects were brought in, hooded and manacled. Those with the most interesting stories were taken to Chaklala, the Pakistan Air Force base next to Islamabad airport, where they were strip-searched; put in orange jumpsuits, goggles, and earphones; and shackled and loaded onto military transports bound for U.S. detention facilities at Bagram or Kandahar. The only indication of something serious and secretive at the Nizamuddin address was the number of SUVs with diplomatic plates and Pakistani government–issue white Toyota Corollas turning up day and night.

Grenier had plenty of resources to call on, with material developed inside Pakistan augmented by files dispatched from the specialist Counterterrorism Center (CTC) in Langley. There, targeters were trying desperately to match tips from agents and assets to technical data coming from satellite intercepts, mobile phone masts, drone footage, and information provided by other intelligences services.

In a sixth-floor office at Langley that was manned around the clock, these targeters experimented with algorithms that could supposedly sift through billions of digital files, searching for keywords and coded phrases. Thousands of phone numbers, names, and addresses were generated and forwarded to the teams working under Grenier or Dave in the hope that something might lead to Osama, Abu Zubaydah, or identify the elusive Mokhtar. The information was overwhelming. Grenier's team was brimming with new staff, generalists now outnumbering specialists. Operating successfully in Pakistan required an understanding of how the country *worked*. The agency was struggling to feel its way into a campaign that required local knowledge it did not have.

To make everyone feel like they had some kind of control of the situation, a template for raids was worked out with the ISI's chief of internal security, General Etesham Zameer, a jovial, balding officer whose father had been a famed Urdu poet. Addresses distributed from the Clubhouse were parceled up and dispatched to provincial ISI chiefs for action. For legal reasons, the Pakistani police had to lead the raids; but the identity of who or what might be picked up was withheld from them. In most cases, one of Grenier's officers and an FBI representative, often legal attaché Jennifer Keenan, waited across the street or in a parked car until the fuss had died down. Any Pakistanis found inside were dealt with by the domestic authorities, while the foreigners belonged to the Americans, who would also gather up mobile phones, laptops, hard drives, USB drives, passports, and notebooks. Original documents went back via Keenan to FBI headquarters, with copies given to the CIA. "Night after night, data streams from hard drives deemed of priority value would be shot skywards from our roof to satellites overhead," recalled Grenier, who later described it as one of the largest intelligence operations in the world.[54]

Grenier worried that most of those being arrested as a result of these raids were only low-level facilitators at best. Months had passed since 9/11 and not one senior Al Qaeda leader had been run to ground in Pakistan—while eavesdropped communications suggested that hundreds were sheltering there. He was under huge pressure.

Only when the ISI began tapping one particular mobile phone number in late January did something more interesting turn up. The number had come from the cell phone of an Al Qaeda fighter detained at Tora Bora. He claimed it was for one of Al Qaeda's most trusted couriers, a man he knew as Abu Ahmad al-Kuwaiti. Listening in, the CIA heard a man talking in Kuwaiti Arabic. When he was connected to a non-Arabic speaker, he switched to fluent Pashto or less confident Urdu. Although he was always careful to speak in code, occasionally he made a passing reference to "the Teacher" or to "Abu Abdullah," two known cyphers for Osama bin Laden.

The more they listened, the more certain Grenier's team was that the caller was closely connected to Osama bin Laden. Sometimes he spoke to a young Arab who spoke too much and giggled—and was using a Pakistani mobile phone in Karachi.

The abduction of Pearl, which remained a mystery and had seen the CIA trip over Al Qaeda's sanctuary network, had opened up a view of Al Qaeda that no one had seen before.[55] And it centered on Karachi.

January 29, 2002, Washington, D.C.

In his first State of the Union address since 9/11, and with nothing much yet to report of the war against Al Qaeda, President George W. Bush zeroed in on nation states that supported terrorism, many of which, he said, were also seeking weapons of mass destruction. North Korea was "a regime arming with missiles and weapons of mass destruction, while starving its citizens." Iraq "continues to flaunt its hostility toward America and to support terror."

Then the president turned on Iran, which, he said, "aggressively pursues these weapons and exports terror, while an unelected few repress the Iranian people's hope for freedom." Bush concluded: "States like these and their terrorist allies constitute an Axis of Evil, arming to threaten the peace of the world."

In Kabul, veteran diplomat Ryan Crocker, who had been sent there to reopen the U.S. embassy, was dumbstruck.[56] All the delicate diplomacy of recent times—the meetings in Geneva, the intelligence and maps locating Taliban and Al Qaeda positions, the haggling at the Bonn conference that had elevated Hamid Karzai into power in Afghanistan—had been swept away by three ill-judged words: "Axis of Evil."

Tehran was currently negotiating the transfer of Afghan warlord Gulbuddin Hekmatyar from his Iranian home into Afghan custody "and ultimately to American control." According to Crocker's CIA acquaintances, Hekmatyar was one of the few people in the world who probably knew where Osama bin Laden was hiding. Why ruin all this delicate maneuvering for the sake of a highly politicized speech?

Crocker could see how this was going to play out. The Iranian leadership was going to conclude that "in spite of their bountiful cooperation with the American war effort, the United States remained implacably hostile."[57]

Bush's Axis of Evil was a "stupid, gratuitous phrase" that "didn't advance anything that the U.S. was trying to do in the region" and that "effectively [sabotaged] cooperation with Iran," said Crocker, who was at that stage unaware of the Al Qaeda factor—which the CIA *had* got wind of and which had in part contributed to the president's decision to include Iran in his naming and shaming.

"For most Americans, it probably sounded like a throwaway line, and for some it may have sounded like the sort of 'tough' rhetoric that they think 'strong' presidents use," he recalled. "But instead of conveying strength, it reflected the clumsy incompetence that would define the administration in the years to come."[58]

February 2002, Tehran

In his office at the old U.S. embassy on Taleqani Street, General Qassem Suleimani was furious. He had the Hekmatyar folder delivered to his office and issued new instructions. The warlord should be secretly transported back to Afghanistan and into the arms of his vast Hezb-i-Islami network, from where he should be encouraged and helped to wreak maximum damage along the Pakistan border in retaliation for Bush's stance.

When the Mauritanian, who was also in Tehran, read the news about President Bush's speech, he was worried but also sensed an opportunity. In alienating Iran, Al Qaeda might become, he thought, a principal beneficiary. Clearly, the Reformists had failed in their attempts to charm Washington, leaving General Suleimani ascendant. Mahfouz would milk this safe haven for all it was worth, and with some careful planning Osama's caravan could separate itself from the erratic Mokhtar, whose recent actions had placed it in harm's way, and travel to Iran freely.

Without thinking through the longer-term consequences of placing Al Qaeda's future in the hands of an Iranian Shia archstrategist, Mahfouz took out his secret phone and made a call. Within a week, he was inundated with requests from Arab families, which "required the hiring of a great number of houses, huge daily and monthly expenses, plane tickets, and other expenses."[59] So sure was he that this was the right thing to do that he sent for his own family to come, too.

A Mercedes met them at the Taftan crossing; the younger children were presented with toys that they stared at blankly, as they no longer remembered how to play. When the family reached Tehran, they were taken to a spacious apartment with food in the fridge, a shower and a bath, soft mattresses, even a TV.

The following day the debriefings began with Quds Force agents asking the Mauritanian direct questions about Al Qaeda, its history, and its future. They were curious about the whereabouts of Osama bin Laden and Mullah Omar. He said he had no idea about Osama's movements. "I told them that some data could be released since it doesn't harm anybody but there is some information I will never disclose."

As the interrogation evolved, the Mauritanian was struck by a significant detail. The men who came to see him said they were certain that Al Qaeda was not responsible for 9/11. "They believed the USA had carried out the September Eleventh attacks, and that an Israeli American pilot and American missiles had brought down the Twin Towers," he recalled, amazed that such a proudly intelligent race could be so stupid. What he did not appreciate was that the Iranians might simply be spinning him a line.[60]

February 21, 2002, Karachi

The gruesome, juddering video had been auctioned off to Pakistani reporters for a few hundred dollars.[61] Its title was self-explanatory: "The Slaughter of the Spy-Journalist, the Jew Daniel Pearl."

Raids to find Pearl's kidnappers began again across Karachi. Doors were kicked down, the police oblivious to how close they were to Osama bin Laden—who fled back to Afghanistan.

The pressure of mass arrests and house-to-house searches did get to Omar Sheikh, who gave himself up—but not to the authorities. He contacted his maternal uncle Ijaz Shah, a brigadier in the ISI, who kept him hidden in the Punjab for a week, coaching him on what to say, before handing him over to the ISI proper—which allowed U.S. investigators to see him.

When the FBI asked Omar Sheikh why Pearl had been killed, his answers were vague. Someone high up in the Al Qaeda hierarchy had ordered it. Sheikh didn't know the identity of that person, only that the leadership had taken over his abductee.

His group was never a group, he said. Nothing it did was planned. Sheikh's collaborators, when they were arrested and questioned, had nothing to lose. Pearl's killer? It was Mokhtar, they all said. What the ISI and CIA did not know was that they were closer to Osama bin Laden than they realized. He had stayed at the safe houses recently raided in Karachi. On one occasion they had missed him by a whisper. But now there was no trace of him.

CHAPTER FOUR

*"Poor ones, this is not how revenge is, or will
be."*

—ABU ZUBAYDAH, WRITING IN
HIS DIARY, FEBRUARY 2002

February 2002, Lahore, Pakistan

ABU ZUBAYDAH WAS COMFORTABLY EMBEDDED in the Punjab, helping to
prepare an alternative bolt-hole with Lashkar-e-Taiba's assistance, should
the Iran plan fail.

For Abu Zubaydah, who was unaware of Osama's recent visits to Karachi
or the specifics of Al Qaeda's future operational plans, Pakistan was a logical
place to regroup. Given that it was permanently chaotic and home to an estimated six hundred thousand mujahid veterans of conflicts in Afghanistan
and Kashmir, plus one hundred thousand active younger members of jihad
groups and one million or more enrolled in radical seminaries, he did not
have to search too hard to find people willing to assist him.

However, after a decade in the country, Zubaydah, like Mullah Omar, had
learned to be wary of his Pakistani hosts. Lashkar-e-Taiba had been guarding
him since early February in an operation personally supervised by its founder
and emir, Hafiz Saeed, who knew Osama and counted one former ISI director
general among his closest friends.[1] Zubaydah appreciated Saeed's help but
suspected that if the ISI leadership knew his business, then wily President
Musharraf probably did too. So he took precautions: moving every few weeks,
changing his guards, and keeping communications to the bare minimum.

In early March, Zubaydah arrived at an empty house on the outskirts of
Faisalabad, a former British cantonment city three hours west of Lahore. A
decade earlier, his older brother Mahir had studied medicine here and had
described it as a backwater.[2] Tucked out of the way down Canal Road and
surrounded by paddy fields, Zubaydah felt safe.

Nominally in charge of a war chest of $100,000 to prepare the ground for the possible arrival of Saif al-Adel and Al Qaeda's military committee that had just outflanked U.S. and British forces in Afghanistan's Shahikot Valley, and eager to move forward with "special programs," Zubaydah was instructed to sit tight.

Mulling over the brutal scenes he had witnessed in Kandahar, he imagined these future plans in his diary, writing nightly before he went to bed: "a general war, non-stop and without mercy," one that would attack "all sectors of life." Every kind of target and method was on the table, from remote-controlled exploding mobile phones to using fissile material in dirty bombs. "If nuclear is available, no problem, in fact, it would be a lot better," Zubaydah proclaimed.

What he did not know was that Saif's deputies were already pursuing the fissile option from the safety of the Tribal Areas.[3] In their sights was America and "those who stood with America (Pakistan is first, Britain is second)." Other countries, too, would get their share "at the right time," wrote Zubaydah.

As he sat waiting for updates and those guarding him strung up sheets over doors and outside spaces to stop neighbors from looking in, Zubaydah contemplated the creeping threat of capture. "News keeps coming . . . the shadow of Ibn al-Sheikh is still around me, may God release him from captivity," he wrote of his friend, the Khaldan commander, who had been seized in Parachinar and sold to the CIA.[4] "God only knows how sad it made me that they caught him, imprisoned him, and whoever is with him. May God enable us to release them from captivity and avenge them."

Sometimes good news outweighed the bad: Zubaydah recorded how on March 20 a suicide bomber had brazenly walked into Islamabad's diplomatic zone, blowing himself up inside a church, killing an American diplomat's wife and daughter.

"Some expected that this is the beginning of Al-Qa'ida's revenge in Pakistan," Zubaydah wrote, thinking of the women and children U.S. fighter jets had blown up on the bridge at Panjwai. "Poor ones, this is not how revenge is, or will be."

February 2002, CIA Station, U.S. Embassy, Islamabad, Pakistan

"Deuce" Martinez, an analyst with a passion for tessellating statistics, was not typical "war on terror" fodder. A staunch Catholic who did not speak

Urdu or Arabic, Martinez had never been to Pakistan and had no idea about its geography when Jose Rodriguez, the chief of staff at the Counterterrorism Center (CTC), sent him there in January 2002.

Martinez had never been a clandestine operative. Cold drops, legends, and burner phones were alien to him. But Rodriguez, who had spent much of his career to date running the CIA's Latin America division, had watched Martinez, who was then posted to the Crime and Narcotics Center, transform the agency's record of interdicting Latin American cartels.

His specialty was numbers, addresses, grid references, and waypoints—any kind of obscure, mistakenly generated, unseen, discarded data, gathered any which way, from which he could emulsify a target.[5]

Now using the same techniques to track Al Qaeda, Martinez focused on one particular cell phone number. Dozens of fighters seized as they crossed over from Tora Bora had it written down on scraps of paper. So many Al Qaeda recruits spoke of the man who owned it and of his legendary logistics hub in Peshawar that he appeared to be a senior member of Al Qaeda's leadership. Shortly before 9/11, his name had appeared in the President's Daily Brief warning of Osama bin Laden's imminent plans to attack the United States.[6] The phone belonged to Abu Zubaydah, and he kept it in his briefcase alongside his contacts book and his diary.

As far as the CIA was concerned, Zubaydah was a "High Value Target," "bin Laden's lieutenant," and Number Three in Al Qaeda. The CIA believed that he was one of the planners of 9/11 and that catching him would strike an existential blow to the terror network.

Martinez wrote Zubaydah's number on a large piece of paper pinned to the wall of his new office in Islamabad, next to old ID photographs obtained from Saudi intelligence. But the pictures—which showed the suspect wearing glasses, a mustache, and a neatly clipped beard—posed their own set of problems.

Zubaydah's younger brother, Hesham Abu Zubaydah, had been recently tracked down to Portland, Oregon, where he had lived since 1998, emigrating from Saudi Arabia to pursue the American dream. Arrested by the FBI after 9/11, he insisted that the photographs were of someone else. "The person just didn't look anything like the brother I grew up with," he recalled.

Referring to his older brother as "Hani," his old pet name from childhood which means "sweet" in Arabic, Hesham told the FBI that he remembered him as a "fun, good guy" who had worn blue jeans, putting him on a collision course with their religious and overbearing father. As a teenager growing up in Riyadh, Hani had smoked, chased "cute" girls, watched romantic movies, and listened to Arab and Western love songs, his favorite singer being Chris de Burgh. But after he went to Pakistan in 1990 he had become estranged from the family.

Hesham told the FBI that he had not seen his brother for a decade, although they had talked on the phone a year before 9/11 when he had been in financial trouble and Hani had helped him out. As far as his brother being the 9/11 mastermind, Hesham doubted it. "I told the FBI, 'The guy you're talking about, I don't *know* that guy.' "[7]

Putting Hesham's denials to one side, and unable to glean any information from other family members who still lived in Saudi Arabia, Martinez concentrated on the phone number, adding lines radiating outward that represented data provided by the National Security Agency on calls made and received, cell towers picked up, and signals relayed. Laid over the top were e-mails received and sent that referenced Zubaydah or his associates. It made, according to those who watched it grow, "a pretty diagram."[8]

By early March, Martinez developed "clear indications" that Zubaydah or someone close to him was in Lahore or Faisalabad.

Robert Grenier, who had watched Martinez's quiet, methodical approach with initial skepticism, began to get excited. Zubaydah's "underground railroad" had been the CIA station chief's personal obsession for two and a half years.[9] By Grenier's estimation, Zubaydah knew more about the network than anyone else. Getting to him would open up many possibilities.

Putting Karachi on the back burner, the CTC system went into overdrive, generating even more addresses across the Punjab. Grenier sent operatives down to Faisalabad and Lahore, where, working with the ISI, they captured mobile phone signals close-up using a phone intercept machine they called the "magic box." But whoever was using the "Zubaydah" phone was on their guard and countersurveillance-aware. They turned it on only to make brief calls or collect messages, which made it difficult to pin the phone down to a specific address.

After two weeks and with fourteen possible locations, Grenier made a decision to hit them all simultaneously. It would be a complex operation requiring considerable political support from Islamabad—and Washington—so Grenier sent his deputy Dave to lobby members of the Senate Select Committee on Intelligence who happened to be visiting Pakistan. Martinez, accompanied by Jennifer Keenan, the FBI's legal attaché, estimated their chances were fifty-fifty: odds that further down the road would shut down an operation like this. However, in need of results right now, Grenier thought the chances good enough.

March 29, 2002, 1:20 A.M., Canal Road, Faisal Town, Faisalabad, Pakistan

Exhausted after a long day's digging, Shafiq Ghani, an agricultural laborer, had gone to bed early, looking forward to an uninterrupted night's sleep as his wife and children were away. But he was woken by voices out in the street.[10]

The clattering around was unusual for this quiet, new development, and when he looked through his gate, he was frightened to see heavily armed police officers, Punjab Rangers—and several Westerners in cargo pants, including a woman, standing in the road.

"There are people living here," he called out nervously, worried about being injured in a shoot-out.

Two Rangers stomped over and pushed him back inside his courtyard. "Keep out of the way," they hissed.

Shafiq began praying as the police piled into his neighbor's ugly gray cement villa, a building called Shahbaz Cottage but that resembled a bullion vault protected by barbed wire and spikes. Shafiq had watched as eight young, clean-shaven men had recently taken up residence. Initially, he had presumed they were students, but when they draped curtains over all the windows and doors and made canopies from rugs to cover outside spaces, he had begun to worry. One of them never went out, although Shafiq overheard him speaking.

At one thirty A.M., the Rangers broke through the gate of Shahbaz Cottage and piled in. Shafiq heard a fierce gun battle start up almost immediately as furniture was tossed about. Men screamed. Others cursed and threatened. Inside Shahbaz Cottage, Constable Mubashir of the Punjab police was wrestling with three men armed with kitchen knives who stabbed him in the neck and back as six of his comrades rushed upstairs.[11]

Shafiq heard running footsteps over the flat rooftops and counted a dozen shots. He opened a window and saw blood dripping down the walls. He heard an American woman shouting in English: "Stop firing!" He crept outside and watched as five injured men were slung into a police pickup, along with three limp corpses.

The Americans clustered around their haul with flashlights, taking photographs and recording video, a practice that Jennifer Keenan had introduced on all raids to ensure transparency. She also used the pictures to compile a database, just as the FBI had done with the Mafia. Now, as everyone stood over the blood-spattered haul, the Americans debated what they had.

One by one they inspected the prisoners, reaching the most seriously injured last: a heavy, clean-shaven man with a square jaw and mop of wild, corkscrew hair.

"It could be *him*," Shafiq heard an American agent say.

Another disagreed.

A third produced a camera. Someone else produced the Zubaydah mug shots that had created confusion. The man lying prone before them was much larger, and his face, although now bloated and flecked with blood, looked completely different. But then again, according to Hesham Abu Zubaydah, the photographs were wrong.

Shot in the thigh, with shrapnel wounds in his groin and stomach, the suspect was bleeding profusely.

A decision was taken to keep him alive in case he was Zubaydah, and he was flown under police escort to a Pakistani military hospital, where one of several CIA agents who took turns sitting watch became so concerned about the lack of security that he tied the prisoner to the bed with a sheet. As word spread that Abu Zubaydah had possibly been arrested, the Pakistanis "started bringing in V.I.P.s just to gawk at him," the former agent recalled.[12]

Over the next twenty-four hours, the prisoner slipped in and out of consciousness. "When he was able to speak, it was practically breathless," the agent recalled. "Our conversations were very short. The first thing he said—he was clearly out of it—was to ask for a glass of red wine." Later, he wept and begged the American to smother him with a pillow.

March 31, 2002, Detention Site Green, Thailand

Hooded and immobile, the prisoner lay handcuffed to a gurney, watched by a doctor and an anesthesiologist from Johns Hopkins Hospital who had been sent over by the CIA. When the bag was ripped from his head, his eyes flickered, adjusting to the light, the left eye clouded green with an infection. He had cuts and dried blood on his face and no idea that he had been flown more than two thousand miles by private charter to a disused military camp deep in the Thai jungle.[13]

The precise location of this makeshift interrogation center cum medical facility remains classified, but sources who worked on the program suggested that it was a crumbling Royal Thai Air Force facility called Ramasun.[14] Developed and used as a signals station by the United States during the Vietnam War, it had lain empty for years and was overgrown with weeds. Situated deep inside the country's northeastern Udon Thani Province, close to the border with Laos and far enough away from Bangkok for no one to question what was happening inside, it was the perfect place to hide a high-profile suspect. Those aware of its existence code-named it Cat's Eye.[15]

Only a handful of the U.S. intelligence and military personnel posted there at short notice knew who the prisoner was thought to be, while none of those who had arrested him in Pakistan had been told where he had gone. And since he was defined as an enemy combatant and not a prisoner of war, the International Committee for the Red Cross had also not been informed. Abu Zubaydah was about to be sucked into a black hole.

When he came to, a pale-skinned FBI agent loomed over him, speaking Arabic. He acknowledged that the prisoner was in terrible shape as he read from the medical notes: "The bullet hit him in his left thigh and shattered coins in his pocket. Some of this freak shrapnel entered his abdomen."[16]

When the prisoner mustered a weak response, the FBI visitor recorded his voice, took fingerprints, swabbed his mouth for DNA, and cut a lock of hair.

The Johns Hopkins team then sedated him before cutting open stitches to drain his wounds, warning that if they did not work fast, the wounds would become septic and, given his weak condition, probably kill him.

Anxious, the FBI visitor placed blocks of ice on Zubaydah's lips and, seeing that the prisoner had soiled himself, reached for a flannel, cleaning him up before dressing him in an incontinence pad.

This was not what Special Agent Ali Soufan had planned for his Easter vacation. He had been packing for a family holiday when he got the call to assist the CIA in the interrogation of what the Bush administration hoped was America's first High Value Detainee (HVD).

Reaching a private airstrip at Dulles International Airport, near Washington, D.C., Soufan had been surprised to find no CIA interrogation team there, only the Johns Hopkins doctors, one of whom had never worked for the CIA before and so was taken off to a telephone booth where he was asked to sign a nondisclosure agreement.[17] "No one else is coming," a crew member told Soufan as they boarded the plane.

The reason for the CIA's sudden about-face was that the CTC had shown the detainee's arrest photographs to an anonymous source in Afghanistan who told them it was *not* Abu Zubaydah. In Portland, his younger brother Hesham had also dismissed the photo as being another man. As far as the CIA was concerned, Ali Soufan was on a wild-goose chase.

Now that he was in the room with the prisoner, Soufan suspected that the CIA was wrong. He was also horrified by the condition Zubaydah was in, wondering at how the CIA could have certified him as being fit to fly after forty-eight hours in intensive care. This broken-down jungle camp infested with snakes was no place for a man near death. That first night, while other members of the local CIA team, who had flown up from Bangkok, left for their hotel, Soufan pulled an old military cot into an adjacent room, wondering about the hall of mirrors that saw an American "fighting to keep alive a terrorist dedicated to killing Americans."

At three A.M., the Johns Hopkins doctor woke him. "You should ask your questions straightaway," he urged. The prisoner had developed septicemia and would likely be dead by morning. An old shrapnel injury to his skull was also causing brain swelling. After Soufan contacted the CIA in-country team, they sent word to Langley, and a sharply worded cable came back: "Death is not an option." The prisoner would have to be disguised and admitted into intensive care at the nearest public hospital.

Soufan and his CIA colleagues donned U.S. military uniforms and put one on the prisoner. Posing as U.S. troops on assignment with the Royal Thai Air Force, they would, if asked, pretend that he was a fellow officer injured on a training exercise. But during the journey, Zubaydah's condition worsened, his larynx swelling. He was suffocating, rasping, struggling for breath. The Johns Hopkins doctors performed an emergency tracheotomy, assisted by Soufan, who pumped air into the prisoner's lungs.

When the bloodied party arrived at the hospital in Udon Thani, a crowd gathered. "People stared, trying to understand why all these 'American' soldiers were wheeling in an injured and handcuffed man." After an emergency assessment, the prisoner was put on life support.

The delirious patient woke up and found himself surrounded by female nurses. He began jabbering, thinking they were *houris* (virgins) and that he was in paradise. When he saw Ali Soufan and realized he was still alive, he tried to get out of bed.

"Don't make a scene," the FBI agent urged.

While the prisoner remained on life support, Soufan spent his time going through his briefcase, recovered from Shahbaz Cottage.

Here were bank statements, a twenty-seven-page contact book listing phone numbers and names, videos of Zubaydah praising the 9/11 attacks, and six volumes of diaries going back to 1991. Soufan was engrossed and hoped that the trove would bring them closer to Al Qaeda and its emir, his deputies, and the operatives out in the field preparing for the next round of attacks—if only he could make sense of it.

"Who," Soufan wondered, as he started reading the diaries "is Hani?" Many of the entries were addressed to this individual.

Soon his pad was filled with notes, one of which he highlighted. On page eight of the phone book, a number and a partial reference to a name struck a chord: "Abu Ahmad K."

Soufan cross-referenced the name with the FBI database and found that it probably belonged to an Al Qaeda courier whom the CIA had been tracking since January 2002. Attention to this man had peaked when Riyadh the Facilitator (determined to distance himself from the abduction of Daniel Pearl) had named Abu Ahmad al-Kuwaiti as a bagman for Osama. If Abu Ahmad al-Kuwaiti and Abu Ahmad K were the same man, they now had his phone number, bringing them much nearer to Osama's family, who was most possibly located in the megalopolis of Karachi.

On April 8, the prisoner came off life support. He still could not speak because of the tracheotomy tube, so Soufan brought in an Arabic alphabet chart.[18]

"Who is Abu Ahmad K?"

"I can't recall," the prisoner spelled out.

Soufan nodded. He would circle back to this. "Okay. Who is Hani?"

Abu Zubaydah managed a smile. He pointed to himself, before explaining with the help of the alphabet chart that this was his childhood pet name and he had adopted it again when he began writing a diary in 1990. That year he had left Saudi Arabia to study computer science at a college in India—much to the annoyance of his father. Far from home, lonely and aged just nineteen, he had adopted a nom de plume, recording a view of his life in a strange land as "Hani1," entries he planned to review ten years later with a new, wiser persona, "Hani2," who would reflect on where life had led him.

"Today I have decided to write my memoirs and these words to you," Zubaydah had written in the first entry, dated June 1990. "So this will be the letter in which I complain . . . get things off my chest, and cry in your arms whenever I feel the need to share my burden from this silly world." Fearing someone would read it and think him crazy, he also noted that he was not "schizophrenic" or "paranoid" but simply "reflective."

Back then waging jihad had been the last thing on the young Zubaydah's mind, and his writing showed how naïve he was on his first journey away from home. Studying in the southern Indian city of Mysore, where one third of the population was Muslim, he ranted about his rude Hindu neighbors and complained about his disappointed father, who had wanted him to train as a medical doctor.

Lonely and sexually frustrated, he also obsessed about women, dismissing them as "clay virgins . . . a passing evil that excite me for a moment then disappear or a wet dream that I shower after having." He would rather hold out for the seventy-two *houris* waiting for him in heaven, he confided, than consign himself to what he saw as an embarrassing role in a cheap "Indian movie."

However, unable to hold out, he began a frustrating relationship with his maid, an Indian Christian woman called Philomena, with whom he experimented sexually, although he would not allow himself to have full intercourse. After six months of sharing a bed, Philomena, unable to understand Zubaydah, began drinking heavily. Believing that he was cheating on her, she concocted a rumor about him sleeping with the wife of his closest friend, an inflammatory allegation of adultery, a crime that according to the Indian penal code carries a five-year jail sentence.[19] Arrested and investigated by the Mysore police, Zubaydah began to loathe India and by December 1990, he had decided to leave.

In January 1991, he abandoned his studies and went with another friend to Pakistan. When they reached Peshawar, they headed for Osama bin Laden's Services Office and then the House of Martyrs, prepared to volunteer.

But the sight of so many amputees and war-wounded mujahideen turned Zubaydah's stomach, as did the short-term goals of jihad. "If I become handicapped, with my leg amputated, or any other type of obstacle—God forbid! Also, what would I do if the party ends and there is no more jihad in Afghanistan! Where would I go as I have no job and no college degree? Oh, what a life!"

By February 1991 he was in Afghanistan and had become a camp rat. "I sit down next to the fire, embracing myself," he wrote. "It's not sunrise, yet, and I smell the aromatic smell . . . and the scent of the wet wood logs as they burn . . . the scent of the ground and the rainwater . . . And I breathe and I breathe and I breathe . . ." Overcoming his fears, Abu Zubaydah had begun jihad training at Khaldan camp under the legendary Al Qaeda commander Ibn Sheikh: "Hani, I feel happiness . . . Oh God!" His transformation was complete: no more smoking or listening to music, and finally he could run without wheezing.

The only things he truly missed were his mother, Malika, who, doting on her distant son, sent him plastic boxes of pastries from the family home in Riyadh when she discovered where he had gone, and his younger brother, Hesham, who he learned had become critically ill with testicular cancer.[20]

But instead of returning home, Zubaydah volunteered for the front line in Gardez. That summer, Afghanistan became a darker place, as the realities of an irregular insurgency battered him, taking the lives of good friends. "Death walks with every person here like his own shadow, awake or asleep, even in a place of solitude or in the bathroom to do the necessary," he wrote. "By God the ghost of death is feared."

In December 1991, it was Abu Zubaydah's turn: a shrapnel injury to the head bringing his war to a sudden halt. It left him traumatized and unable to speak, write, or read, and he spent the next few months in a Peshawar hospital. Six months later, discharged but unable to fight, he volunteered to work as a logistics assistant for Ibn Sheikh, basing himself at the House of Martyrs.

The Zubaydah diaries ran to six volumes and reached right up to the day before his eventual arrest. After reading them, Soufan now had no doubt that they had the right man and, watched over by the local CIA team, who could not speak Arabic and so missed much of what was going on, he intensified his questioning, asking about Osama, his family, and Al Qaeda's senior leadership.

Who is Sheikh Saeed al-Masri?

Where is Saad bin Laden?

Who is Saif al-Adel?

Zubaydah qualified his answers. He knew the head of Al Qaeda's military committee, but as he had never served in Al Qaeda he could not be sure about Saif al-Adel's's duties.

Soufan kept at it. One day, when he used a *kunya* for Saif that did not tally with the one in Soufan's notebook, the agent asked a colleague to call up

Saif's photo from the FBI Most Wanted Terrorist list on his BlackBerry, to make sure they were talking about the same person. He handed the phone to Zubaydah while the image was still loading.

"Tsk. That's not *him*," Zubaydah snapped, handing back the phone. "That's *Mokhtar*."

Soufan looked at the screen and froze. "What?"

Image 20, the photo he had intended for Zubaydah to study of "Saif al-Adel," had not come up. Instead what had loaded was Image 5 on the FBI list: a man indicted for the 1996 Bojinka Plot in which terrorists planned to bring down twelve United States–bound aircraft over the Pacific. Here was a photo identified by the FBI as Khalid Shaikh Mohammad. But Zubaydah knew him by another name.

Soufan felt fit to burst: "Mokhtar?" He hoped he could keep it bottled up. Stunned, he tried to keep his excitement hidden and let Abu Zubaydah continue.

Mokhtar was an ethnic Pakistani, the injured prisoner revealed, but had grown up in Kuwait City. He was uncle to Ramzi Yousef, who was in an American jail. Surely the Americans knew all this already? Soufan nodded dumbly.

The name Khalid Shaikh Mohammad was etched into Soufan's memory, as he had studied the first World Trade Center bombing and Mokhtar was a code name they had been trying to crack for months now. But he had never considered them to be one and the same.

Zubaydah revealed enticing details. Khalid/Mokhtar spoke English and at thirty-four was responsible for many of Al Qaeda's operations outside of Afghanistan. In fact, Mokhtar had trained the 9/11 hijackers.

Astonished, Soufan made his excuses to ring FBI headquarters. Mokhtar was Khalid Shaikh Mohammad—or KSM, as American investigators called him.

Going back to the prisoner, Zubaydah described how, like himself, this man was also not a member of Al Qaeda but was working on a twin track. He was too vain to swear fealty to another man, was always on the lookout for an opportunity to create mayhem, and saw himself as a leader among sheep, always "*the better person*." There were other juicy details. Although Mokhtar used a pocketful of cheap Nokias for innocuous communications and e-mails, he sent all operational messages via couriers. Nothing was left to the eaves-dropped airways. Chief among these couriers was Abu Ahmad K, an old friend from his Kuwait City days.

Soufan inhaled. That name again: the courier for whom Soufan now had a number.

Still, Abu Zubaydah had not finished. There was one more messenger whom Osama and Mokhtar trusted equally—and he was called Hassan Ghul.[21]

Ali Soufan's humanity was paying off. Ghul, Mokhtar, and the Kuwaiti were coming into view.

April 11, 2002, Karachi, Pakistan

Mokhtar, aka Khalid Shaikh Mohammad, had so many plans in progress that they circled like planes. There were operations being plotted, others put on hold, and some running so slowly that he had virtually forgotten about them until, *ping*, they popped up when the media reported them.

And then Khalid, as his close friends knew him, would remember and say: "That's one of mine."[22]

In the absence of a real Al Qaeda *shura*, which was now scattered across several time zones, and of the military council, which was with Saif al-Adel charting the mountains between Pakistan and Afghanistan, there was only ravenous Khalid—and insecure Osama. The two men communicated with increasing ferocity by way of letters, carried great distances by couriers Hassan Ghul and Abu Ahmad al-Kuwaiti, that were increasingly filled with plots that were tested by no one, and that had no Koranic seal.

Even after Osama had come so close to being caught in Karachi, Khalid—a jack-in-the-box with an unbounded ego—was courting a marooned emir who had won the world's attention and wanted more fame, not to hide away. To remind the world of Osama's existence, Khalid was more than happy to conduct brutal abductions and bombings of an increasingly haphazard nature in his name, each one destabilizing Al Qaeda even as it tried to find its feet after the fall of Afghanistan.

On the Tunisian resort island of Djerba, newspapers reported that a natural gas truck collided into the ancient El Ghriba Synagogue, the fireball engulfing sixteen tourists who were burned to death, alongside three local residents, with thirty people seriously injured. Nizar Nawar, identifiable only by his dental records, was named as the driver. Although not much was written about him, Khalid Shaikh Mohammad recalled the name. Nizar had rung him moments before he had detonated a bomb, igniting the gas and immolating the sightseers inside the synagogue.

"That's one of mine," Khalid had told Ramzi bin al-Shibh when he called him over to crow and to mull a controversial new idea.[23] What was the point of infamy if there was no legacy?

Khalid wanted to write his own story rather than see it surmised by others. What he had dreamed up was a three-part documentary that needed to be slick and independent enough to be transmitted by a major network, which discounted As Sahab, Al Qaeda's rudimentary in-house production company. For maximum impact it should be aired on the first anniversary of 9/11, and he knew just who could make it: a keen young Egyptian correspondent named Yosri Fouda who worked for Al Jazeera.[24]

April 2002, London

Recently appointed as Al Jazeera's bureau chief in London, Fouda was admiring the view from his office overlooking Thames House, the home of MI5, when a caller rang in.

"Brother Yosri?"

He did not recognize the voice.

"I hope you are thinking of preparing something special for the first *anniversary*," the caller suggested cryptically.[25]

Fouda probed the matter, and the man offered to provide some exclusive and "top-secret" information about 9/11.

Four days later, with Fouda having forgotten all about the call, an outline arrived by fax. It was certainly a tempting document: suggesting which sources to interview, locations to film, and questions to ask. One part of the film should focus on the life story of Mohamed Atta, the lead hijacker, the fax suggested. "If you are interested, we will provide you with addresses of people and locations," someone had written at the bottom. But first Fouda would have to travel to Pakistan. He took a gamble and agreed.

When he stepped off the plane at Quaid-e-Azam International Airport in Karachi, the remains of *Wall Street Journal* reporter Daniel Pearl had just been discovered in nearby Ahsanabad, with the BBC reporting: "Police sources said the head had been severed from the body, which had itself been dismembered." Inside the cinder-block outhouse, buttons had been found that matched those on clothes Pearl had been wearing when he disappeared. Reading about it in a local newspaper, Fouda was extremely nervous by the time a monosyllabic driver greeted him, instructing him to get into a car with blacked-out windows.

The driver took him to the Regent Plaza Hotel, where he was told to register and wait for a phone call. Instead, he received a visitor. The man, who did not introduce himself, entered Fouda's room and took a shower before ordering room service.

Fouda, bemused, waited politely until the man finished eating, before his curiosity got the better of him. Who he would be interviewing? Was it Osama, he asked, hopefully?

"Sheikh Osama, God protect him, is alive and well," the visitor said, adding that he was "an avid viewer of your channel." *That means he is living somewhere with electricity and a satellite connection,* Fouda noted to himself.

They sat up all night as if waiting for someone or something. No one came. The next morning, April 19, the visitor rose and told Fouda to stay in his room until five P.M. Then he should leave the hotel through a rear entrance and take a taxi. He scribbled down the address of a commercial block. "Wait by the stairs on the second floor."

Later that day, as Fouda stood in the shadows as instructed, he became increasingly paranoid. "I have thrown myself into the unknown with no clue whatsoever," he told himself.

After a few minutes, a Pakistani approached and addressed him: "I have just given my mother-in-law a lift home. We can go now."

It was the prearranged code and Fouda got into another stranger's car, thinking of severed heads and shirt buttons.

Someone slipped a blindfold over his face. He gasped. A hand grabbed his and squeezed it. Then the car stopped. A door opened. He was walked into a building and Fouda counted as he was led up four flights of stairs. He heard a doorbell ringing before he was led into an apartment.

"It's okay, you can take the blindfold off," said a high-pitched voice, as a door closed behind him.

Fouda found himself standing face-to-face with a short, hairy man with a huge protruding belly under his *shalwar kameez.* He led the reporter into a back room where a younger man in a *keffiyah* was sitting on the floor surrounded by laptops and mobile phones.

"Recognize us yet?" the fat man joked, as his friend jumped up and shook Fouda's hand warmly. "You will when intelligence dogs turn up at your door," said the younger man, giving him a toothy grin.

Fouda didn't know what to say as the men introduced themselves as Khalid Shaikh Mohammad and Ramzi bin al-Shibh, two of the most wanted men in the world.

He blurted out: "They say that you are *terrorists*."

"They are right," Khalid, aka Mokhtar, replied, smiling proudly. "We like to terrorize disbelievers. That is what we do for a living."

Khalid asked the journalist to place his right hand on a copy of the Koran and swear an oath. They would tell Fouda everything he wanted to know, and in return Fouda would not talk about how they communicated or where they met.

"When they ask you what we now look like, you will say we have not changed at all since the photos they will show you were taken," Khalid instructed.

Fouda could wait no longer: "Did you do it?"

Khalid smiled triumphantly: "I am the head of the Al Qaeda military committee," he began, "and Ramzi is the coordinator of the Planes Operation. And yes, we did it."

Fouda was stunned. No one had yet claimed direct responsibility for 9/11. He needed to tape this conversation but as instructed he had left his electronic equipment behind in the hotel.

Khalid asked to see Fouda's passport. "Nice one," he said, noting down the serial number of the Pakistani visa. Document forgers would find it useful to know the latest numbering system used by the High Commission in London. When Khalid spotted Fouda's mobile phone he snatched it. He tore out the battery and SIM card, snapping: "*Careless!*"

Fouda could see his attention to detail, as well as his paranoia, and how Khalid's temper could boil over. There would be no filming that night, Khalid ruled. Nervous, Fouda asked to go out onto the balcony for a cigarette. Khalid chided him for being weak-willed.

When he came back inside, Khalid said: "Come on: let's pray."

They prostrated themselves and when they were done Khalid patted the carpet beside him. "Now we sleep."

Lying between a snoring Khalid and al-Shibh, who was curled up like a child, Fouda stared at the ceiling, fretting about what would happen next.

At dawn, a tapping on his shoulder woke him. "It's time to pray," whispered al-Shibh. Khalid joined them, drying his hairy, wet arms on the tail of his *kameez*.

Shortly after breakfast an assistant arrived with a Sony MiniDV Handycam, a microphone, and five tapes, the same equipment they had used to document the decapitation of Daniel Pearl.

Khalid yelled at the assistant to bring a brown shawl that he and al-Shibh pinned to the wall. Nothing in the apartment should be visible. Then he went out and returned wearing a similar wrap, covering his bulky body like a fly sheet. Eventually, having balanced the camera on a cardboard box, he sat down.

"It is okay now," he said, smoothing down the fabric. "We can begin."

Gone was the aggressive, overconfident, bullying Khalid, replaced by a man who was considered and quietly spoken, although tripping over his words as he tried to speak in classical Arabic. He was aping Osama, Fouda thought. But he was sweating profusely and several times they stopped so he could dry himself.

He described the planning for 9/11 in so much detail that Fouda was certain that he truly was the architect.

Next, al-Shibh sat down to be interviewed, announcing he would not need a disguise as "natural is better" and anyhow, they would doctor the tapes before giving them to Al Jazeera.

Fouda hesitated. These tapes would be taken away from him when he flew back to London? "Al Jazeera can do this doctoring in the studio," he tried, knowing he would probably never see them again.

Khalid shook his head. "You guys usually use a mosaic and it can easily be decoded. We have our own production company, As Sahab, that will do a better job."

He went into another room and returned with a handful of CDs. "This is the beheading of Pearl the Zionist," he said, handing one to Fouda. "You can use as much as you wish."

Fouda nodded dumbly.[26]

By Sunday afternoon, they had spent almost forty-eight hours together, praying, eating, and discussing the ethics of mass murder. Fouda was mentally and physically exhausted. After he gathered up his things, al-Shibh hugged him deeply, and as he broke away Khalid handed him a statement about the Djerba synagogue attack. "That's one of mine," he said.

At the door, an assistant tied a blindfold on Fouda. Khalid guided him down the stairs, talking all the way. "You know what?" he said. "You would make the perfect terrorist. I mean look at yourself! You are young, intelligent, highly educated, well organized, you speak good English, you live in London, and you are single. You remind me in a sense of brother Atta."

Fouda struggled to find any words, let alone the right ones, eventually blurting out: "One of Allah's dearest blessings is that no human being can read the minds of their fellow human beings."

Fouda heard a car door open and he felt Khalid's hand on his. "You are such a good man," Khalid said. "God bless you and protect you."

April 2002, CIA Station, U.S. Embassy, Islamabad

Robert Grenier was at a crossroads. Abu Zubaydah was being monopolized by the FBI, a rival agency, in another country. The ISI Clubhouse might as well not have existed, as all potent foreign suspects were shipped out before CIA's Islamabad station had a chance to build any lines of inquiry, while local detainees went off to Pakistan's jails, where they were housed in communal cells and colluded to create bogus leads or were kept away from the agency altogether. Permission to enter any prison had to go through General Javed Alam Khan, and these days the ISI chief was distracted by the new Karzai administration in Kabul that was perceived to lean toward New Delhi.

But Grenier knew that the CIA was also to blame. More than six months had passed since 9/11 and his agency was still not geared up to the scale of the task at hand, having insufficient linguists, targeters, analysts, interrogators, or even counterterrorism experts to ask smart questions in the right languages.

Intelligence chiefs in Langley were thinking the same. Revelations about the CIA's failure to follow up on multiple warnings about Al Qaeda's intentions before 9/11 had been compounded by the fact that Zubaydah's explosive intelligence—identifying Mokhtar and exposing the courier network—had been elicited by the FBI after the CIA had concluded he was not the right man.

Final confirmation of Zubaydah's identity had come a few days after he was transferred to Thailand, putting the FBI firmly in the driving seat. The

Bureau tasked a special agent in Portland to take saliva samples from Abu Zubaydah's younger brother, Hesham. When his DNA matched that of his brother in Thailand, Hesham was accused of being part of an Al Qaeda sleeper cell and placed into solitary confinement, charged with violating the conditions of his student visa, as removal proceedings were initiated to expel him from the United States.

"The [FBI] was really, really mad," Hesham remembered. "They said, 'You lied to us. We showed you the pictures and you said it's not your brother. You're hiding something.' I was like, 'I'm not hiding anything. I'd not seen the guy for years.'"[27]

While the FBI bore down on the unfortunate Hesham, President Bush confirmed the news that his brother had been caught, telling a Republican gathering in Greenwich, Connecticut, that the United States had captured "one of the top operatives plotting and planning death and destruction on the United States." Abu Zubaydah was now "not plotting and planning anymore. He's where he belongs."[28]

Behind the scenes, Zubaydah's case was debated at several White House meetings attended by Defense Secretary Donald Rumsfeld, National Security Advisor Condoleezza Rice, and Attorney General John Ashcroft.[29] A decision was made to put him back into CIA custody and to radically alter the nature of his interrogation. Jose Rodriguez, the chief of staff at the CTC, would supervise this covert program.

A memo signed by Bush shortly after 9/11 had already given the CIA the power to secretly imprison and interrogate war on terror detainees outside the protection of the Geneva Conventions. For now, the Bush White House was advised, Zubaydah could continue be legally held at the undeclared CIA "black site" in Thailand while a full interrogation plan was devised.

CIA director George Tenet needed to take back control of the 9/11 investigation and stop Al Qaeda before it committed any more atrocities, and Rodriguez believed he had found the means to do it.[30]

Tenet was happy for Rodriguez to take the lead as he was also under significant pressure from the Bush administration to find links between Al Qaeda and the Iraqi dictator Saddam Hussein. A plan was already forming, mooted by Vice President Dick Cheney and backed by Defense Secretary Donald Rumsfeld, to use the 9/11 tragedy as a pretext to finish off some old business in Iraq.[31]

*   *   *

April 10, 2002, Detention Site Green, Thailand

A cable arrived for Ali Soufan. "CTC Legal" had recommended that "a psychologist working on contract in the CIA's Office of Technical Services (OTS)" be dispatched to Thailand along with a new team to "provide real-time recommendations to overcome Abu Zubaydah's resistance to interrogation."[32]

Soufan was pleased. Handling Zubaydah alone was exhausting, and he knew one of the CIA operatives slated to join him, as they had worked together on a previous investigation into Al Qaeda's bombing of the USS *Cole*.

However, when the new team arrived, Soufan instinctively disliked the contracted psychologist. Dr. James Mitchell, a veteran of the U.S. Air Force's Survival, Evasion, Resistance and Escape (SERE) program, based at Fairchild Air Force Base in Spokane, Washington, was well known and well regarded in the U.S. military. He had retired a month before 9/11 but after the attacks had volunteered his services to the CIA.

Accustomed to being listened to, Mitchell informed Soufan that Al Qaeda commanders had been specially trained in resistance techniques using stolen U.S. Special Forces manuals and that the CIA had decided only a program focused on tailor-made countermeasures would get someone of Zubaydah's seniority to tell the truth.[33] Mitchell had been contracted to come up with these measures, based on his SERE training.[34]

After his earlier success with Zubaydah, Soufan was irked at being lectured. But Mitchell came with the full authorization of CTC chief of staff Jose Rodriguez: a point emphasized by the fact that a senior CTC official now accompanied him. Zubaydah was to be discharged from the hospital and returned to the jungle camp, Soufan was informed. After that, the new CIA interrogation team would have exclusive access to him.

Coached by Mitchell, the team would work on Zubaydah for as long as it took for him to develop a sense of "learned helplessness," a procedure based on research conducted in the 1960s and that Mitchell had studied carefully. Experiments back then had shown that when dogs realized they could do nothing to avoid small electric shocks, they would become listless and simply whine, enduring the shocks even after being given a chance to escape.[35]

At home, on the shelves of Mitchell's personal library, books on psychology jostled for space with Islamic texts and he had a particularly personal reason for studying the mindset of violent Islamist extremists. Back in 1995, a close friend from Spokane, a psychiatrist and fellow extreme sports enthusiast called Donald Hutchings, had been kidnapped in Kashmir along with five other Westerners by an offshoot of the Pakistani terror group Harkat-ul-Ansar. One of the hostages was beheaded and one escaped, but Hutchings and three others were never seen again.[36]

Soufan was unconvinced by Mitchell's pitch and questioned the senior CTC official who had accompanied him from Washington. But it was useless. The program and Mitchell had backing at the highest level.

"Washington feels that Abu Zubaydah knows much more than he's telling you," the CTC official told Soufan, explaining that Langley was convinced Zubaydah was still hiding intimate knowledge about future attacks on the United States.[37] The CTC also believed Zubaydah to be a senior Al Qaeda lieutenant and confidant of Osama bin Laden, and it wanted him to admit to having played a critical role in planning the 9/11 attacks.[38] "[Mitchell] here has a method that will get that information quickly," said the CTC official.[39]

"What is this *method*?" Soufan asked Mitchell directly, pointing out that he had already obtained crucial intelligence from Zubaydah on couriers, Mokhtar, and Al Qaeda's military council just by talking to him.

Mitchell launched into a prepared speech about taking away privileges, including clothes, food, and his chair. Zubaydah would come to see his interrogator as "a god" who controlled his suffering. "Pretty quickly you'll see Abu Zubaydah buckle and become compliant," Mitchell assured.[40]

Soufan needed to do only one further thing: inform Zubaydah that Mitchell's "boss," the senior CTC official, was taking over, and that this person would determine whether he lived or died. "After that you will never see him again," said Mitchell.[41]

Soufan was upset and angry. "These things won't work on people committed to dying for a cause," he insisted. "They expect to be sodomized and to have family members raped in front of them!"[42] Would taking away Zubaydah's chair make him more cooperative?

This was science, Mitchell condescended. "He will fold quickly."

But Zubaydah had already *folded*, Soufan countered. Had Mitchell ever questioned an Islamic terrorist before?

"No," he replied.[43]

"Have you ever conducted *any* interrogations?"

"No."

Soufan was furious that someone he regarded as having no field experience was pulling rank on him.[44] Mitchell later defended his level of expertise, saying: "In survival school, you have to understand the various interrogation approaches. Oddly enough, if you spend years and years and years watching people try to lie and tell the truth under various circumstances where coercion exists, you get some sense of what people are like when they're lying or telling the truth."[45]

Soufan contacted a senior: "Is this a joke?"

He fired off a cable to FBI headquarters. "I have spent an un-calculable amount of hours at [Zubaydah's] bedside assisting with medical help, holding his hand and comforting him through various medical procedures, even assisting him in going [to] the bathroom ... We have built tremendous report [sic] ... with AZ and now that we are on the eve of 'regular' interviews to get threat information, we have been 'written out.' "[46]

An unequivocal message came back from New York: Dr. Mitchell had full authorization from Jose Rodriguez. The psychologist would later say: "I'm just a guy who got asked to do something for his country by people at the highest level of government, and I did the best that I could."[47]

Soufan was also told that the president had recently signed an executive order that excluded Al Qaeda or Taliban detainees from protection under Common Article 3 of the Geneva Conventions, which prohibited "mutilation, cruel treatment and torture." The CTC had free rein to do whatever was deemed necessary to get Zubaydah to confess what it believed him to be guilty of.[48]

On April 13, 2002, the "new interrogation program" started while Zubaydah was still in the hospital.[49] Briefed by the CTC psychological team, a CIA interrogator sat by Zubaydah's bed and quietly advised that he should cooperate and inform them of "a most important secret that [they] needed to know": when were the next Al Qaeda attacks planned for and was the U.S. mainland a target?[50]

Zubaydah, who was more focused on the pain in his stomach and his seeping wounds, nodded but said nothing.

Two days later, with Zubaydah still not speaking, a "pre-move message" was delivered according to Mitchell's advice, informing him that "time is running out."[51] Zubaydah was then sedated, discharged from the hospital, and moved back to his old cell in the jungle camp. He woke up four hours later.

"I found myself chained to this steel bed in this white room," he wrote in his diary, a record that Mitchell later said he allowed Zubaydah to write in detention so they would know what the detainee was thinking.[52] Most of the entries were undated and some are hard to understand, but the diary, which was later confiscated from Zubaydah and classified, gives a frightening insight into the brutality of the new interrogation program.[53]

Though he was desperate for sleep, cold water was repeatedly thrown over him to keep him awake. Shivering, he tried to take in his new surroundings. "There was nobody, nothing, except for the three walls that reflected the light as if they were lights . . . At the end of the panel of bars there was a metal door mostly made of metal bars as well . . . So I am in a prison and not in a hospital."

Eventually, he met his new jailers. "I saw a black object," he recalled. "The black object turned out to be a man all dressed in black. Even his face, his nose and his mouth were all covered." His eyes were covered with what looked like diving goggles. "And yet too these were black." Each time Zubaydah closed his eyes to sleep, the man in black threw cold water on him.

Once Zubaydah had been softened up, the interrogators filed into the room and questioned him about his Al Qaeda links.

Zubaydah recalled repeating the same words over and over: "I'm not from Al Qaeda, I'm not from Al Qaeda."[54]

One of the interrogators responded: "Don't go there." The words would ring in Zubaydah's ears after they came to be repeated thousands of times over.

More interrogators and guards filled up the cell. Unlike Mitchell, who had spent twenty years in the military, they were mostly newly employed contractors or inexperienced agency operatives, who were no longer "individuals who [Zubaydah] could attempt to establish a relationship or dialogue with."[55]

Someone shouted another question about Al Qaeda.

"I am not from Al Qaeda . . ."[56]

"Don't go there."

One black-clad guard produced handcuffs and leg shackles, while another switched on a "noise generator," filling the cell with ear-shattering sounds, another method designed to amplify Zubaydah's "sense of hopelessness."[57]

Next, they cut off his clothes and shaved his head, leaving clumps of hair lying on the floor where they would soon get mixed up with his urine and excrement. "They sat me on a plastic chair totally naked and they chained me very tight," Zubaydah wrote later. "I don't know how long I was chained to the chair. It felt like one and a half months."[58]

The chair became his world. "As to urinating I would do it on the first chair in a special can. However the chains were so tight to the chair to the point that many times I found myself urinating all over myself and on the bandages that were still wrapped around my left wounded thigh."[59]

Whatever happened, according to the program, he wasn't to sleep. "I was deprived . . . for a long period of time; I don't even know for how long: maybe two or three weeks or even more and it felt like an eternity to the point that I found myself falling asleep despite the water being thrown at me by the guard who found himself with no choice but to strongly and constantly shake me in order to keep me awake."[60]

Soufan watched horrified, wondering how, when a nation's expectations were invested in them, departmental rivalry between the CIA and FBI as well as a vengeful hardening of views inside the Bush White House were resulting in their best lead since 9/11 being subjected to an unproven, brutal, and likely illegal set of procedures. "We could only imagine what Abu Zubaydah was going through," he recalled.[61]

A doctor was sent for. "He gave me the injection and I woke up from the pain," recalled Zubaydah. "He examined me and then he started making signals to them without saying anything as if he was trying to tell them: 'he needs to sleep, otherwise he would go crazy.' "

Briefly, Zubaydah was allowed to fall asleep on the chair. "My chained hands were hanging," he recalled. "I laid my chest on my thigh and slept. My hanging arms became like a cushion for my head. Sometimes the pain would wake me up, other times I would wake up from the cold but most of the time I would wake up because I was hungry."[62]

Then came more noise. "Boum! Boum! Boum! . . . then zen, then zzzz, then wezzzz."

Zubaydah felt crushed by sound waves. "I felt my brain was going up and down, left and right . . . The song would last 5 to 10 minutes and was played again and again non stop to the point that on the first day I became afraid to reach the moment when the song would end, for the end sounded like a screaming. I started trying to distract my mind in order to avoid feeling the end of the song coming and I finally found myself screaming along with it."[63]

He was barbered again. "They kept shaving my head and my face with an electrical razor and they did it in such a quick and violent manner," recalled Zubaydah, whose hands and nails became totally black from the buildup of dirt. He began vomiting and a nurse was sent in. "I couldn't cover my genitals in an appropriate manner."

"Why are you naked?" she asked.

"Ask them," he replied.

She said: "I'll see what I can do."

Perhaps she complained or was part of the pageant, he could not decide, but the guards returned and clothed him.

"Praise God, I am finally able to cover my genitals," he thought just as another, or was it the same guard who resembled a frogman, rushed in and smothered his face in a rough hood covered in vomit. "Someone started screaming loudly and shoving me violently and started violently and quickly cutting my clothes. I felt at that moment he was cutting my skin." He was shaved again, "like you shave a sheep and not a human being."

Zubaydah was naked again, covered in his own hair and vomit, and "unable to control my urination."[64]

After several sessions Ali Soufan confronted Mitchell.[65] He and other members of the on-site CIA team were becoming worried about the "science" that lay behind Mitchell's methods. Several, along with Soufan, wrote confidential e-mails to their superiors in the United States, requesting an intervention.

After much debate at headquarters level, Soufan was given temporary permission to reengage with the detainee on April 17, while the CTC reassessed its position. "I poured a cup of tea and walked back into Zubaydah's cell."

Zubaydah spluttered: "Hello, Ali."[66]

At the end of April 2002, despite mounting protests from Soufan, he was pulled out of the interrogation room again while CIA headquarters introduced the most coercive of new interrogation strategies proposed and supported by Mitchell.[67] They included sensory deprivation and involved "a single-minded, consistent, totally focused questioning of current threat information." The procedures had the full backing of Jose Rodriguez and were supervised on the ground by a senior CTC official.

First, the interrogators removed Zubaydah's hood and produced his jihad address book. "You're a liar and you have ways of getting in touch with these people," someone hissed.[68]

Zubaydah laughed hysterically. Recalling this moment in his diary, he wrote: "If it were not for God's protection, I could have officially declared myself psychotic."

Next, they chained him down and questioned him around the clock: two teams who took turns at resting while he was kept permanently awake. One man in particular terrified Zubaydah. "I saw a man wearing black clothes, but he was also wearing a military jacket," he wrote. "His face was uncovered. He had no mask or big glasses, like the other guards usually had." It was Mitchell.[69]

In Islamabad, the ISI's foreign intelligence liaison boss General Javed Alam Khan was furious. Not only had high-profile prisoners his men had helped capture in Pakistan vanished into another country's intelligence-gathering program, but the CIA's Robert Grenier, irritated by the length of time it took to gain approvals for operations, had gone over his head and asked the ISI chief General Ehsan ul-Haq for permission to speak directly to ISI field agents without a chaperone. The general had agreed.

This undermined Khan's authority and set a dangerous precedent, he told his director general. "It was a strategic mistake," he recalled. "We just gave the Americans the signal they could just run around Pakistan willy-nilly, talking to whoever they wanted."[70]

It had not escaped Khan's attention that newly trained CIA operatives and contractors were converging on the Islamic Republic in ever-larger numbers—many of them without any accreditation, leaving the ISI with little grasp of who was who, where they went, and what they were up to. They were taking photos of sensitive locations, intercepting ISI phones, and reading his e-mail traffic.

What was Pakistan getting out of this collaboration, Khan asked General ul-Haq, pointing to their experience with Abu Zubaydah, who his men had not got to interrogate? Would Pakistan ever have anything to show for all this assistance?

The next time Grenier met Khan, he was cold. "You can run me on a polygraph and you won't get a blip," he said. "I can tell lies. It's part of my job."[71]

At the end of April, Khan was out, reassigned back into the regular army as a corps commander. And he let rip about the spy agency. About 90 percent of ISI staff were military officers, but since top-scoring graduates always went into operations or training, the spy directorate received third-rate recruits. "Garbage in garbage out," he thundered from his new position in Mangla, in Pakistan-held Kashmir. The First Strike Corps, which General Pervez Musharraf had once commanded, had the most fearsome reputation in the army. "Its only job is to attack," said Khan, who was delighted to forget about Osama bin Laden and get back to fighting Pakistan's *real* enemy: India.

Two months later, at the end of a three-year assignment, Robert Grenier left Pakistan for America's coming war, reassigned to be the CIA's mission manager in Iraq.[72] The hunt for Osama would now be left in the hands of relative newcomers.

March 2002, Iran

The Al Qaeda exodus to Iran was at its height, with the Pakistani portal firmly shut and General Qassem Suleimani's open-door policy having been rejuvenated by President Bush's Axis of Evil speech. Quds Force agents had set up a refugee camp in the no-man's-land just beyond the Iranian border with Afghanistan. Most of the families that arrived in buses and beaten-up taxis, on foot, or by pony were connected in one way or another to Al Qaeda. Taliban guards barred foreign aid workers, reporters, and any other unwanted visitors, while every few days a group of smartly dressed officials came to the camp from the Iranian side to select those it was willing to assist.[73] The lucky ones were escorted in small groups to Tehran.

There they were put up at the white monolith of the four-star Howeyzeh Hotel on Taleqani Street, just down from General Suleimani's headquarters in the former U.S. embassy. To maintain family modesty, husbands and unmarried brothers stayed across the road at the Amir Hotel. Compared to where they had come from, the hotels felt like holiday camps.[74] At the Howeyzeh, there was room service, a ladies-only gym, movies, and a swimming pool for the children. In the Amir, former fighters sat down together in comfort for the first time since 9/11. At both hotels, the Quds Force set up information points where advice was offered on getting home. For those without papers, the Quds Force drew up special "passports" that would represent the Arabs as Iraqi Shia refugees from the Iran-Iraq War. They escorted them onto flights, some choosing to relocate to Muslim majority states in Southeast Asia, including Indonesia and Malaysia. The agents were always careful to take the false identity documents back with them to cover Tehran's tracks.[75]

However, the most high-ranking Al Qaeda brothers stayed separately, their numbers swelled by those who took more secretive routes in, assisted by Saif al-Adel's Jordanian protégé, Abu Musab al-Zarqawi. Working with Gulbuddin Hekmatyar's forces, he had set up a reception point in the desert outside the Iranian city of Mashhad. Seeking out like-minded mujahideen and mercantile criminals, he established connections with local militias running illegal smuggling routes on either side of the official border at Islam Qala.

Zarqawi brought over men so senior the Quds Force could not be trusted with them, among them Saif al-Adel, who traveled under the pseudonym Ibrahim.[76] His friend, fellow Egyptian and Al Qaeda *shura* member Abu Mohammed al-Masri, a former professional soccer player who had helped coordinate the 1998 U.S. embassy attacks, arrived with papers that identified him as Daoud Shirizi. A third member of their group was Abu Musab al-Suri, the redheaded tactician who had joined Osama bin Laden in Tora Bora in 1996 and argued against the 9/11 attack during Al Qaeda's last *shura* meeting. Al-Suri was still furious with Osama for bringing about the downfall of the Taliban and squandering Al Qaeda's refuge, leaving them with a "meager" future, as he saw it, which they would have to spend as fugitives, dodging the international dragnet and constantly "moving between safe houses and hideouts."[77]

As more significant figures arrived, Saif, who assumed a leadership role, suggested that the *shura* coalesce in Mashhad, Iran's second largest city and one of the holiest sites in Shia Islam. If not there, Zabol—an Iranian border town located several hundred miles to the south, midway between the dried-out Lake Hamun and the Hirwan River—which was mainly inhabited by Arab nationals and where Arabic was the lingua franca.[78] Whatever their choice, they had to keep the Quds Force at arm's length while they consolidated in communities they could trust, gathered their strength, and prepared for new attacks on Western targets.

"We began to converge on Iran one after the other," Saif recalled.[79] "We set up a central leadership and working groups. We began to rent apartments for the brothers and some of their families." They also began to prepare for the arrival of the most precious and sensitive group of all: Osama bin Laden's family.

They were presently lurching in a bus across the emptiness of Afghanistan's Desert of Death, Dasht-e-Margo, the driver craning to see through a dust-covered windshield as the man sitting next to him studied a map searching for coordinates that had been transmitted in a letter disguised as a religious edict.

Starting in Karachi, the bus had picked up more passengers in Quetta before skimming around the bottom of Afghanistan and had taken more than a week to reach the border. Death in the desert came on like a *haboob*, the sandstorms that regularly darkened the skies to the northeast. In the faceless, roadless terrain, several times when the sand covered everything, they got lost and had to double back. The children, who slept fitfully in abandoned buildings or shepherd's huts, were ragged.

Only the man in the passenger seat seemed alert. He was Saudi fighter Abu Abdallah al-Hallabi—better known by his *kunya* Daood and for the fact he was married to Osama's daughter Khadija. He clutched a pocket Koran, hoping it would ward off every kind of accident that however minor in this environment could prove fatal. Bandits preyed on travelers forced to cross this unforgiving area of western Nimruz Province, and the food the women in the group had brought from Pakistan was long eaten. Empty water bottles rattled about on the floor as the bus plunged through potholes and groaned over dry riverbeds.

Eventually, they reached a scruffy border outpost. The women stepped down, clinging to their robes as they were whipped by a violent storm. They watched nervously as Daood handed over a bundle of dollars and the family's well-worn Sudanese passports.[80] They had left their real Saudi documents behind in Karachi with Khalid Shaikh Mohammad, who had helped them invent cover stories: their husbands and fathers had been martyred fighting the Americans. They were to invoke Iranian generosity to get home. The border guards, who, over the past six months had seen plenty of families like these, waved them through.

The women and children bade farewell to Daood, who got back on the bus to begin a long return journey to Quetta.

Waiting on the Iranian side were Sunni families loyal to Hekmatyar's network. As instructed by General Suleimani, the Quds Force had smuggled the veteran warlord back into Afghanistan, where he immediately galvanized forces to attack America, before traveling to Kunar to meet Osama and further secure his hideout.

Hekmatyar's Iranian network would transport the bin Laden caravan in two old trucks to a remote farm he owned east of Zabol.

As the oldest son present, Saad was nominally head of the bin Laden family party; but given his mental issues his aunt, Osama's wife Khairiah, took charge, trailed by her hotheaded teenage son, Hamzah. Accompanying them were Saad's wife and son and Najwa's married daughter, Fatima, whose husband had vanished at the border when the family party had been ambushed on its way into Pakistan. With Fatima were her younger siblings, Iman and Ladin. There were also the young families of Othman and

Mohammed bin Laden. The sons themselves continued to hide, Othman shadowing Dr. Ayman al-Zawahiri and Mohammed with his father.

Those in the family who had elected to stay behind in Pakistan with what was now being described in Washington as "Al Qaeda Central" were Osama's third wife, Seham, and three of her children, Khalid, Miriam, and Sumaiya. Her married eldest daughter, Khadija, had also insisted on remaining in Pakistan and was now waiting anxiously in Quetta for the return of her husband, Daood, the Saudi fighter who had escorted the women and children to Iran.

The Zabol farmhouse was a fortress in the desert. The younger women tried to settle the children, while Khairiah sent word of their arrival to Saif al-Adel. He was shuttling between Al Qaeda cells hiding in Mashhad, Zahidan, Shiraz, Tehran, and small towns on the Caspian Sea.[81] It took him several days to reach the families, taking with him whatever he could find en route— dried dates and small gifts including books on jurisprudence and hadiths supplied by the Mauritanian.

Saif had news for everyone. His own wife, Asma, and children had reached Tehran and had been reunited with Asma's father, the former Al Jazeera bureau chief.[82] The widow and children of the martyred Abu Hafs the Commander were also there, but Dr. al-Zawahiri's wife and two children were dead. Khairiah, who knew the woman well, was horrified.

Anxious, Saad, a creature of habit who found every small change in his routine alarming, nervously asked about their safety. Would they be spending the rest of their lives like this? He wanted to go home to his grandmother, Osama's mother, Allia, who lived in the exclusive bin Laden family compound in Jeddah.

Saif gently reminded Saad that their Saudi citizenship had been rescinded long ago, and that Riyadh's proximity to the Bush administration ruled out any rapprochement. There was another problem. The Sudanese passports had now lapsed, meaning they had no travel documents with which to fly.[83]

When someone suggested traveling overland to Turkey and then crossing into Syria, where they could reach out to Saad's estranged mother, Najwa, and their brother Omar, Saad became enthusiastic.

Again, Saif tempered his expectations. According to news reports in the Arab press, President Bashar al-Assad's intelligence agencies had been cooperating with the United States in its 9/11 investigation, providing information about lead 9/11 hijacker Mohamed Atta, who had worked in Aleppo in the mid-1990s. Saif advised everyone to stay here for now and keep their heads down, which meant no phone calls.

The advice was of no comfort to Hamzah, who still carried the string of prayer beads his father had given him in the olive groves of Melawa, a moment so painful that he had written about it, saying he "remembered every smile that my father smiled at me, every word that he spoke to me, and every look that he gave me."[84]

When Saif made it clear to the family that he was directly in touch with the Sheikh, Hamzah brightened up. Khairiah suggested that he write a letter.

He began immediately.

"Oh father!" he wrote. "Where is the escape and when will we have a home? Oh father! I see spheres of danger everywhere I look." Born into jihad, Hamzah had never known peace. Now that he was in Iran, he could see no future. "Tell me father something useful about what I see," he pleaded. "What has happened to us?"[85]

A few weeks later, Osama, incredibly, replied: "Oh son! Suffice it to say that I am full of grief and sighs. Pardon me my son but I can only see a very steep path ahead."[86] There was a message for all the family in these words. Even though they had reached Iran, they were still not safe. "Security has gone, but danger remains," Osama warned.

Even in hiding, he saw himself as a vengeful savior. "For how long will real men be in short supply? I have sworn by God Almighty to fight the infidel."

Khairiah comforted her son and told him to heed his father's message. Hamzah's time in the Iranian wilderness should not be wasted. Instead, he should study and prepare for the day he could "march with the mujahideen legions."

April 2002, Iran

Alarming news arrived at the Zabol fort. Furious at being labeled as part of Bush's Axis of Evil, the reformers in the Iranian government had ordered the intelligence ministry to round up all Al Qaeda families and expel them. President Khatami, who had come to power promising to take on the unelected Iranian state and reduce the power of the military, was determined to show Washington he was in charge.

General Qassem Suleimani, who was known for his unwavering loyalty to Iran, loved a fight and had the support of Iran's supreme leader, Ayatollah Ali Khamenei, who described him as "a living martyr of the revolution." But at this juncture Qassem could do nothing but watch as Al Qaeda wives and daughters were detained and sent to an abandoned Iraqi refugee camp in the desert outside Arak, a city in the parched center of the country. Former fighters that Khatami's agents arrested were transported to Rajai Shahr, a prison for political detainees in Karaj, where they were photographed and fingerprinted, being made ready to be bartered.[87]

Khatami had a plan. Arabs fleeing Afghanistan and Pakistan would be handed over to their respective governments or offered to the United States. To show that he was serious, and in a sideswipe at General Suleimani, Khatami had sixteen Saudi fighters deported to Riyadh and handed another low-level Al Qaeda group to Afghan president Hamid Karzai, who turned them over to America, after which they were transported en masse to Guantánamo Bay. Several Al Qaeda foot soldiers were issued with Iraqi refugee passports and put on flights to Southeast Asia, the authorities at the other end having been tipped off about their arrival. The net was being gathered in.

But in Iran every high corresponded to a low, and the guests hiding out at Hekmatyar's Iranian farmhouse learned from Saif al-Adel that the Quds Force had become emboldened. Senior Al Qaeda figures from bomb makers to former camp commanders, biological weapons specialists, operational planners, and financial chiefs were once more being smuggled into Iran through Abu Musab al-Zarqawi's northerly route. The fight was far from over.

Saif, feeling more confident, started to plan a new campaign for Al Qaeda. "We formed some groups of fighters to return to Afghanistan to carry out well-prepared missions there," he wrote.[88] "We began to examine the situation, looking for new places to hide the fraternal brothers." For months he had been carefully monitoring the U.S. campaign for a war against Saddam Hussein, with President Bush telling the BBC in April 2002, "I made up my mind that Saddam needs to go." Surprised that the U.S. had taken such a turn as a result of 9/11, but happy to have been handed such an opportunity, Saif determined that Al Qaeda should begin building up a force on the Iran-Iraq border, ready to take on the Americans whenever they arrived. What he did not realize was that the person he entrusted to scope out this critical new mission—Abu Musab al-Zarqawi—was one of the reasons Bush was citing for taking out Saddam.

In late 2001, Zarqawi had traveled to the Iraqi border town of Khurmal to negotiate an allegiance with a hard-line Kurdish fighting group called Ansar ul-Islam. It was led by a Kurdish veteran of the Afghan jihad who, taking the lead from Saddam Hussein, had used poison gas against the Kurds in 1988 and was developing cyanide gas, toxic poisons, and ricin for potential use against Europe and the United States.[89] Zarqawi found himself at home among these harsh ideologues, who strictly observed the ancient *hudud* punishments of execution, beheading, stoning, and amputation. Local Sufi shrines were desecrated, singing was banned, and the only girls' school in the area had been destroyed. In his present location, Zarqawi was also safe, since Khurmal was in Kurdish territory and so in a U.S. no-fly zone, established at the end of the first Gulf War. But that did not stop the United States from watching.

That winter, Zarqawi and Ansar ul-Islam's activities were observed by a CIA forward-deploy team, which reported back to Langley that a group of Islamists who might or might not be linked to Al Qaeda was playing with ricin and bioweapons in a small factory in the Khurmal hills.[90] When the team cabled back to the CIA's Counterterrorism Center (CTC) in Langley recommending an operational strike, the intelligence was fast-tracked over to the White House.

Defense Secretary Rumsfeld was keen to go ahead, but Secretary of State Colin Powell argued against it. The United States was not yet ready to declare war with Iraq, although plans were advancing. Why take out one small faction now when Zarqawi and his group could be used to justify the war?[91] In June 2002, Bush vetoed the Pentagon plan for military action, enabling Zarqawi to slip down into Baghdad with Ansar's help and to seed more sleeper cells ready to greet the Americans in the Iraqi capital.

As plans for "regime change" in Iraq advanced in Washington, the CTC went into overdrive on Zarqawi, mapping his background in Zarqa, his religious conversion in prison with Maqdisi, and his troubled relationship with Osama.[92]

Unaware of this mounting attention, Zarqawi sent word to Saif al-Adel in Iran that he needed more cash, more fighters, and Al Qaeda's official approval. Saif would have to convince the *shura* to endorse a man it despised. He called a "consultative council" in which he drilled those present on the need to focus on Iraq, describing how Zarqawi was inspired by reading about

Nur al-Din Zengi, who in the twelfth century had repelled the European Crusaders from the Levant, and his protégé, Saladin, who had battled Richard the Lionheart. In Saif's eyes, the Jordanian mujahid was a totally different man from the one he had first met in Kandahar in 1999, someone who back then had been "not really very good with words" and whose "life experience was not very rich." Now, he was "one of the best lions and heroes," reading as many books about Zengi and Saladin as could be found in the remote border region.[93] Zarqawi had matured, argued Saif. He now understood his place in history. "His hatred and enmity against the Americans shaped his new character," reasoned Saif, whose own attitude toward America had also significantly hardened. Gone was his fervent opposition to random attacks that caused civilian casualties, a position he had voiced during the final *shura* meeting with Osama in Kandahar, prior to 9/11. Now Saif talked of how Al Qaeda needed to strike at "the head of the snake" to "smash its arrogance" and to "prompt it to come out of its hole." They should deal "consecutive blows to undermine it and tear it apart." Zarqawi's activities in Iraq—aided by Ansar ul-Islam—would foster Al Qaeda's "credibility in front of our nation and the beleaguered people of the world."[94]

Saif gained the *shura*'s consensus and issued a stark warning: "Woe unto the Americans, British, and everyone who supports them when our nation wakes up."

Now that he had official backing, Zarqawi plotted to use Iranian president Khatami's repatriation program to channel hundreds of Al Qaeda fighters from Iran to Iraq so as to expand his own group—Tawhid al-Jihad—and assist Ansar ul-Islam.

The first company of men bound for Iraq converged on the Amir Hotel in Tehran, where the Quds Force, also keen to see the United States bled in Iraq, issued them with fake travel documents and cash. They would travel by air, while a second group made its way overland, through Kurdish-held territory. According to Saif, they "would then spread south to the areas of our fraternal Sunni brothers."

During the next fourteen months, Zarqawi traveled widely, through Iran, Kurdistan and northern Iraq, Turkey, Syria, and Lebanon, where he visited the Ayn al-Hilwah Palestinian refugee camp in the south, which became another recruiting ground.[95] Saif al-Adel saw this growing brigade of Jordanian, Syrian, Iraqi, and Palestinian volunteers as a perfect tool to use against U.S. forces, as their "skin color and tongue enabled them to integrate into the Iraqi society easily."

Zarqawi's plan became ever clearer, he explained in couriered messages to Saif. He would focus his energies on the Sunni Triangle—a densely populated region lying to the north and west of Baghdad bounded by Baqubah to the northeast, Tikrit to the north, and Ramadi to the west. He had already begun training fighters and setting up safe houses and military camps there, using funds from Gulf supporters channeled through Iran.

Despite President Khatami's best efforts, Al Qaeda, working with the Quds Force, had turned Iran into its main supply artery for the coming war in Iraq.[96]

April 2002, Tehran, Iran

As he sauntered along wide-open boulevards, enjoying the cool evening air, no one noticed the Mauritanian. What had been a long beard was now closely cropped and the Afghan desert robes he had worn for years had been swapped for a tidy pair of suit trousers and a buttoned-up shirt. These days everyone addressed him as Dr. Abdullah, a scholarly aesthete.

Although a team of Quds Force "hosts" guarded him and his family around the clock, he was able to take a constitutional stroll most days. He claimed it was for health reasons, but he used these free moments to duck into Internet cafés. After the roundups of Arab families had begun in Tehran and elsewhere, he had received dozens of calls from Pakistan from concerned brothers wondering if it was still safe to travel.

Unlike Saif al-Adel, who dealt directly with senior Quds Force officers on a regular basis, some of whom he had known since 1995, the Mauritanian had felt personally "shocked and embarrassed" by the arrests and unsure how to react to them. "I was the one who had concluded the contract on their behalf with the Iranians," he recalled. Now he felt a duty to keep everyone abreast of the rapidly developing situation. He demanded a meeting with one of General Suleimani's officers, a conversation that was "unpleasant and angry."

The Quds Force had been taken by surprise by the reformers and by the Ministry of Intelligence and Security, which wanted to take over the Al Qaeda operation. General Suleimani was not used to losing political ground and his man shifted the blame to Mahfouz: "The root cause of the arrests is mainly due to your people's phone calls, which are now being tracked in Iran." Why couldn't the Arabs learn to shut up?

The Mauritanian bridled.[97]

Soon after, intelligence officials barged into his home and demanded his cell phone, claiming they were doing it for his own security as they had intelligence that "foreign spy networks" were monitoring his number. From now on he had to resort to Internet cafés, from which he Skyped Quetta. "No one else should come," he told everyone. "Until Iran decides where it stands."

One day, as he emerged from a café, a man in civilian dress stopped him and asked to see his papers. "Police!" the officer barked. The Mauritanian demanded to speak to his superior, and as the man turned away to make a call, the Mauritanian tossed a bag filled with CDs and documents into a rubbish bin. Minutes later, a police car arrived, lights flashing. "We like to do things quietly," said the officer. "But you want it all out in the open?"

At the police station, a seemingly well-prepared investigator who spoke fluent Arabic quizzed the Mauritanian. Who had he been meeting? Where had he gone? Who did he represent? Who was he calling?

When he said nothing, the investigator produced a ledger of all the places he had traveled to and the people he had called and met since arriving the previous December.

"You are from Al Qaeda," the officer said coldly, "and we will hand you over to the intelligence service. You will be given the death sentence as a terrorist and a spy. Or be given to the Americans."

The Mauritanian was shaken, but he stood his ground. He hoped the officer was bluffing. "I came legally to Iran and if you want proof—call my Iranian host," he said, asking for a pen and scribbling down a telephone number. Would the man dial it? He prayed for his plan to work.

The investigator dialed and handed the receiver to the Mauritanian.

"I've been arrested," he whispered into the handset to his Quds Force liaison officer, Ali.

"I'll call back," Ali muttered, ending the call.[98]

The next morning, the Mauritanian was released without explanation, although the police looked furious. When he reached home he discovered that his laptop, notebooks, and CDs had been taken.

The phone rang. It was Ali. "You have two hours to pack. Then take a taxi to the tomb of Ayatollah Khameini." At the huge green and white marble complex on the outskirts of the city, he should wait for further instructions. The Quds Force could no longer guarantee his safety and he had to move.

The Mauritanian, his wife, and their children fled. Reaching the tomb, they spent the night out in the open, mingling with pilgrims. The next morning, he rang Ali, who told him to take another taxi south to the holy city of Qom, where Iran's ayatollahs lived. "It is a pure Shia city without any single Sunni family since the dawn of history," Ali explained, making it the best place in Iran for a Sunni Al Qaeda leader to hide.

When the Mauritanian and his family arrived, he took his children shopping in the main bazaar. It was the first time they had been in an Arab market and they raced about excitedly. He gently chided them for spending too much money until he saw a leather-bound copy of *Under the Shade of the Koran* by Sayyid Qutb, Osama bin Laden's inspiration. He had to buy it.

Two days later, Ali called again with more instructions. "Pack. Move again. This time head north toward Karaj." This was where Al Qaeda brothers had been imprisoned.

At Karaj, he made another call to Ali, who told him to travel on to Ramsar, a small town on the Caspian Sea, and rent a tourist lodge.

The children were delighted. They swam and paddled canoes. The Mauritanian twiddled his thumbs, becoming ever more stressed. He had no phone or Internet connection, so no way of sending messages back to Dr. Ayman al-Zawahiri or his deputy, Al Qaeda's finance chief Sheikh Saeed al-Masri.

He wondered what the brothers in Quetta would make of his silence.

June 2002, Shiraz, Iran

Saif al-Adel was unnerved by Iran's maneuverings, but Khalid Shaikh Mohammad's unauthorized activities disturbed him more. From his vantage point "in the exterior," Al Qaeda looked like a disjointed and scattered movement with an absent emir, a group being taken advantage of by someone bent on committing wild acts.

Khalid's foolhardiness infuriated Saif. A private message he had entrusted to Khalid's nephew Ammar al-Balochi, with instructions to deliver it to his family in Tehran, had ended up on the Internet. "It ends with greetings and kisses to my children," complained Saif, adding that the whole world now knew their names. The interior world was Al Qaeda's biggest secret. KSM was slapdash.

On June 13, 2002, Saif wrote a letter.[99] "My beloved brother," he wrote to Khalid. "I love you in God, and Allah knows that I care for you." They had known each other for "more than seven years" and he needed to say something important. "Stop all foreign actions, stop sending people into captivity, stop devising new operations." Above all, "Stop rushing into action." Many had already paid the price: Abu Zubaydah, Riyadh the Facilitator, and all those others recently "rendered" by the CIA to secret detention sites around the globe, a story that was just beginning to emerge. What was Khalid thinking when he had allowed Osama to go to Karachi at a time when much of the local network there was being rolled up?

"Regrettably my brother, if you look back, you will find that you are the person solely responsible for all this," Saif wrote. In sidelining the *shura*, Khalid had undertaken a mission—9/11—that had lost Al Qaeda its refuge and support. Now he was driving the movement into the dirt.

Saif pointed out the source of Khalid's recklessness. "[Sheikh Osama] pushes you relentlessly and without consideration as if he has not heard the news and as if he does not comprehend the events," he wrote. "It is his absolute habit that he will not abandon. If someone opposes him, he immediately puts forward another person to render an opinion in his support." In favoring people like Khalid over the Mauritanian, Osama had irreparably damaged Al Qaeda.

Saif suspected that in Kunar Province, Osama was recklessly dreaming again. The 9/11 attacks had made him, but he needed more. Although he had agreed that Dr. Ayman al-Zawahiri would run day-to-day affairs, he and Khalid came up with ever-wilder plots: smashing hijacked planes into Big Ben, Canary Wharf, and Heathrow Airport in London; blowing up nightclubs and hotels in Bali, Bangkok, and Mombasa; targeting gas stations, skyscrapers, and suspension bridges across the United States. Everyone had noticed that "there is a new hand that is managing affairs and driving forcefully," Saif continued. "Every time it falters, it gets up and rushes again, without understanding or awareness."[100]

Many of the operations led by Khalid, like Richard Reid's failed shoe-bombing, had provoked ridicule. If Khalid did not stop, Al Qaeda would "become a story and an example of people who do not learn," Saif warned.

Khalid's cavalier attitude to security was also costing lives. The Pakistani security forces had recently raided the factory where the shoe-bombs had been put together and several brothers had been shot dead. But rather than closing down the operation, Khalid had simply shifted to another address.

Saif got to the point. He asked Khalid to resign and hand his duties to others. Pakistan and southern Afghanistan would be handed to a Libyan brother called Abu Faraj al-Libi and northern Afghanistan to Abdul Hadi al-Iraqi, one of Zarqawi's deputies. Saif would write to Osama to get his rubber stamp. He hoped that Khalid would abide by his wishes "so as to preserve the organization, its families, its cadres, and its money until we meet."[101]

July 2002, Karachi

The man who delivered Saif's slap-down was a young, wispy-bearded Libyan brother called Atiyah Abd al-Rahman who was responsible for maintaining communications between Iran and Pakistan. He had joined Al Qaeda as a teenager and trained under Saif. Loyal and ambitious, he had first come to the leadership's attention when he lived at the bachelors' dorm at Tarnak Qila in the late 1990s. Since 9/11, Atiyah, whose *kunya* meant "gift," had acted as a crucial go-between with Zarqawi and Al Qaeda Central.

There is no surviving record of Khalid Shaikh Mohammad's reply or even evidence he wrote one; but soon after receiving Saif's letter he informed Amal bin Laden, who had spent months shuttling between Karachi safe houses, to pack up and leave Karachi.

It was her seventh move in as many months, but she was resigned to living out of a suitcase. This time she and her nine-month-old daughter, Safiyah, were taking a flight and heading north to Peshawar, accompanied by Maryam and her husband, Ibrahim, the courier working under the *kunya* Abu Ahmad al-Kuwaiti.

If anyone tried to speak to Amal at the airport or during the flight, she was to pretend to be *goongi* (deaf and mute). Ibrahim carried fake Pakistani identity cards for everyone and removed the batteries and SIM cards from his phones. Knowing that no Pakistani official would ever dare to question a covered woman, Ibrahim told Amal and Maryam to dress in dowdy *shalwar kameez* and wrap *dupattas* around their faces.

Amal, who had grown accustomed to her strange, isolated existence, walked through Karachi's thronged airport feeling frightened and exposed. She spent the flight feeding Safiyah. Maryam, who sat beside her carrying her baby daughter, Rehma, wondered why her silent husband had deliberately changed his appearance by shaving off his beard and cutting short his long hair.[102]

All Ibrahim had told them was that they were going to Peshawar to "fix a problem with Amal's passport." The visa she had entered Pakistan on in June 2000 had long run out, but the women did not understand the sudden urgency. When they exited the airport, a private minibus with curtained windows pulled up. Amal watched as Pakistan's vibrant North-West Frontier Province flashed by: painted *jinga* trucks, traffic policemen in white gloves, fruit markets, smartly turned-out schoolchildren, and green minarets.[103] Passing orange and honey sellers, Maryam whispered in broken Arabic: "We're not going to Peshawar." She was sure they were heading to Swat.

Beyond Dargai, a garrison town that housed a major Pakistani military base, and before the road began to climb, the party stopped off briefly at a roadside hotel to use the toilet. When they got back into the minibus, two new passengers were seated inside: a policeman and a tall, pale, bearded man with a scarf wrapped around his face, his long legs stretched out between the seats.

Ibrahim greeted the tall man deferentially. Maryam, who was exhausted, fell asleep. Amal felt the hitchhiker's liquid brown eyes burrowing into the back of her neck.

The road climbed to Malakand Fort, a British colonial outpost where Winston Churchill had once spent the night. Ahead, lush green terraces and fruit orchards unfurled, sliced in half by the aquamarine Swat River and overlooked by the distant snow-covered peaks of the White Mountains. The left side of the valley was sparsely inhabited, but the right side was dotted with bazaars, empty tourist hotels, and ski resorts built during the 1980s. At the next town, Chakdara, the minibus crossed the bridge and took a complicated series of hairpin bends, following the left bank of the river to avoid Mingora, the bustling capital of Swat.

Maryam woke up. Seeing they were heading north she became frightened. This was a deeply conservative and religious area ruled by firebrand *maulvis* (clerics), where village women stayed at home and every boy above the age of ten carried a weapon. For a few nights they lodged in a house overlooking a tributary of the Swat River, with Ibrahim and the strangers ensconced in another room.

When they set off again, it was to cross back to the right bank of the valley at Khwazakhela. Maryam knew the way from here. They were heading toward Shangla, where she had grown up. At nightfall, they slipped into

Martung, her home *tehsil* (district), and finally pulled up in the tiny hamlet of Kutkey.

The low-slung redbrick house where Maryam's parents lived was closed up. Her father, Naeemuddin, was away working in Kuwait and her mother had gone to visit.

After the gate shut behind them, the women and babies got out. Amal took in her new surroundings: terraced hills all around and with a river bubbling down in the valley bottom. There were no neighbors to speak of, but she noted with relief that the house had electricity.

As the silent passenger emerged from the minibus, Maryam looked away but not before she had noticed his height—several inches taller than most Swat natives. He went inside, followed by the guard and Ibrahim, who beckoned to Amal.

Follow, he urged.

Amal tensed. Excited and a little scared, she followed her husband into the house.

September 10, 2002, Karachi

A new round of ISI raids unfolded and led to an address in the upmarket Gulshan-e-Iqbal district. Hiding behind their vehicles, the police prayed the tip-off was right. They had mobilized everyone. The ISI and their U.S. counterparts were there, as well as the Sindh Rangers, drawn by a claim that this was the home of Hassan Ghul, Khalid Shaikh Mohammad's main courier.[104]

"In!" the Rangers screamed, lifting a door off its hinges.

At first no one they grabbed would talk. Then, a driver who had nothing to gain broke down and revealed that his boss was Ahmed Rabbani, one of the two Saudi-Burmese brothers who were in Khalid Shaikh Mohammad's *shura*. They were not here but at another property on Tariq Road, close to Dunkin' Donuts.

The convoy moved out.

"In!" a Ranger shouted at the new location.

Rabbani's brother, Abdul, was inside with a sixteen-year-old boy who they later identified as the younger brother of Khalid Shaikh Mohammad's bagman, Silver. When police recovered a prosthetic limb, too, they realized they had just missed Silver himself and they radioed the perimeter to look out for a man hobbling on crutches.

There was no sign of Khalid. But in a bedroom, the FBI discovered a box of SEGA game consoles filled with explosives and twenty sealed envelopes containing the bin Laden family's Saudi passports. The ISI wondered if this proved that Osama's family was still in Pakistan, as it was unlikely they could have left the country without their documents.

Cowering behind a wardrobe, the intelligence agents found two young boys who gave their names as Yusuf al-Khalid, aged nine, and Abed al-Khalid, aged seven. A group of women found hiding in another room explained that they were the children's nannies and the boys were the sons of Khalid Shaikh Mohammad. The raiding party was astonished.[105]

Khalid and his wife were always busy and came and went often, the women explained, leaving their children behind. Questioned about his present whereabouts they gave another address: 63C, Fifteenth Commercial Street, Defense Housing Authority Phase (DHA) II Extension: an apartment block in the heart of a neighborhood of textile factories and machine shops.

Early on the morning of September 11, 2002, a year to the day since the Planes Operation, ISI agents and Rangers poured into DHA, observed by the FBI and CIA. After dawn, the caretaker of 63C was picked up coming back from morning prayers and under duress admitted that two adjoining top-floor apartments were "filled with Arabs."

By seven A.M., the area was locked down.

"In!" screamed the Rangers.

At nine thirty A.M., paramilitaries and intelligence agents stormed the building. A mechanic working several streets away heard a blast. "It sounded like a bomb had gone off."[106] Halfway up the stairs, the ISI crashed into two men running down, who they wrestled to the floor before dragging them out of the building, blindfolded and with their hands tied behind their backs.

Minutes later, gunshots rang out. A male voice could be heard shouting up above: "Allahu Akbar!" Ranger snipers fired down from adjoining rooftops, and police shot up from the pavement. Tear-gas canisters skittled across the street. Flash-bangs were hurled inside as a coughing, spluttering woman emerged from the fug in a red *shalwar kameez*, carrying an unconscious child.

By midday, several Arabs lay dead in the stairwell and five Rangers had broken through onto the top floor. Three men were still alive, and as the Rangers closed in, the sounds of gunfire bounced around the lanes below.

"Surrender!" the Rangers screamed.

A voice shouted back in English: "Bastards, fucking bastards."

"One down," a Ranger radioed down. "Now just two left, in the kitchen."

The Arabs started hurling pots and pans. The Rangers, bedded in behind a sofa, lobbed in a grenade, forcing their quarry into the hall, where the men held kitchen knives against their own throats, muttering prayers.

One lunged for a gun. As the Rangers piled on top of him, he shouted: "You're going to hell!" Pulled up on his feet, the prisoner was taken to the window. "Got one alive!"

Police started shooting in the air in celebration as the blindfolded and cuffed prisoner was led out of the block. They all gathered around for a photograph as someone with a mug-shot chart noticed his buckteeth and screamed his name. "Ramzi bin al-Shibh! We got him!" Later claims in the Pakistani press that this was a staged encounter and that al-Shibh had been caught earlier by the ISI and subjected to several days of illegal interrogation were quickly dismissed as irrelevant.

However, there was no sign of Khalid Shaikh Mohammad.

September 12, 2002, Doha, Qatar

Yosri Fouda was asleep at his hotel when a night editor called. "Please come. People have been ringing in, saying you have turned in Ramzi bin al-Shibh."

Fouda was horrified. The second part of his documentary, *The Road to 11 September*, had aired on Al Jazeera on September 10, and although he had never gotten back the tapes of his interview with Khalid Shaikh Mohammad, the program had featured audio recordings of al-Shibh's admission that they were the masterminds of 9/11.[107] The Arabic-language press was pointing a finger, accusing Fouda of betraying al-Shibh and hinting that he was a pro-American turncoat—a dangerous suggestion that was likely to inspire someone to take a shot at him. He also faced accusations from some Western media outlets of having tipped off Khalid, enabling him to escape from the DHA raid.

After news broke that both Rabbani brothers had been captured, online death threats against Fouda started.

The desperate journalist needed to send out a clear message that he was not guilty. Suspecting that Khalid would be watching Al Jazeera, he appeared on air and deliberately lied about the timing and locations of their meetings earlier in the year.

The following morning, a statement appeared on jihad.net: "To put an end to speculations and rumors, Al Qaeda's media office would like to assure everyone that neither Al Jazeera channel nor Mr. Yosri Fouda had anything to do with the recent events in Karachi."

It was the "criminal role" of Pakistan's president Musharraf that should be blamed for the unraveling, said a statement almost certainly written by Khalid.

During the DHA raid, the FBI found automatic weapons, grenades, and ammunition. They also a recovered a letter signed "Mukh," advising someone about a future attack on two hotels.

Family photos found at Tariq Road showed Khalid dressed in Kuwaiti robes and standing with "at least one wife" and several children. The pictures were a bonus as they were much more recent than those the FBI and CIA had on file. The search team also recovered a satellite phone, several laptops and mobile phones, CDs, travel documents, more passports, and instructions on how to evade attention when boarding an aircraft.

On the kitchen wall they found a message scrawled in blood: "There is no God except Allah, Mohammed is his messenger."[108]

The Pakistanis were given three days to question al-Shibh at an ISI detention facility in Karachi, with the CIA observing. He had only one thing to say, over and again: "My name is Abdullah, servant of Allah."[109]

On September 15, he was shipped out of Pakistan as Musharraf's press secretary told reporters, "Al Qaeda is either in hiding or on the run. Their back is breaking and we are getting constant leads, more and more with each arrest. It's snowballing."[110]

The ISI bore down on the Rabbani brothers, convinced that Ahmed, despite his slight stature and Burmese features, was Khalid's courier Hassan Ghul. Khalid's sons were also questioned and given Coca-Colas. "You have to help us out for the sake of the kids," an ISI colonel warned the Rabbanis.

When they refused, the ISI handed the children to the CIA, which transferred them to an adult detention center. When they refused to talk, food and water were withheld although an American official told one newspaper: "We are handling them with kid gloves. After all, they are only little children, but we need to know as much about their father's recent activities as possible."[111] The CIA later claimed to have had "child psychologists on hand at all times" and that the two boys had been "given the best of care"; but according to adult detainees held with them, ants and other insects were put on the boys' legs before both were locked up in small containers, similar to the treatment meted out to Abu Zubaydah.[112] When the boys still remained silent, the CIA flew them out of Pakistan and into the secret detention program along with the Rabbani brothers.[113]

However, material gathered from the raids was exposing Khalid's life. One of the prizes was a battered suitcase, held together with tape, that contained bank records, letters, and his framed diploma from North Carolina Agricultural and Technical State University. The certificate became a political football in the ever-growing turf war between FBI and CIA agents, with the FBI wanting to keep it as evidence while a senior CIA officer wanted to put it on his wall as a trophy. As the two security departments fought over prisoners and methods of interrogation, Islamabad's new CIA station chief tried to keep details of raids and seizures away from the FBI's legal attaché, Jennifer Keenan, whose confrontations with the agency grew ever more bitter.[114] What the suitcase and the belief they had captured courier Hassan Ghul told everyone was that Khalid Shaikh Mohammad was on the move and in regular touch with Osama bin Laden.

Zalmay Khalilzad was East meets West: a Pashtun in a smart business suit with Afghan and U.S. flag lapel badges. He had left Afghanistan as a teen-ager, benefited from some expensive education (the American University of Beirut and University of Chicago) and cut his teeth in Washington as an aide to Zbigniew Brzezinski, an architect of America's support of the Afghan mujahideen.

Recently appointed as President George W. Bush's special presidential envoy for Afghanistan, he was the highest-ranking Muslim in the adminis-tration.[115] Afghans, who joked that he, and not Karzai, was the real presi-dent, were frequently starstruck by him.

In May, Khalilzad joined the U.S. National Security Council and became part of a team laying down the foundations for the White House's Iraq campaign. He also reached out to Iran, believing it had to be won over rather than attacked.[116]

If the Bonn conference had represented the "pinnacle of cooperation," the Axis of Evil speech had sunk the relationship. President Bush had been wrong to pillory Iran, he said. Washington had to think more creatively. "There was not one but two Irans," Khalilzad advised U.S. secretary of state Condoleezza Rice. One was pro-engagement, steered by President Khatami, and the other—the fiefdom of General Qassem Suleimani, the Ministry of Intelligence and Security, and the Revolutionary Guard—was "belligerent, unpredictable, anti-American, and bloodthirsty."[117]

The president's State of the Union address had denigrated both, weakening Khatami, who was portrayed by his enemies as having failed in his pointless mission, and emboldening General Suleimani—thereby dropping a daisy cutter on U.S.-Iran relations.

Khalilzad, a self-styled crusader who could express himself in Dari, Pashto, and English, would fix this, and he also needed to broach a sensitive intelligence issue. Following the Iranians' surprise delivery to Kabul of a group of low-level Al Qaeda prisoners, the CIA had reported back some startling news. In a highly classified cable, the White House had been informed that most of Al Qaeda's leadership, in particular its military and religious committees, had slipped into Iran, although it was not clear whether this had been done with the knowledge of the government in Tehran or not. It was "likely that Osama's family, including his sons, [were there] too." The cable continued: "Members of this group are in *regular contact* with OBL, and his network in Quetta, Peshawar, and Karachi, by mobile phone and also via couriers. Need deft attempt to extract/penetrate/manipulate."[118]

Khalilzad set off for Geneva intent on buttonholing Mohammad Javad Zarif, the Iranian diplomat who had turned around the Bonn conference and was now Iran's representative at the United Nations. He took along State Department official Ryan Crocker, who already had a warm relationship with Zarif thanks to their secret discussions on mutual assistance between the United States and Iran in the early days after 9/11.

When they met, Khalilzad got straight to the point. He had a proposal to make: "Look," he said, "you hand them over to us directly. Or, assuming this is sensitive, you send the Al Qaeda leadership et cetera to their respective countries. Deport them. Extradite them. Give it whatever name you will. Or if this won't work, hand them to the Afghans—as you did before."

Zarif listened intently but was uncharacteristically silent. He left the meeting saying he would seek advice from Tehran.

By the time they met again in November 2002, the Iranian position seemed to have calcified. Crocker concluded that the damage wrought by the State of the Union address was insurmountable, with Iran and the United

States now, again, rivals in the region. "We just never knew what Zarif was thinking or what he actually knew about the Al Qaeda issue," Khalilzad later reflected.

Both men were frustrated. "We were at a turning point," Khalilzad recalled. "Iran could have helped us end this Al Qaeda crisis. But we spent the time we should have been negotiating the end of Al Qaeda in trying to heal wounds, and frankly, there was simply not the appetite in the White House to reach out to Tehran warmly and constructively—even though the prize was a massive one. 'Let them rot in hell' was the message coming out of Vice President Cheney's office. And it was not just Iran that was being cold-shouldered. By taking this aggressive approach, the U.S. was committing itself to war over peace."[119]

November 2002, Ramsar, Iran

The Mauritanian had watched Yosri Fouda's 9/11 documentary at his tourist lodge on the Caspian Sea. He and his family had been living there unobtrusively for several months—in a large house on the beach that felt comfortably far from the gaze of intelligence officials. He had obtained permission from the local Quds Force agent, who visited weekly, to put up a satellite dish—his wife throwing a sheet over it to conceal it from neighbors—ostensibly so his children could watch Iranian educational programs, as they still could not speak Farsi. But most of the time he hogged it for himself.

When he wasn't following the news, he tried to bring some routine back into his children's lives by giving them lessons. He put on a brave face, but when he watched news about the arrests in Karachi he realized just how insecure Al Qaeda really was.

One day he became certain that the Ministry of Intelligence and Security was trying to hack into his laptop "to see whether I was communicating with others without their knowledge." He shared his fear with his wife. Iran was now positively hostile, plotting against Al Qaeda. Of equal concern was the fact that prisoners handed over to the Americans were disappearing once they reached U.S. custody.

In November, the Mauritanian learned from the agent that the standoff between General Qassem Suleimani, the intelligence ministry, and Khatami's

Reformists had reached such a crisis point that Iran was no longer going to host Al Qaeda's leaders. They all would have to leave the country.

The Mauritanian was appalled and terrified. He had to think fast. On November 28, he and his family dismantled their home in Ramsar, leaving everything behind except for a few toys, clothes, his pocket Koran, and a laptop. An official car drove them to Tehran, where he had one last brief meeting with Ali before returning to Qom, where he and his family were put up in a guesthouse. The following morning, they were deposited at the long-distance bus station in Arak. "I thanked my escort for his kindness and gentleness over the past months and bade him a final farewell," said the Mauritanian, who had been advised to make his own way across the border. The Iranians did not want to know where they were heading, only that they had gone.[120]

His family stood helplessly, watching travelers milling around, while he bought a SIM card and a mobile phone, convinced that the minute he left Iran the Americans would seize him. None of them could leave. Taking his family to a café, he began calling Al Qaeda brothers, eventually reaching a son-in-law of Dr. Ayman al-Zawahiri who directed him to a safe house in Karaj.[121]

The Mauritanian was relieved to hear that many senior figures remained concealed in Iran. Osama's adult sons were with Saif al-Adel in Shiraz, accompanied by the operational planner Abu Mohammed al-Masri and by Mohammed al-Islambouli, whose brother Khalid had been executed for his part in the murder of the Egyptian president Anwar Sadat and whose daughter was married to Othman bin Laden.

Osama's reluctant spokesman Sulaiman Abu Ghaith was hiding with a Sunni family in Zahidan. Also in Iran were the paramilitary commander Abu Laith al-Libi and Thirwat Shihata, an aide to Dr. al-Zawahiri.[122]

They all kept in touch with Al Qaeda Central in Shakai through Yasin al-Suri, a young Syrian courier who delivered messages from Iran and brought back cash and new recruits for Zarqawi.

However, within a day of settling in Karaj, disturbing news blurred the picture. Hetmatyar's safe house in Zabol had been raided. Khairiah, Saad, Hamzah, and the younger children had been taken into protective custody, where intelligence agents were questioning them.

Al Qaeda in Iran needed to regroup. They needed to free Osama's family. But Karaj did not feel at all hospitable. "I noticed suspicious people all the time," the Mauritanian recalled. He sent word to Saif al-Adel, who knew the Quds Force and intelligence ministry better than anyone else in Al Qaeda, asking for advice.

In the third week of December he got a reply. He should join Saif's group in Shiraz. Using the code word "honey," they told him that they were stockpiling fissile material for a new attack on an as yet unspecified American target. Abu al-Khayr al-Masri, chairman of Al Qaeda's foreign relations committee and an explosives expert who had helped build the bombs used in the 1998 U.S. embassy attacks, was busy designing the device.[123]

On December 25, shortly before the Mauritanian was due to move, a loud knocking woke the family. As he opened up, an Iranian intelligence officer barged in, followed by a half dozen armed men who rushed around the house pulling out books and drawers, filming as they ransacked.

The Mauritanian's family was ordered upstairs, while he was led into his living room. They knew he was Al Qaeda, they said. He feigned ignorance, but he could see they were well briefed. "Get dressed and bring your things," one of them ordered. "We are taking you into custody."

As he was led out, the wives and children of other brothers were brought in. Karaj was being turned over house by house. He called out to his wife as he was bundled into a car. "There's money hidden. You will find it. This problem will end soon, God willing." This was no way to leave them, he thought, worrying that he was about to vanish like Abu Zubaydah. Or would he be paraded before the cameras like Ramzi bin al-Shibh?

The car started up and there was no mistaking the route they took. They were heading back to Tehran. And to what? Deportation into the hands of the United States? He had to try something. He could not fight his way out. But he could talk. "Is not America the Great Satan?" he asked the driver and his guard, smiling nervously.

The broad-shouldered man in the passenger seat turned and glared. "You destroyed Afghanistan and you came here to destroy the Islamic Republic of Iran," he hissed. "We will not risk the future of more than seventy million Iranians for ants like *you*."[124]

CHAPTER FIVE

"The banging was so strong that I felt at some
point that my skull was in pieces."
— ABU ZUBAYDAH, WRITING IN
HIS PRISON DIARY, 2002[1]

August 4, 2002, Detention Site Green, Thailand

FOLLOWING WARNINGS THAT "COUNTLESS MORE Americans may die unless we can persuade AZ to tell us what he knows," Abu Zubaydah had been held in isolation for forty-seven days while the interrogation program designed by U.S. Air Force survival school psychologist Dr. Mitchell was upgraded and refined in Washington.[2]

Several meetings took place at CIA headquarters to discuss the possible use of "novel interrogation methods" and Mitchell provided a list of twelve SERE techniques: (1) attention grasp, (2) walling, (3) facial hold, (4) facial slap (insult slap), (5) cramped confinement, (6) wall standing, (7) stress positions, (8) sleep deprivation, (9) waterboarding, (10) use of diapers, (11) use of insects, and (12) mock burial.[3]

Mitchell recommended that the CIA enter into a contract with Dr. Bruce Jessen, his co-author of a report written the previous December on potential Al Qaeda resistance and his former colleague at Fairchild Air Force Base in Spokane. Like Mitchell, Jessen, who had grown up in a Mormon community in Utah, had no practical experience of interrogation, but his reputation at Fairchild was legendary and his CIA appointment was approved.[4]

Evidence that the CIA team on the ground in Thailand felt that the new "aggressive methods" under discussion might cross the red line and cause permanent damage to Zubaydah was contained in a cable sent to headquarters on July 15, 2002: "We need to get reasonable assurance that [Zubaydah] will remain in isolation and incommunicado for the remainder of his life."

If the worst-case scenario happened and Zubaydah died, "we need to be prepared to act accordingly, keeping in mind the liaison equities involving our hosts."[5] His body should be cremated.[6]

Officers from Langley responded several days later, stating, "The interrogation process takes precedence over preventative medical procedures" and confirming that "all major players are in concurrence that Zubaydah should remain incommunicado for the remainder of his life."[7]

On July 24, Attorney General John Ashcroft had verbally approved the use of ten interrogation techniques, which included walling, cramped confinement, and the use of diapers and insects. When the interrogation team indicated that they intended to wait for the approval of waterboarding, the attorney general verbally approved it on July 26.[8] Soon after, Dr. Mitchell flew back to Thailand, where he was joined by Dr. Jessen, while the FBI's Ali Soufan was ordered to permanently withdraw from the case.[9]

The new process started at eleven fifty A.M. on August 4, 2002, after a decision was taken that it would be continued on a near twenty-four-hour-per-day basis.[10] A medical officer wrote an e-mail updating Langley, subject heading: "So it begins."[11] A number of guards entered Zubaydah's cell accompanied by two CIA interrogators. One of them pointed to a large wooden box that looked like a coffin. They flipped it upright and beckoned Zubaydah over. "From now on this is going to be your home."[12]

The vertical casket was just about big enough for him if he sat on the bucket placed inside for human waste, Zubaydah later wrote in his diary.[13] He didn't know how long he was inside when he "heard the click of a lock" and light flooded in. "I felt something was being wrapped around my neck. I suddenly saw another man . . . He was twisting a thick towel, which was wrapped with a plastic tape so it could be given the shape of a noose. He wrapped it around my neck and dragged me. I fell on the floor along with the bucket, with all its content that fell on me."

Without uttering any words, the interrogator slammed Zubaydah's head against a concrete wall. This was the CIA-approved technique of "walling," but it immediately became obvious to Zubaydah that he would sustain serious injury if it continued without some kind of modification.[14] The next time he saw the wall a plywood skin had been placed on top of the concrete wall and the procedure then continued.[15]

To Zubaydah, it still felt like his skull was shattering. "He started banging my head against the wall with both his hands. The banging was so strong that I felt at some point that my skull was in pieces, or that the artificial bone in my open head was falling apart. I don't know how to describe that feeling. The feeling was abnormal . . . It lasted forever and that guy . . . was not getting tired from beating me."[16]

The beating intensified as the man yelled at Zubaydah: "You think you have pride? I will show you now what pride is about." Zubaydah felt his back was breaking due to the intensity of the banging. "He started slapping my face again and . . . yelling."[17]

Later, Zubaydah glimpsed another wooden box, much smaller than the first and barely the dimensions of a child's coffin. "With the help of the guards, he shoved me inside."[18]

It was twenty-one inches wide, two and a half feet high, and two and a half feet deep. Zubaydah called it the dog box. "The stress on my legs . . . meant my wounds both in the leg and stomach became very painful. It was hot and sweaty inside. The wound on my leg began to open and started to bleed. I don't know how long I remained in the small box, I think I may have slept or maybe fainted."[19] Cramped and immobile, Zubaydah was soon in agony. "I felt I was going to explode."[20]

The waterboarding came next. "I didn't hear or feel them come nor heard them turn the lock," Zubaydah recalled. Hauled out of the box, he saw that before him was a metal bed "that had many belts in every direction." It looked like a medieval rack.

"I was totally restrained to the point that I was unable to make any movement whatsoever. They restrained me in a lying down position. Obviously, even the wounded thigh was strongly restrained under the gauze. I felt the wounds were opening . . . After they restrained my body, they restrained my head as well with the help of strong plastic cushions on the sides, which made it impossible for me to move it, not even for one centimeter to the left or one centimeter to the right, and obviously neither upward nor downward." Zubaydah felt a black cloth being pulled over his head. Then water was poured onto his face.

"It shocked me because it was very cold," he recalled. The water didn't stop but continuously poured and flowed over his mouth and nose. "So the idea was . . . aimed at giving me the feeling of drowning." And it worked. "They kept pouring water and concentrating on my nose and my mouth until I really felt I was drowning and my chest was just about to explode from the lack of oxygen. Indeed that was the first time and the first day that I felt I was going to die from drowning . . . All I know or remember is that I started vomiting water but also rice and string beans."

One of the CIA interrogators would later tell the CIA's Office of the Inspector General that Mitchell and Jessen's SERE school model was based on resisting North Vietnamese "physical torture" methods, which had included waterboarding. But doing it in the classroom and for real were not the same, according to the interrogator, who said that the CIA "needed a different working model for interrogating terrorists."[21]

After a pause, a second wave of waterboarding started. "They performed the same operation three times on [the first day]," Zubaydah later wrote in his diary. "And every time they were deflating the cushion that was holding my head a little bit and so I would feel my head lowered a little bit, which made it ever more difficult for me to bear water flowing inside of me." After they interrupted the operation for a few minutes to allow him to breathe or vomit, they resumed. "After the third time on that day, they kept the hood, soaked in water, on my head and started asking me questions . . . Then, they removed me from the bed and dragged me to the box; they shoved me inside and locked the door."[22] The procedure lasted in total two and a half hours, during which, according to the official report, Zubaydah suffered "involuntary spasms of the torso and extremities."[23]

Mitchell would later confirm that he had taken part in that first waterboarding session and that Jessen had helped him, although he claimed he had tried to calm everything down.[24] "The [Justice Department legal] memo says that in a waterboarding session, you can pour an application of water for 20 to 40 seconds to give that person a chance to breathe, then another 20 to 40 seconds, and you can do that for 20 minutes," he said.[25] According to Mitchell, it became clear early in the first session that too much water was being poured. "We decided we would do two 20-second sessions and one 40-second session, and the rest would be from 1 to 10 seconds. The CIA [Inspector General] sent a lawyer out with a stopwatch and a counter to measure the average amount of time water was poured in a single waterboarding session. The average amount of time was 10 seconds."

For Zubaydah, even when he was recovering in one of the boxes, there was no letup. "I suddenly felt a strong strike that shook the box from outside followed by several other stronger strikes," he recalled.[26] "They shook the box so heavily, which made me fall from the bucket. The strikes continued. There were probably ten strikes. Then every quarter of an hour they would bang again ten times, maybe to make sure I am unable to sleep. Yet with the time, the fatigue, the headache and the pain it seemed to me I was able to sleep for a very short time. And I started hearing the bangs as in a dream. They would wake me, I would count them and then fall asleep again."[27]

A CIA cameraman recorded every minute, creating a complete record that would ultimately run to ninety-two tapes.[28] "The little box, the water bed, the long box," it went round and round.

The waterboarding increased "from three to four and sometimes five sessions," as, according to Zubaydah's diary, the CIA team added new twists. "1) Keeping me on my feet tied up for long hours, wet with water and urine to the point where I felt my legs, especially the wounded one, were just about to explode from pressure, and my back as well. 2) They kept me lying down on the water bed for long hours . . . This time, my head was tied up and restrained in one direction and the wet black cloth was entirely covering my head which added to the pain resulting from the contraction in the neck, the back, the limbs, the joints, the muscles and the nerves . . . 3) They increased the amount of cold water that was being poured over my naked cold body."[29]

To further humiliate Zubaydah, medical personnel contracted to the CIA's Office of Medical Staff (OMS) recommended the intake of just 1,500 calories per day. As little as 1,000 calories a day was still "safe and sustainable for weeks on end."[30] Food mainly consisted of the high-protein shake Ensure, and the preferred method to forcibly feed a detainee refusing to eat was "rectally."

The questioning continued, an interrogator demanding to know about future terrorist operations against the United States: names, phone numbers, e-mail addresses, weapons caches, and safe houses. "I tried to speak or yell with my head covered, shouting 'I don't know anything,' but I suddenly felt the water flowing again," recalled Zubaydah. Every time Zubaydah denied he was in Al Qaeda or knew anything, an interrogator banged his head against the wall. "Before I could finish my sentence the beating started again and my head and back were brutally banged against the wall."

During one especially grueling session, Zubaydah felt his body was being ripped apart. "There were tears in my eyes, my nose was leaking and even my genital organ was involuntarily discharging," he recalled.[31]

In total, Zubaydah spent more than eleven days inside the large coffin-size box and twenty-nine hours inside the smaller one, his interrogators telling him that the only way he would leave the facility was "in a box."[32] "They did the same thing again and again: the banging against the wall, the little box, the water bed, the long box," he recalled. During at least one waterboarding session, he "became completely unresponsive, with bubbles rising through his open, full mouth."[33]

Despite this, Zubaydah offered up "no useful information."

The log from Detention Site Green recorded that the Enhanced Interrogation Techniques continued in "varying combinations, 24 hours a day" for seventeen straight days through to August 20.[34] During the interrogators' downtime, Zubaydah was left strapped with a cloth over his face, or locked in one of the coffins. He tried to place himself somewhere else, reciting the lyrics to "Sailor," his favorite Chris de Burgh song, about being lost at sea and dreaming of going home.

But Chris de Burgh did not work. A cable noted that Zubaydah "cried," "begged," "pleaded," "whimpered," and denied knowledge of any ongoing Al Qaeda plans.[35] "I vomited each time I was put in the vertical position between the suffocation," Zubaydah recalled.[36] He began losing control of his body. "This is very similar to the shaking I noticed years ago after I was wounded in my head and lost my memory." He would go to sleep shaking and wake up shaking. He also began uncontrollable mumbling.

Some CIA staff at Detention Site Green were by now chafing. On August 5, 2002, one official cable read: "Want to caution [medical officer] that this is almost certainly not a place he's ever been before in his medical career . . . It is visually and psychologically very uncomfortable."[37]

On August 8, another noted: "Today's first session . . . had a profound effect on all staff members present . . . It seems the collective opinion that we should not go much further."[38]

A third cable written on the same day reported: "Several on the team profoundly affected . . . some to the point of tears and choking up."[39]

The next day another cable stated that two, possibly three, personnel were likely to elect to transfer away from the detention site if a decision was made to continue.[40]

Dr. Mitchell later claimed that he was one of those raising concerns and that he and Jessen considered resigning after they were told to continue waterboarding Zubaydah despite the fact that they said it was no longer necessary to do so.[41] According to the Senate report on CIA torture, the chief of support services at Detention Site Green said that Mitchell and Jessen were "frustrated that they kept beating Zubaydah up on the same question while getting the same physiologic response from him."[42]

By August 9, the sixth day of enhanced interrogations, the CIA in-country team informed Langley that they had come to the "collective preliminary assessment" that it was unlikely Abu Zubaydah "had actionable new information about current threats to the United States." The following day they sent another cable reinforcing the message: it was "highly unlikely" that Zubaydah possessed the information they were seeking.[43]

Officials at CTC headquarters led by Jose Rodriguez insisted the procedures continue.[44] The subject was still withholding information, in their assessment. In his filthy cell, surrounded by excrement, vomit, urine, and hair, Zubaydah was by now so conditioned by his treatment that all the interrogator had to do was snap his fingers twice to get him to lie down on the waterboard.[45] His sense of "learned helplessness" was fully developed.

"The torture continued using the same methods during the period of drowning that was not limited to water but also urine, in addition to the heavy vomiting that was breaking my head in two and tearing apart my stomach—that was already wounded," Zubaydah later wrote in his prison diary. "The long closed wound that goes through my belly and appears a little under the chest . . . seemed as if it opened internally during every episode of vomiting or after drowning or during long standings or even by just sitting down."

An interrogation tape recorded on August 11 was labeled with a warning to "prepare for something not seen previously."[46] At times Zubaydah became so hysterical that he was unable to communicate.

The interrogation team demanded that someone come from headquarters for a "first-hand on-the-ground look" as the treatment was "approaching the legal limit."[47] After reviewing "quite graphic" videotapes of Zubaydah's recent sessions on a conference call, headquarters agreed to send a team.[48]

Zubaydah recalled the day that the visitors from Langley arrived. "The hood was lifted and I saw two other individuals: a man and a woman in civilian clothes," he wrote later in his diary. "It took minutes before I realized that I was completely naked in front of a woman. For moral and religious reasons I covered my genitals with my hands."

The man threw Zubaydah against the wall. "Don't start getting angry again otherwise we'll start again from zero. Understood?" At this point, the woman started reading questions from a piece of paper she was holding. Zubaydah noticed that her hands were trembling.

After the visitors went back to the United States, the interrogations continued. No one stopped it, although one interrogator came who was better than the rest. In his head Zubaydah called him "Mr. Its-gonna-be-fine."[49]

That month, Mitchell and Jessen sent a cable to CIA headquarters describing Zubaydah's interrogation as a success and recommending that the "aggressive phase at [DETENTION SITE GREEN] should be used as a template for future interrogation of high value captives."[50]

October 30, 2002, 2 A.M., Islamabad, Pakistan

In his sharp, starched *shalwar kameez*, pinstriped waistcoat, and moonstone-colored *pakul*, Dr. Ghairat Baheer was a famous face about town. An Afghan national living openly in Islamabad, he was the son-in-law and spokesman for warlord Gulbuddin Hekmatyar. Everyone—from his neighbors to the police posted at the bottom of his street and the ISI agents who hung about outside his house—knew he was a portal into the Afghan jihad movement. But because he had never taken part in any militant activities, Dr. Baheer thought he was safe.

On October 29, 2002, an acquaintance named Gul Rahman, a father of four daughters who lived in Peshawar, stopped overnight. Formerly an assistant to Dr. Baheer's father-in-law, Rahman needed to stay due to a postponed medical appointment and, after calling Peshawar to warn his wife he would not be home until the following day, he joined Dr. Baheer for dinner.

At just before two A.M., with everyone asleep, Dr. Baheer's doorbell rang. Then a group of men barged in. "Without any explanation, they just grabbed me, put a hood over my head, tied my hands with plastic cuffs, and threw me into a van," Dr. Baheer recalled.[51] After being interrogated for a week in Islamabad, he and Rahman, who had also been seized, were taken blindfolded and cuffed to the airport. "Men with American accents grabbed me under the arms, threw me on the floor, cut off my clothes, and tossed my Koran against the wall," said Dr. Baheer.

When he started weeping at the desecration of his holy book, the Americans mocked him. "You're a very brave man, why are you crying?" He was dressed in an orange jumpsuit, with a hood and goggles, before being dragged onto a military transporter and strapped to a chair, with an American contractor sitting on his chest.

Dr. Baheer and Rahman were told they were being flown to Peshawar, but instead they were taken to an abandoned brick factory northeast of Kabul. As a result of the experimentations in Thailand and a recent report to President Bush that Abu Zubaydah's enhanced interrogations had provided "key intelligence," the CIA secret prisons and torture program were growing. Detention Site Cobalt—as the brick factory was now renamed—was the latest grim addition.[52] Below ground and completely out of sight was a second holding area that was dubbed "the Salt Pit."

Clinical psychologist Dr. Bruce Jessen was already there when Dr. Baheer and Rahman arrived, working in a prison where noncompliant detainees were kept naked or in diapers and were chained in darkness to a rail above their heads or to the floor.[53] Loud music was pumped into cells day and night.

As the winter temperatures plummeted, the cells dropped to a few degrees below zero and detainees were subjected to freezing blasts of water that the guards called "the shower from hell" and that brought on severe convulsions.[54]

The guards also performed mock executions by firing handguns outside, then parading detainees past a cell to view hooded guards lying on the floor as if they were dead.[55]

Like many others held there, Dr. Baheer described his new home as "the dark prison." He recalled, "All I saw for months was the end of a [flashlight]," explaining how he spent his time in a six-foot-square cement cell with Michael Jackson songs pumping in so loudly that his captors wore ear protectors. The Americans suspected that as Hekmatyar's son-in-law, he could reveal Osama bin Laden's location. They also wanted to know about a $1 million *hawala* payment from unnamed Arab donors to his father-in-law's group, Hezb-i-Islami Gulbuddin (an offshoot of the Hezb-i-Islami network). Had it also been used to fund the Al Qaeda leader's life in exile after he fled Tora Bora?

When he wasn't being interrogated, Dr. Baheer listened to the whimpers of other detainees, who whispered messages into the water pipes connecting their cells—one of them telling him he was Abu Yahya al-Libi, the Mauritanian's former pupil, and that he had been betrayed by Pashtun villagers in the tribal belt.

One day, interrogators locked Dr. Baheer inside a coffin-size box. Dr. James Mitchell was also at the Detention Site Cobalt around this time, but Dr. Baheer does not know if he met him.

Dr. Baheer struggled to breathe as an American voice screamed through the lid. "Where is Mullah Omar? Where is Hekmatyar? Where is Osama bin Laden? We won't let you out until you tell us."

Dr. Baheer recited his prayers.

"Where is Hekmatyar? Do you know?" the American shouted, banging on the lid.

Exhausted and in pain, Dr. Baheer yelled back. "Yes," he spluttered. "I know where they all are."

The lid was flipped open. "Do you *know* Osama?"

"Yes, I've met him *twenty times*. And I'm not telling *you*." The lid slammed shut.

Later, Dr. Baheer was hauled out naked, carried to the shower room, and blasted with freezing-cold water.   ·

"It kept pouring. So cold."

Convulsing and still naked, he was taken back to his cell and manacled into a crucifixion position. A female interrogator began to question him as two male interrogators beat him from both sides.

Dr. Baheer later claimed that he lost almost ninety pounds in the first month.[56] But his friend Gul Rahman suffered even worse. One day, Dr. Baheer had no idea which day, the whispers along the pipes carried worrying news: guards had been seen carrying a body bag out of Rahman's cell.

Rahman's wife would not find out her husband's fate until a reporter called her seven years later and informed her that Rahman had been found dead in his cell on November 20, 2002.[57]

According to a subsequent report by the CIA Inspector General, Dr. Bruce Jessen was involved in Rahman's interrogation, conducting six sessions with him, including one in which he had deployed the "insult slap."

In another session, Dr. Jessen witnessed but was not involved in a "hard takedown" of Rahman, which involved a team of four or five guards cutting off his clothes, securing his hands with Mylar tape, and putting a hood over his head. Now naked, Rahman was slapped and punched in the stomach and made to run up and down the corridor outside his cell.

According to the Inspector General's report: "Jessen saw a value in the hard takedown in order to make Rahman uncomfortable and experience a lack of control. Jessen recognized, however, that the technique was not approved and recommended to [redacted] that he obtain written approval for employing the technique."

Jessen left Cobalt after preparing an interrogation plan for Rahman that stated: "It will be important to manage the [proposed interrogation] deprivations so as to allow [Rahman] adequate rest and nourishment so he remains coherent and capable of providing accurate information."[58]

Noting that Dr. Jessen and Dr. Mitchell had left the site some days before Rahman died and that ten student interrogators still in training had taken over, the CIA Inspector General reported that Rahman had been found dead, naked and lying on his side, with his hands and feet shackled together and chained to a grate on the wall. His hips, shoulders, and wrists were all marked by abrasions.[59]

December 4, 2002, Detention Site Green, Thailand

Two weeks after Gul Rahman's death, the CIA decided to "render" Abu Zubaydah to a new location after the *Washington Post* picked up rumors that he was in Thailand.[60]

On December 4, Zubaydah, who had by now lost his left eye, was dressed in an orange jumpsuit, with opaque goggles tightened around his face, a hood pulled down over his head, and his legs shackled and wrists cuffed.[61] He was shoved into the back of a vehicle, where two guards forced him down in the footwell by placing their feet on his head.

Before he boarded the Gulfstream jet, the guards told him it would be a long journey. "They . . . took out my genital organ and held it and although I felt I was going to explode from controlling my urination it took me some time to start urinating and in fact it was like it was exploding from pressure. The pain was so strong I couldn't help but screaming or moaning until I was done. They then undid my slacks and sat me down on the bucket; at this point I said: 'no, there is no need', although I really needed to do it, but!!! The wait was long after which they took us to the car and then the plane."

Inside the plane, they conducted an anal cavity search. Then they tried to put him in a diaper, which he refused. "They chained us to the floor. And I started counting the hours that go very slowly when you want them to go fast and you find yourself begging the hours to go by fast. The plane stopped for a long period of time and then took off and I was destroyed and felt that was the end."

Zubaydah's journey concluded at the end of a snowy landing strip at Szymany in northern Poland. The plane in which he arrived was screened off from the airport control tower before he and another prisoner were led out and bundled onto Polish military vehicles. From Szymany, the prisoners were taken to the village of Stare Kiejkuty, an SS outpost during World War

Two and now a Polish intelligence training base.[62] It had been co-opted as the CIA's new Detention Site Blue. "I was carried up to a location where they sat me down on a seat," Zubaydah later recalled, "chained me for some time and then they removed the hood, the blindfolds and the earplugs. I found myself in a new place that I will call Prison 2."

Zubaydah was placed in a cage, and he asked for a pad of paper so he could continue writing his diary. "When I asked them in the outset if there was a problem writing down what was happening to me, their response was: 'no, none of the things we did to you was considered illegal.' I was surprised to hear that, for I have a different understanding."[63]

Addressing his alter ego, Hani, Zubaydah wrote in the third person: "Since they tortured him, he began having nightmares. Of people messing w/ his sisters or his small brothers & he is wanting to help, but cannot. He wakes up in a start. Not afraid, as a child, but very, very angry. Sometimes thinking about his situation is distressing enough to trigger a seizure."

One night in March 2003, Zubaydah wrote, he was kept awake by the sound of a power drill and someone screaming.[64] After nine months in secret CIA detention, all that was left of Abu Zubaydah was "Hani."

After Zubaydah's rendition to Poland and the investigation into the death of Gul Rahman, Dr. Bruce Jessen and Dr. James Mitchell formed a company, Mitchell Jessen and Associates, whose principal officers included former CIA and Defense Department officials. It was awarded a sole-source multimillion-dollar contract to manage the CIA's global Enhanced Interrogation Program.

Dr. Mitchell and Dr. Jessen continued to be employed by the CIA long after the torture program and use of black sites was exposed in 2006 and President Bush ordered the secret prison system to be closed down.[65]

By the time that newly elected president Barack Obama terminated Jessen and Mitchell's contract in 2009, their Spokane-based company had reportedly been paid $71 million.[66] Mitchell later claimed that most of the cash was earmarked for "overhead, operating expenses, and salaries for employees" and that he had been paid by the hour and only when he worked.[67]

November 12, 2002, Islamabad

Al Jazeera's Pakistan bureau chief Ahmad Zaidan had been enjoying a rare evening off. It was a state holiday, he was tired, and when his cell phone began buzzing at ten P.M. he did not answer it. But the caller was persistent, and Zaidan was an inveterate story-getter. When it rang for the third time he pressed *accept*. *"Salaam Alaikum."*

"I have a scoop for you," an unidentified man said in English. The language was not the caller's birth tongue, but he was a proficient speaker, suggesting someone who had lived among English-speaking people. "Come to Melody Market, behind the Islamabad Hotel."[68]

Zaidan glanced outside. Cold rain fell in squalls. Throwing on a jacket, he ran to his car. Melody Market, crammed with cafés and outdoor restaurants, was desolate. As he pulled up, a man with his face obscured behind a woolen shawl knocked on the car window and slid a plastic bag through the gap. Ripping it open, Zaidan found an audiocassette. He listened to it on his car's player on the way back home.

First there was a mournful *nasheed* (chant) and then a distinctive voice rang out eulogizing Khalid Shaikh Mohammad's suicide attack on the Djerba synagogue. It then praised a second, more recent attack: the slaughter of more than two hundred tourists on the Indonesian island of Bali on October 12.[69] A suicide bomber had detonated his backpack inside an Irish bar in the resort town of Kuta, and when the crowd of young clubbers and staff had stampeded, a bomb in a Mitsubishi van parked outside had scythed through them and through drinkers at a second, open-air club in a sadistic attack on the softest of targets. Was Al Qaeda really claiming these acts of hypercruelty?

Zaidan closed his eyes and listened to that unmistakable Saudi diction used only by the elite of the kingdom. It was not Al Qaeda claiming the incidents; it was Al Qaeda's missing emir. In Osama bin Laden's last video after Tora Bora he had looked gaunt and injured. "We say that the end of the United States is imminent," he had declared. That was the last the world had heard of him, and recent ISI-fueled speculation had suggested that he was gravely ill or possibly dead. But here he was on tape making pronouncements about events that had occurred in the past four weeks.

Racing back to his office, he pinged the sound file to his news editor in Doha as he prepared his exclusive: OSAMA BIN LADEN ALIVE.

December 2002, Malir Town, Karachi, Pakistan

Khalid Shaikh Mohammad was busier than ever. There was no news about his two young sons, Yusuf and Abed, who had been picked up in the ISI raids that had snagged the Burmese brothers and spirited out of Pakistan by the CIA. But his wife was pregnant again and his plots abroad, carried out in Al Qaeda's name, were coming to fruition, some spectacularly. Recently, he had arranged for a prize of $130,000 to be sent to Hambali, the jihadi mastermind of the Bali bombing, who had once been his partner in Southeast Asia.

Then he received his own reward.

Courier Hassan Ghul, who was still at-large despite the arrest of his brother-in-law Abdul Rabbani, arrived with a message from Osama. He had decided to appoint Khalid as chief of external operations for Al Qaeda, putting him on a par with Saif al-Adel, whose sternly worded warning that Khalid and Osama were out of control had done nothing to dampen either man's ardor for terror. The appointment came with one proviso: Osama wanted to confer the title face-to-face.

The Sheikh also wanted to see Khalid to discuss new operations, especially those advancing in Britain and Spain. Despite the heightened security, the capture of Abu Zubaydah, the arrest of Khalid's sidekick Ramzi bin al-Shibh, the operation that had wrapped up the Burmese brothers and seen Khalid's two young sons taken, the interrogation of Riyadh the Facilitator, and the ongoing waves of unknowable chaos in Iran, Al Qaeda's emir could not bear to stay under wraps for long.

December 2002, Kutkey, Martung Tehsil, Shangla, Pakistan

Osama bin Laden was seriously ill. Despite having obtained medication from a specialist and possibly having had an operation, his kidneys continued to plague him, resulting in long periods of extreme tiredness and occasional blackouts.[70] The few people who saw him could not fail to notice it, along with the fact that he appeared frustrated and more ill-tempered than before. Gone were the caves of war, the attentive circle of admirers, and the heart-stopping radio broadsides. He was now living as his wives did—in a kind of purdah. A man who craved attention spent most of his time alone.

The cat-and-mouse games with the media had dried up, as had the ego-stroking audiences with visiting mullahs and mujahideen—and the covert trips to Karachi. No one could be trusted when a $25 million bounty had been placed on his head.

Instead, Osama shared a house with two nursing mothers and their squalling tots. His aide Ibrahim Saeed Ahmad, aka Abu Ahmad al-Kuwaiti, was his only sparring partner, and according to Amal, he was also feeling the stress.

Most of those with words—the clerics, lawyers, and military strategists who continued to run Al Qaeda—were gathered in Iran. The rest were hundreds of miles away in Shakai, regrouping under the protection of the egotistical young mujahid Nek Muhammad Wazir, whose handsome profile and notoriety caused jealous Osama to feel threatened. Dr. Ayman al-Zawahiri and others in Al Qaeda Central had taken a unilateral decision to buff Osama as the outfit's totem, an untouchable but mesmerizing figurehead who would draw in funds and recruits but would be kept away from the action.

Too sick to live in the Tribal Areas, a place where brothers were often required to shift locations at short notice and had infrequent access to medical facilities, Osama had had no choice but to go along with these decisions. But nothing could stop him from writing. Daily, he sat at his laptop in his bedroom overlooking the terraced Shangla hills, typing up letters for Ibrahim to dispatch down the courier chain, often signing them with his favorite moniker, Azmaray (the Lion).[71]

Nightly, he pestered Ibrahim to bring replies, demanding to know when he was next going down to Peshawar or Mardan, where he met the couriers coming up from Waziristan. When Osama felt well enough, he attempted to get Ibrahim to walk with him through the mountains, and on one occasion he asked to be taken to a local mosque, as he wanted to make a donation.

Ibrahim tried to stand firm. Osama's face adorned posters in Mingora's markets, he said. His name was sprayed on rock faces and Al Qaeda was written about daily in newspapers sold in shops across Swat and Shangla. To distract his companion, he arranged for a satellite dish to be delivered, at great expense, beaming Al Jazeera into the home. The news reported that Al Qaeda facilitators were being picked up all over Pakistan, and some were giving up compromising information about how they worked and communicated. This was not the right time to make a public appearance, Ibrahim constantly reminded Osama. With Abu Zubaydah apprehended and being interrogated by the CIA in an unknown location, a crucial phone book and diaries had also been captured, which meant that the CIA was folding things up.

But the recalcitrant Al Qaeda leader would not listen. Eventually, Ibrahim became so worn down that he took Osama and Amal on a day trip to a nearby bazaar in a curtained van, silently cursing as they drove. Wanting to get it over with, he drove fast and ran into one of the rarest things in the area: a police speed trap. The constable who pulled him over asked to see his documents. Terrified, Ibrahim produced a roll of rupees, while Osama shrank beneath a shawl in the back. They crawled home that night so ashen that Maryam asked if she should call a doctor.[72]

In a house where everyone was lying to each other, it was difficult to mask the tension. When she was not attending to baby Safiyah or her husband, Amal did her best to maintain her friendship with Maryam, without being able to explain where she spent her nights.

Maryam wondered constantly about the tall, thin, beardless man who lived like a ghost upstairs and who was always deferentially referred to as "the Sheikh." One day, when she asked Ibrahim directly, he exploded like a pinwheel and beat her.

Nursing her bruises, Maryam pleaded with him to allow her to visit Alpuri, where her sister lived. Ibrahim locked her in her room. He charged around the house, shouting at everyone, and took away her cell phone. Great danger would befall all of them if she gossiped. *Stop asking me questions, or making demands, and focus on your housework*, he hissed.

Ibrahim was falling apart, Maryam thought.

What he could not tell her was that unbreakable family ties bound him to a man he called "the mujahid of the Islamic World"—otherwise he would have already run away. This job was killing him.[73]

Ibrahim's father, Ahmad Saeed, had studied at the same Pakistani madrassa as Taliban leader Mullah Omar, after which he had migrated with his family to Kuwait to work as a honey trader. The business brought him into contact with Khalid Shaikh Mohammad's father, who, aside from his religious duties, imported honey from Pakistan's Tribal Areas.

Soon, Ahmad Saeed and his sons were frequenting the mosque in Al Ahmadi, on the southernmost edge of Kuwait City, where Khalid's father was imam. The fathers and their sons became close, and when Khalid's father extolled the Afghan jihad, Ahmad Saeed had felt compelled to send several of his boys back home to join.[74]

In early 2002, when Khalid first asked Ibrahim to become Osama's companion in exile, he had felt honored as he was taught how to communicate safely with the outfit's couriers and was shown basic countersurveillance craft. He should use a different alias with each contact, as they would with him. "Make sure neither side knows any other name, be it your true name or another alias," Khalid had said. He had stuck with Abu Ahmad al-Kuwaiti, a name he had chosen when he first volunteered for Al Qaeda.

But no one had talked about how to manage stress or claustrophobia, and after nearly a year with Osama in Shangla the situation was made even harder by the nine thousand rupees a month (then about $150) Ibrahim was paid, which was barely enough to cover the food, fuel, and electricity for a household of eight, let alone run the courier network. When they ran short, Ibrahim was forced into the humiliation of asking for credit from shop-keepers, while Osama remained oblivious to their daily struggle.

The threat was grinding and continuous. Any journey Ibrahim made was perilous. Every time he left the valley with the Sheikh's messages or met a courier bringing notes from Waziristan or cash from Khalid in Karachi, he had to pass through a phalanx of army and ISI checkpoints: outside the Pakistan Army cantonment at Dargai, on the way in to Peshawar, and every other place he visited. He varied his route. He took the back roads. He changed vehicles when he could. He bought different clothes, cut his hair, and shaved or grew a beard. He sought new rendezvous points: a pome-granate juice stall in Charsadda, the covered mall in Hayatabad, Peshawar.

But these things—the pressure of a clandestine life—began to build, until one afternoon he announced that he was leaving. He packed a small bag and headed for his ancestral village of Suleman Talaab, on the outskirts of Kohat, a city southwest of Kutkey. His parents remained in Kuwait, but several brothers had migrated back to Pakistan to marry and, according to Maryam's later account, upon arriving in the village, Ibrahim partly confided in them.

Ibrahim had a special guest, he explained, a famous mujahid, staying at his wife's home in Kutkey, and he was this man's guardian. It was an irksome task and he needed support. Sometimes, when he had to go to the bazaar or take the women and children to the doctor, he had to leave this guest alone, contrary to his instructions. Then there was his wife, Maryam. She was becoming nosy and in a fit of rage he had lashed out at her, making things even worse.

The family had to shoulder this responsibility, he said. He needed help. After a long discussion, Abrar Saeed, Ibrahim's unmarried older brother, was volunteered. A weather-beaten, puffy-cheeked man with greasy hair, a tuft of hair on his chin, and a drooping mustache that gave him the look of an unlucky matador, Abrar was the black sheep of the family.

Ibrahim asked Khalid for approval. The instructions that came back were that Abrar would have to marry so that there was a credible reason for him to move into the house. But getting Abrar hitched was a challenge. He had a storied past and it was well known by residents in the district. Addicted to heroin in his teens, Abrar had had a history of intoxication and warring with his neighbors before he had fled to fight jihad, as if he were some kind of foreign legionnaire.

The only wife they could find for Abrar was fourteen-year-old Bushra, the daughter of a desperately poor relative. With the wedding agreed, Ibrahim asked Khalid for extra funding only to be told that the winding up of Al Qaeda networks combined with the on-off Iranian crisis had choked the outfit's cash flow.

Maryam took Bushra in without questions. They would find a way to feed everyone. Maryam asked Amal to help prepare for the marriage in the same way that Khalid's Balochi wife had coached them. On the day of the celebration, a few families from across the valley were press-ganged into sharing a meal, while Osama stayed upstairs. Afterward, the house was split into four: one area for Abrar and Bushra, a second for Maryam and Ibrahim, a third for Amal and her daughter Safiyah, and the fourth for the mysterious Sheikh.

Ibrahim spread the message through the villages. The Saeed brothers had changed their ways. Happily married, they were enjoying a new start in Shangla. Family, children, and making a living from their small farm was all that mattered now.

But the small house was fit to burst. And then Amal announced to Osama that she was pregnant. She tried to hide it for as long as she could, wearing loose clothes and concealing her morning sickness as fatigue. When Maryam inevitably found out, confirming her suspicions that Amal spent her nights with the Sheikh, Ibrahim panicked.

Maryam's meddling had to be dealt with and he needed to cater to Amal's medical needs. But he was not from the area and did not know which midwife or clinic could be trusted to keep quiet about an Arab patient in these days of roundups. Ibrahim resorted to a ruse he had used once before. He and Maryam would accompany Amal to the hospital and tell doctors that she was deaf and mute. Unless there were serious complications, she would discharge herself immediately after the birth and if they had to register the child, they would record its father as Abu Abdullah.

When the baby arrived in early January 2003 without any problems, everyone in the house rejoiced, especially Osama, who chewed a date and placed the softened pulp against his new daughter's lips, naming her Aasia, meaning "hope."

But there was no sense of hope for Ibrahim; Osama advised him that more people were coming. He should prepare for important visitors. They would celebrate an *aqeeqah*—an Islamic tradition of making a sacrifice to honor the birth of a child—and then conduct a high-level meeting. Aasia's birth hair would be shaved and weighed, with the equivalent weight in silver gifted to a local mosque. An *aqeeqah*. Another risky visit. Elaborate gifts. Ibrahim was outraged. How could the Sheikh arrange a baby shower in a time of war? he complained to Maryam. From where would the money come?

He demanded to know who the guests were, but all Osama said was that they would bring new identity documents for Ibrahim and Abrar, who were to become Tariq and Arshad Khan, two Pashtun brothers from Charsadda, east of Peshawar.

In the second week of January 2003, Khalid Shaikh Mohammad arrived at the small house in Kutkey, alongside his pregnant wife and several other children. It was the first time he and Osama had seen one another since Karachi.

February 5, 2003, United Nations Security Council, New York City

America was finally ready to take on Saddam Hussein. In his blue suit and liverwurst tie, U.S. secretary of state Colin Powell looked tense and nervous as he prepared to present Washington's case that the Iraqi dictator was in breach of Security Council resolutions and that war was the only viable option.

The Security Council remained deeply divided, so the speech Powell was about to deliver, which had been finessed right up until the last moment, needed to quash dissent and also accelerate the process. The Bush administration needed backing from a "coalition of the willing": nations that would join the hunt for Al Qaeda in Iraq—and for weapons of mass destruction (WMDs).

Powell needed to stanch the ambivalence that had so far met Washington's call to arms. He wanted to prove that he was in the business of delivering incontrovertible facts. "My colleagues," he said gravely, setting the tone, "every statement I make today is backed up by sources, solid sources. These are not assertions. What we're giving you are facts and conclusions based on solid intelligence."

After running through a seemingly impressive body of evidence to show that Iraq did in fact possess WMDs, Powell introduced Abu Musab al-Zarqawi and his suspicious activities in the Khurmal hills, transforming him into a tool to make the crucial Al Qaeda–Saddam connection. "What I want to bring to your attention today," Powell declared, "is the potentially much more sinister nexus between Iraq and the Al Qaeda terrorist network, a nexus that combines classic terrorist organizations and modern methods of murder . . . Iraq today harbors a deadly terrorist network headed by Abu Musab al-Zarqawi, an associated collaborator of Osama bin Laden and his Al Qaeda lieutenants."[75]

Powell went on to highlight intelligence that firmly placed Zarqawi in Saddam's pay. There was no mention of other known facts such as that Zarqawi's real backers in Iraq were Ansar ul-Islam, a group opposed to Saddam Hussein's regime, or that the WMD production facility was little more than a shack and had been established by Ansar long before Zarqawi arrived.[76]

Iraq was playing everyone, Powell warned. "After we swept Al Qaeda from Afghanistan, some of its members accepted this safe haven [in Iraq]. They remain there today. Iraqi officials protest that they are not aware of the whereabouts of Zarqawi or of any of his associates. Again, these protests are not credible."

The ties between the Iraqi government and Al Qaeda went back decades, he insisted.[77] "Going back to the early and mid-nineteen nineties, when bin Laden was based in Sudan, an Al Qaeda source tells us that Saddam and bin Laden reached an understanding that Al Qaeda would no longer support activities against Baghdad," Powell claimed.[78]

Inside a reinforced room at the CIA's Counterterrorism Center that the analysts called "the vault," the team tasked with compiling evidence to connect Zarqawi and Al Qaeda to Saddam Hussein watched Powell mount his case with a growing sense of disbelief.[79] In a paper they had submitted the previous June entitled "Iraq and Al Qaeda: Interpreting a Murky Relationship" they had explicitly reported no evidence of Zarqawi having any connection to Saddam Hussein, concluding that Zarqawi was not a member of Al Qaeda, would not have known about 9/11 in advance, and so neither did Saddam Hussein. As a result of this paper, the CTC team had been called to an urgent meeting with Vice President Cheney and his chief of staff, Scooter Libby, who made it clear that Cheney was looking for another conclusion. "It was intense," recalled Nada Bakos, a young CTC targeting officer who attended and had been on the Zarqawi case for more than a year.

Now, as Powell talked and she desperately flipped through a draft of the speech that she thought the CTC had agreed with senior White House officials, she felt the panic rising in her throat. "When he got to our portion, it went off our script fairly quickly, and we were looking around at each other, saying: 'Where's he at? Where's he at?'" Bakos continued: "We were very, very, very careful about describing the relationship as we saw it, and it seemed to overinflate and not reflect our analysis . . . I don't know how it was changed or by who."

Despite these private misgivings, a *New York Times* editorial stated the next day that President Bush's decision to dispatch Powell showed a wise concern with winning international opinion. The paper congratulated the secretary of state for ditching the "apocalyptic invocations of a struggle of good and evil" to focus "on shaping a sober, factual case against Mr. Hussein's regime." And it rounded off: "It may not have produced a 'smoking gun,' but it left little question that Mr. Hussein had tried hard to conceal one."[80]

As far as Bakos and many other CTC colleagues saw it, the Powell speech, in which Zarqawi's name had been mentioned twenty-one times, was a disaster and had catapulted him from being a low-level jihadist who Osama bin Laden did not trust or like into one of the world's most dangerous men. "I can't even imagine what this did for Zarqawi's ego," recalled Bakos. "Here he is; his name is spoken at the UN. Now he's showing bin Laden and Al Qaeda who he really is, right?" Rather than going after a real threat coming from Al Qaeda in Iran, Powell had created a monster.

Bakos and her CTC colleagues suspected that recruits and funding would soon be flowing toward Zarqawi from everywhere, and back home in the dusty, working-class Zarqa suburb of Hai Masoom, where Zarqawi had grown up, within hours of the speech he was crowned a hero. As his name appeared spray-painted on walls around the city, a steady stream of volunteers and well-wishers gathered at his innocuous concrete house set back from the street with its rusty white painted iron gate.[81]

February 28, 2003, 5 P.M., CIA Headquarters, Langley, Virginia

Three weeks after the Powell speech and with recriminations still flying back and forth, Marty Martin, the unpredictable chief of the Counterterrorism Center's Sunni Extremist Group, bowled excitedly into the conference room. "Boss?" George Tenet was running the daily meeting of the executive staff. "Where are you going to be this weekend?"[82]

Tenet regarded him quizzically. Martin had had a lengthy clandestine career, but he had a way of rewriting the world in his own image that would later lead some colleagues to describe him as the "Jack Bauer of the bayou."[83] Maybe that was the trick of surviving for so many years inside the rabbit warren of Islamism.

An asset code-named X had surfaced, Martin said.

Tenet waited, accustomed to the way Martin drip-fed his stories.

"And he is on his way to meet *Khalid Shaikh Mohammad*."

Tenet puckered his lips.

"Stay in touch," Martin added, deliberately underselling his product. "I just might get some good news."

Others in the loop were more skeptical. Small, undernourished, and resembling a subsistence farmer, Asset X was an Iranian Balochi whose uncle was a well-known cleric in London. He maintained that his family, whose origins lay in Zahidan, was intertwined with KSM's, making him a distant relative.

But up until now things had not gone smoothly in his career as a CIA source.

When Asset X had first come forward in the spring of 2001, no one in Washington was giving much attention to Islamist terrorists. After 9/11, an urgent review of all CIA sources had led to a Farsi-speaking CIA case officer being assigned to Asset X. After KSM was named among the FBI's twenty-two Most Wanted Terrorists, accused of masterminding the failed Bojinka plot, the CIA officer was authorized to make small payments that were hand-delivered to Asset X in paper envelopes. However, Asset X proved to be greedy and when one expense claim was refused for being falsified, he had taken offense and cut off all contact.

The CIA would not see Asset X again for nine months, during which time the agency learned through Special Agent Ali Soufan that Khalid Shaikh Mohammad was the architect of 9/11.

As they hastily tried to rebuild relations with Asset X, his handler was reassigned, leaving before he could fully explain the importance of his source to his successor. The arrangements with Asset X were on the verge of being terminated again—as he cost too much—until an overheard conversation at the CIA station in Islamabad brought him back into focus. Assigned a new case officer, Asset X was made a lucrative offer. "Look, Brother," his new handler said, "there are twenty-five million frigging reasons why you need to find Khalid," meaning that getting KSM would inevitably lead to Osama, on whose head was placed a $25 million bounty. Having agreed to give the operation one last shot, the agency had to fashion the right bait. Estimating that the raids all over Pakistan had made Al Qaeda feel the pinch, they plumped for hard cash. Asset X was told to float an offer by KSM of $3 million donated from friends in the Gulf and London. He wanted to hand over the money personally and Khalid agreed to meet him, as he desperately needed the cash.[84] Getting the real culprit behind 9/11 could not have come at a better time for the CIA, which was still reeling from the implications of the Powell speech.

February 28, 2003, 10 P.M., 18A Nisar Road, Westridge, Rawalpindi, Pakistan

The text message was brief: "I M W KSM." It was sent from a villa in a well-to-do suburb of Rawalpindi, the army cantonment twinned with Islamabad. Asset X was texting from the bathroom, while Khalid Shaikh Mohammad held forth in the lounge.

The house, located in a district dense with soldiers and spies, was a five-minute drive from the Pakistan Army's general headquarters (GHQ) and belonged to a well-respected scientist and his wife, who was politically active in the women's wing of Jamaat-e-Islami, Pakistan's largest religious political party and one that was frequently accused of having links to militant groups.

The householders were out at a wedding, but Khalid, who had been on the road for days returning from seeing Osama in Shangla and Dr. al-Zawahiri in Shakai, had dropped in at the invitation of Adil Qadoos, the scientist's son, who was a major in the Pakistan Army.

This was the kind of nexus that had come to antagonize the CIA and that many in the Islamabad station had become convinced the White House was blind to as it ramped up for a war in Iraq. A wanted terrorist, sheltering in a property whose residents' papers melded religion, politics, and the Pakistan Army: was there a more potent symbol for how the nuclear-armed Islamic Republic was playing all sides?

Exhausted by juggling his pregnant wife's demands with multiple new terrorist plots, Khalid had broken two of his golden rules in coming to Westridge. This was not the first time he had stayed in the house. And Asset X had not been searched, enabling him to enter with a cell phone in his pocket.

After midnight, the CIA and ISI converged on the villa, although the Pakistanis had not been informed of the identity of their target. They waited in the dark for Asset X to leave and to be certain that Khalid, who was a night owl, had fallen asleep.

At two thirty A.M., Pakistani police and ISI went in through the doors and windows. The police cuffed Qadoos's brother, who was at home, and escorted his wife and their children outside. Khalid had taken sleeping pills and the ISI had trouble waking him. When he realized what was happening, he immediately offered a deal. "Why are you doing this for the Americans?" he asked an officer. "*We'll* give you what you want."[85]

In another room, the search team hauled up a cowering figure. His papers showed he was a Saudi national who would shortly be identified as Mustafa Ahmad al-Hawsawi, Khalid's 9/11 financier. In his briefcase, the CIA found a nineteen-page phone directory of Al Qaeda facilitators, and on his laptop were several letters and details of wire payments to the 9/11 hijackers. Seemingly small details homed in on later would come to mean the most in the hunt for bin Laden, including an e-mail address for Abu Ahmad al-Kuwaiti, a man whose real name still eluded them but whose *kunya* had been identified by Riyadh the Facilitator and confirmed by Abu Zubaydah, whose address book contained a phone number for him.

The next day, the ISI raided an army billet in Kohat cantonment and took away Major Adil Qadoos of the Forty-fifth Signals Regiment.[86]

March 1, 2003

Two hours after Khalid's capture, the chief of interrogations at the Salt Pit sent an e-mail to headquarters: "Subject: Let's roll with the new guy."[87]

The chief asked for permission to use the new OMS-approved Enhanced Interrogation Techniques that had already been deployed on Abu Zubaydah and Ramzi bin al-Shibh.[88] He also checked that he could use rectal rehydration in order to "assert total control over the detainee."[89]

Shortly after, Marty Martin called the ISI safe house in Rawalpindi where Khalid was being held. The first media reports of the extraordinary raid were already out and he was buzzing. But news channels were using the old FBI picture of Khalid neatly barbered and suited, looking like a Kuwaiti plutocrat.

"Boss, this ain't right," Martin complained to George Tenet, seeking his approval to make a change before calling the Pakistan spies. "The media are making this bum look like a hero." The ISI interrogators in Rawalpindi must have something better. With his hair still mussed up from sleep and wearing only his undergarments, Khalid was snapped by the ISI looking doped-up, hirsute, and bedraggled.

Back in Washington, KSM's detention was greeted with applause, Porter Goss, the chairman of the House Permanent Select Committee on Intelligence, declaring it a war-winning moment—comparing it to the liberation of Paris in 1944.[90] All talk of Abu Musab al-Zarqawi was temporarily forgotten.

Observing the first phase of the interrogation inside the Rawalpindi safe house was Brigadier Asad Munir, the ISI's Peshawar station chief. Munir was hard to handle and had a vicious bite. A man whose tight, open-neck shirts, slicked-back hair, and chain-smoking gave him the appearance of a pool-hall hustler, Munir had been on Khalid Shaikh Mohammad's trail for months.

He had tracked him to the Amin Hotel in Peshawar and intercepted calls that suggested he was using addresses in Quetta. But Khalid always flitted before any raid. In a joint operation with the ISI in Islamabad, Munir had also pursued Khalid's couriers, eavesdropping on their calls and watching as they delivered messages at dead-drops on the outskirts of Kohat. That town felt especially important to Munir—as was one particular phone number whose user traveled to Kohat and then down to Rawalpindi, only for the ISI to lose him.[91]

Now that Khalid had been found in affluent Westridge, Munir felt he should have been in on the raid. All he could do was go through the recovered documents from Hawsawi's laptop, which included three letters from Osama.[92] For him, the standout was a letter to his son Hamzah that had almost certainly been given to Khalid during his visit to Kutkey. The Peshawar station chief did not have long to make copies of the data, as everything recovered from Westridge was shipped back to Washington, where one official described it as the "mother lode of information that leads to the inner workings of Al Qaeda."[93] That trove included a list of people Khalid was running—assets, agents, couriers, and fighters, including those he intended to deploy abroad—and constituted a roadmap of sleeper cells, some of which had been in the United States, the United Kingdom, or mainland Europe for years, but no connections to Saddam Hussein or Iraq.

While the interrogation continued in Rawalpindi, Munir wondered how the CIA had finally got to the finish line. That had not been explained. But

Asset X was rarefied intelligence and he had no idea that George Tenet was on his way to Pakistan to personally thank the informer and usher him into a witness protection program with a huge reward.

March 3, 1:20 A.M., ISI Safe House, Rawalpindi

Khalid Shaikh Mohammad had not slept for forty-eight hours. A videotape shot from above showed him sitting at a table in the interrogation room, swaying from side to side like a drunk.[94]

"You say you are going to do something," he mumbled, squinting at an American interrogator. Technically, Khalid was still in ISI custody, but a CIA agent was running the show—a man who would later be accused of punching the detainee in the head and stamping on his face.

"Maybe you can . . ." Khalid began.

The American cut him off: "I haven't promised you anything."

"Same thing, different night," Khalid continued, popping the occasional line that revealed he was still compos mentis. "Maybe go to sleep until night, you come back the next night." He nodded off midsentence: "I cannot make sure. You make sure . . ."

The American pointed to a clock on the wall. "It's one twenty A.M.," he said, addressing Khalid but looking at the ISI officer. "He said you would be talking by one twenty A.M. It's now one twenty A.M."

The interrogation team knew the Al Qaeda rule that anyone who got caught would say nothing for forty-eight hours to allow brothers outside to go underground. Time was up.

Khalid roused himself and looked at the ISI officer. Did he want to speak to the American alone, the ISI officer asked, keen to break the deadlock?

Khalid shook his head, surely thinking of all the disappearances. "Other people know about the matter . . . the word is already out, on BBC . . . CNN."

The CIA officer pushed on, referring to an earlier conversation. "Somebody was talking—yesterday, actually," he said, hoping to hoodwink Khalid into spilling.

The detainee's head sank back down on the table next to an overflowing ashtray.

He was not ready to spill anything.

*   *   *

March 3, 2003, Kutkey Village, Martung Tehsil, Shangla

Maryam and Ibrahim were watching the news on Al Jazeera when the arrest photograph of Khalid Shaikh Mohammad flashed up on the screen. Maryam froze and grabbed Ibrahim's arm. "It's Hafeez," she spluttered, referring to their recent houseguest.

She glanced at her husband, who was clearly in shock.

After a long silence, he spoke. "He *was* a great mujahid." Then he rose and disappeared into the forbidden section of the house.

When Ibrahim returned, he told his wife that no one should go near the tall guest. Coming so soon after the laughable reports about Zarqawi and Al Qaeda's links to Saddam Hussein, Osama was dumbfounded at the sudden loss of his real chief of external operations.

Ibrahim called his brother Abrar. Khalid had become exceptionally cautious in recent months. Someone in the movement must have betrayed him. Who was it—and would they be next? Khalid had recently visited this house, which placed all of them in jeopardy. They had to move out.

For the first time, there was no one the brothers could ask for advice. Khalid was detained; Dr. al-Zawahiri was impossible to reach directly in Waziristan, where he sheltered along with much of the Al Qaeda leadership; and messages to Saif al-Adel and his military committee in Iran took weeks to arrive.

Ibrahim could see danger everywhere. Khalid might well have been carrying Ibrahim's and Abrar's numbers or their e-mail addresses. He certainly had letters with him written in this house just a few days back by Osama. Khalid had said he would never be broken, but surely every man had his limit.

The next morning, they decided to shift Osama to their parents' empty house in Suleman Talaab.[95] The village lay on a floodplain, just south of Tanda Lake, a few miles outside Kohat, where Major Adil Qadoos had been picked up. It was not ideal, but it was safer than staying in Shangla, they reasoned. Ringed on one side by neat rice paddies and by honey-colored ridges on the other, there was nothing to draw the CIA or ISI to the house, and it was officially registered as *be-chiragh* (uninhabited).

Ibrahim, Abrar, and Osama set out in the early hours of March 4 and they drove through the gloom of the predawn Swat Valley in silence. They had told their wives nothing about their plans, only that the women should wait.

With the men gone, Amal, Maryam, and Bushra flew into a panic. Barricading the compound, they turned off all the lights, put the babies back to sleep, and waited. Maryam had overheard her husband talking. He and Abrar were jittery, suggesting a raid. Would the Americans come for them? As they sat waiting, Amal sought courage from her mother's pocket Koran.

March 4, 2003, Detention Site Cobalt, Afghanistan

Shackled, blindfolded, and with a hood over his head, Khalid Shaikh Mohammad arrived at the Salt Pit.

"My clothes were cut off me, the bag and blindfold were removed, and photographs were taken of me naked," he later recalled.[96] After he had been examined by doctors, his hands were chained to a bar suspended from the ceiling in accordance with OMS recommendations. Later, he was moved into a larger room, where three interrogators—a man and two women—began firing questions at him. Ten masked guards took turns punching him in the chest or stomach whenever he refused to cooperate.

Keeping him somewhere between alive and dead seemed to be the goal. Each action was designed to addle, offend, or dislocate. When Khalid stopped drinking, they flipped him around and pumped fluids into him anally. If Khalid needed exercise, he was stripped and made to parade with fellow naked inmates. If anyone complained, all of them were doused in icy water.

One of those who nodded to Khalid was Dr. Ghairat Baheer, Hekmatyar's son-in-law and still a ghost captive. "The cold and the humiliation of relieving yourself naked in front of the other prisoners was far worse than the interrogation," Dr. Baheer said, recalling that he only exchanged glances with Khalid, as talking was prohibited.[97] The worst experience was squatting together naked and knee-to-knee over the toilets, where the skin-rubbing, muscle-tensing proximity and the rising smell conspired to depress them all.

Dr. Baheer recalled that prisoner Khalid quickly disappeared. Three days in and strapped into a high chair by his wrists and ankles and tilted backward, he was rendered on a Gulfstream with tail number N379P. He slept for the first time in five days. He deduced the location of his new detention facility by examining the label on a water bottle and noticing the manufacturer's web address ended in ".po." Site Blue was in Poland, the same location where Abu Zubaydah was being held.

Here at Stare Kiejkuty, Khalid was taken to the "verge of death and back again." When he was uncooperative, he was put against a wall and punched and slapped in the body, head, and face. "A thin flexible plastic collar was placed around my neck so that it could be held at the two ends by a guard who would use it to slam me repeatedly against the wall," he later told the International Committee of the Red Cross (ICRC), the same treatment as described by Abu Zubaydah.[98]

After a CIA-employed doctor fixed a clip to his finger so they could measure his vital signs, the waterboarding began. Khalid remembered being told that the guards would "take me to breaking point" but not beyond. "I struggled in the panic of not being able to breathe," he said. If the doctor intervened, Khalid was given a brief respite in his cell. Photographs had been pinned up of his missing sons, Yusuf and Abed, making it clear they were still in CIA detention, and he was informed that they were now being held in the United States. A former military policeman stationed at Guantánamo Bay detention facility would later claim that there was a secret section of the base called Camp Iguana that was used to house children, some of whom were as "young as twelve and eight."[99]

While the CIA refused to say where Khalid's sons were, a spokesman acknowledged that they were important to him. "The promise of their release and their return to Pakistan may be the psychological lever we need to break him."[100] During at least one interrogation, CIA interrogators pushed that lever to the maximum when they told Khalid: "If anything else happens in the United States, 'We're going to kill your children.'"[101] The interrogators also ignored his multiple requests to know whether his wife had given birth to a boy or a girl.[102]

But however hard he was worked, some things could not be shaken out of Khalid. When asked about the letter to Hamzah bin Laden and how he had it in his possession, he laid a false trail, talking about an Al Qaeda courier he identified as "Abu Khalid," who was also known as "Abu Ahmad al-Balochi."

When the interrogators suggested that this courier was actually Abu Ahmad al-Kuwaiti, Khalid deftly distracted them. Yes, someone called the Kuwaiti had helped move families from Afghanistan to Pakistan after the Tora Bora operation, but this man "was a minor figure who was more interested in earning money than serving Al Qaeda." Now that he thought about it, al-Kuwaiti had married and retired in 2002. Laminating truth with deceit was Khalid's specialty.

Asked again about Abu Ahmad, Khalid, pretending not to hear, said that Abu Ahmad al-Balochi had skipped to Iran. Referring back to al-Kuwaiti, he recalled that that man had worked with Abu Zubaydah in Peshawar prior to 9/11, but he said he did not know him well as he had only met him three or four times. Anyhow, the man was now retired. Each suggestion had to be tested and explored by the CIA. Privately the agency worried that KSM "only ADMITS details when he knows we know them from someone else." Other than that it was obfuscation.[103]

The orders came back to intensify the waterboarding. On one occasion Khalid's belly became so distended that when an interrogator pressed against him, water gushed out of his mouth. "The worst day was when I was beaten for about half an hour," he recalled. "My head was banged so hard against the wall it started to bleed. Cold water was poured over it. This was then repeated with the other interrogators. Finally I was then taken for a session of waterboarding."[104]

During his first month at Detention Site Blue, Khalid was kept naked and given solid food only twice. When he complied, he was force-fed Ensure, a nutrition shake, as a reward.[105] When he was difficult, they administered it anally.

But the interrogators were getting nowhere. A CIA cable warned: "KSM's pattern of behavior over the past three months, trying to control his environment, lying and then admitting things only when pressed that others have been caught and have likely admitted the plot, is a cause for concern."

FBI special agent Ali Soufan had predicted as much, pointing to his experience with Abu Zubaydah. They had all visualized and even rehearsed for this moment, and in KSM's case his limits, and his strategy, remained an unknown.

He started tossing out real names, identifying lower-level supporters, whose arrest and detention he anticipated would be even more complicated and time-consuming, while revealing little of the inner workings of Al Qaeda. One of the first he sacrificed was a woman: the new wife of his nephew Ammar al-Balochi. A talented young Pakistani neuroscientist from Karachi, her name was Aafia Siddiqui and she had volunteered to assist Al Qaeda in America, where she lived. To lock her in, as Osama had done with his own family, Aafia had been secretly married into Khalid's family a few months earlier.

A well-educated and highly intelligent woman, Aafia spoke English with an American accent and had won a scholarship to study biology at the

Massachusetts Institute of Technology (MIT), where she wrote an essay called "How Intercultural Attitudes Help Shape a Multinational World." After graduation, she had enrolled at Brandeis University near Boston for a Ph.D. in neurocognitive science. She married a young Pakistani doctor, who worked in Boston and with whom she had two children.[106]

After 9/11, when Aafia's husband complained of religious and racial discrimination and worried about his wife's increasing extremism, they had returned to Karachi, where they divorced. After giving birth to their third child at a Karachi hospital, she began moving in Khalid's circle, working on a plot to smuggle explosives into America inside containers transporting secondhand clothes. In early 2003, she agreed to marry Ammar al-Balochi to advance the plot.

Within days of Khalid giving up Aafia's name, the FBI issued a global "wanted for questioning" alert that portrayed her as a "courier" and "financial fixer" for Al Qaeda. On March 30, they traced her to Karachi, where she was staying with her mother. She fled the house in a taxi, intending to catch a flight to Islamabad, where her uncle lived; but she vanished on her way to the airport, along with her three children.[107]

At first, Pakistan's interior ministry confirmed that a woman had been taken into custody on terrorism charges. Then it and the FBI issued denials. Later, Pakistani officials contended that Al Qaeda had grabbed Aafia and spirited her away.

In the vacuum, all that was left was a photo of a veiled Muslim mother of three, her youngest son only four months old. The caption most often used when the photo was printed in Arabic newspapers indicated that she was "imprisoned in a CIA secret detention site." The Indian media ran another iteration: "Forced to work incognito for the ISI."

Both stories deepened mistrust in the Bush administration's self-proclaimed war on terror, just as Khalid had intended.

March 2003, Evin Prison, Tehran, Iran

The Mauritanian had been locked up in a cell for three months. After he'd been arrested in Karaj on Christmas Day 2002 and driven through the night across the snow-clad Alborz Mountains, his vehicle had drawn up at the huge, locked iron gates of Evin Prison in Tehran, Iran's most notorious prison.[108]

He recalled quaking as he took in the bleak landscape: guard towers and high walls topped by security cameras and dense coils of electrified barbed wire. Once inside, he had been both relieved and frustrated to see that there were many familiar faces. Once again, Iran had betrayed Al Qaeda.

As a large group of brothers lined up in front of him in the courtyard, exchanging their clothes for prison uniforms bearing the blue logo of the Iranian Ministry of Justice, the guards left them alone just long enough for him to tell them to say that he was "Dr. Abdullah, a visiting Sunni scholar." It was one thing for the Quds Force to know his real identity, but not the Reformists or their allies in the intelligence ministry.

Blindfolded, he was led away to a tiny cell with a floor that looked like it had been trampled by thousands of feet over the years. There was a prayer rug, a metal toilet and basin, and a gas fire. As the days dragged by, the Mauritanian felt as if he was falling into an abyss. His human interactions consisted of food trays slid under his door, and the monotony was punctuated only by the call to prayer, which was broadcast along Evin's humid corridors. By the time he was photographed on the fourth day, he had lost all sense of time. "I did not try to arrange my messy hair, nor arrange my untidy clothes. Nor did the photographer seem keen on anything like that."

"Name?"

"Dr. Abdullah," he replied hoarsely.

Taken back to his cell, the Mauritanian prayed and prayed. "I found myself face-to-face with the Koran, as if I was reading it for the first time," he said. He was overwhelmed by a "haunting concern for my family and the fear of what is waiting for me at the opening of the investigation file."[109]

He had not prepared for this moment, and he wondered how others coped. He created a small routine to distract himself: jogging on the spot for an hour a day, tidying his cell each morning. He watched the ants harvest crumbs from his food tray, envying how happy and satisfied they looked. He explored his new world, examining every inch, identifying small bumps on the walls and minute cracks in the tile, probing every space and texture with his fingertips, discovering tiny messages scraped into the plaster by previous occupants under the bed. Some had written prayers, others had composed letters to lost lovers and absent family members.

Others had scored the bed or the walls to record just how many months they had been locked inside this hutch. The Mauritanian could not bear to count them. They seemed to run into eons.

The Quds Force was not coming to save him this time, he told himself. "Oh God, do not let me suffer," he prayed.

After a week, the Mauritanian heard movement in the next-door cell. He tapped on the water pipe of his basin, which went into the wall: *pik, pik, pik*.

His new neighbor tapped back: *pik, pik, pik*.

They began to exchange messages by whispering down the pipes. The Mauritanian knew this man. He was an Egyptian Al Qaeda explosives expert who had worked on the bombs that destroyed the U.S. embassies in Nairobi and Dar-es-Salaam in 1998. He was one of twenty-two named on the FBI's Most Wanted Terrorist list, and he had a $5 million price tag on his head.[110]

"Mujahideen brothers are being arrested all over Iran," the newcomer said. "Nowhere is safe."

"Anything from Sheikh Osama?" the Mauritanian asked.

"Nothing," replied his neighbor.

Pik, pik, pik.

The Mauritanian leaned in.

"More new arrivals," the man whispered as voices came down the corridor.

Pik, pik, pik.

"Twenty-three members of Abu Musab al-Zarqawi's group."[111]

They had been rounded up at the Amir Hotel on the eve of their departure for Khurmal. Among them was Zarqawi's second-in-command and brother-in-law, Khalid al-Aruri, and his childhood friend, Iyad al-Toubasi, the former ladies' hairdresser from Zarqa. Their capture was an unexpected bonus for the Reformist government but a disaster for the Quds Force, which up until this point had been actively helping Zarqawi's fighters reach Kurdish-held Iraq. Many who had already passed through the Amir Hotel had reached Baghdad, according to British intelligence, and were awaiting reinforcements.[112] Zarqawi had been ranging all over the region, using real Iranian passports made out in the names of Ibrahim Kasimi Ridah and Abdal Rahman Hasan al-Tahihi and communicating with a Swiss satellite phone and two Iranian cell phones provided by the Quds Force.[113] The Mauritanian sensed that the Quds Force could not afford to let these newly captured Zarqawi fighters fester for long in Evin.

He heard nothing more for a few days.

Pik, pik, pik.

"Yes?"

"I have news."

"Tell me! Don't make me wait."

"Zarqawi is here!"

During a trip back into Iran to update Saif al-Adel and other *shura* members about his activities in Iraq, Zarqawi had been caught, putting Al Qaeda's Iraq war plans on hold. Intelligence officials had found at least nine passports and identity cards on him, showing him variously as a citizen of Lebanon, Iran, Palestine, and Yemen. His recent radius of activity was said to cover Iraq, Iran, Syria, Jordan, Turkey, the Pankisi Valley in Georgia, and the northern Caucasus.[114] He had been so emboldened by his assistance from the Quds Force that he had even found time to slip back to Zarqa, where his two wives and children were now living.

"More news."

"Yes?"

"America is about to invade Iraq and it says Saddam backs Al Qaeda!"

The Mauritanian raised his eyebrows, recalling how Osama had sent him and Saif al-Adel to Baghdad to meet with Saddam Hussein during the Sudan years. They had returned empty-handed, complaining that Saddam was "virulently opposed to Osama and Al Qaeda." Instead, they had gone on to Tehran and arranged tentative access to the Hezbollah camps in the Beqaa Valley, where Al Qaeda would receive training in the use of explosives.

Iran—not Iraq—had helped Al Qaeda.[115]

Despite his current predicament, it was still satisfying to catch the Americans lying.

One week later: *Pik, pik, pik.*

"Yes? I am here."

"Zarqawi's gone!"

The Mauritanian leaned closer to the pipe.

"He's been released with all his men."

The Quds Force must have fought tooth and nail with the Iranian Ministry of Justice to secure Zarqawi's release. The Mauritanian was impressed.

Several days later all the cell doors were flung open. A Ministry of Justice investigator was touring Evin and wanted to question the Al Qaeda prisoners. Guided to the governor's office, the Mauritanian spent most of the session focusing on a message a previous inmate had etched into the arm of his chair: "You should endure as YOU are in the right."

Was the prisoner part of Zarqawi's group? the investigator asked. Did he wish to go to Iraq or return to Pakistan?

"Neither," the Mauritanian blustered before being led back to his cell.

Two weeks later the doors were unlocked again. Guards ran down the corridors, shouting: "Prepare yourselves!"

Assembling in the courtyard, the prisoners filed into waiting buses. The Mauritanian was amazed at the voices and faces he recognized. He had not seen so many Al Qaeda cadres since Osama's son Mohammed had got married in Tarnak Qila in January 2001.

"Why are we out?" he asked a guard nervously. Was everyone being shipped to Iraq? "No," said the worried-looking guard. The ICRC had won entry to Evin and was on its way over. All evidence of the secret Al Qaeda prisoners had to be concealed, whether or not they were part of Zarqawi's group.

"Dr. Abdullah?" a guard called out.

Gingerly, he raised his hand.

"Not you," the guard said, marching the Mauritanian to a new, remote wing and an even smaller cell.

March 19, 2003, Shiraz, Iran

Saif al-Adel was still at liberty, reunited with his family, plotting war in Iraq, and surrounded by loyalists including his old friends from Cairo, Abu Mohammed al-Masri and Abu al-Khayr al-Masri. After his release from Evin, Zarqawi's deputy, Khalid al-Aruri, had joined him, along with Sari Shihab, another of Zarqawi's old jihad friends from Zarqa who in more recent times had become an important facilitator for any Iraq-bound brothers traveling through Iran. Sulaiman Abu Ghaith, Al Qaeda's accidental spokesman, had arrived, too. Wanted the world over, as his face loomed large on the 9/11 celebration videos, he had nowhere else to go.

Saif's immediate concern in the wake of Khalid Shaikh Mohammad's arrest was to warn the entire organization against complacency. Al Qaeda Central had been hit hard, and he and the other brothers in Iran needed to help it get back on its feet. He contacted his Syrian courier Yasin and asked him to deliver a message to Dr. al-Zawahiri. Al Qaeda needed to take swift action to overhaul security protocols and examine communication strategies. The Waziristan cells needed to depute a senior Al Qaeda commander to supervise Osama's security, as his current companions were "undoubtedly compromised." Recruited by Khalid Shaikh Mohammad, Abu Ahmad al-Kuwaiti was likely to be tracked and seized.

Saif sent a second messenger, the Pakistani Hassan Ghul, to track down Zarqawi, who he knew through Aruri had been released from Evin. If he had not already done so, he should cross the border back into Kurdish-held territory and the no-fly zone. In the early hours of March 20, news broadcasts had flashed across their TV. U.S. bombers were over Baghdad. Carrying on from Operation Enduring Freedom in Afghanistan, Operation Iraqi Freedom was under way. Al Qaeda had its chance to hit back, Saif told his men. "Zarqawi has to harry the American forces." The moment of retribution had at last arrived.

Others aligned to Al Qaeda were advocating the same. Tactician Abu Musab al-Suri, the redheaded Syrian, who now had a $5 million bounty on his head and was hiding in Marivan, close to the Iraqi border, was finalizing his 1,600-page treatise entitled *The Call for Global Islamic Resistance* that, among other things, considered what had gone wrong with previous failed jihads, including the popular Syrian uprising of the early 1980s.[116] Based on his own experiences and research, and an analysis of Koranic writings, the Syrian was laying out a plan, stage by stage. The aim, he wrote, was to "bring about the largest number of human and material casualties possible for America and its allies." Iraq was one theater—but there were others. Al Qaeda should not focus solely on large-scale spectaculars but should also encourage acts of terrorism by individuals or small groups as a "leaderless resistance" that would wear down the enemy. The "strategic goal" was the declaration of a caliphate.

In the early hours of April 23, Saif, his family members, and his friends were woken by the sound of splintering wood as a column of armed Iranian intelligence officials charged through the door, one of them filming the raid.[117] The women and children were gathered in the living room, while the men were put in a van that drove to Tehran, each one being dropped off at a different location.[118]

A man of action, Saif now found himself in an underground cell with nothing to do but hope that Zarqawi would make good progress in Iraq and that several bombing operations he had set in motion in Saudi Arabia would still come off. When the guards gave him a Koran, Saif thought of the

Mauritanian, his old friend, who he had often ragged about keeping his head stuck in books when he could have been fighting. He tried to pray but could not concentrate.

Eventually, he managed to get a pencil and some yellowing greaseproof paper. He began sketching out a small biography of Zarqawi, on whom he pinned Al Qaeda's future hopes, writing that he had sent Zarqawi firm guidance in the note carried by Hassan Ghul: "In brief, our advice is a clear objective, a sound banner, clear legitimate means, the ability to take advantage of the circumstances and resources."[119]

If he kept these things in mind, Zarqawi would win "victory, power and the satisfaction of the Lord of the Universe."

Although incarcerated, Saif was already looking to the future. "We expect that Syria and Lebanon will face similar circumstances," he advised. "If this takes place, it will give the Islamic action a vast theater to maneuver in." A new leadership for Islamic nations would emerge and "jihad [would] enable this leadership to reestablish the Islamic Caliphate once more."

An Islamic state would overcome injustice. "May God grant us success," he wrote in the gloom of his cell.

May 3, 2003, United Nations Office, Geneva, Switzerland

The fortunes of Zalmay Khalilzad, Bush's special presidential envoy for Afghanistan, continued to rise. Rumors were rife that he would soon be announced as U.S. ambassador to Afghanistan, and with the war in Iraq into its third month there were more reasons than ever to improve relations with neighboring Iran.

Fifteen months had passed since the Axis of Evil speech, and Iran's influence over the emerging Shia militia in Iraq meant that Tehran could no longer be ignored.[120]

Khalilzad had also seen new intelligence reports about Al Qaeda being present in significant numbers in Iraq, wreaking havoc in operations that the CIA believed were being steered from Iran—contrary to Colin Powell's public assertions to the United Nations.

On May 3, Khalilzad and Ryan Crocker, who was by now an interim envoy to Afghanistan, met again with Mohammad Javad Zarif, who had become Iran's deputy foreign minister. This was their fourth meeting in as many months. Al Qaeda fighters should be turned over to the United States, the Americans suggested. The evidence that Iran was still sheltering them and facilitating their Iraq operations was overwhelming.

Zarif informed the Americans that Iran had been ready to offer Al Qaeda's military council and family to the United States only for this extraordinary proposal to be wrecked by President Bush's inflammatory State of the Union address in January 2002.

Khalilzad and Crocker had long suspected this was the case, but this was the first time Zarif had spelled it out. Now, they tried to get Zarif to understand the urgency of the situation. Could they put the past behind them and get the deal back on track? Al Qaeda was not only starting to cause problems for U.S. forces in Iraq; the CIA had intelligence that showed how cells based in Iran were also preparing to attack Western targets in Saudi Arabia. "They were there, under Iranian protection, planning operations," recalled Crocker.[121]

Zarif advised the Americans that Tehran was deeply divided. Reformists were anxious to restart "talks about everything—including Al Qaeda." However, other factions—which Crocker knew referred primarily to the Quds Force—had other plans.

On May 4, there was movement. The Swiss ambassador to Iran, Tim Guldimann, who represented American interests in the country, faxed the U.S. State Department in Washington, claiming to summarize the dominant view inside Iran's government.[122] Shocked by the scenes broadcast from Baghdad, dissenters worried about regime change in Iran were prepared to start wide-ranging talks, in which nothing would be precluded.

Guldimann suggested that a "Grand Bargain" might be possible if Iran received diplomatic recognition, and if some elements of its domestic nuclear-power generation program were legitimized. At their next meeting in Geneva, Zarif would let it be known that this "Bargain" could take the form of a swap: the leaders of Mujahedin-e-Khalq, an Iranian group that the Quds Force said were terrorists and were harbored by Saddam Hussein, in exchange for Al Qaeda's military council and bin Laden's family. This was just what Crocker and Khalilzad had hoped for, and they eagerly referred it up the ladder to Washington, expecting a positive response.

Almost immediately, Washington hawks began circling with senior officials at the Pentagon voicing skepticism that Iran's Reformists actually had the power to conclude such a deal. The U.S. State Department also seemed unimpressed. Khalilzad said: "I asked around and it was made clear to me that no one cared much for this deal. It was seen as the Swiss ambassador's power play rather than a genuine offer."

On May 8, Vice President Dick Cheney's and U.S. Secretary of Defense Donald Rumsfeld's reluctance to strike a deal with Iran appeared to be vindicated when Saif al-Adel's men mounted simultaneous attacks inside Saudi Arabia, hitting three residential compounds popular with Western workers, creating mayhem, killing more than thirty people (including nine Americans), and injuring 160. It was the largest number of U.S citizens killed by Al Qaeda since the 9/11 attacks, and Rumsfeld revealed that the United States had intercepted phone conversations implicating Al Qaeda members in Iran as being behind the bombings. Without any further discussion with Zarif, the Bush administration cut off the back channel to Tehran. The "Grand Bargain" was dead in the water.

June 24, 2003, Camp David (U.S. Presidential Retreat), Maryland

Iran had been rebuffed, but Pakistan was still being promiscuously wooed. President Bush welcomed General Pervez Musharraf to Camp David for a summit at which he credited Pakistan with having apprehended more than five hundred members of Al Qaeda and the Taliban, including Abu Zubaydah, Khalid Shaikh Mohammad, and Khalid's nephew Ammar al-Balochi and his Yemeni thug Silver, who had also been run to ground in Karachi.

"Thanks to President Musharraf's leadership, on the al-Qaeda front we've dismantled the chief operators," Bush said.[123] Although Osama bin Laden was still at large, his lieutenants were "no longer a threat."

For Musharraf, who had left India as a four-year-old Muslim migrant in 1947 and spent his early years in Karachi sharing two barrack rooms with eighteen relatives, this was his proudest moment; and he milked it shamelessly: "Thank you. Thank you very much, Mr. President. I am extremely grateful to President Bush for his gracious invitation to me to visit the United States. I am particularly honored and touched by his special gesture in arranging our meeting in Camp David."

Over whiskey and before an open fire, he pledged Pakistan's ongoing support.[124] The two countries enjoyed a "very close and, indeed, special relationship," he said, departing with a new $3 billion aid package, half of it designated for the military.

"Pure gold," Musharraf said to an aide on the flight back to Islamabad. "And there's more to come."[125]

Summer 2003, Peshawar, Pakistan

Brigadier Asad Munir could not get Osama's letter to his son Hamzah out of his head. He was sure that it proved the Al Qaeda leader was alive somewhere in Pakistan—writing and directing the terror.

Circumstantial evidence pointed toward the Tribal Areas. And as Peshawar station chief, this was close to his fiefdom, a place he nowadays ran in tandem with the CIA. Every day, Munir met agents Julie and Keith, who stayed in suites at the Pearl Continental Hotel, the last vestige of luxury in a shuttered city plagued by bomb threats and kidnappings—the last place one could get a steak and a cold beer.

Together they were compiling a new Al Qaeda almanac that went well beyond the FBI's original 9/11 table of twenty-two names: dozens of pages of couriers, facilitators, and guesthouse managers; foot soldiers, drivers, lookouts; cleaners and cooks.

Each morning Munir and his counterparts would pore over a thick stack of transcripts from conversations intercepted overnight. Hundreds of phones were now being monitored and e-mail accounts sieved. "We'd compare and we would sift," he reflected.[126] Most of these names came from the ISI, which had the better humint (human intelligence derived from interpersonal sources). "Unlike the U.S., we understood how tribal society worked."

Spread across Pakistan, Al Qaeda sometimes had no choice but to resort to cell phones or to Public Call Offices (PCOs), which were located in every village and town. Given the arrest of several important couriers, the outfit's increasing reliance on open channels enabled the CIA to extract a web of interconnected phone numbers and suspect addresses, just as Deuce Martinez had done when he went after Abu Zubaydah. A similar schematic now adorned the wall of Munir's office, beside a detailed map of the North-West Frontier Province—another gift from the United States.

Munir and his American counterparts studied it, measuring journey times between locations, overlaying courier routes, identifying compounds. "Who's new at this guesthouse? Who's staying in that private home? It was my job to know everyone checking in and out within a one-kilometer radius of any given point," he recalled.

Munir and his CIA partners believed Osama was in semipermanent transit.[127] They tried to focus their energies on the Tribal Areas but, administratively independent, the areas were physically off-limits even to the ISI. National laws applied only to highways, government buildings, and installations. One foot either side of the roads was no-man's-land. "We didn't have access. We barely had a presence. If we did a raid, we'd have to mobilize an entire army. We'd have to fight our way in. And out."

Nothing could be done quickly or quietly.[128]

As "close-in" surveillance was impossible, the U.S. National Security Agency (NSA) offered remote solutions. General Michael Hayden, the NSA's director since 1999, was keen to put the agency's 9/11 intelligence failures behind him and had already overseen a total overhaul of the NSA's surveillance operations, farming much of the new work out to private contractors. Now, with the help of the British Government Communications Headquarters and Western intelligence agencies, the NSA draped an electronic blanket over Pakistan's Tribal Areas. "If you wanted huge coverage of the FATA [the Federally Administered Tribal Areas], NSA had ten times the manpower and twenty times the budget," said Munir.

A "listening trawl" saw them scoop up information from satellites and data from cell phone towers and Internet portals. Controversially, the NSA also began tapping communications between suspected terrorists in Pakistan and people in the United States—without obtaining any search warrants—an initiative referred to by the Bush administration as the "terrorist surveillance program" and that would later face legal challenges.

A companion operation on the ground, a "cyber espionage trawl," saw CIA assets seed doctored phones and computers (whole and in parts) into markets across the region. The hope was that one of these tampered-with devices might be purchased and co-opted into the low-budget DIY network run by Al Qaeda. It was a long shot, but it might enable the U.S. intelligence community to enslave a user's computer or phone, even a local village PCO and fax machine. Under the watchful eye of Brigadier Munir, cheap-deal Nokia handsets, refurbished hard drives, motherboards, processors and screens, cable modems, and cut-price USB drives were shipped out to tempt unsuspecting shoppers in Mir Ali, Miram Shah, and other far-flung locations where Al Qaeda supporters were suspected to be hiding out, such as Bara, Bannu, Hangu, and Kohat.

* * *

August 7, 2003, Baghdad, Iraq

Backed by Iranian supply lines and Al Qaeda cash and guided by Saif al-Adel, who was still officially in Iranian detention but had been allowed some freedom to continue with his activities, Abu Musab al-Zarqawi started his offensive in Iraq in bloodthirsty style by attacking his own countrymen. A huge car bomb destroyed much of the Jordanian embassy in Baghdad on August 7, leaving behind scenes of horrific carnage with injured survivors crawling between blackened bodies.[129]

Less than two weeks later he dispatched a colossal truck bomb to blow up the UN headquarters in Baghdad, which flattened a poorly guarded building and much of the neighborhood, killing twenty-two people, including the head of the UN mission in Iraq, Sergio Vieira de Mello.

Ten days later he sent another car bomber to attack the Imam Ali Mosque in Najaf, the third holiest site in Shia Islam. It killed the senior Shia cleric Mohammed Bakr al-Hakim and more than eighty worshippers. Al-Hakim had been the spiritual leader of the Supreme Council of the Islamic Revolution in Iraq and his death struck terror in the country's large Shia population.

In committing his first major offensive against Shias, Zarqawi had made sure to give it a personal touch. The suicide bomber, a Jordanian called Yassin Jarrad, was his own father-in-law, the rabidly jihadist father of his beautiful Palestinian wife.[130]

Soft targets. Sectarian objectives. Family connections. Blood and more blood. Children, women: no one would be spared. Zarqawi knew his actions would be criticized as "hasty and rash." But he had warned Saif that real Muslims had to be brought to their senses. There were many people and parties competing for attention. To get it, Zarqawi had to conceive of actions that would be "revolting." And much "blood has to be spilled."[131]

CHAPTER SIX

"If you bid us plunge into the ocean, we would
follow you."
——INTERCEPTED LETTER FROM ABU MUSAB
AL-ZARQAWI TO OSAMA BIN LADEN,
OCTOBER 2004[1]

June 2003, Suleman Talaab Village, Kohat, Pakistan

MARYAM, BUSHRA, AND AMAL BIN LADEN had been living in limbo on the outskirts of Kohat for more than two months. Occasionally, they were allowed out to the bazaar accompanied by a male householder, but otherwise they were stuck inside with their children. No explanations as to their long-term future had been given and the young women were too scared to ask.

Their departure from isolated Kutkey had been sudden and unsettling. Two days after Ibrahim, Abrar, and Osama had fled from the house, Ibrahim had returned alone, rapping on the door after dark. Thinking that the ISI had come for them, the women froze. *Is it our time?* Amal whispered. Bushra, who was heavily pregnant, started crying.[2]

When Maryam recognized Ibrahim through the shadows, she unlocked the door. "Where have you been?"

Pack, Ibrahim hissed, ignoring her question.

The women were bundled into a vehicle with all they could carry and by midnight they were in Peshawar. Ibrahim pulled into a silent courtyard in the Ganj district of the old city. Before them was an annex of the Ganj madrassa, a feeder school for the jihad and a way station for Al Qaeda.[3]

"Get out," Amal was told.

She stepped down with her two young daughters and, looking over her shoulder, saw that Maryam and Bushra remained in the van.

211

She was shown into an empty office, from where she heard the minibus depart.

Maryam and Bushra were driven on to Suleman Talaab, Ibrahim's ancestral village. "You go here," Ibrahim barked, letting his wife out at his sister's place, while Bushra was dropped at her father's.[4]

In the Ganj madrassa annex, Amal and her two young daughters were hustled into an upstairs room, where a Moroccan woman greeted her.[5]

"A taxi is coming," she explained. "We are going to Kohat. It is for your safety."

July 2003, Peshawar, Pakistan

With hooded eyes that looked as if they were rimmed with kohl, and disfiguring blotches caused by severe vitiligo, the Libyan mujahid was the most unlikely choice for a covert operative working in a shadow organization that was being tracked by the intelligence services of the world. However, despite his unforgettable face, he remained invisible.

Abu Faraj al-Libi enjoyed some kind of social camouflage that made him vanish, a skill he deployed when taking over Khalid Shaikh Mohammad's network in the spring of 2003. Abu Faraj had other skills, although he could not drive and so had to be ferried around the North-West Frontier Province on the back of a distinctive red motorbike. He spoke Arabic, Pashto, and passable Urdu.[6] He also had a well-honed sense of self-preservation, and sensing the growing ISI and CIA joint operation in Peshawar, with Asad Munir's sniffer-dogs going door-to-door in the Faquirabad and Gulbahar neighborhoods—where Al Qaeda and Taliban supporters dispersed themselves among the refugees and travelers—he sought out a new permanent base for himself and his Moroccan wife, Miriam, who had just accompanied Amal bin Laden to Suleman Talaab.

Abu Faraj was drawn to a sleepy bolt-hole where security, relaxation, and retirement were uppermost on people's minds: a hill station in Hazara region, at the eastern corner of the North-West Frontier Province that was popular with tourists, home to three of the army's most well-respected training schools, including the prestigious Pakistan Military Academy, and was named after Major James Abbott, the British Raj officer who founded the town in 1853. Osama bin Laden had rented a house here during the Peshawar days for his wife and children.[7]

These days, smart young Pakistani officers trained in Abbottabad with the military elite who, in their spare time, played golf. Given that the city is just under ninety miles by car from the capital, Islamabad's middle classes descended during the holidays, and they sent their children to its upmarket schools. The air was clean and the wide avenues were lined with flowerbeds, statues, and military memorials. All around, the rugged Sarban hills were thick with pine trees and crisscrossed with walking tracks.

Like any other city in Pakistan, Abbottabad had its share of conservative religious scholars and a sprinkling of Islamist seminaries. It even had a small militant presence in the form of a single unit of Sipah-e-Sahaba, a sectarian outfit formed with the blessing of the deep state to harry and murder religious minorities. Officially, President Musharraf had banned it and several other homegrown militant groups after the United States demanded that Pakistan do something to contain the domestic forces of terror it manipulated. All it and the other banned groups had done was reemerge under new names.

What Abbottabad did not have was the ISI. The spy directorate considered the city to be "too far inland," ISI-speak for far away from the Islamist whirlpool. The nearest ISI field detachment was located at Mardan, a three-hour drive west.[8]

Abu Faraj found a house in historic Nawan Shehr, close to Ban Wali Masjid, the oldest mosque in the area. He also rented two apartments in the busy city center, intending to use them as Al Qaeda guesthouses.

September 2003, Shakai Valley, South Waziristan, Pakistan

Abu Faraj was summoned to the first of several *jirgas* at Shakai. The base was led by an ethnic Kurd called Abdul Hadi al-Iraqi, who had once served as a major in Saddam Hussein's army before defecting to fight the Soviets in Afghanistan. A close associate of Abu Musab al-Zarqawi, Abdul Hadi had fought with Al Qaeda forces at Tora Bora in December 2001 before traveling with Zarqawi's group to Iran.[9]

Under Abdul Hadi's leadership, Shakai had been transformed into Al Qaeda Central's new nerve center, a place for training recruits, planning operations, and manufacturing suicide vests, remote-controlled devices, and car bombs. He had local assistance in the form of Ilyas Kashmiri, a striking Pakistani mujahid famed for his mirrored aviator sunglasses (that hid a missing eye), luxuriant hennaed beard, and long, tangled relationship with Pakistan's security services.

A veteran of the Pakistan Army's elite Special Services Group (President Musharraf's old unit in which Kashmiri occasionally denied he had fought) who had honed his skills during the Afghan jihad (a campaign he often bragged about), Kashmiri had been funded, armed, and trained by the ISI, losing a finger as well as an eye to the Afghan slaughter of the 1980s. During the 1990s, he had been sent over the border to battle Indian forces in Kashmir in operations directly sponsored by Pakistan's spy directorate.

Musharraf's recent crackdown on homegrown militancy had infuriated and disappointed veterans like Kashmiri, who had formed his own jihad unit with funding from S-Wing, the Islamist section of the ISI that ran fundamentalist factions on behalf of the deep state. Called the 313 Brigade, Kashmiri's new outfit was staffed by former ISI agents and mujahideen who, along with him, were allied to Al Qaeda.[10]

Kashmiri joined the *jirga* alongside Al Qaeda financier Sheikh Saeed as the agenda was read out: "Al Qaeda's new priorities." Plans to attack the "far enemy," including Britain and the United States, were in development over the border in Iran, but what about the near enemy? asked Dr. Ayman al-Zawahiri, referring to the regimes it opposed in the Middle East.[11]

Abu Faraj suggested sinking more resources into Al Qaeda's presence in Iraq.

Abu Musab al-Zarqawi already had that region well covered, said Abdul Hadi.

Kashmiri put forward another idea. Al Qaeda Central should attack Pakistan, as its American-loving president was currently doing more damage to the cause of global jihad than anyone else.[12]

December 14, 2003, Rawalpindi, Pakistan

General Pervez Musharraf was driving home from the airport with his military secretary, Major General Nadeem Taj. The officer, who had survived a few near misses with Musharraf, had been in on the plotting to overthrow the civilian government in 1999 and had been rewarded with marriage to the sister of Musharraf's wife.[13]

They were discussing a disturbing photo in the newspapers. U.S. forces, in an operation code-named Red Dawn, had just run Saddam Hussein to ground, pulling him out of a "spider hole" in ad-Dawr, close to Tikrit. The photo released to the newswires showed a broken dictator, with a wild gray beard and mussed-up hair. It was a world away from the striking portrait of Saddam in a three-piece wool suit and homburg, discharging his Ruger rifle like a Mafia don. Musharraf told his military secretary that he was struck by the transformation. What came to mind was how this picture resembled those released of Khalid Shaikh Mohammad after he had been captured in Rawalpindi. They reflected the CIA's modus operandi. Americans diminished the dictators they fell out with while continuing to feather the beds of those they needed, like the princes in Bahrain, Qatar, and Saudi Arabia.[14]

"Even us," Musharraf joked. "Pakistan will always be needed so long as Osama bin Laden remains at large."

A screech. And: *boom.*

Musharraf's stomach flipped and his eardrums popped. He felt the air sucked from the vehicle as he was slammed into the footwell.

"Nadeem!"

The major general groaned from the other footwell. "Alive, sir," he said.

A huge explosion had sent the three-ton armor-plated Mercedes hurtling into the air. As the car, still intact, crashed back down onto the road, bursting all four tires, Musharraf screamed for the driver to hit the accelerator.

Looking back, the president saw a pall of smoke, dust, and debris. They did not pull over, even though the vehicle was riding on its rims, sending up showers of sparks. Arriving at Army House, shaken and enraged, Musharraf charged into his private quarters, showered, changed his clothes, and called for his X Corps commander, General Ashfaq Parvez Kayani, a laconic, chain-smoking and golf-obsessed career officer he regarded as a dependable pair of hands.

"Get the bastard," Musharraf thundered at Kayani. "Imagine trying to take out a head of state!" He could not get over the attack. It was the military's job to deploy terror, not be a target of it.[15]

"I want the ISI to lead this investigation," Musharraf insisted. "The police must be kept out of it." As Kayani got to work, Nadeem Taj was promoted to Director-General of Military Intelligence. Musharraf needed his friends around him.

That night, the president and his wife attended a wedding at the Serena, Islamabad's top five-star hotel, where he regaled guests with his near-death experience and blamed Osama bin Laden.

In Rawalpindi, General Kayani, the son of a noncommissioned officer and a "soldier's soldier," threw everything at the inquiry, knowing that one of the top jobs in the armed forces, the director general's seat at the ISI, was coming up for reappointment in October. If he could substantiate Musharraf's surmise—that this had been an Al Qaeda operation—the post would almost certainly be offered to him.[16]

Intelligence flowed in quickly, but not of the right kind. The jihadi chatter led to a member of Jaish-e-Mohammed, the ISI-sponsored outfit behind the Indian parliament attack, bringing everything uncomfortably close. All clues pointed to the failed assassination as being in response to Musharraf's recent attempts to declaw Jaish and other homegrown Islamist groups.

Kayani's problems deepened when, under interrogation, one mujahid swore that those behind the assassination attempt included religious officers serving in the Pakistan Air Force. The plotters had procured inside knowledge on the route taken by the president's column from sources inside general headquarters in Rawalpindi. The more Kayani dug, the more it looked like a conspiracy, with members of the armed forces siding with the jihad movement over the president and general, demonstrating that infiltration was an unconscionable reality in Pakistan.

But fissures in the ranks was not something Kayani could sell to his president.

He directed his officers to refocus on Al Qaeda. The forensic evidence was laid out. Examining the trigger, the chemical composition of the explosives, and the fragmentation ballast packed around them, officers advised that the bomb was similar to those the ISI taught mujahideen to build and rig in Indian Kashmir, which pointed to this being the handiwork of Ilyas Kashmiri—given his deep links to the ISI and the Kashmir jihad.

December 25, 2003, Rawalpindi

Two weeks later, President Musharraf was traveling along the same stretch of road, on his way home from a meeting in Islamabad, when a minivan slipped out of a petrol station just a few hundred yards ahead. A vigilant police patrol stepped on the gas and placed itself between the convoy and the van as a blinding fireball engulfed the road.

Another minivan entered the curtain of fumes and drove straight at the now almost stationary presidential convoy, detonating only feet away.

"The second bomb was jarring," Musharraf recalled. "Smoke and flames blinded us, but I told the driver to keep on going, and Allah saved us."

When the president's Mercedes lurched into the drive at Army House "plastered with human flesh," his wife, Sebha, screamed. Back at the scene, General Kayani's men counted seventeen bodies, with fifty bystanders seriously injured. Picking through the charred remains, they recovered the face of one of the bombers, which had been peeled off its skull by the force of the blast. Kayani radioed the details to Musharraf, who ordered that a plastic surgeon reconstruct the head.[17] The president appeared on national television and blamed "terrorists and extremists" for the attack.[18]

However, the forensics team combing the scene again found evidence straight out of the military playbook.[19] The drivers had rammed the convoy just beyond the same bridge where the first bomb had been rigged. Whoever designed the first attack was also likely to have been involved in the second and had detailed inside knowledge of how to override jammers that were deployed to block remote detonations.

Kayani ordered his men to intensify their search. Later that day, at three thirty P.M. during raids on a housing complex, the ISI recovered a SIM card. One number on it registered in the ISI database. It belonged to an Al Qaeda courier called Salahuddin. Kayani's men quickly tracked Salahuddin to a Rawalpindi district close to the bridge, and he broke down in an hour, confessing that he was in contact with Abdul Hadi al-Iraqi, the leader of Al Qaeda's Shakai camp, via "a panda-faced Libyan" Al Qaeda operative called Abu Faraj al-Libi.

Salahuddin had met Abu Faraj twice but explained that the Musharraf plots had been designed and implemented by Ilyas Kashmiri and his new outfit, which combined ISI agents and mujahideen.

Al Qaeda flow charts from the Peshawar station suggested Abu Faraj was a middle-ranking operative who worked as a go-between. The ISI station in Peshawar obtained an old photograph of Abu Faraj in his Libyan days, dressed in a suit, and some recent intelligence bulletins that pointed to his possible location: Hassan Abdal, a historic town twenty-eight miles west of Rawalpindi, located at the junction between the Grand Trunk Road and the N5 highway leading north to Abbottabad. Kayani could work on this material and bury the parts of the confession that impacted on the military.

After he briefed his president, Musharraf called CIA director George Tenet. He had identified the man who was trying to kill him: "Abu Faraj al-Libi, he is the third biggest fish in Al Qaeda's pond." Sensing an opportunity, the Pakistani president assured the CIA director that the hunt was already on for Abu Faraj.[20] There was no mention of Ilyas Kashmiri or his new outfit that combined ISI agents and the mujahideen.

January 23, 2004, Kalar, Kurdish Iraq

On a map the route looked forbidding, but Hassan Ghul, Khalid Shaikh Mohammad's overweight courier who wore a shirt with open collar and carried a satchel containing a notebook, three bundles of currency, three cell phones, two computer disks, and a USB drive, knew what to expect.[21] He had made this 1,500-mile journey many times before, traveling with messages from Al Qaeda Central in Waziristan, skirting beneath Afghanistan, crossing the width of Iran, and into the cauldron of Kurdish Iraq, where he would link up with one of Zarqawi's operatives.

This time, however, after Ghul had exited Iran at Khosravi and entered Kalar, a city just twenty miles inside the Iraqi border, chatting on his phones, the CIA and the NSA were watching. Ghul should have been more careful. His Karachi apartment had been one of the addresses searched during the September 2002 raids that had caught the Rabbani brothers and Ramzi bin al-Shibh. Now, the Kurdish security services let him do his business in Kalar and then picked him up. If the investigators had got it right, Ghul would hopefully be carrying correspondence for Osama.

Expecting Ghul to put up a strong resistance, his jailers found instead that he was pliant and polite. One Kurdish agent recalled how he walked the prisoner into a local military garrison and watched as he neatly laid out his possessions on a table. "He didn't want to get hurt. He was a deal maker, a talker," the agent said.

Joining the Kurdish interrogation team as an unofficial observer was Nada Bakos, the young CIA analyst who had been tracking Abu Musab al-Zarqawi's movements across the Iran-Iraq border since late 2001, and who had watched Colin Powell's speech to the United Nations in February 2003 with horror. She was looking for evidence about Zarqawi and his Iraq-based cells.

A CIA technician easily cracked the encryption on Ghul's disks and USB drive, handing Bakos and the Kurdish investigators a gold rush of invaluable data, including a rambling seventeen-page missive from Zarqawi to Osama suggesting a formal joining of forces between his group, Tawhid al-Jihad, and Al Qaeda. "We stand ready as an army for you to work under your guidance and yield to your command," Zarqawi wrote.

The Bush administration, which needed to bolster its weak case that Al Qaeda's Iraq operation was a state-sponsored confabulation, announced Ghul's capture the same day. "We made further progress in making America more secure," President Bush said, "when a fellow named Hassan Ghul was captured in Iraq. Hassan Ghul was reporting directly to Khalid Shaikh Mohammad, who was the mastermind of the September Eleventh attacks. He was a killer."

A sleight of hand had seamlessly moved the Arab nationalist Ba'athist regime of Saddam Hussein a little closer to being the trigger for 9/11, justifying an unpopular war that had been under way for nearly a year and had already cost hundreds of American lives.

In Kalar, Nada Bakos disregarded the White House politicking and watched, fascinated, as Ghul happily discussed his Al Qaeda–linked activities. "He was in a safe house," she said. "He wasn't locked up in a cell. He wasn't handcuffed to anything. He was having a free-flowing chitchat."[22]

Ghul described how he worked as a messenger between Abu Musab al-Zarqawi, Osama bin Laden, and Dr. Ayman al-Zawahiri. He gave interrogators four e-mail addresses through which he communicated with Zarqawi and described the code they used when they spoke on the phone— in Zarqawi's case his Swiss satellite phone (supplied by the Quds Force) and two Iranian numbers registered in Isfahan.[23]

He confirmed that Al Qaeda Central had been "ground down" by the joint CIA and ISI efforts in Pakistan and had regrouped in Shakai Valley, South Waziristan, where they had constructed a new Tarnak Qila–style camp under the protection of the Pashtun mujahid Nek Muhammad Wazir and run by Abdul Hadi al-Iraqi. Ghul estimated that approximately sixty Arabs, 150 to 200 Turks and/or Uzbeks, and a "significant population" of Balochis were there.

Ghul provided important new information about Abdul Hadi. After helping Zarqawi establish relations with Ansar ul-Islam in the Khurmal hills of Kurdistan, Abdul Hadi had headed back east to the Iran-Pakistan border, where he facilitated the movement of Al Qaeda brothers wishing to join Zarqawi's forces.[24] Others he guided down to Shakai, with a plan to launch martyrdom brigades to attack U.S. forces in Afghanistan. According to Ghul, Shakai was a "mini Islamic society."[25] The camp consisted of married quarters, a bachelors' house, a madrassa, and training facilities. Ghul also "identified and decoded phone numbers and e-mail addresses contained in a notebook he was carrying, some of which were associated with Shakai-based operatives."

Probed about Osama's whereabouts, Ghul gave a clear description of how and with whom the Al Qaeda leader lived. He was not in Pakistan's tribal belt or Afghanistan but "living in the Peshawar area . . . in a house with a family."

Nothing seemed too sensitive for the talkative Ghul. It was "well known that the Sheikh was always with Abu Ahmad al-Kuwaiti, his closest assistant," a man who "handled all of Osama's needs" including his security apparatus, which was "minimal." Since fleeing Tora Bora, he had only ever maintained "a small security unit of one or two persons."

This made the couriers responsible for security, finance, welfare, and communications. In his collapsing universe, they were Osama's lifeline. As well as caring for him, Abu Ahmad transported and collected messages, received money, and sent donations, connecting Osama to his new operational chief in Pakistan, who was, according to Ghul, a Libyan brother called Abu Faraj al-Libi.

If the CIA could find these men, they would lead to Osama.

Ghul hoped he had said enough to get himself off the hook since he was deeply concerned about the vanishings of Khalid Shaikh Mohammad, Ramzi bin al-Shibh, his brother-in-law Abdul Rabbani, Khalid's nephew Ammar al-Balochi, and al-Balochi's wife, Aafia Siddiqui.

The last case was particularly worrisome. If they could make a Western-educated scientist and mother of three disappear, along with her three children, there was clearly no limit to the depths to which America was willing to sink.

February 2004, Rawalpindi

Rather than follow up on Hassan Ghul's vital information about Osama, the CIA's Islamabad station contacted the ISI with a pressing request: Pakistan should "undertake to verify" the presence of "a large number of Arabs" in Shakai "as soon as possible."

However, Pakistan was busy focusing on the investigation into Musharraf's assassination attempts, and it quickly became clear to the CIA that extra pressure needed to be applied.

A long-running operation elsewhere provided just the ammunition Western governments were looking for. The British foreign intelligence service MI6 sought out ISI chief General Ehsan ul-Haq to deliver the first warning. It had, he was told, amassed an enormous dossier showing that Pakistan's preeminent nuclear scientist, who was cherished at home as "the father of the bomb," was selling proscribed doomsday technology around the world. Dr. Abdul Qadeer Khan, a Pakistani metallurgist who had steered Pakistan's nuclear program to test blasts in 1998, countering India's status as South Asia's sole nuclear power, had approached Iraq, Iran, Libya, North Korea, and a host of other rogue nations.[26]

Even worse for General ul-Haq and his president, according to the MI6 dossier, Khan was working not alone but as the brand ambassador for the Pakistani intelligence service and armed forces, which had sought to benefit financially and politically from the illicit deals.

Musharraf called a crisis meeting. There was only one path to take: isolate Khan and project him as a traitor.

On February 4, a chastened Dr. Khan appeared on TV to announce that he alone was to blame, which was not true. "There was never ever any kind of authorization for these activities by the government," he said. "I take full responsibility for my actions and seek your pardon."[27] Dr. Khan later claimed that Musharraf had promised that if he took the flak now he would personally oversee his rehabilitation once the dust had settled, an accusation that Musharraf denied.[28]

Seizing the moment, the CIA returned to the issue of Al Qaeda forces hiding in Shakai, urging the ISI to confirm the Arabs' presence in Shakai.

On February 12, George Tenet arrived in Islamabad with a twenty-four-member CIA delegation. The large size of the U.S. team was deliberate. They wanted to use the "shock and awe" of intelligence—photos, intercepts, and charts—to compel Musharraf and ISI chief ul-Haq to act.[29]

However, when Tenet asked the Pakistani military to launch a ground assault on Shakai, Musharraf refused, recalling how ten soldiers had died when, in June 2002, Pakistani troops had attempted to mop up Al Qaeda fighters in South Waziristan at a barren cleft called Kazha Punga.

To head off Tenet, Musharraf claimed he had already sent a delegation to Shakai with an ultimatum for the hardheaded Pashtun mujahid Nek Muhammad Wazir: if they were found to be giving refuge to Al Qaeda, his people's homes and livelihoods would be leveled, like the Israelis did in Gaza.

Tenet dismissed the idea and instead suggested that Pakistan should allow U.S. drones to fly over the Tribal Areas. This was a far simpler way to track down and kill militants hiding in the hills and gullies, he argued. Musharraf was stumped.

He knew that after the incident with Dr. Khan, Pakistan was at a fork in the road, a pariah state whose proximity to terror was all that had saved it from being defanged. He began to lobby general headquarters to support the U.S. plan. Drone technology could whittle away a common enemy, deniably, and without hurting the army, he said.

General ul-Haq vehemently disagreed. It was Pakistan's proximity to Al Qaeda that ensured it would always survive, he said. America and Europe could not afford to cast them out. And drones would compromise Pakistan's sovereignty and curtail their espionage capabilities.[30] The United States would inevitably eavesdrop and see ISI deployments in sensitive areas, further compromising Islamabad's position.

Sensing resistance, Tenet's delegation turned the screw and accused Pakistan's intelligence services of playing a double game by aiding Al Qaeda and the Taliban instead of hunting them down. They also revealed that they had learned the twin assassination attempts on Musharraf had involved the active participation of elements within the armed forces that were demonstrably allied to Al Qaeda.

Hamstrung, General ul-Haq lunged for a pressure point. Washington was spinning a new Al Qaeda narrative to distract attention away from its unjustifiable war in Iraq. Just days before coming to Pakistan, George Tenet had been forced to admit that there had been no imminent threat from weapons of mass destruction before the 2003 invasion and that the CIA had become transfixed by "fabricated" intelligence on WMDs supplied by an "unreliable" Iraqi defector.[31] In ul-Haq's eyes, and to many voters back home in the United States, the war was "tantamount to a policy catastrophe."

Before their next meeting with the Americans, ul-Haq sought out Musharraf. "If the CIA wants to accuse the ISI of misbehaving," he said, "you must tell President Bush that his people need to give names. Incidents. Evidence. They are insulting *us*. I'm a serving lieutenant general and I have some military pride. If they don't trust us, they are going to have to prove that we are disloyal."[32]

Three weeks later Musharraf committed six thousand ground forces to flush foreign fighters out of South Waziristan. He would rather go along with the charade than enrage his friend President Bush. "Success," his spokesmen announced when thirteen suspected Al Qaeda operatives were killed after the army attacked a bus attempting to flee the area. Human rights lawyers quickly identified the dead as civilians and also revealed the real level of military casualties: sixty-four soldiers dead, fifty-eight injured, and fourteen taken hostage. Trained to fight on the plains of the Punjab, Musharraf's men were being hammered in the mountains.

In Islamabad, opposition to Musharraf's decision to crack down on home-grown jihad outfits was also growing. Clerics at the radical Lal Masjid (Red Mosque) put a voice to a rising tide of criticism, characterizing Musharraf as America's lapdog, a man who had turned his army against Muslims. "People of South Waziristan," one cleric exhorted in a fatwa issued against the army, "seize the bodies of dead Pakistani soldiers and do not hand them over."[33] The *faujis* (soldiers)—who had epitomized national pride—were traitors.

In Washington, President Bush seemed oblivious to Pakistan's growing instability. He was busy electioneering and announced that Task Force 121—a special operations force that had played a critical role in the capture of Saddam Hussein—was now being reassigned to Afghanistan to reinvigorate the hunt for the Al Qaeda leader. It would press from one side while Musharraf's forces would push from the other, catching Osama between an American "hammer" and a Pakistani "anvil."

February 2004, Bilal Town, Abbottabad, Pakistan

Abu Faraj had watched the For Sale signs go up over a large tract of agricultural land at the inexpensive end of Bilal Town, a couple of miles northeast of the city center. To make some easy cash for the military elite, the Abbottabad Cantonment Board had decided to sell it off in small parcels and he passed by on his way to Nawan Shehr. In late 2003 he contacted Ibrahim and Abrar, the Kuwaiti brothers who protected Osama, suggesting they take a look. Osama knew and liked the town. Maybe it could provide a semi-permanent refuge for him and his family.

Abrar arrived in the city with $50,000 in cash and a forged national identity card, provided by Khalid Shaikh Mohammad and that described him as Mohammed Arshad, son of Naqab Khan from Charsadda.[34]

He made a bid for three adjacent plots in the middle of a soggy field. Only a dirt track connected it to the nearest paved road. Having bought the land, in January 2004 he started negotiations with farmers who owned adjoining pieces. One of them recalled that he was a "modest, humble type of man," sturdily built, and spoke with a Waziri accent.[35] The only noticeable thing about him was an unusual tuft of hair under his lower lip. Abrar said he was investing on behalf of an uncle, who needed to relocate from the Tribal Areas because of a blood feud.

When Abrar had purchased nine connecting plots covering 38,000 square feet, he employed Mohammed Younis from Modern Associates, a local architectural firm, to draw up plans according to precise specifications: a large two-story villa with a staircase at the rear; four bedrooms, three bathrooms, and a kitchen on the first floor; and four bedrooms and four bathrooms on the second floor, with a narrow balcony out front.[36]

The Abbottabad Cantonment Board approved the plans without verifying the owner, although this was a legal requirement. Afterward, Abrar hired a local builder, who was told to spend "whatever it costs."[37] When the builder queried an instruction to extend the perimeter wall to a height well above the approved plans, Abrar warned him to ask no further questions or he would be fired. Over the months he worked on the site, the builder sometimes heard his employer talking on the phone about the "master." Once he listened to him discussing how the "guest" would arrive soon.

Anyone who asked when the owner was moving in received the same answer: "Only God knows."[38]

April 24, 2004, Shakai Valley, South Waziristan

President Musharraf had at last come up with a solution to the increasing external pressure on him to fight the domestic jihad and pacify the internal forces that constantly warned that such a move would tear down the entire republic. He proposed a truce.[39] If Nek Muhammad Wazir and the foreign fighters living around him in Shakai pledged not to attack Pakistani troops, the military offensive would be called off.

Nek insisted that Musharraf's envoy go to Shakai to personally sign the agreement. Musharraf sent up as his sacrificial lamb the Peshawar Corps commander, enabling Nek to brag: "I did not go to them; they came to my place."[40] In Wana, the main town in South Waziristan, the corps commander was photographed draping a garland of tinsel and plastic flowers around the twenty-nine-year-old warlord's neck. "That should make it clear who surrendered to whom," Nek quipped to his followers, before the Pakistani officer addressed a crowd of tribal leaders (and a smattering of Al Qaeda brothers), telling them America had been foolish to make war against Afghanistan. Pakistan, by brokering this peace deal, was protecting South Waziristan from an American invasion, he said.

When it was his turn to speak, Nek was pugnacious. Al Qaeda had never been in Shakai, he claimed. "Had there been a single Al Qaeda fighter here, the government would have caught one by now."

With the ceremony over, Nek took a second wife in celebration and almost immediately began harrying Pakistani forces once more. Some habits died hard.

Musharraf took in the reports somberly. He grudgingly ordered his men back into Shakai on June 10. The clearance operation was swift, bloody, and, Musharraf argued, successful. Once a "partner," the army was now victor. "We eliminated a major propaganda base and stronghold of the terrorists, including a facility for manufacturing IEDs [improvised explosive device]," Musharraf crowed. The haul from a large underground cellar at one of the targeted compounds included "two truckloads of TV sets, computers, laptops, disks, tape recorders, and tapes." But no Nek and no Al Qaeda fighters.

In a classified cable, the CIA's Islamabad station chief described the Shakai raid as a "fiasco," with the Al Qaeda base having apparently received advanced warning of the operation from S-Wing. This news reached Washington just as counterterrorism officials were forced to rethink their response to the "war on terror." A damning report by the CIA Inspector General suggested that Enhanced Interrogation Techniques tested on Abu Zubaydah and then used on others, including Khalid Shaikh Mohammad, violated the United Nations Convention Against Torture. Unofficial black sites staffed by contractors and where dozens of "High Value Detainees" currently languished were "unauthorized, improvised, inhumane and undocumented." As a result, detainees all over the world were being shuffled around.

Abu Zubaydah—who in September 2003 had been transported to an undeclared black site code-named Strawberry Fields, located out of sight of the main internment camp at Guantánamo Bay—was now at another secret

CIA site in Rabat, Morocco, being fed sachets of tomato ketchup and fixating on the eyebolts in the ceiling that looked "ready for anything that might happen."[41] Khalid Shaikh Mohammad was being questioned at a detention site in Bucharest, Romania.

New methods of remote interdiction were needed and drones began to constitute a major part of the CIA's offensive. Asked for permission for the United States to commence with drone operations in Waziristan, General ul-Haq remained opposed. But pragmatist Musharraf signed off on the deal with the proviso that Pakistani intelligence officials could approve each strike in advance, and that the United States would never acknowledge its hand in any operation.

Would this charade hold up to scrutiny? the CIA's Islamabad station asked, incredulous. It seemed a paper-thin ruse.

No problem, replied Musharraf. "In Pakistan, things fall out of the sky all the time."[42]

Nek Muhammad Wazir, who was enjoying his moment in the limelight and giving regular interviews by satellite phone, was sitting in the yard of his compound in Kari Kot village on June 17 when his eye was drawn to the sky. "Why is that bird following me?" he asked the Al Qaeda brothers surrounding him, before going back to telling the BBC Pashto service that foreigners living in Waziristan were "not terrorists" but "mujahideen who took part in the Afghan jihad." Asked about his ultimate goal, Nek spelled it out: "We want to eradicate the U.S.-installed puppet governments in Pakistan and Afghanistan."

At ten P.M., a Predator's Hellfire missile destroyed the Kari Kot compound.[43]

When Musharraf heard the news, he called his army chief, giddy with excitement. "Claim it," he insisted. "A Pakistani rocket has killed the Taliban commander," said a spokesman, as Nek's newly dug grave instantly became a shrine. "He lived and died like a true Pashtun," the freshly painted inscription declared.

Almost immediately Al Qaeda's commander at Shakai, Abdul Hadi al-Iraqi, began evacuating senior Al Qaeda figures, including financier Sheikh Saeed, who went to join his family in a village near the city of Dera Ismail Khan, on the edge of the Tribal Areas.

Sheikh Saeed's long-term houseguest, Osama's second Saudi wife, Seham, who in 2002 had chosen not to accompany the rest of the family to Iran, dispatched a message for the Kuwaiti brothers asking if she could be reunited with her husband.[44] When the answer came back "yes," she and three of her four children set out from Shakai on a grueling three-hundred-mile journey—with Khalid, Osama's fifteen-year-old son, fully veiled and posing as a girl. No one knew their final destination.

Their escorts, a Pashtun couple related to the recently deceased Nek, would take them as far as Mattani, a settlement on the Kohat–Peshawar road that the Taliban had transformed into a ruddy Islamist fistula, where they would be handed over to one of Ibrahim's contacts and taken to Peshawar.

The move would take Seham far away from her oldest daughter, Khadija, who was married to Daood, the Saudi fighter. Still only seventeen, Khadija was pregnant for the third time and living on the border with Afghanistan, where her husband remained on active Al Qaeda duty.

Dr. Ayman al-Zawahiri, Osama's deputy and the linchpin of Al Qaeda Central, headed deeper into the hills, settling on Bajaur, the smallest and most inaccessible of Pakistan's seven tribal agencies. There, in Damadola, a town just four miles from the Afghan border, he lodged with a local family. They had promised to let al-Zawahiri marry their daughter to replace the wife who had died along with two of their children during the retreat from Afghanistan.[45] Marrying into the local community meant no one would inform on him; and in any event, remote and cantankerous Bajaur was off-limits to the Pakistan Army and even the Frontier Constabulary, a paramilitary police force.[46]

Summer 2004, Haripur, Pakistan

After nearly three years apart, Osama bin Laden and Seham were reunited in a rented house in a nondescript Pakistan town—a temporary bolt-hole where they waited for their permanent home in Abbottabad to be finished.

Amal, who now had a son as well as two daughters and had for the past year had Osama to herself, was snubbed, as the rest of the family enjoyed a tearful reunion. The last time Osama had seen Khalid was in the Melawa olive groves before the battle for Tora Bora. Now he was a handsome teen-ager with a downy beard. Seham maintained he "could defend himself in battle, fix up the house and recite the Koran."[47]

Osama's daughters Miriam, fourteen, and Sumaiya, twelve, seemed so grown up he immediately announced a search would begin for husbands.

Seham knew how to deal with Osama. "That can come later," she said, distracting him with news of Khadija's latest pregnancy and photos of their two grandsons.

July 2004, Abbottabad

Musharraf ordered for Abu Faraj's picture to be printed in all national newspapers with a caption that he was "No. 3 man in the terrorist network." The army offered $340,000 for his capture.

NBC News followed up, regurgitating the intelligence spin: "Abu Faraj is also believed to know at least the general whereabouts of bin Laden and al-Zawahiri, and to be the mastermind of the December 14 and 25 assassination attempts against Pakistani president Pervez Musharraf."[48]

Seeing the news, Abu Faraj threw away his SIM cards and fled to Bajaur.[49] But in October 2004, Osama, oblivious to the agreed security protocol, sent Ibrahim to find him. The courier had a package containing a video recording addressing the American electorate ahead of the forthcoming elections. "I tell you in truth, that your security is not in the hands of [Democratic candidate John] Kerry, nor Bush, nor al Qaeda," Osama railed. "No. Your security is in your own hands." If Americans chose Bush at the polls, they would be damned. "The real loser," he concluded, "is . . . you."[50]

Abu Faraj was asked to take the video to Al Jazeera. In an accompanying letter, Osama requested updates about the financial situation in Waziristan, where Al Qaeda commanders and Arab families were now scattered.

Abu Faraj did not turn up at the contact point.

Osama sent Ibrahim to track him down again. But he returned empty-handed.

Abu Faraj had gone to ground.

Summer 2004, Block 100, Quds Force Training Facility, Tehran, Iran

Inside Evin prison, the Al Qaeda prisoners had gone on hunger strike.[51] A small group had rioted, and the International Committee for the Red Cross continued to demand regular access to the jail. If the Quds Force wanted to keep them they would have to move them permanently out of sight.

General Qassem Suleimani ordered a mass transfer to vacant buildings at the Imam Ali University for Army Officers, the main Quds Force training facility in Tehran. Located close to the former Sa'adabad Palace, in the far north of the city, beyond the last metro stop, the site was encircled by security detachments of every kind.

"After driving north through the streets of Tehran, we entered a large military area and stopped in front of one of the buildings before a big gate was opened," recalled the Mauritanian.[52]

After several more gates, they reached a "residential complex" at the heart of the base: a prison within a training facility, concealed in the military university, its layers of security impossible to breach. They were led into a concrete bunker inside which were simple box-like rooms running along a central corridor. Outside was an alley and yard, facing six-foot-high walls topped with barbed wire, and a huge metal gate.

Security cameras and movement sensors had been installed throughout the building, which backed onto a military parade ground. "The whole place seemed to be part of an old training camp built decades ago that had been abandoned," the Mauritanian recalled. "Renovations and repairs for our arrival were still going on."

The walls of their new home—which the Iranians referred to as Block 100—were the thickness of an old oak trunk, and there were no windows, only narrow ducts beneath the eaves. Each of the cells was marked with a number in fluorescent pen. "Perhaps this is the place where Iran is hiding its nuclear bombs," quipped one of the brothers.

After a week, there was a banging at the Mauritanian's cell door. It swung back and standing before him were his wife and children. Stunned and grateful, he sprang to his feet as tears filled his eyes, delighted to see them but embarrassed at the conditions they would have to live in.

At night, the children's cries echoed along the corridor. There was no privacy as the security cameras were monitored around the clock from a closed-circuit-television monitoring room far away in the administration area. There was also no air-conditioning, and the concrete boxes soon felt like "red-hot ovens spewing steam." The prison complex was staffed by Quds Force and Ministry of Intelligence and Security officials, headed up by a man called Mr. Nasseri.

The Mauritanian tried to extract concessions. The cameras offended the women's modesty, he said. Nasseri, a devout Shia, tried to placate the prisoners by allowing them to construct a *majlis* (meeting area) out in the yard.

They hung up sheets to partition off a section for the women and children while the men gathered on the other side beneath a large fig tree, boiling up pots of smoky green tea.

The only thing no one complained about was the food. There was an abundance of lamb, fish, and chicken from which the wives and daughters prepared lavish meals.

But days turned into weeks. Would they be here forever? they wondered, as they listened to the sound of Quds Force recruits being drilled on an unseen parade ground. One day in August, the dam broke.

The Mauritanian was told he had fifteen minutes to prepare to receive "an envoy from the Leader of the Islamic Republic of Iran." He put on his smartest clothes and rushed about, ordering the brothers to sweep the small, windowless box-room they called the mosque, where the meeting would take place.

When the official guests arrived they were led by a bearded ayatollah wearing a robe and white turban. He introduced himself as the security minister, Ali Younsei.[53] The Mauritanian was worried. Although the Al Qaeda phalanx was now under the joint protection of the Quds Force and the Ministry of Intelligence and Security, this man was a graduate of the Haghani school—a Shia academy in Qom that was controlled by hard-line right-wingers. Previously, he had been head of the political ideological bureau of the Revolutionary Guard and had once headed the Islamic Revolutionary Court. What was his agenda?

With his face fixed in a half smile, Younsei informed the Mauritanian of the supreme leader's position. Mahfouz knew enough about how Iran worked to know that Younsei's meeting with Ayatollah Khamenei would have been one-on-one. "The Islamic Republic is going out of its way to be hospitable to Al Qaeda despite its appalling track record," he said, addressing the Mauritanian as Dr. Abdullah. He cited the bombing of Mashhad in 1994, in which twenty-six Shia devotees had died and more than two hundred had been wounded, and the killing of Iranian diplomats in Mazar-e-Sharif in 1998. "The Islamic Republic of Iran endured these *wounds* and worse than these," Younsei said bitterly. "But instead of holding you responsible for these reprehensible acts, we have provided you with hospitality."

The Mauritanian decided to meet Younsei head-on. "It was not us who killed the Iranian diplomats," he countered. It was the Taliban. "And you know very well that we were not responsible for the bombings in Mashhad."

It was Ramzi Yousef who had carried out the attack at the shrine. The Mauritanian also reminded the security minister that Iran had supported the U.S. invasion of Afghanistan in 2001. "We forgive *you* for this crime," he said disingenuously.

After this initial exchange of accusations, the two men studied each other. Younsei clearly detested Al Qaeda, and Mahfouz feared Tehran's complicated agenda. Were he and his brothers really guests, or collateral? he wondered. Who held the upper hand, the Quds Force or the Reformists? Instead of asking, he reeled off a list of grievances. Al Qaeda had been invited to enter the country, he said, and yet here they were locked up again. "Our imprisonment is an injustice that is not permissible under any circumstances."

Younsei cut him off. Iran was under "considerable and continuing international pressure" to deport Al Qaeda prisoners, he explained, in a sideways reference to Javad Zarif's recent discussions with Zalmay Khalilzad and Ryan Crocker, about which the Al Qaeda contingent knew nothing. Now that these talks had failed and the "Grand Bargain" that could have seen them handed over to the United States was off the table, the "guests" had been granted a temporary reprieve. "We are here to reassure you that you and your brothers will not be delivered to any international destination against your will," Younsei continued. He stood to leave. "We will meet those needs we can," he said. "And as for the rest—you can wait and see."

Conditions gradually improved. Khanum Medeni, a female intelligence official who also worked for the foreign ministry, was appointed to deal with women's affairs. She recruited a team of female escorts, who accompanied the wives and daughters to hospital. A television was installed broadcasting Al Jazeera and an Islamic prayer channel. On Friday afternoons the children were allowed to watch cartoons. A snack shop opened up next to the mosque, where the families could buy basic groceries, and a clinic staffed by a medic, Dr. Jamali, offered treatment.

After three years on the run or in prison on their own, several women became pregnant at the same time. "One baby was born every few months," said the Mauritanian, who officiated at *aqeeqah* ceremonies, wondering when, if ever, these children of Block 100 would experience freedom.[54]

More settled than they had been since their arrival in Iran, the prisoners were now wooed. Dr. Jamali from the clinic offered the Mauritanian a deal to leave the compound and settle in a villa if he also worked for Iran. "Your family will live a happy life and enjoy many great advantages," he suggested, adding that several Al Qaeda brothers had already taken up this offer and were now "living a normal life in Tehran."[55]

Other brothers? The Mauritanian wondered if some brothers had been forced to make compromises in exchange for benefiting from such special treatment, but there was no way of knowing for sure. Nervous, he refused, claiming that he was needed here to teach the children and lead prayers.

He warned the others to be wary. "They want to draw me into cooperating with them on matters that may be initially acceptable but then would commence with other things I would have to reject."

He continued to push for more privileges, negotiating for the wives and children to go on chaperoned trips. Being cooped up for so long was taking its toll, he said. He couldn't guarantee compliance unless they were allowed to let off steam. The Iranians agreed after a wrangle over appearances.

The Mauritanian insisted that the wives could only visit public places with their faces covered. The officials pointed out that while all Iranian women had to wear a scarf, *niqabs* were a rarity on Tehran's streets and so would draw unnecessary attention.

Al Qaeda refused to move. Ground down, the Iranians agreed to a trial run, with *niqabs* in place.

Khanum Medeni's female officers took the Al Qaeda wives and daughters to the zoo, a park, and a games arcade on the top floor of a smart shopping mall popular with diplomats. They began to swap stories and realized they had much in common. Most of the escorts were Iraqi Shias who had migrated from Baghdad during the Iran-Iraq War and now worked for the Ministry of Intelligence and Security. They, too, considered themselves to be stateless.

They also complained about being overworked: "When we finish with *you* we have to tend to the *other* group, and they are a lot more trouble."

The Mauritanian's wife resisted the urge to jump on the comments and instead reported them back to her husband: There were other Al Qaeda prisoners being held in another location.

A few days later, Dr. Jamali asked the Mauritanian for help. He revealed that Al Qaeda prisoners were being held at Rajai Shahr prison in Karaj, and they were rioting over the right to have conjugal visits. Some were bent on starving themselves to death. Would he intervene?

The Mauritanian agreed to write a letter, passing on an Iranian proposal: if they called off the strike, wives and children would be allowed to visit the men while permanent family accommodation was built adjoining the prison.

Rajai Shahr Prison, Karaj, Tehran

Families staying at the Quds Force holding center in Arak arrived on buses, among them the wife of Abdullah Saeed al-Libi, a member of the Libyan Islamic Fighting Group. Her husband, who in Afghanistan had been a close confidant of Saif al-Adel, spent a night with his wife in a family room. With the security cameras switched off, he slipped out a razor with which to shave his beard. He then put on his wife's black *chador* and *niqab*, reminding himself that a similar incident written of in the Koran made this maneuver permissible in the eyes of the Prophet.

When the departure bell rang, Abdullah and a Moroccan friend who had done the same boarded the women's bus.

It was only when the prison authorities discovered two women dressed in men's clothes that they realized their mistake. Furious, the Ministry of Intelligence and Security ordered a lockdown. The hunger strike restarted, then rioting, which led to an Iranian guard being taken hostage and lynched.

When the ringleaders were transferred to Block 100 in Tehran, they brought with them a story about how Abdullah was planning to head back to Al Qaeda Central in Waziristan, determined to update Dr. Ayman al-Zawahiri about Al Qaeda's predicament in Iran. He would know how to get them out.

Spring 2005, Damadola, Bajaur Agency, Federally Administered Tribal Areas, Pakistan

Dr. Ayman al-Zawahiri was feeling comfortable. Married to a local Pashtun girl, he had been given a new home, a large mud-brick compound up in the hills. He wrote that it was a "good place" owned by his new father-in-law, "a simple old man," originally from Mohmand. Recently, his young wife had given birth to a daughter, who they named Nawwar, meaning "the timid female gazelle" and "a woman who is free from suspicion."[56] Dressed in tribal robes, Al Qaeda's deputy leader was practically indistinguishable from locals, and he roamed among a dozen or more compounds in the area, where he was secretly welcomed as a hero.

"The real danger," he wrote in a couriered update to Abu Musab al-Zarqawi that was intercepted by the Americans on its way to Iraq, "comes from the agent Pakistani army that is carrying out operations in the Tribal Areas looking for mujahideen."

As a result of Dr. al-Zawahiri's move to Damadola, Al Qaeda had followed suit, under the command of Abdul Hadi al-Iraqi, who had fled fallen Shakai and was creating a new heavily fortified base along two ridges west of Damadola, straddling the Afghanistan-Pakistan border. A deep warren of 156 subterranean bunkers was hewed into an area of three square miles. Stocking up on food, sleeping bags, and weapons, Abdul Hadi's men were reinforced by brothers serving with Qari Zia-ur-Rehman, an Afghan warlord from neighboring Kunar Province.

May 2, 2005, Ghazi Baba Shrine, Mardan, Pakistan

After months of false starts and near misses, the ISI's prisoner Salahuddin finally persuaded Abu Faraj to emerge from his hiding place, exploiting Al Qaeda's cash crisis just as the CIA had done when they put Asset X into play with Khalid Shaikh Mohammad. A wary Abu Faraj agreed to a rendezvous to discuss "a significant new donor."

They would get together at four thirty P.M. outside the shrine of a popular Sufi saint on the outskirts of Mardan. The ISI took up positions, with several officers dressed up as women in burqas as they mingled with the worshippers, and waited for Abu Faraj's red motorbike to appear.[57]

As the meeting time approached, Abu Faraj called. "Is everything set?" he asked nervously.

Salahuddin, who had been dragged out of his detention cell to a nearby bazaar so that Abu Faraj could hear suitable background noise, mumbled: "Everything is fine."

But no one showed and the ISI stood its team down.

Everyone was dejected.

Early the next morning Salahuddin's phone rang. It was Abu Faraj. "Nine thirty A.M.—same place."

The ISI called it through. "Rendezvous is back on!"

Knowing the habits of Pakistani officials, Abu Faraj had deliberately rescheduled when most of them would still be in bed. Pulling in a skeleton team at short notice, the ISI again took up positions around the shrine, and at exactly nine thirty A.M. a red motorbike pulled up. The man sitting on the back was wearing large sunglasses and a hat, but the ISI surveillance team spied his distinctive facial markings.

As Abu Faraj walked toward the shrine, followed at a discreet distance by his gunman, *burqa*-wearing ISI agents closed in. One got a hand on Abu Faraj before his bodyguard pulled out an AK-47 and let rip, emptying the clip into the crowd. A second ISI agent tried to wrestle him to the ground, but Abu Faraj broke free, jumped back onto the motorbike, and tore off down the road.

After a chase and a standoff, Abu Faraj was cornered and arrested. Musharraf could barely contain himself. "Al Qaeda's Number Three. We've got him," he told General John Abizaid on May 3, 2005, when the CENTCOM commander arrived in Islamabad for a surprise visit. "Please tell President Bush—or should I?" In Washington, Bush was lavish with his praise. The capture of Abu Faraj was "a critical victory in the war on terror." Both presidents had caught a lucky break.

Osama bin Laden, who was in Haripur, saw the report on Al Jazeera. He railed about the "dictator tyrant" Musharraf, who allowed "the FBI to frolic in his country with freedoms that they cannot even enjoy in America." The president was a "traitor" who sought to "annihilate Pakistan" in a campaign that would "only benefit Americans, Jews and Indians."[58]

In Damadola, Dr. al-Zawahiri was also apoplectic. "The enemy struck a blow against us with the arrest of Abu al-Faraj. May God break his bonds," he wrote, complaining that "many of the lines have been cut." How would they get funds distributed now, and their letters? He instructed the brothers "to contain the fall as much as they could."[59]

The analysis of Abu Faraj's network started immediately, with Pakistani interrogators pummeling him at a secret ISI interrogation facility in Islamabad while the CIA observed. ISI chief Kayani wanted details on the assassination attempts on Musharraf, while the Americans wanted to chart his role in terrorist operations in Afghanistan, Iraq, and Europe. Both sides wanted to know about Osama and Dr. al-Zawahiri. Where were they?

Abu Faraj had prepared for this moment with a fake story, saying that he had once met al-Zawahiri at the home of a tribal elder called Bakhtpur

Khan, who lived in Damadola. It would take the ISI months to locate this man, but he had no connections to the jihad.

Frustrated with Abu Faraj, the CIA dispatched him to Detention Site Orange in Afghanistan, where permission was given to use Enhanced Interrogation Techniques on him.

After he had been softened up, Abu Faraj was flown to a secret CIA detention facility in Romania, becoming another ghost in the machine.

Soon after, Osama received news about two more significant losses. His friend, the fugitive red-haired strategist Abu Musab the Syrian, had sneaked back into Pakistan after several years in Iran, only to be caught by the ISI at a safe house in Quetta, along with his deputy, Abu Khalid al-Suri. Handed over to the CIA, both men were rendered to their native Syria, where they faced an uncertain fate.[60] Both Abu Musab and Abu Khalid stood accused of inspiring and helping to finance the Madrid train bombings of March 2004 in which 192 people died, among many other operations.[61] They disappeared into the notorious Sednaya prison complex north of Damascus, where more than fifteen thousand of Assad's political enemies and Islamists were incarcerated, starved, beaten, or injected with life-threatening doses of medicines by prison doctors.

Summer 2005, CIA Detention Site Bright Light, Bucharest, Romania

Hassan Ghul, the trusted courier who had worked for Khalid Shaikh Mohammad and taken messages to Zarqawi, had been in U.S. custody since January 2004. After agent Nada Bakos questioned him in Iraqi Kurdistan, reporting back that he had "opened up right away and was cooperative from the outset," the CIA had ordered that he be turned over to another team for a more thorough grilling, much as it had done with Abu Zubaydah.[62]

The new team recorded the same intelligence but attributed it to enhanced interrogations, leading James Pavitt, the CIA's deputy director, to congratulate them and ignore the work done already by Bakos. "This is exactly the type of effort with a detainee that will win the war against Al Qaeda," Pavitt wrote. "With the intelligence Station has obtained from Ghul, we will be able to do much damage to the enemy."[63]

Now, Ghul was dispatched on an invisible journey that was later partially illuminated in a series of declassified government cables. According to a

May 2005 Justice Department memo, a detainee named "Gul [*sic*]" was held for two days in Afghanistan and subjected to interrogation methods such as "attention grasp, walling, facial grasp, facial slap, wall standing, stress positions and sleep deprivation." Afterward, he was rendered to another secret CIA detention facility in Bucharest, Romania.[64]

Housed in the former National Registry Office for Classified Information (known as ORNISS), an anonymous office building in the heart of a busy residential district in the capital, the site was code-named Bright Light. From the outside, the white and cream plaster building looked like just another unloved Romanian government bunker. But in the basement, the CIA jail consisted of just six cells, mounted on large iron springs to keep inmates literally off-balance.[65]

Ghul's former boss, Khalid Shaikh Mohammad, had been there since late 2003 and was a physical wreck after almost a year of enhanced interrogations that saw him waterboarded 183 times. Ghul remained relatively laid-back and cocky. "His earlier experiences with U.S. military interrogators have convinced him there are limits to the physical contact interrogators can have with him," wrote one of his new interrogators, taking another sideswipe at Bakos.

After CIA personnel requested permission to "shift his paradigm of what he expects to happen," Ghul was "shaved, barbered, stripped and placed in the standing position."[66] He was spared the waterboard because he was considered too fat and unhealthy to survive the experience.[67] The interrogators focused on "beatings, rectal examinations and water dousing," but did not pick up on the relationship Ghul had with Khalid or detect the notes they wrote for each other, dropped behind toilets and placed under shower mats.

When Abu Faraj joined them that summer they conspired, rehearsing what each would say, passing around letters while on toilet visits, communicating in knocks and whispers through the cell walls. Ghul had last seen Abu Faraj two years earlier when he had brought money from Saudi Arabia to Shakai. Between the three of them, they could draw a snapshot of the entire support system surrounding Osama and Dr. al-Zawahiri.

In July 2005, after two months of brutal interrogation, Abu Faraj claimed never to have heard of Abu Ahmad al-Kuwaiti. The following month, Khalid said he could recall a brother called "Abu Ahmad" but that he was a very junior member of Al Qaeda who had married and retired from the jihad in 2002.

Abu Faraj "swore to God" that he had never heard of Abu Ahmad, saying, "I would never forget anyone who worked for me." He also threw a bogus name into the mix. The outfit's key courier was Abu Abd al-Khaliq Jan, who had been his "go-between with bin Laden since mid-2003."

As "the last detainee to maintain contact with [Osama]," Jan would surely be best placed to know the truth about couriers, the CIA duly reported. Had the al-Kuwaiti name been a ruse all along? They went back to Hassan Ghul. But after being tortured, he was now playing dumb.

The agency eased off. All three prisoners were assigned "homework" in their cells. This included writing up lists of contacts with their code names and phone numbers, drawing diagrams of safe houses and training camp layouts, and detailing bank accounts. They were rewarded with Snickers chocolate bars or allowed to read books, which they shared, concealing notes inside. The guards found one written by Khalid in J. K. Rowling's *Harry Potter and the Philosopher's Stone*, instructing the others to stop talking about couriers altogether.[68]

July 2005, Block 100, Tehran

The Mauritanian's wife had been watching the lights going on and off in a neighboring block for more than a month, wondering if it was some kind of interrogation center. Al Jazeera was full of stories about U.S.-operated black sites to where people they had known in Afghanistan were being rendered. Was Iran doing the same? she wondered.[69]

Sometimes she heard a distant call to prayer that wafted over the wall. Might it have been screaming? She wasn't the only detainee to notice. One brother had been spying through a hole in the gate, watching as guards brought in shopping bags that were delivered to a neighboring building. One day the Mauritanian called on Dr. Jamali in the medical center and saw some documents on his desk that addressed treatment programs for prisoners in "Block 200."

He called a *shura* under the fig tree. "I think our *mujahideen* brothers are next door," he whispered. High walls, solid gates, barbed wire, guard towers, and a dozen cameras lay between.

Urwah al-Libi, a hothead from the Libyan Islamic Fighting Group, volunteered to make contact. He waited until nine P.M., when the guards changed over, then slipped into the yard and shouted out a greeting in Arabic.

A call came back.

Excited, Urwah asked the neighbors to turn their lights on and off.

They did.

Over the next few nights, Urwah and the Mauritanian stood by the wall and called out questions, establishing that one Egyptian and two Libyan brothers were there, along with their families. They shared the same escorts and guards as those in Block 100 but their conditions were far worse. Desperate to learn more but fearing they would be overheard, they decided to wait a couple of days to see if the Iranians were watching.

When nothing was said, they resumed the dialogue by wrenching off a metal grille from a wooden gate that separated the two compounds. The Mauritanian fetched his son, who wriggled through the hole to call out questions, relaying the answers back to his father.

The three families in Block 200 had evaded capture until late 2003, they said, meaning they had much more up-to-date news about others in Iran. They were certain that Osama's family was also imprisoned elsewhere on this base, as were the army council chief Saif al-Adel, his deputies Abu al-Khayr al-Masri and Abu Mohammed al-Masri, and several Jordanians.

Fearful for his son's safety, the Mauritanian hauled him back by his ankles and replaced the grille.

August 2005, House No. 3, Street No. 8-A, Garga Road, Bilal Town, Abbottabad

The Kuwaiti brothers contemplated the implications of Abu Faraj's arrest. Abrar was at the new house in Abbottabad, fixing anti-snooping film onto the windows of the upper floor. He told his brother that too much money had been spent for them to abandon the building, even though Abu Faraj could lead the authorities there if he broke under pressure.

Ibrahim, who was fatigued by three years at Osama's side, remained worried; but the rental house in Haripur was bursting.[70] Both Maryam and Bushra had new babies. The neighbors were nosy. The Sheikh was so excited about moving home, he couldn't bear to disappoint him.

Once they were settled, Ibrahim was hoping to broach the subject of handing over the reins to a new companion. He wanted his life back. He already had an eye on his middleman in Peshawar, a Pashtun brother named Mohammed Aslam who he met once a month to exchange letters at one of the city's covered markets.

Ibrahim and Abrar were decided. They could not afford to change the plan.

A disguised Osama and his family arrived in Abbottabad at the end of August, settling on the second floor, with Amal, Seham, and the children taking rooms on either side of the corridor, while one bedroom was set aside as the Sheikh's "media studio." No children or women were allowed in there.

Abrar, Bushra, Maryam, and Ibrahim lived downstairs in a self-contained apartment cut off from the rest of the house by a locked metal gate. Their entrance was at the front of the house, under the balcony, while Osama's was to the rear. A patch of garden to the left of the house was separated from the lawn at the front by a high wall to give Osama's family some outside space.

As everyone settled in, Osama began to regrow his beard for the first time since 2001, and he organized his work, filing hundreds of audio- and videotapes in immaculate rows, hanging his golden *thobe* on the back of the door, ready for his next recording.[71] He spent many hours locked away, watching news from Iraq and Afghanistan on Al Jazeera or composing speeches to "my Muslim *Ummah*" and letters to commanders out in the "mother arena" of Waziristan. These days he had good spells and bad, sometimes confined to bed by ongoing health problems. The room was shaded by yellow flowered curtains, and on a high shelf above the door he kept his good-luck totem from the Jaji battle of 1987, the snub-nosed Kalashnikov.

Whenever he rallied, he pestered Ibrahim to find a new route out for his thoughts, tapes, and letters. Ibrahim took a risk and drove across to Peshawar to train up a new courier, Abu Faraj's deputy, Abu Hamza Rabia. He lived in Asoray, a village close to Miram Shah, the commercial hub of North Waziristan, from where he had easy access to Dr. al-Zawahiri in Damadola and to Al Qaeda financier Sheikh Saeed, who was living in Mir Ali.

When Ibrahim received his first message back from Dr. al-Zawahiri and informed Osama that the lines were open, the Sheikh immediately began writing to everyone, and the subject matter was nearly always the same: Abu Musab al-Zarqawi.

Saif al-Adel's protégé dominated the news from Iraq. His videotaped beheadings of Western hostages had made him notorious. One after another they appeared on jihadist websites: Nicholas Berg, Eugene Armstrong, Jack Hensley, Kenneth Bigley. In the background was the trademark black banner of Zarqawi's group, and in the foreground, a blindfolded prisoner pleading for life, dressed in an orange jumpsuit like those worn by prisoners rendered to Guantánamo Bay.

Osama dealt with the rising sense of disgust at Zarqawi's behavior by asking everyone in the movement to be patient. He had distrusted Zarqawi when Saif al-Adel had introduced them in Kandahar in 1999. His tattoo scars, lack of education, and swagger were the warning signs. Five times during 2000 and 2001 Osama had called Zarqawi to Kandahar to swear *bayat* and every time the Jordanian had refused. He was disrespectful, rude, and narcissistic.

But during the Tora Bora battle of December 2001 and in the months before the U.S. invasion of Iraq in 2003, Zarqawi had proved his mettle, helping coordinate the entry into Iraq, through Iran and Syria, of hundreds of Al Qaeda operatives—mujahideen who were now dependent on him for intelligence and support. To command the respect of an ever-growing army of fighters who joined Tawhid al-Jihad, Zarqawi demanded more support from Al Qaeda.

In the letter found on courier Hassan Ghul in January 2004, Zarqawi had requested a formal merger, promising: "We will be your readied soldiers, working under your banner, complying with your orders, and indeed swearing fealty to you publicly and in the news media."[72]

Unable to respond directly, Osama had asked Dr. al-Zawahiri to post a reply on an Islamic website, announcing that such a merger would take place. Afterward, Zarqawi wrote Osama back, pledging loyalty: "By Allah, O sheikh of the mujahideen, if you bade us plunge into the ocean, we would follow you . . . For what a fine commander of the armies of Islam you are, facing down the inveterate infidels and apostates!"[73]

Three months later, Al Jazeera broadcast an audiotape in which Osama reciprocated, describing Zarqawi as "the prince of Al Qaeda in Iraq" and asking "all our organization brethren to listen to him and obey him in his good deeds." Buoyed, Zarqawi began talking about himself as the "Emir of Al Qaeda's Operations in the Land of Mesopotamia." With Osama's endorsement and Al Qaeda cash, he felt invincible.

In February 2005, Zarqawi condemned the Iraqi elections as an "American game" and claimed responsibility for a series of horrifying suicide attacks, including the detonation of a massive car bomb at Hillah that wiped out 125 police recruits. He confirmed his men had kidnapped Riyadh Katei Aliwi, a colonel in the interior ministry; and the following month he was sentenced in absentia by a Jordanian court for blowing up its embassy in Baghdad in 2003. In April 2005, his men launched a rocket and mortar attack on Baghdad's Abu Ghraib prison and tried to assassinate the Iraqi prime minister. In May, Al Qaeda in Mesopotamia prayed for Zarqawi's recovery after he was injured in fighting. The hard man sent an audiotape to Osama reassuring him that he would pull through.

Summer 2005, Amman, Jordan

Not everyone was pleased with Zarqawi.

Abu Muhammad al-Maqdisi, once his spiritual mentor, a man who was widely respected as a leading light in the world of jihad theory and whose writings were cited by Osama bin Laden, was furious with his former pupil.[74]

The straggly bearded Palestinian-born Salafist, who lived in Zarqawi's home town of Zarqa but was then jailed on charges of inciting terrorism, wrote to him in blunt terms, a message smuggled out of prison and posted on a jihad website: "The pure hands of jihad fighters must not be stained by shedding inviolable blood. There is no point in vengeful acts that terrify people [and] provoke the entire world against mujahideen."

These were strong words from someone widely recognized as the intellectual godfather of Al Qaeda.

Maqdisi and Zarqawi had first met in Peshawar at the end of the Soviet war. After they returned home to Jordan they had launched an insurgency there. Arrested for possessing a gun and a grenade, the two became close during their four years interned at the Swaqa correction center south of Amman.

Maqdisi had comforted Zarqawi, who, feeling maudlin, composed poems to his mother and drew her pictures of hearts and flowers, declaring "Ummy [Mommy] I will never forget you."[75]

What had happened to that rough but emotionally sensitive young man? Maqdisi wondered. To get his attention, he now issued a devastating ruling that he knew would be picked up and publicized by jihadists everywhere. Mujahideen should not join his former pupil on his murderous journey through Iraq, Maqdisi concluded: "It will be an inferno for them. This is, by God, the biggest catastrophe."[76]

When news of the ruling reached Zarqawi, he was furious and took time away from the battlefield to write back. Maqdisi had "misrepresented me and misrepresented the facts," he said, sniping that these days he only took orders from God. Although he thanked the cleric for showing him the path, "he does not and should not have a monopoly on knowledge, and not everything he says is correct." Times had changed and he now regarded himself as "a soldier in the army of Sheikh Osama." He urged his followers to ignore Maqdisi and "seek the scholars and leaders of mujahideen, such as Osama."[77]

However, by the summer of 2005, Osama had also begun to worry about the direction in which Zarqawi was heading. Having followed Zarqawi's heated exchanges with Maqdisi, Osama recognized that Zarqawi's hotheadedness was having a negative impact on the greater outfit's reputation. In Iraq, he now had a $25 million reward on his head, matching Osama's. In addition to the videotaped beheadings of Western hostages, he had declared an "all-out war" on Iraq's Shia minority, killing hundreds and horrifying Muslims worldwide. The violence was debilitating, unauthorized, and it had to be stopped.

Dr. al-Zawahiri stepped in. From Damadola, he reached out to Zarqawi through Al Jazeera, recording a subtle message that was broadcast in June 2005. When Osama heard it, he was furious with his deputy. Advertising internal squabbles publicly gave the enemy a dangerous advantage, he warned. They had to communicate by private means.

The unrestrained violence continued. Zarqawi claimed the assassination of Iraq's oldest member of parliament, and in August his group pledged to kill anyone involved in drafting Iraq's new constitution, while launching a rocket attack in Jordan that narrowly missed a U.S. warship.[78] In correspondence with Al Qaeda Central, he reminded al-Zawahiri and Osama that when he had sworn loyalty in October 2004 he had done so on the basis that they had agreed to him "fighting the sects of apostasy," in other words, Shias. Were they now reneging on that deal?

Dr. al-Zawahiri sent a couriered letter, explaining to Zarqawi that the primary goals of the outfit's mission were being put in danger by his folly.[79] In order for Al Qaeda to establish the caliphate in Iraq, it first had to expel the United States, while at the same time keeping Muslim support on its side. Right now "the scenes of slaughtering the hostages" and indiscriminate attacks on Shia targets were doing the opposite. "This matter won't be acceptable to the Muslim populace," wrote al-Zawahiri. In the absence of popular support, "the Islamic mujahid movement would be crushed in the shadows," he continued. Zarqawi shouldn't be deceived by the praise of zealous younger men who had dubbed him "the sheikh of slaughterers."

Al-Zawahiri, too, had reason to seek unbridled revenge. "The author of these lines has tasted the bitterness of American brutality," he wrote. "My favorite wife's chest was crushed by a concrete ceiling and she went on calling for aid to lift the stone block off her chest until she breathed her last." His young daughter had suffered a cerebral hemorrhage during the airstrike on Gardez and "for a whole day suffered pain until she expired." To this day, he did not know where they were buried. Despite these losses, he had to constantly remind himself that the war they were fighting also took place in the "battlefield of the media." Al Qaeda was in a race "for the hearts and minds of our *Ummah*," he wrote.

Al-Zawahiri ended with a plea. Al Qaeda Central was short of funds, so could Zarqawi send $100,000 to tide them over? After all, Osama had kept him afloat for years.

Suspecting that his letter would fall on deaf ears, al-Zawahiri began to train up a new spokesman. The man's first foray into the public arena had come in October 2004, when ABC News broadcast a seventy-five-minute speech in which he kept his face covered but identified himself as "Azzam the American." Soon afterward, someone from his old mosque in the United States identified him as Adam Gadahn, a tech-savvy Caucasian convert from Orange County, California, who had turned his back on baseball, Christianity, and death metal to run Al Qaeda's media empire As Sahab from a cave in Damadola.[80]

October 8, 2005, 8:50 A.M., Abbottabad

Sheikh Osama woke to find the ground moving beneath him. A huge earthquake had struck the heart of Pakistani-administered Kashmir fifty miles to the northeast, killing more than eighty thousand people in the region and leveling the protective wall around his compound. Exposed and frightened, Osama fretted until he realized that chaos had engulfed the whole area, with rescue workers trying to reach thousands of villages entombed in mud, putting Pakistani security forces on the back foot.

Ibrahim suggested they should use this opportunity to increase the height of the perimeter wall in places where the house was overlooked, building it up to more than eighteen feet.[81] Others, too, made use of the mayhem, with mujahideen from banned Pakistani militant groups like Lashkar-e-Taiba and Jaish-e-Mohammed flooding into the area, delivering aid and simultaneously recruiting the families of victims.

As Abbottabad filled up with Islamists, Osama began to feel more secure; and when the founder of Harkat-ul-Mujahideen asked for a meeting he agreed, breaking a promise he had made to Ibrahim after Khalid Shaikh Mohammad's arrest never to meet anyone again.

But Fazlur Rehman Khalil was not just anyone. He and Osama knew each other from fighting the Soviets in Afghanistan, at which time Khalil, a Punjabi by birth, had been a popular commander, fluent in Arabic and a skilled operator with a Stinger missile.[82] His group had gained notoriety in 1995 when mujahideen loyal to him kidnapped six Western backpackers in Indian Kashmir, including the best friend of Dr. James Mitchell.

In 1998, Khalil became a signatory to Osama's famous fatwa against "Jews and Crusaders," and in 1999 his group orchestrated the hijacking of an Indian passenger jet to secure the release of another old friend, Masood Azhar, the leader of Jaish-e-Mohammed. Also freed was Omar Sheikh, the British-Pakistani who went on to lure Daniel Pearl to his death.

In Afghanistan, Khalil had acted as a go-between with Mullah Omar, and his forces had helped Al Qaeda infiltrate Pakistan after 9/11. These days, he operated training camps in the Tribal Areas, which he now hoped to shift closer to Abbottabad. He was in hiding himself, after being tipped off that the Americans—sick of the license given him by the ISI—wanted to kill him.[83]

They could not take the risk of meeting at Osama's new home. Instead, as the earthquake rescue operation mushroomed, they chose a supporter's house on the fringes of the Tribal Areas.[84] It was the Al Qaeda leader's first trip out of Abbottabad, and as he clipped short his beard, he told Amal he was nervous.

When the two men sat down together that night, they shared a meal of goat and rice as Khalil revealed the purpose of this risky meeting: he had brought with him a highly sensitive proposal that could secure Osama's long-term position in Pakistan. It came from a mutual, high-wattage friend: the former ISI chief, General Hamid Gul.

During his tenure as head of the ISI from 1987 to 1989, Gul had culti-vated deep ties with the Taliban, Al Qaeda, and other jihadists then fighting in Afghanistan. Legend had it that Osama had been introduced to Gul by Milt Bearden, the CIA station chief in Islamabad, as a "prince who left every-thing for jihad."[85] Out of the most powerful Afghan warlords (who the CIA referred to as "the Seven Dwarfs"), Gul favored Osama's old friend Gulbuddin Hekmatyar and he channeled an estimated $600 million to him.[86]

After the Soviets were defeated, Gul had become one of Osama's most outspoken advocates, supporting Mullah Omar, too. They met twice in Sudan, with Gul later bragging about these get-togethers—although some-times he denied them.[87]

A mischievous and belligerent contrarian and inveterate plotter, always ready with a scheme in each pocket and another in his sock, Gul champi-oned the cause of Pakistani national interest.

Mostly, Gul liked to dish it out. Ad hoc Islamist lectures and provocative anti-Semitic pronouncements were his daily routine. He was especially fond of riling American reporters by insisting that 9/11 had been a Mossad operation.[88] One of his favorite possessions was a chunk of the Berlin Wall that he told new visitors had been presented by the East Germans—although in truth President George H. W. Bush had gifted it to him in gratitude for "delivering the first blow" against the Soviet empire. But however hyper-bolic he sounded, Gul was consistent and entertaining, and he continued to be well connected inside Pakistan's security apparatus.

Khalil told Osama that powerful friends backed the controversial general. He pointed to the ISI's S-Wing, the 313 Brigade formed with ISI cadre, and the assassination attempts this unit had made on Musharraf that had been assisted by members of the Pakistan armed forces, using IEDs fashioned the old ISI way.

This cabal had had an idea, Khalil said. They wanted to revive an old rumor, passing Osama off as having died from a chronic condition. It was a typical ISI smoke screen, modeled on the protective cordon thrown up around Taliban leader Mullah Omar, who had been allowed to reestablish his *shura* in Quetta before heading down to Karachi, where he remained hidden in an ISI safe house, sick with diabetes.[89]

With Osama "killed off," Gul would use his deep contacts within the spy directorate to make sure that no one came sniffing around Bilal Town. All other arms of intelligence and security, from the regular police to the Special Branch, Military Intelligence, the Intelligence Bureau, and the Federal

Investigation Agency (FIA; Pakistan's equivalent of the FBI), would be kept away. Any intelligence that related to Arabs or the search for Al Qaeda would be funneled through the ISI's S-Wing, to which Gul had direct access.[90] Tangible proof of this deal came almost right away, with the FIA's director general warned to "not touch any case involving Arabs."[91]

Osama was not yet convinced. In an undated letter to Atiyah Abd al-Rahman listing significant Al Qaeda losses since 9/11, he had blamed Abu Zubaydah's capture on "our opening up so much to Lashkar-e-Taiba," something he still believed.[92] Lashkar was pro–Al Qaeda, but ultimately it was a creature of the ISI that was only for itself. Khalil tried to convince him otherwise, pointing out that he would not be alone in receiving such protection. They had many friends in common who survived in Pakistan only because of their connections with the security establishment. Beside Mullah Omar, there were warlord Hekmatyar, tribal chieftain Jalaluddin Haqqani and his sons, radical cleric (maulana) Sami ul-Haq, and, most important, Lashkar boss Hafiz Saaed and Jaish emir Masood Azhar.[93]

Gul and Khalil had Osama's back, and if anyone in Pakistan's security establishment needed to reach him directly, they would act as intermediaries.

When Osama returned to Abbottabad, having agreed to Khalil's plan, he became bolder. His letter writing increased and he got to work improving his image. Having learned that Dr. al-Zawahiri and Azzam the American were putting together a documentary for distribution to American networks, he demanded a role.

"Knowledge Is for Acting Upon: The Manhattan Raid" was to present Al Qaeda's philosophy and feature the martyrdom videos of the 9/11 hijackers. Osama was not sure that Azzam was the best man for the job. A brash video recorded in Damadola, in which Azzam praised the "echo of explosions and the slitting of the throats of the infidels," had recently appeared on *Good Morning America*, and Osama had felt compelled to write a private letter instructing al-Zawahiri to present a more considered impression.

Osama also had to address family matters. According to a recent letter from his eighteen-year-old daughter Khadija in Waziristan, the harsh environment of the tribal areas was taking its toll on her health.[94] She had suffered a miscarriage, several bouts of typhoid and malaria, and had recently given birth to a daughter, Aisha, ignoring doctor's advice against any more pregnancies. Seham badgered Osama to let her and the children join them in Abbottabad and had already decorated a room for them. The chaos of the earthquake could provide cover for their journey. Khadija and the children would travel first and her husband, the Saudi mujahid Daood, could follow soon after. "I prepared myself and the explosives belt," Daood said in a letter to Osama on the matter, referring to the standard travel procedure for a senior Al Qaeda operative.[95]

However, a downed bridge and roads ripped up by the quake forced Khadija to turn back after Haripur. Traveling in a private car, those bringing her to Abbottabad needed to think quickly, and they headed west, via Peshawar, to the outskirts of Miram Shah, the capital of North Waziristan, where numerous Al Qaeda families were living. Once she was settled with a host family, she wrote to her parents.

"My dear Dad. How are you?" she began. "I hope my message reaches you and that you are well, as we are, praise God."[96] Recently, she had learned that she had two new siblings, Amal's children Aasia and Ibrahim. "May God bless you with them and make them righteous."

She was bitterly disappointed that she had been unable to come. "We constantly yearn for you and delight in hearing your voice in messages," she said, reminding everyone that her eldest son, Abdallah, who had been born in Kandahar shortly before 9/11, had never known his grandfather, other than what he saw on Al Jazeera. Abdallah was working hard to learn how to read and write, "so he can send you a letter himself."

This was not the end of the road, said Khadija, promising to try to reach them again. "We are constantly ready, God willing."

Khadija's letter got Osama thinking about the marriage prospects of the three teenage children who had made it to Abbottabad: Seham's son, Khalid, and their other daughters, Miriam and Sumaiya. He did not want them marrying Pakistanis. Someone would have to find suitable Arab partners, which was not an easy matter given that the family was in hiding.

Seham had an idea. Her daughter Khadija was now better placed to help than most. Arabs had converged on the villages around Miram Shah, where she was now living. Lying in a hollow below a crucial pass over the mountains, the town had once acted as a staging post for the mujahideen, and it remained a personal fiefdom for Osama's and the ISI's long-term partner in jihad Jalaluddin Haqqani. His mosque and a huge religious school still dominated its outskirts.

These days, Haqqani's son Sirajuddin had taken over the family business, and his network stretched to neighboring Mir Ali and across the border into

Ghazni and down to Uruzgan. According to Dr. al-Zawahiri's vision of having multiple fortresses dotted around the tribal zone, so that if one was attacked many others could continue, dozens of Al Qaeda's operational commanders had also taken up residence in the area, many of them marrying into local families.

Khadija and her children were lodging with the family of an Egyptian brother who had been killed in Afghanistan, leaving behind several unmarried daughters.[97] His widow had taken Khadija under her wing—helping with her new baby, Aisha. Khadija had also befriended one of the daughters, Karima, who was "pious and beautiful." She was, Khadija thought, a perfect match for her younger brother, Khalid, in Abbottabad.

Seham was delighted. If Khalid wed Karima, the bride's family would be indebted to Osama for life; and if Khalid moved to Waziristan, that would free up space for Khadija to come to them. Daood could take over Khalid's job of running Osama's media studio.

To get the ball rolling, Seham wrote to Karima's mother. While they waited for her reply, Khalid asked his father for permission to travel to Waziristan to meet his future wife.

Osama was reluctant. There was still plenty for Khalid to do in Abbottabad. Bathroom pipes needed fixing and he wanted window blinds replaced. He told his son to buy a cow and a chicken so they could have milk and eggs without going to the market, and to start a vegetable plot in the empty courtyard to the far right of the house. Osama wanted to reestablish the self-sufficient and frugal lifestyle he had adopted in Sudan and Kandahar. He had one more job for Khalid. His son was to purchase a wide-brimmed hat from Abbottabad's main bazaar and construct a makeshift gazebo in the family garden. Osama was sick of staying indoors.

Osama's companion Ibrahim was exhausted. He had to cover vast distances to connect disparate brothers, and back home there was no peace. Abrar was suffering from chronic depression brought on by stress. The main house was chaotic, with boxed-up possessions spilling out everywhere. The only order was in the Sheikh's private realm. Inside his wooden wardrobe, his clothes hung on hangers or were folded into neat squares and piled up. His taped speeches sat in alphabetical rows. A large cupboard in his bathroom was filled with carefully labeled medical supplies.

Amal, Bushra, and Maryam were all pregnant again. If Khadija reached Abbottabad, that would mean three more children in the house. Where would they all sleep?

Even at home, Ibrahim felt as if he was at war, arguing with children and wives who were not allowed outside. Although a heavy double gate on the first floor separated his family from the bin Ladens, children, ever curious, pushed notes underneath and peeked through the gaps. Amal's children, who were four, two, and one and cooped up on the second floor, wanted to play too, and they jealously watched Ibrahim's and Abrar's children running around in the yard.

Although the nearest neighbors were several hundred yards away, Ibrahim worried constantly about what they might overhear and say, not to mention the local shopkeepers, farmers, the imam, and the doctors and nurses at the local hospital.

He was also concerned about maintaining his own far-fetched cover story—a blood feud, warring brothers from the Tribal Areas. He tried several times to engage the Sheikh, but Osama wasn't interested. With Fazlur Rehman Khalil's plan on his mind, Osama was proposing to build another story on the house with an annex in the garden so the couriers and their families could move out of the main house. He wanted Al Qaeda Central in Waziristan to fund it, which meant delivering yet another letter.

Asoray Village, North Waziristan, Pakistan

The Kuwaiti brothers were safer than they thought. A CIA report from September 1, 2005, disclosed that couriers "remain largely invisible to us until a detainee reveals them." Interrogations were going badly and even those who had previously cooperated, like Hassan Ghul, who had confirmed to the CIA Ibrahim's nom de guerre Abu Ahmad al-Kuwaiti, saying he was Osama's "closest companion," were no longer trusted. "We have to consider the possibility that they are creating fictitious characters to distract us or to absolve themselves of direct knowledge about bin Laden," the report concluded.[98]

With no luck on the ground, the United States was reliant on fire from up above. When Hellfire missiles struck a house in the village close to Miram Shah on November 5, eight people were killed instantly, including the three children and the wife of Dr. al-Zawahiri's new courier, Abu Hamza Rabia, the successor to Abu Faraj. Abu Hamza escaped with a leg wound and went into hiding. A TV reporter who lived next door described the scene: "I grabbed my Kalashnikov because I thought somebody fired a rocket at my house." Poking his head inside the ruined building, he saw "nothing left but body parts."[99]

On November 30, a drone struck again, this time killing Abu Hamza Rabia and four others. Musharraf welcomed the news by announcing the death of "Al Qaeda's new Number Three."

To conceal the role of the CIA, Musharraf's spokesman told reporters that Abu Hamza had blown himself up while constructing a bomb. But another gutsy tribal journalist, who went to the compound and photographed pieces of shrapnel that appeared to be from a Hellfire missile, published his story in the Urdu daily *Ausaf*, causing an outcry.

"Let's enjoy the fact that Al Qaeda has lost another key person," said an irritated Pakistani government official as he tried to dismiss talk of American drones. When the tribal reporter continued to investigate, five gunmen abducted him. Six months later, his corpse was dumped in a marketplace in Miram Shah, his family alerted to it by a man who claimed to be from the intelligence services.[100]

Reassessing their position from the relative safety of the Damadola trench complex, Dr. al-Zawahiri's commanders concluded that the mounting drone strikes were, in part, a response to Zarqawi's savagery. Al Qaeda was his sponsor and had to be crushed.

On November 18, Zarqawi had sent bombers into three popular hotels in Amman, killing at least fifty-seven people.[101] Al-Zawahiri tried again to rein him in via a letter written by Zarqawi's friend and collaborator Atiyah Abd al-Rahman. "I am with them," Atiyah wrote to Zarqawi of the high command, "and they have some comments about some of your circumstances."[102] Explaining that direct communications between Waziristan and Iraq were difficult and that it was easier for Zarqawi to send a courier to Pakistan rather than the other way around, he advised his Jordanian friend that the brothers "wish that they had a way to talk to you and to advise you, and to guide and instruct you; however, they too are occupied with vicious enemies here."

Al Qaeda Central was weak, he admitted, "and we ask God that He strengthen them and mend their fractures. They have many of their own problems, but they are people of reason, experience and sound, beneficial knowledge." Zarqawi should listen to his seniors.

He had to improve his relationships with other Sunni insurgent groups in Iraq, be more judicious in using the Al Qaeda name, and, perhaps, consider standing down as leader.

"It is a possibility," Atiyah suggested politely, "if you find at some point someone who is better and more suitable than you." He added: "Know that we, like all mujahideen, . . . have not yet reached a level of stability. We have no alternative but not to squander any element of the foundations of strength or any helper or supporter." Before the letter was dispatched in December 2005, the state security court in Amman, Jordan, sentenced Zarqawi to his third death sentence in absentia.

A surprise visitor to Waziristan lifted the gloom: Abdullah Saeed al-Libi, the Al Qaeda prisoner who had sneaked out of Rajai Shahr prison dressed in his wife's chador. He had spent the best part of a year trying to reach Al Qaeda Central's new bolt-hole, and he reported that the Al Qaeda army council and its *shura*, as well as Osama's missing family members, were alive—and imprisoned in Iran.[103]

Atiyah immediately wrote to Abbottabad, where Osama's house was clad in bamboo scaffolding while his home improvements were carried out. It was the first confirmation Osama had that his family was still alive, and he was delighted. But how to get them back?

Al Qaeda Central came up with several suggestions, including kidnapping an Iranian VIP. Yusuf al-Balochi, a relative of Khalid Shaikh Mohammad who, because he had both an Iranian and a Pakistani passport, was able to come and go between the two countries freely, could lead the negotiations.

Osama sounded out his wife Seham. Her sister-wife Khairiah, Khairiah's son Hamzah, and Najwa's children Saad, Othman, Mohammed, Fatima, Iman, and Ladin were all being held, along with several spouses and grandchildren. Also imprisoned was Saif al-Adel and the Mauritanian, to name but two on the *shura*. Perhaps they should first appeal to the supreme leader of Iran, Ayatollah Khamenei, and his radical new president, Mahmoud Ahmadinejad, who had taken up office in August and was ushering in a new age of cooperation with the Quds Force, marking a downturn in the fortunes of the Reformers. Osama asked his son Khalid to draft a suitable letter— yet more correspondence for the nervous Ibrahim to transport to Al Qaeda Central.[104]

*   *   *

January 13, 2006, Damadola

The mud-brick compound had been brim-full since Eid, with elders traveling from miles around to listen to two local firebrand clerics, both renowned for their extreme views and ash-black *pakuls*.[105] One carried an AK-47 with a red wood stock on his shoulder that lent him the air of Osama. They were both on the run, having been charged with being heralds for Al Qaeda; but in a lawless land being an outlaw was something of a tautology. When the Frontier Corps came to Damadola, which was infrequently, it was cap in hand. The Corps always knew where the clerics would be, as they spent their days running a jihad seminary in Chinagai village.

The gathered elders relaxed, watching their teenage sons slaughtering goats, as younger children raced about in holiday clothes. Despite the festivities, their host, a local jeweler, was unnerved.[106] Up above, tiny glinting slivers hovered, and since the previous November, when rockets had pounded Miram Shah, killing the latest Al Qaeda courier, any unidentified flying objects were a cause for concern.

Unable to sleep that night, the host woke before dawn, put on his beige anorak, and climbed up a hill above the town to find his friends wakeful, too. "There are three of them now," they said, pointing.

Arrow-shaped and metallic, they circled on the thermals far up in the sky.

Moments later, the men were blown off their feet as missiles slammed into the compound below, shaking the hillside.

When the jeweler came to, his house was gone. "Where are my children?" he croaked, staggering back into the village.

In Washington, the CIA briefed that Dr. al-Zawahiri had been holding a "terror summit" in the compound. In Rawalpindi, President Musharraf told journalists that "at least two high-profile Al Qaeda targets" had been killed, including Abu Khabab al-Masri, the chemist and bomb maker, who had a $5 million bounty on his head and was credited with manufacturing Richard Reid's shoe-bomb.[107] Pentagon sources suggested that Dr. al-Zawahiri had left "only minutes before the strike" and that a son-in-law had died.

On the ground, residents laid out on winding sheets the bodies of ten villagers and children who had no connections to terror. The people of Damadola came to pay their respects, and the firebrand clerics, who had escaped unscathed, led the funerals.

When local journalists arrived, they were presented with shrapnel wrapped in tissue like take-home cake at a children's party.[108] Afterward, they were escorted to a nearby clinic to photograph dying children on metal gurneys.

Back at the crater, the jeweler—who had lost two sons and a daughter—denied he had ever met al-Zawahiri. "I don't *know* him," he hissed. "No foreigner was ever at my home."[109]

To prove he was still alive, Dr. al-Zawahiri issued a mocking audiotape. "Bush, do you know where I am? I am among the Muslim masses!" he taunted. "The whole world has discovered the extent of America's lies, failures, and savagery."

Bomb maker Abu Khabab also contacted a reporter in Peshawar to correct a published obituary.

In Islamabad, ISI chiefs stirred the pot by suggesting that the FBI had illegally taken some bodies away from the blast scene for DNA testing. In response, a local office of the United States Agency for International Development (USAID) was attacked and the border region boiled, while in Karachi and Islamabad tens of thousands of people took to the streets, chanting "Death to America." Reacting to the darkening public mood, Pakistan's information minister announced an inquiry, as the government wanted "to assure the people, we will not allow such incidents to reoccur."

Despite the heartfelt bluster, the inquiry was never opened.

May 2006, Block 100, Tehran

A rock thumped down into the dirt, and the Mauritanian retrieved the piece of paper wrapped around it. It was the third such message he had received in as many days, and it contained more updates from the Egyptian and Libyan brothers incarcerated on the other side of the wall.

Brother Urwah decided the rock telegraph was too slow. He would try to climb into Block 200 through an air-conditioning duct. The Mauritanian tried to dissuade him. "The ceilings are old and frail," he warned. Urwah went ahead anyway. Armed with a flashlight and some tools, he set off down the tube. "We kept praying for him," the Mauritanian said.

After Urwah's voice could no longer be heard, they strained for sounds of his feet and fists. Finally, they heard a howling and saw a gust of black soot, as Urwah shot back out of the duct "looking like he had come out of a grave." He had reached a narrower section of the tube, turned back, and lost his footing.

Frustrated, the Mauritanian waited until morning and then confronted the Iranian block chief, Mr. Nasseri, telling him that they knew brothers were being held next door. He listed names. Embarrassed, Nasseri allowed some of the brothers and their wives from Block 200 to visit Block 100.

But the exchange program did nothing to alleviate building tensions that were predominantly fueled by a troubled mujahid from the Libyan Islamic Fighting Group, Abu Anas al-Libi. A fluent English speaker, he had been sent to the United Kingdom by Al Qaeda in 1995. The following year, he was granted political asylum, moved to Manchester, and was recruited by the British security services to kill Colonel Muammar Gaddafi. But the plot had failed without Anas even leaving Britain. Afterward, he fled, leaving behind in his apartment a 180-page terrorist manual that would become known as the Manchester Manual, the most important tome on Al Qaeda field craft to be recovered pre-9/11.

After making it back to Afghanistan, tall and slender Abu Anas had worked as a body double for Osama. He also helped Khalid Shaikh Mohammad manage the Al Qaeda's IT needs. In late 2001, he was placed on the FBI's Most Wanted Terrorist list, after being charged with playing a significant role in the 1998 embassy bombings. Now, imprisoned, he was a constant source of friction, and the Mauritanian, who had known him since the Sudan days, was running out of patience.

When a child broke both legs as a result of a fall in the garden and had to wait for several hours before being taken to hospital, Anas set fire to his room and whipped others into a riot.[110]

The Iranians drew weapons and after locking the families up, fired stun grenades and rubber bullets. Abu Anas was carted off to Evin prison, an action that triggered a hunger strike that degenerated into another riot. "The complex was transformed into a war zone," recalled the Mauritanian.

The Libyan brothers voted to bring the entire building down, brick by brick, gathering whatever they could from the corridors and setting it on fire, before kicking through walls and smashing glass.[111]

An internal phone rang. The Mauritanian grabbed the handset.

It was block chief Nasseri. "Make *peace*," he urged.

"What's in it for me?" the Mauritanian shouted.

A pause. "Okay. There is another camp. We call it Block Three Hundred."

The Mauritanian bit his lip.

The silence drew Nasseri out. "There are people held there . . ." A pause. "Who are *more like you* . . ."

The Mauritanian was desperate to ask more but sensed he should not.

"Make peace," Nasseri begged.

The Mauritanian walked out into the smoke-logged corridors. "We need to stop," he shouted. "We need to find another way." Stunned by seeing a quiet man turning purple with rage, one by one men who respected him downed their burning torches.

"Ahmadenijad's appointment means we will never be handed over to the Americans. We are safe here," the Mauritanian insisted. "We should make the most of this time."

The men walked back to their cells and he returned to his family.

"Pack," he whispered to his wife. "We are leaving."

CHAPTER SEVEN

"The reprisals of the mujahideen shall come like lightning bolts."
—ELEGY FOR ZARQAWI, WRITTEN BY
ABU YAHYA AL-LIBI, AL QAEDA CLERIC[1]

Summer 2006, Damadola, Bajaur Agency, Federally Administered Tribal Areas, Pakistan

ALONG THE AFGHAN BORDER, A DEATH-STRIP of fortifications neared completion, and fighters bedded down in trenches in Razmak, Mir Ali, Miram Shah, and Dande-Darpa Khel as well as Damadola. Villages and towns were sown with preachers who beat a drum for the Taliban and Al Qaeda.

While Abu Musab al-Zarqawi kept the black flags aloft in Iraq, and Osama (whose anonymous existence was being safeguarded by mujahid outfits cloaked by the intelligence service) did the same from Abbottabad, his life force drawing in funds and recruits from around the world, Dr. al-Zawahiri reshaped Al Qaeda's ideology and set a course for war against American troops in Afghanistan.

Money was flowing in once more. After the recent years of fame, Al Qaeda was attracting cash, recruits, and prestige like no other jihad group in history. Hundreds of thousands of U.S. dollars were pledged by supporters in the Gulf states who were inspired by American atrocities in Iraq and drone strikes that killed innocent civilians in Pakistan, and who wanted to see more action from an organization that had inspired the London public transport bombings of July 2005. Its network reached around the globe and through the heart of Iran.

As Al Qaeda's chief strategist, Dr. al-Zawahiri briefed a new generation of two hundred operational commanders, men entrusted with driving events out in the field without recourse to the center. Beneath grew a standing army

257

of impoverished peasants, madrassa graduates, unemployed farmhands, orphans and the children of broken families, local ruffians, and Taliban fighters who crossed the border every month to attend training workshops run by visiting Al Qaeda commanders from the front lines of Iraq.[2]

Huge swathes of the impoverished Tribal Areas had been sucked into a Taliban–Al Qaeda vortex that transformed the lands-beyond-reach into a vision drawn by Hieronymus Bosch. The most courageous tribal journalists photographed the beheading of spies and the crucifixions of heretics, nailed to telegraph poles in Miram Shah, while in Mir Ali the guilty were flayed, chained alive to pickups, and dragged through the streets until they disintegrated.

From the center of the maelstrom, Dr. al-Zawahiri issued a new edict. Believing the intelligence that had led the CIA to bomb the Damadola compound had come from the eavesdropping of loose-lipped couriers, he fired them, ordering media-savvy Azzam the American to upgrade Al Qaeda's delivery methods. Instead of sending out traceable men with cumbersome tapes and letters in plastic shopping bags to be dumped at discoverable dead-drops under bushes in Islamabad, announcements and speeches would in the future be uploaded invisibly onto password-protected websites, accessed by a new distribution network called Al-Fajr Media Center. It comprised hundreds of anonymous webmasters scattered around the globe whose job was to decrypt the material, repost it on popular Islamist forums, and encourage like-minded armchair mujahideen to enlist.

Content was streamlined, too, with Azzam producing broadcast-quality quasi-documentaries on his Sony Vaio, editing together high-definition footage and cell-phone videos, underscored by easy-to-understand Islamic dogma. In his makeshift studio, he had mastered a version of "green screen" that enabled him to transport Dr. al-Zawahiri to a backdrop of his choosing.[3]

Osama kept a close eye on their prolific output. He was pleased at the progress the doctor made in representing Al Qaeda, but he disliked his deputy's hectoring and pedantic tone. He preferred the poetic and ambiguous Arabic phonemes of the old days. Looking forward to a time when he could seize back control of the message, he had expanded his own media center in Abbottabad into two bedrooms, ordering the children whose space he took to squash up.

Osama's silence was a cause for worry, especially among *shura* members trapped in Iran who wondered if he was ill or even dead, as the ISI maintained in its dealings with the CIA. "I want to criticize you the same way a younger brother would criticize his older brother for not letting us know how you are doing," wrote one of the Mauritanian's comrades in a letter that was smuggled over the border and reached courier Ibrahim, who took it to Abbottabad. "I hope you know how much you mean to us."[4]

Supporters in the Arabian Peninsula also wrote: "How true is it that Shaykh Ayman [al-Zawahiri] is the most influential man in the organization and that Abu Abdullah [bin Laden] is like a puppet on his hand?" Had Osama ceded all authority to Dr. al-Zawahiri? The writer worried Al Qaeda was now "tinged" with the ideology of Egyptian Islamic Jihad "to the detriment of the whole movement."[5]

Osama dispatched polite replies stating that he was well and remained the captain of the ship, but privately he had become fixated on his inability to rein in Abu Musab al-Zarqawi, whose theater of death continued unabated.

One particular act got Osama riled: the fallout from Zarqawi's November 2005 hotel bombings in Amman, as video and eyewitness accounts emerged from the Radisson SAS Hotel, where husband and wife suicide bombers, Ali and Sajida al-Rishawi, had invaded a wedding in the Philadelphia Ballroom.[6] Sajida, the sister of one of Zarqawi's closest aides, was unable to make her belt work. Ali screamed at her to run, while he leaped onto a table and flicked his switch, bringing down the ceiling and a wall of plate-glass windows, killing thirty-eight Jordanian partygoers, including the fathers of the bride and groom.[7]

Failed bomber Sajida was made to confess her crimes on TV. The attack triggered immediate and ferocious condemnation from mujahideen, clerics, and influential Saudi sheikhs. It also spurred President Bush to deploy a secret military unit, Task Force 145, to run Zarqawi to ground any way it could.[8]

Emboldened by his cheerleaders, Zarqawi released a provocative video in which he strutted about dressed in black fatigues with ammunition pouches strapped to his chest, while swearing allegiance to Osama and surrounded by heavily armed companions who obscured their faces. He made a surprise announcement. He intended to declare an Islamic state or caliphate in Iraq within three months. Whoever remained would have to submit to living under the ancient *hudud* punishments of execution, beheading, stoning, and amputation.[9] Those who rejected him would be hunted down and killed.

However, Zarqawi was running out of time. Nine days before the video was released, Task Force 145 killed five of his men, captured another five, and almost grabbed Zarqawi himself. The previous February, they had come so close that they had glimpsed his face through a car windshield, but rules of engagement in a densely inhabited neighborhood had prevented them from firing. After the video emerged, on May 13 and 14, Task Force 145 killed one of Zarqawi's lieutenants and fifteen others. Two days later another two were dead.

In Damadola, a new arrival came with a tale so exhilarating that it temporarily pricked the bubble of paranoia and fear triggered by the drones. He was a young Libyan theologian, Abu Yahya al-Libi, who had once been the Mauritanian's student in Nouakchott and when last heard of had been embedded at the battle of Kandahar airport.

Abu Yahya revealed that not only had he survived, but U.S. forces had captured him and taken him to Bagram air base, where he had undergone months of torture. Recently, he and three others had slipped their shackles, discarded their orange jumpsuits, and sprinted away. A manhunt had been launched, with thermal-imaging cameras slung beneath a U.S. military helicopter that sought a heat signature in a frozen landscape, but Afghan families had taken them in.

"They gave us a hero's welcome," Abu Yahya told a rapt audience. "As soon as we showed up at a compound, they would ask, 'You're the four who escaped from Bagram?' Despite their fear and poverty, they—by Allah—helped us with everything they possibly could." Some offered their shirts. Old women insisted on shaking and kissing their hands "out of love and support for the mujahideen."

Dr. al-Zawahiri realized that Abu Yahya's was a great story of survival and that the power of this firsthand testimony of American torture—and bettering it—could draw attention away from Zarqawi's excesses. An account was uploaded into As Sahab by Azzam that concluded with a rousing quote from Abu Yahya that aped U.S. Marine–speak: everyone should fight "for the captive brothers who we left behind."

Abu Yahya's broadcast contained detailed descriptions from his time in custody, revealing that he had been tortured in a place dubbed the Salt Pit, an experience he described as "being put in the grave while you're still alive." He had made friends there with Dr. Ghairat Baheer, son-in-law of

Gulbuddin Hekmatyar, whom everyone also presumed was dead. He had also met Ibn Sheikh al-Libi, the camp commander seized at Tora Bora, but this giant had been reduced to "skin and bones."

Life in the Salt Pit had been bleak, and when Abu Yahya overheard a rumor that the Americans were holding in permanent isolation and raping a female prisoner, he had staged a hunger strike. She was, Abu Yahya discovered, a forty-year-old American-sounding Pakistani who had "lost her mind," someone the other inmates called the "gray lady of Bagram." Some concluded she was Aafia Siddiqui, the Pakistani neuroscientist who had been abducted in Karachi in 2003. It was impossible to confirm whether this or the rape claims were true, but nevertheless the "gray lady" conjured by Abu Yahya would become a potent symbol.[10]

June 7, 2006, 6:12 P.M., Hibhib Village, Baqubah, Iraq

Task Force 145 was following a compelling nugget of actionable intelligence. Zarqawi's most frequent visitor was his spiritual adviser, Sheikh Abd al-Rahman, who made an elaborate series of vehicle switches but always ended up in a small blue car when he was visiting the Tawhid al-Jihad leader. *A small blue car.* It seemed too obvious. But they watched out for it anyhow. Even the most security-minded had mental blocks.

Watching drone feeds throughout May, they spotted al-Rahman twice but then lost him. Task Force 145 found him a third time in a small blue car on June 7 and trailed him to an isolated compound in a palm grove five miles from Baqubah—a war-scarred city north of Baghdad that had witnessed heavy insurgent activity.

After the Jordanian General Intelligence Directorate (GID)—which had been monitoring Zarqawi since 1990, longer than anyone else, and particularly wanted him dead after the Amman bombings—provided map coordinates confirming that this was a location known to be connected to Zarqawi's third wife, an Iraqi woman with whom he had several small children, a five-hundred-pound guided bomb was called in and it smashed into the compound, throwing up star-shaped plumes, the first overwhelming strike quickly followed by a second.[11]

When the Americans arrived and pulled Zarqawi from the rubble, he was still alive, although close to death. He tried to get up but fell back, lost consciousness, and died in the vehicle he was hauled into.

"Today is a great day in Iraq," said a spokesman for the Multi-National Force in Iraq.[12] "Today, Iraq takes a giant step forward." Uncompromising images were shared of the dead Zarqawi's swollen and bloodied face. No pictures were released of his Iraqi wife or children, who also died in the blast alongside preacher Sheikh Abd al-Rahman.

With Zarqawi out of the way, Al Qaeda Central jumped in to reassert control of jihad forces in Iraq after storyteller Abu Yahya recorded a glowing elegy that gave away none of the relief some must have felt that the uncontrollable Jordanian was gone. At al-Zawahiri's insistence, Abu Yahya had written to Zarqawi during the second half of 2005, repeatedly asking him to stop committing atrocities. But now he talked of him as one of "the lions of Islam," describing him as "an igniter of wars" and "the man who split the Romans' heads."[13] Soon, Zarqawi's successors would "[cleave] the darkness of the enemy like meteors." Abu Yahya rounded off with a Koranic flourish: "Let the worshippers of the cross, dynasties of treason, suckers of depravity and agents of the Jews . . . know that their swaggering won't be for long and that the reprisals of the mujahideen shall come like lightning bolts."

Charged with leading these reprisals was Zarqawi's old friend, the veteran Kurdish commander Abdul Hadi al-Iraqi, from the Shakai camp. Osama and al-Zawahiri had chosen him as the new commander of Al Qaeda in Iraq. Already known to the CIA and FBI, Abdul Hadi would have to take extreme care on the long journey from Waziristan to northern Iraq, and knowing he would probably be gone for a long time, he took along his wife and four young children. They would travel via Quetta, across Iran, and into Turkey using fake Iranian passports provided by the Quds Force.[14] From there, he planned to drop down across the border into Mosul. His appointment as leader of Al Qaeda in Iraq would be announced once he sent confirmation of his arrival.

While they waited for updates from Abdul Hadi, Al Qaeda Central refocused on Afghanistan, where Dr. al-Zawahiri had launched a new offensive against NATO forces. On June 6, an IED in Nangarhar Province had killed two U.S. soldiers. On June 15, a bus bomb killed ten workers at an American base, and on July 1, two British troops died when their compound was attacked with RPGs. Dozens more attacks were in the pipeline.

* * *

Summer 2006, Islamabad, Pakistan

Since 9/11, Pakistan had received almost $10 billion in U.S. government aid, most of it paid directly to the military. However, President Musharraf was at his lowest ebb.[15] Constantly pressured by the United States to do more to rein in the Taliban and Al Qaeda, he had committed seventy thousand soldiers to the Tribal Areas, where they were virtually under siege and unable to leave their bases for fear of attacks.

In March, the Taliban had taken over the telephone exchange and government buildings in Miram Shah and established in plain sight a recruitment office in Wana. By late July, barbers were being shot in Tank, wedding music was outlawed in Dera Ismail Khan, and even peaceable Swat, where Osama had once sheltered, was roiling, with clerics burning television sets. The military death toll was rising daily, with eight hundred troops lost so far.

Musharraf was struck by a fear that Pakistan was heading toward all-out civil war. Wondering if the Islamic Republic would disintegrate like Iraq had, he suspected that what was needed was a big policy idea that would eclipse troop deaths and the drone program while satisfying the demands of an American paymaster—and securing his own future office. The attacks came from all sides. Islamists portrayed him as an American puppet, Western-leaning secular Pakistanis characterized him as a tool of the jihad, and democrats criticized him for suspending the country's constitution.

He called Lieutenant General Ali Jan Aurakzai, the uncompromising former head of Western Command who had been in charge of Pakistan's force at Tora Bora.

Aurakzai, who was now the governor of North-West Frontier Province, had good connections inside the Federally Administered Tribal Areas (FATA), which translated in Washington simply as being a "Taliban sympathizer." Asked by Musharraf to come up with a "holistic approach" to solving the current crisis, he was clear. "There can be no *military* solution," he told the president, thinking of a vast area governed by ancient feudal rules, where the people were literally disenfranchised, having no voting rights, meaning they had no investment in the greater vision of Pakistan. "There has to be a *political* solution," the retired general stressed. "It's time for dialogue."[16]

In an elaborately staged spectacle, the ISI prompted influential warlord Sirajuddin Haqqani to issue a decree on June 26, 2006, that it was not

Taliban policy to fight the Pakistan Army, while Aurakzai began drawing up a formal agreement. The government pledged to put an end to airstrikes and ground operations. It also committed, woollily, to resolve the issue of foreign militants hiding in FATA, "while respecting local traditions and customs."

Musharraf wondered, privately, at this. These *customs* required the tribes of FATA to respect the code of hospitality, meaning that evicting a guest was tantamount to bringing dishonor on an entire community. Aurakzai tweaked the wording so that foreign fighters who had married into local families would be allowed to remain if they agreed to "live peacefully, respecting the law of the land and the agreement." That included high-value targets like Dr. Ayman al-Zawahiri. But hopefully no one outside Pakistan would spot this.

Crucially, the army pledged to withdraw from all FATA checkpoints and retreat to its bases in the main towns like Mir Ali, Razmak, and Miram Shah. For their part, the elders and tribal commanders agreed to cease their support for foreign militants and halt cross-border operations.

Robert Grenier, who had been sacked from the CIA in January for opposing the secret detention system and the use of interrogation practices he likened to torture, read about the accord while at home in Virginia. "It's a rout," he said to himself, referring to the Pakistan Army. "Now we know where *they* stand."[17]

Running so hard on ideology, the Bush administration, which had invaded Afghanistan, deposed Saddam in Iraq, and cold-shouldered Tehran, was not going to stand by and allow this to happen, Grenier thought.

September 5, 2006, Government Degree College,
Miram Shah, North Waziristan

A grand *jirga* of more than five hundred tribesmen gathered on the football pitch under a brightly colored *shamiana* (wedding tent).[18] Commanders, elders, and military officials exchanged bear hugs as *chapli* kebabs were dished out. Officeholders in the Taliban and Al Qaeda stayed away. Journalists were barred, too, although Syed Saleem Shahzad, bureau chief for *Asia Times Online*, who made it a policy to disregard the army's rules, had sneaked in, noticing how someone had slung Al Qaeda's black standard over the stadium's scoreboard.

"Fire and blood were in the air," he wrote in an article headlined THE KNIFE AT PAKISTAN'S THROAT. Unlike the Pakistani journalists who were happy to remain in Islamabad and Rawalpindi and print whatever they were told by the establishment, Shahzad was unafraid to meet Taliban representatives and publish reports that took in the views of Pakistan's jihad networks.

However, on this day Shahzad was worried, and he concluded that "momentous events loom over the Pakistani Tribal Areas of North and South Waziristan where the Taliban are in complete control."

General Aurakzai welcomed the peace agreement as "unprecedented in tribal history" and commissioned a celebratory painting of himself handing a ceremonial pen to tribal elders, although he did not attend the official ceremony. "They were armed to the teeth," he said, recalling their private meeting. "I showed them the pen and I said this fellow is stronger than the Kalashnikov you carry."[19]

Only a few signatures remained outstanding, including those of the extremist preachers Faqir Mohammad and Liaqat Ali, who had escaped the drone strike at Damadola back in January 2006 and were to be pardoned as part of the new deal.

General Aurakzai's representatives negotiated to meet with them separately on their home turf in Chinagai village, where the walls of Ali's seminary were adorned with the slogan "Come unto Jihad."[20]

Once agreement had been reached, Aurakzai and Musharraf planned to fly to Washington and seek President George W. Bush's approval of their peace plan.

September 6, 2006, White House, Washington, D.C.

Making friends with Al Qaeda and the Taliban was the last thing on Bush's mind. Since the previous November, when the *Washington Post* revealed that the CIA was holding Al Qaeda prisoners in secret jails around the world, his administration had been under huge pressure to explain the clandestine detention and interrogation program. While senior White House staff scrambled to find suitable responses, the CIA sought to place its so-called ghost detainees elsewhere.

The most dangerous and those who could not be released for fear of what they would say about their treatment would be transferred to Guantánamo

Bay. Others were sent back to their home countries against their will, including the former Al Qaeda commander and friend of Abu Zubaydah, Ibn Sheikh al-Libi, who was deported to Libya, where he would later die of wounds sustained in his prison cell.[21]

Incriminating evidence was destroyed on the orders of Jose Rodriguez, who in November 2004 had been promoted to deputy director of operations at the CIA. In November 2005, he was directly involved in the decision to destroy video recordings of Abu Zubaydah's torture that had been stored in a safe at the U.S. embassy in Bangkok.[22] Officially, Rodriguez claimed he had made the decision to protect agents in the field from terrorist reprisals. But, according to one unnamed official in a declassified e-mail, there was also deep concern about a public backlash. The official claimed that Rodriguez had said, "Heat from destroying is nothing compared to what it would be if the tapes ever got into [the] public domain." The e-mail continued: "He said that out of context, they would make us look terrible: it would be 'devastating' to us."[23]

On one of the destroyed tapes, an interrogator verbally threatened Abu Zubaydah: "If one child dies in America, and I find out you knew something about it, I will personally cut your mother's throat." In a subsequent investigation by the Department of Justice, the Inspector General found that there was also a twenty-one-hour gap in the taped record, which included two of Zubaydah's waterboarding sessions.[24] The tapes had been removed from the catalog of videotapes much earlier.[25]

On September 6, after a series of hastily arranged late night CIA charter flights into Cuba, the president was ready to front his new plan. Surrounded by the families of 9/11 victims, he announced that over the past forty-eight hours, fourteen captives whose names had become synonymous with the "war on terror" had been transferred into Defense Department custody in Guantánamo, where "military commissions" would try them.

They included Al Qaeda courier Abu Faraj al-Libi, Abu Zubaydah, 9/11 mastermind Khalid Shaikh Mohammad, and Mustafa Ahmad al-Hawsawi, who was suffering from "chronic hemorrhoids, an anal fissure, and symptomatic rectal prolapse" as a result of the anal-rehydration program.[26] Also there was Khalid's sidekick Ramzi bin al-Shibh; his nephew Ammar al-Balochi and his Karachi-based assistant, Walid bin Attash (Silver); and Abd al-Rahim al-Nashiri, who had been waterboarded and subjected to mock executions by CIA interrogators, one of whom had cocked an unloaded pistol against his head and revved up a power drill as if preparing to drill into him.[27]

After several minutes of applause, Bush defended the CIA program as "one of the most vital tools in our war against the terrorists," one that was "invaluable to America and to our allies."[28] To show how well it had worked, he revealed details about Abu Zubaydah's capture and subsequent treatment. "Zubaydah was severely wounded during the firefight that brought him into custody," he explained gravely to the families. "And he survived only because of the medical care arranged by the CIA." After he recovered, Zubaydah had been defiant and evasive, Bush continued. "He declared his hatred of America. During questioning, he at first disclosed what he thought was nominal information—and then stopped all cooperation."

Revising history, Bush said: "We knew that Zubaydah had more information that could save innocent lives . . . As his questioning proceeded, it became clear that he had received training on how to resist interrogation." Referring to the torture program first tested out in Thailand in 2002, the president continued: "And so the CIA used an alternative set of procedures. These procedures were designed to be safe, to comply with our laws, our Constitution, and our treaty obligations. The Department of Justice reviewed the authorized methods extensively and determined them to be lawful." There was no mention of the coffins and dog boxes, the waterboarding and mock executions, but Bush was able to confirm that "the procedures were tough, and they were safe, and lawful, and necessary."

Quashing accusations that the techniques were illegal and immoral, he said that the program had been subjected to "multiple legal reviews" and conducted by a "pool of experienced CIA officers." Those selected to conduct the most sensitive questioning had to complete more than 250 additional hours of specialized training before they were allowed to have contact with a captured terrorist, he said. "I want to be absolutely clear with our people, and the world," the president concluded. "The United States does not torture. It's against our laws, and it's against our values. I have not authorized it—and I will not authorize it."

Bush did not reveal that one of Abu Zubaydah's former torturers had recently visited him in his current location and apologized. "He said that he was sorry for what they had done to me," Zubaydah wrote in his diary. "That they had been acting without rules, giving me no rights, trying to get information from me in any way they could, and that he realized I did not know anything . . . He then began to cry."

Inside Guantánamo, tensions were running high even before the new arrivals landed. To date, more than a hundred inmates had attempted suicide, including one mass suicide attempt in August 2003 and three—two Saudis and a Yemeni—who had succeeded in June 2006.

When Zubaydah, Khalid, and the others reached the base, they did not join the 455 men housed in the main jail but were taken to a newly constructed facility on a wooded hillside above the base, accessed by a heavily guarded single-track road. Camp 7 was a fortress that had been designed to house the "worst of the worst," as Defense Secretary Donald Rumsfeld described them.

Inside their cells, the fourteen new detainees would be watched around the clock on monitors. Their guard—Task Force Platinum—had the authority to conduct cell searches and remove personal letters or legal papers at will.[29] Some of those held in Camp 7 would later complain of constant noise being pumped into their cells, which vibrated and frequently smelled of noxious fumes.[30]

For some of the new arrivals, including Abu Zubaydah, it was not their first visit to Cuba.[31] He and others had been secretly incarcerated there at a Defense Department facility known as Strawberry Fields in 2003. But in March 2004, as concern mounted that a pending Supreme Court decision over another prisoner might go against the Bush administration and force it to provide detainees with a counsel who would hear details of their treatment, the CIA had taken them back into custody. In Zubaydah's case, he was transported to a black site in Morocco.[32]

Now, after four years and five months in limbo, and seven different renditions, Zubaydah found himself on a long flight from an unofficial CIA detention facility he suspected was in Afghanistan, followed by a journey over water and then a bumpy ride in a hard-sprung military vehicle.[33] A black patch covered the eye that he had lost during his time in Thailand, although the precise circumstances of that loss remained "classified."[34]

He still had his writing pad, and he assessed his condition, writing that he had become prone to episodes of random fainting. "I would lose my writing capabilities as well, or I would mix up things when I wrote. However this condition would usually last for hours or few days until I would reach a point where I would totally lose my writing capabilities. That time it lasted for a long period of time. It lasted for over an entire year."

On paper, this transfer appeared to be a significant improvement in his prospects. But given that the detainees' new home was offshore and therefore also free from U.S. laws, they could still be held without proper access to lawyers and interrogated as the military saw fit.

Zubaydah documented the impact of his new interrogation sessions at Guantánamo. "The people in charge would tell me: '. . . you are probably bluffing us.' I started urinating on myself every time I fainted. I started to become afraid that, or feel like I am not even able to control my feces, so I decided not to drink or eat anything to preserve my dignity. They thought I was on a hunger strike and started inflicting on me the hunger strike punishment."

He poured it all into his diary. "Hani has experienced his entire time since capture as [one] experience. On the one hand, there are 5 things that are changed—better food, gym, etc. On the other hand, there are 5 things that are constant—hopelessness, etc. Sometimes thinking about his situation is distressing enough to trigger a seizure."[35]

September 21, 2006, Washington, D.C.

When Musharraf arrived in Washington, D.C., for his first state visit in more than a year, President Bush was basking in the glow of the Guantánamo transfers and in no mood for ratifying deals with Taliban and Al Qaeda representatives in Pakistan.

Musharraf had brought along General Aurakzai to explain the brilliance of their new Waziristan Accord.[36] He gave a sharp fifteen-minute presentation to Pentagon and CIA officials, only to be rounded on.

The Bush administration would do all that it could to undermine the deal, they were told.

Musharraf appeared on CBS, clearly unsettled, and hit out, randomly, wildly, regurgitating evidence of having been wronged, wherever he could find it, revealing how in September 2001 Richard Armitage, the deputy secretary of state, had threatened to bomb Pakistan "back to the Stone Age" if it did not toe the line. It had been, Musharraf said primly, "*a very rude remark*" and demonstrated how Washington infantilized Islamabad.

Every time he came to the United States he felt as if someone was going to tell him off, when the Islamic Republic had lost so much blood in the fight.[37]

What about the accord? Musharraf no longer appeared to be so sure. It was not about *peace*, he said, distractedly. It might be about *war*, he added. "This treaty is not to *deal* with the Taliban. It is actually to *fight* the Taliban. The misperception [is] in the media." There would be no more Al Qaeda or Taliban activity in FATA or across the border in Afghanistan, and no "Talibanization" of Pakistan, he declared.

When Musharraf met President Bush, he handed over a signed copy of his new memoir, *In the Line of Fire*, which had been ghostwritten by several subordinates, including his staff officer Brigadier Asim Bajwa, who had narrowly survived one of the assassination attempts on Musharraf's presidential convoy in 2003.[38]

"He holds the single most crucial job in the global war on terror," declared the jacket blurb. "He is transforming Pakistan from a third-world nation to a democratic, enlightened, prosperous state . . . the entire world depends upon him to succeed."

October 30, 2006, 5 A.M., Zai-ul Uloom Taleemal Qu'ran Seminary, Chinagai Village, Bajaur Agency, Federally Administered Tribal Areas, Pakistan

A brigade of cooks busied themselves, preparing to feed the one-hundred-plus guests due at nine A.M. "Curd and milk," Maulvi Liaqat Ali reminded them, as he strutted around in his black *pakul* and woolen waistcoat. "Make sure not to burn the bread."

"Line up," Faqir Mohammad instructed the students as orderly boys knelt to perform dawn prayers. They had just returned from Eid al-Fitr holidays, and they were excited that their seminary was hosting a historic *jirga* that would write them into the history books.

Daylight shimmered on the horizon when the missiles slammed into the madrassa. Afterward, there was silence for a moment, until the survivors began to scream. As the smoke cleared, villagers who charged over recovered shrapnel from American projectiles that they laid out beside eighty-one corpses, sixty-nine of them under the age of seventeen. Among the dead was Liaqat Ali.

By midmorning, an armed militia of thousands massed, men who had come to celebrate but now vowed to wage war. Two days after the funerals, preacher Faqir Mohammad resurfaced at a rally and denounced the governments of Pakistan and America, before praising Dr. al-Zawahiri and Osama. He was cheered on by a gun-toting mob.[39]

In Islamabad, grim-faced government officials who no longer knew if they were making peace or going on the offensive hunkered down. On November 8, two men wrapped in shawls talked their way into the Punjab Regiment Centre at Dargai and blew themselves up, killing forty-two trainee soldiers. "Body parts, hats, shoes, and pieces of military uniforms were scattered all around the parade grounds," reported an eyewitness.

Days later, General Aurakzai's convoy was attacked at Wana, with RPGs clattering off his roof. Shaken but unhurt, Aurakzai emerged to denounce the Chinagai attack, and he hit out at Musharraf, too. It had been a U.S. drone strike, he fumed, designed "to stop the agreement from going ahead." Aurakzai recalled: "We went overboard in supporting the Americans. We crossed the red line when we should have concentrated on our national interests."[40] The painting on his study wall showing him at the signing ceremony with tribal elders in Khyber Agency now filled him with bitterness every time he passed it. "Maybe the gun is more powerful than the pen after all," he muttered.

Musharraf publicly distanced himself from the massacre, but privately ISI chief Ashfaq Parvez Kayani was ordered to tighten up procedures for advance vetting of U.S. raids and come up with a plan to extricate Pakistan from the drone program altogether, without losing Washington's largesse.[41]

At the same time the CIA debated how to expand its drone program and focus on the more senior targets, such as Osama and Dr. al-Zawahiri, concluding that the only certain way to reach them was to groom a traitor.

The agency wanted the impossible. They needed a person in the room, an individual with a high-ranking jihadist pedigree who was accessible, cooperative, and had the will to turn on Al Qaeda. It would be an extraordinarily perilous mission, as the outfit was already on its guard. Al Qaeda Central now suspected everyone. "Be especially wary of newly-joined members," said one intercepted communication.[42] "No matter their status or capabilities, they must not be placed in leadership positions, as there are many dangers lurking. Victory lies ahead, so one must remain on the lookout for penetrations and be extremely wary."

News had just reached Dr. al-Zawahiri that Abdul Hadi al-Iraqi, the Shakai commander and his chosen successor to lead Al Qaeda in Iraq, had been arrested in the Turkish city of Gaziantep as he prepared to cross into Syria. After keeping him for two weeks in detention, along with his wife and children, the Turkish authorities deported the family to Afghanistan and into the arms of the CIA, which took them to Bagram.[43] Al Qaeda in Iraq was once again leaderless as Dr. al-Zawahiri fretted about who else was qualified to fill the void.

* * *

November 2006, ISI Safe House, Islamabad

Al Qaeda courier Hassan Ghul, a man who Bush had once called a killer, and whose capture had meant "one less enemy we have to worry about," had been transferred back into ISI custody with instructions that he should be set loose in the Tribal Areas to search for Osama bin Laden.

Confirmation of this came from Rangzieb Ahmed, a British Pakistani from Manchester who was arrested by the ISI in Haripur around the same time and met Ghul in November 2006, when they were held in adjoining cells.[44] "I talked to him when no guards were around and he told me that the CIA had kept him in a secret location for two years," said Ahmed.

He described how he and Ghul were taken for questioning at an interrogation center, where the treatment worsened by the day, culminating in his fingernails being pulled out with pliers.[45] Both, Ahmed claimed, were regularly beaten and threatened, while Western intelligence agents watched.

Ghul's situation deteriorated, the prisoner becoming rambling and incoherent. However, the British prisoner's situation improved after a smartly dressed ISI officer came one day and asked him to fill out some forms stamped Security Act of Pakistan 1952. "He congratulated me and said I was now a legal detainee and that the government of Pakistan knew about me," Ahmed said. "He stated that there were many people who did not even have that recognition."

They included Ghul. One day in January 2007, Ahmed returned from an interrogation session to find him gone from the safe house. A year later Ahmed was deported back to the United Kingdom, where he would be convicted of terrorism offenses, never to see Ghul again.[46]

Shortly after Ahmed's departure, the ISI appeared to put the CIA's plan into action. They told Ghul they would release him too, but only if he became their asset and reported back regularly through two cut-outs (intermediaries) in Waziristan called Malik and Khalid who answered to an ISI major in the Peshawar station.

Apparently Ghul agreed, the ISI reported back to the CIA, and a pseudonym was created for him: Asset Imtiaz. He had the perfect cover story. An Al Qaeda administrator and courier with several years' experience, he had served time with Khalid Shaikh Mohammad and Abu Faraj—and could prove it. He had been told to use the stories of his capture and torture at the hands of the Americans and the ISI to leverage a good position for himself.

He was to claim that he had escaped custody, like Abu Yahya, who had legged it out of Bagram and become a jihad media sensation.

Once he had been readmitted and his freedom had been celebrated, he should ask to move to a role that would bring him closer to Dr. al-Zawahiri or even Osama. There was a warning. If Asset Imtiaz cut ties with his handler or otherwise deceived the ISI, his family would pay the price. Past masters at turning the screw, the ISI advised that his sister, Nabila, his wife, and his children, as well as other family members who lived in Pakistan, were under constant surveillance and could be picked up in minutes.

In May 2007, Asset Imtiaz was driven to Karachi Company, a bus depot on the outskirts of Islamabad, and dropped off with a bag of cash, a secondhand Nokia brick, and a fake national identity card. He could not carry any kind of tracking or communication device for fear of being uncovered as a spy.

From now on he would use coded e-mails sent from cyber cafés dotted around the main towns of FATA. "I have reached Miram Shah," he wrote in his first message. "I am being vetted so you may not hear from me for some time."

June 2007, Abbottabad, Pakistan

The CIA was reviewing what it had learned over the years about Al Qaeda couriers. After interrogating more than a dozen suspects, they decided that the absence of new and building profiles on Abu Ahmad al-Kuwaiti—a name they believed to be reliable—was indicative and might be just as significant as the information itself.

A CIA targeting study dated May 20, 2007, laid it out: "KSM described Abu Ahmad as a relatively minor figure and Abu Faraj al-Libi denied all knowledge of Abu Ahmad. Station assesses that KSM and Abu Faraj's reporting is not credible on this topic and their attempts to downplay Abu Ahmad's importance or deny knowledge of Abu Ahmad are likely part of an effort to withhold information on [Osama] or his close associates. These denials, combined with reporting from other detainees indicating that Abu Ahmad worked closely with KSM and Abu Faraj add to our belief that Abu Ahmad is a High Value Target courier or facilitator."

The *kunya* was likely right as was information as to his role and seniority, but how, the study asked, could the authorities find the individual himself?

Out in the field, the man they were discussing was exhausted.

Ibrahim had new letters to deliver to Atiyah in Waziristan, Osama's responses to massing critics in the Arabian Peninsula, who were oblivious to Al Qaeda Central's thwarted attempt to appoint Abdul Hadi al-Iraqi as successor to dead Zarqawi and railed about his legacy of violence in Iraq.

A writer who called himself "the one who loves you in Riyadh" accused Osama of making "colossal strategic errors" and causing a crisis in the movement by supporting Al Qaeda in Iraq. "Being besieged and distant is not the best environment for thinking and for forming the right opinion and decision. In this case, one should seek the opinion of brothers who are outside of the hardship."[47] Did Osama only care to protect himself and "let the entire world burn down?"

Supporting Zarqawi's bloodthirsty reign of terror in Iraq had "turned people against you, especially scholars and intellectuals." For supporters it was not enough that Zarqawi was dead; they wanted to know why he had been supported while he was alive and how the terror he had fomented would be stilled.

The only way out of this crisis was for the Sheikh to conduct an audit. "It is not appropriate for an honest person to think that he is always right and that those who disagree with him are ignorant," the writer continued, identifying the same weakness in Osama that the Mauritanian and many others had zeroed in on.

The writer finished with an ultimatum: "Focus on the head of the snake [America] in its home or in areas that it occupies, such as Afghanistan and Iraq." There could be no more repeats of the wedding day massacre in Jordan. No more needless killings of Shia in Iraq or elsewhere.

What "the one who loves you in Riyadh" did not appreciate was the crisis propagated by Abdul Hadi al-Iraqi's arrest. With no strong leader representing Al Qaeda's interests in Iraq, a bloodthirsty and ambitious mujahid called Abu Ayyub al-Masri, also known as Abu Hamza, an old comrade of al-Zawahiri from the Egyptian Islamic Jihad days, had seized control of the group and was taking it down a dangerous new route.

During the 1990s, Abu Ayyub had made bombs at Al Qaeda training camps. After meeting Zarqawi in Afghanistan, he had accompanied him to Iraq, where he was put in charge of recruiting suicide bombers. Abu Ayyub shared Zarqawi's obsession with "end of days" revelations and Naeed bin Hamed's *Book of Tribulations*. Since taking control in Iraq, he had declared that the Mahdi, the Muslim savior, would soon come to alleviate Iraq's suffering.

Surrounded by the horror of a war that was costing almost a thousand Iraqi lives a month, hundreds of new supporters were drawn by Abu Ayyub's arguments that doomsday was approaching, and in October 2006 he formally took over the group and renamed it Islamic State of Iraq.[48] Sometimes he referred to it as Islamic State *in* Iraq, suggesting that it was a caliphate. However, as an Egyptian he knew he would always be regarded as a foreigner and so while he took the role of "minister of war," he had cast around for an Iraqi front man, settling on Abu Umar al-Baghdadi, who grandly claimed descent from one of the Prophet's grandsons although he was in reality nothing more than a former police officer who had been dismissed from the force for his ultraconservative views. Now he was proclaimed as the "commander of the faithful," a title traditionally held by the Taliban's Mullah Omar.[49]

From the letters flowing to Osama it was clear that Al Qaeda supporters around the world were confused. Was the new Islamic State in Iraq part of Al Qaeda or something different? Was it a caliphate or an emirate? Were Osama bin Laden's and Dr. Ayman al-Zawahiri's oaths of allegiance to Mullah Omar now redundant, given that Abu Umar was the new commander of the faithful? "How can we pledge allegiance to Abu Umar al-Baghdadi when we have pledged allegiance to Mullah Omar?" asked one. Was it Islamic State *of* Iraq or *in* Iraq? Was a former policeman who had made ends meet before the U.S. war by repairing televisions and dishwashers really now more important than Osama bin Laden? "What do we do with the pledge of allegiance to Shaykh Osama?"

Al-Zawahiri and Osama wrote a complaint to Abu Umar, and Islamic State's shadow leader Abu Ayyub wrote back, telling them that Abu Umar had pledged an oath to Al Qaeda Central in front of the jihad brothers in Iraq but that they did not want to announce it publicly "due to some political considerations."[50]

Abu Ayyub then addressed the Iraqi people, predicting that the Mahdi would come within the year. A caliphate needed to be in place to help the Mahdi fight the final battle on Iraqi soil, he said.

Because the incipient Islamic State needed to beef up its membership, many people were allowed to join without proper vetting and the ranks were soon filled with former Saddam Hussein loyalists and intelligence cadres. Rivals were kidnapped, tortured, and killed, as scores were settled that had nothing to do with the outfit. The putative figurehead, Abu Umar was kept out of the loop and "didn't know what [was] going on around him."[51] If anyone doubted the new group's virility, insurgent attacks were soon averaging more than ninety a day. But most of the casualties were Muslims.

Those outside the group could see only chaos. The situation in Iraq was "escalating," one letter writer warned Osama, talking of "imminent catastrophe" and advising: "This is your last chance to remedy the jihad breakdown that is about to take place in Iraq."[52] Osama should take back control of the Iraq situation "through a speech that you air via the satellite TV stations" or be damned. "You should be aware that on the day of reckoning, you are responsible in front of God for blessing the work done by Al Qaeda in Iraq without disavowing the scandals they are committing in your name."[53] Abu Ayyub and his madness had to be stopped.

Before Osama had a chance to respond, Abu Umar, the shadow commander of the faithful in Iraq, announced the complete dissolution of Al Qaeda in Iraq. All its fighters would be reassigned to Islamic State of Iraq or punished. "Al Qaeda is but one of the groups in Islamic State," he declared. His media department followed up: "The brothers previously in the organization of Al-Qaeda in Iraq became part of the 'army of the State.'"[54] Soon after, Abu Umar emerged to decry the "lies" circulating about the group's brutality and to lay down nineteen new laws that Islamic State's subjects would have to abide by. Those who refused would be crucified, beheaded, stoned, or flogged.[55]

The apocalyptic messages undermined Osama's authority, but he could not distance himself completely as Al Qaeda needed to keep a hand in the Iraq game. However, after reports filtered back to Abbottabad that an Al Qaeda fighter who had flipped to Islamic State had beheaded an eight-year-old girl, he asked al-Zawahiri to address the issue through As Sahab.[56] After weeks of to-ing and fro-ing, al-Zawahiri decided to announce his official support, saying, "It is a legitimate emirate established on a legitimate and sound method."[57]

Soon after, a mujahid who until recently had acted as chief justice to Islamic State arrived in Damadola and warned al-Zawahiri he had made a serious mistake. They could not contain the Iraqi storm. It was not an emirate but a rolling war crimes machine. Islamic State was "approaching the abyss." More than 2,500 civilians were being killed by the month, many of these executions posted online like serial snuff films. Al Qaeda's brand was bloodied and battered.[58]

Frustrated at his inability to influence Islamic State in Iraq, Osama turned his attention to something he could control, his wives and children. The compound had been overhauled as a result of the 2005 earthquake; a third floor had been added with a terrace protected by a huge seven-foot-high privacy wall. The bedroom on the right facing the balcony was Osama's private domain, shared most nights with Amal, while Seham and her children occupied the bedroom opposite. The younger children slept downstairs in bedrooms opposite the vast "media center," which now took up three rooms and was filled with neat desks, computers, and tidily filed boxes filled with thumb drives, videotapes, and audiotapes—a situation room waiting for a war.[59]

Much of the time Osama complained of feeling ill, describing his symptoms as dehydration and a lack of energy. He spent hours sitting crosslegged on the floor wrapped in a woolen shawl and watching reruns of the 9/11 footage, saved programs about the ongoing search for him, and daily news on Al Jazeera and BBC World.

During the day, Amal and Seham stayed out of his way and kept the children busy. Seham had set up a classroom, while Amal cooked with Seham and Osama's daughters Sumaiya and Miriam. Ibrahim, fearful of discovery, had banned the women from throwing anything away, so the common areas were filled up with boxes of broken shoes, old clothes, and disused kitchen and electrical equipment. Because none of the many members of the household ever went out and all meals had to be prepared on two ring burners, the kitchens stank and were filthy.[60]

On Osama's suggestion, a builder had cut off the far end of the main garden and erected a small, box-like, single-story annex inside a tight triangular courtyard. This was where Ibrahim now lived with Maryam, their children sleeping on cots lined up along the walls, the other half of the building taken up by a kitchen. To complete the separation between the two households, a lockable gate was fitted between the two courtyards to which only Ibrahim had the keys. Abrar and Bushra still lived on the ground floor of the main house.

Bushra and Maryam were the main security problem, Osama warned, as they frequently left the compound and used their cell phones. He worried about them being tracked, their calls being eavesdropped on, or what they might say should they be arrested. Although he tried to keep them inside as much as he could, Ibrahim was unable to stop them from going out to meet other family members, shopping or visiting the pharmacist.

When it came to managing his own family, the years of exile had not softened Osama. Amal's children were now old enough to question their confines and frequently asked to go outside to meet their "cousins," who they watched playing with balls and waterpistols.[61] Osama would not budge, forcing his children into long hours of religious study, rapping their knuckles with a cane if they looked out of a window or made too much noise. Only the youngest were allowed outside with him when he made his daily perambulations under the gazebo Khalid had erected, Osama walking with his wide-brimmed hat shielding his face. Seham, Sumaiya, and Miriam only went out if there was a medical emergency, in which case they were driven in a red Suzuki van, their faces obscured by *dupattas*.

Most frustrated was Khalid. Eighteen years old but still a virgin, he was ensconced all day with his father, typing up his speeches and filing papers. The boy had grown up hoping to become a mujahid but now he was a secretary. The only time he got to go outside was to attend to the family cow or work in his vegetable garden, an enclosed and muddy patch of land to the west of the main house.

Respite came in June 2007 when his sister Khadija wrote. "I want to relay to you good news."[62] The family of the martyred Egyptian had finally agreed to him marrying their pretty daughter Karima. "They do not object," she said. The reason for the long delay was that Karima had been busy memorizing the Koran. Now that she had finished, she had one question to ask her future husband. Would she be expected to move to Abbottabad or would he go to Waziristan where she was? "If the marriage happens, God willing, come here for jihad?"

Suspecting that her brother would prefer the second option, Khadija continued: "Pray to Allah you join us soon."

Karima was to be Khalid's ticket out of Abbottabad.

July 2007, Lal Masjid (Red Mosque), Islamabad

Nothing was going right for Pervez Musharraf. His hoped-for grand policy idea, the Waziristan Accord, had been shot down by America in Chinagai, and the ISI had still not wrested control of the drone program from the CIA. To democrats the president remained a bugbear. For Islamists he was a traitor, and the clerical brothers who ran the Lal Masjid in Islamabad, preachers who had single-handedly demoralized the army by calling for the corpses of soldiers killed in Waziristan to be concealed, now upped the rhetoric. They drummed up a following that looked and acted like the Taliban, and their prayers and catcalls rang out across the capital.

Maulana Abdul Aziz Ghazi and his brother Maulana Abdul Rashid Ghazi began advocating for imposition of *sharia* law across Pakistan, sending out groups of male and female students who resembled the Taliban's "Vice and Virtue" brigades. Armed with sticks and knives, they attacked massage parlors, kidnapped Chinese prostitutes, and burned down restaurants accused of serving alcohol. Shops selling CDs were ransacked.

At the beginning of July, Musharraf snapped. Accusing the mosque authorities of harboring militants connected to the London transport bombings of July 2005—an attack said to have been inspired but not commissioned by Al Qaeda—the police raided the mosque, only to be beaten back on live television by baton-wielding female students. On July 3, a fresh battle erupted, as police tried to lay barbed wire around the mosque's precinct. In firing that started from inside the mosque, nine people were killed and 150 injured before the students bolted the doors.

As worried parents gathered by the roadside, the ISI cut off all live TV and brought in Osama's ally Fazlur Rehman Khalil of Harkat-ul-Mujahideen to negotiate a cease-fire. But Khalil would not, or could not, bring the two sides together, leaving Musharraf to call up his old unit, the Special Services Group (SSG)—in which Ilyas Kashmiri had once served.

The interior of the mosque had been booby-trapped, and the SSG commander was killed. Charging down into the basement, his men encountered militants armed with machine guns, shoulder-fired rockets, and Molotov cocktails.

The battle raged on for eight days until July 11, when officials reported that the bullet-ridden Lal Masjid complex had been cleared and that suicide belts, night-vision goggles, and antitank and antipersonnel land mines had been recovered, along with the bodies of dozens of foreign militants allied to Al Qaeda itself. How they or their arms cache had reached the capital unseen was never answered, and how many had actually died was never verified.

Official figures put the dead at one hundred, including Maulana Abdul Rashid Ghazi, his mother, and his nephew. The brother, Maulana Abdul Aziz Ghazi, was caught trying to flee the complex dressed in an oversized *burqa*, just as other Al Qaeda members had done to escape the post-9/11 bombardment of Afghanistan and prison in Iran.

Musharraf did not crow, as he knew that the sight of soldiers smashing up a mosque was incendiary news in Pakistan. But Dr. al-Zawahiri capitalized, issuing a video calling for a holy war against Pakistan's security forces. "Muslims of Pakistan: your salvation is only through Jihad," he declared, dressed in white like a saint against one of Azzam the American's green-screen backgrounds. "Rigged elections will not save you, politics will not save you, and bargaining, bootlicking, negotiations with the criminals, and political maneuvers will not save you." Turning his attention to the president, he accused him of having committed "a dirty, despicable crime" in killing Abdul Rashid Ghazi. "Musharraf and his hunting dogs have rubbed your honor in the dirt in the service of the Crusaders and the Jews."

Rumors spread that Dr. al-Zawahiri felt so emboldened he visited Islamabad to see the wrecked mosque for himself.[63] His battalions were soon raging across Pakistan. By the end of the month the country had been rocked by seven huge suicide-bomb blasts, most of them directed against military and police targets. More than 150 officers died in attacks at police training centers in Dera Ismail Khan and Hangu. A military convoy was confronted in Miram Shah. Lawyers in Islamabad were bombed and shot at, while a mosque used by soldiers in Kohat collapsed after a colossal blast, as Al Qaeda fought on three fronts: Afghanistan, Iraq, and Pakistan.

August 2007, Block 300, Quds Force Training Facility, Tehran, Iran

The car had been fitted with opaque glass windows and drove them out of Block 100 and on a circuitous tour of Tehran, before pulling back into the training facility and eventually stopping at a new gate marked Block 300. The charade had fooled no one, including the other inmates of Block 100, who soon realized the Mauritanian had left them, having bargained to get himself out.[64]

As they entered Block 300, the family was stopped in its tracks by a huge crowd of smiling faces—women and young children on one side, men and teenage boys on the other. "The joy was overwhelming," the Mauritanian said. "Happiness, excitement, and pleasure beyond description."

He caught sight of Osama's sons Saad, Mohammed, Othman, Hamzah, and Ladin. In the six years since he had last seen them they had all grown up. Saad, now twenty-eight, was the father of three children, a boy named

Osama and two little girls, Asma and Duha. He was anxious to inform the Mauritanian that a few months back his wife had had another son who had died because the Iranians had refused a hospital visit. In tears, Saad had held the dead baby up to the security cameras so the administrators could see the consequences of their actions.[65]

Mahfouz noted that Othman, twenty-three, most resembled his father in appearance and stature. He wore a thick beard and had a reputation for punching walls. He had taken a second wife, Sofia, one of Saif al-Adel's daughters, and was standing beside his other father-in-law, Mohammed al-Islambouli, who had remained with Osama's family throughout their Iranian sojourn. Islambouli told the Mauritanian that his wife had died for want of medical treatment while they had been held in Block 200, cut off from the world.

Mohammed bin Laden, who the Mauritanian had not seen since his wedding day in January 2001, was now twenty-two and the father of two little boys. He appeared to be the sanest of Najwa's sons. He was quiet, polite, and well-read. His shy wife, Khadija, stood at the back of the crowd.

The biggest surprise was Hamzah. The last time they had met in Afghanistan in November 2001 he had been a child. Now he was a strapping eighteen-year-old with a beard, married to a daughter of Abu Mohammed al-Masri, Al Qaeda's Egyptian head of training and the builder of the bombs that had been used to attack the U.S. embassies in East Africa. Hamzah had already fathered a boy, yet another Osama.

Ladin, once the baby of the family, stood alone, glaring. Aged fifteen and already six feet tall, he spent most of his time in bed. Had the Mauritanian heard from his mother, Najwa? he asked gruffly. Mahfouz shook his head. As far as she was concerned, he said, they were all dead, killed during the U.S. invasion of Afghanistan after 9/11.

An older man wearing steel-rimmed glasses and a cotton skullcap stepped forward and took the Mauritanian's hand. Suddenly Mahfouz was transported back to Tarnak Qila and the day of Mohammed's wedding, when, deeply troubled over the brewing Planes Operation, he had sought out this man to shoulder the burden: Saif al-Adel. Al Qaeda's military supremo and number twenty on the FBI's original Most Wanted Terrorist list was more gaunt and aged, but the Mauritanian could see that he still burned with ambition.

Al Qaeda's chief of foreign relations, Abu al-Khayr al-Masri, who had known Osama and al-Zawahiri longer than anyone, was also here, as was Sulaiman Abu Ghaith, who had been thrust into the limelight in the days after 9/11. He had never managed to cut free, and as a result had had no contact with his wife and seven children in four years.

From what the Mauritanian could see, the entirety of Al Qaeda's military council minus Dr. al-Zawahiri and Sheikh Saeed al-Masri was here in Block 300.[66]

On the far side of the courtyard, crying women, their *niqabs* pulled askew in the rush to kiss each other, surrounded the Mauritanian's wife and daughters. Matriarch Khairiah bin Laden greeted them stoically. The bad food and unsanitary accommodations had taken their toll on her. She now walked with a cane, assisted by Najwa's daughter Fatima, who was desperate for news of her siblings. Where was her half sister Khadija? How many children did she have now? Was she still in Waziristan? Had anyone heard from Fatima's husband, who had vanished at the Pakistan border in 2001?

Osama's beautiful daughter Iman, now sixteen, listened in. She was eager for news of her "twin," Seham's daughter Miriam. They had been born on the same day in the same hospital in Jeddah. Although they had smuggled out letters, no one in Block 300 had received anything back from Pakistan.

The Al Qaeda brothers laid carpets out in the yard to create an impromptu *majlis*, while Osama's daughters moved mattresses and rearranged furniture inside to make space for the Mauritanian's family.[67]

Saif al-Adel began to recount. After his arrest in Shiraz in April 2003, he, Sulaiman Abu Ghaith, Abu Mohammed, and Abu al-Khayr had been incarcerated in "secret underground prisons" run by the intelligence ministry. They had been allowed to maintain some communication.

After twenty months, Saad and Hamzah, who had been separated from the women on the day that they were discovered in Zabol, had joined them. Khairiah, Fatima and Iman, and Saad's wife and children had spent two years in detention at a large housing complex in Tehran that the Iranian guards referred to as Block Six.[68]

Mohammed and Othman, who had accompanied their father at Tora Bora and Kunar, explained how they had joined their brothers and the military council members at the underground prison after entering Iran in late 2003.

In December 2005, all of them had been brought to the Quds Force training center, where initially they were penned inside Block 200. They had watched the Mauritanian and his family "playing ball, strolling in the garden, and enjoying the sun." But the windows were soundproofed and sealed, so even though they had banged repeatedly it became obvious that they could not be heard.

The conditions had been bleak. To see one's friends and not be able to talk to them had been frustrating, Saif said. At one stage, the families had found listening devices in their bedrooms, which horrified those who were married. After months of complaining, in June 2006 they had been shifted to Block 300.

The Mauritanian felt ashamed that he had not pressed harder and earlier to chase down rumors of other prisoners. How had he missed them waving behind the thick glass? Osama's caravan and the army council had been under his nose all this time.

He entered his new quarters on the ground floor and saw that his family had been allocated two rooms on either side of a corridor, the last free space in the compound. Sensing the Mauritanian's discomfort—he had two unmarried daughters—Hamzah bin Laden offered to switch apartments as his was far larger.

"He had seen since he was a child the strong brotherly relationship that I had with his father," reported the delighted Mauritanian. When he eventually got to bed, his mind wandered. He began to think about Osama's daughter Fatima. She must be twenty, he thought, and she had lived without husband for six years. Although his death had never been confirmed, she needed to remarry.[69]

After the residents of Block 300 appointed the Mauritanian as their official spokesman, an Iranian emissary arrived to meet him. The visitor explained that the welfare of Osama's family was the personal responsibility of General Qassem Suleimani, the commander of Quds Force. Osama's sons, who had met him a few times already and called him "Hajji Qassem," said he was "very dynamic and positive." They had much in common, Hajji Qassem had told them, given that the United States had designated him as a terrorist two years previously and the United Nations had sanctioned him for supporting terrorist activity.

Now the emissary assured the Mauritanian that their mission was to "correct all the mistakes made over the past years."

The compound's residents listened with interest to news that the United States and Europe were ganging up on Iran with President Bush talking of a third world war, while the French foreign minister warned: "We have to prepare for the worst."

President Ahmadinejad, seen by Western powers as a dangerous demagogue and a holocaust denier, compounded the country's building sense of panic with ever more antagonistic outbursts. The Quds Force was flexing its muscles and Al Qaeda was becoming useful once more, the Mauritanian calculated, either as collateral or as a bargaining tool.

Qassem assigned two senior Quds Force officers to Block 300. Their job was to provide "the guests with whatever they needed." Furniture, kitchen appliances, new fridges, and wide-screen televisions arrived. The Mauritanian was given an "unlimited budget" with which to furnish a new religious library. To show they were serious, the Iranians announced day trips for the families. Gone were the opaque windows, blindfolds, and circuitous car journeys. Now they were taken aboard luxury coaches to visit "green orchards, flowing rivers, high mountains, beautiful parks and zoos"—even the most famous landmarks in Tehran, where they mingled with American tourists. When Saad tried to practice his rudimentary English, his younger brothers had to physically restrain him.

Then came gym memberships. Once a week, the families were taken to a sports complex in Elahieh, where Saif al-Adel, who had a $5 million bounty on his head, swam in lanes alongside foreign diplomats.

General Suleimani also arranged shopping trips for the Al Qaeda women, who took along their younger children and walked around the markets and bazaars freely.[70]

The Mauritanian could not get over the strange idea of shopping, something he had never really done before. "We had an unnatural lust to buy, just buying to buy, rather than needing what we bought." Mostly it was toys for the children, he said, noting that it was "as if we wanted to compensate them for the loss of freedom."

A clinic was installed at the compound fitted with imported diagnostic equipment and a specialist dentistry section staffed by foreign-trained doctors. Khairiah was in there almost weekly. Anyone needing more advanced treatment was taken to a prestigious private hospital in Tehran for Iran's religious and political leaders.

Where, the Mauritanian wondered, was all this largesse leading? Being courted by the Quds Force would not preclude Hajji Qassem from giving them up if the price was right. Staying one step ahead of this Machiavellian officer bothered him daily and he was not privy to the regular discussions Qassem had with Saif.

Mahfouz tested the waters, asking for access to the Internet. When Qassem's agents agreed, he was stunned. "After all those years of harassment and deprivation I had not believed I will be allowed to sit in front of a computer ever again," he said. But a few days later, he was duly escorted out of the complex to a nearby cyber café, where "the staff turned on a computer and handed me the mouse."

He sat there, transfixed by it. What should he search for first? He felt sick with excitement and also fearful of what he might discover.[71]

To begin, he followed the escort's rules, reading "public sites" and not sending e-mails. He was also barred from social media, which his escort pointed out was restricted for Iranians, too. However, when the escort turned away to check his own messages, the Mauritanian took his chance, accessing forums and news sites that reported on Al Qaeda, reading, incredulously, behind-the-scenes material about the demise of Zarqawi and about Dr. al-Zawahiri's support for Islamic State of Iraq, which had officially formed in October 2006 under the leadership of Abu Umar al-Baghdadi, with the hated Abu Ayyub, made his deputy.

There was too much to take in: mounting attacks against the security establishment in Pakistan and an Al Qaeda–backed Taliban offensive in Afghanistan. He would share it all with the rest of the compound. Was Al Qaeda making a mistake in backing the Islamic State? he pondered. Or was jihad marching toward its final goal?

A group of senior Iranian officials arrived at Block 300 to discuss Al Qaeda's "future cooperation." The meeting took place at the Mauritanian's apartment, with the discussion focusing on "the issue of the war in Iraq"—especially the fact that a movement endorsed by Osama was conducting a sectarian war against Shias.

Tehran was "extremely involved in the support of the government regime in Baghdad," they continued, and was funding militias battling Abu Umar al-Baghdadi's forces. They were on opposing sides of the war from Al Qaeda. When one of al-Zawahiri's recent speeches came up for discussion, the Iranians made no effort to disguise their displeasure. The conversation turned to Al Qaeda's "mistaken" endorsement of Abu Musab al-Zarqawi's successor. Could Al Qaeda be brought around?

The Mauritanian turned the tables on his visitors. When he had been at Evin prison, Zarqawi had also been jailed there before the Iranians arranged "special" passports for him and his fighters "to slip into Iraq without a visa."

He knew that the Quds Force had also supplied Zarqawi with weapons, false documents, even money. If Osama was responsible for financing the butchers of Baghdad, so was Tehran. Both of them had been wrong, he ventured. There was no shared vision between Osama and the Jordanian. While Zarqawi had considered it legitimate to slaughter Shias, this was "not the opinion of Al Qaeda and Sheikh Osama," he said.

The officials nodded. One of them, Hajji Ali Akbari, stood up. He wanted to invite the Mauritanian on "an entertaining cultural visit" to Qom, the exclusively Shia city, and the next day he was shown around the shrine of Fatima and a huge new mosque President Ahmadinejad was building around a sacred well. They went shopping, again, the Mauritanian buying religious books, Arab clothes and perfume for the women, sweets for the children. On the way back to Tehran, they talked about the schism between Shias and Sunnis and how Iran and Al Qaeda could help each other.

The meetings would continue, some argumentative, others agreeable, and when Ramadan came in October, the *shura* and Osama's sons invited Qassem's officials to break their fast with them, with Sulaiman Abu Ghaith supervising preparations for the feast. "We put our best carpets and mattresses in the yard and laid the tables. We prepared different types of food, beverages, and fruit," the Mauritanian recalled.

The Iranians responded by taking the Al Qaeda *shura* on coaches for an *iftar* meal at a five-star restaurant. A few days later, General Qassem Suleimani turned up in person to celebrate Eid with Osama's sons, sitting down with the heirs of the world's most infamous terrorist to break the fast.

The following Friday, the general sent a car for Osama's sons that drove them toward Tehran University, where the crowds became so dense they had to stop and walk. They were greeted by a senior Quds Force official and two clerics who guided them through security gates and around the back of a prayer hall into a small waiting area carpeted with prayer mats, a small TV set fixed on the wall.[72]

A roar rose up outside, and the TV flickered on, focusing on rows of devotees, scholars, clerics, and officials standing for the supreme leader, Ayatollah Ali Khamenei, who was about to speak. The sons of Osama bin Laden, children of a rabidly anti-Shia terrorist movement, were in a private prayer room behind the Ayatollah's pulpit, his personal guests at Friday prayers that were being broadcast around the world on Press TV. A man gestured from the door, and the nervous young men got to their feet, transfixed by the screen and the rising roar, as the chanting began: "*Marg Bar Amrika*—Death to

America." Back in Block 300, Saif received a message from the Syrian courier Yasin: Al Qaeda's Iran pipeline, sending funds and recruits from the Middle East to Pakistan, was up and running once more.

December 2007, Bilal Town, Abbottabad

Osama woke his wife Seham with a new letter delivered by Ibrahim. It concerned family matters, and as he was busy with Khalid in the media center, he asked her to read it first.

Osama dictated as Khalid wrote. He wanted to promote his favorite deputy, Atiyah, to be Al Qaeda's general manager and spokesman. Atiyah should take immediate charge of "the preaching, provoking jihad, and supporting the mujahideen in hot spots such as Palestine, Iraq, Afghanistan, Somalia, and the Islamic Maghreb."

He needed to issue statements that "support[ed] the Islamic State of Iraq and defend[ed] it from any disproval and rumors."[73] He also needed to settle a score.

Osama wanted to quash the "nonsense criticism" being spouted by the son-in-law of Abdullah Azzam, the co-founder of Al Qaeda, a man who had once been his inspiration (although the two had fallen out bitterly after Dr. Ayman al-Zawahiri turned up in Peshawar and stole Osama's attention, leading to some blaming al-Zawahiri for Azzam's death in a car bombing).[74] Son-in-law Abdullah Anas had also once been Osama's friend, having taken him into the desert outside Jeddah where Osama had first played at being a jihadi. These days Anas lived in northwest London, from where he mounted sporadic attacks on Al Qaeda—and it made Osama's blood boil.[75]

Finally, there was the bookkeeping. Osama was a renowned penny-pincher and kept a close tally on all expenses, but most of the actual cash was banked by Al Qaeda Central into an account in Miram Shah. Atiyah needed to contact Abu Uthman, the head of Pakistan operations, and ask him to withdraw 15,000 rupees from the "mujahideen account" to buy three sacrificial goats. Eid al-Adha was approaching on December 19. Uthman also needed to transfer $10,000 from Osama's personal account to the "mujahideen account," and then deposit a new cash donation of €12,000 that had come in from the Gulf. The money was being sent with this letter.[76]

Sitting with Amal in another room, Seham opened her letter and froze. It brought the news that her eldest daughter, Khadija, had died in Waziristan giving birth to twins. After suffering a miscarriage three years earlier,

288 THE EXILE

doctors had advised Khadija to undergo a dilation and curettage procedure
to cleanse her womb. However, as medical facilities in the tribal areas were
not suitably equipped and as she was the daughter of Osama bin Laden, she
had been unable to travel to a city, so the problem had been left unresolved.[77]
Although the tragedy had happened three months back, this was the first
time anyone had been able to get a message through to Abbottabad. One
baby had died. The other, a girl, was critically ill.

Seham asked to be on her own, reaching for a pen and paper to write a
poetic tribute to a child she had not seen for four years. "My precious
daughter," she began, "She is my mature daughter. She is the flower of the
field. She is my smile and my wish . . . O how painful the agony of separation. If only I could be at your side again."

Seham, too, had suffered a premature birth in her youth: her second
daughter, Miriam, had almost died. But that was when they had lived in
Jeddah, and Osama had driven in his gold Mercedes at breakneck speed to
the city's most exclusive private clinic. Khadija's delivery had taken place in a
mud-walled compound with no medical treatment available. Her husband,
Daood, had been far away on the front lines.

Seham called Amal back and asked her to help compose a letter to Karima's
mother, who had arranged Khadija's funeral.[78] "My dear sister, I love you,"
she wrote. "We cannot say thank you enough for the effort you gave in
washing, preparing, and covering the body. God was wise to make sure that
I did not attend or see her." Referring to the surviving baby, she thanked her
for "explaining to me the trying details of the little girl."

As for Khadija's three older children, they could not travel to Abbottabad
as Daood wished since the house was full and Ibrahim and his brother
were at their wit's end. Perhaps Osama's elder brother Bakr would have
them. He lived in Jeddah, where he ran the family's multibillion-dollar
construction empire and paid the rent for aunties and cousins who occupied
neighboring villas in an exclusive housing complex. But he had disowned
Osama years earlier.

Seham had another worry. Khadija's shocking death would cause problems
for Khalid, too. His marriage would have to be put on hold while everyone
decided on the fate of her four surviving children. Karima, his intended,
was still young and could wait. The only way to speed things up would be
for Khalid to travel to Waziristan. But Osama would not allow that unless
someone came to replace him in the media office.

A few days later, Seham received a letter from Daood.[79] Khadija had been the "best wife and the best mother," he said. The three months since her death had "passed by as thirty years." The worst for him was that his youngest son, also called Osama, barely knew him because he had spent so much time away from the family and even now was insisting on calling him uncle.

"If it wasn't for my religious restrictions, I would have worn her clothes and jewelry," he said, wanting to wrap himself up in his wife's memory. The best he could do for the children was to find a new wife as soon as possible. "Dear Mother," he continued, "pass on your valuable advice."

When Seham and Amal broke the news about Khadija's death to Osama, he showed no emotion but offered a practical suggestion. Miriam, Seham's second daughter, was old enough to marry the widower Daood in Waziristan. She could take her dead sister's place.[80]

CHAPTER EIGHT

*"We will get you, CIA team, inshallah, we will
bring you down."*
—DR. HUMAM AL-BALAWI, SPEAKING
IN A VIDEO RECORDED AHEAD OF HIS
SUICIDE ATTACK ON U.S. FORWARD
OPERATING BASE CHAPMAN[1]

December 2007, Mir Ali, North Waziristan, Pakistan

DAOOD WAS FRANTIC. THE MISSILE STRIKES were relentless, his Al Qaeda
duties were mounting, and he was struggling to cope with three young children on his own. Khadija's surviving baby was in the care of a wet nurse, but
things had come to a head during Eid when five-year-old Aisha would not
stop crying for her dead mother. He could not find the right words to
comfort her. As a hard-bitten mujahid, he had spent so little time with his
children to date he barely knew them.

He wrote to the children's grandfather, Osama. "Most of the time I remain
in the house and it is very difficult for me and for them," he noted.[2] During
the holiday, he had taken them to their old home, where they had lived with
their mother, and he had bathed and dressed them in their holiday clothes.
He attached a photo—three mournful children with plastered-down hair.

He hoped the image would spur Osama into action. "They are your grandchildren," he pleaded. "God knows that I understand that all of you miss
them dearly."

Abdallah, the oldest boy, had another semester to complete in the madrassa,
and the baby "still has a year of breast-feeding." While he waited for Osama's
reply, he would try to find a temporary solution: marrying another woman
so she could at least enter the house and help him. "I decided to begin
searching for any widow so that I wouldn't be living in sin for the sake of my
children."

Seham called a family summit. The situation in Waziristan was deplorable. The grandchildren should come to them. Osama reluctantly agreed on the condition that Miriam marry Daood. He dispatched instructions to his Pakistan operations chief to get the children ready.[3] Daood should bring them up to the Kohat Tunnel, a strategically important mile-long stretch under the mountains, where Miriam and her brother Khalid would wait in another vehicle. Located three quarters of the way from Mir Ali to Peshawar, it was one of the few places where U.S. drones could not spy. Entering in one car as a tribal family on their way to the city, they would emerge at the other end in another vehicle as urban travelers returning to Peshawar from a sightseeing trip.[4]

Conveniently, the tunnel was also a well-known intelligence dead-spot. The southern half of the tunnel came under the jurisdiction of ISI Kohat, while the northern half was the responsibility of ISI Peshawar. The spy agency maintained checkpoints at either end but rarely bothered to go inside.

January 2008, Block 300, Quds Force Training Facility, Tehran, Iran

Sulaiman Abu Ghaith was at a breaking point. More than six years had passed since he had last seen his family. He had sent them off to Kuwait just before 9/11, only to be roused by a midnight door-knock in Kabul and frog-marched to a cave above Khost, where he had been compelled to voice Osama's 9/11 vision—which had then enveloped him like a noxious cloud. From Afghanistan, via a cellar somewhere in Tehran, he had ended up in the hands of the Quds Force, as far away from his family as a man could be. When he learned on the TV news that the Kuwaitis had canceled his passport, another door slammed shut. What he thought of most often was how he had never met his son, born as the Twin Towers fell.

A stateless prisoner in a nameless jail, Abu Ghaith felt as if his heart would burst every time Block 300 celebrated the arrival of a new baby—Othman bin Laden's second wife Sofia being the latest to give birth.[5] At night, he retreated to his room, which was bereft of ornamentation, with no children's drawings to brighten up the rough concrete walls.

Before his capture in Shiraz in April 2003, Abu Ghaith had snatched two brief phone conversations with his wife, Fatima, explaining that he had fled

Afghanistan for another country. But since then there had been no contact, and an unhappy second marriage to the daughter of one of the Egyptian brothers had not eased his pain. "No lawyers, no charges, no rights," he would chant under his breath whenever an Iranian administrator crossed his path in the yard. That his children's last sight of him had been the video-taped threats he had made to bring down more mayhem on the West tore at his heart. Every waking moment, he regretted those recordings.[6] He hoped that his first wife had explained that it was not their real father speaking but someone compelled to serve a man drunk on fervor.

He resented having been press-ganged into supporting "the project of one individual using the blood of others to act out what seem[ed] correct to him."[7] He hated those around him who were reunited with their families and bragged about their roles in a war he had not fought in.[8]

Over the past five years, he had begged to be allowed to make a phone call, post a letter, or send an e-mail. He tried to distract himself through study, spending most days with the Mauritanian, the only man in the compound he still trusted.

After the Eid decorations were put away at the end of 2007, Abu Ghaith decided to take things up a notch and refused to eat or get out of bed. The women cooked up bowls of mutton-bone broth but he would not touch them. In two weeks, he lost many pounds, but an Iranian doctor concluded that he needed to diet and ruled out any intervention.

After twenty-one days, the Mauritanian sought out a senior official—Abu Ghaith was weakening. Worried by the repercussions of a death in the compound, a Quds Force agent brought in a voice recorder and asked him to compile a message for his family. They would do their best to deliver it via the Iranian embassy in Kuwait City.

After several weeks, a small envelope arrived. Abu Ghaith played the audiocassette inside, and when he heard his brother's voice, he felt joyful. There were updates about brothers and cousins, and personal greetings from aunties and uncles. But nothing from his wife and children. Abu Ghaith replayed the cassette. Omission, he told himself, was an admission.

He wandered around mournfully, asking for a second opinion. Was his wife sick? Maybe she had died. For three weeks he pestered the compound directors for a phone call.[9] Finally, they relented.

Since Abu Ghaith had a $5 million bounty on his head and Iranian intel-ligence could not afford for anyone to eavesdrop, they drove him ten hours east to Mashhad and then for two more hours to get him over the Afghan border, a deserted place close to where Osama's family had crossed in March 2002. He was given a Thuraya satellite phone and instructions to say nothing about his location or his fellow prisoners.

Standing in sand-blasted western Afghanistan, Abu Ghaith called home with trepidation. There was no answer. He tried all the numbers he could remember, eventually getting his brother. *Where was his wife?* His brother fell silent.

There was no good way to break it: she had waited for four years, but in line with the Islamic principle of *idah* (the waiting period), she had then submitted a case to a magistrate who had granted her a divorce.[10] *Divorce?* He could not believe what he was hearing.

There was more. His wife had married one of his closest friends, with whom she now had a child. Their other children had been sent to live with in-laws.

"The news was like a lightning strike," recalled the Mauritanian, who consoled Abu Ghaith when he got back.[11]

January 22, 2008, Islamabad, Pakistan

In a quiet cul-de-sac in the Pakistani capital, another long-dead relative reappeared. Aafia Siddiqui's elderly uncle, Shams ul-Hassan Faruqi, a spritely government geologist with a huge white beard, was drinking tea with guests when his doorbell rang.[12] A white car had pulled up at the gate and the driver beckoned him over. A *burqa*-clad woman in the back leaned forward and rolled down the window. "Uncle, I'm Aafia," she whispered.

He stepped back, barely able to believe it. This woman who refused to show her face was his missing niece, a woman who had since become an Islamic cause célèbre as Prisoner 650 or "the gray lady of Bagram"—one of America's famous "ghost prisoners."

Aafia had been on her way to visit him when she vanished in March 2003, nabbed by the ISI, with the CIA looking on, as a result of Khalid Shaikh Mohammad's tip-off. Since then nothing more had been heard of her, although Pakistan's extremist outfits claimed her as their own, citing her case as an example of the worst excesses of the U.S. administration and plastering her photograph on their posters and banners.

"Where have you been all this time?" asked Faruqi.

The woman, still veiled, shook her head. "Three people are watching me," she whispered. "Get in the car."

They drove to Captain Cook's, a fish-and-chips restaurant in nearby Jinnah Supermarket, a middle-class shopping bazaar. Aafia, still whispering, told him a story that in another country would have seemed extraordinary. "I was kept in cells, people wore gloves and masks when they gave me food," she muttered. Maybe it was Bagram, or an ISI facility in Pakistan, she did not know. Some of the guards were Americans, the others Pakistanis. "They kept shifting me."

Her jailers' goal had only recently become clear. Certain that she was broken and without hope, they had ordered her to infiltrate Al Qaeda. Willing to say anything to get out, Aafia had agreed, and she had been set free that morning and put on a bus heading for the Tribal Areas. Taking a risk, she had jumped off the bus at a rest stop and hailed a taxi.[13]

Aafia had rare potential as the perfect double agent. She had the right pedigree: related to Khalid Shaikh Mohammad through marriage and demonstrably connected to several Al Qaeda plots before and after 9/11. Like Hassan Ghul, she also had family in Pakistan, which meant the ISI could turn the screw. Agents had warned that she would never see her children again if she failed to go along with the plan, she told her uncle; and as of now, she had no idea where they were.[14]

As she became more agitated, Faruqi found himself backing away.

"I have money," she rasped. "Help me get to Afghanistan."

Why was she was in such a hurry? Faruqi thought. What was it she needed? "Where will you go?" he asked.

A pause. "Ta-li-ban."

Faruqi recalled: "She was desperate to reach the Taliban, who she believed were essentially moral and would not stand by while her children were held hostage. ISI, Taliban, holding cells—all of this felt so alien and wrong to me."[15]

He thought back to the last time he had seen his niece. It had been in November 2001, when she had also turned up unexpectedly, begging for assistance. Back then, she had asked him to help her buy a house in Gilgit, a remote and picturesque area of Pakistan. The attacks in New York were on her mind and she wanted to disappear, she said. At the time, Faruqi had wondered whether she was paranoid or perhaps complicit in something he did not understand.

Now, unable to decide what to do, Faruqi called Aafia's mother in Karachi. "Come quickly, your *daughter* is here," he said.[16]

His sister did not seem at all pleased, and when she arrived that night she launched herself at Aafia, telling her she was a troublemaker.[17] The family had already suffered, with the ISI holding them under house arrest for months after she vanished. Aafia was on her own, her mother said.

Faruqi could not stand his sister's coldness. "She is my blood. She trusted me at a time of calamity. I cannot throw her out."

Aafia sat in a corner, silently observing the row.

They eventually went to bed, with Aafia sleeping on a prayer mat in the lounge. When they woke the next morning, she was gone.

January 2008, Bilal Town, Abbottabad, Pakistan

Seham bin Laden had turned the second-floor bedroom she had set aside for her daughter Khadija into a shrine. At least she now had three of the grandchildren with her. They had been brought out of Waziristan in December, much to their father Daood's relief. However, his relocation to Abbottabad had been canceled after one of the senior Al Qaeda brothers with him said he was too fair-skinnd and Arab-looking to get away with traveling as a local. He wrote to Osama, apologizing for being "incapable of assisting you" and saying for the first and last time he "wished I was an Afghani or a Pakistani."[18] Osama was disappointed, but his daughter Miriam was secretly delighted she would not now have to marry him.

Seham described the boys as "little heroes" and the girl as a "sweet rose" and "little chick."[19] Abdallah, born before 9/11, was the only one to have met his grandfather before, and he regarded him silently, this great mujahid leader who sat on the floor under a blanket and shooed the children away.

To cheer things up, the women stitched matching pink dresses for the girls and braided their hair with pink ribbons, while the boys took over the hallway, flying paper airplanes and floating paper boats in a plastic basin.[20] Having grown up in the relative freedom of a Pashtun village, they had no concept of a confined life and filled the house with noise, infuriating Ibrahim and Abrar.[21]

Seham wrote to Daood, who had returned to his Al Qaeda duties in Waziristan: "Do not worry about the children, they are in our hearts and eyes, they will be surrounded by kindness, affection and care."[22] But "we cannot compare your affliction to mine," she wrote dejectedly, mentioning that she had not seen her "precious and beloved" daughter Khadija for five years before her death.

Seham wanted Daood to "send the name of the region where our precious was buried, and the address of the graveyard." He should go to visit on Eid al-Adha and take the family's prayers. One day, she intended to visit, too.

Then she came to a bone of contention. A decision had been made to leave her daughter's baby behind with the wet nurse in Mir Ali. Seham wanted the girl to be sent to Abbottabad directly, along with Khadija's last remaining possessions. "Send me whatever my daughter was wearing, even her wristwatch, where I can smell her." He could keep the gold and any other valuables. They did not matter.

Daood wrote back.[23] "My dear Abdallah, Aisha, and Osama [Daood's younger son had been named after his grandfather] kiss the forehead of your grandfather, grandmother, and your [new] mother [Miriam]." They should listen, study, and not forget to do physical exercise. They should always kneel when saying their prayers. He would never forget them, he said, updating them with disturbing news from their old life that evidently was a fast-changing scenario. "The rabbits we used to have in the house gave birth, but the cat ate the little ones and after that, the infidels entered the place." Addressing them as his "little fighters," he signed off: "My dears, please pray for victory for the mujahideen."

Spring 2008, Rawalpindi, Pakistan

Pervez Musharraf was falling into a political abyss, but, as a canny survivor, he still believed he could pull himself out by his fingernails.

After cycles of increasingly brutal violence by Islamist groups, including those manipulated by the ISI, dovetailed with growing protests by the middle classes, who were infuriated by the president's sidelining of democracy, he had announced that he would stand for the presidency again when his first term finished in October 2007. To alleviate the increasing pressure, he had conceded to a general election that was slated for February 2008. But given that his popularity was at an all-time low, he doubted that even a massive vote-rigging exercise would save his political party in the polls. It would take something more.

Desperate for allies, the outgoing president had held secret talks with erstwhile enemies, including his nemesis Benazir Bhutto. Their relationship was rancorous. Former prime minister Bhutto had been exiled from Pakistan for eight years, charged along with her husband with having stolen millions from the state purse and secreting it in Swiss bank accounts and property in England. In Pakistan, it was customary for an incoming leader to ambush the outgoing one in a legal minefield, sown with corruption and theft charges; and these surrounded Bhutto and her husband, Asif Ali Zardari, by the dozen, courtesy of Musharraf and of Nawaz Sharif, the prime minister who had succeeded her—and who also faced similar charges thanks to Bhutto and Musharraf.

The president resented Bhutto's gender, her dynastic power, and her liberal inclinations—which stuck in his throat. She had experienced his wiles and games directly when she had been prime minister in 1993 and he, as her director general of military operations, had unsuccessfully lobbied her to order the Pakistan Army to invade Indian-administered Kashmir, claiming she would be able to "wear its crown like a queen."

More recently, Musharraf had offered Bhutto a quid pro quo. If she backed his bid for another term as president, he would ease her legal problems, enabling her to return to Pakistan and run in the February 2008 elections as the head of her Pakistan Peoples Party (PPP).

They had discussed a deal in Dubai in the summer of 2007, after which her team and his had surreptitiously got together in Duke Street, in London's Mayfair, and in Dupont Circle, in Washington, D.C.[24] But, having been warned by her advisers that dealing with a dictator would tarnish her last remaining democratic credentials, Bhutto had pulled back, instead seeking broader support from the U.S. and British governments. She had returned to Pakistan in October 2007, daring Musharraf to jail her, ignoring the warnings from the CIA and British MI6 that he might stand by while elements within the ISI and Islamist groups, stoked by Al Qaeda, placed her in their sights.[25] Within hours of arrival, her homecoming cavalcade was blown up as it wound its way through the streets of Karachi, resulting in more than 150 deaths.

Bhutto agonized over the maimed and murdered.[26] "I have to press on, for them," she concluded, failing to appreciate how much Pakistan had changed.[27] The drone campaign, the raid on the Red Mosque in Islamabad, and the burgeoning presence of Al Qaeda and the Taliban that had merged with tribal levies had transformed politics. The mood of the whole country was far darker than when she had last lived in Pakistan.

Bhutto's return augmented the simmering unrest about Musharraf's long rule, with the country's lawyers taking a stance against him, deepening his problems. The Supreme Court of Pakistan was persuaded to investigate the constitutionality of his twin roles as army chief and president. On November 2, 2007, with only days before his term ran out, and with judges threatening his future, he declared a state of emergency, fired the chief justice, and sent troops clattering into the Supreme Court. Taking to TV, he warned that the country was facing an existential crisis and that uncertainty over its leadership would only make matters worse. What was needed, he said, was a firm hand, someone who could face down the forces that Al Qaeda had unleashed.[28] "The extremists are trying to take the authority and power of the government into their own hands," he said. He was the only man strong enough to resist them.

However, Musharraf's support had evaporated, with many believing the extremists were being enabled by those in power—who themselves were lawless. Demonstrators massed in cities across the country as a patchy media blackout was implemented. Leading human rights activists were jailed, international correspondents were deported, and Bhutto was placed under house arrest, twice, as lawyers began to march in protest.

Musharraf temporarily stepped down as army chief in order to be elected president for the second time in November, backed by a tame parliament facing reelection itself in February.

Up in the Tribal Areas, more than thirteen armed tribal groups came together to form the Tehrik-i-Taliban Pakistan (TTP), a leathery coalition of Islamists, warlords, robber barons, and cutthroats that would become better known as the Pakistan Taliban and sought Islamabad's submission through suicide bombs, IEDs, kidnappings, and beheadings. Baitullah Mehsud led it, as a successor to hardheaded highwayman Nek Muhammad Wazir, who had been killed by a drone strike in 2004. And he had Bhutto in his sights.

The TTP's charter had been shaped and honed by Al Qaeda, which regarded it as an affiliate. Both Osama's general manager, Atiyah Abd al-Rahman, and Abu Yahya al-Libi, who now served as a religious adviser to Al Qaeda Central, had sent detailed suggestions on how the new movement should be run, pointing out flaws in its governing documents and making requests for more information so that new wording could be added.[29] The TTP should "trust the rule of the Amir of the Believers Mullah Muhammad Omar Mujahid, and consider him as their emir."[30]

At dusk on December 27, 2007, after a huge PPP rally in Rawalpindi, Benazir Bhutto drove off through cheering crowds. Her staff commented that the electricity in the area seemed to have been switched off, throwing a pall over everything. As she stood up out of her Land Cruiser's sunroof to bid farewell to supporters, gunshots rang out. A split second later, a suicide bomber detonated himself beside the car. Bhutto was thrown back into her bulletproof vehicle, hitting her head on the way down.

Evacuated to a Rawalpindi hospital, she was declared dead at six sixteen P.M.[31] Whether she died from a bullet wound or a neck fracture was a mystery that would never be solved, as Zardari refused to allow a post-mortem. He squarely blamed Musharraf for her death, claiming that the president had rejected her requests for foreign security contractors and her demands that her domestic security be upgraded. He cited the fact that emergency crews had hosed down the crime scene before the police arrived.

When the case was eventually unraveled, a filament of it appeared to lead back to Baitullah Mehsud, the new emir of the Pakistan Taliban, who had been encouraged by Musharraf to take out his rival. Although the link was never proven, the fact that most people believed it underscored yet again how the Pakistan Army both thrived on and was corroded by the forces of terror spawning inside the country.

When the February elections came, widower Zardari, who had previously been known by many Pakistanis as Mr. Ten Percent—a reference to his alleged slice of all contracts awarded during his wife's two tenures as prime minister—campaigned noisily in the name of his martyred wife, and the PPP swept to power in parliament with a landslide win. Musharraf clung on as president for another six months, but in August 2008, facing impeachment for suspending the constitution and conspiracy charges concerning Bhutto's murder, a dejected man whose reign had come to define an epoch of terror as much as that of George W. Bush was finally forced from office.[32]

March 2008, Block 300, Tehran

Sulaiman Abu Ghaith was driven to the Afghan border for another phone call, but this time standing in the whistling desert he rang a different number. It was the eldest of his six daughters, who sounded as tearful as he was.

Did he know that she, her sisters, and her brother had been consigned to their grandparents after their mother remarried, and had been told that their father was dead? "Are you ever coming back?" she wept.

With the call on an open line, listened in on by the Quds Force and whoever else, all Abu Ghaith could do was promise he would never stop *trying* to reach them.

As soon as he got back to Block 300, he took root in the *majlis* again and commenced another hunger strike, spending his waking hours writing what he described as his "book of regrets," a scrawl of sorrows that coalesced into an embittered rejection of Osama's jihad.[33] "Those who think that jihad means carrying arms and fighting the enemy are mistaken," he wrote, pointing to the Sheikh and his lieutenants. "They think that they are right all the time and they are encircled by a bunch of advisers who do not qualify to give advice," he said, echoing the hundreds of complaint letters Osama had received from the Middle East about Zarqawi. Now all he wanted to do was "stop the chaos" introduced by second-generation Al Qaeda thugs like Zarqawi and his successors. He rejected violence, favoring working to "secure a better life for all who live with Islam and in the Islamic state."

He wrote and wrote. Spilling blood was against God's wishes, he railed, explaining that his only wish was for his book to be published so that his children could see he was a good man.

Abu Ghaith's obsessive behavior eventually caused the Iranians to snap. When the guards tried to manhandle him back inside Block 300, a tussle turned into a thrown punch, which degenerated into a fight that exploded into a full-blown prison riot. Egyptians and Libyans ripped up sheets and shattered wooden beds, setting fires, hurling petrol bombs made with secretly stockpiled heating fuel, and daubing anti-Shia messages on the walls. Abu Ghaith's rage was infectious. Everyone wanted out. Osama's sons pelted guards with stones. The director of the compound stood in the yard, hands on hips, declaring: "Could you all please calm down."

According to the Mauritanian, he "participated in their protest as a sign of sympathy." When the exasperated director withdrew, Abu Ghaith stomped back into the *majlis*. Osama's grandsons acted as lookouts, watching the main gate. "Car!" they shouted, seeing a brand-new Peugeot drive in. Abu Ghaith shot out, armed with "his weapons and tools." The Iranian driver fled, leaving the keys in the ignition, and Abu Ghaith jumped in, revving the engine and slamming the vehicle into a fence before leaping onto the hood

Osama bin Laden at Tora Bora in November 1996. PHOTOGRAPH COURTESY OF ABDEL BARI ATWAN, PRESENTED AS EVIDENCE IN THE 2015 TRIAL OF KHALID AL-FAWWAZ

Road to Tora Bora in 1996. PHOTOGRAPH COURTESY OF ABDEL BARI ATWAN, PRESENTED AS EVIDENCE IN THE 2015 TRIAL OF KHALID AL-FAWWAZ

Cave entrance at Tora Bora next to family huts in 1996. PHOTOGRAPH COURTESY OF ABDEL BARI ATWAN, PRESENTED AS EVIDENCE IN THE 2015 TRIAL OF KHALID AL-FAWWAZ

Children of Al Qaeda members at Tora Bora in 1996.
PHOTOGRAPH BY ABDEL BARI ATWAN, PRESENTED AS EVIDENCE IN THE 2015 TRIAL OF KHALID AL-FAWWAZ

Abu Musab al-Suri at Tora Bora in 1996.
PHOTOGRAPH BY ABDEL BARI ATWAN, PRESENTED AS
EVIDENCE IN THE 2015 TRIAL OF KHALID AL-FAWWAZ

Mullah Omar as a young man.
PICTURE RELEASED BY THE TALIBAN IN 2015

Huthaifa Azzam with the jacket his father, Al Qaeda co-founder Abdullah Azzam, was wearing when he was assassinated in 1989. PHOTOGRAPH BY CATHY SCOTT-CLARK

Sulaiman Abu Ghaith and Osama making their first video statement after 9/11. PRESENTED AS EVIDENCE IN THE TRIAL OF ABU GHAITH IN 2014; SOURCED FROM GETTY IMAGES

Hamzah and Ladin bin Laden with what Al Qaeda claimed to be a downed U.S. helicopter in November 2001. ASSOCIATED PRESS

Dr. Amin al-Haq, who helped Osama flee from Tora Bora in December 2001. PHOTOGRAPH BY CATHY SCOTT-CLARK

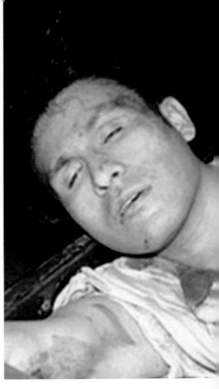

Abu Zubaydah as a young man in Saudi Arabia.
ZUBAYDAH FAMILY ARCHIVE

Abu Zubaydah's capture in Faisalabad in 200
INTER-SERVICES PUBLIC RELATIONS,
PAKISTAN ARMED FORCES

Jody and Hesham Abu Zubaydah.
AUTHOR COLLECTION

Hesham Abu Zubaydah with his daughter En
in Florida. AUTHOR COLLECTION

ft: Ramzi bin al-Shibh wanted photograph. FEDERAL BUREAU OF INVESTIGATION

nter and right: Khalid Shaikh Mohammad (two views). GETTY IMAGES

MOST WANTED TERRORIST

SAIF AL-ADEL

Conspiracy to Kill United States Nationals, to Murder, to Destroy Buildings and Property of the United States, and to Destroy the National Defense Utilities of the United States

DESCRIPTION

Aliases: Muhamad Ibrahim Makkawi, Seif Al Adel, Ibrahim Al-Madani			
Date(s) of Birth Used: April 11, 1963, April 11, 1960		Place of Birth: Egypt	
Hair: Dark		Eyes: Dark	
Height: Unknown		Weight: Unknown	
Build: Unknown		Complexion: Olive	
Sex: Male		Citizenship: Egyptian	
Languages: Arabic		Scars and Marks: None known	

REWARD

The Rewards For Justice Program, United States Department of State, is offering a reward of up to $5 million for information leading directly to the apprehension or conviction of Saif Al-Adel.

REMARKS

Al-Adel is thought to be affiliated with the Egyptian Islamic Jihad (EIJ), and is believed to be a high-ranking member of the Al-Qaeda organization.

CAUTION

Saif Al-Adel is wanted in connection with the August 7, 1998, bombings of the United States Embassies in Dar es Salaam, Tanzania, and Nairobi, Kenya.

SHOULD BE CONSIDERED ARMED AND DANGEROUS

If you have any information concerning this person, please contact your local FBI office or the nearest American Embassy or Consulate.

Field Office: New York

bu Faraj al-Libi.
WEL SAMAD/AFP/GETTY IMAGES

Saif al-Adel wanted poster.
FEDERAL BUREAU OF INVESTIGATION

Aafia Siddiqui (center) with her siblings. AUTHOR COLLECTION

Aafia Siddiqui's uncle Shams ul-Hassan Faruqi, who spent five years looking for her after she disappeared in 2003. PHOTOGRAPH BY CATHY SCOTT-CLARK

Rewards for Justice

Seeking Information Against International Terrorism

Wanted
Atiyah Abd al-Rahman
Up to $1 Million Reward

Nationality : Libyan
Age : late 30s
Hair : Black
Eyes : Brown
Height : 5'5" (165cm)
Build : Medium
Comments : Atiyah Abd al-Rahman may have a thin mustache. He has a light complexion.

Atiyah is the al-Qa'ida emissary in Iran as

Atiyah Abd al-Rahman wanted poster.
FEDERAL BUREAU OF INVESTIGATION

REWARD
Up to $10,000,000 USD
ABU MUSAB AL ZARQAWI

This man is wanted for murdering innocent women and children.

This terrorist born in Jordan also goes by the names:
Ahmed Al Kalaylah,
Fadel Nazzal Al Khalayleh,
Abu Mussab Al Zarqawi,
Abu Mussa Al Zarkawi

778-4076 Inside Bagdad
01-778-4076 Inside Iraq
964-01-778-4076 Outside Iraq
Email: tips@orha.centcom.mil

Your identity will remain secret

IZ C0825

Abu Musab al-Zarqawi wanted poster.
FEDERAL BUREAU OF INVESTIGATION

General Javed Alam Khan (left) with General Pervez Musharraf. AUTHOR COLLECTION

General Ashfaq Kayani meeting tribal elders shortly before Abbottabad raid in 2011.
INTER-SERVICES PUBLIC RELATIONS, ARMED FORCES OF PAKISTAN

Osama's protector Fazlur Rehman Khalil.
PHOTOGRAPH BY CATHY SCOTT-CLARK

Former ISI director general and Osama's protector
Hamid Gul. PHOTOGRAPH BY CATHY SCOTT-CLARK

Dr. Ghairat Baheer, son-in-law of Gulbuddin
Hekmatyar. Baheer was captured in 2002.
PHOTOGRAPH BY CATHY SCOTT-CLARK

Abu Zubaydah in February 2017. AUTHOR COLLECTION

The Mauritanian, Sheikh
Mahfoud Ibn El Waleed,
in Nouakchott, 2015.

General Qassem Suleima
(right) with Ayatollah Al
Khamenei, the Supreme
Leader of Iran.

hotograph of Khalid bin Laden.
ECTION

Ladin bin Laden with his children.
AUTHOR COLLECTION

eneral Qassem Suleimani's Quds Force headquarters, located in the former U.S. embassy
Tehran. PHOTOGRAPH BY CATHY SCOTT-CLARK

Saudi passports of Khadija bin Laden (left) and Hamzah bin Laden, recovered during a raid in Karachi in 2002. RELEASED BY THE UNITED STATES ARMED FORCES DOCUMENT EXPLOITATION TEAM

Omar and Zaina bin Laden. AUTHOR COLLECTION

Zaina bin Laden. PHOTOGRAPH BY CATHY SCOTT-C

...bdul Rahman and Omar bin Laden. AUTHOR COLLECTION

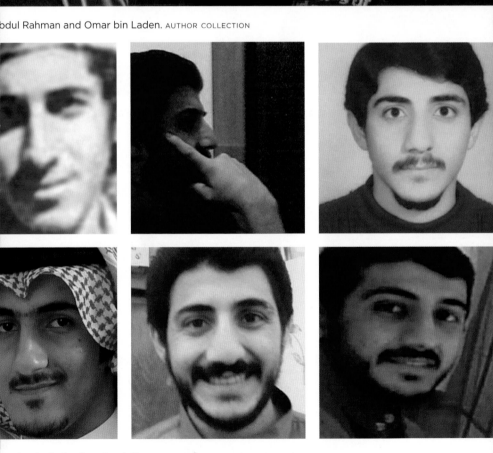

...ounterclockwise from top left:
...thman bin Laden, Ladin bin Laden, Saad bin Laden (four views). AUTHOR COLLECTION

NAME: USAMA BIN LADIN
ALIASES: SHAYKH
SIGNIFICANCE:
POSSIBLE DESCRIPTION
- NATIONALITY: ARAB/SAUDI
- AGE: 54
- HT: 6'4" – 6'6"
- WT: ~180 LBS
- EYES: BROWN
- HAIR: BROWN
- CLOTHING: 3RD MALE OBSERVED ON CMPD ALWAYS WEARS LIGHT COLORED
SHAWAL KAMEEZ WITH A DARK VEST. OCCASIONALLY
WEARS LIGHT COLORED PRAYER CAP.
FAMILY MEMBERS: CMPD AC1, COURTYARD A, 2ND AND 3RD FLOOR
- 1ST WIFE: AMAL AL FATTAH AL BADAH (28 YRS OLD)
- DAUGHTER: SAFIYAH (3YRS OLD)
* 2 UNIDENTIFIED CHILDREN BORN SINCE 2011 (UNK IF IN "A" COMPOUND

- 2ND WIFE: SIHAM ABDULLAH BIN HUSAYN AL SHARIF (54 YRS OLD)
- SON: KHALID (23 YRS OLD)
- DAUGHTERS: MIRIAM (20 YRS OLD), SUMAYA (10 YRS OLD)

- 3RD WIFE: KHAYRIYA HUSAYN TAHA HAMZA (62 YRS OLD) aka UMM HAMZA
- SON: HAMZA (21 YRS OLD)
  - WIFE: MARYAM
    - SON: USAMA (4 YRS OLD)
    - DAUGHTER: KHAYRIYA (1 YR OLD)
* 3RD WIFE KHAYRIYA AND SON RELEASED FROM IRANIAN CUSTODY IN JUL
2010

NAME: IBRAHIM SAID AHMAD ABD AL HAMID
ALIASES: ARSHAD, ASIF KHAN, TARIQ, HAJI NADEEM, SARDAR AISHAD
(OWNER OF AC1)
SIGNIFICANCE: COURIER AND ASSESSED
AS ONE OF 3 INDIVIDUALS
RESPONSIBLE FOR HVT #1's CARE
POSSIBLE DESCRIPTION
- NATIONALITY: ARAB/KUWAITI
- AGE: 33
- HT: 5'9" – 5'11"
- WT: UNK
- EYES: UNK
- HAIR: UNK
- SKIN: UNK
- CLOTHING: TYPICALLY A WHITE SHAWAL KAMEEZ
- OTHER: MOVED FROM MARDAN CITY TO TARGET CMPD IN 2006 WITH
BROTHER ABRAR
FAMILY MEMBERS: CMPD AC1, COURTYARD C
- WIFE: MARYAM (31 YRS OLD)
- SONS: KHALID (5-7 YRS OLD), AHMAD (1-4 YRS OLD), HABIB (18 MONTHS)
- DAUGHTER: RAHMA (8 YRS OLD)
* WIFE AND KIDS RETURNED TO C CMPD ON 26 APR 2011
- BROTHER: ABRAR
- FATHER: AHMAD SAID (DECEASED)
- MOTHER: HAMIDA AHMAD SAID (46 YRS OLD)

NAME: ABRAR AHMAD SAID ABD AL HAMID
ALIASES: ARSHAD, ASIF KHAN,
SARDAR ASHAD (OWNER OF AC1)
SIGNIFICANCE: FACILITATOR FOR HVT #1
POSSIBLE DESCRIPTION
- NATIONALITY: ARAB/KUWAITI
- AGE: 33
- HT: UNK
- WT: UNK
- EYES: UNK
- HAIR: DARK
- SKIN: UNK
- CLOTHING: WEARS GLASSES
- OTHER: MOVED FROM MARDAN CITY TO TARGET CMPD IN 2006 WITH
BROTHER ABRAR
FAMILY MEMBERS: CMPD AC1, COURTYARD A, FIRST FLOOR
- WIFE: BUSHRA (~35 YRS OLD)
- SONS: IBRAHIM (4 MONTHS), ABD AL RAHMAN (1-4 YRS OLD), MUHAMMAD
(6-7 YRS OLD, ATTENDS MADRASSA AWAY FROM FAMILY)
- DAUGHTER: KHADIJA (1-4 YRS OLD)
- BROTHER: ABU AHMAD
- FATHER: AHMAD SAID (DECEASED)
- MOTHER: HAMIDA AHMAD SAID (46 YRS OLD)

AMAL BIN LADEN
WIFE

KHALID
SON

Sensitive Site
Exploitation card
given to U.S. Navy
SEALs conducting
the Abbottabad raid
in May 2011.
AUTHOR COLLECTION

Abbottabad annex
where Maryam and
Ibrahim lived with
their children.
PHOTOGRAPH BY
SHAUKAT QADIR

Abbottabad
staircase to the
second floor, where
Khalid bin Laden
was fatally shot.
PHOTOGRAPH BY
SHAUKAT QADIR

Abbottabad main
house with front
door visible.
PHOTOGRAPH BY
SHAUKAT QADIR

nal's bed and entrance at the Islamabad villa where Osama's family was kept by the ISI after his death. OTOGRAPHS BY CATHY SCOTT-CLARK

ontage created by Zakariya -Sadeh, brother of Amal bin den, of himself with two of s sister's children, Hussein d Ibrahim. AUTHOR COLLECTION

Osama's children and grandchildren in ISI custody after the Abbottabad raid: (left to right) grandchildren Fatima, 5, Abdullah, 12, and Osama, 7 or 8, and children Hussein, 3, Zainab, 5, and Ibrahim, 8. AUTHOR COLLECTION

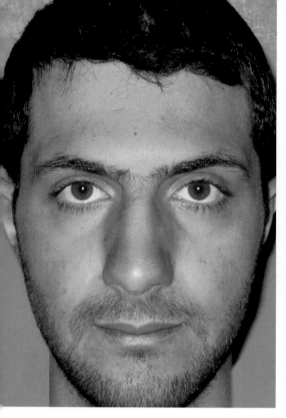

U.S. prison photograph of Abu Mohammad al-Julani, leader of Jabhat Fateh al-Sham, who was held at Camp Bucca in Iraq in 2004. U.S. DEPARTMENT OF DEFENSE

U.S. prison photograph of Abu Bakr al-Baghᵈ leader of Islamic State, who was held at Camⁱ Bucca in Iraq in 2004. U.S. DEPARTMENT OF DEF

Abu Qatada (left) and Abu Muhammad al-Maqdisi. PHOTOGRAPH BY CATHY SCOTT-CLARK

and scratching a message: "This is for your sake, my dear children!" Jumping down, he poured heating fuel on the vehicle before setting it alight. Children stood around whooping.

That night, General Qassem Suleimani sent somber-faced and neatly uniformed "military judicial officials" into Block 300 to take Abu Ghaith off to Evin prison.

Then Qassem arrived in person to address Osama's family and the others. He was furious: "I did my best to serve *you*," he told them, incredulous. "I turned a deaf ear to your unrest. I stopped those who wanted to hurt you. But things have gone too far."[34]

Osama's hotheaded sons boiled over. "We have been illegally kidnapped and concealed in this secret jail," they shouted, thumping the wall. "For five years we have had no legal rights. We have been prevented from contacting our families. Our children were born and have grown up in prison. Our ongoing incarceration goes against international law." They said they would rather be prosecuted in open court than remain in this "living cemetery."

When Qassem offered to appoint a magistrate to hear the case, everyone calmed down. If this process was truly to be judicial, then the Mauritanian offered to pay $10,000 for the damaged car, so that the slate would be clean when they began.

Osama's sons returned to the *majlis*. After days turned into weeks, they began a series of heated discussions. "We need to get out from under the infidel's fist," railed a furious Othman, who suggested they try to contact their father in Pakistan. Ladin pointed out they had tried to do this a hundred times already with no success. Hamzah wanted to sign up for the jihad. His mother, Khairiah, wanted to return to her husband's side, whatever the risks. Iman and Ladin wished to go to their mother, Najwa, in Syria. However, to make any of these dreams a reality, someone would have to escape.

Escape. Now that someone had uttered the word, Osama's sons hesitated. Despite the tough talking, they had been so institutionalized by their long incarceration that they were secretly fearful of the outside world. Perhaps there was a less dangerous option? The safest way might be to get transferred to a place where the security was less stringent and then send a message. Everyone agreed, relieved to procrastinate.

The next day, the Mauritanian approached the administrators, complaining that Block 300 was too volatile. The fighting got in the way of study and prayer, he said, and the children and women were all suffering

from depression. Surprisingly, the Iranians offered alternative accommodation in residential villas outside the complex and took the Mauritanian to
visit. But the new apartments had bars on the windows, movement sensors
in every room, and a complex electronic gate-locking mechanism, monitored
with night-vision cameras. They stayed put.

Reconvening in the *majlis*, autistic Saad suggested they should all dress
up as women. Military chief Saif al-Adel wearily shook his head. This ruse
had been used already, so the Iranians were wise to it. Someone else recommended sending word to Saif's father-in-law, Abu Walid al-Masri, who lived
semi-freely in a government villa elsewhere in Tehran. Saif disagreed. In
order to get his deal, his father-in-law had likely agreed to work for the
Iranians, which meant no one could trust him.

Amid the discussions, the Mauritanian pointed out another problem. If
everyone ran away, who would care for Fatima, who had no husband and
could not travel unaccompanied? A couple of days later he came up with a
ready-made solution. Why not marry Fatima to Sulaiman Abu Ghaith? He
could do with the distraction.

The family agreed, although Fatima had no say in the matter. After Abu
Ghaith consented (even though this marriage would be seen from the outside
as further evidence that he was still wedded to the movement), the Mauritanian
performed a quick ceremony. A muted celebration followed and then
everyone sank back into a funk.

In May 2008, ministry officials arrived on a détente mission, carrying
boxes of sweets and cakes. Saad spotted that the gate had been left open,
and, speaking fast in Arabic, ordered his nephews and nieces to make a run
for it. They hurtled out toward the main entrance, surprising the Quds
Force guards, who stood by openmouthed, not wanting to fire on children.
Soon they were joined by their mothers, who sat down by the main entrance
to the complex, through which they could see the shadows of members of
the public strolling by.

"We want freedom, we want human rights," the women chanted, exhilarated by their sudden action. The Al Qaeda party remained immovable for
the next thirty-six hours. They began shouting to the pedestrians on the
other side. Confronted with a top secret cache of Al Qaeda hostages calling
out for help, General Suleimani sent in negotiators. Ice creams were handed
around for the children and a lavish meal was prepared for the adults, served
out on the gravel. Sated, the Mauritanian recommended they negotiate, but

Saif al-Adel overruled him, supported by Osama's sons. After years of stasis, they were in a stronger position than ever before to demand change.[35]

The talking lasted for hours with no resolution. Exasperated and deeply worried, the Iranians eventually sent soldiers dressed in black overalls and wearing ski masks. They fired tear gas and pushed the families back toward Block 300. In the melee, women and children were hit with sticks and rifles. Abu Ghaith was beaten unconscious. He and others accused of being ringleaders—including the Mauritanian—were sent to Evin prison as their wives launched a hunger strike.[36]

June 2008, Secret Al Quds Detention Facility, Yazd, Central Iran

Osama's family was given twenty-four-hours' notice to pack. Since the Iranians could no longer control their Al Qaeda guests, they would have to be split up. Only Fatima bin Laden, who was now married to Abu Ghaith, and the Military Council stayed behind; the rest were marched onto buses and driven out into the country's central desert, where the temperature topped one hundred degrees Fahrenheit. After many hours of travel, they pulled up at Yazd, one of Iran's most historic cities and a center for Zoroastrian culture.

The bin Ladens' new home was a huge, sand-colored villa surrounded by a low mud-brick wall. Saad, Othman, Mohammed, and Hamzah, together with their young families, as well as Khairiah and Najwa's two unmarried children, Iman and Ladin, hurried inside to escape the glare of the sun.

The Iranian escorts took rooms closest to the main gate. There would be no trips out to Yazd's stunning central bazaar, with its vaulted ceiling, or to the dazzling blue-tiled twelfth-century grand mosque, they said. Such privileges had been lost as a result of everyone's recent behavior. Each family unit was asked to provide a shopping list. As they wandered around the villa allocating the rooms, one thing struck them: there were no security cameras at the rear, and only a low wall. They had been moved in such haste that the villa was not ready for them.

When they learned from news reports that Khalid Shaikh Mohammad and four others were about to go on trial for aiding the 9/11 attacks and would receive the death sentence if convicted, their discussions about escaping resumed with more vigor. Khalid was quoted as saying that he welcomed the death penalty. "Yes, this is what I wish, to be a martyr for a long time."[37] Osama's family had no such wishes.

But they would have to move fast, as technicians came daily to upgrade security. Hamzah volunteered to hop over the wall. Khairiah vetoed it. At nineteen, he was too young and would never survive on his own. Besides, his wife, Asma, had just given birth to a baby daughter, who they had named Khairiah, after her grandmother. She needed him here.

Saad, who at twenty-nine was the nominal head of the household, piped up.[38] He would do it in memory of his dead son, he said solemnly as his siblings shook their heads in disbelief. Saad, who couldn't even tie his own shoelaces, would never make it out. Othman stepped forward. He would go.

He would head for his father's "land of jihad" and search for their half sister Khadija, who, as far as he knew, was still living in Waziristan within the tight-knit Al Qaeda group, along with Al Qaeda Number Three Sheikh Saaed al-Masri and their father's chief spokesman, Atiyah.

If that failed, he would try to locate Abdullah al-Sindi, a young Saudi courier who had once worked for Khalid Shaikh Mohammad and who Osama's sons had got to know in early 2002 while in Karachi.[39] Back then al-Sindi had networks that straddled the border and reached into Zahidan, a city with a large Arab community. Maybe he was still active?

The plan felt too rushed and not well thought through. The family retired to discuss it again the next morning.

That night, Saad sat on the carpet in his room, playing bedtime games with his son, Osama, and two daughters, Asma and Duha, as an idea formed in his befuddled mind. After he put the children to bed and his wife, Wafa, fell asleep, he quietly packed up his laptop.

In the early hours, when he was sure everyone was asleep, he kissed his sleeping children, climbed out of a window, and slipped over the wall into the desert night. He would rescue them all.

The alley behind the house was silent. He crouched in the shadows trying to sort through a jumble of thoughts until he realized he had not said farewell to his wife. He climbed back over the wall and crept into the bedroom, waking a confused Wafa. "I am leaving," he whispered as he kissed her. "I am doing this for you." Before she could say anything, he climbed out again, driven by a strong desire to prove himself, rewriting his past as the family joker.

By the time an alarmed Wafa woke other members of the family, he was gone.[40]

At first light, a lone taxi trundled along the desert road carrying a young Arab man who would not stop talking. At Kerman, a city two hundred miles to the southeast, the driver dropped him at the bus station. Telling other waiting passengers of his desire to travel to Iranian Balochistan, Saad was put on a bus heading for Zahidan, a place where Othman had said the Taliban still had a secure footing and where members of Khalid Shaikh Mohammad's old network still lived. During the years they had been incarcerated with Saif al-Adel, Osama's sons had been made to memorize details for helpful contacts in case they ever got out. But despite his best efforts, Saad could not recall a single telephone number.

Dusty, confused, and bedraggled, at Zahidan he hung around at the bus station and then a local mosque, unsure of where to go next, until a Sunni family took him in out of pity. When he announced over dinner that he was the son of Osama bin Laden and had been imprisoned by the Iranian authorities for the past five years, the head of the household froze. The city was rife with rumors about a Zahidan-born man who still had relatives living locally but who had become a prized asset for the CIA, to whom he had given up Khalid Shaikh Mohammad in return for a king's ransom.[41]

Locking Saad inside the house, the reluctant host called around the city's radical Sunni clerics until one of them turned up an old Pakistani cell phone number for Abu Uthman, Al Qaeda's Pakistan operations chief. When he dialed and a voice answered, he explained the bare bones of the young man's far-fetched story. Saad bin Laden, if this was who he really was, had escaped an Iranian prison and was insistent that he could not go back. Could Al Qaeda come to collect him?

Uthman ordered the caller to stop speaking. The line was insecure, and if they could be heard, a drone could see them, too. He told him to sit tight.

As soon as he finished the call, Uthman sent word to Osama that someone claiming to be his son had turned up in Zahidan. Until they had proof, they had broken off communications, he said. "The link between us and Sa'ad is disconnected for now and we think that the best way for [the plan to continue] is with the people that he is with (we will call them the West)."[42]

Despite Saad's perilous situation, Abu Uthman could not risk making the journey himself. A local connection would have to be found. There was one Balochi "supporter" in Zahidan he still trusted. Uthman sent him a message that concluded: "May God grant you success so that you can complete the matter and make your hands accomplish good things."[43] This Balochi agreed to ask for help from a Taliban-supporting Zahidan cleric who sheltered the families of several Quetta *shura* members, including relatives of Mullah Omar.[44] In 2002, this cleric had helped facilitate the movement of hundreds of Al Qaeda brothers into Iran; and after Khalid Shaikh Mohammad was sent to Guantánamo Bay in 2006, he had also helped Khalid's wife and five of his seven children resettle in Zahidan. These days she raised goats and sold trinkets in Zahidan to get by, but her sons, Yusuf and Abed, who had been captured by the ISI in Karachi in 2002 and turned over to the CIA, had never been seen again.

When the cleric saw Saad several days later, he recognized him immediately. They had met once before, at Mohammed bin Laden's wedding in Kandahar in January 2001. Over tea, the young bin Laden babbled, insisting that he was going to Pakistan to find his father. When the cleric said this was impossible, Saad became angry. Seeing that he would be unable to stop him, or keep him, the cleric gave Saad a phone and an old Pakistani SIM card and dropped him off at the border point of Mirjaveh. From here, he should get a bus to Quetta, the home of Mullah Omar's Taliban *shura*. Someone would be waiting at the other end to guide him, the cleric said, telling Saad not to talk to anyone. The bounty for a bin Laden son was high, he warned, pressing a box of dates into Saad's hands, something to keep his mind off the road ahead.

August 2008, Pakistan-Iran Border

The bus pulled up to the stand in Quetta and Abu Uthman's man stood watching as the passengers stepped off one by one. When the young Arab man in the white prayer cap failed to appear, he casually asked the driver about him. The driver knew immediately who he meant: a youthful man who had talked so much that he had upset other passengers. He had got off several stops back.

Unaware of the true identity of his missing charge, Abu Uthman's agent quickly relayed the news to his boss. Somewhere along the N40 highway, a road that everyone knew was watched from above by American drones, the

Arab guest had gone AWOL. Abu Uthman sent an urgent message to Abbottabad.

Osama was deeply worried. Almost seven years had passed since he had last seen Saad, and it had been four years since he had heard anything from the family in Iran. Now his son, an adult with a childish demeanor, was wandering around a tribal battleground, almost certainly lost and definitely confused. Knowing his son's limited faculties would hold him back and worried that his incessant chatter would let slip something about his father's whereabouts, and wondering if Saad's reappearance was actually a trap sprung by the Iranians, he dispatched Ibrahim with an urgent message for the brothers in Waziristan. They had to find Saad before he compromised everyone. Above all, he had to be stopped from coming to Abbottabad.

Several hundred miles to the south, on the Balochistan-Waziristan border, Saad had talked his way into a Pashtun family's compound, telling anyone who would listen who he was and where he had come from, making the householders, who were bound by Pashtunwali to take him in, queasy with fear.

Saad, too, was jittery and, believing his life was in danger, he asked the family's teenage son—the only one in the family who could read and write Arabic—to compose a couple of letters, something he was unable to do himself.

He wanted to send his last will and testament to his wife back in Yazd and a message to his father. The Iranians could come after him at any moment, he said. There was no time to waste.

August 15: "My dear wife," Saad began, addressing Wafa through his teenage ghostwriter. "How are you doing?" How were the children? He was praying daily. "I ask God . . . that he expedites your release and all the prisoners of the mujahideen to the shores of safety." But as a result of his present predicament, which he did not go into, he was not confident he was going to be able to help them.[45]

The spelling errors and crossings-out on the pages of the schoolboy's spiral-bound notebook evoked the state of fear and haste in which the letter was composed. At moments it also became mawkish. Wafa, who he had married when she was sixteen and he was nineteen, was "the apple of my eye, the most precious thing that I have in this world," said Saad, who also dictated compromising details about what he had done in Iran. "My dear wife, you know I escaped from prison for my sister, you, [Khairiah,] and Hamzah." But whatever had happened since his departure was going to hold him up. It may take "a long time" to get them out, he wrote, and he was evidently feeling the burden. "I know you are in a psychological crisis," Saad continued, referring to his unexpected midnight flit. He was sorry for causing additional stress. "Know that you fill my heart with love, beautiful memories." Every time he thought about her, tears sprang to his eyes, he said. He was praying for the day when God brought them together again and he could "enjoy looking at you and at my children." Then he would "compensate you for the kindness and love you missed in prison."

Now that he had entered the land of drones, darker thoughts also preoccupied him. "If meeting in the world is not possible, then I will see you in the thereafter and that will suffice." In the event of his death, Wafa could return to her family in Sudan if she wished, he said. "But you have to raise my children properly, and watch them and be careful of bad company for them, especially after puberty, especially the girls Asma and Duha." She should find them husbands who were mujahideen, he said, "that is best," or otherwise "good people."

As for his son, he wanted only one thing for him. Without considering the need for secrecy he instructed his teenage ghostwriter to continue: "Send him to the battlefield at his grandfather's." Wafa should only trust the boy to Osama and no other, "because his path is clear and true without qualms." Finally, he gave Wafa permission to remarry in the event of his death, so long as she came back to him in paradise. He felt so imperiled that he had to set her free. "Please forgive me for my shortcomings," he ended, "pray for me and remind my children to pray for me. So, so long either in this world or in the hereafter." He signed the letter in his own name.

The next letter. "What a father you are, you are the greatest," Saad dictated. "I do not forget your kindness in raising us and for deepening the meaning of jihad in our hearts." If he were to die, he hoped his father would take care of Wafa and the children. Saad also wanted to set the record straight. "My dear father, I counted myself as a mujahid and an immigrant on God's path." He was in a fix right now, and he asked his father to "please pray a lot for me, and do continuous charities in my memory, as I will need all the push I can get to reach that everlasting home."

There were financial accounts that needed to be settled—a dead man's dealings. He owed money to a friend who had underwritten his marriage in

Sudan in 1998.[46] "Please pay him back so that I will not be imprisoned in my grave." Mostly, he wished his father triumph. "I ask [God] to make you victorious over your enemies" and to establish the caliphate "sooner and not later." Once again he signed it with his own name.

A few days later, after the son who had acted as the scribe for Saad revealed the existence of the letters to his parents, they asked the Arab visitor to leave. Exhausted by his emotional journey, Saad took the boy's notebook with him. At some stage over the next couple of months he or someone else propped it up on a Sony Vaio laptop and filmed the letters with a cell phone. Enticing glimpses of the videographer's location could be seen around the edges of the screen—a window ledge, a clear blue early evening sky above a band of vivid green. There was no sign of houses, trees, or people.

July 18, 2008, Ghazni, Afghanistan

Across the border in Afghanistan another missing piece of the 9/11 years had recently come together inside an out-of-the-way police station filled with sweating officers and local reporters.

The focus of everyone's attention was a delicate woman with her face wrapped up in her black scarf.[47] According to the local police chief, who addressed the media pack summoned at short notice, she had been caught the previous day with enough chemicals in her bag to build a powerful explosive device. Beside her sat a thirteen-year-old boy, who she was accused of recruiting as the suicide bomber.[48]

Later that day, the woman, who the police chief falsely identified as "a Pakistani from Sindh" although he knew that her real identity was Aafia Siddiqui, was resting on a bed behind a curtain at the police station when an Afghan translator and four Americans—two FBI special agents and two soldiers—came to pick her up. Hopeful of winning a reward, the Ghazni police chief had agreed to hand her over. One soldier laid his M4 on the floor not realizing that Siddiqui was resting just behind the curtain. Moments later, according to statements taken later from the Americans, the curtain swung back and Siddiqui stood, pointing the assault rifle in their faces. One witness alleged that she fired twice. Another alleged that she shouted in English, "Get the fuck out of here!" and "Allahu Akhbar!" before being wrestled to the floor, where she was shot twice in the stomach.[49]

Barely alive, she only survived because a U.S. Army surgeon cut her open from clavicle to belly button. One kidney and several teeth were removed, while her broken nose was reset. While still recovering from her wounds, she was flown on an FBI jet to the United States, where, seventeen days later, she was officially identified as Aafia Siddiqui, "a fugitive Al Qaeda operative."

While Aafia awaited charges in a Manhattan detention center, the boy arrested with her, who the Afghan authorities claimed had been groomed to be a human bomb, was named as her missing eldest son, Ahmed. He was taken to Islamabad and put in the temporary care of his great-uncle Faruqi, who tried to be welcoming but could not get the thought out of his head that the boy bore little resemblance to old photos he had of Ahmed from before 9/11. This boy's habits and demeanor were all Pashtun, not middle-class Karachi, and when he began to probe gently, "Ahmed" made some startling claims.

"He said that his real name was Ali Hasan and he came from a remote hill village beyond Mansehra," Faruqi recalled.[50] "He told me his family had died during the earthquake of 2005."

Initially picked up by the Pakistani police, the boy said he had spent two years inside children's jails and had been used several times by the ISI as a dummy witness to mount false cases.

"Eventually, he had ended up in Kabul at a prison run by Americans," said the uncle. "He was moved every two months and periodically given a new name and a new story to recite." He was used by U.S. intelligence to penetrate and inform on groups of prisoners: Al Qaeda, Taliban, and those from other jihad fronts. It was not the first time that children had been enveloped in U.S. counterterrorism operations: Khalid Shaikh Mohammad's two sons had been captured and then threatened with beatings and had had insects placed on them, before vanishing into the U.S. detention program.

Ahmed aka Ali Hasan also claimed he had met Aafia Siddiqui for the first time when he was taken to Ghazni on the morning of the press conference.

Despite concerns that the boy was an imposter, Aafia's sister and mother, who lived in Karachi, accepted him as one of the family, while they accused the uncle of being senile. After the boy was flown to Karachi to live with them, Aafia's sister, a strident and outspoken U.S.-trained scientist, claimed that Aafia had been in U.S. detention for the entirety of the past five years, distancing the ISI from the story. Even Aafia's ex-husband came out of hiding to back this version of the story.

"That was part of the deal when they gave him to us," Aafia's sister admitted later, without expanding on who "they" were.[51] A child who they would all say was Aafia's, and the United States to blame: it was a tragically familiar story in Pakistan—a family riven apart under pressure from the spy agencies.

When a frail-looking and faltering Aafia Siddiqui appeared in a New York court charged with seven counts of assault and attempted murder, hundreds of thousands of people in Pakistan who thought they could guess what had really happened to her took to the streets in protest.

After a shocking photograph taken shortly after her tussle with U.S. soldiers in Ghazni was released, Moazzam Begg, a British-Pakistani former Guantánamo Bay detainee, who now ran CAGE, a London-based group campaigning for detainees' rights, took up her case. Aafia became a poster girl for American excess, even though it was Pakistani forces in the deep state and the world of jihad that had nurtured her.[52]

September 2008, Islamabad

Pervez Musharraf was in no mood for sympathy for Pakistan's "daughter," as Aafia was described in the domestic press. Instead, he watched horrified from his Zamzama bungalow in Karachi as Bhutto's widower, Asif Ali Zardari, rode a wave of pity to election victory as president.[53] Soon afterward, the former president-dictator exiled himself to Edgware Road in Central London, from where he could reconsider his future surrounded by wealthy acolytes and without fear of assassination.

One of his legacies was the aerial drone campaign against Al Qaeda and the Pakistan Taliban that during his last eight months in office had been ratcheted up, something that Zardari would now have to confront along with a long-promised military campaign in Waziristan. As insurance, Zardari had kept on Musharraf's army chief, General Ashfaq Parvez Kayani, who was practically the only man in the new administration with any experience dealing with the Taliban and Al Qaeda. As a graduate of the U.S. Army's staff college at Fort Leavenworth and infantry school at Fort Benning, Kayani also provided crucial contacts within the Bush administration.

By 2008, the drone war had a new flavor to it. The United States was now conducting operations without Pakistan's cooperation, and four senior Al Qaeda figures had been killed since the beginning of the year, including

Abu Laith al-Libi, who had been commander of Al Qaeda operations in eastern Afghanistan and central to Dr. al-Zawahiri's fight against NATO.[54]

An internal Pakistani military assessment on the campaign in the Tribal Areas made for stark reading, with 1,140 insurgents killed or wounded and 197 captured. More than 800 civilians had been killed or seriously injured.[55]

In the face of the omnipresent drones, Al Qaeda Central shuttered safe houses, closed down communications, and relocated families in a scramble to regroup. Couriers went into hiding. The network went dark, just as Saad bin Laden most needed help.

November 2008, Peshawar, Pakistan

Desperate to locate his son and to elicit news about family members he now knew were still being held against their will in Iran, Osama bin Laden issued orders for the screw to be turned on Tehran.

Heshmatollah Attarzadeh, the commercial attaché at the Iranian consulate in Peshawar, was targeted on his way to work on the morning of November 13.[56] Based in Peshawar for three years, he was already jittery, as just the previous day an American aid worker had been shot dead by unknown gunmen on a busy street.[57] Now, as his vehicle drove through the upmarket Hayatabad neighborhood, two cars rammed it and gunmen, lying in wait, stepped out and sprayed the vehicle with bullets, killing his police escort. Attarzadeh was bundled into a pickup and driven away, thinking, he would reveal later, he was about to be executed.

By dawn the next morning he was deep in the mountains of South Waziristan, being held inside a stone house by an angry-looking Arab and Pashtun-speaking masked gunmen from Al Qaeda's new allies in the Pakistan Taliban.[58]

The questioning of Attarzadeh, who was blindfolded and manacled, centered on Osama bin Laden's family. Where were they? What had happened to Saad? What about the Al Qaeda *shura* members? Unless everyone was located and released, he would be beheaded.

When the diplomat explained that he was far too junior to be a party to such high-grade intelligence, his jailers grew sullen. They recorded a video, in which they threatened to kill him if Osama's family was not freed. Over the course of the next few weeks, they kept him permanently on the move, as the TTP guards tried to outsmart U.S. drones. Eventually, the diplomat found himself in an isolated village near Mir Ali, sharing a room with the Afghan consul general to Peshawar, who had been kidnapped by Al Qaeda the previous September and was by now "half dead." The two prisoners remained locked up together, whispering to each other in the dark through a thick curtain as Al Qaeda tried to extract some kind of benefit from its captives.[59]

When Tehran demanded that the Pakistani government open a channel with the kidnappers, the case was referred to the new ISI chief, General Ahmed Shuja Pasha, a diminutive infantryman with a taste for tailored suits. Army chief General Kayani had appointed him in September, anxious to replace Musharraf's brother-in-law, General Nadeem Taj, and usher in a new era.

Trained at the Pakistan Military Academy in Kakul, Abbottabad, and with the British Army on Salisbury Plain, and having once headed up United Nations peacekeeping troops in Sierra Leone, Pasha was reasonably global, and knowledgeable about the West, as well as being a savvy political strategist.[60] Behind the wisecracks and amenability—Pasha liked to say he was the first soldier in Pakistan to own a sleeping bag, something he had bought in England at the end of a military training course in 1979—he was also deeply patriotic. He was a staunch supporter of Pakistan's strategic depth policy of secretly backing the Taliban and homegrown jihad groups through the ISI's S-Wing, all of which put him on a direct collision course with Washington.[61]

Initially, the U.S. government had high hopes for Pasha. For the past two years he had played a key role in Waziristan as director general of military operations and seemed, genuinely, to be seeking engagement with jihad fronts that the United States also wanted gone. Kayani had taken him along to six meetings with the U.S. chairman of the Joint Chiefs of Staff, Admiral Mike Mullen, who was impressed with their talk on tackling the Taliban through counterinsurgency rather than conventional warfare. However, General Michael Hayden, the CIA director, remained skeptical. "PAKMIL was big, artillery heavy, and road-bound and ill-suited to navigating mountain trails or dealing with insurgents," he recalled.[62] The idea that it knew how to fight any kind of war other than a front-on collision with a force it hoped was weaker was naïve.

Hayden, who had taken serious flak for surveillance failures over 9/11, as he had been director of the National Security Agency (NSA) at the time, and who as a result of 9/11 had ushered in controversial new NSA surveillance methods for technological communications, was also doubtful that the ISI could change course. For him, the test would be Pasha's willingness to tackle S-Wing. Hayden knew enough about the ISI's internal workings to know that S-Wing's contractors and field operatives dealt directly with armed Islamist outfits without referral back to headquarters to ensure plausible deniability for the ISI chief.[63]

The U.S. government hoped that the ISI's newly revamped facilities might influence future thinking on the matter. The gray hulk of Aabpara had been completely rebuilt thanks to U.S. tax dollars—both aid cash and secretly paid reward money for culling Al Qaeda scalps. That the figure ran into many millions was evidenced in the ambition that lay behind the new building. Standing behind five layers of security, it more resembled a five-star hotel than a ministry, and it towered over squat, peeling old structures that still housed junior officers.[64] Inside, everything had been finished off to the highest specifications (especially Pasha's office).[65]

In reality, whatever Hayden thought, General Pasha told his closest colleagues that he believed that Pakistan had no choice but to reform.[66] The Islamic Republic had been rocked by more than forty suicide-bomb blasts since the beginning of the year, most of them orchestrated by the TTP, whose men got behind security cordons and into sensitive areas, making some official complicity undeniable. Only it was not inexplicable to Pasha, who had read the files on the Musharraf assassination attempts and knew that the Pakistan military itself was heavily infiltrated by allies of Al Qaeda or the Taliban. Unless he got them under control, which would take considerable time and dexterity, the force he had dedicated his life to would buckle.

The new ISI chief's greatest problem was the mountain he had to climb every day. He was already inundated by investigations. Shortly before he walked through the doors at Aabpara, a truck had crashed through the security barrier outside the Islamabad Marriott, a five-star hotel redolent of a more affluent and peaceful age—a brazen attack on a much-loved institution that had shocked everyone.

Security guards had opened fire, stopping the driver, but the truck was carrying at least 1,300 pounds of explosives, military and commercial, muddled with mortar ammunition and aluminum powder, and it gouged a sixty-foot crater into the driveway, blowing off the front of the hotel. Hundreds were injured, and picking through the ruins of the charred building, at least fifty-four bodies were recovered, with five foreign diplomats among them.

The target—with its much-cherished vestige of lounge suits, sherwanis, and the softer, brighter era of Pakistan's founding father Mohammed Ali Jinnah—was emotionally significant, and the plot had been constructed to demoralize, demonstrating how febrile state security was and how fragile the last vestiges of secular Pakistan.[67] The timing was also purposeful, as the attack took place just hours after President Zardari had made his maiden speech to parliament. Pasha had his work cut out in trying to pin down the perpetrators. But almost immediately there were new distractions. On November 26, three weeks after the U.S. presidential election ushered in a new era in Washington, ten Pakistani gunmen sailed out of the night to lay siege to the Indian megalopolis of Mumbai, killing 164 people, an act of terrorism that brought Pakistan and India once again close to nuclear war.[68]

Evidence quickly emerged that the attack had been orchestrated by the ISI-backed Lashkar-e-Taiba—with compelling evidence pointing to elements within the directorate as also being complicit. Pasha pleaded ignorance. "I was asking everyone, you need to tell me if you know something," he recalled.[69] When the answer came back "no," he told the CIA's Islamabad station the same.

In Washington, Michael Hayden remained unconvinced. "I began routinely harassing my counterpart in Pakistan . . . on the phone, urging him to get to the bottom of the attack and to discuss it frankly with us," he recalled.[70] "We had no doubt that the attack was the work of [Lashkar-e-Taiba], and there was mounting evidence that preparation for and direction of the attack took place from within Pakistan, where LeT enjoyed the protection and support of ISI."

Hayden took to describing Pakistan as "the ally from hell," citing as evidence a previous incident when he had gone to Islamabad during Musharraf's tenure only for the president to refuse to refuel his aircraft to take him back to the United States. "The [U.S.] crew had forgotten their government credit card—you can't make this stuff up—and the Pakistanis wouldn't budge," Hayden recalled.[71] Having been paid millions, they would not lend the United States thousands to get the jet back home. Someone would have to front the cash.

The Mumbai postmortem rumbled on for weeks, with hard evidence against the ISI mounting. Pasha was summoned to Washington on Christmas

Day for a showdown with Hayden. Working carefully from handwritten notes—as was his style—Pasha's rebuttal was a delicate affair. One of those who attended recalled how he gave some ground, admitting that "some" former ISI agents may have been engaged in "some broad training of the attackers." But he refused to name names and insisted that serving ISI officers were not connected to the plot. Afterward, Pasha visited Pakistan's ambassador, Husain Haqqani, and told him that the planners of Mumbai were "our people" but it wasn't "our operation."[72]

Another high-ranking ISI official went further, concluding: "We lost track of this."[73] Pressed to explain, the officer said that a similar plan had been in the offing for many months and had been given "tacit support from the intelligence service." However, it was supposed to remain "shuttered." Instead, elements of the intelligence service, allied with the Pakistan Taliban and keen to undermine Zardari, who had offered India his "hand in peace," had given the green light.[74]

With Mumbai, the Marriott bombing, and dozens more smaller terrorist incidents to investigate, a war to fight against the Pakistan Taliban, and Hayden breathing down his neck about homegrown Islamists, especially the Lashkar-e-Taiba and the ISI-sponsored Haqqani network—which was accused of escalating attacks inside Afghanistan—the last thing General Pasha needed was to help out Osama bin Laden or go searching in the Tribal Areas for a minor Iranian diplomat.

January 2009, Bilal Town, Abbottabad

Saad bin Laden had crossed into Pakistan five months earlier and still there was no news from him. Osama's long-suffering companion and protector, Ibrahim, prayed that Saad would never find his way to Abbottabad as he fretted about a house that echoed to the sound of ever more children. He had signed up to care for the Sheikh as a favor to his friend Khalid Shaikh Mohammad at a time when there had been one wife and one child only. Now, there were so many people living in the house that neighbors had dubbed it the Waziristan *kothi* (palace). Despite the women's best efforts, it was impossible to keep the children subdued around the clock. To make matters worse, Amal, Maryam, and Abrar's wife, Bushra, were all pregnant again.

After discussing with Abrar, Ibrahim gave Osama an ultimatum: no more relatives.[75] No more guests. No more traffic in and out of the building. In the future it would be one out and one in. Secretly, he and Abrar, whose nerves were shot, began discussing their exit strategy.

Both of them were bound to Osama by a *bayat*—their oath—but also by the Islamic notion of *fard* (obligation). More practically, they had stuck by him in the hope of receiving a generous nest egg, enough to buy a villa or two in Saudi Arabia, where they intended to retire. But whenever Ibrahim tried to commence a discussion about the future, suggesting that it was time for the family to move elsewhere, or tried to ascertain what their compensation might be, the Sheikh rounded on him, saying that the brothers' selfishness was endangering "the jihad and the nation's issues."[76]

Riskier still was the endless messaging, Osama even recruiting members of Ibrahim's family in Kohat to keep his covert postal service functioning. So many letters passed between Abbottabad and Waziristan these days that Ibrahim's family in Suleman Talaab acted as a postbox. Both his brother-in-law and two teenage nephews went to Peshawar to collect thumb drives, meeting with trusted Pashtun middleman Mohammed Aslam.[77]

Ibrahim's sister, Haleema, was agitating for change, too. The Saeed family had done more than enough to help the mystery sheikh over the years, she said—although she did not know it was Osama. "It's time for someone else to carry the burden."

Ibrahim tackled Osama again, and finally he agreed to a new system.

Khadija bin Laden's widower, Daood, who was still in Mir Ali, knew a talented document forger, and he was commissioned to prepare fake Pakistani ID cards for Osama and his son Khalid, so that they could begin traveling themselves. Khalid sent a personal letter to Mir Ali with photographs and all relevant details, requesting that Daood keep an eye on the work "because we need them quickly."[78] Even though his father refused to contemplate it, he knew that if they did not make an effort to ease the pressure, the situation with the companions was in danger of spinning out of control.

When no news came back from Daood, Seham also wrote to him. Unaware of her husband's arguments with Ibrahim, she was still lobbying for Daood to join them. "My precious son," she began. "I pray day and night to join you with your children. They have not forgotten you, and they always ask about you. They are fine and well and we surround them with our love."[79] Daood's eldest son, Abdallah, had finished the third chapter of his book and his daughter, Aisha, was studying. The surviving baby, who was named Fatima after dead Khadija's favorite sister in Iran, was now walking and spent most of her time running away from her foster mother—Khadija's nineteen-year-old sister, Miriam. Turning to the still raw memory of her daughter's death, Seham became emotional again, recounting a dream Khadija had had when she was a child. "Ten years ago she told me, 'Do not be sad. I see myself standing in the door of Paradise and knocking on the door. *He* asked who [goes there]? And I said, "I am Khadija." And then I entered, [beneath the bows of] a beautiful tree and all of you came with me.'"

Her daughter had foreseen that she would die before her family, said Seham. "But we will follow her to heaven, God willing."

A few days later, with still no news from Daood, Khalid wrote again, reassuring him and also urging him into action. "Regarding our security situation after the kids' arrival right over here, I would like to let you know that it is good."[80] As soon as the ID cards arrived, he and his father would start traveling.

Ignoring Ibrahim's concerns, Khalid also rekindled discussions about his long-delayed betrothal to Karima—as Daood was the only one still in regular touch with her family. "You, my brother, have gotten me a fiancée and an agreement was granted. You also have asked for a fiancée from my dad, and an agreement was granted," he wrote, referring to the news that Miriam had been promised to Daood. But when would he meet his wife-to-be? Many times before his sister's death, Khalid had tried to bring his intended over to Abbottabad only for security or an earthquake to get in the way. "It is the same problem that is preventing me from getting married now," he complained, a sideways reference to Ibrahim's ultimatum that no new people could come. He had heard that Karima's jaded mother was threatening to look for another husband for her daughter.

Daood replied and addressed Khalid man-to-man, promising to reason with Karima's family. Marrying within the mujahideen was every young person's duty, he said. "And God willing, I will continue [canvassing on your behalf] until God grants you a good woman."[81]

Despite that good news, there was no update about the counterfeit ID cards.

January 2009, Washington, D.C.

On January 20, 2009, Barack Obama was inaugurated as the forty-fourth president of the United States, promising "a new birth of freedom" in his

address. But beyond the "can-do" attitude and the goodwill, beyond the promises to close Guantánamo within a year, end wars in Iraq and Afghanistan,
and build a more inclusive world, the new president told his closest national
security advisers that he suspected he had to strike hard at Al Qaeda if the
never-ending war was to be diminished.

Within days, CIA director Michael Hayden was out, and Obama met
with his successor, Leon Panetta, to discuss the ongoing hunt for Osama
bin Laden, asking him: "How's the trail? Has it gone completely cold?"[82]
Despite the successes of the drone program, the search for the Al Qaeda
emir had barely progressed since the closure of "Alec" station, the CIA unit
that had run from 1996 to 2005 and was dedicated to hunting Osama and
his deputies.[83]

In May 2009, after receiving a briefing from counterterrorism officials,
Obama and Panetta sat down to plot a new strategy.[84] "We really need to
intensify this effort," said the president. On June 2, he signed a memo for
the CIA chief: "In order to ensure that we have expended every effort, I direct
you to provide me within 30 days a detailed operation plan for locating and
bringing to justice" Osama bin Laden and to "destroy, dismantle, and defeat
Al Qaeda."

Panetta's team did a lot of blue-sky thinking. They rewatched all the
Al Qaeda videos, scouring every inch of every frame for potential clues,
studying types of vegetation and even rock formations.[85] An obvious starting
point was to examine how Osama's written and audio communications
reached the outside world. This in-and-out contact with an otherwise closed
system was a fissure to be exploited. The CIA recommended refocusing its
energies on identifying and following Osama's couriers. At the top of the list
was Abu Ahmad al-Kuwaiti, who had been named by several Al Qaeda
prisoners.

One of the first things Panetta's new team did was conduct a thorough
review of detainees' statements, discovering several nuggets of information
about bin Laden's Kuwaiti courier that had been previously overlooked.[86]

A CIA intelligence report entitled "Probable Identification of Suspected
Bin Laden Facilitator Abu Ahmad al-Kuwaiti" noted that the review of old
data had determined that his real name might be Habib al-Rahman and that
he was "living in Pakistan, probably in the greater Peshawar area."[87]

Back in 2002, a young Saudi detainee named Mohammed al-Qahtani,
who had been recruited as a 9/11 hijacker but failed to gain entry to the

United States, had told interrogators that he had been introduced to an Al Qaeda official called Abu Ahmad al-Kuwaiti in the summer of 2001, when he had been sent to Karachi to prepare for his mission.[88] The Kuwaiti had taken al-Qahtani to an Internet café and shown him how to use a computer and how to send "dead-drop" e-mails, whereby two correspondents who shared the same e-mail address and password logged in and wrote messages to each other that they saved as drafts, allowing each of them to read the other's messages before erasing them.

During their time together, the Kuwaiti told al-Qahtani that his main job was working as a courier for Khalid Shaikh Mohammad.[89] If he was telling the truth, al-Qahtani's evidence, long overlooked by the CIA, directly contradicted that given by KSM, who had said that the Kuwaiti was a low-level operative who he did not know well and who had never worked as a courier.

The data-review produced more leads. Another Guantánamo detainee, a Mauritanian called Mohamedou Ould Slahi, had also mentioned the Kuwaiti. Slahi, who was married to a sister of Mahfouz the Mauritanian's wife, said that "Abu Ahmad al-Kuwaiti was a mid-level Al Qaeda operative who facilitated the movement and safe haven of senior Al Qaeda members and families." Slahi had gone on to say that the Kuwaiti was dead, killed during the battle for Tora Bora, at which point the CIA's inquiry into him had paused.[90]

Now, matching Slahi's story with others, the CIA realized that some of these accounts, or at least the ones that were not trying to misdirect them, contained kernels of useful truths.

According to other detainees, the Kuwaiti courier came from a large family of brothers, several of whom were involved in the jihad, and one of whom—named Habib Ahmad Saeed—*had* died at Tora Bora. Maybe Slahi had deliberately mixed up the Kuwaiti brothers, opening up a possibility that the brother working for Osama was still alive.

CIA reports from early 2008 drew out some common denominators. "Debriefings of the senior most detainees who were involved in caring for Osama have produced little locational information," the cables reported.[91] The true identity of the Kuwaiti was "the final nugget that detainees hold on to in debriefings (over threat info and even al-Zawahiri LOINT [Location Intelligence]) given their loyalty to the Al Qaeda leader." One cable noted: "We assess that Abu Ahmad would likely be in the same category as Khalid Shaikh Mohammad and Abu Faraj al-Libi, so we advocate building as much of a targeting picture of where and when Habib/Abu Ahmad travels to flesh out current leads to bin Laden."[92]

In order to pursue their quarry, President Obama was told, what the CIA really needed was a phone number, an address, a confirmed sighting, or, ideally, an asset inside the network. The only problem was that the ISI had lost both of its prime contenders—Aafia Siddiqui, who was now in U.S. detention, and the former Al Qaeda courier Hassan Ghul, who, according to the ISI, was AWOL. Had he returned to the Al Qaeda fold? the CIA repeatedly asked. The ISI would not comment, but it appeased the Americans by promising to track him down in the Tribal Areas. It was actively monitoring all e-mails and calls received by Ghul's wife, who was a sister of the Rabbani brothers now in Guantánamo, and by Ghul's own sister, Nabila, who lived in Karachi.[93]

Sooner or later he was going to have to contact one of his old friends or his family, the ISI promised the CIA, and then they would have him. In the meantime, the CIA let it be known that finding a suitable asset, and fast, was priority for all stations.

One candidate immediately floated to the top: a Jordanian doctor who by night was a digital jihadi. He had recently been arrested in Amman by local spies who had monitored him writing increasingly extreme postings, exhorting his brothers worldwide to commit acts of violence. His name was Humam al-Balawi, and it fell to the Jordanian General Intelligence Directorate (GID) to flip him and set him in play in Pakistan.

June 2009, Mir Ali, North Waziristan

Saad bin Laden had been crisscrossing Pakistan's Tribal Areas on foot and in shared rides for months, unable to locate his father and rejected by frightened villagers whenever he tried to ask for help, often unmasking himself. In the heightened paranoia of living with the drones, with at least one strike a week, no one wanted to help a bin Laden.

Traveling alone, carrying a small battered suitcase and his laptop, Saad sometimes returned to Quetta, which was beyond the drones' area of activity and was thronged with young Taliban recruits who strutted about in black turbans and openly bore arms. The reality of Al Qaeda's pact with the Taliban was visible everywhere, from the jihad recruiting posters papering the walls of the mosques to the boarded-up DVD shops.

Eventually, Saad located a Pashtun "supporter" to whom he had previously been introduced in Karachi in 2002. The man informed Saad that his half sister Khadija was dead and her children had been sent to join Osama at an undisclosed location.[94] For security reasons, no one knew where this was, only that it was somewhere in Pakistan's settled areas. There is no record of how Saad reacted to the news, but armed with jotted-down notes of the safest routes to follow, he set a course for Al Qaeda Central in Damadola.

Over the past couple of years, the movement had mapped the entire district, with brothers surveying routes to be used during "tightening periods" (of drone activity or an army crackdown) and dirt roads or mule paths for times of "extreme tightening." There were lists of secure rest stops, way stations, and safe houses, unmanned checkpoints where a traveler could sneak through unnoticed, and known flashpoints that should be avoided, such as hidden military positions. Friendly Pashtun "seekers of knowledge" were videoed or photographed so those on the road would have a "facial recognition" of who they could trust. They were listed by number rather than name: Figure 5 was okay because he had fought at Lal Masjid and was usefully "fluent in Arabic," but the deputy to Figure 26 was not okay, because he "thins out his beard," a sure sign of weakness. There were some useful generalizations. The people of Orakzai and Khyber should generally be avoided since they "plant hashish and some plant opium."[95]

Eventually, Saad showed up at a shopfront in the village of Mir Khon Khel, a raggedy village halfway along the main road connecting Mir Ali to Miram Shah. The shop was one of several locations from where As Sahab videos were distributed, and someone alerted Khadija bin Laden's widower, Daood, who came to check Saad out.

The two had not seen each other since Daood had accompanied the family to the Iranian border in 2002, and Saad was overwhelmed to see a familiar face. In his excitement, Daood got out his cell phone and took several photographs, ignoring established protocol.[96] Sitting in the back of the shop over tea and *parathas*, Saad updated him as best he could, a rambling story that Daood struggled to follow. In turn, Daood recounted how Khadija had died giving birth to twins, and that one had died, while their surviving children had gone to live with their grandfather, wherever he was hiding. Even he did not know the precise location. There were things to celebrate: Osama was well and Daood had recently married a Pashtun girl called Sarah, who was already pregnant.[97]

When Saad said he was desperate to be reunited with his father, Daood warned him against it. He also sent word to Osama that his son had risen from the dead. The instruction that came back was perfunctory. Saad should stay put, working in the shop and pretending to be deaf and mute.[98] Knowing his son's mental proclivities, and his loose lips, Osama instructed Daood to keep a close eye on him. He could not afford to have Saad come until someone had thoroughly checked out if he had been tracked or bugged.

July 2009, Yazd

Hamzah bin Laden could not wait any longer. A low-level Al Qaeda brother released by the Iranians carried a letter describing his pain at watching on Al Jazeera as the jihad progressed without being able to play his part.

"My beloved father, when you left me, my brother Khalid, and my brother [Ladin], at the foot of the mountain, near the olive farm, I could not imagine the length of this bitter separation," Hamzah wrote.[99] Eight years had passed. "My eyes still remember the last time they saw you, when you were under the olive tree and you gave every one of us a Muslim rosary."

Much was different, not least Hamzah himself. "You might not recognize me when you meet me, as my features have changed." Still, he cherished the old memories most. "I remember every smile that you smiled, every word that you spoke to me, and every look that you gave me." But now he needed his father's wisdom. "I wish that I could see you, if only for a minute, to get your pertinent opinion."

Hamzah had not wasted his time, he assured his father, but had studied hard with the Mauritanian. "I have been taught by the learned brothers, one who helps me, directs me, and guides me on the path." He had married a "pious wife," Maryam, the daughter of Al Qaeda *shura* member Abu Mohammed al-Masri. They had two children: "a son who I gave your name Osama and a daughter who I named after [my] mother Khairiah." As he could not send photographs, he asked for God to "place their image in your eye. He created them to serve you." Rounding off, he told his father that he ached to join the world of jihad. "We will leave soon, with glorious God's permission . . . I consider myself to be forged in steel."

*   *   *

July 2009, Bilal Town, Abbottabad

Sheikh Osama told Amal that he was most worried for his easily confused son Saad.[100] The drones over Waziristan were so plentiful with their incessant buzzing that locals called them *machays* (wasps). The worst days were when the skies were blue, allowing for clear views over the target area. Those who had money had relocated to Balochistan, while the rest stayed at home and prayed. Some slept on the roof, fearing being buried beneath rubble, while others planted trees around their homes, hoping to shield themselves.

Osama wrote to Atiyah, telling him to start thinking of getting the brothers out of the tribal areas and over the border into Afghanistan. Zabil and Ghazni provinces should be considered as alternative bases as well as Kunar, which he knew from his own experiences was well-fortified due to its rough terrain and inaccessible, with many mountains, rivers, and trees.[101]

Only the senior leaders should remain in Waziristan "and take the necessary precautions" such as moving regularly but only "on a cloudy day," avoiding the main roads "because many of them got targeted when they were meeting on them." Atiyah had to take charge of Saad, who had a habit of getting into trouble and as a child had once been run over and almost died in Sudan.[102] Osama asked Atiyah to go to Mir Khon Khel to retrieve him.

Atiyah had not used the highway for many months. He and his men trekked along smuggling routes and mule trails, traveling at night and on foot. The main problem besides the drones, he complained, was spies. There were traitors among them who were providing the Americans with such accurate targeting information that they had killed more than four hundred Al Qaeda figures and civilians in just eighteen months.

The Arabs had become so paranoid they also believed invisible ink was sprayed on target vehicles that could be spied from the sky, and that special microchips had been scattered about, disguised as stones. News of the CIA's attempt to turn Aafia Siddiqui had reached them and filled them with dread. Dozens of suspects were seized, including several foreign journalists who came to interview Taliban commanders. Among them were Sean Langan from Britain's Channel 4, who had been held for three months the previous year and had been threatened with mock executions; and David Rohde from the *New York Times*, who had been abducted near Kabul in November 2008 and held at a succession of Haqqani safe houses around Miram Shah until June 2009, when he escaped.[103]

Hassan Ghul had also reemerged with an alarming tale to tell. Arriving in Mir Ali, he met Atiyah and told him how the CIA and ISI had tried to recruit him to infiltrate the inner circle. Soon after that, Abu Yahya al-Libi, the famous Bagram escapee who now worked closely with Atiyah, wrote a manual, *Guidance on the Ruling of the Muslim Spy*.[104] With a foreword by Dr. al-Zawahiri, it offered legal advice regarding the correct punishment for informants. Local Taliban commanders took immediate action. Five Pakistanis accused of leading U.S. intelligence to Abu Laith al-Libi's hideout shortly before he was killed were forced to make videotaped confessions, before one of them was beheaded, the footage released by Al-Fajr Media Center.

July 17, 2009, Garyom District, North Waziristan

Dusty and tired, the Al Qaeda guests arrived at Maulana Abdul Majeed's compound in the hills outside Razmak. Majeed was an influential Islamist cleric, and his security had been especially tight since the Pakistani government had accused him of links to the Tehrik-i-Taliban Pakistan. Nevertheless, shortly after ten A.M., missiles screamed down, scattering rice and stainless-steel plates. It was the twenty-eighth drone strike of the year, and at least six people died, with another four seriously wounded.[105]

Speaking on National Public Radio in the United States five days later, an unnamed senior counterterrorism official announced that they were "eighty to eighty-five percent" certain that Saad bin Laden was among the dead. A photograph was circulating that appeared to show his body. Osama's son, who had survived President Clinton's 1998 Cruise missile attacks on Afghanistan and President Bush's invasion three years later, only to vanish into the Iranian wilderness, had not been the target. He had simply been in the wrong place at the wrong time.[106]

The news came as a jolt to Osama, who described Saad as the most soft-hearted of his sons, an unlikely mujahid who had been regarded within the family as "incapable of harming a soul," a practical joker who in the camps had liked to feed baked hedgehog to his friends, telling them it was chicken.[107] It was "impossible for him to plan or commit any crime or violation," said his siblings—unlike Hamzah, who everyone felt sure would follow in his father's footsteps one day.

Osama sent an urgent letter to Atiyah demanding a moratorium on the "leakage of the news." His immediate concern was that Saad's death would demoralize the troops and somehow lead back to him.[108] "Regarding what you mentioned about the picture of Saad (may God rest his soul)," he wrote to Atiyah, "his after-death picture should be deleted."[109]

A shamefaced Atiyah wrote back to Sheikh Osama, confirming he would destroy the image and sending details of Saad's demise.[110] While working in the As Sahab archive, filing tapes, Saad had stayed at a house near Mir Khon Khel village, closely monitored by Pashtun "supporters," who had all been apprised of his willfulness. When he had tried to engage any of them in a conversation about taking up an operational position in Al Qaeda, they had gently rebuffed him. Frustrated, he had befriended a visiting Al Qaeda commander who was unaware of his vulnerability. Flattered to receive attention from a genuine bin Laden, the commander, unbeknownst to Atiyah, had agreed to take Saad to Maulana Abdul Majeed's lunch. By the time anyone realized he was missing, it was too late.

Osama wrote back, furious. His son deserved peace in his death and his grave, an unmarked plot on the edge of a martyrs' cemetery outside Razmak, had to be kept secret. Atiyah could never make such a mistake again and should find some way to avenge Saad.

August 2009, Wana, South Waziristan, Pakistan

When Humam al-Balawi, a baby-faced Jordanian doctor, had first turned up in Wana seeking to contact Al Qaeda Central in March 2009, everyone suspected him of being another spy.[111] Although he demonstrably had a secret double life as a fearsome online jihadist called Abu Dujana al-Khorasani, a self-styled "scourge of the West," in the flesh he was effeminate and bookish.

Balawi came from a stable middle-class family in Amman, the Jordanian capital, where he worked in a clinic treating refugees, and he was married with two young daughters. However, while they slept, his avatar took over as he embarked on an online crusade to inform Muslims worldwide about the brave actions of his hero, the martyred Jordanian hardman Abu Musab al-Zarqawi.[112] Night after night, Balawi aka Abu Dujana posted grisly videos of insurgent attacks on U.S. troops in Iraq as he tried to rehabilitate Zarqawi's reputation among those who had been previously alienated by his excesses.

Balawi's arrival in Wana, where he attracted a curious but cautious crowd of Taliban and Al Qaeda supporters, was not completely unexpected. Atiyah had already heard of him, since he and Balawi had begun corresponding by e-mail in 2008, with Atiyah promising to help if he ever came to Pakistan. The Jordanian had flown to Peshawar in March 2009 with two small suitcases containing medical equipment, initially intending to volunteer his services to Al Qaeda as a field doctor.

Balawi had a list of contacts, including several Pakistani jihadists who had written to him through his website, but with the drone war having intensified, it took nearly five months for him to gain anyone's trust. One of the first to take a chance on him was TTP emir Baitullah Mehsud, who in mid-May 2009 invited the Jordanian doctor to join him and his band of Mehsud fighters.[113] Baitullah, who suffered from diabetes and several other ailments, welcomed the opportunity to have a personal medic, someone who could also treat his fighters, who shifted daily from house to house. To thank him, Balawi presented Baitullah with a large roll of dollars he had brought from Amman.[114]

On August 5, when Baitullah Mehsud was killed in a drone strike, Waziristan rose up in fury and pledged to avenge the TTP leader's assassination.[115] Balawi, who was accused of having called in the strike with devices hidden in his medical equipment, fled north. When he reached Mir Ali on August 8, he wrote a note to Atiyah. He desperately needed to call in that favor. "By Allah, I have yearned to meet you, Sheikh," he wrote. "When I meet you I will squeeze you to my chest."[116] Atiyah decided to take a risk and meet him.

Balawi told Atiyah a staggering story that he immediately understood as the foundations of a plan. The CIA *had* sent the baby-faced doctor to Waziristan to spy on Al Qaeda, but he had no intention of becoming an American asset.

Balawi explained how when, in January 2009, the CIA had unmasked him as Abu Dujana, the Americans had asked their colleagues in the Jordanian GID to arrest him. After two months in GID custody, he had been offered a stark choice. Either he would become a double agent, a job for which the Americans would reward him with "millions upon millions of dollars," or he would spend the rest of his life in jail.

Balawi, who was both physically and emotionally weak, had pretended to choose the first option and over the following weeks he was coached by Ali bin Zeid, a young GID captain, who angered Balawi by bragging that his agency had been the source of critical location intelligence that had led to the killing of Abu Musab al-Zarqawi in Iraq.[117]

Balawi, who regarded Zarqawi as a hero, decided to play along with the young captain's plan but betray him at the first opportunity. He told Atiyah that Captain bin Zeid was "an idiotic man" and a "hired dog" of the CIA. His attempt to "brainwash" Balawi was "a dream come true," a chance to fulfill a pledge he had made to his followers on social media to make his "words drip with blood."[118]

The too-trustful bin Zeid "was digging his own grave," said Balawi, explaining that now that he had linked up with Al Qaeda in North Waziristan all he needed to do was to send tangible proof back to Amman. Then Atiyah could spring a trap.[119]

Atiyah introduced Balawi to moneyman Sheikh Saeed al-Masri, who, after asking more searching questions, grasped something everyone else had missed. Captain bin Zeid was a cousin of King Abdullah of Jordan. Killing such a man, who had conspired against Zarqawi and was in cahoots with the CIA, was a ripe opportunity to avenge the death of Saad bin Laden and strike at Jordan, which Al Qaeda regarded as an American lackey that had made peace with Israel.

They decided to lure the captain to Peshawar with a video of Balawi debating with Atiyah, whose face was well known to Western intelligence agencies. They shot it near Mir Ali: the two men sat in a room filled with wood smoke and Pashtun mujahideen. Balawi encrypted the file, e-mailed it to bin Zeid, and waited.

The GID captain was astounded. "You have lifted our heads in front of the Americans," he wrote back.

The CIA was equally impressed, although some worried about the motives of a man who no one in the agency had ever met, and who had got close to ever-vigilant Al Qaeda Central unfeasibly quickly.

"The bait fell in the right spot," Balawi reported back to Atiyah. "They went head over heels with excitement."

Over the next few weeks more tantalizing information streamed out of Mir Ali.[120] In November, when Balawi claimed to be treating Dr. al-Zawahiri and by way of proof provided intimate medical details, the CIA ordered Amman to take things to the next level.

In the eight years since 9/11, no one had ever got this close to al-Zawahiri, and everything Balawi reported matched what the CIA already knew about the fifty-eight-year-old Egyptian physician. But before launching any kind of "kill or capture" operation, the CIA needed to be sure. The only way was to meet Balawi face-to-face, and preferably out of the treacherous, overly eavesdropped death strip of Pakistan. The meet had to be fixed in Afghanistan.

November 2009, Tourist Complex, Quds Force
Training Facility, Tehran

After Saad's escape from Yazd, Osama's family had been transported back to Tehran, where they found a new kind of prison waiting for them at the heart of the Quds Force complex. It consisted of large and newly constructed apartments with a shaded garden for each family, a school, *majlis*, mosque, soccer pitch, even a swimming pool and a gym. Fatima bin Laden, who had just given birth to a daughter fathered by her new husband, Sulaiman Abu Ghaith; Saif al-Adel and his family; and Abu al-Khayr, Abu Mohammed, and the Mauritanian were already installed. As a joke, they called it the Tourist Complex.[121] But with tall walls topped with barbed wire and security cameras, this was clearly no holiday camp. The Iranians were obviously not planning to give up their Al Qaeda "guests" any time soon but were trying to lure them with better facilities.

At the end of the first month, several brothers were offered the chance to call home. Flown to Mashhad, they were whisked to the border through the empty desert in a fleet of cars, in a well-established routine. Standing in the white furnace of the midday sun, Othman bin Laden tried an old number for his brother Omar.[122] Over the years, Omar and his mother, Najwa (who still lived in Syria), had written to the International Red Cross and the United Nations in search of news of their family but had learned nothing certain.

The number still worked, and when Omar picked up he heard the unmistakable sound of his younger brother's voice.

Rapt, Omar listened as Othman recounted their situation. Then, all the horror of his father's "mad world" came flooding back and Omar was overcome as he recalled one repellant episode when Dr. al-Zawahiri had adjudicated over a grisly homosexual gang rape: Omar's childhood friend had been assaulted by a group of men, and the doctor had ruled that it *had not been the assailants' fault*—as the victim was gay. Picking up a sidearm, the doctor had shot Omar's erstwhile school pal in the head.

Omar came around to find Othman was still talking. *"Where are you?"*

Othman could not say. But he asked Omar to make discreet approaches to the Saudi authorities to see if they would be allowed to return home. Frightened and reluctant to reopen old wounds, Omar said he would consult his wife. She handled all the tricky stuff. She was his guide and counsel. A British woman twice his age, she had met Omar in 2006 through her work as a psychoanalyst based in Egypt at a time when he was broken and dejected after six years living back in the real world.

After returning to Saudi Arabia from Afghanistan in late 2001 and assuming he would slide easily into a playboy life of private jets and luxurious homes as part of the larger bin Laden clan, Omar instead had found himself rejected by his family and put to work as a real estate agent—earning commission. Seven different Saudi women, including cousins, turned down his proposals of marriage. In 2006, he had left again, heading for Egypt and seeking a fresh start. While horse trekking around the pyramids, twenty-five-year-old Omar had bonded with British-born Zaina, aged fifty-one. She could see he was an absolute mess. But something about Omar intrigued her and she took him under her wing. When he revealed his true identity, and told stories of his upbringing, instead of being rapt, she was appalled. Osama had been a terrible father, she commented. Omar reacted furiously. "He is a prince," he responded defensively. It was the start of a combative relationship.[123]

Within months they had married and settled at her expat villa in Cairo. But after neighbors contacted British newspapers and revealed the identity of her new husband, his outlaw status cost her a residency visa and they spent the next couple of years bouncing around Europe, looking for asylum.

Deported, followed, questioned, and confined inside various immigration holding facilities, Omar, like his father before him, searched for asylum, with Zaina leading the way. In frustration, Zaina rang the United Nations and asked to be put through to the "refugee section." A well-educated fighter, she wrote to George W. Bush, Tony Blair, and Amnesty International. But in the end, only New Zealand and Qatar had responded, Omar now told his younger brother.[124] The previous year they had moved to Doha, where they were sharing a government compound filled with exiles—families ostracized by revolutions, insurgencies, and wars, or the wives and children of those who had started them. It was a fantasy housing geopolitical cul-de-sac and their current neighbors included several members of Saddam Hussein's family (including his imposing widow Sajida), Yasser Arafat's daughter, and Yusuf al-Qaradawi, a controversial Egyptian cleric who had been barred from entering the United States and several European countries after being described by some in the West as the "sheikh of death."

Maybe the liberally minded Qatar was the answer. "Maybe they will welcome the rest of the bin Ladens," Omar told Othman.

His head swirling with Omar's story and convinced that Zaina was a British spy, Othman hung up, and the party returned to Tehran to reflect on what they had learned.[125] Days later, they were still debating when a photograph flicked up on Al Jazeera that all of them instantly recognized. It was a snap of Saad, taken in Iran.

What followed was a story of a drone strike in Waziristan. Wafa, who was also watching in the women's section of the apartment, froze. One of the victims had been identified as Saad. He was not missing after all, rambling through the badlands, an infuriating houseguest, but dead.

That night, Othman, Mohammed, Ladin, and Hamzah gathered in the *majlis*. None of them had expected Saad to get far, but when they had heard nothing after his midnight flight from Yazd they had convinced each other that he had succeeded in being reunited with their father.

However unlikely, he had become a reason to hope. Now with that thread severed, a furious row blew up. All of them were desperate to go. Pakistan was clearly out of the question. But someone—one of them—had to try another escape.[126]

They eyed one another but no one volunteered.

The women whispered that Saad's death was on Iran's hands and that its intelligence agencies had surely followed him and tipped off the CIA as they had done so many times before. "No one else should try to leave," they said.

By the time they heard that a Pakistani working at the Iranian consulate in Peshawar had been shot dead on November 12, 2009, in retribution for Saad's killing, the family was deeply divided.

November 20, 2009, Tehran

The Mauritanian was deep into his Koran when he heard a gentle knocking at the door late at night. He opened it a sliver, to see a covered girl standing in the shadows. It was Iman, Osama's eighteen-year-old daughter, asking to see his daughter Khadija, her best friend. When they were alone, Iman took off a gold ring and handed it to Khadija. "This was a gift from my father," Iman said. "Why are you giving away something so precious?" a puzzled Khadija asked. Her friend hugged her. Something was about to happen that would "hit the compound like an earthquake," Iman said. Khadija suddenly knew what that was. Iman was preparing to escape. Khadija fetched her father. The Mauritanian knew not to intervene but instead gave Iman a thumb drive containing a copy of Sulaiman Abu Ghaith's anti–bin Laden treatise, *Twenty Guidelines on the Path to Jihad*.

"If you get out, please ensure to get this published," he said.[127]

The following morning, the Al Qaeda women gathered in the yard for a special Eid shopping trip—their first outing in more than six months. Iman was chatty as ever, and she and Khadija sat together on the bus that took them to Shahrvand, a Western-style supermarket on Argentine Square. It was thronged with diplomats who worked in nearby embassies.

While Khairiah and the other mothers filled their trolleys, with a dozen excited young children trailing behind demanding sweets, Iman pulled Khadija into the toy section.

Weren't they too old for this, Khadija asked?

When Iman was sure no one was looking, she grabbed a life-size baby doll from the shelf and took out some sunglasses and clothes she had snatched elsewhere in the store. Khadija watched, stunned and amused, as her friend transformed herself by slipping out of her black *chador* and *niqab*, putting on an Iranian chemise and a pair of jeans and wrapping a colorful headscarf around her hair in the Iranian style. She then swaddled the doll in a blanket, as if it were a baby.

She gave her friend an embrace and set off for the main entrance, showing her face to the world for the first time since she was a three-year-old child in Kandahar. *What are you doing?* hissed Khadija.

What does it look like? Iman called back with a grin, before she disappeared into the crowd.

Casting around, increasingly panicked, the escorts realized a few minutes later that Iman had gone. Shouting to one another, they shut the shop and corralled the remaining women and children back onto the bus, wondering who among them had collaborated in the escape. Within minutes, Iranian soldiers swarmed into Argentine Square to lock it down. But Iman had been too quick for them and had asked the first woman she saw with a phone if she could borrow it.

She rang her oldest brother, Abdullah, a respectable family man in Jeddah who had rejected his father's lifestyle back in 1995. Unable to believe he was talking to someone he thought was long dead, he told Iman to make her way to the Saudi embassy. He would call ahead to let them know she was coming—and to warn them to check she was not an imposter.

Back in the Tourist Complex everyone was grilled but nobody talked. When the questioners had gone, Mohammed, Othman, and Hamzah argued among themselves. Over the years, they had all discussed trying to reach the Saudi embassy and plead for assistance. They had looked up its location on local maps. But after Saad's death, their enthusiasm had waned. Now their baby sister had shown them up as cowards.

For three days there was no news. Then, while the Mauritanian and his family were watching a local cable channel, they spotted something odd on a ticker tape running at the bottom of the screen. Normally it carried service updates or advertisements for a local kebab restaurant, and for a small fee customers could display a message about a birthday or marriage. Tonight it read: "Iman is fine. She has come."[128]

Everyone sat up. Was this their Iman? Who had posted the message? Had they imagined it? Then it came again. "Iman is fine. She has come."

Saudi Embassy, Pasdaran Avenue, Tehran

Dumbfounded Saudi diplomats listened to Iman's story and checked it out as best they could before allowing her to call her mother in Syria. She appeared to be telling the truth. In Latakia, Najwa, who had believed her children to be dead or in hiding with Osama, was overjoyed and immediately called her mother-in-law Allia in Jeddah and Omar in Qatar.[129]

Omar flew to join his mother in Syria. Within days, the family received a call from an Iranian woman claiming to work for the foreign ministry in Tehran. They should come to collect Iman, she said.

The instructions made Omar fearful. He often said that when he was put under stress, he got "a mess" in his head."[130] Najwa had gained some confidence in the years since leaving Kandahar, but she was also not accustomed to dealing with the authorities or doing anything for herself.

Everyone in the family relied on Omar's worldly and savvy wife, Zaina, who when she argued with Najwa was jokingly denounced as "the British spy."

Najwa could not get over her extraordinary daughter-in-law, who was five years her senior. Brought up in the United Kingdom, she claimed to have a Kuwaiti Arab father and a Jewish mother. Her original name was Jane Felix Browne.

Eschewing the *hijab* and *abaya*, she mostly dressed in drainpipe trousers, crepe-soled shoes, and tailored jackets that she designed herself. Her hair was dyed jet-black, sometimes shaved on one side, and she had striking blue eyes. She rode a motorbike, swore like a Marine, and had reportedly been married five times already (once to a Hells Angel). Zaina was ready to take on the world. She talked with a broad Cheshire accent, had multiple tattoos, had a flesh tunnel in one ear, and treated the sensitive and under-confident Omar like the child he really was, helping him daily to overcome his autistic tendencies.

In the three years since their marriage, Omar had come to rely on Zaina for practically everything, and she acted as his dresser and interpreter. Their relationship had endured a blizzard of negative publicity led by the British tabloids, which accused her of marrying a bin Laden just for the notoriety or even in a misfired bid to get rich.

Among the more outlandish claims were that wild Zaina had once dated the British soccer superstar George Best, that Omar wanted to leave her and marry Drew Barrymore, and that in a bid to save her marriage she had hired a surrogate mother to carry her and Omar's babies. Sylvester Stallone, who briefly met the couple when they stayed at the same hotel in Rome, fueled the flames by spinning a story that Omar was "the son of Hitler" who had an "old grandmother wife." He was disgusted to stand in the same room as them, he said.[131] But Zaina, who had always been her own woman, liked to shock; she was naturally drawn to outsiders and underdogs, and she loved Omar deeply. She was, also, the only person allowed to call him "babe."

Now, with Zaina's help, Najwa and Omar applied for Iranian visas. But when they tried to call the Saudi embassy in Tehran to confirm they were coming, they could not get through. Zaina told them not to worry. Admitting that Osama bin Laden's family was in Iran was a huge embarrassment for President Ahmadinejad, who, she argued, was probably doing everything he could to keep the story under wraps. To date, the state media had issued only one vague statement, saying that a member of Osama bin Laden's family had been in Tehran but had already left the country, smuggled in a truck.

After the *Asharq Al-Awsat* newspaper discovered more of the truth and asked if the relative was Osama's daughter, Iranian foreign minister Manouchehr Mottaki was forced to issue a clarification. Yes, the family member was actually still in Iran, but "we are not able to confirm her identity," he said.

While Najwa and Omar waited for updates, Zaina piled on the pressure, meeting with Saudi and Syrian officials, who promised to help but did little. She also lobbied the Iranian foreign ministry to release Iman's younger brother Ladin, who was now aged seventeen. Both had been minors when they entered the country, they had committed no crime, and they should be released together, she argued.

Surprisingly, and after lengthy discussions, Ladin was brought out of the Tourist Complex. He was not taken to join his sister at the embassy but driven straight to the airport and put on a commercial flight to Damascus, arriving alone in the early hours of Christmas Day. That afternoon, he turned up at Najwa's home in Latakia trailing a small carry-on case. When Zaina opened the door, she thought he was an Arabic-speaking salesman. Only when Ladin, who didn't speak English, uttered her name did she invite him inside.[132]

Najwa smothered her child in kisses, while Omar called the press, reading a statement written by Zaina.

"My youngest brother, [Ladin,] arrived from Tehran," he told *Asharq Al-Awsat*. "The family is overjoyed, and my mother wiped away many tears . . . However, this joy will not be complete until the safe return of the rest of my siblings, God willing, from the Iranian capital."

The parallel world was being revealed as Najwa caught up on all she had missed: Hamzah's marriage, the death of Saad's second son, Fatima's second marriage to Abu Ghaith and her new baby, and the death of her niece Khadija, not to mention the plight of those others still trapped in the Tourist Complex.

Assisted by Zaina, she once more tried to dislodge Iman.

Playing for time, the Iranians demanded legal proof of the teenager's identity.

Saudi Arabia had revoked Iman's citizenship. Officially the girl had nowhere to go.

* * *

December 30, 2009, U.S. Forward Operating
Base Chapman, Khost, Afghanistan

The CIA agents and American security contractors stood waiting nervously with the GID's Captain Ali bin Zeid as a red Subaru station wagon drove across the desert toward the base.

After several false starts, Humam al-Balawi, their Al Qaeda double agent, who had leveraged his way into treating Dr. al-Zawahiri and counseling Atiyah, was on his way to meet them. But everyone was on tenterhooks as he was twenty-four hours late.[133]

Wrapped in a thick woolen blanket and wearing a *pakul*, his face obscured by a thick black beard, Balawi was sitting in the rear seat of the Subaru, behind an Afghan driver who worked at the American base and had met him at the Pakistan border.[134]

Bin Zeid and his CIA partner were worried even before they saw Balawi get out of the car. They had flown to Afghanistan in early December for a quick visit to give him more training and had ended up staying for more than three weeks. Senior CIA officials in Khost and Langley had taken over the operation, and, greedy to capture Dr. al-Zawahiri, they had not listened to the junior officers' mounting reservations.

Things were moving too fast, the captain feared. The operation had been taken out of his hands; it involved too many people and they had allowed Balawi to dictate the pace and determine locations.

So keen were his handlers to make him feel at home that no one even searched him as he drove through the outer security checkpoints at Camp Chapman. Now sixteen people waited to greet him in the glare of the winter sun.

As a U.S. contractor, who had served as a Navy SEAL, opened the passenger door of the Subaru, Balawi slid away from him across the seat, stepping out of the far door.

Balawi was late because Hakimullah Mehsud, the new emir of the Pakistan Taliban, had insisted on one last video to record his sweetest triumph. The two men had sat side by side, surrounded by weapons and sticks of explosives. Balawi was a man "who wants to go on a martyrdom mission" that would be remembered for "a hundred years," declared Hakimullah.[135] When he spoke, Balawi cited the imprisonment of Aafia Siddiqui as one of his motivations.

Balawi was weighed down by more than thirty pounds of explosives and shrapnel worn in a suicide vest that had been stitched by Al Qaeda's tailor in the North Waziristan town of Datta Khel. He had paid for that vest, and for this moment, with money given him nine months earlier by bin Zeid.

In the past few days, Balawi had recorded a dozen martyrdom statements as Al Qaeda's revenge attack on the U.S. security establishment came together. "We will get you, CIA team, *inshallah*, we will bring you down," he said in one clip, filmed as he got into the Taliban car taking him to the border. "This is my goal: to kill you, and to kill your Jordanian partner."

Raising his left hand and addressing the camera in English, Balawi revealed a wristwatch beneath his sleeve. "Look, this is for you: It's not a watch, it's a detonator."[136] Although there was fear in his eyes and he flubbed some of his lines, he pressed on. It was a blessing from Allah, he said, to have "my limbs, my bones and my teeth turned into shrapnel." He would go to paradise, while those he killed would go to hell.[137]

"Do you not fear to be cowardly at the last moment . . . unable to press the button?" Balawi's online avatar Abu Dujana had once asked supporters. "I have often wished to know what is going on in the head of a martyr before a martyrdom operation."[138] Now he knew.

Captain bin Zeid stepped forward as a percussive cloud swept over all of them, shaking their chests and squeezing their hearts, before a fireball tore through Camp Chapman.

Ali bin Zeid, his CIA partner, and three security contractors were killed outright, while shrapnel, bone, and teeth fragments hit eleven others, just as Balawi had imagined. By the end of the day, seven CIA officers were dead—the worst loss for the agency in twenty-five years—two of them women who had played vital roles in the search for Osama bin Laden.

At a somber meeting of stunned seniors in Langley the following Monday, all Leon Panetta could do was pledge revenge. The CIA would fight back, he said, as one family.

CHAPTER NINE

"I'm back with the people I was with before."
—ABU AHMAD AL-KUWAITI[1]

January 2010, New York City

AAFIA SIDDIQUI, THE PAKISTANI NEUROSCIENTIST and alleged Al Qaeda agent, had been in U.S. detention for eighteen months when her trial began in New York in January 2010. Unofficially, she had been detained far longer. She took to the stand with most of her face hidden behind a cream scarf and delivered a series of outbursts as government lawyers laid out their case against her: that she had grabbed a gun and deliberately tried to kill the U.S. military personnel who had gone to arrest her in Afghanistan in July 2008, the incident in which only she had suffered gunshot wounds. The judge expelled Aafia from the courtroom for "disrespecting proceedings" as government lawyers did their best to steer clear of the five missing years in her story—from her disappearance in 2003 to her arrest in 2008—a period during which she claimed she had been held in secret U.S. detention facilities and tortured, while being coerced to act as an agent for the CIA and ISI.

Even before she was formally allowed to give evidence, the case against her appeared inconsistent and troubling.[2]

An FBI firearms expert testified that it was unlikely the U.S. Army–issue M4 assault rifle that she had allegedly picked up off the floor at Ghazni police station had been fired at the scene. The nine government witnesses who took the stand (including the army warrant officer whose weapon allegedly had been discharged by Aafia) offered incomplete and conflicting accounts of what had happened. No trace of her fingerprints was found on the rifle.

When Siddiqui testified, she admitted that she had tried to escape but denied taking the rifle or firing any shots. "Your president wants to make peace, but you guys are not acting on it," she said bitterly.

Turning to her own experiences, specifically the spectral five years, she maintained she had been "tortured in secret prisons" before her arrest by a "group of people pretending to be Americans, doing bad things in America's name."[3] She alleged that her children had been tortured too and that she had been framed for plotting acts of mass terrorism—when in reality she was so squeamish that she "couldn't kill a rat myself."

It took the jury three days to reach a guilty verdict in February 2010. One of her former attorneys described her as "the ultimate victim of the American dark side."[4]

March 2010, Saudi Embassy, Pasdaran Avenue, Tehran, Iran

Iman bin Laden had spent almost one hundred days inside the embassy, staying in a diplomatic apartment lent to her by the ambassador, where she watched TV reports about Aafia's case with mounting fear.

Although Iman had never met Aafia, they knew people in common from the Al Qaeda world, including Khalid Shaikh Mohammad, and she was mesmerized and appalled by what had happened. Still unsure if she would even be allowed to leave Iran, Iman worried what kind of reception awaited her in the outside world. Would she too be shot and end up on trial in New York?[5]

A few weeks after Aafia was found guilty, Iman learned from the state-run Press TV channel that she had clearance to leave Iran. This was how Tehran broke the news. No calls or explanations; just a TV anchor delivering the news, deadpan.

Iman nervously waited for the next bulletin. It carried an update: she could go where she pleased, so long as it was not Saudi Arabia. The daughter of the world's most wanted man would have to find another country to take her.[6] Feeling panicked, Iman waited nervously for the Saudi diplomats to guide her.

Najwa flew to Tehran a few days later, Omar staying behind for fear he would be abducted. Aafia Siddiqui's trial in New York had been a wakeup call to everyone in the family that almost nine years after 9/11 the United States was still vengeful. Greeted at the airport by intelligence agents who silently confiscated her passport and cell phone, Najwa was terrified as she was escorted to the five-star Parsian Esteghlal Hotel, a huge complex near the Tehran International Exhibition Center.[7] Was this to be *her* prison, she wondered?

"Wait," they told her.

Eventually, someone knocked on the door. Opening it nervously, half expecting to be arrested, she saw a tall teenager she barely recognized, accompanied by a Saudi diplomat and an Iranian escort. The last time she and Iman had seen each other had been in Kandahar just before 9/11 when, as an inconsolable mother, she had been forced to say good-bye to her distraught then eleven-year-old daughter as a punishment for her desertion. Before they could catch up on nine lost years, Iman was taken back to the embassy. She would only be produced when the family had secured citizenship for her, Najwa was informed. While Zaina bin Laden worked the phones in Damascus, speaking to the Saudi foreign minister, Saud al-Faisal, and Syrian leader Bashar al-Assad, neither of whom was willing to help, Najwa gazed out at the lights of Tehran from her hotel room and thought about the rest of her family still stuck inside a compound somewhere else in the city. She was desperate to see her oldest daughter, Fatima, and her baby. Saad, Mohammed, Othman, and Hamzah had eleven children among them, most of whom she had never met. She was desperate to comfort Saad's widow, Wafa, and even wanted to catch up with her sister-wife Khairiah. Even though there was no love lost between them, together they had endured so much.[8]

She worked herself up to call the Ministry of Foreign Affairs, demanding visits. When she got no reply, she called Zaina, who rang them every day. She found numbers for the ministries of interior and justice, ringing them, too. But even a determined mother and her feisty British daughter-in-law made barely a mark on the ice face of the Iranian establishment. "No visits," they were told.

Inside the Tourist Complex, the Mauritanian was as usual thinking about himself, wondering if Iman still had the thumb drive he had given her. He had penned a foreword to Sulaiman Abu Ghaith's book and as the first critique of Sheikh Osama by a former member of the inner circle he hoped it would cause controversy. Nine years had passed since 9/11, and he badly wanted to make an impact on what came next: "Al-Qaeda 2.0."[9]

*　*　*

March 18, 2010, Damascus, Syria

Iman was floored by her first glimpse of the Syrian capital when she flew in with her mother: women in Western clothes, with uncovered heads and faces, walking by bars selling alcohol and nightclubs catering to every sexual predilection. Her older brother Omar, who wore a leather biker jacket and his hair in cornrows, smoked cigars, and ate American burgers, terrified her. For Iman, whose life had always been minutely controlled, Zaina was the most extraordinary person she had ever met. She found her chutzpah, disregard for authority, and love of the outlandish mesmerizing and shocking.

While Zaina and Omar appealed for a royal decree to restore Iman's Saudi citizenship, she was reunited with her younger sisters Rukaiya, twelve, and Nour, ten, who like their mother wore Western clothes and wore their hair long and styled. They took her to the beach, ate pizza, and painted her nails.

Irritated by Riyadh's sluggish response to her request, Zaina called up influential Arab newspapers and broke the family's code of silence, revealing that more than a dozen bin Laden siblings, nephews, and nieces, as well as Osama's eldest wife, Khairiah, were in secret jails in Tehran. To build a case for them all to be allowed to go temporarily to Doha, where Zaina and Omar still lived, they revealed details of his former life, saying that he had almost died on more than one occasion during the years that he lived with his father in Sudan and Afghanistan.[10] None of this made Omar a terrorist, he maintained, in a wide-ranging interview, conducted with Zaina at his elbow, prompting him when he faltered and interrupting when he said something compromising. Like those still trapped in Iran, Omar was an unfortunate bystander with a "danger dad" who risked his family's lives by dragging them into his wars.

Then, in the middle of these delicate negotiations, a letter purportedly from Omar's half brother Khalid was uploaded to a pro–Al Qaeda website. Addressed to Supreme Leader Ayatollah Khamenei, it claimed family members in Iran had been "beaten and silenced" after being tricked into entering the country. "We communicated with the Tehran government many times," Khalid wrote. "We asked scholars and dignitaries to mediate their release promising they won't return to Iran. But to no avail."[11]

Cursing Khalid's bad timing, Najwa won herself a small victory: a call to the Tourist Complex. She spoke to her sons and to Saad's widow, Wafa, who begged her to find out if her husband was really dead. Zaina took up Wafa's pleas, writing to the *Asharq Al-Awsat* newspaper, saying, "We have no idea where he is, or if what the media says is true about him being killed." The intelligence agencies had "got it wrong when they said that Hamzah and Saad were or are connected to Al Qaeda," since the two had been imprisoned in Iran. "None of the siblings liked war or violence; all they ever wanted was a normal life with a normal family."[12]

March 2010, Bilal Town, Abbottabad, Pakistan

Osama bin Laden opened the file to find a letter from his dead son Saad.[13] It had been dictated to a ghostwriter and saved on a thumb drive before Saad died in the drone strike. It detailed some of what he and other family members, as well as the Al Qaeda *shura*, had endured in Iranian custody.

Osama instructed Atiyah to issue a rebuke to the Iranians. In it he focused on the death of Saad's baby and Mohammed al-Islambouli's wife and the beatings endured by Sulaiman Abu Ghaith, the Mauritanian, and others. "As you may know Iran is very concerned about its reputation in the Islamic world," Osama informed Atiyah, keen to turn the screw.[14]

Unaware of the behind-the-scenes efforts to free his family being made from Syria by Zaina, Omar, and Najwa, Osama reached out to his estranged oldest brother, Bakr bin Laden, who lived in Jeddah, where, maintaining a close personal relationship with the Saudi royal family, he was one of the richest men in the kingdom. Bakr had disowned Osama after the 1998 embassy attacks, but now the errant younger brother exhorted his elder sibling that it was his *duty* to help to secure the release of "the grandsons and granddaughters of our father" from the Iranians, who in his opinion were a pack of wolves. "If you do this, you will be doing good for your father," Osama continued, using a condescending tone he deployed when sending Al Qaeda recruits on suicide missions. "Allah have mercy on his soul, and you will be doing good for your kin."

But even now, when he truly needed assistance, Osama could not resist having a dig at old enemies, sniping about the kingdom of Saudi Arabia's reluctance to stand up to the Americans waging war in Iraq. "Your sitting back from supporting the mujahideen in Iraq is a great sin," he berated Bakr, "and your delay in suppressing the rebellion of the rejectionists [Shias] until their danger overcomes everyone is a shameful issue."[15]

Bakr did not reply.

In Latakia, Damascus, Tehran, Riyadh, and Doha, negotiations to free the bin Ladens crawled on. On March 30, 2010, the Iranian diplomat kidnapped in Peshawar was released after being held by Al Qaeda for more than a year. Tehran had made a significant concession: a promise to free Khairiah, Othman, Mohammed, and Hamzah bin Laden, plus all their families.[16]

Thrilled at the news, even though no dates or exit routes had been provided, Osama sent instructions via Atiyah. His family should head for Syria or the Gulf states. He issued specific instructions for Hamzah to be dispatched to Qatar, where he was to study "religious sciences" and take up Al Qaeda duties. Hamzah was "one of the mujahideen and he bears their thoughts and worries."[17]

To distract from the embarrassment it felt at having capitulated to Al Qaeda, the Iranian intelligence ministry started an unnecessary row with Pakistan, accusing it of having failed to help secure the diplomat's release. Iran's first vice president boasted that the Tehran-led operation "shows the all-out might of the Islamic Republic of Iran and its all-around dominance in the realm of intelligence."[18]

However, behind the scenes, Iran had agreed to lubricate the Al Qaeda deal by supplying unspecified "anti-drone technology," some of which had already been sent ahead of the diplomat's release as a gesture of goodwill.

When the U.S. intelligence community picked up on the Iranian shipment, CIA analysts went back over recent drone flight plans. Several aerial assets had inexplicably vanished or crashed, including one that had fallen near Hamzoni village in North Waziristan on January 24. At the time, the CIA had struck back, targeting an antiaircraft position at Dande-Darpa Khel in North Waziristan, killing one of the sons of the famous Afghan warlord Jalaluddin Haqqani—a figure who the CIA had once courted and who was still closely aligned to the ISI.[19] A later intercept suggested that the Haqqanis received a replacement consignment from Iran days after the diplomat was freed.[20]

* * *

May 21, 2010, 10:30 P.M., Deegan, North Waziristan, Pakistan

The Iranian gift of anti-drone assistance did not help Sheikh Saaed al-Masri, the real Number Three of Al Qaeda. He had been on the road working with Azzam the American on a celebratory video about a suicide attack on Bagram air base in which one U.S. contractor had been killed and nine soldiers injured. The journey from the shoot-and-edit had been long, and after several exhausting days on the road he had arrived at a house overlooking the Tochi River, where he enjoyed a warm meal and a heartfelt reunion with his wife, children, and grandchildren.[21]

Sheikh Saeed, whose program was normally well choreographed, should have departed the *hujra* (guest room) at dusk. The house, located five miles west of Miram Shah, was in the middle of a well-known kill zone and was owned by vocal supporters of Al Qaeda. Several brothers who had previously stayed there had been subsequently targeted by U.S. Predator drones.[22] The *machays* (wasps) circled ominously and Atiyah, who presumed the compound was on a U.S. strike list, had instructed everyone that it should never be used as a refuge.

But shortly before ten P.M., Sheikh Saeed fell asleep. When his son came to wake him, eager to move on, their hosts protested.[23] "He is tired, let him rest."

Less than an hour later, missiles pounded the compound, in the ninety-fourth strike of the year. When villagers came to inspect the ruins, they pulled from the rubble the bodies of Sheikh Saeed, his Egyptian wife, three daughters, and young granddaughter, Hafsah. Another daughter was critically injured.[24]

In the United States, where CIA director Leon Panetta described President Obama's escalating drone campaign in Pakistan's Tribal Areas as "the only game in town," there was little sympathy for the civilian toll. Financier Sheikh Saeed had been on the radar ever since 9/11.[25] Recently, he had described the Camp Chapman attack that killed seven CIA operatives as an "epic" operation and he had feted bomber Humam al-Balawi as "a hero."[26]

Sheikh Saeed's surviving family members were taken in by Atiyah, who delivered a letter from Osama mourning the loss of one of his oldest and most loyal aides. "My deepest condolences for myself and for all of you for the death of your noble father," he wrote. After nearly three decades on the battlefield, the great Sheikh Saeed, the "prince of financial princes," had died a hero. "He was persistent in his resistance upon the highest mountains of Waziristan," Osama said, not missing a beat to remind them also of their duty to honor his death by keeping on the path of jihad. Al Qaeda would inflict "a severe curse . . . upon the infidels."[27]

But finding a replacement for Sheikh Saeed would be a tricky task.

July 2010, Bilal Town, Abbottabad

After Dr. al-Zawahiri, Sheikh Saeed had been Osama's most important deputy.[28] In the weeks leading up to his death, they had corresponded about several clandestine missions, including a plot to assassinate President Obama in Pakistan or Afghanistan.[29] Now he was gone, Osama sent a weighty forty-nine-page manifesto and to-do list to Atiyah, appointing him as Number Three.[30]

Osama expected to be heartily thanked. However, this position was fast becoming one of the most unpopular jobs in the organization and Atiyah was alarmed when he received the news, knowing that he had no choice but to accept.

Atiyah's new duties would be wide-ranging, Osama's essay explained, from corralling Al Qaeda franchises abroad to promoting the Sheikh's primary message. His first priority was to tackle the wayward Islamic State of Iraq, which had recently lost both its leaders, Abu Umar al-Baghdadi and Abu Ayyub al-Masri, who had been killed in a U.S. operation near Tikrit on April 18.[31]

Atiyah's brief was to take advantage of the consequent disarray as the outfit coalesced around a newly declared but as yet unproven figurehead, a religious scholar who called himself Abu Bakr al-Baghdadi. Like his predecessor, virtually nothing was known about Abu Bakr in jihadist circles, and although Islamic State of Iraq had recently pledged allegiance to Al Qaeda, no effort had been made to bring Osama into the discussion concerning his appointment.

The affronted Al Qaeda leader intended to spell out this egregious mistake in a polite but firm letter that stressed the "importance of unity and collectiveness" as well as stating overtly who was in charge. But before writing to Abu Bakr, he needed to know who he was dealing with and so he asked Atiyah to dig around.[32] For a man constantly on the run from American drones, staying in compounds with little electricity and no Internet access, this was a tall order.

*   *   *

Summer 2010, Mosul, Iraq

Abu Bakr al-Baghdadi, who officially became leader of Islamic State of Iraq in May 2010, had been born Ibrahim Awwad Ibrahim al-Badri into a farming family in Samarra in 1971. Shortsighted and compulsively religious, as a child he had been nicknamed "the Believer." Rather than completing his military service, he had enrolled in endless college courses, editing a medieval book on Koranic recitation for his master's thesis. For several years, he lived a quiet life in a room attached to a mosque in Tobchi, on the outskirts of Baghdad.[33]

In June 2004, as war invaded his clerical world, Ibrahim had disappeared, with one of his professors noting that "he has not attended class." Arrested at a friend's house, Ibrahim ended up in Camp Bucca, a mega U.S. internment facility in southern Iraq filled with Islamists, Ba'athist mercenaries, and innocent men recently transferred from the notorious Abu Ghraib. Bucca was known as "the Academy," and its American commander would later admit that it was "a pressure cooker for extremism."[34] A U.S. military report found that the prison's unofficial *sharia* courts, not U.S guards, enforced discipline.[35] During his time there, Ibrahim built a reputation for resolving disputes, and he enjoyed the attention and respect of a judge.

After his release, Ibrahim joined forces with Jordanian hardman Abu Musab al-Zarqawi, who appointed him emir of Rawa, a town near the Syrian border.[36] When Zarqawi was killed in June 2006, Ibrahim quickly transferred his allegiance to Abu Umar al-Baghdadi, a move that was rewarded with a promotion to being his religious adviser. After Ibrahim began writing some of Abu Umar's letters to Osama, he advanced rapidly, until he became chief justice of Islamic State of Iraq.

When Abu Umar and Abu Ayyub were both killed, Ibrahim suddenly found himself with surprising proximity to the throne; but as a relative unknown, he would need a powerful backer to champion his case.

Assuming the *kunya* Abu Bakr, after the first caliph in Islam, Ibrahim sought out a veteran battlefield commander, Hajji Bakr. A former colonel in Saddam Hussein's army and sometime adherent of the ancient Chinese military strategist Sun Tzu, Hajji Bakr was more widely known by his nom de guerre: "the Prince of Shadows." Successful jihadists needed a powerful "avatar" behind which to rally, wrote Hajji Bakr: someone who had won battles and lost friends fighting them and was seen as heroic and evenhanded.

The white-bearded Hajji Bakr drew up a strategy paper that championed Abu Bakr, distanced him from his predecessors, and blamed the United States for Islamic State's previous failings, such as its propensity to massacre civilians. "When it was at the pinnacle of its power and influence, [the Americans] bombed markets, public places and mosques." They "killed the opponent of the State so that the mujahideen were blamed." He recommended that the time to strike back would be when the Americans began their withdrawal from Iraq.[37] Many aspects of his war plan seemed to have been lifted from *The Management of Savagery*, an Al Qaeda–linked prophetic book that suggested that what was needed was "naught but violence, crudeness, terrorism, frightening others, and massacres." Even women and children could be targeted.[38]

With the Prince of Shadows at his side and determined to get his CV into shape to assume leadership of the movement, Abu Bakr also appointed a youthful religious adviser who came from a wealthy family close to the Bahraini royals and had been taught by the famous Palestinian cleric Abu Muhammad al-Maqdisi. After being arrested in Dubai in 2005 for "expressing extremist ideals," Turki al-Bin'ali had fled to Iraq, where he had come to Abu Bakr's attention after whipping up a large following in refugee camps. Turki al-Bin'ali was, according to some of those who knew him, malleable, ambitious, and keen to attach his name to a viable cause.

Summer 2010, Bilal Town, Abbottabad

Osama bin Laden was determined not to be drowned out by Abu Bakr al-Baghdadi, and he instructed Atiyah to highlight Al Qaeda's impact "on all fronts and in all territories" by launching a new campaign that focused on "bleeding the American enemy."[39] Funds were flowing in from supporters and other enterprises. The Afghan politician held hostage by Al Qaeda for eighteen months had recently been released, netting an incredible $5 million.[40]

Buoyed by this huge windfall, Osama instructed Atiyah to revisit Khalid Shaikh Mohammad's concept of deploying passenger-filled aircraft as flying bombs. The outfit needed to launch another "large operation in the US," Osama wrote, instructing his new Number Three to identify young volunteers who could be sent to their home to "study aviation"—preferably at their own country's expense. Meanwhile, one brother with "good manners, integrity, courage, and secretiveness" should settle in the United States to act as coordinator.[41]

Atiyah was also told to prepare for commando-style terror attacks in France, the United Kingdom, and Germany, where undetectable sleepers should select multiple targets. He would be assisted by Younis al-Mauritani, a protégé of his former spiritual adviser, Mahfouz the Mauritanian. Younis was a founding member of Al Qaeda in the Islamic Maghreb (AQIM) and since 2005 had been shuttling between Pakistan, Afghanistan, and Iran, acting as a courier and conduit for Al Qaeda's financial pipeline through Iran. His new job was to become "external operations chief," a post that had once been held by Khalid Shaikh Mohammad. Younis was ordered to encourage lone wolves to migrate to Europe to plot attacks and spread Al Qaeda's message.

Next, Osama turned his attention to the other unwieldy Al Qaeda franchises, some of which were trying to follow Zarqawi's lead, declaring caliphates in their regions, adopting too the black flag of Islamic State and imposing severe *hudud* punishments of execution, stoning, crucifixion, and amputation without prior approval from Al Qaeda Central. Al Shabaab in Somalia tried to establish a caliphate in 2009. Al Qaeda in the Arabian Peninsula (AQAP), based in Yemen, and AQIM were threatening to follow suit.

Through Atiyah, Osama issued a stern message to the leader of AQAP, Nasir al-Wuhayshi, a loyalist who had once been his personal secretary but who had recently come under the influence of an upstart Yemeni-American scholar called Anwar al-Awlaki.

"Establishing the [caliphate] before the elements necessary for success are put in place most often will lead to aborting the effort," Osama lectured Wuhayshi. "Weighing people down with something that exceeds their expectations is fraught with negative results."[42] While Yemen could one day become the ideal place for the caliphate to flourish, the time was not yet right; and when it was, Osama would declare it—not Wuhayshi or Awlaki.[43]

Next, he turned to internal housekeeping. He wanted to send a complaint to Abu Walid al-Masri, the former Al Jazeera journalist and father-in-law of Saif al-Adel, who officially remained under detention in Iran but had somehow been able to publish a book online called *A Cross in the Sky of Qandahar*.[44] Those who had read it had been "shaken" by the "hate-mongering and treachery" it contained as well as the "random attacks" on Osama's character and authority. While everyone in Al Qaeda was familiar with Abu

Walid's propensity for straight talking, this book had "no connection with reality or any semblance of truth," according to Osama loyalists.

Key among the complainants was Al Qaeda's foreign relations chief Abu al-Khayr, who lived in the Tourist Complex with Saif and had already written to the author, castigating him for "slaughtering truth and fabricating history" and making a "sweeping attack on one of the most important groups of mujahideen." How could someone they had lived with, and whose daughter had married into the leadership, betray them and still claim to be a "personal friend of Shaykh Osama"?[45] The only logical explanation, given that Abu Walid lived in a government villa in the smartest part of Tehran, was that he had been persuaded to "adopt the view of the Iranian intelligence agencies."[46]

Closer to home, the Tehrik-i-Taliban Pakistan (TTP) leader Hakimullah Mehsud, supposedly an Al Qaeda loyalist and therefore subject to the outfit's discipline, was also chafing against the outfit's disciplinary code. Having slaughtered hundreds of Muslims from minority communities in brutal assaults across Pakistan, Mehsud was fast becoming a Pashtun version of Zarqawi.

There were so many incidents, but Osama was most incensed by an attack on a mosque of the Ahmadi sect, which Hakimullah regarded as heretical, that had killed eighty-two worshippers. The slaughter, in Lahore, was followed by a botched attempt to detonate a bomb in New York's Times Square—an operation so poorly planned and executed, and without Osama's say-so, that it enabled U.S. officials to portray Al Qaeda as clowns.

Atiyah was asked to remind Hakimullah that the TTP did not have authorization to conduct operations in Al Qaeda's name and that Al Qaeda had a right to veto its operations.[47] It should return to its core domestic business of targeting Pakistani security forces and politicians, as set out in its foundation charter, edited and shaped by Al Qaeda.

Osama turned to the most sensitive issue. Since the release of the Iranian diplomat in March 2010, there had been no updates about the promised release of his family. Why had they not been freed? he asked Atiyah. If the treacherous Iranians were reneging on the deal, Al Qaeda Central would have to consider more kidnappings. Whatever the cost, he wanted his family back.

*   *   *

July 2010, North Waziristan, Pakistan

Constantly on the move, often in the dead of night, with a laptop in his pack and a generator in the pickup, Atiyah shuttled between mud-brick compounds. His world was rapidly shrinking. The frequent trips he had once made to Quetta to consult with the Taliban *shura*, send e-mails, and take some respite from the drones, which did not operate over Balochistan, were now too dangerous. Al Qaeda's local support was also hemorrhaging. The villages inhabited by "supporters" were almost all ghostly ruins, and on the roads twitchy young TTP militants shot anyone muttering the wrong password.[48] Spies and the threat from the skies had worn everyone down. Pashtun codes of honor and protection had been eroded by aerial intimidation.

When Atiyah finally replied to the Sheikh's long missive, it was with a surprise announcement of his own: his resignation. "I ask God to relieve me and quickly," he wrote to Osama, his mental state revealed in his description of himself as "the weakest servant."[49] He was not going to leave Osama in the lurch, as he had already thought of a replacement, Abu Yahya al-Libi, the hero escapee from Bagram, who had served as a deputy to the deceased financier Sheikh Saeed. "I think he is the most prepared of the brothers," Atiyah wrote.[50]

Atiyah was exhausted, stressed, scared, and frustrated, and his biggest bugbear was having to continually lean on the Pakistan Taliban for security, given that Hakimullah's attitude to internal discipline was at best slipshod.

"They do as they wish and roam around in the markets," he complained, drawing a pen portrait of mercenaries and thugs who robbed and kidnapped in the name of religion. "They have no obedience." The most violent and unpredictable among them exacted summary punishments. The beheading in February 2009 of a Polish engineer, kidnapped on his way to work—the first execution of a Western hostage in Pakistan since Daniel Pearl—had enraged Atiyah.[51]

The Pakistan Taliban—largely responsible for the cascading, random suicide attacks that had claimed 3,500 lives in Pakistan over the past three years—was making Atiyah's job of enabling Osama's vision of an Islamic emirate practically impossible.[52] The TTP's martyrdom operations took place without letup in "marketplaces, mosques, roads, assembly places," he complained. It would also be impossible to dispatch these wild brothers abroad to carry out complex operations in sophisticated Western settings, as Osama was demanding.[53]

The Sheikh would do best to let his foreign franchises get on with that job and keep the Al Qaeda brand alive, Atiyah suggested, taking a significant risk in criticizing his leader. He disagreed with the way Osama was choking the foreign franchises. Why oppose a call by AQAP in Yemen to declare a caliphate? Al Qaeda should seize the opportunity to back its most loyal affiliate, rather than muzzle it. "War [in Yemen] has become a reality," he argued presciently, acutely aware of the Islamic etiquette of only praising one's teacher even when he is wrong. The brothers from Al Shabaab also craved the Sheikh's approval to deepen the insurgency in Somalia. "It would be nice if you could do something, especially for them—that would convey we are happy," Atiyah wrote.[54]

Turning to family matters, there was more bad news: Atiyah had nothing to report from Iran. "Shaykh, perhaps the matter is more difficult than you imagine," he advised. Even if he was released, Hamzah could not simply fly to the Gulf, as Osama had suggested. "The Americans will definitely take him! The matter requires that we study it in detail and be careful and take precautions."

Only one person had reached them from Iran, Abu Anas al-Libi, the Al Qaeda veteran who had once lived in Manchester and who arrived just a few days before Sheikh Saeed was killed. He had negotiated his way out of the Tehran compound, possibly as he was identified by the Iranian authorities as a troublemaker who had sparked many of the riots. Atiyah reported that Anas was "in bad psychological shape." He was "very agitated, showing signs of anxiety and depression." Atiyah had found him secretly phoning his family in Libya, oblivious to those who would be listening in and in contravention of direct orders that warned that use of phones exposed Al Qaeda to drones. "Even though it was known that he is a dangerous man and wanted by the Americans, he contacted them by telephone repeatedly!" Atiyah protested.[55]

The prognosis was not good. He estimated that it would take months for Anas to be rehabilitated, and if that was his fate, what, he wondered, had become of legends like Saif al-Adel and others on the army council, whose return he had hoped would revive the outfit.

Atiyah was also horrified by the security crackdown that the Pakistan Taliban had provoked. Roadblocks were being thrown up sporadically and surveillance had become more pervasive. There was even talk of war in

North Waziristan. Al Qaeda needed quiet and discipline to consolidate, but Atiyah was faced with the prospect of a leader who refused to keep quiet. Osama's output remained prolific. In these volatile days, ferrying video and audio recordings from Abbottabad placed everyone in harm's way. "I consulted with the brothers and we think that at this time and for the indefinite future we should not be present in the media, owing to our remaining hidden and . . . to avoid the monitoring by spies," Atiyah suggested, wondering if they would not be better to correspond by e-mail, using "Mujahideen Secrets," a software encryption program developed by Al Qaeda supporters in the West.[56] "Our circumstances are difficult, Shaykh, and we are trying, but this war of espionage has really worn us down. Take excessive caution and care, especially this year."

Would he listen?

There was one more outstanding issue that required the utmost care, and Atiyah could not decide how to tackle it. The "Pakistani enemy"—even at this time when Al Qaeda was on the run—was secretly and incredibly offering peace talks.

Heavyweight covert mediators had emerged in the form of two of Osama's old allies: Fazlur Rehman Khalil and Hamid Gul. The former, the emir of Harkat-ul-Mujahideen, who had met Osama several times, had been "consulting back and forth" with Islamabad.[57] On his most recent visit to the Tribal Areas he had been accompanied by Gul, the former ISI director, who had promised to shield Osama in 2005.

Recently, Khalil and Gul had delivered a message to Atiyah from the ISI's director general, Ahmed Shuja Pasha: "We are trying to convince the Americans and pressure them to negotiate with Al Qaeda and to convince them, as well, that negotiating with the Taliban side and without Al-Qaeda is of no use."

"Just wait a little bit," Pasha had apparently said. "If we are able to convince the Americans, then we have no objection to . . . sitting down with you."[58]

Atiyah did not know what to make of this olive branch. "Are the Pakistanis serious, or are they just playing with us?" he asked Osama.[59] "We must be cautious." The army and the civilian government of President Asif Ali Zardari were under constant pressure from their "lords and masters" in the United States to eradicate Al Qaeda. Sensitive to "enemy tricks," Atiyah wondered if this ISI approach was just another ruse designed to entrap Osama.

Perhaps Khalil and Gul were being used, he suggested. While the ISI had paid Khalil handsomely to run a proxy force that waged war secretly in Indian-held Kashmir, it also had a history of turning on him when he refused to do the ISI's bidding. In 2006, he had been abducted and beaten by ISI thugs after refusing to tell one faction within the spy agency what he knew of Osama's whereabouts. "I was asked to help arrest the key leaders including Osama," Khalil later recalled.[60] "I refused to provide such help, due to which I was badly tortured."[61]

"So I ask you," Atiyah wrote to Osama, "what is your opinion?"

August 2010, Bilal Town, Abbottabad

In earlier times, Osama would have spoken to Khalil and Gul personally. But their phones were tapped and in Khalil's case a shipping container was permanently parked outside his madrassa in Islamabad with a phalanx of ISI officers sitting inside, listening to his every conversation.[62]

Osama's companion Ibrahim would have to test the water. After driving down to Hassan Abdal, Ibrahim turned on his cell phone and made some calls, before popping into a public phone booth in Mansehra to make some more. He returned with interesting news. Veteran Al Qaeda supporters believed the negotiations offered by General Pasha were in good faith. The Sheikh should advance—but with caution. These were confusing times and opportunists were everywhere.[63]

Osama wrote back to Atiyah, giving him permission to proceed with the ISI talks "in a fashion that . . . is in the interest of the al-mujahidin [sic]."[64] But he turned down Atiyah's suggestion to use encrypted e-mail. "We should be careful not to send big secrets by email," he wrote. "We should assume that the enemy can see these e-mails." Encryption was not a guaranteed fail-safe. "Computer science is not our science," he concluded warily, "as we are not the ones who invented it." Besides, the Abbottabad compound did not have an Internet connection.

To demonstrate his point, he referred to some recent correspondence from the brothers in Yemen, in which they had recommended that American-Yemeni cleric Anwar al-Awlaki be declared "the top man." Although Osama had vetoed the proposal, the U.S. government had started referring to Awlaki as Al Qaeda's "top man" in Yemen, echoing these intercepted words.

Osama also ignored Atiyah's request to maintain a lower profile. Instead, he recorded a new video, his first in several years, something he described as a "visual statement to the American people." For it, he wore his favorite golden robe and a new turban. His beard had been neatly clipped and the gray hairs dyed back to black, but the shadows under his eyes and his sagging cheeks spoke to his bottled-up and stressful existence. When he was finished, he copied the file to a USB drive and sent it off in Ibrahim's next batch, with instructions that Atiyah should give it to Al Jazeera for a forthcoming film on the anniversary of 9/11. If the channel agreed to use it, he would answer their questions and provide "real information." He would not interfere with their editorial freedom, but he did want a promise "not to interview anyone in my family."

Although he was keen for Atiyah to get the conversation started as soon as possible, he advised him to be cautious in his dealings with Al Jazeera. The last person to interview Sheikh Saeed had been the station's Pakistan bureau chief, Ahmad Zaidan and, although Osama liked Zaidan, he wondered whether the reporter had inadvertently led the CIA to the financier, with some "tracking chip" placed inside his camera or laptop.[65]

August 10, 2010, Ramadan Eve, Bilal Town, Abbottabad

It was a truly auspicious day. Osama at last received news that Khairiah, his favorite wife, had, after eight years, "got out of the infidel's fist" in Tehran. Even more uplifting was to hear that she had not gone to Syria or Qatar but was coming his way. Quds Force agents had flown her to Zahidan and then driven her to the Pakistan border. But fearful of what had happened to Saad, she was refusing to cross until she received some confirmation from her husband or an Al Qaeda representative that others who had been set free by the same route were still alive. Abu Uthman, Al Qaeda's Pakistan's operations chief, was suggesting they record a video "showing the released brothers or some of them" to prove that she was not walking into a trap.[66]

Immediately, Osama wrote to assure her she would be safe inside Pakistan. "It comforts me to hear your news, which I have waited and longed for." She should cross with "the mediator" and then go with him to Quetta, where "supporters" would shelter her until it was safe to come to Abbottabad. Privately, he worried about these last-minute changes instigated by Tehran, and when he told Ibrahim to make preparations for Khairiah's unexpected arrival, Osama's companion dug in his heels.

Osama wrote about the showdown to Atiyah. Unable to cope with the large number of Arabs they were already protecting, and concerned that the new arrival might have been bugged, Ibrahim and Abrar had resigned. Abrar had suffered a nervous breakdown and Ibrahim was also sick; the corner annex where he, Maryam, and four children lived was dank and cramped.[67] He was permanently stressed by the superhuman efforts required to keep his family quiet and out of the main courtyard.

The situation between the two families was now so tense that Osama—who rarely stopped to consider others—sent orders for Atiyah to start looking for replacements.

What Osama wanted Atiyah to find was a Pakistani citizen with an ID card, preferably someone who was of Pashtun descent and who would be willing to give up everything to become the new factotum.[68] He was clear about what type of person he preferred. The candidate should be "well mannered, quiet, patient, aware and knowledgeable of the enemy tricks" and willing to stay away from his family for as long as the job demanded it. The right person would have to be "tested until there is no doubt," have no visible criminal or jihadi record, and be smart enough in his intellect and appearance that he could rent houses and carry out a mass of secretarial duties.

But it was not as if Atiyah, who himself was looking to quit, could place an ad on some Al Qaeda bulletin board or pin a note to shop counters in Miram Shah or Mir Ali. However, Osama seemed not to care. "Inform me within two months," he demanded, revealing that "the notice that my companion has given me is limited." If they did not move quickly, he was sure that Ibrahim and Abrar would walk, leaving the bin Ladens to fend for themselves.

August 15, 2010, Bilal Town, Abbottabad

Osama and Ibrahim met again to work out their differences. There was some movement. Khairiah could come to Abbottabad, Ibrahim suggested, seeming to relent a little, but only if her possessions were thoroughly inspected for bugs and if Osama's son Khalid left first. One in and one out. That was the rule he had previously imposed. Osama needed to think fast.

Khalid had been agitating to go to Waziristan to marry his long-term fiancée Karima and join Atiyah. But Osama could not decide whether it was worth risking a son, who transcribed all of his work and was his link to the outside world, to win back a wife whose unexpected arrival in Pakistan he, too, was starting to worry about.

He sent more instructions to Atiyah: Khairiah should head north into Waziristan, traveling incognito, while they observed her from afar to see if she was being tailed. They should presume that "the adversaries," meaning the CIA, listened to all Iranian government chatter concerning bin Laden's family—or had been covertly consulted by Tehran—and would be following their movements.

Khairiah should jettison everything she had brought with her, even her clothes, in case the Iranians had implanted tracking devices for their American clients. And then there was the added risk the Pakistanis might pick up on her arrival in the country. "If the intelligence commander in the area is aware, he will think that they are headed to me and will survey them to find the place that they will settle in," Osama wrote.[69]

To confuse the watchers, he recommended that his wife should come via the Kohat Tunnel—using the same car-switching trick that had worked with the grandchildren—and then head for Peshawar, where she would be met by Ibrahim's trusted Peshawar representative, Mohammed Aslam. If the coast remained clear, Khalid could fetch her before leaving for Waziristan.

An excited Sumaiya, the youngest of Seham's daughters, wrote to the aunt she missed: "My heart is filled with joy for the happy news for which we have been waiting for many years."[70] Had Khairiah heard about the tragic deaths in Waziristan—Saad by drone and Khadija in childbirth? "I pray to God Almighty to have mercy [and] accept them with the martyrs and to gather them in the highest paradise," Sumaiya wrote.

She shared happier news about Khadija's children. After two years in Abbottabad they had come to regard Miriam as their mother. In fact, "the only mother Fatima [the youngest] knows is Miriam." The children were now all mixed up with Amal's, whose second daughter, Aasia, was only a few months younger than her niece Aisha. Amal's son Ibrahim was a few months older than his nephew Osama. Amal's youngest daughter, Zainab, was a few months older than Fatima. The baby of the family, born to Osama and Amal in 2008, was Hussein.

Turning to the siblings still in Tehran, Sumaiya asked for news of Saad's widow, Wafa, and her children. How were they coping? What about Iman and Ladin, who she had heard had been freed? "Also, tell me about my brother Hamzah, and Maryam [his wife] and their children." Every night since her aunt Najwa had left in September 2001, Sumaiya had prayed that they would all be reunited, and now that day was almost upon them.

In his next letter to Osama, Atiyah sent news that Hamzah, too, had left the Tourist Complex. Osama wrote to his son immediately: "We are longing to meet you and hear your news. We are getting ready in upcoming days to receive Umm Hamzah [Khairiah] over here, with God's permission."[71]

After so many years of stasis, things were moving fast—a little too fast, Osama thought. He sent detailed instructions for Khairiah to follow on her journey: "Leave everything behind, including clothes, books, everything she had in Iran . . . everything that a needle might possibly penetrate." She should also be checked out by a doctor and a dentist. Khalid had been doing some research and discovered that it was possible to plant a bug under a person's skin or inside their mouth without them knowing.

He issued new instructions for Hamzah. If his son was released and brought to the Iran-Pakistan border as his mother had been, then he, too, should enter Pakistan. However, due to the "situation"—code for Ibrahim's threat of resignation—he could not come to Abbottabad but should head for Mir Ali, where his mother, Khairiah, was already staying with Daood, the widower of Khadija bin Laden.

There was room in Daood's compound for Hamzah and his family, too. Daood would take care of their security and Atiyah their finances, as he had access to the Sheikh's personal accounts.[72] Two sums had been set aside: €10,500 and $10,000.[73] Khairiah, Hamzah's wife Maryam, and her two children would find Sarah, Daood's second wife, most welcoming, Osama wrote. Since Khadija's death he had come to regard Sarah as a daughter, too.

But staying in Mir Ali had its own associated risks. A few days back they had received a letter from Daood, sending happy Ramadan greetings.[74] In it, he had mentioned a terrifying dream that the family initially puzzled over, not knowing if it had been real or just a rhetorical flourish to entertain the children. "I saw that I had been chased by a huge black snake," Daood had written them. "Next thing I was grabbing its head. I opened its mouth and I saw as if all the teeth had shattered."

In a separate letter to Khalid, Daood revealed that he had just survived a double-tap drone strike in which several supporters were killed, and then their family members, too, when they came to evacuate the injured and dead. Clearly shaken, Daood told Khalid: "My brother was in front of me in a car with three others. Another car came ahead of them. Both cars stopped and the passengers were talking. They were about 400 meters ahead of me. The air strike started and they were killed."

Daood knew the risks he was taking by staying in Waziristan and he told Khalid that he believed spies living along the Datta Khel–Miram Shah road had been spray-painting Al Qaeda vehicles with invisible ink that could only be seen by the *machays* in the sky.

Back in his media suite, Osama was concerned about leaving his wife and son in the kill zone. But he was more worried that until she had been checked over, Khairah might inadvertently lead the enemy to his door.

He made a difficult decision. He wrote again to his wife, saying that he had no choice but to advise her to remain for now at Sarah's compound, in the strike zone of Waziristan. He had to keep them away from Abbottabad.

August 2010, Aabpara, Islamabad, Pakistan

Hillary Clinton, the U.S. secretary of state, had been steadily increasing the pressure on Pakistan to locate Osama bin Laden since the beginning of the year. In May 2010, shortly after the arrest of Times Square bomber Faisal Shahzad, she made her strongest statement yet: "I believe that somewhere in this government are people who know where Osama bin Laden and al-Qaeda is . . . and we expect more co-operation to help us bring to justice, capture or kill those who attacked us on 9/11," she said.[75]

General Pasha, whose agents were engaged in secret talks with Al Qaeda, swatted aside Clinton's threats. The ISI had already helped America hunt down hundreds of Al Qaeda targets, he said, sloughing "blood, sweat and time." He was sick and tired of being harangued by what he described as Washington's "psychological warfare." Had Clinton caught a whisper about the ISI cease-fire overtures? he wondered as he composed a vague response to her complaints.[76]

Before becoming director general of the ISI, Pasha had described attacks by foreign intelligence agencies as a "compliment to our achievements." But now that he had been in the hot seat for two years he doubted there could ever be trust between the CIA and ISI. As far as he was concerned, America nakedly expressed its national interest, projecting itself through Hollywood movies (which rewrote the outcomes of wars it lost), while Pakistan dissembled so it could secretly pursue its own course. The United States and Pakistan would rub along, but theirs would always be a fraught relationship enriched only by occasional overlapping interests.[77]

One memorable conversation with a U.S. intelligence official had underscored how each nation regarded the other. "You are so cheap," the official told Pasha, laughing. "We can buy you with a visa, with a visit to the US, even with a dinner . . . we can buy anyone."[78]

Pasha had told friends, "We will take anything and rarely respond." Like most senior army officers, he blamed Pakistan woes on corrupt, low-grade governance rather than military incompetence. "The thinking process [is] nonexistent," he said of the Zardari administration. In government circles it was common knowledge that the president did not like to read official documents and instead deployed aides to recite them to him.[79]

Pasha had only once briefed Prime Minister Yousaf Raza Gilani and had never gone back.[80] At the time of Pasha's appointment, Gilani had been attempting to put the ISI under the authority of the interior ministry, giving civilians control of the spies for the first time in the history of the ISI—a bid that failed.

Pasha believed there was "elite complacency, lack of capacity, inadequate knowledge and wrong attitudes" and apathy at every level, in every sector of national life. Society was "deeply penetrated." The media was "practically bought up." Nearly "everyone of our elite was purchasable." Accordingly, "we are a failing state if we are not yet a failed state," he railed as he quietly coached cricketer turned politician Imran Khan, telling him he was "a future prime minister."[81]

Duplicity was everywhere. Pasha was especially aggrieved by America's army of undercover operatives, people who gave only vague explanations and incomplete information when they demanded visas at the Pakistani embassy in Washington, and then had the cheek to complain of ISI harassment when they arrived. His country was "crawling with foreigners all over the place acting as the eyes and ears of foreign intelligence services."[82] Not to mention the unilateral drone strikes, which had killed thousands of civilians.

For that Pasha blamed former president Musharraf, who "had caved in too easily to American demands." Someone had to say: "Enough was enough."

*   *   *

August 2010, Washington, D.C.

According to the official U.S. story, the CIA had known that Abu Ahmad al-Kuwaiti was Ibrahim Saeed Ahmad for three years. They also had a rough idea of where he operated. But not much more until a sister agency picked up a phone call Ibrahim received from an old friend in the Persian Gulf during a random sweep.

"We've missed you," said the friend. "Where have you been?"

"I'm back with the people I was with before," Ibrahim replied, his distinct lisp identifying him.

There was a pause in the conversation as the caller mulled over the meaning. "May God facilitate," he said finally, understanding that Ibrahim was back working with Osama.[83]

After analyzing this conversation, the CIA began to focus even more closely on Ibrahim, trying to scoop up his signal when he reached the usual calling points at Hassan Abdal, Mansehra, or Peshawar. It could only be locked on to for a few seconds at a time, enabling analysts to record the numbers Ibrahim dialed but not to fix his position.

More ears were needed. A decision was taken to partially involve the ISI. Four numbers were shared—Ibrahim's, his brother Abrar's, Ibrahim's wife Maryam's, and Abrar's wife Bushra's. The CIA deliberately did not tell the ISI to whom they would be listening. Given that the numbers were often switched off and that the team of officers whose job it was to monitor cell phone calls across the country consisted of only eighteen people, the ISI did not eavesdrop as often as it should.[84]

However, in late August 2010, according to the official U.S. version of events, there was a stroke of luck. A signal from Ibrahim's phone enabled a CIA asset working in Pakistan to lock on to a white Suzuki Potohar jeep as it made its way through Peshawar. The operative rang it through, excited. The jeep was easy to follow as it had a distinctive rhino symbol on its spare tire cover.

The news brought more services online. The National Security Agency's spatial and digital net, and CIA informants on the ground, tracked the jeep two hours east to a large compound in Abbottabad, at which point all intelligence sharing with Pasha's men was switched off.

The CIA reported that the Abbottabad compound was prosaic but also peculiar: it was eight times larger than any other home in the area and sat in the middle of a large plot of private land.[85] Despite the obvious wealth of the occupants, who had been there for about five years, there were no phone or Internet connections. They never came out and they burned all their rubbish inside. In a breach of local planning regulations, parts of the perimeter wall were eighteen feet high and topped with another two feet of barbed wire. The outside windows were tiny and mirrored. And a seven-foot privacy screen obscured a view into the second floor—the only part of the house visible from the street.

On the other hand, the compound was less than a mile away from Pakistan's premier military academy—making it a bold location for a hideaway. There were no guards or security cameras, which surely there would be if Osama was inside. There was also a dog, which was surprising in a strict Muslim household.

In late August, a female analyst from the CIA's Counterterrorism Center (CTC) briefed director Leon Panetta in an e-mail: "Closing In on Usama [sic] bin Laden's Courier."[86] In a follow-up meeting with CTC officers, Panetta was told: "We've been tracking suspected couriers, people who've got historical ties to bin Laden, and we tracked them back to a place that looks like a fortress."[87]

The Abbottabad compound had been "custom built," the analysts said.

Panetta gave permission for a deeper investigation. "I want every possible operational avenue explored to get inside the compound," he said.[88]

September 2010, White House, Washington, D.C.

Leon Panetta briefed President Obama and showed him NSA overheads of the compound: "Maybe, just maybe, bin Laden might be there . . ."[89]

During his 2008 presidential campaign, Barack Obama had told supporters that if he ever got Osama bin Laden in his sights and the "Pakistani government [were] unable, or unwilling" to take him out, he would be willing to act alone. "We will kill bin Laden. We will crush Al Qaeda," Obama had said.[90]

Now that he had been presented with what was described by the CIA briefers as "the best lead that we have seen since Tora Bora," he asked for more solid proof.[91]

Speaking later, Obama recalled: "My feeling at the time was *interested*, but *cautious*." He did not want a rerun of the Aafia Siddiqui fiasco, which had finally ended with a New York court sentencing her to eighty-six years in prison amid cries that she had been badly mistreated by the U.S. military and then setup.[92] Despite the court's decision, questions about what had really happened to Aafia during the years of secret detention and then in a Ghazni police station refused to go away, and her sentencing only served to confirm her cult status among jihadists. Her case would be cited as the main reason behind several subsequent high-profile kidnappings of Western aid workers, oil company employees, and journalists in Pakistan, Algeria, and Syria.[93]

But all this had happened under the Bush administration, and Obama was sick of paying for his predecessor's mistakes. He wanted to draw a line under the era of renditions, torture, and black sites. It was time for a cleaner story, a simpler hit. And the president knew full well that killing or capturing Osama would silence his critics.

The principal investigator, who was the deputy chief of the CTC's Afghanistan-Pakistan desk, an intelligence official known only as John, compiled a detailed assessment of everything the CIA had on al-Kuwaiti. The document, entitled "Anatomy of a Lead," was put on a "close hold," which meant only a rarefied circle had access to it—and none of them was from Pakistan.

As the weeks progressed, more clues emerged as the NSA and CIA did what Osama had long feared they would: fixed on phone calls made by Maryam and Bushra. When they spoke to relatives, they lied about where they lived. For several years, the two women had pretended to their families that they were in Kuwait. They went to great lengths to shore up the lie, even taking gifts of expensive foreign clothes and cloth whenever they went home to Shangla or Kohat.

Maryam had recently told her mother that she had "returned to Pakistan." However, she said she was living in Peshawar.[94]

Neither of them even mentioned Abbottabad. But where they said they were was not where the phone calls were ever made from.

September 2010, Bilal Town, Abbottabad

The compound was steeped in fear and paranoia but not because anyone had any inkling of America's plans. The funk set in after Osama received a shocking letter from Daood's new wife Sarah in Mir Ali.

"Please forgive my poor sentences," she began. On September 19, Daood had left home after dawn prayers and driven along the dangerous road between Datta Khel and Miram Shah to meet Atiyah's representative, who had money to pay for Khairiah bin Laden's ongoing stay at his home.

It was a notorious route along which hundreds of Al Qaeda brothers had been killed, including Sheikh Saeed al-Masri. But the minor roads were so backbreaking and so much longer that many fighters took the risk.

On his return journey he had stopped at Deegan, the halfway point, when a drone targeted his vehicle, killing Daood and his driver outright. "He was killed before breaking the fast, right before sunset prayer, on his way [back] to us. The loss is bigger than can be expressed in just a few lines," a distraught Sarah wrote.[95]

Osama panicked. Whether the strike had been opportunistic or had deliberately targeted his former son-in-law, Daood's death made his home unsafe for any bin Laden family member. It also brought any observers one step closer to Osama. Security had to be tightened up and Khairiah had to move.

Osama held a series of urgent meetings with Ibrahim and Abrar, asking them to speed up Khairiah's arrival, while they pointed out she had not yet had the requisite checks to make sure she was not bugged. Meanwhile, Seham, Miriam, and Sumaiya agonized over how to break the news to Daood's children.

Sarah sent another update. Going through her husband's possessions she had found many items that belonged to the family in Abbottabad, including two boxes of Khadija's gold jewelry and gifts for Aisha and Seham.[96]

There was a computer, a pistol, and notebooks containing Daood's will, as well as his ring, which now belonged by rights to his eldest son, Abdallah, along with an iPod.

She had also found Khadija's old diary, inside which all the family birthdays had been marked. There was also a handwritten poem from Seham commemorating Khadija's wedding to Daood in 2000.

The most tragic relic was Saad bin Laden's suitcase and possessions from Iran. There were clothes, notebooks, and photographs of his children. On Saad's cell phone they had found the two video files that comprised his will and a letter to his father.[97]

Sarah wanted to send all these possessions on with Khairiah.

Tempering all the bad, there was one piece of good news. Sarah was seven months pregnant with her second child. If it was a girl, she intended to name it Khadija, after Osama's dead daughter. Her first child had been named after Saad.

Seham wrote back immediately. "Misfortune has enveloped us," she began, saying that the children were standing around her, crying and blowing kisses. Trying to be positive, she wrote that their "mother," Miriam, had had a dream in which she saw God calling to Daood to rise up with the martyrs. When she told the children that Sarah was pregnant, they had "divided into two teams," guessing whether she would have a boy or a girl. Miriam had scolded them not to be silly but to "pray to God for her to be safe, whether a girl or boy."[98]

Whatever happened, Sarah had to stay in touch. "Saad and the newborn are brothers to Abdallah and his sisters, as there is no difference between them all," Seham wrote. Family was family. The children were planning to write their own letters when things settled down.

November 2010, White House, Washington, D.C.

Panetta, John, and the bin Laden team went back to the president. There was a "strong possibility" that the Al Qaeda leader was in the compound, they reported. When he asked each of them to quantify their degree of certainty, John said 90 percent. His team went for 80 percent, while Michael Morell, the deputy director of the CIA, was at 60 percent.

The president remained skeptical, thinking of the many previous leads over the years that had turned out to be "Elvis sightings." Among the most embarrassing was a photograph of Osama bin Laden sitting in an open-top jeep in Chitral that Dick Cheney had gleefully presented to Musharraf in 2007. The president of Pakistan had come back a few days later beaming with the news that the man in the picture was a well-known smuggler from Khost who liked to dress up as his hero.[99]

To avoid a repeat, presidential advisers began an "interrogation of data," testing the CIA theory.[100] Among the possibilities they conjured was that the Abbottabad compound did house a senior Al Qaeda figure, but *not* Osama. Perhaps it was another Gulf sheikh on the run, or members of Osama's family—but not the man himself.

To take a closer look, the CIA needed an observation post and someone fireproof in the field. It reached out to a retired Pakistan Army officer, Lieutenant Colonel Saeed Iqbal. A former commanding officer of the 408th Military Intelligence Battalion, he had once held a prestigious position reporting directly to the chief of army staff and had been responsible for his personal security.[101]

He also had a checkered record—which made him gettable. The officer had been accused by a government inquiry of torturing a man to death, allegations that had summarily ended his military career in 1993.[102] Afterward, he had sought to maintain important military, establishment, and intelligence connections, with one of his sons working as a private secretary to Pakistan's former president Pervez Musharraf.

The family bought an elegant home in the upmarket Defense Housing Authority, where his neighbors were all senior officers.

In 1994, Iqbal had started a private security business, staffed by ex-ISI officers, and according to some of those who worked for him, he had almost immediately turned a profit by winning prestigious security contracts with embassies in Islamabad. His relations with the West deepened when in 1997 he was introduced to the CIA station in Islamabad.[103]

Within a decade that relationship had blossomed. Iqbal regularly supplied "contractors" to work with the CIA in-country: drivers, muscle, street surveillance and pickpockets, logistics, and armorers.[104]

In the fall of 2010, he set off for Abbottabad, where he approached Dr. Amir Aziz, a young major in the Army Medical Corps. Aziz was not related in any way to Osama bin Laden's doctor from Lahore, although they shared the same name. Iqbal's interest was that Dr. Aziz's elaborate house with fake Doric columns sat fewer than eighty yards away from the mysterious Abbottabad compound and had a clear view of it.

Iqbal expressed interest in land Aziz was selling, saying he wanted to build a retirement home for himself and his wife. He returned several times, according to Aziz, always driving an expensive bulletproof "silenced" car that Aziz described as creeping up on people.

Aziz recalled that Iqbal was keen to look around, climbing up onto the flat roof of the building to "take pictures of Aziz's pets"—with the mysterious compound in the background.[105] Eventually, he moved on, finding other homes in the neighborhood.

President Obama was informed that the CIA had "eyes on" the house. As well as Iqbal's photographs, a team of locally recruited informants had been installed in one nearby building, from where they watched through curtained windows. They photographed everything that could be seen, copied down the license plates of cars that came and went, and used infrared cameras to capture any movement at night. They planned to insert listening devices into a row of young poplar trees that grew close to the outside wall—until a gardener cut them all down, in a move that spooked the observation post.

Iqbal took a backseat, renting an office in his company's name at Jadoon Plaza in downtown Abbottabad. A mile away from the compound, the "camp office," as he called it, became a forward operating station from where his men could come and go for debriefings without fear of being spotted.[106]

His operation began to accumulate useful data, sufficient for the CIA to put together a "pattern of life" study that reported that about a dozen women and children lived in the compound, the group consisting of at least two families, with between six to eight children among them. They would buy sweets and soft drinks for the children at Rasheed's corner store, about a one-minute walk from the house, while the adults got their bulkier supplies from Sajid General Store down the road. Occasionally they bought naan bread from a shop with a tandoor oven that was nearby, but most baking was done at home.[107]

The close observation post homed in on yet more strange elements in the house's setup. Four separate electricity meters had been wired up, along with four gas meters, all listed in just one name—Sahib Khan, son of Noor Hussain—who was not the registered owner of the property.[108]

There were other oddities, small but pronounced. Only one of the children, a boy aged about seven, went to school, at a madrassa outside the city. The rest spent their days inside, only occasionally emerging to play cricket in the street. Local children reported they were "unfriendly."

But still there was nothing that the CIA or its assets could offer to firm up the presence of Osama.

Analysts came up with increasingly imaginative proposals. The CIA could dig a tunnel underneath, or hack into the large satellite dish that sat on the roof of a small sunroom in the yard. Perhaps a high-powered telescope placed on a nearby mountain could pick up activity at the house.

None of these proposals was practical, leaving agents to return to the compound and inveigle themselves into the families who lived around it.

The closest described their secretive neighbors as "polite people who did not make small talk." The only residents they had ever met were two brothers—Arshad and Tariq Khan—who had built the house in 2005 for an elderly relative fleeing from a "blood feud" in their native Waziristan, which explained the high walls.[109]

Others gossiped that the Khan brothers were shifting heroin. How else could two men with no obvious source of wealth afford such a lavish home? One complained that the Khans were miserly as they rarely gave charity to the poor of the area, as was customary.

The best eyewitness was Shamraiz Khan, a laborer who lived in a low-slung mud-brick home directly opposite the compound's main gate. He had only ever noticed one visitor, he said, someone who came to the compound in the summer of 2010 in a white Toyota Corolla.[110] Shamraiz had also been inside the compound: the Khan brothers paid him a few hundred rupees to plow the soil in the field next to the house. But he never went into the residential courtyard where Osama lived or saw anyone from the main house.

The only sight of the compound's female residents came when they occasionally emerged, fully covered, and were driven out in the white jeep or the compound's other vehicle, a red Suzuki van. Sometimes they went to the hospital. Other times they went to Shangla or Kohat, where they stayed for several days.

A young man also lived at the compound and, according to Shamraiz, had bought a cow from him and was attempting to grow vegetables.

Eventually, after scrutinizing the pieces of laundry that went up on a washing line in the yard, the CIA concluded that a third family was living on the top floor that never went out at all. It consisted of at least three adult women, two men, and ten children—figures that were roughly consistent with what was known about Osama's family.

All attention was now focused on identifying one figure. He emerged most days from the back door of the main house to stroll around the courtyard for an hour or two, walking back and forth in tight circles like a prisoner in an exercise yard. Sometimes a woman and child accompanied him.

By magnifying satellite images of the figure and measuring the length of his shadow, officials determined he was tall, roughly Osama's height.[111] However, since he always stayed under an awning and wore a wide-brimmed hat, no one had seen his face.

September 26, 2010, Bilal Town, Abbottabad

Inside the compound, Osama waited anxiously for Khairiah, filling his time by reading a biography of Abu Musab al-Zarqawi that Atiyah had found on a jihadist website.

It was attributed to Saif al-Adel in Tehran and was ultimately a damning critique. It detailed secret Al Qaeda smuggling points into Iran, and how the Quds Force had assisted in Zarqawi's passage to Iraq and continued to allow the through-flow of financing.

Osama was furious that such sensitive material about their crucial Iran network had been published, and he could not believe that Saif would have been so indiscreet. Atiyah was instructed to mount a damage-limitation exercise. Saif was not the author, everyone should be told. "Remind them he is in jail."[112]

October 21, 2010, Bilal Town, Abbottabad

More than two months had passed since Khairiah bin Laden's arrival in Pakistan and there was still no clearance for her travel to Abbottabad. Daood's death continued to hang over the house, with the children bursting into tears while Osama ignored them and spent most of his time writing letters or in front of the television news. The United States, he argued, was flailing: a record number of American soldiers had been killed in Afghanistan and a financial crisis of their own making threatened to impact Pentagon budgets. "Anyone who looks at the enemies in NATO, especially America, will know that they are in big trouble," he wrote to Atiyah.[113] The "local enemies" were also in crisis, he said, referring to Pakistan's worsening security situation and recent floods that had affected more than twenty million people.

Through the "generosity of God, the situation is moving in the direction of the mujahideen," he wrote. Be patient and strong, and God would reward them, Osama told Atiyah, who still remained in office unable to leave, having narrowly survived a drone strike earlier in the month—something the CIA crowed about in the media, mistakenly believing that he was dead.[114]

Family members, still in Waziristan, should "move only when the clouds are heavy," and not use the Datta Khel–Miram Shah road, instructed Osama.[115]

Unsure about the Ibrahim situation, Atiyah informed Osama that he had been working up a contingency plan to find temporary accommodation for Hamzah in Balochistan. A son of the dead Al Qaeda financial chief Sheikh Saeed al-Masri and another brother had gone there to secure a suitable location.

Osama wrote back that the emissaries should be wary of certain Balochi brothers who had once been loyal to Khalid Shaikh Mohammad but were now known to "work for Pakistani intelligence."[116] Hamzah should "not leave the house" until Atiyah was ready to send him to Peshawar with a "trusted Pakistani brother." What about the "new companion"? Had any person been hired? Osama asked.

Frustrated, he turned on Atiyah, accusing him of throttling his public voice as his latest video had still not been aired. "It seems there is a misunderstanding regarding the issue of jihadi media," he said, sarcastically. "It is a main piece of the war and I did not mean that it should be abandoned." Atiyah needed to "do better," he needled, ignoring the fact that his Number Three wanted to quit.

The tenth anniversary of 9/11 was coming and "attention should be paid to start preparing for [it] now," Osama railed. Al Qaeda needed to "benefit from this event" and present "our just cause to the world, especially to the European people." Atiyah should reach out to the right people. He suggested Ahmad Zaidan at Al Jazeera, Robert Fisk of the *Independent*, and the prominent Arab newspaper editor Abdel Bari Atwan, based in London.

Osama had an idea. "Ask Brother Azzam about which U.S. channel you should send the tape to." On the USB stick were yet more audio recordings, to be broadcast "before the American congressional election."

One thing that had made Osama contented was a letter from Mullah Omar— the first direct correspondence since 9/11. "I have received your kind letter," Osama replied. "I was so happy reading it. We are your soldiers and we are with you heart and soul in supporting the religion of God Almighty."[117]

November 24, 2010, Bilal Town, Abbottabad

Ibrahim was far sicker than he realized. According to family members, the doctor's diagnosis was cancer. As a result, the thirty-two-year-old was incapable of making scheduled courier exchanges, so it took almost a month for letters from Waziristan to reach Abbottabad. When Atiyah's reply to Osama's entreaties finally arrived, it contained bad news.

The two emissaries he had sent to Balochistan to find a safe house for Osama's family had been picked off in a drone strike. They included Sheikh Saeed's last remaining adult son.

Atiyah confirmed that Hamzah, his family, and Khairiah were now staying with him in North Waziristan, although he was careful not to identify their precise location.[118] Khairiah still intended to go to Abbottabad, he continued. They were just waiting for a "cloudy day" and a "green light" from the Sheikh. The fear that she was somehow a dupe of the Iranians, or even the CIA, was being taken so seriously that Atiyah worried "they are even overdoing it." Someone had ordered a female recruit to examine

Khairiah's teeth, as Osama had become paranoid that a chip could have been inserted into a filling by the Quds Force during one of her frequent dental appointments at the Tourist Complex. "I doubt—with God's help—that there would be anything [hidden in her teeth]," Atiyah added. "Nevertheless I preferred to mention this to you just so you know."

There was news about Hamzah. Over recent weeks, Atiyah had got to know him and liked what he saw. He described the boy to his doting father as being "very sweet and good." Osama would be pleased to know that his son had wisdom and politeness, was easygoing and warm, and had requested that he receive no special treatment just because he was the son of "someone."

However, Atiyah was worried that Osama was expecting too much of Hamzah. "Beloved Sheikh, he is a young man who lived years in prison."

Although Hamzah was already asking for military training, Atiyah warned that he needed to spend time getting used to his new environment first. "I calm him down as we pray together . . . I reminded him of what happened to Saad, because he was impatient and persistent." In Atiyah's opinion, Hamzah could become a great mujahid but first needed time to mature. "I promised to plan some safe training for him: firing various weapons. Perhaps I will get to do this in the coming days." Osama should write "something proper" to him, finding some encouraging words.

There was better news about finding a replacement companion, a subject that Atiyah referred to as "the special issue." Finally, he had identified someone: a mujahid who was thirty-five years old and married with small children. Presently, he managed shops in Lahore and so knew how to behave in cities. "He is a savvy person, mature, confident, and understands the subject matter of renting, selling, and purchasing homes," wrote Atiyah. There was only one hitch: he was an Urdu-speaking Punjabi, not a Pashtun. "What is your opinion?" he asked, adding that this candidate was the best he could find and that he wanted to resolve the issue as it had been dragging on for far too long.

Next, Atiyah addressed future operations. Things were looking up. Abu Yahya's Libyan group had formally merged with Al Qaeda, bringing in more money and recruits. The list of commanders under training was swelling once more, Atiyah naming them all individually, using their *kunyas*. "The good news is we are in one heart, loving, confident, and cooperating," he said. He had also been in touch with the elusive Dr. Ayman al-Zawahiri, who was "very happy" in his tribal bolt-hole with his young wife.

Even Younis al-Mauritani, the new external operations chief, was working out. Despite his relative youth he was galvanizing support. Currently he was on the Balochistan border with six brothers, preparing to enter Iran. From there they planned to disperse across Europe to monitor the growth of cells in Western cities.

Days later more family news reached the compound. Osama's sons Mohammed and Othman has also been released by the Iranians and brought to the Pakistan border. They had already crossed over into Waziristan and were on their way to Karachi with their families.[119] Buoyed by the news but worried that some Iranian double-game was afoot, Osama wrote immediately to Atiyah, sending Ibrahim to meet Atiyah's courier in double-quick time. All family members and their luggage had to be thoroughly checked for spying devices. Not a moment could be spared.

But then outside life reached inside. One night while the women and children were watching Al Jazeera, a recent demand by Maryam and Bushra, who had complained of being bored, Maryam's eldest daughter, Rehma, nine, saw a picture of Osama bin Laden on the screen and exclaimed that "this is the man upstairs!"[120]

Maryam demanded an explanation from her husband. "Don't you trust us?" she yelled at him, with all the children listening, after he stonewalled and refused to comment.[121]

"It's none of your business," Ibrahim finally hissed.

She stopped talking to him. They sat sullenly.

"Yes," he eventually said, "the man we have been protecting all these years is Osama bin Laden."

Although it was not a complete surprise, Maryam was still shocked. How could he have taken on such an arduous responsibility? And what would they gain from it? she asked. What about the children? Their lives were being played with. "Don't *you* worry about being arrested or tortured?" she asked, reminding him of the Aafia Siddiqui story.

"It's the will of God," Ibrahim replied blithely. "He gave me this mission."

Maryam looked him in the eye. "Well in that case there is no stopping you and I wish you are martyred rather than captured," she said, storming out of the annex, "because at least that will be a quick death."

Ibrahim called after her. "Come back. For now we all have to find a way to live together—with the Sheikh," he said. "But I have given notice. Soon I will be free of my duties."

The Sheikh was planning to give him some money as compensation for the years of service, he revealed. They could make a fresh start in Saudi Arabia. "You need to stay calm," he hollered, "and keep the children quiet."

Maryam stormed back into the room. "I am leaving unless you give him a deadline," she spat. "How much longer?"

Ibrahim hesitated. "Six more months and then it is over. I will tell him tonight."

The meeting went badly. Osama talked over Ibrahim and Abrar, telling them that he had changed his mind and that instead of emptying out his household, five new family members were coming to join him. Hamzah, his wife and two children, and Khairiah were coming to Abbottabad. Khalid was staying and they had to find a safe house for his sons Mohammed and Othman in Peshawar, who would soon be arriving with their wives and children. He was sick of being blackmailed.

As a sop, Osama suggested limply that Ibrahim and Abrar tell their wives and children that the family upstairs had "gone away."

The Kuwaiti brothers despaired. With their children growing older it was impossible to keep Osama's existence concealed. It would only get worse if yet more Arabs moved in. Their children heard every footstep and scraping chair above them. Lives were in the balance, Ibrahim said. He had just come back from a doctor who had diagnosed his cancer as terminal and he did not want to spend his dying days caring for the Sheikh.[122]

Osama would not budge. His organization had rallied, it was solvent and busy plotting new attacks, and he was not going to be pushed around by a Pakistani. He, too, was "suffering from a long-term and life threatening condition." Did they not understand how he had sacrificed everything and never stolen even a moment for himself?

The Kuwaiti brothers looked at each other and rose as one. "We quit," Ibrahim said. Abrar nodded.

There was one final matter. Given how much time they had invested in building the Abbottabad villa, and the fact that Abrar's name was on all the paperwork, the brothers regarded the compound as theirs. They would not be moving out but Sheikh Osama and his family would have to go.

On December 4, a shaken Osama wrote to Khairiah. "I have been living for years in the company of some of the brothers of the area and they are getting exhausted—security wise—from me staying with them."[123] He had done everything he could to win Ibrahim's support for his plan to receive the family from Iran but to no avail. "I have used all my energy and I have tried so hard . . . to convince them to agree," he wrote.

But the companions would not budge. "They are down, and they asked us all to leave," he revealed. "Our number is large and beyond what they can handle, and so we started telling them that you will come alone. They still refused. That's how much they are in a state of shut down."

Even Osama's suggestion that Khalid would leave so Khairiah could stay had been rejected. "I have to leave," a dejected Osama wrote. And if this was the case he was in no rush. "It will take a few months to arrange another place."[124]

Osama became so sullen that he barely spoke to anyone.[125] He had been banking on Khairiah's arrival. She was the only one capable of helping him prepare for the tenth anniversary of 9/11. During the first years in Pakistan, Seham had tried to assist as best she could, editing his statements. But she did not have Khairiah's clarity or literary skills, and after the deaths of her daughter Khadija, Saad, and her son-in-law Daood, her fervor for jihad had dwindled.

These days, she was at war with Maryam and Bushra. Blaming them for the brothers' decision to evict Osama, she could not bear to be around them. She also feared for Khalid. Her twenty-one-year-old son was, she thought, coming to the end of his tether, partly because of his enforced monastic lifestyle. Nothing was going to change fast. Khalid's marriage to Karima was still some way off because of Ibrahim and Abrar's demands. All Seham could do, as a prospective mother-in-law, was write to her future sister-in-law asking for yet another postponement.[126]

Osama decided to get around his companions. If Khairiah could not come to him, he would send his writings to her for review via Atiyah. "I sent you all the statements and ideas I have on my computer to contribute to putting together the statements for this important anniversary," he wrote. "While waiting for God Almighty to facilitate your return and fill our hearts with joy," could she please take a look and "assist me in my path and in my messages?"[127]

He dispatched a separate message to Atiyah to buy Khairiah a computer and USB drives on which to record her responses. Osama hoped she could also look over the video statement he had recorded more than two months back that had still not been aired. "I plan to redo it before broadcasting."

At the back of his mind, he continued to worry about Iran and the CIA. He just could not stop himself. He had one more piece of advice for his wife. Inspecting her teeth was just not good enough. She should get all of her Iranian fillings replaced. And while she waited she should also learn Pashto, and take care of all her medical needs "as our security situation here does not allow us to go to the doctors." Hamzah had to do the same.

He rounded off his letter to his wife obliquely. "Tell me again one thing," he wrote. "What was the reason [the Iranians] told you they were releasing you?"[128]

Days later, Osama pushed the plan on. He wrote another letter to Atiyah checking up on an older request to arrange for fake ID cards to be manufactured for himself and Khalid. He would do what needed to be done. The Sheikh could not wait any longer. He was coming out to meet Khairiah.

This was not the first time Osama had ventured out. Contrary to popular belief, he had left the compound several times before. In 2008, according to two former aides to the Lashkar-e-Taiba leader Hafiz Saeed, Osama had traveled to Mansehra to attend an extraordinary planning meeting for the Mumbai operation of November 26, 2008 (which had become known as 26/11).[129] It had been facilitated by Lashkar, overseen by the ISI's S-Wing, and sponsored by Al Qaeda.

In August 2009, he traveled to Kohat to meet up with Qari Saifullah Akhtar, the leader of the banned Islamist group Harkat ul-Jihad al-Islami (HUJI).[130] Akhtar, a prominent figure in Osama's closed circle of protectors, had wanted Al Qaeda's help with a planned attack on the Pakistan Army's general headquarters in Rawalpindi. Instead of giving his blessing, Osama had tried to talk Akhtar out of it, requesting that HUJI and other jihad fronts concentrate their firepower on America. But Akhtar had gone ahead anyway, launching a savage and surprising broadside on October 10 that had killed nine soldiers and two civilians, shaking the Pakistan Army establishment to its core.[131] At one point in the siege, reporters claimed that several senior ranking officers were being held captive, and regardless of whether the hostage taking actually took place, the fact that the public believed it did demonstrated how low was the standing of the army.

Osama's most recent trip out had come in the summer of 2010, when Fazlur Rehman Khalil arranged a meeting with Hakimullah Mehsud so they could discuss TTP–Al Qaeda differences face-to-face. The Sheikh had left Abbottabad at sunset and arrived on the edge of the Tribal Areas around eleven P.M. "We were dumb-struck," said the elder of the compound that had been selected as the venue at the last minute. "We all knew his face. He was the last person we'd expected to turn up at our doorstep."[132]

After discussions sustained over a dinner of lamb chops and rice, Osama's entourage left the village via a different route, seemingly able to pass through several army checkpoints without any trouble, showing chits of paper as if they were working for the chief of the army staff.

This time, Osama planned another venture. Reassured that important ISI-linked figures like Khalil were watching his back, his only concern was running into impromptu patrols. "Are there any permanent, nightly or time to time checkpoints there in the place where you deliver and receive messages from your area?" he asked Atiyah in a letter discussing logistics.[133]

When was the best time for him to travel? Just after sunrise "when movement is weak because of the extreme cold" or after sunset, when roads became deserted?

As for a rendezvous point, he suggested to Atiyah the "place where you all meet customarily," which was possibly somewhere near Kohat, close to or even in the tunnel, or possibly near Ibrahim's sister's place. If not any of these, they could arrange it at "the other place where I met with the brother from our side a while ago," Osama said, referring to his trip to see Hakimullah in the summer. To make sure that he and Atiyah were on the same page, he mentioned another landmark. The place he was thinking of was where "I prepared the goods in a bag for him."

Osama would not be going alone. He decided to use his wife Amal as cover, along with their two youngest sons, Ibrahim and Hussein. Using innocent family members to shield behind came as second nature to a man who had once happily dragged his young sons across the battlefields of Afghanistan. Amal had no say in the matter. She comforted herself in the knowledge that as always Osama would be carrying five hundred euros sewn into his undergarments and two phone numbers, one for a handset held by Atiyah that was only ever to be rung in a dire emergency. The other number linked through to a close aide of Dr. Ayman al-Zawahiri.

There was a brief postscript. He had taken the precautionary measure of instructing his son Khalid of what to do "in case any mishap should befall my two companions." In the event of Ibrahim or Abrar being arrested, or running away, leaving them all dangerously exposed, Khalid was to contact Atiyah with prearranged details of an emergency safe house in Peshawar, where the family temporarily could hide.

Atiyah needed to acknowledge the plan. Could he do that, Osama asked?

* * *

December 14, 2010, Washington, D.C.

Analysts called him "the Pacer," and this image intrigued John Brennan, the president's counterterrorism chief, whose gut told him that Osama bin Laden was likely in the Abbottabad compound.[134]

Shortly before the president left for his annual Christmas holiday in Hawaii, Panetta and Brennan briefed him again. They discussed the mysterious third family who lived on the top floor of the house and similarities between the Pacer and old Predator footage of Osama walking across the parade ground at his former headquarters in Tarnak Qila in Kandahar.

This man's gait and poise were similar, Brennan argued.

The president was still not ready. "I want to hear back from you, Director Panetta, when I get back from the holidays," he said. "Let's make sure that we pull this string as quickly as possible. If he's there, time is of the essence."[135]

That month, the CIA requested tens of millions of dollars in extra funding from Congress. It was skimmed off other agency budgets and plowed into various schemes that sought more tangible proof that the Al Qaeda leader and his family were inside the compound.

One idea involved setting up a fake National Literacy Program inside Shamraiz's house in an attempt to lure out the children living opposite.[136] Another was a phony Save the Children vaccination scheme. If the doctors got to meet Osama's children, they could sneak a few DNA samples and check them against those of a sister of Osama's who had died of brain cancer in the United States. The hospital in Boston that had treated her in 2010 had kept tissue samples—at the request of the CIA.

CHAPTER TEN

*"We go to a house, we fuck with some people,
and we leave. This is just a longer flight."*
—SEAL TEAM MEMBER ROBERT O'NEILL[1]

January 13, 2011, Bilal Town, Abbottabad, Pakistan

OSAMA CALLED A SUMMIT WITH IBRAHIM and Abrar. Still at loggerheads, they all needed a way out.

"We have been friends on this great path for more than eight years," he began, choosing a somber tone. "You have given us a great gift that we will never forget as long as we live," he tried. He needed to buy a few weeks of their time. After that, he agreed to move out with his family. They were ready to pack everything and leave.

He understood the pressures the Kuwaitis were under, he said, and was disturbed by their sicknesses—Ibrahim's cancer and Abrar's chronic depression.[2]

He wanted to reassure them that he was actively seeking a new companion and a new place to live. It might all happen very quickly indeed. He pulled out his Koran: "Help ye one another in righteousness and piety."[3]

The brothers were not impressed. A "long and strenuous discussion" followed that involved shouting, "petulance," and "irritation" and carried on into the next day. However, finally an agreement was hammered out and Osama must have been relieved by the concessions he won: Khairiah could come after all, so long as she completed any outstanding medical treatment first. Once in the house, she would not be able to leave until they all departed for their new bolt-hole.

For his part, the Sheikh signed a new written promise to move out of Abbottabad after the tenth anniversary of 9/11. The property could then be sold, meaning Ibrahim and Abrar would cash in and could spend their money on buying their retirement homes in Jeddah, where no one could

377

touch them. The moving date for the caravan of Osama bin Laden was set. The Abbottabad epoch was, in Osama's mind, almost over. To avoid any further misunderstandings, he wrote it all down. "We do appreciate the amount of pressure you have been under and the importance of lessening the pressure, so I have suggested decreasing the number [of people] to nearly half."

Who was going to be asked to leave, and where they would go, he didn't say.[4]

A couple of days later, Ibrahim delivered a missive to Khairiah telling her that she was, after all, to go to Peshawar, where the wife of Mohammed Aslam was ready to take her to a doctor and a dentist.

Osama was not sure about the exact date of her journey to Abbottabad, but it would probably be a Thursday afternoon or a Friday, he wrote, days that Pakistani police and soldiers often took off, leaving many security checkpoints unmanned.

However, not everything he had agreed with the Kuwaiti brothers was set in stone. Osama had already penned two secret messages for Atiyah, one instructing Hamzah to come to Abbottabad along with his family and another asking his sons Mohammed and Othman to travel to Peshawar and meet a contact who would rendezvous with them either in the Lady Reading Hospital or Paradise Square. From there they would be taken to a Peshawar safe house until it was safe to come to Abbottabad.[5]

Osama updated Atiyah about tensions inside the compound. "Eight years and months have passed accompanied by Ahmad [Ibrahim] and his brother. They accepted the job a short time before the arrest of Hafith [Khalid Shaikh Mohammad]. The length of companionship and the security pressure have affected [Ibrahim's] health and his nerves. And his condition [impacts on Abrar], who is now suffering from a dangerous disease that hit him a few weeks back, and his illness is the reason *we* did not communicate with *you*."[6]

Osama had a sensitive announcement: a crisis to reveal that could put the kibosh on all other decisions. The candidate who Atiyah had found in Lahore to replace Ibrahim and his brother as companion had got cold feet and dropped out. They would have to start again. "Inform me of the developments in every message," Osama wrote, his exhaustion and frustration that the move from Abbottabad may be further delayed evident from the text.

The Sheikh tidied up loose ends, writing directly to Mohammed Aslam to thank him for agreeing to host his family when they arrived in Peshawar. He used this letter as a chance to ask Aslam if he knew anyone in Peshawar suitable for the companion job. "It's been eight years and a few months in the company of the brothers," he explained. "But with the length of time they have suffered serious fatigue. Do you have brothers from Pakistan who you know and trust and are fully confident?"[7]

If the answer was yes, then Aslam should act fast and brief whoever he proposed as to how the bin Laden caravan was run: "We are in two separated houses, inside and out, and we are making our bread by ourselves, and we buy grain wholesale." Medical needs were minimal as they kept stocks in-house. At most, the adults went out once a year. His son Khalid was the only one who spoke to neighbors and he "knows Pashtu 70 percent and now would endeavor to speak Urdu."[8]

The upheavals had had one positive consequence. Even though Osama had no idea where they would all live after the 9/11 anniversary, their getting out of Abbottabad would finally free up Khalid, who was keen once more to fix a marriage date for September 2011—if his bride-to-be could be persuaded that the stop-start engagement was really back on.

In a letter that was probably dispatched on the same thumb drive as Osama's missives, Seham updated Karima's mother. "I want to assure you that this is the last and final appointment, no more and no less, God willing," she assured her. "My son says he will compensate [Karima] for waiting for him."[9]

January 2011, Washington, D.C.

CIA director Leon Panetta and his deputy Michael Morell were exploring possible courses of action. Some were suggesting "over-kill," meaning an aerial bombing raid that would obliterate the compound and everyone in it, or a precision drone strike to take out the Pacer as he made his daily circuit. "I'd rather just push the easy button," said Gina Bennett, an analyst who had become a key figure in the CIA's hunt for Osama bin Laden over more than a decade.

After Admiral William McRaven, a former Navy SEAL who now led the Joint Special Operations Command (JSOC), was brought into the conversation, the focus switched to a ground operation. A bunker-buster strike would make it almost impossible to verify that they had hit the main target, he warned, and collateral damage to women and children in the compound as well as those living in neighboring houses would probably be substantial, causing aftershocks, real and psychological, that the United States might not be able to contain or ride out. Besides, there was no way of knowing whether the surgical strike had hit or missed its target, meaning Osama;

and if he survived, he could go to ground, possibly forever. They had to go in person to kill or capture him.[10]

McRaven pointed out that during the past decade JSOC had conducted thousands of such raids against compounds much harder to penetrate than Abbottabad. It would not be the first time SEALs had operated inside Pakistani territory, either. At least ten covert forays had been made into Waziristan, without Pakistan's knowledge, and many more had been planned, including an aborted parasail operation to nab Dr. al-Zawahiri from Damadola in 2006.[11]

This swoop, however, was far trickier and the political fallout potentially catastrophic. Abbottabad was more than 150 miles inside Pakistani airspace, which meant a covert mission that involved flying temperamental helicopters—notoriously difficult to cloak—beneath Pakistan's radar, unless they brought Islamabad into the discussion.

In Virginia, no one could see that working.

In Aabpara, the ISI had never felt more alienated from Langley. General Ahmed Shuja Pasha told friends that relations with the CIA had reached their "lowest ebb" as a result of a private lawsuit lodged in New York the previous November that had named him as complicit in the Mumbai attacks of 2008, alongside Hafiz Saeed, emir of Lashkar-e-Taiba.[12] Pasha told friends that he suspected the CIA had had a hand in pursuing the case.

Langley had sent a succession of station chiefs to Islamabad who had spent far less time building up goodwill than had their predecessors. Jaded case officers cycled through the capital, with each one leaving Pakistan more embittered or disengaged than the last.

Pasha believed that "the main agenda of the CIA is to have the ISI declared as a terrorist organization," and he had responded to the Mumbai court case by leaking the name of the CIA Islamabad station chief, Jonathan Bank, thereby forcing Bank to pull out.[13]

His replacement, Mark Kelton, an acerbic old-school type who was coming straight from Russia, had yet to arrive, although CIA director Panetta had concluded that years of engaging in adversarial espionage in Moscow could be a significant asset in Islamabad.[14]

Everyone in the know at Langley was worried by the consequences of a hostile ISI and an unsettled Islamabad CIA station on the building Abbottabad plan.

For Obama administration veterans like Defense Secretary Robert Gates, history, rather than Pakistan, was also a potent issue. The emerging proposal to dispatch helicopters into hostile territory evoked a vision of the Black Hawk Down episode, referring to the disastrous 1993 mission to Mogadishu in which two U.S. helicopters had been shot down and eighteen soldiers killed.[15]

Admiral McRaven's job was to find workable solutions, and he profiled the unit he intended to use: SEAL Team Six. Its commander had led an audacious mission in 2009 to rescue Richard Phillips, the captain of an American freighter that had been seized by Somali pirates. The operation had been so successful that Tom Hanks was already in talks with major Hollywood studios to star in a cinematic retelling of the story.

What was needed was detail. McRaven appointed a JSOC official known as Brian, an officer who had previously been an operational commander, to prepare a meticulous raid schematic.

Brian moved into an unmarked office on the first floor of the CIA's printing plant at Langley, which he filled with topographical maps and overheads of Osama's home, which was officially identified as AC1—or Abbottabad Compound 1. Some jocularly referred to the proposed raid as "a trip to Atlantic City."[16]

January 25, 2011, Abbottabad

Post office clerk Tahir Shehzad's luck had run out in November when he failed to waive a customer's bill at the counter where he worked, a squat building across the road from Abbottabad's British-era St. Luke's Church. The customer owed a handful of rupees, not enough to buy a plate of biryani, but Shehzad was a zealot and with his supervisor always breathing down his neck he felt obliged to threaten the customer.

After an argument, the embarrassed customer—a former army officer—stomped out, waiting outside for Shehzad to finish his shift so he could rough him up. But instead of jumping him, he had instead followed him to a deadbeat corner in an otherwise smart army town, where he saw Shehzad chitchatting with a fair-skinned man who was unmistakably an Arab. The retired officer watched intrigued as the two men dived inside a religious bookshop. Suspicious, he called a police contact to say he had witnessed what looked like "an Arab plot" unfolding.

The cops, who were under ISI instructions not to touch any cases involving Arabs—just as former ISI chief Hamid Gul had told Osama would happen—gave the tidbit to the ISI station that had opened in town after the 2005 earthquake so as to keep an eye on the jihad outfits disguised as aid groups.

The spooks had just changed roster, and an energetic new chief took up the tip, ordering his men to tail clerk Shehzad, eventually following him to Lahore International Airport on January 23. They surprised him as he greeted two men off a flight who turned out to be French nationals—one of Pakistani descent and the other a Caucasian convert to Islam.

Terrified, the jet-lagged men admitted they were on their way to North Waziristan to join Al Qaeda. Clerk Shehzad did not put up much of a struggle either and confessed to being a low-level Al Qaeda foot soldier. He offered to trade his way out of a lifetime off the grid, in an ISI cell, by leading spooks back to his senior contacts in Abbottabad.

Two days later, he pointed out an apartment where another foreign couple he had also recently met off an international flight was now staying. An ISI raiding party swooped on the property, firing off rounds before going in and bringing down a bloodied prisoner. In pain, the bleeding man—clearly not a Pakistani—confessed, to the amazement of the ISI team, that he was the notorious Indonesian mujahid Umar Patek, on the run for the Bali bombings of 2002.

Sought by U.S., Indonesian, and Australian intelligence for almost a decade, Patek described how he had fled his hiding place in the Philippines the previous May, stopping off in Saudi Arabia, where an Al Qaeda connect had set him up with a contact in Pakistan.

ISI Abbottabad was incredulous. They had bumped into a terrific score. The cash reward for Patek, offered by the U.S. Department of Justice, was $1 million.[17] The cachet was even greater since the CIA's new station chief, Mark Kelton, had arrived in-country that very morning.

General Athar Abbas, head of the combined ISI and army press bureau, the Inter-Services Public Relations (ISPR), was delighted. Accustomed to dealing with endless black news days, Athar sent a congratulatory text message to ISI director General Pasha, suggesting they exploit this rare event and publicize the arrest of Patek. "This is a project Pakistan enabled to happen and we should trumpet it from upon high."

However, there was no response from Pasha, and Athar watched, frustrated, as the air was sucked out of the story.[18]

* * *

January 27, 2011, Lahore, Pakistan

General Pasha was not being idle. He quietly contacted the ISI's secretive S-Wing—the section of the spy agency charged with maintaining relations with outlawed extremist groups—and asked for "comments, clarifications and a plan to develop intelligence derived from the raid." He heard nothing back, and he meant to chase it up, but cascading events rolled over him.

Just two days later, Raymond Davis, a former U.S. Special Forces soldier and security contractor, shot dead two Pakistani men in front of hundreds of eyewitnesses at a red stop light in Lahore. As a crowd grew, colleagues racing to Davis's rescue sped down the wrong side of the road and killed a third Pakistani.

Davis was beaten, arrested, and taken to Kot Lakhpat prison, while in his car the Pakistani authorities found a collection of gear that could be used for espionage. When Davis was charged with double murder and accused of covertly chasing down links between the ISI and the banned terrorist outfit Lashkar-e-Taiba, Mark Kelton issued instructions to the U.S. ambassador, Cameron Munter. "Don't tell them anything."[19]

As news of Davis's arrest spread, Lashkar's Hafiz Saeed and cronies working for former ISI chief Hamid Gul and Fazlur Rehman Khalil organized street protests, demanding that the American be sentenced to death. When Munter's spokesman stubbornly backed Davis's claim that he was an "administrative and technical official" at the American consulate in Lahore and had acted in self-defense as he feared he was about to be robbed, the fatal street fight became a major diplomatic incident. The United States required deniability, and Pakistan feared it could no longer furnish it.

A senior Pakistani official briefed reporters that Davis worked for XE Services, an American private security firm that had until 2009 been named Blackwater and had been linked to the killing of civilians and torturing of detainees in Iraq.[20] President Obama hit back, describing Davis as "our diplomat" and citing the Vienna Convention on Diplomatic Relations. On Capitol Hill, angry Republicans proposed slashing Islamabad's $1.5 billion annual aid budget.

In an attempt to calm things, Admiral Mike Mullen, the U.S. chairman of the Joint Chiefs of Staff, called up his old friend General Ashfaq Parvez Kayani, Pakistan's army chief. Mullen had had a significant say in Kayani's appointment as army chief, and the two men shared a close working relationship, with Mullen vising Pakistan twenty-seven times during his tenure.[21]

They spoke about Davis three times on the phone before Kayani promised to refer the case to his ISI chief General Pasha.

Pasha was duty bound to intervene in the Davis affair, but he was deeply worried about the implications of doing so. Already furious but unable to do anything about the ever-increasing number of U.S. government contractors arriving on remote airstrips all over Pakistan with visas issued by the Pakistani embassy in Washington, he was amazed that the United States had become so lax that it had entrusted a spying mission in the heart of the Punjab to a Caucasian agent with no languages who tooled around Lahore apparently armed with everything except a cool head and tradecraft.[22] Now that one of the "CIA's secret sniffer dogs" had been caught in the act, Pasha was incredulous that Kayani had asked him to save Davis on America's behalf. He preferred jailing Davis and launching an investigation into which other Western spies were in Pakistan working against Pakistan. Instead, his boss was bending over backward to pacify a country whose arrogance already "knew no limits."[23]

But Pasha was nothing if not loyal. Having received a direct order, he called Leon Panetta on February 23, suggesting that they try to resolve the matter. Out of all the Americans he had come across, Pasha liked Panetta better than most. He was the only U.S. official he had ever invited to his house, introducing him to his wife and son.[24] Now, Panetta proved stand-offish. The U.S. State Department was taking the lead on Davis, he said, and the CIA would not intervene.

Surprised, Pasha posed a direct question. "Was Davis working for CIA?"

"No, he's not one of ours," Panetta replied before hanging up.

Believing that he was being lied to, Pasha backed off, instructing the ISI station in Lahore to leave Davis's fate in the hands of the Punjab police and the courts, the former brutal and the latter unpredictable.[25] The United States had just lost its only chance to end the dispute safely and quickly, he told friends.

The ISI continued to milk the case, leaking to local newspapers details of Davis's presumed mission: "tracing links between the ISI and Lashkar-e-Taiba." Video footage of Davis's arrest and interrogation played on national broadcaster PTV, clips that showed Davis reaching beneath his flannel shirt and producing a jumble of identifications.[26] "This is an old badge," the American can be heard saying. "This is Islamabad." He showed the badge to the man across the desk and then a more recent one proving his employment in the American consulate in Lahore.

"You are working at the consulate general in Lahore?" a policeman asked.
"Yes."
"As a . . . ?"
"I, I just work as a consultant there."

The equipment confiscated from his car was also paraded on PTV: an unlicensed pistol, a long-range radio, a GPS device, an infrared flashlight, and a camera with pictures of buildings around Lahore. "He was doing espionage and surveillance activities," said the Punjab law minister.[27]

President Obama's chief diplomatic troubleshooter, Senator John Kerry, was dispatched to Islamabad to secure Davis's release but returned empty-handed.

Before SEAL Team Six set out for Abbottabad, someone had to get Davis back to the United States.

Early February 2011, Bilal Town, Abbottabad

Osama sent a flurry of letters to Khairiah when she reached Peshawar. Things were finally on track for her arrival, he said, but he warned that she should not be surprised if Ibrahim or Abrar were unfriendly: "They are exhausted . . . It is hard for them to do some of the things I ask them to. One of the hardest things is to ask them to bring one of my family members."[28] The fact that three of Osama's sons and their families were also now in Pakistan made that job even harder.

Although Osama was desperate to see her, writing, "Please trust me that I am working very hard to live with you," he still remained fixated on the possibility of a sophisticated Iranian-CIA plot. Why had the Iranians released Khairiah, Hamzah, Mohammed, and Othman at the Pakistan border, rather than allowing them to fly to Syria or Qatar as had been previously discussed? He asked her again, "Did you ask to go to Qatar?" drilling down for details. "Were they afraid if you and Hamzah went to Syria you would not stay there, but instead that you would go to Saudi Arabia and that you would embarrass them through the media?"

Doubt was undermining truth. "Did you hear anything that forced them to release you . . . to Waziristan? We need to know if they intended to send you in this direction so they can follow your movement." Did Hamzah think this was a trap? Had Khairiah had her teeth x-rayed yet? Had anything shown up in her medical examination, like a tracking chip that, according to Khalid's recent research, could be implanted under the skin and be "the length of a grain of wheat and the width of a fine piece of vermicelli"? Could she remember the date of her last dental treatment? Or the last time an Iranian doctor had seen her? Osama demanded "every detail to help me from the security point of view."

While Mohammed and Othman were now safely in Karachi, he wrote of his concern that Hamzah was still in Waziristan, a dangerous region where two of his children had already perished. "What gives me solace is that they died in the land of jihad," Osama wrote, "and that was their destiny." As far as his own survival, almost a decade after 9/11: "God has been generous to me." Hamzah had to be moved immediately.

Returning to Khairiah's transportation to Abbottabad, Osama finished off: "In the coming days the brother will come from our side [Ibrahim]. He will ask Mohammed Aslam if you are ready to come . . . if you have finished your treatment and are sure about the security matters that worry you."

Along with the letter, the Sheikh sent 25,000 Pakistani rupees and a box of Saudi dates to sustain Khairiah on her journey.[29] But he remained worried.

Wrapped up in several *dupattas*, Khairiah bin Laden entered Bilal Town after dark on February 12, driving past banners promoting a FREE MEDICAL CAMP AND POLIO CAMPAIGN featuring a Save the Children logo and the beaming face of a well-regarded local doctor.[30] Ibrahim had gone to collect her from Peshawar, taking Khalid along as the rules of purdah had to be strictly observed, even in times of war.

As the huge metal gates of the compound opened and swallowed up the white Suzuki jeep, everyone inside the vehicle must have exhaled with relief.

Ibrahim's and Abrar's families had been sent away for the night so their children would not see the new arrival, and the only sound came from bull-frogs croaking in the fields.

Waiting on the second floor of the main house, Osama was on tenter-hooks. He had many things to discuss with Khairiah, his voice of reason and sounding board, who he had last seen in September 2001. In January 2011, the government of Tunisia had been overthrown and Egyptian president Hosni Mubarak had resigned just the previous day. Signs that the mujahi-deen were gaining ground globally could be seen everywhere.

This was "the beginning of a new era," she declared as she greeted family members who respectfully lined up. She kissed the foreheads of grandchil-dren she had never met. She tried to hug Seham but her sister-wife stiffened.

An age had passed since they had parted in Quetta in early 2002. Seham was deeply worried about Khairiah's arrival and by the possibility that she had been followed or used. Several times she had tried to talk her husband out of letting Khairiah come, but he had not listened. Amal, to whom Khairiah had been so unwelcoming in Kandahar, watched in silence as the older woman, who everyone greeted as Umm Hamzah (mother of Hamzah), immediately began bossing them about.

Osama had organized a modest celebration—a meal of chicken and vegetables from Khalid's garden. After the plates were cleared he asked Khairiah to share her news.

She started with Hamzah, who she had left behind at Sarah's house near Mir Ali, passed on what little she knew of Mohammed and Othman's journey to Karachi, and ended with Iran, where some family members remained.

Osama asked one question. In the past few days, Atiyah had told him that *Time* magazine was reporting the release of more family members from the Tehran compound.[31] Was it Fatima and her husband, Sulaiman Abu Ghaith?

Khairiah had no idea. She made no mention of the fact that there had been a falling-out in Iran and that, before she left, Osama's children and the Al Qaeda *shura* had all tried to stop her from going to Abbottabad. Fierce arguments had broken out. "The Quds Force will follow you," they had complained. "Our father will be compromised." She had disagreed. She was Osama's eldest and most senior wife and would do what she pleased. She was smarter than all of them.[32]

Khairiah tried to rally the family. She noticed Khalid was looking wan and asked about his forthcoming marriage. She offered to write to Karima's mother, suggesting that her voice could add authority to the message that the bin Laden family wanted it to go ahead despite the interminable delays.

Without waiting for a reply, she demanded pen and paper. "We rejoice after meeting," Khairiah wrote, "and seeing Khalid, the mujahid, who still has the hope to urgently marry into your family. He is trying very hard to reach you: finding a brother who can help him take the necessary steps to set up a meeting."[33]

This match was meant to be, she declared, informing Karima's mother that Khalid had had a vision that all of them would be reunited. Look on the bright side, she continued: the delays had furnished Khalid and Karima with more "intellectual maturity" with which to face their future together.

Seham wanted to ask more about the circumstances surrounding Khairiah's release but the elder woman looked exhausted.[34] As she showed her upstairs, Khairiah took in the mess. The women's quarters were filled with dirty bolsters, broken kitchen appliances, and old clothes—filthy compared to their husband's pristine domain. Since Bushra and Maryam never came inside, the kitchen areas and bathrooms were rarely cleaned. How far their standards had slipped from the Jeddah days, when they had been surrounded by servants.

Khairiah was more worried about her personal Koran, which, as she unpacked, she realized she had left behind at Sarah's house in Waziristan. Certain that this was a bad omen, Seham asked Osama to send for it as soon as he could.[35]

That night Osama and Khairiah shared a bedroom for the first time in a decade and talked about their son Hamzah. He was deeply frustrated in Sarah's house, Khairiah warned. For him, it was simply a "new prison." The boy was eager to train with the other mujahideen. But Atiyah, ever protective and mindful of the tragic Saad episode, kept him inside the house, warning that he would have to obtain his father's written approval before commencing military training. Khairiah had tried to impress patience on her son, but like his father he would not listen. Osama penned a brief letter. Hamzah had to stay hidden inside the compound, "unless it is absolutely necessary" to go out. He needed distractions. Perhaps he should correspond with his older brother Mohammed, who was thinking of heading to Qatar rather than staying at a safe house in Peshawar.[36] "Write details no one but he is privy to, so that he knows that the letter is in fact written by Hamzah," Osama instructed via Atiyah.[37]

A few days later, the Sheikh received a reply.

"Dear Father, I have a strong desire to meet with you," Hamzah wrote, adding that now that mujahideen and mountains surrounded him, his urge to join the jihad was stronger than ever. "I would like to come and spend some time with you, after which I will serve the religion. This is my aspiration." He was eager to receive training. "I need to join the brothers serving in Afghanistan to fight the enemies of Allah." Until that day came, he felt only frustration, although he was mature enough to understand that Atiyah's primary concern was his safety. "Bless them, they are very careful, which keeps me from doing anything." He was caught between needing to learn and wanting to fight. "I do not want to work without planning or security and I do not want to stay without work."[38]

Hamzah had news about possessions that had once belonged to his dead half siblings, Khadija and Saad. They had just arrived at Sarah's house and included a box containing gold bars bought in Jeddah.[39] Inside another box was

Khadija's jewelry and two gold and emerald lockets bought in Jeddah by Daood for his daughters Aisha and Seham.[40] He would bring everything to Abbottabad.

As the new arrival settled in, everyone began to relax. There were no Quds Force agents knocking at the door, no reports of Khairiah's journey from the border having been tracked. Putting all his worries behind him, Osama was keen to get started on his 9/11 documentary. What were his wife's thoughts? Had she written anything down? She gave him a message from Atiyah, who still had not followed through on his notice to quit. Something more pressing needed to be composed first, he had told Khairiah.

Osama needed to address the recent dramatic events in other parts of the Muslim world, one "showing solidarity"and to "demonstrate your pleasure" in the uprisings that had rippled across North Africa and even the Gulf. Atiyah had jotted down the main points.

Osama and Khairiah got to work. "To my Muslim *Ummah*," he dictated. "The people of the world who were previously held prisoner have succeeded in escaping from the slavery of their tyrant rulers." Just as his wife had escaped the "tyrant's fist" in Tehran, the entire *ummah* should look forward to freedom. "We have to take charge of the reins and free ourselves . . . With the Muslim revolution in Egypt, this shall ignite the sentiments felt by the Islamic Arab World."[41]

The speech ranged from betrayal to death. "The Arabs say that killing prevents death," Osama wrote, predicting that more blood would have to be shed. "I understand completely that exposing the Children of the *Ummah* to battle/death is extremely difficult, however there is no other means to rescue them. There is no one that may go into battle without being exposed to death."

As a result of the $5 million ransom paid by Hamid Karzai's government for the kidnapped Afghan diplomat, Al Qaeda had settled its debts, and Atiyah was buying new weapons in preparation for an offensive, should peace talks with the ISI collapse.[42] Al Qaeda scouts had already been sent out and reportedly had penetrated a Pakistani naval base in Karachi, where they were biding their time.[43]

Younis al-Mauritani's recruits were also on their way to Europe, ready to set off whatever plans were incubating there.

That still left Hamzah. How was he to reach Abbottabad?

He sent a letter to his mother, asking for updates: "Dear Mother, how are you? I miss you. I hope that your trip was not bad and the cold did not bother you."[44] He signed it with a code name, Abu Ma'adh. He was writing while everyone was asleep, he said, adding that he could not rest until he knew when he was coming. "If you have a chance to write tell me what I can take and what is too dangerous to take; you know how important books are to me. Can I take them or not?"

Maryam, his wife, added her own note. "Say hello to everybody, we miss you, it's empty around here without you. The Pashtuns ask about you a lot and Imad's wife was mad that she did not see you. Please write back . . . Tell Miriam and Sumaiya that I miss them a lot."

But Hamzah was not moving just yet.

Emboldened by Khairiah's seamless arrival, Osama dispatched new orders to Atiyah. "Upon your receipt of my letter, your administrative work in Waziristan will end." Leaving Hamzah for now in the care of Sarah, Atiyah was to relocate to Peshawar, while Osama planned to "arrange for you a quiet house in the area that we are in." Together, they could map out Al Qaeda's response "to the monumental event that is taking place."

His time was now. America was suffering its worst financial crisis in living memory. Pakistan was wracked by unrest. So was the Arab world. Leadership was needed. Together they would "reinstate the rule of the Caliphate." Osama's life in exile was coming to an end.[45]

February 25, 2011, CIA Headquarters, Langley, Virginia

The meeting was planned after dusk on a Friday to minimize the chances of anyone finding out. Joining CIA director Panetta, Admiral McRaven, and Mike Mullen's deputy, James Cartwright, in the windowless conference room were the Pentagon's chief counterterrorism adviser, Michael Vickers, and a row of senior CTC officials.

A four-foot-square scale model of the Abbottabad compound dominated the oval table in front of them. The National Geospatial-Intelligence Agency had built it out of clay and Styrofoam, and it was accurate down to the mirrored film masking the second- and third-floor windows, the satellite dish on the roof of the sunroom, and the Pacer's tarpaulin-covered circuit to the east of the main house. There was even a tiny model of Ibrahim's red minivan parked outside.[46]

The analysts, some of whom had worked on tracking Osama for most of their careers, walked the visitors through the layout and their intelligence assessments. Then the military took the floor and went through a spreadsheet

listing possible courses of action, most of them described as "kinetic"—
which was Pentagon-speak for lethal combat. The gathering was a dress
rehearsal for the first National Security Council meeting with the president.[47] They needed to have an answer to every question.

When the team met again in the White House Situation Room on March
14, President Obama reminded everyone that Pakistan had to be kept out of
the loop. After listening to the presentations and studying the scale model,
he asked Admiral McRaven how long it would take to finesse a raid option.
When McRaven replied "three weeks," the president interjected: "Then
you'd better get moving."[48]

Two days later, as McRaven and two senior JSOC officers discussed
whether to drop the SEAL team some distance from the compound and
allow them to proceed on foot across the fields or insert them directly onto
the roof of AC1, a closed-court hearing took place inside Kot Lakhpat prison
in Lahore to decide Raymond Davis's fate. General Pasha was in attendance,
sitting at the back silently, with his cell phone in hand, while a judge decided
what to do about the American prisoners.

Early March 2011, Lahore

U.S. ambassador to Pakistan Cameron Munter, a pragmatist who had also
served in Iraq, had come clean. Davis was with the CIA, he had told Pasha,
trying to unblock negotiations. And the United States wanted Davis out
of Kot Lakhpat as quickly as possible because several inmates had died
there under suspicious circumstances.[49] Intelligence suggested Davis might
be poisoned, too.

Pasha smiled stiffly. Privately, he was delighted that Munter was asking for
his help, as this put him in a rare position of power.[50] Afterward, he contacted
Pakistan's ambassador in Washington, D.C., Husain Haqqani: "What should
they do?" President Zardari had asked Haqqani the same question, as had officials in the CIA. "The Pakistan military wanted him to go. He was a problem,
getting in the way of the U.S.-Pakistan relationship. At the same time it was
important to act within Pakistan law as Davis had committed a crime."

Haqqani realized the only legal way to settle the matter so domestic law
was not broken was by raising blood money. "It is a legitimate strategy in
Pakistan," Haqqani recalled. "I gave the idea to Leon Panetta. And I gave the
idea to Pasha."

A week later, Pasha returned to the negotiating table saying he had a possible solution based on the *sharia* tradition of *diyat*, or blood money. If the families of the dead men agreed to take it, the matter could be settled outside the jurisdiction of the Lahore High Court.[51]

The ISI made sure the families made the right decision. "There is a padlock on their door. Their phones are all switched off," said a cousin of one of the parties involved, who revealed that their lawyers had been detained.[52] At any other time, America might have excoriated Pakistan for resorting to brutal tactics. But Washington, mindful of the building AC1 operation, needed to get Davis out of the country.

After the families of the dead men filed into the temporary courtroom and agreed to accept a total of two hundred million Pakistani rupees (approximately $2.34 million), Pasha sent a text message to Munter, who relayed the sentiments to Washington.[53] The matter was settled. Davis was a free man.[54]

News about his release was kept bottled up until the contractor was airborne. Only then did anti-American protests flare in several cities across Pakistan, rallies addressed by Hamid Gul, Fazlur Rehman Khalil, and Hafiz Saeed, who whipped up instant crowds.

I AM RAYMOND DAVIS, GIVE ME A BREAK, I AM JUST A CIA HIT MAN, declared the freshly painted banners.

Asked whether relations with the CIA were now improving, General Pasha told acquaintances, "It hasn't deteriorated." But privately he was still furious and refused to take Mark Kelton's calls, referring to him as "the cadaver."

Many in Washington had been counting down the days to March 18, the official date of General Pasha's retirement as ISI director, only to learn that General Kayani was giving his spy chief a year's extension. No one else was as experienced or sufficiently wily to do this job, Kayani told his corps commanders.[55]

When the official announcement was made, declaring the intention as "ensuring continuity," the decision—made behind closed doors, in contravention of rules or etiquette—was in reality a reflection of the ISI's determination to maintain continuity with its takeover of the Pakistani military elite.[56]

Concerned with the prospect of another twelve months of animosity— even without taking into account the forthcoming Abbottabad raid—in early April, General Pasha was summoned to "DC to discuss the issue" of deteriorating relations. Before he left for the United States, he deliberately put a positive spin on Pakistan's domestic security situation. "You can see things are much better," he told a friend in the media. Attacks were down and limited to the Tribal Areas. His only regret was that the army had not gone into North Waziristan many years back, when he was director general of military operations, and taken on Al Qaeda and the Taliban face-to-face. It was a bone of contention between himself and Kayani that they had missed their chance there. Now, the only way to reach Al Qaeda and the Pakistan Taliban was through South Waziristan, where the army was busy building roads but slow on resettling residents.

By the time General Pasha met Leon Panetta on April 11, his mood had darkened. With Davis freed, drone strikes had resumed—immediately. One blitzkrieg on the Nomada bus depot, in Datta Khel, had obliterated an entire *jirga* of forty-four tribal elders who had nothing to do with Al Qaeda, triggering anti-American demonstrations all over Pakistan when photographs of the carnage were published.

Pasha described it as a "kick in the teeth."[57] Even after Pakistan's prime minister, president, and army chief all condemned the attack, belligerent U.S. officials still refused to apologize. "These people weren't gathering for a bake sale. They were terrorists," was the official Washington line.[58]

Pasha carried a personal message from General Kayani, who was infuriated by a damning new White House report to Congress on Pakistan's domestic efforts to stamp out terrorism that had concluded that "there remains no clear path to defeating the insurgency in Pakistan."[59] Putting the focus back on the CIA, Pasha complained that the United States had far too many undeclared officers in-country. According to his tally, more than 330 contractors and staff had been identified as working under the radar and would have to quit Pakistan. "If the purpose of their coming was consistent with the interests of Pakistan, there was no good reason for Americans not to disclose all the required information," Pasha said.[60] The United States needed to come clean and treat Pakistan as a partner, or perhaps all parties should go their own way, he told Panetta.

In Islamabad, U.S. ambassador Munter appeared to back the latter course. At a think tank event entitled "Pakistan–United States: A Way Forward" he suggested that it was time to "change the nature of our help." In the future, America must be "wise enough to build the relationship outside of the military."[61]

* * *

April 11, 2011, Bilal Town, Abbottabad

Ibrahim's wife, Maryam, was packing, taking her daughter, Rehma, and the three boys off to her parents' place in Shangla. After hearing about Al Qaeda roundups in Abbottabad (although the ISI had never confirmed it had seized Bali bomber Umar Patek, the news of his capture had spread like wildfire among local residents) and fearing further crackdowns, she needed air. She had to get out of the compound, a place she found stifling, especially since Ibrahim had tried to convince her that the Sheikh and his entourage had "gone away." Rehma, too, needed a break. Since the television incident she had barely spoken. She was frightened of the man upstairs and of what his continued presence meant for her family's safety.

Osama watched from his third-floor balcony as Maryam was driven out in the red Suzuki minivan, glad to see the back of her.[62] Her absence would provide him with a timely opportunity to work on Ibrahim, winning more time before he and his family would have to move.

Osama was determined for Hamzah to come before they quit the house. He had already dispatched Khalid's fake ID card and driver's license with letters to Atiyah, hoping that Hamzah bore a close enough resemblance to his half brother to be able to use them on his journey. All they had to agree on now was the safest route. Hamzah's wife and children would come separately, as they did not need any special security measures.

In North Waziristan, where Hamzah was still staying, Atiyah remained deeply worried about security and still believed that Khairiah, Hamzah, Mohammed, and Othman bin Laden had all been tracked from Iran. His fears and frustration bubbled over in a letter written to Osama on April 5: "I am still upset with you about this. I want you to understand my point of view and . . . deal with the issue without rushing." Unless they moved carefully, Hamzah could succumb to a drone strike like his half brother Saad or be picked up by Pakistani security forces. "All I want is for . . . us to have safety and success," Atiyah explained, beseeching his leader to remain cautious. "You are his father. He belongs to you. You are our leader, and we will obey you."[63]

There was another problem. Bored with Atiyah's "prison," Hamzah had taken off with Abu Khalil, a brother who supervised explosives training. Now Atiyah's charge was in the most dangerous location of all: a designated Al Qaeda training camp. The last time Atiyah had lost control of one of the Sheikh's sons there had been tragic consequences.[64]

Getting Hamzah to the safety of Abbottabad would take guile. But did the Sheikh understand how appalling the security situation really was? Atiyah asked. "Searches on the road have increased and become more intense. This is very dangerous and applies to travel on the highway." If something were to happen to Hamzah—"God forbid"—then the intermediary who brought him would also be compromised, and Osama, too. "So the danger is multiplied!"

Atiyah had two suggestions: send Hamzah by the mujahideen smuggling route that went from North Waziristan into Khyber Agency, down to the town of Bara, and on to Peshawar, or send him to Quetta, from where he could fly up to Peshawar using Khalid's ID card.

The first option was the most problematic, as Hamzah would have to be guided. "Do we tell the brothers we recruit to accompany him to Peshawar who their passenger is?" asked Atiyah. If they kept his identity secret, then Hamzah would have to fend for himself when he reached Peshawar, using addresses and telephone numbers provided. Perhaps Khalid could meet him?

For Atiyah the second option was better: Quetta to Karachi to Peshawar by air or train. "This is the least dangerous . . . We have the means (through southern Waziristan) and we would introduce him to people there."[65]

Still jittery, he reminded the Sheikh to review all communication methods. "I got rid of the [SIM] cards that I used to use between us," he confided. "I broke them. I am using new cards now. Please do the same."

A few days later, as the plan advanced, Khairiah wrote to Hamzah's wife, Maryam.[66] "Everyone misses you and hopes to see you." She wanted to pass on some practical advice. "It is preferable to travel light." And she added an apology for leaving them alone in Waziristan: "Please forgive me if I made you mad." She also had a message for the grandchildren: "I miss you very much. May God unite us soon. Listen to and obey your mother and father and do not anger them. Peace and God's mercy and blessings be upon you."

She was sorry the letter was brief but "the power keeps going on and off." Even leafy, peaceable Abbottabad had its problems.[67]

As Osama plotted new arrivals, worrying mainly about dangers posed by the "wicked Rafidahs [Iran]," the Americans were getting closer by the day, analyzing and watching. As well as establishing an observation post within sight of the compound, the CIA had also recruited local help to confirm Osama's presence there. It came in the form of Dr. Shakil Afridi, a well-regarded local district health officer, who had been secretly tasked with obtaining DNA evidence from the women and children living inside AC1.[68]

Dr. Afridi had first turned up at the family planning office in Ayub Medical College, Abbottabad, in early February 2011, asking to recruit female nurses to work on a hepatitis B vaccination campaign. Dressed in a black suit and carrying a new laptop and satellite phone, he explained that Save the Children (STC) and USAID were footing the bill, so he could afford to pay higher-than-normal wages. Successful candidates only needed to have a good working knowledge of the local community.

As nurses queued up to put their names down, the doctor cheerfully mapped out a program that would concentrate on Abbottabad's poorer fringes, particularly the parts of Nawan Shehr and Bilal Town inhabited by Pashtuns. He told the nurses that STC international colleagues Sue and Toni, who had set up an office in Abbottabad for the duration of the campaign, would supervise their work.

With nine nurses recruited, Dr. Afridi explained that each resident should be given a blood test to check if they had hepatitis B. If their results were negative, a vaccination would be administered. All blood samples should be kept and handed over to him. After treating those who came voluntarily, the nurses would knock on other doors. What he did not tell them was that the project had come about in a rather unorthodox manner.

An American STC staffer called Kate had first approached Dr. Afridi at a seminar in Peshawar in November 2009. The project had been green-lit the following year and, aware of the security implications for a Pakistani working on a USAID project, Kate had always picked up Dr. Afridi in an SUV with blacked-out windows and hid him under a blanket before driving him to a location that she described as "a USAID warehouse" but that was actually part of the U.S. embassy in Islamabad's diplomatic zone.[69]

Dr. Afridi understood the need for heightened security. He had been kidnapped by the Tehrik-i-Taliban Pakistan in 2008, the fighters hoping to extract money from his in-laws. It had been a terrifying experience that had led to his family relocating temporarily to California. After he signed on to Kate's project, she had given him a satellite phone. The signal, she explained, was always on and could be tracked, unlike with the temperamental Pakistani cell phone network.

At the end of 2010, Kate had passed Dr. Afridi on to another American colleague, Sue, at Save the Children. To ensure his cooperation, Sue paid the equivalent of $55,000 into his private bank account. He had not questioned the surprisingly generous size of the sum but had gone on to recruit local helpers, following Sue's instructions.

After the first medical camp in February, Dr. Afridi had come back to Abbottabad on March 19 to retrieve the blood samples—so that the DNA of everyone who had taken part could be tested. Dr. Afridi's nurses had checked a significant percentage of the four thousand people who lived in Bilal Town, and a second camp took place between April 13 and 18.

Four days later, Afridi received a call from Sue, who asked him to extend the program farther into the "Pashtun area," concentrating on the lanes closest to the Waziristan Palace, as locals nowadays called the Abbottabad compound. This time he should monitor the nurses' progress personally, she said.

On April 21, 2011, Dr. Afridi, accompanied by two nurses, Amna and Bakhto, arrived in a gray jeep bearing the logo of the provincial health department outside the Waziristan Palace. It was the only house in the area the vaccination team had not yet visited. The local nursing supervisor had informed Dr. Afridi that her two workers had tried but had not been able to get in as the family had "had a feud" and told them to go away.[70] He had been encouraged by Sue to give it another try.[71]

When nobody answered the doorbell, nurse Amna realized she had been to the house once before, administering polio vaccines to ten children shortly after the earthquake of 2005. At the time, Ibrahim and Abrar had had at most four children between them, so she must have treated Amal's children, too.

But the nurse had no idea about names and identities. Finding Shamraiz Khan, the farm laborer who lived opposite and had once been inside the compound, Dr. Afridi extracted a phone number for the owner.[72] The nurse called it. Ibrahim the companion answered and claimed that the residents were away. Unsure what to say next, the nurse gave the phone to Dr. Afridi, who explained that a new batch of high-quality hepatitis B doses was available. He was offering a cut-price deal. Ibrahim said he would consult his wife when she returned and hung up.

Later that day, Dr. Afridi reported back to Sue, who asked him to ring the palace again. He did so the next morning but the phone was switched off.

The following day, Osama, who had been inside the compound throughout this exchange—although Ibrahim had not informed him of the calls—received an update from Atiyah about a possible new companion. The Punjabi shopkeeper with cold feet was now back on, but he was having trouble extricating himself from his current job.

Atiyah was apologetic. Osama might have to remain in Abbottabad a while longer. In his reply, Osama came up with some suggestions as to how to break the deadlock.

"Propose to [the new companion] that he [quit his job and] be self employed," he wrote, advising that the man would need a cover story to tell to relatives and neighbors whose curiosity would be pricked by his movements. "He convinces his relatives that self employment is better than a position and that he [has] found a partner to work with." Perhaps the new companion could tell them he has set up "a real estate office," "an automobile spare parts store," "a household appliance store," "a grocery story," or "a small chicken farm."

Osama was insistent. This maneuver had been brought on by Ibrahim, but he was ready to move in September. He wanted Hamzah with him when they ventured out.[73]

April 2011, CIA Headquarters, Langley, Virginia

The Sensitive Site Exploitation (SSE) booklet for AC1—a compendium of everyone living inside the Abbottabad compound and its probable layout— was brimming with information. One of its compilers was Gina Bennett, a veteran CIA analyst with a remarkably honed attention to detail who had authored the first strategic warning about Osama bin Laden and Al Qaeda while employed by the State Department in 1993.

Over the course of ten years, she had worked day and night inside a windowless office at CIA headquarters chasing bad guys, "people who are trying to kill lots of people in horrendous, painful ways."[74] By 2011, getting Osama had become personal. Her all-encompassing mission had contributed to the breakdown of her marriage, caused ructions with her children, and led to the loss of friends and colleagues, including Jennifer Matthews, who had been killed by Humam al-Balawi at Camp Chapman in 2009.

Matthews and Bennett had first bonded when they were both pregnant and throwing up with morning sickness in an agency bathroom. They joked that they were like the cartoon character Elastigirl from the Pixar Animation Studio film *The Incredibles* who declared: "I'm at the top of my game. I'm right up there with the big dogs. Girls, c'mon. Leave the saving the world to men? I don't think so."[75]

Reviewing all the available data, Bennett was now "100 percent sure" that Osama was living on the top floor of AC1.[76] Although there was no reference to any assistance having come from the Iranian authorities, she knew that sixty-two-year-old "Khayriya Husayn Taha Sabir aka Umm Hamza" had recently moved in, and she believed that son Hamzah had arrived, too.

In the SSE booklet, "Hamza" was listed, correctly, as being twenty-one years old and was marked as having come to the house accompanied by his wife and children, whose names were recorded, correctly, as "wife: Maryam, son: Usama (4 yrs old), daughter: Khayriya (1 yr old)."

Given that the first names of Al Qaeda wives and children were almost as sacrosanct within the movement as the real names of mujahideen, Bennett and her "Band of Sisters" at the CTC had been dexterous in getting this information. It could only have come from the authorities in Tehran or from reading private bin Laden family correspondence, which meant there was possibly a mole somewhere inside the courier network or Osama's Pakistani protection ring, something that the CIA never admitted to.

Bennett's team noticeably knew far less about Amal bin Laden, who had never been in Iran. The best piece of intelligence was a grainy picture of her as a teenager—smiling and with a shaggy mop of black hair, the young bride who Osama would marry—a photo that had been sold to the CIA by a relative in Yemen. According to the SSE booklet, Amal lived on the "2nd and 3rd floor" of AC1 and was thought to be twenty-eight years old and to have one daughter "Safiyah (9 yrs old)" and "2 unidentified children born since 2001." Bennett could only presume that they were in the compound, too, although she had no actual information about them.

She was better informed about "Siham Abdullah bin Husayn Al Sharif (54 yrs old)." Osama's third wife was also living on the second or third floor along with her daughters, "Miriam (20 yrs old) and Sumaya (16 yrs old)." Also confirmed as a resident was "Siham's son, Khalid (23 yrs old)." The CIA had digitally aged a photo from his old Saudi passport, seized in a raid in Karachi. He was thought to be living on the second floor.

Bennett had struck gold with a passport photograph of Abrar, which showed him floppy-haired, jowly, discontented, and stubbly. According to Bennett's information, his full name was "Abrar Ahmad Said Abd al Hamid." He was thirty-three years old and had moved to the compound with his brother from "Mardan city" in 2006. His known pseudonyms were "Arshad,

Asif Khan and Sardar Ashad" and together with his brother he was the "Owner of AC1." His oldest son, "Muhammad," attended "madrassa away from family" while he, Bushra, and three other children, "Ibrahim (4 months), Abd al-Rahman (1–4 yrs old), and Khadija (1–4 yrs old)" lived on the first floor of the main house. The agency suspected the house was split into a duplex with different entrances, Abrar and family using the door at the front of the house while Osama exited at the back.

On the CIA mock-ups, the main house was located in "Courtyard A."

There was no photograph of Ibrahim.[77] He was described as "Courier and assessed as one of 3 individuals responsible for HVT #1's care"—the others being Abrar and Osama's son Khalid.

Ibrahim had several pseudonyms—"Arshad, Asif Khan, Tariq, Haji Nadeem and Sardar Ashad"—and typically wore "a white *shalwar kameez*." His children were "Khalid (5–7 yrs), Ahmad (1–4 yrs), Habib (18 months) and Rahma (8 yrs old)," who lived with their parents in the annex. The CIA labeled it C1, locating it in the smaller "Courtyard C."[78] There was no mention of Mohammed or Othman bin Laden, who were both in Karachi with their families.

In Washington, things were coming together. The president had chaired several National Security Council meetings about AC1 and by the time the final plan was brought to him for approval on March 29, analysis of the water table around the compound had discounted the possibility of tunneling in. It also meant there were no tunnels out.[79] If he was in there, and they went in to get him, Osama bin Laden would be trapped.

Early April 2011, Naval Special Warfare Development Group Headquarters, Virginia Beach, Virginia

The Red Squadron of SEAL Team Six (ST6) had received an unexpected recall to the garrison. They had just got back from a deployment in Afghanistan, after which they had been on a training trip, diving off the coast of Miami, according to Robert O'Neill, a decorated sniper and former assault team leader who had been on the Captain Phillips Somali pirate mission.

At the end of their first day back at base they were no wiser. Some of the team speculated that they were being deployed to Libya, where Muammar Gaddafi's regime was in free fall. "The first day's briefing, they actually kind of lied to us," recalled O'Neill.[80]

On April 10, Red Squadron reported to a CIA facility in a densely forested area of North Carolina. On the way down, they learned that senior officers from JSOC would be joining them along with staff from the Afghanistan-Pakistan desk at the CIA. "That's when the wheels started spinning for me: This is big," said O'Neill.

The following morning the SEALs filed into a secure room where the commander, the CIA staff, and a two-star JSOC general briefed them. "Okay, we're as close as we ever have been to UBL," said the commander, as he showed them around the Styrofoam-and-clay model of AC1.

"There was none of that cheering bullshit," said O'Neill. "We were thinking, 'Yeah, okay, good. It's about time we kill this motherfucker.'" Over the next few hours, CIA analysts including Gina Bennett briefed them about the compound: how they had found it, who was thought to be inside, and the likely security.

"We've got him," Bennett said. "This is my life's work. I'm positive."

Over the next five days, Red Squadron rehearsed in a full-scale mock-up of the compound. It occurred to them that while swooping in would be relatively easy, the chances of all of them getting out were slim. "We're gonna die, so let's do this right," O'Neill said to the others.

On April 18, the team shifted to Nevada, where the heat and elevation approximated Abbottabad. Here, another life-size set had been constructed, and they spent a week fast-roping down from two helicopters that hovered low over the ground. The evolving plan was for one team of SEALs to drop onto the roof and clear the house from the top down, while a second, accompanied by a dog and a Pashto translator, would enter at ground level and hold back any neighbors and Pakistani security forces who turned up. Satellite footage of the Pacer showed a man who did not flinch on the few occasions when a Pakistani military chopper flew over the compound on its way to the military academy. "We might actually be able to get on the deck before [the family] really figure out what is going on," said another operator on the team.[81]

The SEALs went over the plan again and again, punctuated by briefings from military top brass. As far as O'Neill was concerned it was only ever a kill mission. "But try not to shoot this motherfucker in the face," said one of his colleagues. "Everyone is going to want to see this picture."[82]

If they got caught they were to fight to the death. O'Neill spoke for everyone when he said, "If we get arrested, we're going to spend the rest of our lives in a Pakistani prison."[83]

To ease the tension, they joked about who would play them in the Hollywood version; after all, Tom Hanks had signed up to play Captain Phillips. Some voted for Brad Pitt or George Clooney. At the end, the commander asked if they were ready.

"Yeah, absolutely," said O'Neill. "This is going to be easy."

April 24, 2011, Abbottabad

Security in the city was tight. Given the recent apprehension of the Bali bomber in Abbottabad, extra checkpoints had been set up on all main roads in and out as the streets around Bilal Town and Pakistan Military Academy at Kakul were swept for roadside bombs. Militant madrassas had been shut since Friday afternoon and likely terrorist hideouts had been searched.

The reason for this heightened state of alert was that Pakistan's army chief General Kayani was addressing a parade of graduating cadets at the academy, whose boundary wall was just about visible from Osama's compound.

The enhanced security measures were a necessary show of force as much as anything else. Kayani told the cadets that the country had broken the "back of terrorism" in Pakistan thanks to the sacrifices of Pakistan's soldiers.[84] He reminded cadets that the previous August the ISI had declared Al Qaeda the top internal threat to the country. Now that the men before him were full-fledged warriors, it would be their job to assist in the fight.

Less than a mile away, Sheikh Osama composed his latest missive to Atiyah, another huge document that ranged from how Al Qaeda should respond to the Arab Spring ("the most important events that the nation has witnessed for centuries") to what to do about an approach from the British security services in London. MI5 had sent a message through a Libyan brother living in London, suggesting a deal in which British forces would withdraw from Afghanistan in return for a commitment from Al Qaeda not to attack "England or her interests." But Atiyah wasn't convinced it was genuine.[85]

On the domestic front, Hamzah remained the most important issue. Atiyah was told to get him to Karachi, where he should remain for as short a time as possible before flying to Peshawar. Ibrahim would meet him there, but in disguise. "His name will be Ahmad Khan." The USB drive Osama was sending with his latest monthly batch of letters saved on it also had a file with "Ahmad's" new number.[86]

There was a short letter from Khalid, too. He and Hamzah had been born just weeks apart and had grown up together. But they had not seen each other since they were thirteen. Now Hamzah was married with two children, while Khalid remained in marital limbo. Khalid was excited that the time had finally come for them to be reunited.

"To start with, thanks God for saving you from the prisons of the Rejectionists, the wicked Magi," he wrote of the Iranians. "We were following your exit with great patience." Moving on to practical instructions, he continued: "Immediately after arriving at Balochistan, inquire about the security situation in the place where you are; be very cautious and say many prayers."

If there was time, Hamzah should send his photo to Al Qaeda's document forger so he could make a new ID.[87] If not, "then use my ID, with God's blessing to [move to] Karachi, then to Peshawar by air or train."

When his brother arrived in Peshawar he was to call "Ahmad Khan." Khalid wrote: "Inform him that you are Hamzah and stay with him." From there, they would arrange the last leg of the journey.[88]

Khalid also penned a quick message to Karima's family, anxious to finalize wedding plans during his coming visit to Peshawar. "We [will be] calling you from Peshawar, and the brother who is with me will conduct the phone call with you and we [will] agree to a place to meet," he noted.[89]

The marriage finally seemed real. The USB drive also contained a message from Seham to her future sister-in-law. "My beloved sister, I give you the good news that a new dawn has shone on us and the stress of [being unable to] meet you . . . has been removed," she wrote. "My son will be in a safe location in Peshawar area ready to receive you and complete our reunion."[90]

Seham painted a picture of her anxious son: "He waits impatiently for the day when we meet, when the matter is complete, and our two homes and our two lives are illuminated." She hoped this would be the "last message that precedes meeting you." Addressing the delays in a sentence that conjured all of their worries about Khairiah without mentioning her or Iran, she added: "We have been through difficult security circumstances; God only knows it. However, by the grace of Allah, things changed and every day that goes by our situation is from good to better." But just to be on the safe side, Karima's mother should as usual "destroy this message after reading it."

Osama saved a letter to the same USB drive, with a pronouncement about safety. He referenced his earlier suggestion that Atiyah should move out of Waziristan. Thinking about it, and the deteriorating security there, he had decided that all senior brothers should move out to the cities. Atiyah should "arrange homes for them on the outskirts . . . to distance them from the people, which reduces the security dangers, and they will be with trusted companions," meaning Pakistani supporters with real ID cards.

Drawing on his own experiences in Abbottabad, Osama added that all such companions would have to have some cover story for how they earned a living, a story that could check out, "especially for those who live close by and have observing neighbors." With his own experience in mind, he advised that they needed to think about "controlling children."

If the brothers had family accompanying them, they should be made to follow strict rules. "Not leaving the house except for extreme necessity like medical care, and teaching [children] the local languages," Osama wrote.[91] "They do not get into the yard of the house without an adult who will control the volume of their voices."

Any mujahid brother who followed these simple precautions would always be safe, he assured Atiyah.

April 29, 2011, Bilal Town, Abbottabad

Maryam and her children returned home after dark to find that a new guest had arrived. She did not see them as she retreated to the damp annex and unpacked. But when Bushra came to welcome her back, she confirmed that another bin Laden family member was in the main house.

Extra food had been purchased. There was a new voice upstairs. Tired after her journey from Shangla, Maryam could not face another showdown with Ibrahim. The children were exhausted. He was twitchy and distracted.[92]

That night she could not sleep and she spied the guest: a young Arab man who looked a lot like Khalid bin Laden. He emerged from under the carport with a heavy bag. Maryam wondered who he was and what he wanted.

Ibrahim had assured her that there would be no more visitors to the house, which was bursting at the seams. Osama had also given his written assurance. She sneaked up to the roof of the annex to spy, and to listen in, a bitter rage filling her head and heart.

Inside the main house the young man—Hamzah bin Laden—produced things one by one to the delight of Osama's family. They made for curious gifts: old notebooks, jewelry, some secondhand iPods, and an old suitcase as well as camera-phone footage of Saad's will.

Sheikh Osama filed the material away in a locked security box covered with a pink-and-white, flower-patterned scarf as he explained to his long-lost son how, with Ibrahim and Abrar sick, two more adults and their two children could not be accommodated.

Maryam climbed back down and slipped into bed, meaning to confront Ibrahim in the morning.

Shortly before dawn, the sound of a car engine starting up woke her. She heard whispering under the carport and the clang of the big gate.

The visitor was leaving.[93]

April 29, 2011, Washington, D.C.

President Obama had finished his National Security Council meeting on April 28 by saying that before making a final decision about the Abbottabad raid he wanted to sleep on it. To make sure they were ready should he decide to proceed, the SEALs flew to Jalalabad, Afghanistan, that night.

At eight twenty the next morning, Obama, surrounded by advisers, consented.[94]

The next few nights there would be no moon over Abbottabad. If they did not go in, they would have to wait another month. Now that the SEALs were in situ, it would also be hard to keep this kind of operation secret for long.

When word came back from JSOC that there was not enough time to scramble SEAL Team Six for a raid right away, they delayed for twenty-four hours.

However, the following day, Saturday April 30, was the night of the annual White House correspondents' dinner in Washington. The president decided to attend anyway. Pulling out at such short notice would be bound to make reporters suspicious. On Saturday afternoon, he called McRaven in Jalalabad, not expecting to speak to him again before the SEALs set out: "Godspeed to you and your forces," he said. "Please pass on to them my personal thanks for their service. I will personally be following this mission very closely."[95]

When weather forecasts for the Abbottabad region predicted fog on Saturday night, McRaven decided to postpone until Sunday night, enabling Obama to make a trademark urbane, gently barbed, and self-deprecating speech to journalists gathered at the Washington Hilton without the distraction of knowing that thousands of miles away U.S. operatives were risking their lives.

May 1, 11 P.M. Jalalabad, Afghanistan

On Sunday, just minutes after President Obama met with his principals in the White House Situation Room to review final preparations, two Black Hawks lifted off from Jalalabad airfield, the twenty-four-man team split into two units code-named Chalk One and Chalk Two.

"A group of guys knew time on Earth was up, so you could be honest with each other," recalled Robert O'Neill. "We all accepted and nobody was afraid. It was really cool."

The CIA analyst Gina Bennett, who had also flown to Jalalabad, had handed each of them a copy of the laminated Sensitive Site Exploitation (SSE) booklet for AC1, containing photographs and biographical information on the occupants of the compound and schematics of its layout. If the mission went according to plan—Osama killed and the others neutralized—it would be the job of several specialists on the SEAL team to seize all the documentation and digital material they could find in the house, vital intelligence that would be shipped back to the U.S. for deep analysis, a procedure the CIA called "documentation exploitation," which helped the U.S. military plan its future wars.

As Obama sat down in the White House Situation Room around two P.M. local time to review final preparations, in Islamabad CIA station chief Mark Kelton and Ambassador Cameron Munter gathered in a secure room at the embassy. They had made preparations for possible Pakistani reprisals, drafting evacuation plans for employees scattered across the country to either flee to the Indian border or head for Karachi, where they would board the USS *Carl Vinson*, which was patrolling offshore. Those at the embassy would have to hunker down.

Three Chinooks carrying backup fuel and forces took the same flight path as the Black Hawks, two crossing into Pakistani airspace between army checkpoints twenty miles apart, while one hung back at the border.

Far ahead, the Black Hawks pursued a "nap-of-the-earth" course (military speak for flying at a very low altitude), without lights, over Khyber Agency, down to Chakdara and Kala Dakka and toward AC1.

They had scheduled thirty minutes for the operation.[96] On the ground, one SEAL's job would include calling out the time.

O'Neill, who wore a noise-canceling headset in the helicopter so all he could hear was his heart beating, ran through his last conversation with Gina Bennett. "She asked me why I was so calm. I told her, 'We do this every night. We go to a house, we fuck with some people, and we leave. This is just a longer flight.'"

Around three thirty P.M. in the basement of the White House, in a conference suite across from the Situation Room, Obama's team began to watch the live feed from a drone circling fifteen thousand feet above Abbottabad.

CHAPTER ELEVEN

*"What really happened doesn't matter if there
is an official story behind it that 99.999% of
the world would believe."*

—@ReallyVirtual[1]

May 1, 2011, Bilal Town, Abbottabad, Pakistan

THE GUEST WAS GONE, his twenty-four-hour stopover far shorter than Osama had hoped for and Amal had expected. After eating dinner and clearing away, they all prayed, before Amal and the Sheikh went to bed. She carried two-year-old Hussein, their youngest son, while Osama cradled his Koran.

By eleven P.M., the Sheikh was deep in sleep. Outside, the streets of Abbottabad were plunged into darkness as the electricity went out all over the city.[2] Power shortages were so common that no one in the Waziristan Palace even noticed.[3]

Just past midnight, Amal woke, her head buzzing with worries about Hamzah's brief visit and their future.

Something caught her ear at twelve twenty A.M.: a thrumming up above.

Chop, chop chop.

It sounded like a storm and she thought she glimpsed a shadow passing across the curtained balcony window.[4]

The noise was too mechanical to be thunder, and she looked across to her husband for reassurance. Occasionally, Pakistan Air Force helicopters passed overhead—but never in the middle of the night.

It became more powerful, swirling the air and the yellow flowered curtains at the windows.

Osama awoke, a fearful look on his face. Whatever was out there was coming in fast, although too slowly to be some kind of drone strike.[5] Amal clutched him. The object that had been hovering above swung violently to the right and then the sound panned to the left. They both jumped when a sickening screech tore through the compound. The walls of the house shuddered. Amal thought it sounded like "something extremely heavy and metallic crashing down."

Now the noise was more like a grinding sound. They slipped from their bed and crept through the darkness to the balcony door. "It was a moonless night and difficult to see," Amal recalled. What popped into her mind was Khairiah's unsettling arrival from Iran.

Could the family's shrill-voiced emira who always thought she knew best have inadvertently overlooked *something*, or someone, leading the enemy to their door? Had she, after all of those years in exile, lost her edge or been corrupted by the Iranians or the Americans? Or maybe it had been Hamzah? Had he been a willing or unwilling stooge?

Amal glanced at Osama, who appeared to be paralyzed by fear.

From the window the thing they could hear could not be seen.

Out of sight, 150 feet away to the west a U.S. military Black Hawk had ditched into the yard, its tail fin bent out of shape and lying across the perimeter wall, with its rotors churning up soil and stones in Khalid's vegetable garden.

May 1, 2011, Washington, D.C.

In the conference suite across the corridor from the White House Situation Room, President Obama slipped in, motioned for everyone to stay as they were, and pulled up a chair, announcing that he "should be watching this." Moments later a White House photographer captured him and other senior members of his team as they watched the live drone feed, Secretary of State Hillary Clinton pictured with a hand clapped over her mouth.[6] One chopper had dropped out of the sky and appeared to have landed on the compound wall. To those gathered in the room it looked like a carefully rehearsed mission gone awry before the first boots had even hit the ground.[7]

For several agonizing minutes, mission commander Admiral William McRaven in Jalalabad, who could see from the chat line that the president was present, remained silent while he searched for a live update from the unfolding crisis. McRaven, who had seen choppers go down many times before and missions survive the blowout, remained calm; but he knew that some of those watching in Washington would be panicking.[8]

Moments later, Clinton and Obama saw the SEALs scrambling from both Black Hawks. "We will now be amending the mission," McRaven explained calmly.

Chalk One's bird was down but the unit was improvising, knowing that they had only thirty minutes to pull it off. Chalk Two's chopper had set down in a nearby field. Its operators were supposed to guard the perimeter. Now they would have to blast their way through the gate and lead the search for Osama from the ground up.

May 2, 2011, Bilal Town, Abbottabad, Pakistan

"We opened the doors, and I looked out," said Robert O'Neill, who was in the chopper that landed in the field. Over the radio he had caught wind in the last few moments that something had gone wrong with Chalk One's landing, but he needed to stay focused.

As his feet hit the ground, O'Neill's mind turned to George W. Bush's words on 9/11: "Freedom will be defended." He sprinted across the mud hoping that his teammates in the other chopper were unhurt.

Behind him, Chalk Two's Black Hawk took off again.

"This is some serious Navy SEAL shit we're going to do," O'Neill said to himself. He liked to narrate his journey, his mind a camera. It was a great way to settle the nerves. "This is so badass."[9]

O'Neill's team pounded across the mud toward the compound. There was no sign of the other chopper. "I looked to the left," he said. "The mock-up had been dead-on. To actually be there and see the house with the three stories, the blacked-out windows, high walls, and barbed wire . . . just like the satellite photos. I was like, this is really cool I'm here."

Sohaib Athar, a coffee shop owner and IT consultant who lived a mile away from Bilal Town was working late at his computer. He had heard the sound of the arriving Black Hawks, too.

"Helicopter hovering above Abbottabad at 1 AM (is a rare event)," he tweeted as his handle, @ReallyVirtual.

Chalk Two kept circling.

Sohaib tweeted again. "Go away helicopter—before I take out my giant swatter :-/"[10]

Inside the Waziristan Palace, up on the third floor, Hussein was crying. Amal went to turn on a light. "No," commanded the Sheikh, grabbing her arm, unaware there was a power outage. He appeared disoriented. Fear made him hostile. This was not how Amal had imagined her hero behaving in a tight spot.

"*Come up!*" Osama called out hoarsely for Khalid.

From a second-floor window, Khalid and his mother, Seham, had seen the SEALs that made up Chalk Two piling out of their Black Hawk and sprinting across the field toward them.

Osama's son ran upstairs. "*Americans* are coming," Khalid panted, clutching a loaded AK-47 but still dressed in his pajamas.[11]

Amal recalled thinking that Osama had told her the last time Khalid had fired a weapon was at the age of thirteen. If the Americans got past Ibrahim and Abrar, he would be his father's last line of defense.

She shuddered.

She and Seham went downstairs to comfort the children, who were crying in their bunk beds, terrified by the unprecedented commotion. Occasionally, their father had allowed them into his studio to play a boot-legged copy of *Delta Force: Xtreme 2*, a first-person shooter video game, but experiencing the real thing was an unknown.[12] What should she say to them? Amal thought. They glanced fearfully toward Khairiah's room, across the corridor. The door was firmly shut. Amal now felt certain she had been right. They had been betrayed by one of their own.

A blast shook the house as the gate to the annex courtyard was blown open.

@*ReallyVirtual* heard it, too: "OMG:S Bomb Blasts in Abbottabad. I hope everyone is fine :(."

Five minutes down: out in Khalid's vegetable patch, the SEALs inside Chalk One had emerged unscathed from their damaged chopper and were impro-vising, their plans to rappel onto the roof of the main house now aban-doned. After blasting through a gate into the main compound, they had fanned out, some heading for the main house while two of them approached the annex where Ibrahim and Maryam lived and that was labeled on the SSE charts as C1. Chalk One team member Matthew Bissonnette and another SEAL identified by the pseudonym Will crept toward the glass doors of C1, their boots crunching the gravel.

Inside, Ibrahim and Maryam were sitting in the dark, having already been woken by the helicopter crash landing, a sound she later described as a "noise of a magnitude I had never heard before."

Just as Ibrahim went to fetch their daughter, Rehma, who was crying in her bed, his cell phone rang. He stifled it before answering. "*Salaam?*" When nobody spoke, Ibrahim guessed it was his brother. "Abrar? I cannot hear you. I'm coming," he whispered, grabbing his AK-47 and heading for the door. He stopped short when he heard a sound.

Someone was trying to open the door from the outside.

"Is that you, Abrar?" he whispered, slipping the safety catch off his weapon.

The door was locked from the inside.

This is it, Maryam thought; the night she had long feared was unfolding. She wrapped herself around her eighteen-month-old son, Habib, as Ibrahim let off a volley of shots. The glass in the door shattered as his assault rifle arched through the air, the recoil catching him by surprise.

From outside, a man speaking Arabic ordered Ibrahim to open up. "Ahmad al-Kuwaiti come out!" shouted Will as Bissonnette pumped rounds through the door toward his likely position.

Inside, Maryam watched as Ibrahim fell backward, blood pooling on the cement floor around him. She stared at his twitching body and watched as her volatile husband bled out.

Rounds whizzed around her, clattering across the kitchen, carving up bags of pasta and splitting the rice sack. Heating oil glugged all over the floor, filling the room with fumes.

A burning feeling hit Maryam's shoulder as a round struck her. A second bullet pierced her cheek.

Judging by Rehma's horrified expression, Maryam realized that she must be bleeding. "Mother, don't die!" the girl cried, shielding her brothers Khalid, six, and Ahmed, three.

"I'm not dying," Maryam rasped, as a strange silence filled the darkened room. Boots sounded outside.

Maryam crawled forward, in agony, trying not to show it. Desperate for the firing to stop, she cracked open the broken door and screamed in Arabic: "You have *killed* my husband and now only I and my children are in the room."

"We'll blow the whole building if you don't open up," barked back Will from the other side, also speaking Arabic.

Bissonnette was beside him, catching his breath, when he spied something through the night-vision goggles. He slid a finger over the trigger. "I could just make out the figure of a woman in the green glow," he recalled. She had something in her arms. Bissonnette began applying pressure to the trigger. If he could discern the four and a half pounds of pressure needed to loose a round, and he thought he could, he was about a quarter of the way down. "I could see our lasers dancing around a head."[13]

He was ready to fire when he suddenly realized it was a woman holding a baby. He relaxed a gloved digit as three more children shuffled into view behind her.

"He is dead!" Maryam screamed. "*You* shot him. He is *dead*. You killed him."

Will strode over and lay hands on her, searching for a suicide vest or concealed weapon. They had to be sure, after Camp Chapman. Everyone was a belligerent until proved otherwise.

"*Allahu Akbar Aleikum!* [The great God is against you!]," Maryam screamed, as he touched her.

Both SEALs held her down, stifling her cries, pushing aside the sobbing children. When she was still, they poked around the annex. It was slippery, the floor slicked with Ibrahim's blood.[14]

Maryam heard the second helicopter as her wrists were cuffed with nylon cord. Chalk Two's Black Hawk was still circling.

Eight minutes down: The family on the third floor gathered to pray, all eyes on Osama. "They want me, not you," he said, his voice trembling as he told his wives to go downstairs with the children.

Amal refused to move from his side, while Miriam and Sumaiya hid out on the outside balcony with some of the children. Seham and Khalid obeyed and went down, bumping into Khairiah, who was watching through a window as silent silhouettes advanced on the house.

Khalid, who was at her shoulder, urged her to move. "They'll see you and shoot," he said. She seemed unafraid.

One floor below, Abrar, Bushra, and their three children sheltered behind their bedroom door, in the first room to the left of the entrance, unable to see anything clearly.

Chalk One was clearing the ground-floor apartment first, before going upstairs. A C-4 charge went off and the south door cracked open. As SEALs poured inside, Abrar popped up to see what was going on, and the point-man took the shot.

Abrar fell back onto a lilac and pink flowered bed sheet, arms raised. Bushra jumped forward through the darkness, shouting curses, hoping her husband had just been winged as more rounds spun toward her. She crumpled dead in the doorway.

As operators shouted that the corridor was clear, they saw through the green glow what looked like a woman and several children huddled in the corner.[15]

O'Neill was still outside. "I heard gunfire from two different places nearby," he remembered. "One of our guys told me, 'Jesus, these women are jumping in front of these guys. They're trying to martyr themselves.'" He was crossing to the back of the house when he ran into another team member. "Hey, man, I just shot a woman," the SEAL said, clearly surprised, recounting Bushra's death.

O'Neill told him to snap out of it. They could worry about the consequences later.

When he entered the north door, O'Neill glimpsed Bushra's daughter, Khadija, in the "first room on the right as we were going in." He reached down, picked her up, and put her in the room on the left "with another woman," so she was not on her own. "She seemed too out of it to be scared."

They had to keep on target: Osama, the Kuwaitis, Hamzah, Khalid—the names in Gina Bennett's SSE booklet.

Upstairs, Amal, Osama, and Hussein were alone, listening to the pings of rounds and pops of charges being detonated around the house.

Osama was muttering prayers. After six years of total isolation, the children having constantly been berated for making the smallest noise or complaining, Amal realized with cold dread that Americans were swarming in their home, readying to kill them all, and there was no emergency procedure aside from the euros sewn into her husband's underwear along with the numbers for Atiyah and Dr. al-Zawahiri. Since neither she nor her husband had a cell phone, what use were those numbers now?

Their safe house was a death trap.

Ten minutes down: Bissonnette was still outside, advancing on the main house. "Through my night vision I could see multiple lasers tracking along the windows and balconies . . . I didn't see any movement." The film on the windows made it impossible to see in.[16]

Inside, O'Neill's team prepared to go upstairs. "So we're looking down the hallway at the door to the stairwell," he said. "I figured this was the only door to get upstairs, which means the people upstairs can't get down."[17]

The breacher had to blast it twice. Whoever was behind here was better protected. "We started rolling up," said O'Neill.

Bissonnette, now inside the building, was not far behind. "Nice and slow," he recalled. No talking. No yelling. No running. "We have a saying, Don't run to your death."

Khalid was hiding on the second landing. O'Neill was four men back in the stack when he saw the point-man hold up the line. A face had just popped up over the balcony before pulling back. O'Neill had seen the jack-in-the-box too, and he listened as the point-man whispered, "Khalid . . . come here . . ." in Arabic, then in Pashto. It was an old bushman's trick. "That confused Khalid," recalled O'Neill. "He's probably thinking, 'I just heard shitty Arabic and shitty Pashto. Who the fuck is this?'"

O'Neill watched as Khalid leaned out just far enough for someone to take the shot. He fell back, out of sight to the advancing SEALs.

Those in front of O'Neill peeled off to clear the second-floor rooms. Climbing over Khalid's body, Bissonnette noticed his cold AK-47 on a step. "Glad he didn't man up and use that thing," he told himself.

Up above, the point-man pushed on and up with another operator. "One hundred percent he's on the third floor," Gina Bennett had told them in Jalalabad. "So get to there if you can."

Thirteen minutes down: the advancing SEALs reached the third floor. O'Neill later claimed he was the second man in the stack. So did Matthew Bissonnette.

Whoever was second turned to check his rear just as the point-man reached the top step and caught sight of a ghostly face peeking out from a doorway ten feet ahead and diagonally to the right: Osama bin Laden.

He fired and the head jerked back, as if he'd been shot. Swinging around, the second SEAL put his hand on the point-man's shoulder and squeezed, "Go."

The point-man and his number two strode across the top landing and clattered into two young screaming women. "Jesus!" It was Sumaiya and

Miriam, lunging at the Americans through the darkness. The point-man grabbed one under each arm and propelled them backward against a wall. Everyone in the house was presumed to be strapped into vests, and in that moment he had to shield the rest of the team.

It was the first time the girls had ever been touched by a man outside the family and they instantly became hysterical.

"It was the most heroic thing I've ever seen," said O'Neill, who claimed to still be number two in the stack and appreciated the point-man's thinking.

With the girls (and any explosives they might have been carrying) covered, O'Neill recalled the point-man turning to say to him, "These bitches is [sic] getting truculent," before O'Neill rolled past him and on into the bedroom, where he came face-to-face with a very tall and very skinny Arab in a white prayer cap looking blindly through the darkness.

According to O'Neill's version, his $65,000 night-vision goggles gave him an extraordinary view of Osama bin Laden, who stood, uninjured, ten inches away, unable to see what was coming at him.

"I was amazed how tall he was, taller than all of us, and it didn't seem like he would be, because all those guys were always smaller than you think."

Recovering his composure, O'Neill noticed there was someone in front of Osama—a woman—Amal. "He had his hands on a woman's shoulders, pushing her ahead, not exactly toward me but by me, in the direction of the hallway commotion." Before their marriage she had said she wanted to go down in history, but she had never expected it to end like this.

For a split second, O'Neill wavered. Who posed the greater threat? The woman or Osama?

"He's moving forward. I don't know if she's got a vest and she's being pushed to martyr them both and me." The hundreds of hours of training kicked in. "He's a threat. I need to get a head shot."

Amal saw O'Neill raise his weapon, and she instinctively rushed him.

He shouted, "No! No!" and, *zing.*

Amal felt the searing pain in her leg and collapsed onto the bed bleeding. The last thing she remembered before passing out was "a red beam of light but I heard no sound."[18]

O'Neill raised his weapon extra high to meet the main target's head. "He's going down," he thought as he loosed off a round. "He crumpled onto the floor in front of his bed and I hit him again, *Bap!* Same place. That time I used my EOTech red-dot holo sight."

The target's tongue was lolling. O'Neill watched him suck in a last breath. "He died afraid, and he knew we were there to kill him. And that's closure."

Matthew Bissonnette entered the room. He recalled it differently. Osama bin Laden had already been injured by the point-man's shot and was lying prone with his daughters standing over him. "Both women were dressed in long gowns and their hair was a tangled mess like they had been sleeping," he said.

According to Bissonnette's version, he and the second SEAL shot Osama "a handful of times," without knowing who it was, reacting instinctively to a twitching body. "The bullets tore into him, slamming his body into the floor until he was motionless."

Bissonnette dropped down to take a closer look. "The man's face was mangled from at least one bullet and covered in blood," he recalled.

More SEALs thumped up the stairs to take a look. A volley of muffled shots rang out as commemorative, vengeful rounds were pumped into the body, everyone wanting to take a shot.

Amal came to and knew she needed to play dead on the bed. She closed her eyes and slowed her breathing.

O'Neill turned around to look at the bed and paused. He thought he heard or saw something moving.

Amal remained as still as she could.

O'Neill saw a young boy watching from the other side of the bed. It was Hussein, and he had witnessed everything. "I didn't like it that he was scared," O'Neill said. He picked him up, threw water from a CamelBak on his face, and put him down next to his mother. *"He's a kid, and had nothing to do with this."*[19]

Bissonnette saw "at least three children huddled in the far corner" beside the sliding doors to the balcony. He pulled them all into the center of the room.

"Get them out."

It was fifteen minutes into the operation but no one wanted to call it in— until they were sure.

Amal, still motionless, listened horrified as the SEALs held Sumaiya and Miriam over their dead father. O'Neill towered above them, demanding they confirm the dead man's identity. Bissonnette, who had put on latex gloves and was wiping blood from the corpse's face using a blanket from the bed, compared the profile against pictures of Osama bin Laden in Gina Bennett's laminated SSE booklet.

He was still not convinced.

The nose looked right but the face was "way younger" than expected, he said as he began to take photographs with a camera he had used on dozens of previous raids. He pulled the beard this way and that, turning the head to get a better look at the famous profile and noting that the beard was black not gray, and very short.[20]

One eye was shot through, but Bissonnette asked another SEAL to pull the good eyelid open so he could get a picture of the dark brown iris. The room was filled with the noise of Amal, who was now screaming hysterically, and the sounds of the other women sobbing. But from outside there was utter silence: no police or army response, no neighbors coming out of their houses.

Sumaiya and Miriam wanted to turn their father's body toward Mecca as was traditional after death, but the Americans only had one thing on their minds.

"What's his name?" barked a SEAL in Arabic.

"The Sheikh."

"The Sheikh who?" he asked.

Miriam whispered: "Abdullah bin Muhammed."

O'Neill shrugged. He did not understand.

Sumaiya spoke in Arabic to her sister. "Tell them the truth, they are not Pakistanis."[21]

Miriam could not speak.

Bissonnette was still busy cleaning Osama. "With each swipe, the face became more familiar," he said.

Sumaiya piped up. "My father," she said at last. "Osama bin Laden."

Still not certain, the Arabic-speaking SEAL grabbed Amal's eleven-year-old daughter, Safiyah, from the balcony.

"Who's that?" he asked, gesturing to the body.

Safiyah was hysterical. "Osama bin Laden."

Another SEAL grabbed Khairiah, who was in the hallway.

"Stop fucking with me now," said the SEAL, shaking her. "Who's that?"

Khairiah started to cry. "Osama," she blurted out.

"Osama what?" he asked, still holding her arm.

"Osama bin Laden."

"Hey, dual confirmation," said the Arabic-speaking SEAL, Will. "Confirmed it with the kid. Confirmed it with the old lady."[22]

Twenty minutes down: The SEAL team leader, who was known by the pseudonym Jay, left the room to call mission commander Admiral McRaven on the satellite. "For God and country, I pass Geronimo," he said. "Geronimo EKIA." Enemy Killed In Action.

Bissonnette took more photos.[23] "Lying in front of me was the reason we had been fighting for the last decade," he thought.[24]

Sumaiya, who had been cuffed and placed in a far corner, listened to the sound of what she presumed was her father's head bumping on every step as his body was dragged down the stairs. A minute later, she and Miriam were taken down, too, following the streak of blood, stepping over her dead brother.

Seham came next, trying to negotiate steps made slippery with his and Osama's blood. Her son Khalid was still wearing his pajama trousers and an old vest. She whispered a prayer and knelt to kiss his forehead but the SEALs pulled her away.[25]

Khairiah, who had braced the door of her room from the inside before a SEAL forced his way in, was also taken down.[26]

Everyone was cuffed as SEALs charged about, stuffing whatever they could into bags—cell phones, DVDs, paperwork, hard drives, thumb drives, cameras—leaving behind what appeared to be a large haul of raw opium stuffed into duffel bags under a bed.

"There was so much stuff in this house," recalled Bissonnette, who was struck by the order of Osama's media center as compared to the disorder of his wives' quarters. He rifled through Osama's wardrobe. It "could have passed a Marine Corps boot camp inspection." As he exited the bedroom he noticed the narrow shelf above the door with the Sheikh's famous snub-nosed AK and a Makarov pistol lying on it. Osama had spent his whole life with the AK never more than an arm's reach away—even when visiting his mother, Allia. But now, when he had needed it most, it had been left on the shelf unloaded. "We routinely saw the phenomenon," Bissonnette noted. "The higher up the food chain the targeted individual was, the bigger the pussy."

Drop-dead time: Before departing, the SEALs tried to corral the women and children and take them out of the house to a corner of Khalid's vegetable plot. "It was like herding cats," said Bissonnette. "None of them wanted to move."

To get them to stay inside the compound, the Arabic-speaking SEAL told them they would return for them in two hours.

The SEALs were now five minutes past their drop-dead time and Bissonnette was getting nervous. "We're running outta time, we got to get going," he urged as he and three others stumbled across a plowed field hauling a body bag containing Osama's corpse. Some SEALs were still inside the house and another was setting charges on the downed helicopter. Any plan to take bin Laden's family with them had been abandoned the moment the first Black Hawk went down.[27] The bodies of Khalid, the two Kuwaiti brothers, and Bushra were left where they fell.

Five minutes later the body of Osama had been loaded onto the still-functioning Black Hawk and the Chalk Two team was ready to go. "We're done, we're clean from the target," said Bissonnette as he clambered into Chalk Two's chopper.

Up in the top-floor bedroom, Amal lay gazing up at the blood-spattered ceiling, thinking about her dead husband. After six years cooped up in this airtight place, the end they had never dared discuss had come and gone in just a few seconds.[28] If only he had dealt sooner with the change of companion instead of endlessly delaying the issue, then they would not have even been in Abbottabad at all—and he would probably still be alive.

She felt Hussein trembling beside her, but her leg was throbbing and she could not find the strength to sit up. Where was everyone else? There was not a sound in the house.

An orange brilliance filled the room and lit up the yellow flowered curtains as a huge explosion shattered the windows, scattering glass over them. The remaining SEAL team had detonated the stricken Black Hawk before departing.

@ReallyVirtual tweeted: "A huge window shaking bang here in Abbottabad Cantt. I hope its not the start of something nasty :-S." He added, "Funny, moving to Abbottabad was part of the 'being safe' strategy." A native of Lahore, he had moved to this quiet resort city because he had thought it offered peace and order. Now the whole valley was awake to a major incident.

Amal's heart was throbbing. A replacement U.S. helicopter was arriving, a Chinook that came down to scoop up the remaining SEAL team. After only a few seconds on the ground, it skimmed off down the valley.

@*Really Virtual* tweeted: "All silent after the blast, but a friend heard it 6 km away . . . the helicopter is gone too."

After a few minutes, Amal heard chatter outside, as frightened neighbors began coming out of their houses. They shouted out, asking who was inside and needed help. Was everyone else in the family dead? she wondered, clutching Hussein closer.

A few streets away, @*Really Virtual* tweeted: "Since taliban (probably) don't have helicopters, and since they're saying it was not 'ours,' so must be a complicated situation #abbottabad."

For the first time ever, the gates of the Waziristan Palace stood wide open. Among the curious neighbors stepping inside the compound was a local busybody who had come out of his house when he first heard the helicopter crashing, only to retreat when the SEAL's Pashto translator threatened to shoot him.[29] The only security official in sight was a thin constable from nearby Nawan Shehr police station who made no effort to disperse the rapidly growing crowd who were filming on cell phones as something large, black, and foreign-made burned brightly beside the wall of Khalid's vegetable plot.[30]

While the nervous policeman held back, an off-duty clerk from the Abbottabad provincial administration entered the buildings. He quickly found Maryam, lying in the annex with blood oozing from her wounds. Speaking in her native Pashto and broken Urdu, she told him that "foreigners" had killed her husband. "Some of the Arabs, too," she said, motioning to the main house.

Climbing the stairs, the clerk stepped over a pool of blood congealing around Khalid bin Laden's lifeless body.

In their frenzied search for evidence, the SEALs had scattered belongings everywhere.

When the clerk reached the top bedroom, through the chaos of clothes, upturned boxes, and paper he found Amal weeping. "They have killed Hamzah's father," she whispered.

She pointed to a blood smear on the concrete floor. The clerk had no idea to whom she was referring.[31]

By the time he went back downstairs, an ISI colonel had arrived, accompanied by the deputy inspector general of police and a commander from the

Pakistan Military Academy.[32] Together they cleared everyone out and roughly questioned the survivors in Osama's family. Everyone heard the shouting. The authorities seemed panicked, eyewitnesses said, as the truth dawned on them.

On the family side, the only one who spoke with any coherence was Khairiah, the eyewitnesses said, and she confirmed in broken English that the body on the stairs was that of "Khalid, son of Osama bin Laden."[33]

Khairiah broke into furious screams: "Heli come, heli go and take away one or two."

Jabbing her finger in their faces, she shouted: "Now you come, when everything over."

Shortly after one forty A.M., the ISI colonel received a call from General Pasha, the ISI director general, who was at home inside the heavily guarded Chaklala garrison in Rawalpindi, trying to get ahead of unconfirmed reports spewing out of Abbottabad.

After the explosion that blew up the damaged Black Hawk, the Pakistan Air Force had scrambled two F16 fighters armed with 30mm cannons and air-to-air missiles.[34] "What the hell has happened?" he thundered. He had spoken to General Kayani but the only thing they were able to conclude was that there had been no military exercises scheduled to take place in the early hours of May 2. Whatever this was, it was *live and fluid*. Their natural inclination was to blame their most deadly enemy—India. Had Indian helicopters crossed the Line of Control?

The ISI was Pakistan's "first line of national defense," stormed Pasha. Until more details of what had occurred in Abbottabad were established, it should take the lead as the "core institution" of the state. The police always bungled operations, got in the way, and "did not know the basics of intelligence work," so the ISI colonel should get them out of the compound before they discovered anything compromising.

Pasha also called the garrison commander of the Pakistan Military Academy in Abbottabad and told him to rouse his unit and help the ISI colonel lock down the site.

Over in the cantonment area, @ReallyVirtual tweeted: "A Major of the #Pakistan #Army's 19 FF, Platoon CO says incident at #Abbottabad where #helicopter crashed is accidental and not an 'attack.'"

Before long he tweeted an update: "Report from a taxi driver: The army has cordoned off the crash area and is conducting door-to-door search in the surrounding area."

Inside the compound, around an hour after the SEALs had departed, ISI officers photographed the bodies of Khalid, Ibrahim, Abrar, and Bushra, recovering whatever documents, weapons, and computers had been left behind. The police would be the last to search the crime scene. No First Information Report, the initial stage of any criminal inquiry in Pakistan, would ever be lodged.

@ReallyVirtual tweeted: "What really happened doesn't matter if there is an official story behind it that 99.999% of the world would believe."

May 2, 2011, 3 A.M., Jalalabad, Afghanistan

Mission commander Admiral McRaven was standing just inside the hangar with his hands in his pockets when the SEALs delivered the body bag. "Let's see him," he said drily, as the corpse thudded onto the concrete floor, where the bag was unzipped. Blood had drained to the bottom of the bag and the skin had a powdery pall.[35]

Matthew Bissonnette pulled the beard to the left and right to give McRaven a clear look at the profile, as others crowded around. Osama bin Laden was not quite as they had imagined, and one of the SEALs who was six feet four inches tall lay down to check his height.

After taking in the scrawny frame, the unexpected crew cut, and the large number of posthumous gunshots, someone brought over Gina Bennett, the CIA analyst who had put it all together. Before the raid she had said she was not interested in seeing the body, but now she approached hesitantly.

"I still had all my stuff on," said Robert O'Neill, who took her by the shoulder and ushered her forward. "I asked her, 'Is that your guy?'"

Bennett looked down and nodded without saying a word.

He took the magazine out of his gun and gave it to her as a souvenir. "I hope you have room in your backpack for this?" he said. It had twenty-seven of the original thirty rounds left in it.

When they stripped the body, the SEALs found five hundred euros and two phone numbers sewn into Osama's clothes, including the special number the Al Qaeda leader had given to his son Khalid for use in emergencies.[36] It connected to a phone carried by Atiyah, his Number Three, who knew that if it ever rang Osama was in serious trouble. To the Americans, it appeared to be a paltry effort at emergency protocol. But after two decades in exile, Osama had still believed he knew best what he needed to survive.

Shortly before leaving Jalalabad, O'Neill glimpsed Bennett sitting alone on the floor of the hangar hugging her legs to her chest and crying. Searching for Osama bin Laden had become her life's work and now that it was actually over the emotion was overwhelming.

Bissonnette went over to speak to a team of CIA and military "document exploitation" specialists who were already sifting through material recovered from the compound, preparing for it to be shipped back to the United States for analysis. Thinking of a stack of boxes on the second floor of Osama's house that he had not had time to pick up, he wanted to apologize. "We could have done better."

The analyst laughed. "Stop worrying about it. Look at all this shit. We've got more here than we've gotten in the past ten years." Later, the president's national security advisor, Thomas Donilon, would comment that the material could fill "a small college library."[37]

Twenty-four hours later, the SEALs flew home. As they landed at their base in Virginia Beach, they turned on their phones for the first time in days and were inundated with messages. It had taken less than four hours for the news to break that the Navy SEALs based at Naval Special Warfare Development Group (DEV-GRU) had led the Abbottabad raid, and reporters were already crawling all over the base looking for someone to interview.

After two days' leave, the team was back at work and listened as their commander, Jay, ordered them to act and speak as though the raid had never happened. To talk, even to close relatives, would violate their code as "quiet professionals," he said.[38]

May 2, 2011, 3:45 A.M., Bilal Town, Abbottabad

Osama's surviving family members were brought out of the compound in a fleet of ambulances just as the *azam* called *fajr* prayer, the first of the day.[39] Streets that would normally be bustling into life remained empty—cleared by the army and ISI. By now the city's residents didn't need any encouragement to stay inside. With so many intelligence agents descending on Abbottabad, nobody wanted to catch the ISI's attention.

As the first rays of dawn doused Abbottabad in pale sunlight, Amal was hustled into a private room at the army's Combined Military Hospital on Karakoram Highway. Son Hussein and daughter Safiyah were at her side. Her other three children and relatives were on their way to Islamabad, driven in a bus with curtained windows, armed ISI officers riding up front.

Maryam was being treated at another hospital, with eight stunned children sitting silently beside her bed—hers and Bushra's. She had watched in horror as the bodies of her husband, sister-in-law, and brother-in-law had been taken out of the compound, knowing that as the lone adult Pakistani survivor of the raid she would face the brunt of the authorities' vengeance. All she could think was that if Ibrahim had pressed the Sheikh harder to move out, they might all have got away with it.[40]

@Really Virtual, who was confined to the cantonment by the roadblocks, tweeted: "I think I should take out my big blower to blow the fog of war away and see the clearer picture." He gave up on going to bed and watched Pakistani anchors reporting the first sketchy details of a U.S. operation over camera-phone footage of a burning Black Hawk.[41]

Over the next couple of hours his Twitter account attracted thousands of new followers and so many foreign journalists tried to reach him that he turned off Skype. "Uh oh, now I'm the guy who live-blogged the Osama raid without knowing it," he tweeted at five forty-one A.M., by which time everyone had heard the rumors about who had been killed. A few minutes later he added: "I need to sleep, but Osama had to pick this day to die :-/."

Rawalpindi, Pakistan

General Pasha was with General Kayani at Army House taking in the fallout from what he was already describing as the "American sting operation." Admiral Mike Mullen had called Kayani around three A.M. to confirm who had been killed. It had been a terse infogram. Shortly after, the ISI colonel inside the Abbottabad compound had called Pasha to confirm the news—extracted from Seham.[42]

"This was a game we all missed because of bad work by all of us, including the police, local government institutions," Pasha said ruefully. The national security of Pakistan had never been "as critically challenged as it was today," he added.

What had happened was a "systemic failure." Raymond Davis should have been a wake-up call to Washington's disregard for Pakistani sovereignty. The fact that Pasha had intervened to allow Davis to leave Pakistan made him feel all the more bitter now.

Suspecting that everyone at the U.S. embassy in Islamabad would soon be out for blood, finger-pointing after their big score in Abbottabad and accusing Pakistan's military of having concealed Osama bin Laden, generals Kayani and Pasha were deeply worried. They went into default position and ordered a lockdown.

The inspector general of police for Khyber Pakhtunkhwa (as the North-West Frontier Province had been renamed in 2010), the most senior police official in the Abbottabad region, was told to back off as "everything was being handled by the ISI."

This was an "intelligence failure" of the greatest proportions, Pasha offered, as he desperately cast around for a scapegoat, asking for a full briefing from S-Wing—the untamable jihad section of the ISI.[43]

May 2, 2011, 8:35 A.M., Inter-Services Public Relations (ISPR), Rawalpindi

An ISI colleague had woken the ISPR chief, General Athar Abbas, at four A.M. "Sir, there's a rumor going around that Osama bin Laden is *dead*."[44] He arrived at his office next to GHQ (general headquarters) in Rawalpindi to find his staff "in a total state of paralysis." And he could not help but wonder why no one more senior had called him. By five A.M., the whole of Pakistan was live to the news and the ISPR had no handle on it.[45]

President Obama appeared live on TV at eight thirty-five A.M. Pakistan time. The power had come back on in Abbottabad, so the residents of Bilal Town watched amazed as he confirmed what had taken place on their doorstep. "Going forward, it is essential that Pakistan continues to join us in the fight against al Qaeda and its affiliates," Obama said, trying to soften the blow.[46]

General Athar was inundated with calls from the world's press. "It was so hot," he remembered. "I didn't know what to say." Hearing nothing from up the chain, he asked Kayani and Pasha for permission to issue a statement.

"I said that we had to face the brunt and then at least nobody would question us. But the clearance wasn't coming." At three P.M. he sent more text messages. "The press is going to eat us up if we don't interact. We should say it was a security lapse," he advised the army chiefs. "We should be up front about it. It will at least take some steam out." Neither of them replied.[47]

That night, with Pakistan having made no comment, Athar returned home and confided in his wife: "There is a great anger and frustration in the army." It would find a vent in the civilian world, he feared, and this conflict would feed an age-old cycle of attrition—the rhythm of life in Pakistan since 1947.[48]

Peshawar, Pakistan

Dr. Shakil Afridi watched the events unfold with horror. Until today he had been fully intending to return to Abbottabad to continue with his next round of vaccinations for Save the Children. While working for Kate, Sue, and Toni, he had never questioned their demands or voiced suspicions, thinking instead of the $55,000 prize in his bank account and more money to come. Now as he watched footage of the Waziristan Palace and learned that this was where Osama bin Laden had lived, he felt sick to his stomach.

Dr. Afridi could see how it looked. The CIA had used him to determine whether Osama was living in the house, a treasonable act that would condemn him in the eyes of the nation, especially the ISI.[49] He was terrified.

He tried to call his expat STC colleagues. All the phone numbers he had for them were disconnected. Should he tell his wife, Imrana, or keep quiet? Should he see if their old U.S. visas were still valid? Running would imply guilt, he told himself. He decided to stay put. Maybe Kate or Sue would surface to help extract him from Pakistan. It was the least they owed him.

May 2, 2011, 2 P.M., Washington, D.C.

As Pakistan went to bed, John Brennan addressed the American press at the White House. Obama's counterterrorism adviser had some direct things to say that seemed like common sense. It was "inconceivable that Osama did not have a support system in the country that allowed him to remain there for an extended period of time."[50] Brennan had pointed to what many were thinking, even though it clashed with the White House's more concilia-tory tone. They had got their man, and in the president's view they did not need to throw Pakistan under the bus.

Having just got off to sleep, General Pasha was woken with the news. He was furious, but he and Kayani still held off issuing a statement.[51] In the absence of any official Pakistani reaction or explanation, a global media scrum had converged on Bilal Town, with reporters looking to find answers for themselves.

@ReallyVirtual was there, too. "Watching the watchers watching the watchmen watching the compound . . . or something like that . . ." he tweeted over a picture of the house that he referred to as "la Den."

At ISPR, General Athar faced a deluge of questions he was unable to answer. "Why had the army been so slow to respond to the operation?" "Why had radars not picked up the helicopters flying in?" "Had the electricity supply been deliberately disabled to assist the U.S. operation?" "How had Osama bin Laden been able to live beside the country's premier military academy for almost six years?" "Had the ISI known he was there all along?"

Pakistan was either complicit, or wretched, was General Athar's private judgment. He kept thinking back to January, when the ISI had caught the Bali bomber Umar Patek in Abbottabad and Athar had sent a congratula-tory message to General Pasha, suggesting they make something of it. At the time, he had not understood why Pasha had not even replied. Now he suspected there was a connection between the two incidents and that Pasha had not wanted ISPR to blunder into a much more sensitive situation.

"The ISI missed very glaring evidence about Umar Patek," Athar later recalled.[52] "What was he doing in Abbottabad? Why did he come? He was the golden goose. He was caught and arrested but the intelligence people failed to connect why he was there."

Or had Athar missed something? Pasha, too, had demanded answers from S-Wing but they had declined to explain Patek's presence or what it meant.

In the absence of any guidance from ISPR, conspiracy theories burgeoned that Kayani and Pasha had been in on the operation, and that the ISI had kept Osama prisoner for years. In the United States, several expat Pakistani "intelligence experts" emerged to claim that presidents George W. Bush and Pervez Musharraf had agreed back in 2003 to keep Osama bin Laden alive and imprisoned in Pakistan. One went further and suggested that the Obama administration had commissioned the killing to improve its ratings in a preelection year. Pakistani president Asif Ali Zardari had been in on the plot and had kept quiet in the hope that the army chief and his ISI director would be forced to resign. None of this was backed up by the emerging facts.[53]

Thinking he was helping his country, Wajid Shamsul Hasan, Pakistan's high commissioner in London, appeared on British TV. "Whatever has happened, has happened with *our consent*," he improvised, having been unable to raise anyone in the presidency or the prime minister's office.[54] But when he ventured that the ISI had helped lay the trap for Osama, he received threatening phone calls from Aabpara.[55] "You need to shut up," he was warned. Being seen as having assisted in the raid was almost worse than being accused of not having known about it in advance as far as the ISI and army were concerned.

In Hasan's Knightsbridge office, a siege mentality set in, with officials sharing a Photoshop-altered image of President Obama, Mike Mullen, Hillary Clinton, and others watching the live drone feed from the Abbottabad operation with Osama's face inserted among them. Gallows humor made more sense than the mess Pakistan was in.

The White House tried to take the sting out of Brennan's scorched-earth statement by announcing that pictures of Osama bin Laden's dead body would not be made public and that his remains had been buried at sea.

In Pakistan, where the generals continued to stay silent as they struggled to get their stories straight, a subtle reframing of the argument started from the grassroots up. A subordinate of the ISI colonel who had been one of the first into the compound sold bloody crime-scene photographs of dead Ibrahim, Abrar, and Khalid bin Laden to Reuters, undercutting the sanitized version of a "smart raid" that the Obama administration was spinning.

General Kayani finally issued a statement through ISPR on May 5, but it fell short, dabbling with issues of pride and doling out threats. "Any similar action violating the sovereignty of Pakistan will warrant a review on the level of military/intelligence cooperation with the United States," he thundered. The ISI had provided "initial information," but the CIA had not shared further developments of intelligence on the case with the ISI, "contrary to the existing practice between the two services."[56]

Paltry penalties followed. The number of American troops in Pakistan was to be reduced "to the minimum essential." General Athar at ISPR fretted. Army chief Kayani was on the attack but had not addressed the central issue that everyone was asking: was the military complicit or diminished? "Something that should have gone into examining our intelligence failure was redirected instead into anger at the U.S.," Athar recalled.[57] "Nobody would buy this story." While a select group of Pakistani reporters known for their loyalty to the military was invited to a private briefing with Kayani, the international media and others began probing conspiracy theories.

Reporter Syed Saleem Shahzad of *Asia Times Online* claimed to have evidence of official Pakistani collusion, writing that U.S. helicopters had stopped off en route to Abbottabad at Ghazi air base near Haripur, an important facility from where ISI covert operations were staged.[58] The CIA and ISI had planned the raid together, Shahzad concluded, although the Americans so mistrusted the Pakistanis that they had not revealed the identity of the target.

Najam Sethi, one of Pakistan's most prominent newspaper editors, said on his political talk show what many people were thinking: the military must have been "complicit or incompetent."[59] Kamran Khan, a TV pundit normally respectful to the military, questioned Kayani's and Pasha's competence. "We have become the biggest haven of terrorism in the world and we have failed to stop it," he said.[60]

General Pasha fumed. Part of his reticence was explained by the fact that he had yet to receive a full briefing from S-Wing. He issued a holding statement: "Incomplete information and lack of technical details have resulted in speculations and misreporting."[61] This was the first truth spoken by anyone in the armed forces.

But in the face of the actual gory, surreal news of the world's most wanted man being run to ground in a military garrison town in Pakistan, and the competing wild stories that were being spawned all over the world, no one was listening to Pasha.

Writing in the *Washington Post*, Fareed Zakaria tried to characterize the dreadful misfiring going on in Aabpara when he quoted an unnamed Pakistani scholar who described the military as "like a person, caught in bed with another man's wife, who is indignant that someone entered his house."[62]

ISPR ordered all foreign press out of Abbottabad, citing the need for reporters to obtain "no objection certificates" before entering a military cantonment city. However, none of these were being issued as ISI checkpoints sprung up on all roads leading into the area.

@ReallyVirtual was intrigued: "Question to international journalists in Abbottabad: Are you guys being told to leave because of the CIA safe house discovery?"

Over the previous twenty-four hours, mischievous CIA sources hoping to press home their advantage had leaked details of their surveillance operation in Abbottabad, making reference to "support it had received on the ground," hinting that it had not been the ISI that had pitched in, but assets recruited by the agency.

The ISI responded by unmasking the CIA's station chief in Islamabad to the local press, shattering decades-long accords that allowed state secrets to remain so. Days later, the official, Mark Kelton, began to experience severe stomach pain. At first he put it down to bad food, but as the symptoms worsened he was forced to take time off work and eventually he left the country for medical treatment. By July 2011, he was suffering from a "severe medical crisis" and told Langley he could no longer function in the job, leading some colleagues to speculate that Kelton, who had withstood the cold, tightening towel of Putin's counterintelligence game, had been poisoned by the ISI. He survived after undergoing abdominal surgery but retired from the CIA soon after. His only public comment on the affair was that the cause of his illness "was never clarified."[63]

May 9, 2011, Washington, D.C.

The CIA quietly reached out to those who had helped them, a dozen Pakistanis who were advised to quit the country immediately lest they be accused of collusion with the United States.[64] At the top of the list was Lieutenant Colonel Saeed Iqbal, the former ISI officer. He and his wife, a former steward for Pakistan International Airways, were relocated to California, while his properties and businesses were put up for sale.[65]

Another to arrive in the United States was Osama bin Laden's architect Mohammed Younis, whose paperwork was seen by Western intelligence agencies before it was seized by the ISI and suggested that Lashkar-e-Taiba had helped the Kuwaiti brothers purchase the plot on which the Waziristan Palace was built.[66] As Lashkar-e-Taiba reported to S-Wing, the implications were dangerous and unsettling.[67]

In the immediate aftermath of the raid, U.S. officials also reached out to Dr. Shakil Afridi to warn that his life could be in danger, but he sat at home in Peshawar, refusing to move, telling family members, "I have done nothing wrong."[68]

Pakistan's ambassador Husain Haqqani, a political jouster who once had been a close adviser to Benazir Bhutto, had been on a scheduled trip from Washington to Islamabad as the raid unfurled and learned of it during a stopover in London. He was told to get straight back on the plane to the United States and plump up the media so that it did not blame Pakistan's government, armed forces, or intelligence services for having allowed Osama's presence in the country, as that would have been a violation of UN Security Council resolutions 1267 and 1373.[69] Haqqani was also instructed to seek an official apology from the United States for violating Pakistani sovereignty but, when he got back, all officials wanted to talk about was how and when Pakistan was going to return the wrecked Black Hawk. It had been removed from the compound and taken to general headquarters in Rawalpindi, where it was being closely inspected.

In Pakistan, a ferocious game of musical chairs had begun. A few days after the raid, John Kerry, the chairman of the Senate Foreign Relations Committee, flew into Islamabad and was persuaded by General Kayani to emphasize Pakistan's ongoing role as an ally in the war on terror. As a quid pro quo, General Pasha agreed to go to Washington. "Most of the ISI" had had no knowledge of bin Laden being in Pakistan, he maintained.[70] He asked for time to run his own investigation into the raid, aware how low the military's popularity was inside the country and how remote Rawalpindi was from Washington. Some civilian officials were now arguing that this might be the time to contain the khaki behemoth.

To prepare for Pasha's Washington showdown, Kayani ordered a board of inquiry into the Abbottabad raid led by the adjutant general, a senior military officer. Even before it began, Pasha said that he was confident it "would not uncover any support network within the military and intelligence establishment."[71]

Behind the scenes, the ISI began an urgent cleanup operation. In Kohat, two of Ibrahim's nephews and his brother-in-law were taken away by the ISI.[72] In Shangla, relatives of Maryam were also picked up.[73]

Commentator Najam Sethi, among Pakistan's most respected media stars, who had accused the army of being complicit or incompetent, was called to what he described as a "stormy" face-to-face confrontation with a senior ISI official. "He accused me of everything, anti-Pakistan, anti-army, anti-everything," Sethi recalled.[74] When he was tipped off that his name had been maliciously added to a terrorist hit list, he and his wife temporarily left the country.

Osama's once-helpful neighbor Shamraiz Khan vanished, as did first-on-the-scene Constable Nazar Mohammad. Next to disappear were two of the men who had built the house, one of the female nurses who had accompanied Dr. Shakil Afridi during his vaccination program, a doctor who had treated Ibrahim's children at his clinic, a mechanic who had repaired Ibrahim's vehicles, a man who had cut down trees in the compound just before the raid—even the milkman.[75]

According to written ISI procedures, everyone would be interrogated and rated for reliability on a scale of A to E, while the quality of his or her information was marked from 1 to 5.[76] Those who were scored as A1 had the most to fear.

@ReallyVirtual, somehow still free, tweeted: "Ever heard of locking the door after the horse has bolted?"[77]

On May 23, the ISI came for Dr. Afridi, announcing to the media that he had been arrested while trying to flee to Afghanistan. His incredulous wife, Imrana, who feared the black hole her husband had fallen into, contested the ISI's account, saying: "He was picked up while shopping in the market in Peshawar." It was now well beyond anyone's capability in the United States to assist him.

In detention, somewhere unspecified, Dr. Afridi pleaded ignorance, saying that he had been as shocked as everyone else to see the compound on TV, never having been told that Osama was in the crosshairs. The health campaign he had worked on was genuine as far as he was concerned. He was more sorry than they could imagine.

Protesting his client's innocence, and invoking habeas corpus, which in Pakistan was tantamount to an invitation for sensitive agencies to fast-track a back-alley killing and sling the body into a gutter, Dr. Afridi's lawyer pointed out that the family still had valid U.S. visas and if they had had something to hide they would have run already.

General Pasha beat the courts to make a judgment: Afridi "was a hero for the Americans and a traitor for us."[78] The doctor's lawyer was threatened and withdrew from the case.

General Pasha then went after Save the Children, claiming that it had "a history of involvement with the CIA." Despite strong denials from the nongovernmental organization (NGO) that it had any such links, six expats employed in Pakistan by Save the Children were expelled, its main office in Islamabad was forced to temporarily close, and its polio campaign, which had saved thousands of lives across Pakistan, ground to a virtual halt. Dozens of female health workers were killed in retaliatory attacks that broadened out to all NGOs, whose ability to work in the country was eroded.[79]

Asked about the ISI's murderous reputation, General Pasha conceded that in the past many "decent people" had been harmed. But he added that prior to Abbottabad he had ushered in a new era, making "changes to its mind-set, culture and methodology." Those who criticized and still feared the ISI were people "who should fear the ISI," as they were more often than not "working against the national interest."

May 22, 2011, 8:30 p.m., Pakistan Naval Air Station Mehran, Karachi, Pakistan

The attackers wore black overalls. They cut through the naval base's perimeter fence at a security camera blind spot and stole across the tarmac before shooting off volleys of rocket-propelled grenades to destroy $80 million in warplanes and marine surveillance aircraft.

Pakistani commandos took sixteen hours to seize back control of the base, by which time a dozen military personnel were dead in the most significant attack on a Pakistani military target since the raid on the GHQ in 2009. The assault appeared even more perilous when it was revealed that the components of several nuclear warheads were housed nearby. It was the second incident in under a month that underscored the apparent lack of preparedness on the part of Pakistan's military chiefs, and it caused fury across the country, both inside the military and in the wider civilian community.

The lower ranks questioned the competence of Kayani and Pasha. Some officers privately demanded they resign, as intelligence came to the fore appearing to show that Al Qaeda sleepers inside the base had planned the raid.

The story was quickly picked up by Syed Saleem Shahzad, the *Asia Times Online* Pakistan bureau chief, who chose this tense moment to identify Ilyas Kashmiri—an Al Qaeda militant who had once been an army commando and then an ISI hired hand—as the mastermind of the attack. According to Shahzad, Kashmiri blamed the army for having failed to protect Osama in Abbottabad and he had mounted the Mehran raid in retaliation.[80] For generals Kayani and Pasha, a claim that Al Qaeda had infiltrated a major naval station was the worst story combination imaginable. But to get ahead of his rivals in the international media, Shahzad deliberately courted danger these days.

Since his coverage of the Waziristan Accord conference in 2006, the reporter had built a reputation for his risky exposés. He went further than most other journalists, building up contacts within militant circles while speaking regularly to the ISI. Some stories proved wildly inaccurate. But he was right enough of the time to have become an irritant for the military and intelligence services, which had threatened him verbally on several occasions.

Friends of Shahzad warned him that maintaining a relationship with the ISI created dangerous expectations of loyalty and that it was best not to talk to them at all so they could not accuse him of betrayal.[81] But he disregarded the advice.

Five weeks before Abbottabad, he had written a story claiming Osama had recently met Gulbuddin Hekmatyar, who also had once been deeply connected to the ISI. Shahzad claimed that he had been summoned to the ISI headquarters at Aabpara the day after his article appeared and ordered to retract his story. A senior ISI official allegedly informed him that the ISI "want the world to believe that Osama is dead." Shahzad refused to retract his story and left Aabpara, telling friends that the ISI was "trying to protect bin Laden."[82]

A vicious attack the previous year on his colleague, investigative reporter Umar Cheema, should have served as another warning that the ISI was in no mood for public criticism.[83] Men in commando outfits who made clear they were acting on behalf of the ISI had abducted Cheema in Islamabad after he wrote pieces critical of the army. He was filmed being sodomized with a metal rod. When they had finished with him, they shaved off his mustache and eyebrows before dumping him in a ditch ten miles outside Islamabad.

Two days after Shahzad broke the Mehran naval base story, he was driving through one of Islamabad's most secure neighborhoods on his way to a TV panel discussion about how Al Qaeda had infiltrated the navy, when he, too, vanished.[84] The next morning, a farmer clearing debris from the Upper Jhelum Canal, ninety miles southeast of the capital, retrieved his battered body from a storm drain.[85]

According to the postmortem, the reporter, who was wearing his best suit and tie, had been beaten to death with a metal rod, his rib cage smashed on both sides, his lungs and liver ruptured. He was the forty-sixth Pakistani journalist to be killed since 2001.

Zafar Sheikh, his friend and colleague, who had accompanied him on trips into the Tribal Areas, spelled it out. "I used to be a brave journalist," he said.[86] "But I will be frank with you. I don't want to get killed like Saleem. I am just writing stereotypical bullshit stories [now]—and no one is angry."

Two days after Shahzad's body was identified, a perturbed Admiral Mike Mullen gave an outspoken media briefing on the incident, saying that Shahzad's killing had been "sanctioned by the government" of Pakistan and that the order to kill him had come from a senior officer on General Kayani's staff.

Shocked, Kayani ordered General Athar Abbas at ISPR to issue a response. The ISI denied any responsibility and declared that "baseless accusations against the country's sensitive agencies . . . are totally unfounded."[87]

On June 3, Ilyas Kashmiri, who up until then had been protected as a former spook and contemporary asset, was killed in a U.S. drone attack near Wana in South Waziristan. For the first time, the Pakistani military admitted responsibility for the attack, confirming that it had provided Kashmiri's coordinates to the CIA.[88]

May 20, 2011, G-6 Safe House, Islamabad, Pakistan

That month, bin Laden's wives, children, and grandchildren were reunited on General Pasha's instructions at an ISI safe house in G-6, a middle-class sector of Islamabad close to Aabpara.

Not happy that the army was investigating itself through the adjutant general, the Supreme Court of Pakistan had ordered a judicial inquiry into the circumstances leading up to bin Laden's killing. Dubbed the Abbottabad Commission, it consisted of four senior government officials and had authority to examine official documents and interview all relevant witnesses, including bin Laden's family. The army succeeded in getting one loyalist on the commission, a retired general called Nadeem Ahmed, who set out his position even before interviewing a single witness, telling Australian journalists that he firmly believed "that no intelligence organization in Pakistan would do such a stupid thing" as harbor Osama bin Laden. But still General Pasha was worried about what the commission might turn up and he wanted to ensure that the ISI interrogated the most critical witnesses first.

A date had been fixed for his forthcoming visit to Washington, where he had been invited to present his findings about Osama's presence in Pakistan to the CIA. To pile on the pressure, the White House had announced it was putting on hold $800 million in military assistance to Pakistan. The money would only be released if Pasha's explanations were deemed satisfactory.

However, bin Laden's wives refused to play ball. As soon as she moved into the G-6 villa, Khairiah began complaining about the accommodations. There were no blackout blinds and close neighbors could see in.[89] It was as if she were back in Tehran at the Tourist Complex.

Worried that she would try to arrange some kind of breakout, female officers from the Federal Investigation Agency (FIA) who normally worked at the airport patting down female passengers, were brought in to guard the family around the clock, as the ISI prepared to interrogate them—appointing two retired colonels and a brigadier.[90]

The wives refused to speak to the male officers. Besides their objection to the religious insult, they were too busy dealing with traumatized children who suffered frequent nightmares and wet their beds, they said. The most affected were Hussein, who had seen his father being shot, and Sumaiya, Miriam, and Safiyah, who had been forced to identify the body. While Khairiah guarded the front of the house, Seham, who had lost not only her husband but also her son, Khalid, retreated into her Koran. Amal, whose leg wound had still not healed, spent her days in bed.

With the CIA as well as Saudi and Yemeni intelligence also demanding access to the wives, the ISI's biggest concern was tutoring the women and children to stay quiet about anything incriminating they may have witnessed over the years.

To clear the resistance, the retired ISI officers brought in a female professor from Islamabad's International Islamic University (IIU) to act as an intermediary.[91]

Dr. Zaitoon Begum, a stout, dour woman who wore her *hijab* pulled tightly around her face, had studied for her master's degree in Arabic literature at a university in Mecca and held a Ph.D. in Arabic.[92] At IIU she had a reputation for being deeply patriotic and reportedly scolding female students who refused to wear the *hijab*.[93] She was a perfect fit for Khairiah, who, in exchange for answering Dr. Zaitoon's questions, demanded the return of her religious books and jewelry and "compensation for the loss of the house."[94]

After the ISI agreed to these requests, Khairiah and the other wives consented to answer some questions through Dr. Zaitoon, and the three interrogators set down the bare bones of a version of their story to be presented to the commission and to the CIA in Washington.

However, while the ISI interrogators recorded graphic descriptions of the night of the raid, the wives' accounts of their years spent in Pakistan were extraordinarily incomplete. None of them explained how they had reached Abbottabad or who had protected them there. None of them were asked any questions that touched on collusion and camouflage: how the household had first embedded in Pakistan and what mechanisms had enabled the family to remain cloaked in Abbottabad without detection for so many years.

The ISI reserved its harshest treatment for Maryam, a Pakistani citizen who would be produced in a court if the ISI got its way, and who, like Dr. Shakil Afridi, was threatened with treason and the death penalty. She was held in secret detention, while close family members in Shangla and Kohat were interrogated and threatened.

Rejected by her parents and in-laws, who all wanted to place as much distance between themselves and Abbottabad as possible, Maryam was not only physically scarred but also a widow with no financial means and eight mouths to feed—her own children and Bushra's. "As far as I was concerned my life was already over," she said.

She tried to cooperate but the sessions became increasingly aggressive.[95]

Having ensured that most of those who knew anything about Osama's time in Pakistan were silenced or disappeared, the ISI turned its attention to limiting the powers of investigation granted by Zardari's civilian government to the Abbottabad Commission—the four-man panel of experts who were supposed to examine every facet of the bin Laden case.

While General Pasha knew he could rely on General Nadeem Ahmed, who had overseen the army's relief efforts after the earthquake of 2005, the others would require more persuasion to present a favorable conclusion.

Within weeks of the inquiry getting under way, a panel member, a retired inspector general of police, went off to the United States for a prolonged period of medical treatment, which meant he was not on hand to hear the evidence.

Another panel member, a retired judge, buried himself in legal arguments.

However, the fourth commission member posed a significant problem for Pasha. He was Ashraf Jehangir Qazi, a well-respected former ambassador to some of Pakistan's most challenging posts including the United States, Russia, China, and India. He came from illustrious but deeply principled stock.

His Irish mother, Jennifer, had married his father, the son of a Balochi tribal chief, after meeting at a ball in an Oxford college in 1939.[96] Relocating to the new country of Pakistan in 1948, Jennifer had become the first female member of the national assembly from her province, and she later acted as an intermediary for rebels who staged an armed uprising against the federal government. When she died in 2008, thousands of Pashtun tribesmen and a smattering of Taliban raised cheers for "Mummy Jennifer" as the cortège passed through Pishin, the Qazi family stronghold.

When the ISI tried to fob off Qazi with an edited summary of bin Laden family interrogations, he insisted on meeting the wives face-to-face. For weeks, the ISI resisted, hiding behind a tangle of legalistic and diplomatic discussions about travel documents and to what countries they might be deported once the official case against them had been heard.[97]

To waste more time, the women were moved to different heavily guarded villas around Islamabad, during which times they would be inaccessible to the commission for a requisite "settling in" period.

But Qazi, who had battled with the State Department under George W. Bush's first administration and served as special representative to UN Secretary General Ban Ki-moon in Sudan, was relentless.

July 2011, Washington, D.C.

General Pasha arrived in Washington for his showdown with the CIA on July 13. Leon Panetta had been made defense secretary several days earlier and so Pasha met the acting CIA director, Mike Morell—who he did not know personally and therefore instinctively mistrusted.

Following usual protocol, Pakistan's ambassador Husain Haqqani greeted General Pasha at the airport. In the car, the mood between the two men was tense. Pasha suspected that Haqqani had something to do with a fake memo purportedly written by President Zardari to the U.S. government, warning of a possible military coup in Pakistan after the Abbottabad raid. It had reached Admiral Mike Mullen on May 10, causing Pasha untold problems. Haqqani guessed that Pasha had fueled the rumors that he was a CIA stooge.

When they did talk, Pasha maintained that there was no way the ISI had known Osama's whereabouts. "He talks in metaphors and all these colorful things," Haqqani recalled.

"Look, there are so many intelligence failures; why is everyone blaming us?" Pasha asked. "Don't you realize this is about weakening and undermining Pakistan. We had nothing to do with OBL. It was a failure but it was a failure of the U.S. as well as us. The U.S. would never have been able to do this if they did not have some of the intel we had earlier shared with them."[98]

Haqqani was incredulous. "I had met Pasha a few times. A U.S. senator once said publicly that he was a boldfaced liar and I thought that too. He thought he was really a patriot who represented the military, and what he knew and wanted the world to know is what was relevant. He was pleasant at a personal level but not well-read or knowledgeable, and usually not as clever as he believed he was."[99]

In his meeting with Morell, Pasha went on the offensive, arguing that intelligence gathering was often an imperfect science and that one's enemy could sometimes hide in plain sight. He complained that the CIA had passed on numerous false leads about bin Laden's location that had wasted valuable ISI time. If the CIA had been more honest about its hunt for bin Laden, the ISI would have been better placed to assist.

For his part, Morell refused to apologize for violating Pakistani sovereignty and complained about Pakistan's ongoing support for banned outfits like the Haqqani network, which shared a name with Ambassador Husain Haqqani but had no connection to him. If Pakistan wanted to benefit from the $800 million in withheld U.S. assistance, it would have to demonstrate a genuine willingness to cooperate in the search for high-value targets still in Pakistan: Dr. al-Zawahiri and the rest of Al Qaeda Central, Mullah Omar, and the Haqqanis.

Pasha returned from his Washington trip furious and determined to air his version of the story. Soon after, the ISI decided to preempt the Abbottabad Commission and publish its own version of what had happened. For assistance, it turned to Brigadier Shaukat Qadir, a retired infantry commander who had served above General Kayani when the latter was a younger officer and who now worked as a "risk analyst" and commentator.[100]

Chain-smoking Qadir was commissioned to write a book that he pointedly entitled *Operation Geronimo: The Betrayal and Execution of Osama bin Laden and Its Aftermath.*[101]

He bragged that he had benefited from what he described as "fairly detailed briefings by both senior military officers and ISI officials ranging from high level officers to field operatives" and assured that he had been provided with "all details, with nothing held back."[102] However, he was not a pushover, he maintained, describing his dealings with the ISI as being like trying to "grab an eel in your bare hands."[103]

Qadir made two visits to Osama's house, approved by General Kayani, and his personal connections to an ISI brigadier who interrogated Osama's three wives shortly after the raid ensured he had access to some of what they said, too.[104] Pasha gave permission for him to speak to the ISI's counter-terrorism wing and to the ISI colonel who had been responsible for securing the compound on the night of the raid and whose deputy had sold the pictures of the bodies. There were several other unidentified ISI sources, including an official he called Othman.

Many of his conclusions were highly contentious, including a claim that Amal bin Laden had described how Osama had flown to the Gulf for a kidney transplant operation while she stayed with Ibrahim's relatives in Suleman Talaab in 2002 or 2003. Afterward, he took two medicines for the rest of his life, which Ibrahim picked up in bulk once a month from Peshawar.[105] This explained, Qadir wrote, how a Saudi militant with a known kidney ailment was able to survive, although he did not explore how the world's most wanted man had been able to leave Pakistan and reenter without some kind of official assistance.

Qadir's version of events had the ISI all over Osama in the days after Tora Bora, claiming they had tracked him to Kunar after 9/11 and then to the Shawal Valley, in South Waziristan in the spring of 2003. But after that, "he just faded away." Qadir said the ISI had mainly stopped looking for him after Khalid Shaikh Mohammad informed them that "OBL was very sick and frequently needed treatment."[106]

He also claimed that the Americans had identified the Abbottabad compound with the willing assistance of Osama's senior wife, Khairiah. Upon her arrival in Abbottabad in February 2011, tensions had erupted between her and Amal, who had accused her rival of having betrayed their husband's location to Iranian and American intelligence. He went on to relate how Khairiah's arrival had particularly spooked Osama's son Khalid, who had challenged her only to be told, "I have one final duty to perform for my husband."

According to Qadir, Amal witnessed this scene and then watched as Khalid warned his father that Khairiah was about to betray him. "So be it," Osama had replied fatalistically.[107]

The companions Ibrahim and Abrar had been in on it, too, Qadir claimed. "They wanted bin Laden gone, and they wanted a share of the $25 million [the reward offered by the United States for his capture]."[108] On the night of the raid, the brothers had not reached for their weapons as they knew the Americans were coming, Qadir claimed he was told by official ISI sources.

A glimpse of another narrative was beginning to emerge from the Abbottabad saga, one that put the CIA firmly in the frame as collaborating with Iran. Only one person could confirm the story: Khairiah bin Laden. But she, Qadir revealed, was once again refusing to cooperate. "She is so aggressive, she borders on being intimidating," a "medium high level officer" in the ISI's counterterrorism wing had told him. "Short of torturing her, we cannot get her to admit to anything."[109]

By the time Abbottabad Commission member Ashraf Qazi was allowed to see the wives in September 2011, they had been in ISI custody for five months. "They were desperate to be released and to return to their families," he reported.[110]

Qazi was not allowed to stay long, recording only glimpses of what life had been like inside Osama's compound; and he never got to ask the most important questions, like what had happened to Hamzah bin Laden or what was in the "significant dossier" the Iranian authorities held on the family and that was referred to in other ISI records.[111] Vital questions about Iran's role in the trapping of Osama remained unanswered, such as how much information Iran had shared with the United States about its transfer of several bin Laden family members to Pakistan in the autumn of 2010.[112]

Qazi argued with the ISI about the relevance of Maryam's seemingly important statement that "visitors" had turned up in Abbottabad just days before the raid—a reference to the brief visit made by Hamzah.

The ISI interrogators had simply dismissed this claim as "the nonsense of a woman" and not worthy of further investigation. Qazi disagreed. Maryam's viewpoint from out in the annex was crucial. When he pushed for access to Maryam, he saw her briefly but she was not allowed to speak freely. Huge gaps in her narrative and that of Osama's wives remained unanswered. "The ISI did not ask many more obvious questions like how [the family] moved around, how Khalid, Hamzah and Saad moved around, how Saad was killed," he complained. Where was Saad bin Laden buried, he asked? No response.

The ISI apparently had Osama's diaries but they, too, were withheld from the commission as were the twenty stacked boxes of files that SEAL Matthew Bissonnette had spotted on the second-floor landing but had not had time to take. These were now in the hands of the ISI and presumably contained a large collection of hugely valuable letters and documents from Osama bin Laden. But they would never be published, or seen again outside Aabpara.

Qazi concluded: "There are questions that the Commission did not put to the wives of OBL and that the intelligence agency had the time and expertise to do so if they had wished."[113] As far as he could see, the ISI's main focus over the five months since Osama's death had been to silence all potentially dangerous witnesses and close down all incriminating lines of inquiry, any one of which might have exposed links between the ISI, Osama bin Laden, and the Al Qaeda and Taliban *shuras*.

November 2011, Islamabad

Amal bin Laden's younger brother Zakariya al-Sadeh flew into Islamabad after being informed by the Yemeni embassy that his sister was about to be released. He claimed that until he saw reports about the Abbottabad raid on TV he had lost touch with her and thought her dead.[114]

Zakariya, a twenty-four-year-old student at Sana'a University, who could not speak English or Urdu and had spent all his money on the plane ticket, was at a loss as to what to do. A Yemeni engineering student who doubled as an IT consultant at the Yemeni embassy took him in.[115]

Zakariya and his new friend, Abdul Rahman, were unsuited for dealing with Pakistani bureaucracy or the ISI.[116] It took them several weeks to negotiate a first visit with Amal—a thirty-minute session that took place in a three-bedroom apartment with no windows. Zakariya was horrified at how damaged his nephews and nieces appeared. "I brought them toys, but they did not know how to play," he recalled. "They had not seen the sun. They were just being kept alive."

He was also shocked at the changes in his sister. Gone was the perky teenager who had neglected her studies and forgotten her *hijab*. Here was a prematurely aged and physically weak woman who seemed so overwhelmed by the present situation and the needs of her children that she sought solace in her Koran.[117]

He demanded that the Yemeni ambassador lobby for better treatment for his sister's leg injury, more suitable accommodation, psychiatrists, and a date for their release. But since the family had not been formally arrested and still floated around in an ISI netherworld, they had no legal status.

Zakariya sought out lawyers willing to work pro bono and spoke to anyone he thought might help. Eventually, he found moral backing in the form of Omar bin Laden, who, having dealt with the Iranians in 2009, now assumed the role of family spokesman, as ever prompted by his fearless British wife, Zaina.

Omar had watched the news about the raid that killed his father from his home in Doha, with Zaina by his side. Although he never spoke to his father again after leaving Kandahar in 2001, he had told Zaina when they met in 2006 that he knew his father was still alive. By 2010, Omar also knew his father was in Pakistan. Although he had spoken publicly against his father, he labeled the American operation as a "criminal mission" that had "obliterated an entire defenseless family" and said that he and his siblings were "not convinced on the available evidence in the absence of a dead body, photographs, and video evidence that our natural father is dead."[118]

But his father's death had far wider ramifications than simply one family's grief, said Omar, warning that without the unifying figure of Osama, even more bloodthirsty Islamists would replace him and run amok. As far as Omar was concerned, killing his father had been a terrible mistake: "Without the head, the arms and legs will run wherever."[119]

Now he requested that family members stuck in Pakistan be given temporary travel documents so they could go to Saudi Arabia.[120] Bakr bin Laden, Osama's elder brother and the powerful head of the family clan, had offered to take some of them in temporarily, so long as they signed agreements never to speak about their experiences. Now that his troublesome brother was finally dead, Bakr wanted the connection between Al Qaeda and the bin Laden family name permanently severed.

Pakistan's president, prime minister, and army chief all refused Ashraf Qazi's requests to appear before the Abbottabad Commission. The only willing attendee was the ISI's General Pasha, who turned up for three sittings and gave a smooth performance. First, he attempted to flatter Qazi by describing the commission's deliberations as "of critical importance" to the ISI's functioning as "the first line of national defense." Then he repeated what he had said to acting CIA director Mike Morell: that during the early years after 9/11, the ISI had established an Osama bin Laden cell to follow its own leads; but that the CIA had shared "disjointed and out of context information," sending his operatives chasing false leads in Sargodha, Lahore, Sialkot, and Gilgit.[121]

When U.S. interest waned as a result of the wars in Iraq and Afghanistan, the ISI came to believe Osama had probably died, confided Pasha. This fitted with preexisting reports that his health was declining, Pasha added, repeating the old Hamid Gul excuse. Osama's name never again came up in CIA–ISI discussions, he said. There had been no indications of his presence or existence in Pakistan. Yet the ISI had steadfastly continued the hunt for him even though America and Pakistan's other security agencies had not.

Digging the knife in, he accused Pakistan's Federal Investigation Agency, Special Branch, Military Intelligence, and Intelligence Bureau of all failing in their duties to locate Osama. The regular police, which had "tentacles down" to the local level should have picked up chatter about Osama's presence in Abbottabad, he said, but instead they worked in "pathetic conditions." He reserved the harshest criticism for the Special Branch, which was responsible for conducting sweeps around the area of the Pakistan Military Academy ahead of VIP visits. They—not the ISI—should have located Osama in Bilal Town.

Asked why he thought the United States had gone it alone with the Abbottabad raid and not informed the ISI in advance, Pasha came up with an inventive response. President Barack Obama had not wanted the ISI to claim the glory of finding Osama and win the laurels, he said with a broad smile, before making way for a lieutenant general, who came to inform the commission about the army's own internal review of the raid.

The lieutenant general concluded that he had found no evidence that any religious group or faction within the armed forces had "provided any kind of protection or support to OBL during his stay in Pakistan." The army was "disciplined and organized" and functioned "in accordance with laid down procedures," he commented. A system of checks and monitoring was in place at all tiers of its command structure. It was "possible" that some retired officers could have been involved in a support network. But given that the army had suffered considerably at the hands of Al Qaeda and militants, he believed this to be "unlikely, if not unthinkable."

The ISI had done a tremendous job in "thwarting the enemy and keeping it at bay."

No one mentioned the directorate's links to Lashkar-e-Taiba, Hafiz Saeed, Ilyas Kashmiri, Masood Azhar's Jaish-e-Mohammed, the Haqqani network, or Fazlur Rehman Khalil, the founder of Harkat-ul-Mujahideen. No one talked about the role of former ISI director general Hamid Gul or any of the other outfits he and S-Wing had romanced and nurtured as coins in an Islamist war chest to which Osama also had access.

Diplomat Ashraf Qazi was stunned by the performances of General Pasha and his supporters, and he poured his contempt into the commission's draft conclusions. The ISI had "completely failed to track down OBL," leading foreign and domestic critics to reasonably conclude that its operatives were too close to assets in the field who would "never tolerate a betrayal of OBL." As a result, the Pakistan file "was closed on him." The ISI had "neither briefed the government leadership on the status of its information on OBL, nor was it asked to do so." Even after Hillary Clinton had made her sensational accusation in 2010 that Osama was receiving official protection in Pakistan, the ISI had still not "stepped up its efforts to satisfy itself that there was no basis for such accusations."

The "pretense" that the ISI leadership was in command of its field operatives "was exposed by the fact that they dared not offend their most zealous operatives." The handling of the Raymond Davis case was a "national disgrace in which the ISI played an inglorious role." Pasha had lost control of "both violent jihadi militant extremists on the one hand" and "CIA special operatives and dirty tricks killers on the other." Even after the Abbottabad raid, the ISI had failed to investigate anything about Osama's network of support beyond "two dead Pakistani security guards cum couriers."[122] Who, for example, was Mohammed Aslam, the brother's crucial Peshawar-based deputy who had put up Khairiah and Hamzah and his family? No answer.

It was a damning indictment of Pasha's tenure.

Qazi's conclusions were not that different from those of General Javed Alam Khan, the ISI's former director of analysis who had once assisted the

CIA's Robert Grenier on the Al Qaeda file. Forcibly co-opted into the ISI prior to 9/11, the former intelligence chief had been appalled by what he had seen in the days after Tora Bora. A secret General Khan kept from no one these days was his abiding belief that the ISI, despite the conspiracies and mythmaking, was a bantam fighter punching above its weight. Khan cynically thanked ambitious journalists, who, in their desire to woo news desks, fluffed up grandiose stories about the ISI's legendary spying abilities like feather beds, because, frankly, without this free media, replete with suppositions, Grand Guignol, and make-believe, he was absolutely certain that no one outside Pakistan would ever talk about the ISI at all.[123]

Ashraf Qazi saved his most scathing comments for last. Although the commission had found no smoking gun of ISI complicity in hiding Osama, it concluded that "connivance, collaboration and cooperation at some levels" must have existed "on a plausible deniability basis outside government structures." From start to finish the whole Abbottabad episode was "nothing less than a collective and sustained dereliction of duty by the political, military and intelligence leadership of the country."

Having questioned three hundred witnesses and reviewed three thousand official documents, the Abbottabad Commission wrote a final report that would be classified "top secret" and submitted to the prime minister of Pakistan. Anticipating an adverse reaction from the military leadership, Qazi noted in his closing comments "apprehensions that the Commission's report would be ignored, or even suppressed," and he urged the government to release it. However, no details were made public despite numerous requests.

Qazi's damning findings only saw the light of day when a copy of the report was leaked to Al Jazeera.[124] Within minutes of publishing it, Al Jazeera's website was blocked in Pakistan, and page 197 of the report, which contained part of General Pasha's testimony, was missing. It was thought to contain a list of seven demands made by the United States to President Pervez Musharraf in the aftermath of the 9/11 attacks.

No serving ISI officer would ever be held to account for Abbottabad; and, after he gave evidence to the commission, General Pasha never spoke publicly about the Osama bin Laden affair again.

But influential figures outside Pakistan continued to pile on the pressure. When militants from the Haqqani network attacked the U.S. embassy in Kabul later, Admiral Mike Mullen, who had once regarded Pakistan's army chief General Kayani as a friend, told a Senate panel that the Haqqani network was a "veritable arm" of the ISI, which had played a direct role in the attack.

It was the most serious charge that the United States had leveled against Pakistan in a grinding decade of mealymouthed cooperation and horse trading between the two countries. Mullen, who was about to retire, went on to accuse the Pakistan Army and ISI of "choosing to use violent extremism as an instrument of policy." The army and ISI had "eroded their internal security and their position in the region."[125] To reinforce the message, General Pasha was summoned back to Washington and warned that if the ISI did not rein back its Haqqani thugs, American troops were prepared to cross the Afghan border and attack them.

June 2011, Washington, D.C.

After the Abbottabad raid, John Brennan, the president's counterterrorism adviser, had assured reporters that everything that could be told would be told, as "we want to make sure that not only the American people but the world understand exactly what happened." And by June 2011, the White House, CIA, and Pentagon were working closely with filmmakers on a big-budget Hollywood retelling of the raid, provisionally entitled *Killing bin Laden*.

Oscar-winning director Kathryn Bigelow and scriptwriter Mark Boal, who had made *The Hurt Locker*, a tense blockbuster about a U.S. military bomb disposal unit in Iraq, had been deep into a screenplay on America's Tora Bora operation when Abbottabad happened. Existing contacts at the CIA and Defense Department suggested that instead of making a film about how the U.S. military had lost Osama in 2001, they should regear to show how the military had finished him off in 2011.

"I know we don't pick favorites," wrote CIA spokesperson Marie Harf in an internal e-mail backing the new project, "but it makes sense to get behind a winning horse."

Scheduled to open in October 2012, Bigelow's film would be a timely boost for Barack Obama during the forthcoming presidential elections. "Mark and Kathryn's movie is going to be the first and the biggest," said Harf as she recommended they be given exclusive access.[126]

Bigelow and Boal attended private briefings at Langley, meetings arranged despite the previous warnings given to the SEALs about the need to maintain secrecy. During one forty-minute session with Boal, Mike Morell, who was still the CIA's acting director, gushed about how much he had loved *The Hurt Locker*, a film widely praised for its neutral stance on the war in Iraq and that had won six Oscars in 2010. The CIA, now under investigation by the Senate Intelligence Committee for its use of illegal torture techniques during the war on terror, and the Obama administration, suffering in approval ratings, could both do with a little stardust.[127]

Boal spoke to Leon Panetta, who was now secretary of defense and declared himself "very interested in supporting" the film. Plans were made for Bigelow to have dinner with Panetta once a forthcoming trip to Afghanistan was out of the way. Boal also met John Brennan, who promised to make sure that the team's White House material was "in good shape."[128]

To thrash out more details, the Hollywood team sat down with Michael Vickers, who was now the undersecretary of defense for intelligence, on July 15, 2011. Vickers began by apologizing that Admiral McRaven, the brains behind Abbottabad, and his boss, Admiral Eric Olson, the commander of U.S. Special Operations Command, could not be directly involved in the film. "They're just concerned that as commanders of the force and they're telling [SEALs] all the time—don't you dare talk to anyone—that it's just a bad example if it gets out," said Vickers. Instead, Bigelow and her team would be given access to Jay, the SEAL Team Six commander who had lectured his men on keeping a low profile. He could "give you everything you would want or would get from Admiral Olson or Admiral McRaven," Vickers said.[129]

The only restriction was that Jay would have to remain an anonymous consultant. "This gives him one step removed," Vickers continued, "and he knows what he can and can't say . . . It ought to meet your needs and give you lots of color."[130]

Over the following weeks, Boal interviewed five CIA and military operatives involved in the raid, including the Pashto translator. Everyone signed release forms allowing their material to be used, and Boal was invited to a private ceremony feting SEALs from the raid.[131]

Marie Harf's boss, George Little, the CIA's director of public affairs, wrote to Boal on July 20: "I can't tell you how excited we all are (at DOD and CIA) about the project . . . PS—I want you to know how good I've been not mentioning the premiere tickets.:)."[132]

Soon the movie was retitled *Zero Dark Thirty*, military-speak for the exact time of night that the real mission had started. Boal and his team were given access to classified material and were walked around the original Styrofoam-and-clay model of AC1. They also used CIA staff as fact-checkers.

Asked to examine a floor plan for the compound against official records, Harf was more than happy to help: "Looks legit to us."[133]

Boal needed more help with the third-floor layout as open-source material was missing crucial details. "We will be building a full scale replica of the house," he explained. "Including the inhabitants of the animal pen!"[134]

Harf responded minutes later: "Ha! Of course I don't mind! I'll work on that tomorrow."[135]

The Hollywood team also made liberal use of classified CIA and Pentagon interrogation reports on which to base one of their central characters—"Ammar"—an Al Qaeda suspect (a composite of real-life detainees Mohammed al-Qahtani and Hassan Ghul) who was tortured in a cavernous, windowless hangar (the Salt Pit), waterboarded (as was Khalid Shaikh Mohammad), and kept in a coffin-like wooden box (like Abu Zubaydah). After "Ammar" was subjected to these techniques, he revealed critical details of Osama's courier—a clear narrative that suggested the CIA's Enhanced Interrogation Techniques had led investigators directly to the compound, when in reality the most apposite, precious information about the Kuwaiti brothers and Abbottabad had been given voluntarily, long before the torture had started. The rest had been deduced by sparky analysts like Gina Bennett, whose character would be played in the film by Jessica Chastain, or had come down a top secret pipeline from Tehran to Washington, D.C., thanks in part to the trail left by Khairiah bin Laden, who had led Iranian intelligence officials to Abbottabad. In the real story, torture had only occluded witnesses, leading the agency into a dark cul-de-sac from which it clearly hoped that Bigelow would now pull it.

March 2012, Washington, D.C.

While *Zero Dark Thirty* was being filmed on location in India and Jordan in January 2012, John Kiriakou—a former CIA officer who had participated in the initial twenty-four-hour detention of Abu Zubaydah in a Pakistani military hospital in 2002 and who was the first former U.S. government official to reveal the CIA's use of waterboarding during a December 2007 television interview—was charged with repeatedly disclosing classified information to journalists and sentenced to thirty months in prison.[136] In his initial media interview, Kiriakou had condoned such practices, saying they had disrupted "maybe dozens of attacks" and saved American lives. Later, he spoke out against waterboarding and other enhanced techniques, becoming a terrorism consultant for U.S. news channels.

David Petraeus, who had recently taken over as CIA director, was one of many senior public figures who pressed forward to condemn Kiriakou. "Oaths do matter, and there are indeed consequences for those who believe they are above the laws," he said. Several months later, Petraeus would be forced to resign after his affair with his biographer became public along with evidence that he had passed classified secrets to her and committed adultery—which remains an offense triable by court martial.

On the first anniversary of the Abbottabad raid and with President Obama's reelection campaign in full swing, seventeen letters from Osama bin Laden's compound were cherry-picked for release via the Combating Terrorism Center based at West Point. They were published under the banner *Letters from Abbottabad: Bin Ladin Sidelined?* with an accompanying narrative suggesting a sharp contrast to previous Pentagon briefings in which Osama had been projected as "al-Qaeda's tactical director."[137] It was the first time anyone outside the CIA's document-sifting team based at the National Media Exploitation Center in McLean, Virginia, had seen anything of the million-plus documents recovered from ten hard drives, one hundred thumb drives and data cards, as well as printed material. Most of the published letters appeared to show a man at the end of his useful life.

To reinforce the message that Osama had been a peripheral figure in his twilight days, David Ignatius of the *Washington Post* was given advance sight of the Abbottabad letters and wrote an article, "Osama bin Laden, a Lion in Winter," revealing the Al Qaeda leader's frustration at his inability to control his jihadist "brothers" acting throughout the region.[138]

From then until the president's reelection in November 2012, countless official briefings presented bin Laden as having spent his last years pacing in his courtyard, watching television, and dictating messages to people who no longer listened. A giant of a man had become a frustrated introvert who frittered away his time on domestic dramas, watched porn, dyed his hair and beard back to black, and recorded faltering video statements that were never aired. According to the carefully chosen declassified letters, he had lost his momentum, and he had lost Al Qaeda, too. He had spent the days before his death in bitter reflection.

One of the many high-ranking officials who demanded a fuller picture of what the Abbottabad documents really revealed was Bruce Riedel, a former CIA analyst with three decades' experience who had served as a special assistant to President Clinton at the time of the 1998 U.S. embassy attacks and who President Obama had appointed in 2009 to overhaul U.S. policy on Afghanistan and Pakistan. Riedel was amazed at the material that he saw and shocked by how little was being done to analyze this unique intelligence material. "While I was sensitive to the needs of live operations," he recalled, "it became clear to me that they wanted to edit the story according to the political objectives of the West Wing."[139]

The message that Al Qaeda was finished and that the United States had won the war against Islamist terrorist began to unravel after *Zero Dark Thirty* came out in December 2012, with an opening credit proclaiming that it was "based on firsthand accounts." Almost immediately, it was lambasted for being "a false advertisement for waterboarding" and other banned torture techniques.[140] Senator Dianne Feinstein, who had just submitted a six-thousand-page report on CIA torture to the Senate Intelligence Committee, wrote to Sony Pictures chairman and CEO Michael Lynton, calling the film "grossly inaccurate and misleading" and asking for details of what help the CIA had given to the film's director and screenwriter. A Freedom of Information Act request forced the U.S. government to further open up, and the newly reelected President Obama was also accused of having leaked classified information for political gain during the first exhilarating days after Osama's death, when everything, it seemed, had been up for grabs: the identification of the raid team as SEAL Team Six, how they had traveled to Abbottabad, what weapons and equipment they had used, how they had taken down the building and with what tactics, even down to the name of the attack dog—a Belgian Malinois called Cairo.[141]

Watching the Hollywood-CIA tryst, the president's reelection campaigning, Kiriakou's fall from grace, and the overt reframing of Osama, SEALs also began to break their codes of silence. Writing under the pseudonym Mark Owen, Matthew Bissonnette published a book—*No Easy Day*—in which he described himself as the second man into Osama's bedroom, making no reference to Robert O'Neill or his rival's claims to have fired the fatal shot.[142]

The first that the Pentagon knew of Bissonnette's book was when George Little, now Leon Panetta's chief spokesman, spotted the press release. The author had failed to submit his manuscript for official editing and was "in material breach of his secrecy agreements with the United States government," Little warned, without reference to how he had facilitated Kathryn Bigelow and Mark Boal's access to classified CIA material.

Bissonnette was on the rack. "We believe that sensitive and classified information is in the book," said Little.

The former SEAL reacted furiously, saying that he had felt compelled to speak after watching inaccurate stories about the raid, many of them spun by government officials without the clearance to know the truth. He complained about the "inconsistencies" regarding who was and was not allowed to talk. "Everybody and their brother was talking about this," he said in a later television interview. "How can you be holding it against me?"[143]

Bissonnette and six other SEALs who had participated in the raid had their salaries docked as punishment for working as paid consultants for a video game entitled *Medal of Honor: Warfighter*.

February 2013

Former SEAL Robert O'Neill was the next to break cover, telling *Esquire* magazine that he was speaking out because so many before him had benefited from his story and yet he faced an uncertain future. "No pension, no healthcare for his wife and kids, no protection for himself or his family," wrote interviewer Phil Bronstein, who identified O'Neill not by name but as "the Shooter." The best offer of future employment and protection from any Al Qaeda retaliation that SEAL command had come up with so far was a witness-protection-like scheme in which O'Neill could drive a beer truck in Milwaukee. However, he would never be able to have contact with his family or friends again.

O'Neill decided to go it alone, recasting himself as a motivational speaker, traveling the country giving paid speeches on the unspoken understanding that he was the man who had killed Osama. He would soon become embroiled in a public row with Bissonnette as they clashed over the exact circumstances of Osama's killing. Bissonnette had said it did not matter who had pulled the trigger as it was "not about who that one person was—it was about the team."[144] O'Neill disagreed and finally went public in a Fox News interview in November 2014, sticking to his story that he had fired the fatal shot.

"Two different people telling two different stories for two different reasons," responded Bissonnette in an interview to promote his second book,

No Hero, published in November 2014. "Whatever he says, he says. I don't want to touch that."

Both men received stinging letters from Naval Special Warfare Command: "We do not abide willful or selfish disregard for our core values in return for public notoriety and financial gain," wrote Rear Admiral Brian Losey and Master Chief Michael Magaraci. "A critical [tenet] of our Ethos is 'I do not advertise the nature of my work, nor seek recognition for my actions.' "[145] In 2016, Bissonnette agreed to pay back to the federal government at least $6.8 million in book royalties and other publication profits under a deal to avoid prosecution for not getting prepublication approval for *No Easy Day*.[146] He was also ordered to hand over a photograph he had taken of Osama bin Laden's body and kept on his hard drive.[147]

To O'Neill, Bissonnette, and others who had played integral roles in America's war on terror, it appeared that their paymasters were happy to condone misinformation for political gain at the same time as pursuing a policy to shut down those who wished to tell another version of the story.

One rule to bind them all. But another for the White House. In early 2017, O'Neill revealed that he, too, had written a book that would include his account of the killing of Osama bin Laden. This one had been approved by the U.S. military and was entitled *The Operator*.

CHAPTER TWELVE

*"It is going to be worse when my father dies.
The world is going to be very, very nasty . . . it
will be a disaster."*

—OMAR BIN LADEN,

SPEAKING IN 2010

*May 2011, Tourist Complex, Quds Force
Training Facility, Tehran, Iran*

MAHFOUZ THE MAURITANIAN AND SAIF AL-ADEL had stayed up through the night to watch rolling reports on Osama's killing. After so much uplifting news about the Arab Spring, his death winded them. "Eventually, I had to turn off the TV," Mahfouz said. "We became too angry."

While his wife comforted Osama's daughter Fatima, the Mauritanian reflected on the man who had once been his friend. "As a man of prayer, my neighbor, and a man of spiritual knowledge, I loved him," he recalled.[1] He regretted the harsh words that had marred their last meeting in July 2001. He also worried for himself. Like everyone else in the compound, he was desperate to get back out into the jihad arena and shape Al Qaeda's now uncertain future; but if he did, would the Americans come for him, too?[2]

He fretted over the incriminating material the CIA might recover from Abbottabad: evidence of his failed attempt to relocate Osama's fortune from Sudan in 1997, the counterfeiting operation he had subsequently helped Dr. al-Zawahiri set up, and his undeclared assistance in the East Africa bombings. Whether he had simply run the telephone exchange for the operation or marshaled the funding for it, he had spoken of it to no one. But if he ever left the protective bubble of Iran he would have to confront it.

He wondered if he would end up in Guantánamo like his old friend and brother-in-law, Mohamedou Ould Slahi, who had sworn allegiance to Al

455

Qaeda and joined the jihad with his encouragement. Later, Slahi had left the outfit, only to be arrested weeks after 9/11, accused of involvement in an unsuccessful plot to bomb Los Angeles International Airport in 1999. He had been rendered to Jordan, then taken to Bagram, and eventually moved to Guantánamo, where he was held in extreme isolation, deprived of sleep, and in his waking hours was physically, psychologically, and sexually humiliated.[3] In one incident, he was taken out into the Gulf of Mexico and subjected to a mock execution.

The Tourist Complex became a place of building paranoia. The women suffered particularly, barely able to believe that Osama, Khalid, Saad, and Khadija bin Laden all were dead. Khairiah, Amal, Seham, and their children were still missing as far as they knew—with many of those still in Iran convinced that Khairiah, wittingly or not, had led the Americans to Abbottabad. Finally there was Hamzah, about whom no one had heard anything. The only lucky ones were Osama's sons Othman and Mohammed, who, together with their families, had quietly flown out of Pakistan on commercial flights in the chaotic few days after the killing of their father and now shared a compound with Zaina and Omar bin Laden in Doha, where they had been reunited with their mother, Najwa, and younger siblings.

To cheer up the children who remained in Tehran, their mothers allowed them to bring their pet rabbits into their apartments, dressing them up in necklaces, tinsel, and watches.[4] "As the number of prisoners reduced, the rabbits took over," recalled the Mauritanian ruefully.

Fatima bin Laden, who had been left bereft by the deaths, especially her "twin" Khadija, relentlessly watched the TV for updates about those still trapped in Pakistan, neglecting her small daughter, Najwa, who ran around dressed in a romper decorated with hearts.[5]

Fatima's husband, Sulaiman Abu Ghaith, once Osama's accidental spokesman, was no comfort as he had fallen into a deep, self-absorbed depression, certain that he too would be given the Slahi treatment sooner or later. He was also back to obsessing about his first wife and seven children.[6]

When photographs from Abbottabad—including a gruesome shot of Khalid bin Laden lying dead in a pool of blood—were splashed all over the news, everyone crashed again.

Another disturbing image depicted three of Khadija's four orphaned children—Abdallah, Osama, and Fatima, the twin who had survived her mother's death, holed up in an ISI safe house. Amal's brother Zakariya had managed to sneak the photograph on his phone. They stood beside Amal's youngest three—Ibrahim, Zainab, and Hussein—six children with blank faces whose lives had taken another irrevocable turn into the unknown.[7]

To break the funk that had settled over the compound, Quds Force commander General Qassem Suleimani ordered his deputies to take the Al Qaeda women and children on outings, arranging visits to the zoo, a riding stable, and even an amusement park on the top floor of an upmarket Tehran mall.

While they were away, the Mauritanian, Saif al-Adel, and other members of the Al Qaeda *shura* debated in the *majlis*.[8] The global jihad was morphing. All of them could see it from Al Jazeera and Press TV. The martyrdom of Osama should be seen not as a catastrophic setback but as a springboard, said Saif. Al Qaeda could use the anger to galvanize support. When Osama was alive they had all referred to him as the "Reviving Sheikh," reinvigorating the idea of jihad among the worldwide *ummah*.[9] By constantly reminding Muslims of "the sinful crime committed in Abbottabad by the Crusader Americans," he could still be the Reviving Sheikh. They came up with a campaign: "We Are All Osama."[10]

With regard to mounting fresh attacks, Saif argued, they had the means to do this right in front of them. We, he said, taking in his fellow captives, are best placed to utilize this strategic tool. Between them, they had enough battlefield experience to open up a new front in another country and guide those already started. Al Qaeda's future wars would not be revenge for "Osama the person" but revenge for "all those who defended Islam, its sanctities and honor."

General Suleimani had made it clear on more than one occasion that Iran was ready to help if it, too, benefited. The question was where should they regroup now that Pakistan was a no-go area? They had to assume that every telephone number, safe house, courier, and smuggling route there was compromised given that, since Osama's death, there had been no letup in drone strikes.

Eight days after a video had been posted on jihadi websites officially proclaiming Dr. Ayman al-Zawahiri as Osama's successor and Atiyah as his Number Two, the latter had been killed in a drone strike in North Waziristan along with his entire family.[11] They had been traveling in a car along the same death-run between Mir Ali and Miram Shah where so many others had previously been killed, targeted just as they passed the village of Naurak. Atiyah's fate had been sealed when the CIA discovered clues as to his location in the letters recovered from Abbottabad.

Another reason to leave Iran was that the Iranian government was coming under increased U.S. pressure to act against the Al Qaeda presence there. In July 2011, the U.S. Treasury Department accused Tehran of supporting a network that "serves as the core pipeline through which al-Qa'ida moves money, facilitators and operatives" from the Middle East to its bases in Pakistan and Afghanistan.[12] Since the Iranians were allowing their territory to be used by this network, "I think it stands to reason that Iran is getting something out of this as well," said a senior U.S. official, naming six newly sanctioned individuals including the linchpin, Ezedin Abdel Aziz Khalil— aka Yasin al-Suri.[13] Two of his main funders were based in Qatar, one in Iraq, and another in Kuwait.[14]

To test the Iranian's resolve, Saif suggested that one of them should attempt to leave the country. The only person able to travel freely, as he did not face an international arrest warrant (although he was sanctioned), was the Mauritanian.[15] He could justifiably claim that as a religious adviser he had never been involved in actual terrorist operations. After witnessing an attempt to assassinate Osama in Khartoum in 1994, he had carried a gun; but he had never used it. Dozens of eyewitnesses (many of whom were now in Guantánamo) could attest to how he had publicly disagreed with Osama over the 9/11 attacks. It was his get-out and he would milk it for all it was worth. But although he could see the logic, he was still daunted about leaving ahead of the others.

Urged on by Saif, he tried the simplest way first, asking the authorities if he could fly home to see his father, who was sick. General Suleimani's security officials refused. For the past nine years, the Mauritanian had been their main intermediary with the rest of the troublesome Al Qaeda group. To persuade him to stay, they offered new privileges, moving him and his family out of the compound into a two-story villa located in District 9, a smart residential suburb close to Tehran Imam Khomeini International Airport. They remained under guard—with the escorts living beneath them on the ground floor—but it was their first taste of freedom in almost a decade.

"We could see the street and people walking about," said Mahfouz, who began receiving a steady stream of important visitors: politicians, security officials, and religious scholars who all lectured him on staying put. If Al Qaeda wanted to retain Tehran's backing, he had to play his part, they said.

Concerned about maintaining contact with those still inside the Tourist Complex, he turned to devious means.[16] All detainees were allowed to write e-mails, which were saved on USB sticks so they could be vetted by

Iranian officials before being sent. Since the officials used the same sticks to save the Mauritanian's correspondence and those inside the compound, he found he could read their messages. He also used the trusted old method of logging into shared e-mail accounts and writing mails in draft. He sneaked letters into the Al Qaeda box at Tehran's central post office, where he was taken, weekly, to pick up his own.[17]

"When are you leaving?" Saif wrote repeatedly.

In October 2011, the Mauritanian was informed that his home government had agreed to take him back if he submitted to being tried under local laws. Over there he was famous and he hoped that unlike Slahi, he would be able to cut a deal. Once more he approached his Iranian hosts. He wanted a private charter plane to take him home, as he was too frightened of CIA spies to take a commercial flight. He still had nightmares about his lucky escape from a Khartoum hotel in 1998, when the CIA had sent a team to render him as a result of the Africa embassy bombings, missing him by minutes through the kitchen door. It could have all ended so differently.

The Quds Force refused. To travel by air necessitated the Iranian government issuing temporary identity documents, and that would leave an untidy paper trail. When he insisted, they came back with another suggestion. He could travel overland via Turkey, guided by people smugglers.[18]

The Mauritanian, a cautious man, dithered. The only ID papers he had were his old student cards from Nouakchott and Khartoum, and his children, who had all been born in Afghanistan or Iran, had no passports at all. He dared not entrust their lives to a criminal network.

In November 2011, the Iranian government allowed the Mauritanian's family to fly home on the condition that he stay behind. In an agonizing farewell, he saw his wife and six children off, left alone for the first time since 2002. "I wandered around looking at all their toys and pens and schoolbooks, [and] each time I saw them a wave of frustration came over me."

When he heard they had safely reached Nouakchott, he put all their things into one room of the apartment and locked the door, so as not to be distracted by memories. With limited Internet and phone access, he began contacting old friends outside of Iran, cross-checking with Saif and other *shura* members via secret notes, and discovering that Al Qaeda's Pakistan operation had been pummeled yet again. Younis al-Mauritani, who was responsible for launching new terror plots in Europe via Iran and recruiting for a new Al Qaeda youth wing, had been captured by the ISI in Quetta and handed to the CIA, their first collaboration since Abbottabad.[19]

The spring 2011 edition of Al Qaeda in the Arabian Peninsula's propaganda magazine *Inspire* had carried an article declaring that the Arab Spring "has proved that Al Qaeda's rage is shared by the millions of Muslims across the world."[20] But by the fall of 2011, the outfit was reeling.[21]

To encourage Tehran to tackle its ongoing Al Qaeda connections, the U.S. Rewards for Justice program offered a $10 million bounty for Yasin al-Suri, who was picked up in Tehran in December 2011. The news jolted the Mauritanian into a realization that leaving Iran was now essential, and his escorts sensed his agitation, one of them telling him, "If you are going to flee, don't do it on my watch!"

But after many years together, some of them had become sloppy. During the daily changeover the new man on duty in the District 9 apartment would always come up for a cup of tea, bringing the front door key with him. "I thought about locking him in a room and breaking out," Mahfouz recalled.[22]

In January 2012, he had a better idea. Every afternoon, he and the duty escort visited the nearby Zeytoon-e-Artesh sports center, where they swam and relaxed in a *hammam*. Most escorts took his locker key to ensure that his clothes remained out of reach. However, his favorite guard was more lax.

On January 30, Mahfouz stayed up late, destroying digital files and burning documents. "I recorded all my most precious things onto an orange USB stick." He hid it in his shoe.[23] On the morning of February 1, he took a piece of frozen meat from the fridge and left it on a plate to thaw, "so if I got caught I could say they misunderstood the situation as I'd got my dinner waiting to cook in the evening." To shore up his cover story, he packed a broken radio in with his sports kit. "If they find me in the street," he told himself, "I can say I was heading to get it fixed." He knew in his heart that he would fold if captured and suspected that a life of facing interrogators around the clock in Evin prison would be just as bad as doing time in Guantánamo.

When they set off for the sports center that afternoon, he had a pang of guilt. The escort beside him would be severely punished if he bolted. He asked to go into a store and bought a bottle of expensive aftershave. "I have to give him something *precious*," the Mauritanian told himself.

"This is for you," he said, handing it to the escort.

"Why?" the man said, surprised at the gift.

"Take it *please*," the Mauritanian urged.

"It's not my birthday," the escort replied, laughing.

"*Take it please*," he insisted. "This is to mark your everyday kindness that does not go unnoticed."

The escort smiled. "Okay," he said, taking the package.

As they passed a smart restaurant, the escort stopped again. "Because you bought me this gift," he said, "I will host you at dinner tonight." The Mauritanian felt sick. He was planning to be at the Mauritanian embassy before nightfall.

At the sports center, the two men entered the changing rooms. "I told him I hadn't prayed yet and would go to the mosque inside the complex," he recalled. While the escort went off to the *hammam* and "disappeared into a cloud of steam," the Mauritanian slipped his locker key into the pocket of his trunks and headed the other way.

Moments later he was back in the locker room, dressing as quickly as he could. Walking out through the turnstile with his head lowered, he felt his whole body shaking. He hailed a cab and doubted his chances of success. "Downtown!" he told the driver, thinking of the small matter of the November 2001 interview he had given to Al Jazeera in which he had claimed that the war against America had only just begun: "We are lying in wait for them, *inshallah*."[24]

Who, the Mauritanian wondered, would be lying in wait for him?

Fall 2011, Federally Administered Tribal Areas, Pakistan

Shortly after taking over as Al Qaeda's emir in June 2011, Dr. al-Zawahiri had given a video address warning that Osama would continue to "terrify" the United States from beyond the grave. But with the losses of Atiyah, Younis al-Mauritani, and Yasin al-Suri in Iran, nothing seemed further from the truth at that moment. The franchises in Yemen and North Africa that had announced their intention of declaring their own Islamic states were also suffering setbacks.

Al Shabaab had tried to dominate southern Somalia, but in late 2011 Kenyan forces, backed by U.S drone strikes, isolated the group in a remote corner of the country. Nasir al-Wuhayshi's Al Qaeda in the Arabian Peninsula (AQAP) had come closer to success, declaring several "emirates" after Osama forbade him to create a caliphate. But in truth, most Yemenis were fearful of Wuhayshi's fighters, especially after a man was executed for spying and several women were stoned to death for witchcraft, leading southern tribal militias to rebel. By the time AQAP's Yemeni-American cheerleader Anwar al-Awlaki was killed in September 2011, the nascent state had collapsed.[25]

Soon after, it was the turn of Al Qaeda in the Islamic Maghreb (AQIM), with Wuhayshi writing to his Algerian counterpart, who had seized control of a large chunk of northern Mali, "The places under your control are a model for an Islamic state. The world is waiting to see what you'll do next."[26] But as *hudud* laws bit in northern Mali and AQIM razed the shrines of local Muslim saints, women who previously had been happy to cover up removed their veils in protest. No one wanted Afghanistan in Africa. Crowds gathered outside mosques to bar the jihadists from praying. They intervened to prevent stonings and amputations.

Al Qaeda commentators argued that these failures demonstrated that Osama had been right to discourage his affiliates from establishing Islamic states before they had deep popular support. His erstwhile competitors interpreted them as evidence that Al Qaeda had not been sufficiently brutal.

Now that the real axis for jihad was rapidly shifting thousands of miles away to new theaters in Iraq and Syria, Dr. al-Zawahiri would have to take advantage.

Fall 2011, Mosul, Iraq

Just days after the raid on Abbottabad, Abu Bakr al-Baghdadi, the leader of Islamic State of Iraq, had issued a eulogy for Osama, and his forces appeared to demonstrate their loyalty by launching a wave of suicide bombers and IED blasts that slaughtered hundreds in Mosul and Baghdad. Dr. al-Zawahiri responded by sending Abu Bakr $2 million a month from donors in Qatar.[27] Abu Bakr took every penny, which arrived via the Iran network. But in reality he was actively plotting to undermine the Al Qaeda leader.

First, he asked his religious adviser, the thirty-year-old Turki al-Bin'ali, to provide "proofs" that he was descended from the Prophet, going against

Al Qaeda's instructions that no one should declare themselves a caliph. Second, he issued orders that senior commanders in Iraq who were loyal to Dr. al-Zawahiri should be sidelined or allowed to die in battle.[28] Most of Abu Bakr's brutal street fighters, who were drawn from irreligious Ba'athists who had fought for Saddam Hussein and were paid to be loyal, happily complied. Islamic State's new field commanders had agendas different from al-Zawahiri's: two of Abu Bakr's uncles had served in Saddam's state security apparatus and one of his brothers had been an officer in the Iraqi army. The ground forces were led by Hajji Bakr, the white-bearded former colonel in Saddam's army who had championed Abu Bakr's appointment and was referred to as the Prince of Shadows.

At the end of 2011, when the United States declared Abu Bakr was a Specially Designated Global Terrorist and offered $10 million for his capture, Al Qaeda was still paying the Islamic State to represent its interests there, but al-Zawahiri's influence was shrinking.[29]

January 2012, Syria

Abu Bakr had unilaterally decided to enter the fray in Syria. Late in 2011, he dispatched Abu Mohammad al-Julani, his top commander in Mosul—a Syrian national and former close associate of Abu Musab al-Zarqawi—to recruit two hundred former Al Qaeda members recently released from Sednaya, the country's most notorious military prison. The amnesty had been a deliberate move by President Bashar al-Assad to foster violence among the street protesters. But Abu Bakr had spotted an opportunity too.

Julani, who had grown up in Damascus where his family ran a grocery store, met the Al Qaeda prisoners in the countryside outside Damascus at Reef Dimashq and then again in Homs. To inspire them, he took along veterans from Zarqawi's old Iraq network.[30] The new outfit tested the water in December 2011 with a huge suicide attack in Damascus that killed dozens of people. They were ready, and on January 24, 2012, Julani officially launched his force. Although it was tied to Islamic State and Al Qaeda, it would have its own name: Jabhat al-Nusra (the Nusra Front). Within weeks, funds were flowing in directly from Al Qaeda's Iran-based facilitator Yasin al-Suri (who had somehow talked himself out of Iranian detention).[31]

Although he was personally answerable to Abu Bakr, the handsome, smiling Julani was spiritually closer to Al Qaeda and greatly influenced by the writings of Osama's trusted red-haired Syrian theologian Abu Musab al-Suri, a man Dr. al-Zawahiri had once described as the "professor of the mujahideen."

Al-Suri was out of action, still languishing in Sednaya prison.[32] However, his deputy Abu Khalid, who had been captured with him in Pakistan, had recently been released along with the rest of the Al Qaeda cohort and was Julani's most valued strategist and commander.[33]

Abu Khalid and Julani had plenty of shared history, going back to the Al Qaeda training camps of Afghanistan long before 9/11. During the Iraq war, Julani, Khalid, and al-Suri had all acted as logisticians for Zarqawi, managing a network of "guesthouses" in Syria to channel would-be fighters into Iraq, and harvesting finances, too.

Another key figure in the Nusra Front was Zarqawi's childhood friend Iyad al-Toubasi, the former ladies' hairdresser from Zarqa. He was by now the outfit's emir in Damascus and Deraa and led a large cohort of Palestinian-Jordanian fighters, mostly from Zarqa.[34]

Julani's allegiances to Abu Bakr and Islamic State were superficial by comparison. The two men had met in Camp Bucca, the sprawling U.S. internment facility in southern Iraq where many next-generation fighters were radicalized during the Iraq war. There, Julani had taught classical Arabic and fired up those who were not already committed to the fight against U.S. forces, while Abu Bakr led them all in prayer. When he seized control of Islamic State of Iraq in 2010, Abu Bakr appointed Julani as a senior field commander.

In his first few months as leader of the Nusra Front, Julani mirrored Zarqawi's group, with his foot soldiers mercilessly killing hundreds of innocent civilians to make their mark. However, by the summer of 2012 Julani sought a new direction. He beseeched his fighters to read Abu Musab al-Suri's treatise The Call for Global Islamic Resistance, written in Iran in 2003. He had them watch al-Suri's old training videos from the Al Qaeda camps in which he stood at a whiteboard and lectured on the six stages that would have to be surpassed before a caliphate was declared. There were talks on military strategy, with al-Suri trying to wean Al Qaeda off set-piece attacks with many moving parts in favor of what he called "individualized terrorism." Lone-wolf attacks were much more effective as they were harder to stop, he had said. Sleeper cells should be seeded in all major European cities, where they could remain hidden for years before being activated.[35]

Julani declared that he was against needlessly attacking the West as it alienated the international community and aided Assad.[36] His focus was overthrowing the Syrian government.

The Nusra Front would not abuse or exploit its people but provide services, he said. His fighters should maintain strong relationships with their neighborhoods and other fighting groups based there, and they should put the focus on a united struggle against Assad.

Dr. al-Zawahiri was pleased that Al Qaeda seemed to be gaining a new and focused lease on life in Syria. "He was to me and my brothers such a great adviser," the doctor would later remark about Julani's strategist, Abu Khalid al-Suri.[37]

Spring 2012, Islamabad, Pakistan

The old guard was also changing in Pakistan. After four years as ISI director, overseeing one of Pakistan's most tumultuous periods and causing the nadir of the ISI's relations with the CIA, General Pasha was stepping down after he and his boss, army chief General Kayani, failed to squeeze through a third extension to his tenure.

Even though the CIA and ISI had briefly come together to capture Al Qaeda's Younis al-Mauritani in Quetta, the military's relations with the United States remained in tatters. A U.S.-led NATO skirmish against the Taliban on the Pakistan border in November 2011 had resulted in the killing of twenty-four Pakistani soldiers. Military chief Kayani had flown to Washington to protest, achieved little, and returned to find Pasha moving furniture about at Aabpara and landscaping in Abbottabad. The outgoing ISI chief ordered demolition crews into Bilal Town on February 27 and leaked a series of bizarre stories, including a claim that during one last sweep of Osama's compound before razing it to the ground, bibles had been found hidden in walls. They supposedly contained coded clues about future terror attacks in Europe and America, although Pasha refused to give any further details.

Instead, the ISI began briefing foreign reporters, building up its version of the Abbottabad raid, telling a British tabloid newspaper that Amal and Khairiah had been caught fighting in their safe house, where they were still imprisoned.

"Amal described Khairiah as 'the real killer of bin Laden,'" the newspaper duly reported. "Khairiah accused Amal of sticking to Osama like a prostitute who wanted sex 24 hours a day." Amal had to be "pulled apart from . . . Khairiah after the pair began brawling."[38] Both inside and outside the safe house things were coming to a head.

On the evening of March 2, two weeks before Pasha's formal retirement date, a Pakistani lawyer employed by Amal's brother Zakariya was informed that the wives' cases would now be heard—the following day.[39] After ten months of drifting in unofficial custody, the family's case was suddenly "urgent." A First Information Report (FIR) had been hastily prepared and it accused the women of technical charges including "illegal entry into Pakistan without any valid travel documents" as well as misrepresenting themselves to doctors when they gave birth.[40]

Zakariya was amazed, as for the past three months he had been prevented from having any contact with his sister or her children.[41] When the Islamabad district courts opened at eight the next morning, Zakariya and his lawyer arrived to find Rehman Malik, Pakistan's interior minister, addressing reporters. Zakariya challenged him, as his sister's repatriation order required Malik's signature.[42]

Malik shook Zakariya's hand and smiled for the cameras. General Pasha, who had only just informed Malik that his ministry was now in charge of Osama's family, had caught him out and he was doing what he did best, talking himself out of trouble.

Knowing that the women and children could not be slung in a regular jail, which would be bad publicity, Malik had called up an old acquaintance, Yaqoob Tabani, one of the richest men in Pakistan. Malik knew Tabani owned several luxurious villas in Islamabad, some of which were empty. "I have some foreign friends coming to the city," said Malik casually. "Can you look after them for a few days?"

Tabani agreed. "They turned up with the police that evening, I couldn't believe it," he recalled.[43] That night he learned from the news that Malik's supposed friends were actually the wives and children of Osama bin Laden.

He had already handed over the keys to a house located behind his own villa on Atatürk Avenue in the exclusive G-6 neighborhood, and now he watched as a huge crowd descended on the pavement outside his gates, scanned by the ISI.

The next day he was horrified to learn that his home had been redesignated as a judicial lockup. "Rehman Malik apologized and told me it would be over in a few days. But the women brought furniture, dozens of religious books, and put grilles up on all the windows."

Over the following weeks, judges, lawyers, security officials, and embassy personnel converged on Tabani's villa, all of them put in their place by the grim-faced International Islamic University professor, Dr. Zaitoon Begum, who had befriended Khairiah during the Abbottabad Commission hearings. "A curtain was strung up in the living room and the case against the women was held right there, the women behind it," said Tabani, who watched discreetly from his adjoining property.[44]

While several references had been made in the FIR to "others who made arrangements for securing and facilitating their illegal entry into Pakistan and subsequently harbored them at different places," the temporary court made no attempt to identify these "others."

At the end of the case, the widows and Osama's adult daughters Sumaiya and Miriam were each handed a forty-five-day detention notice and a fine of 10,000 Pakistani rupees ($100).[45] They would serve their short sentences in situ as the villa was now reclassified as a sub-jail.

Barring travel documents that would have to be provided by the Saudi and Yemeni embassies, it was all settled.[46] Distracting attention away from questions about ISI collusion, Pasha's deputies released a video purporting to be of the women, but starring actors dressed up in *abayas* and *niqabs* praying and corralling children who looked nothing like Osama's youngest offspring and were all the wrong ages.[47] The ISI also released "transcripts" of Amal's interrogation. "Osama loved me the most," she allegedly told her questioners. "We used to talk about romance . . . apart from Al Qaeda things." In the last days, "he was ready to face death." Echoing the private fears of *shura* members still in Tehran, the ISI insinuated that it was the Iranians who had found Osama, not the CIA.

Asked about the ongoing search for Dr. Ayman al-Zawahiri, General Pasha lobbed one final grenade: "ISI is working hard to locate him," he said, but the "US is continuing to withhold vital information from the ISI and could be planning another assault somewhere in Pakistan."

Finally, Pasha's successor was announced.[48] For the next three years, the job of guarding Pakistan's tower of secrets would fall to Zahir ul-Islam, a general who had been responsible for the country's internal security during the Abbottabad period.

* * *

April 27, 2012, Islamabad

Almost a year after his killing, Osama's family was deported from Pakistan. As an excited crowd of journalists gathered outside Tabani's villa in G-6, Osama's youngest sons, Hussein and Ibrahim, looked out through curtained windows.

Making efforts to maintain the women's modesty, police and guards strung plastic sheets and blankets across the driveway, and through this impromptu structure that resembled a soccer tunnel, the family trooped onto a curtained bus. Once everyone was on board, it charged off down the Islamabad Highway and deposited the family at the airport, where they boarded a private jet bound for Jeddah.

Waiting at the other end were Omar and his mother, Najwa. Zaina had sensibly decided to stay away. Osama bin Laden's older brother Bakr offered the returning wives three houses in the vast bin Laden family compound on the outskirts of Jeddah.[49] After they settled in, he paid for the whole family to go on *umrah* (pilgrimage) to Mecca, but when they returned, Najwa decided to leave. The day after the Abbottabad raid her mother had died of shock at home in Latakia, and Najwa could not help but associate the bin Ladens with that loss. Having spent time in Mecca with Khairiah, she was also convinced that the "old sourpuss," as she called her elder sister-wife, had cost Osama his life, although she did not understand the intricacies of what had happened. Doha—with its palm-fringed Corniche, smart malls, fancy Western restaurants, and relative-free living—represented a fresh start.

She moved permanently into Omar and Zaina's West Bay Lagoon compound, leaving behind her daughter, Iman, who had recently married a bin Laden cousin.

All that remained of the bin Ladens' time in Pakistan were the religious books, towels, broken teacups, and pieces of discarded furniture that littered Tabani's house.[50] Jewelry held by the ISI was not returned to the wives as promised but sold to a gold dealer in Rawalpindi. The land where the Abbottabad compound had stood reverted to the Cantonment Board—meaning it went back to the military.

But it wasn't all over for everyone.

A few weeks after Osama's family departed, Dr. Shakil Afridi, the doctor who had unwittingly helped the CIA, appealed his thirty-three-year sentence. When Fox News managed to smuggle a phone into his cell, he said he had been kept in an ISI lockup for more than a year and was being tortured.

ISI sources told reporters that Afridi was a hard-drinking womanizer of bad repute who in the past had faced accusations of sexual assault, harassment, and stealing.[51] They said his main obsession was making easy money. Later, in May 2015, Afridi's lawyer was shot dead in Peshawar.[52]

Having cleared his desk, General Pasha walked out of Aabpara in March 2012, securing a lucrative contract to advise the Dubai government on "intelligence matters."[53] Despite the Abbottabad fiasco and the findings of the Abbottabad Commission, that year he was named as among the top one hundred "most powerful and influential people" in the world by *Time* and *Forbes*, ahead of President Barack Obama and CIA director David Petraeus.

April 2012, Nouakchott, Mauritania

From the sports complex in Tehran, the Mauritanian had reached his embassy, where he ran inside and demanded asylum. "My mother tongue was a little shrunk but they brought me a *boubou* [traditional robe]," he recalled. He felt like a character from the Old Testament: "People who lived alone many years in a cave. It was the same for me."

Mauritanian diplomats got him out of Iran on April 4, 2012, flying him on a commercial carrier that made stops in the Middle East and North Africa. Every time he stepped off the plane, he broke into a sweat, expecting to be seized by the CIA. At Nouakchott's tin-roofed international airport, he was welcomed like a homecoming hero and then escorted away by security officials, although no one pretended he was going to jail for long.

"My judgment was based on a mutual understanding between me and the Mauritanian authorities," he recalled. What followed was a lengthy interview with the prosecutor and his deputy. "I answered most questions and refused to answer some others." He trotted out a few old Al Qaeda snippets like his story of opposing 9/11 and resigning, but nothing more.

To maintain the appearance of judicial process he was held for a few weeks in a secret prison in the capital, where he was locked up with Abdullah al-Senusi, Muammar Gaddafi's brother-in-law and until recently Libya's notorious spy chief. He had fled after Gaddafi had been captured and bloodily executed in October 2011, arriving in Nouakchott disguised as a Tuareg chieftain.[54]

The prisoners circled one another for a few hours but soon began debating Al Qaeda, Osama bin Laden, the Arab Spring, and the future of the global jihad.

In May 2012, the authorities announced the Mauritanian's release if he agreed to one condition: meeting a delegation from the U.S. embassy. "It will be a short session," assured a security official. "You are free to say what you want. How about it?"[55] He was shocked. "I came back on the understanding that the only body authorized to consider my case is the Mauritanian judiciary," he replied haughtily.

When the officials made clear that without this meeting he was going nowhere, he consented. But as a matter of pride, he requested the Americans arrive first.

They met on May 26 at a government office. As he shook hands with five U.S. officials, one of them, an FBI officer of Lebanese descent, stepped forward and told him in Arabic that he was the luckiest man alive. "If you knew how many plots there have been to kill you, you would be amazed," he said.[56]

The first question was the kind of thing Osama would have asked: general, sweeping, and thorny. "How can we end the war in Afghanistan?"

He slipped back into his old speechifying. "When you invade great countries like Iraq and kill thousands of innocent people, what consequences do you expect? Billions of violent people will emerge from all over the world to fight you."

It felt good to be lecturing again; but the Americans looked bored. They switched to Iran, asking why Al Qaeda had been allowed to stay there for so long.

"We were their 'trump card,'" he boasted, "ready to wave around and play whenever they needed." Their presence had bought protection for Iran against Al Qaeda attacks and increased Iran's influence in the region. He said nothing about Zarqawi or the funding pipeline. He made no mention of the secret deals with Iran or his personal relationship with General Qassem Suleimani.

When the Americans asked about Saif al-Adel, Sulaiman Abu Ghaith, and other *shura* members still in Iran, he grew irritated. "I don't have contact with them now," he snapped. "They are only allowed to write e-mails to close friends and family. They are censored."

The U.S. delegation became restless. "You're covering up for killers and criminals," an official snapped. Another accused him of deceiving his own government, alleging that his real intention was to assist Al Qaeda in Mali. The Mauritanian shook his head. "I've retired," he said. "I left Al Qaeda because of my religious convictions."

His inquisitors made him an offer. If he cooperated in a detailed, honest way, his name would be taken off the sanctions list. The Mauritanian shrugged. "It's not something I need," he said, dismissing the repercussions of being on that list, something he had never really thought about.

One session extended to four, much to his mounting annoyance, and finally a man he presumed to be in the CIA asked him about Hamzah bin Laden. "How important is Hamzah, and where is he right now?"

"I've not seen him since 2010," the Mauritanian replied truthfully. "Ask Sheikh Osama's family about him."

One of the Americans produced documents from Abbottabad, including a letter Hamzah had written to his father in 2010 in which he mentioned the Mauritanian. He took a look but handed it back. "I can't comment on its authenticity."

They showed him Osama's will, which detailed his intention to pay the Mauritanian for his efforts to launder the $29 million left in Sudan in 1996.[57] They read out a line: "I need you to take 1% from the total and give it to Shaykh Abu Hafs al-Mauritani," Osama had written, using the Mauritanian's old Al Qaeda *kunya*. "By the way, he has already received 20,000–30,000 dollars from it. I promised him that I would reward him." He shrugged.

As the meeting broke up, the CIA officials delivered a warning: "If you wander far from Nouakchott, we cannot guarantee your safety." He nodded. Freed on July 7, he was reunited with his family.[58]

When he felt it was safe, he recovered his Al Qaeda files from the orange USB stick in his shoe, bought a new laptop, and downloaded encryption software to cloak his presence on the dark web, as Al Qaeda began its resurrection.

With tentacles stretching from Nouakchott to Timbuktu, across Algiers to Tunis, and into Niamey and Bamako, Al Qaeda in the Islamic Maghreb and its regional affiliates, Nigeria's Boko Haram, Somalia's Al Shabaab, and Al Qaeda in the Arabian Peninsula in Yemen, flexed their muscles. Far from being shattered by Osama's death, they were galvanizing and growing: attacking beach resorts, the Westgate shopping center, the Amenas gas facility, killing hundreds of innocent people in suicide-bomb blasts, often citing America's mistreatment of Pakistani neuroscientist Aafia Siddiqui or those at Guantánamo as their inspiration, taking dozens of hostages, including Westerners and Christian schoolgirls.

In Nouakchott, the Mauritanian became a star of Friday prayers.

December 2012, Tourist Complex, Tehran

Sulaiman Abu Ghaith also wanted to leave. He was allowed to speak to his brother in Kuwait, who promised to arrange a new passport for him and even a possible reunion with his first wife. His third wife, Fatima bin Laden, who was seven months pregnant, wanted to get away too, from Iran and from Abu Ghaith, who was driving her mad.[59]

The Iranians agreed. Their only proviso was that they should leave as a couple and travel overland via Turkey. Desperate to go, they accepted. In early January 2013, they bade farewell to the remaining *shura* members before they were escorted northwest toward the Turkish border, which was deep in snow.

At the border town of Urmia, they were introduced to people smugglers. As the drifts deepened, Abu Ghaith worried that he had no telephone numbers for the guides who were supposed to meet them on the other side. He urged Fatima to call Abdullah bin Laden, her oldest brother, who promised to fly from Jeddah to meet them in Ankara.[60]

Soon the way became impassable as the temperature dropped. Fatima could not go on. They stayed in a hotel for four restless days waiting for the conditions to improve.

On January 13 there was a letup. They were given fake Iranian passports and told to huddle among fifty Iranian migrants who were being taken to a remote crossing by truck.

From the border gate, they had to struggle on foot through the snow to the Turkish side, where a car was waiting. The driver introduced himself as Naji. He was slim, middle-aged, and clean-shaven, and he chatted easily throughout the twenty-hour drive west to Ankara.

At the Saudi embassy, Fatima was reunited with her brother, who she had not seen for eighteen years.

While she and Abdullah went inside to sort out her passport, Abu Ghaith excitedly checked into a five-star hotel and ordered room service. Fatima called to say she had got her passport and they were set. That just left the driver to deal with. Abu Ghaith went out and told Naji he was no longer needed, before dressing for dinner. Fatima and Abdullah had invited him for a farewell meal. But on his way out of the hotel, the preacher was seized by Turkish intelligence officials after Naji, who was an informer, tipped off the police.

Abu Ghaith remained under house arrest in his hotel room for the next month. Pressured by the United States to hand him over, prickly Turkish officials decided to deport him back to Kuwait. The Americans were furious, but by the time his flight stopped over in Amman on February 28 they had persuaded Jordan's General Intelligence Directorate to arrest him on behalf of the FBI.

By ten P.M. that evening he was aboard an FBI Gulfstream bound for New York. The interrogation began immediately. No mention was made in the official FBI transcript as to whether he was restrained, but he was allowed to "rest, pray, use the bathroom, stretch his legs," and he was regularly checked by an FBI medic.[61]

Speaking mainly in English, Abu Ghaith seemed relieved that it was finally all over. "I will not hold back," he said. "I will be honest with you. You will hear things of Al Qaeda that you never imagined." All he could think about was his first wife and the seven children in Kuwait, whom he was sure the American justice system would allow him to see. He was willing to give up everything and everyone to meet them again.

He began by explaining how the Iranians had arrested him with Saif, Abu al-Khayr, and Abu Mohammed in April 2003. He revealed how Saif and Abu Mohammed had openly admitted to him that they had been behind the 1998 embassy attacks. He spoke of the Mauritanian, who he still loved as a brother even though he had lured him to Afghanistan in the first place. He described how Osama had compelled him to make videos in the days after 9/11, and how hard life had been inside the Quds Force compound. He was an accidental spokesman who had never wanted to be part of Al Qaeda, he insisted.

Abu Ghaith faltered only when he was asked about those still being held in Tehran. Did they want to return to the jihad? asked the FBI special agent. Abu Ghaith trod carefully. Saif, Abu Mohammed, and Abu al-Khayr were "beaten men," he said, and were primarily concerned with the welfare of their families. As for Al Qaeda's volatile relations with Iran, he was unsure if there had been any official relationship. He told the FBI: "Iran doesn't want any Sunni Muslim group to gain power." Shown a photograph of facilitator Yasin al-Suri, he said that he did not know him.

After fourteen hours of questions, in which he hoped he had proffered enough answers, the plane began to descend into New York and Abu Ghaith's interrogation was concluded at noon on March 1, 2013.

But America was not as Abu Ghaith imagined. "There is no corner of the world where you can escape from justice," the U.S. attorney general Eric Holder told him as he was remanded at Manhattan's Metropolitan Correctional Center, which was located just a few blocks from Ground Zero. Former inmates included World Trade Center bomber Ramzi Yousef, the Egyptian hate preacher Abu Hamza, mob boss John Gotti, and failed Times Square bomber Faisal Shahzad. "Lord of War" arms trader Viktor Bout, who spent fourteen months there in solitary, described it as a harsh place, like the jail depicted in the Alexandre Dumas novel *The Count of Monte Cristo*.

Nouakchott

When he saw Abu Ghaith's face on the news, the Mauritanian's heart flipped. The trap was the same that had been sprung for him, but he had had the sense to decline it.

He thought back to a conversation he had had with an Iranian security adviser during the time of the compound protests. "I told him, 'You have to give me assurance that you will never hand my brothers or sisters to the Americans.'" The Iranian had eyed him: "I *can't* give that guarantee," he had said, "in the same way that the human body must sometimes cut out an organ to keep the remaining organs alive."

The Mauritanian was in no doubt that the Iranians had tipped off the U.S. government about Abu Ghaith's departure and that the rest had been contrived play-acting. General Qassem Suleimani wanted to hang on to the *shura*, the only ones in the Tourist Complex who really mattered.

Two months later, in May 2013, Younis al-Mauritani, Al Qaeda's former chief of foreign operations, who had been seized by the ISI in Quetta and then subjected to months of interrogation at Bagram air base, was extradited to Nouakchott. Unlike the Mauritanian, he was not offered a deal. Instead, he endured a long and tortuous period of interrogation at the hands of the security services.[62]

In October 2013, another of the Mauritanian's old friends from the Quds Force compound was also run to ground. Abu Anas al-Libi, who had caused the Iranians so much trouble that they had let him out in 2010, had returned to Libya intent on helping Al Qaeda. Still talking too much on his phone, he was captured by U.S. commandos in Tripoli on October 5, 2013, and interrogated aboard the USS *San Antonio* in the Mediterranean. He stopped eating and drinking, his health deteriorated, and he was flown to New York, where he was locked up in a cell in the same "terrorist wing" where Abu Ghaith was being held.

When al-Libi appeared in court at the end of October 2013, accused of being a mastermind of the 1998 U.S. embassy bombings, a former U.S. intelligence officer described him as one of the "top finds" since the death of Osama bin Laden.

Abu Ghaith, who appeared later in the same court, was described as "the most senior adviser to Osama bin Laden to be tried in a civilian court in the United States since the 9/11 attacks." So few had actually gone on trial that Abu Ghaith was by default a catch. Having taken such care to fashion *Zero Dark Thirty*, Washington required a guilty verdict.

Abu Ghaith's legal team knew they faced an uphill struggle and they tried to take statements from anyone who personally knew the defendant, including the Mauritanian. But U.S. officials based in Nouakchott blocked the lawyers' visit.[63]

The defense team turned to Yemen, where Salim Hamdan and Abu Jandal, "the Father of Death"—Osama's security officer who had been sent to Yemen in 2000 to broker the Sheikh's marriage with Amal—agreed to meet, only for the meetings to also be annulled "at the request of U.S. officials."[64]

As a last resort, Abu Ghaith's lawyers tried to depose the actual mastermind of 9/11—Khalid Shaikh Mohammad. Housed in Camp 7 at Guantánamo Bay since September 2006 and in the early stages of being tried by a military commission along with his four codefendants, Khalid had effected his most dramatic transformation to date. He entered Guantánamo's $12 million Expeditionary Legal Complex flanked by military personnel and sporting a great fanned beard, a stunning white robe, military waistcoat, and a red-and-white-checked headdress, which made him look like the caliph of Cuba. Often seen at loggerheads with his Pentagon-appointed legal team, he tried to frustrate proceedings at every opportunity, complaining on several occasions that his sons Yusuf and Abed had never been returned to their mother.

Unsurprisingly, the attempt to produce Khalid Shaikh Mohammad in New York was struck down, although the lawyers did manage to acquire a fourteen-page statement from him in which he was explicit: "[Abu Ghaith] did not play any military role . . . I do not recall that I ever met him or saw him at a training camp. He did not know me by any name other than the one I was using in Afghanistan [Mokhtar] so he never knew my real name." He "was not part of that fabric and did not participate in jihad at that time."

Nevertheless, Abu Ghaith was found guilty and received a life sentence.[65] Before being taken away, incredulous, he spoke from the dock. "At the same moment where you are shackling my hands and intend to bury me alive," he said, "you are unleashing the hands of hundreds of Muslim youth. And you are removing the dust of their minds."

March 2013, Syria

Abu Bakr al-Baghdadi had a serious problem. Spies working for the Prince of Shadows, his military commander Hajji Bakr, had returned from Syria with the worrying news that Julani's Nusra Front was now the preeminent rebel movement in Syria, eclipsing Islamic State.

As Julani had intended, Syrians dominated his group of five thousand fighters, and he had spies inside government institutions, including the security apparatus. By contrast, Abu Bakr's forces had mostly won ground by wielding rape, torture, and execution and were widely criticized for forcing their extreme Islamism on civilians. The residents of Raqqa, Aleppo, and Homs happily hung Julani's Al Qaeda–style banners from their balconies, but they rejected Abu Bakr and his Islamic State.

Worried that Julani was intending to elevate himself as leader of a new and independent Al Qaeda branch, bypassing Islamic State altogether, Abu Bakr demanded a statement of loyalty.[66] Julani refused. On April 9, Abu Bakr tried to get around his disobedience by announcing the formal merger of both groups into the Islamic State in Iraq and the Levant (Syria): ISIL.

Instead of accepting his fate, Julani sought guidance from Dr. al-Zawahiri, calling him the "sheikh of jihad." He issued a declaration on jihadi websites: "We are not murderers; we are not criminals. We are fighting those who fight us. We are standing against tyranny."

Dr. al-Zawahiri issued a private message asking both commanders to be quiet. Abu Bakr kept at it, warning that Julani was a "traitor." If al-Zawahiri backed him, there would be "no cure except the spilling of more blood."

On May 23, al-Zawahiri declared that ISIL should be abolished, as it had been created without prior approval, and that Abu Bakr should confine his group's activities to Iraq. Leave Syria to Julani and the Nusra Front, he commanded.

Furious, Abu Bakr hit back. "I have to choose between the rule of God and the rule of al-Zawahiri, and I choose the rule of God," he declared before setting his forces against the Nusra Front.[67]

As the two groups began fighting each other in Syria, Al Qaeda commanders, including Muhsin al-Fadhli, who had fought with Zarqawi in Iraq and had helped manage the Iran pipeline, were sent to shore up Julani.[68] He raised a unit of battle-hardened veterans from the Soviet war in Afghanistan that called itself the Khorasan Group—after an ancient name for the Afghan region. Dr. al-Zawahiri also sent one of his oldest deputies, Ahmad Salama Mabruk, whose *kunya* was Abu Faraj al-Masri. The two men had known each other since the killing of Anwar Sadat in 1981 and Abu Faraj now became a top Nusra Front commander.

Keen for a resolution, al-Zawahiri also dispatched Abu Khalid al-Suri to meet with ISIL.[69] He faced a tirade of abuse. "Al Qaeda is gone, it's burned out," Abu Bakr snarled. ISIL was here to stay "as long as we have a pulse or an eye that blinks."[70] Men loyal to Abu Bakr set out to seize control of the five-hundred-mile-long border between Turkey and Syria, in an attempt to cut off the Nusra Front's supply lines.

By the end of December 2013, Abu Bakr's black-clad hordes had absorbed or killed more than 80 percent of Julani's foreign fighters, and they rode into towns previously dominated by their rivals with their black ISIL pennant rippling in the wind. NO GOD BUT GOD screamed the rough lettering of their logo. Underneath, the words MUHAMMAD IS THE MESSENGER OF GOD were arranged inside a circle designed to represent the Prophet's seal ring that was housed in the Topkapi Palace in Istanbul.

In Abu Bakr's eyes, ISIL was living out predictions laid down in the *Book of Tribulations*, a collection of hadiths written down by ninth-century Islamic scholar Naeem bin Hammad that described the civil wars preceding the apocalyptic "Last Days" of humanity: "The black banners will come from the east, led by men like mighty camels, with long hair and long beards; their surnames are taken from the names of their hometowns and their first names are from *kunyas*."[71] The Antichrist would "appear in the empty area between Sham and Iraq" and one of the crucial final battles would take place in Dabiq, a small village north of Aleppo.

Adopting these ancient words, Abu Bakr declared that Syria and Iraq were ground zero for the apocalypse. His fighters went on a rampage, hunting down and executing high-level Nusra Front commanders, along with civilians loyal to them. Bodies were burned, crucified in the street, dragged behind cars until they fell apart, or returned to their families with legs broken or missing, ears severed, the tops of their heads blown off, their bodies eviscerated.

They zeroed in on Dabiq itself, in a ferocious battle that was fought mainly for its symbolic value and the demoralizing effect it would have on Julani's forces.

Sickened, Julani publicly pledged allegiance to al-Zawahiri while Abu Faraj al-Masri ensured that extra funding was coming from Al Qaeda Central via Qatar and the Iran network.[72]

In January 2014, Julani published an online editorial about ISIL, alleging Abu Bakr's movement was corrupting the jihad in Syria, just as it had done in Iraq. Two weeks later, al-Zawahiri formally expelled ISIL from Al Qaeda.[73]

Abu Bakr's response came on February 21, when al-Zawahiri's emissary, Abu Khalid, whose mission had been to stop the internecine fighting, reached Aleppo, his birthplace, and was killed by five ISIL suicide bombers.[74] Photographs of his bulky, bloodied corpse went viral, intensifying the bitter war between ISIL and Al Qaeda. Someone had to bring the two factions back from the brink.

Stepping into the fray was a notorious cleric who so far said nothing publicly at all—feeling that to do so would give succor to the enemies of jihad in the West, and to Assad in Syria. This don of Salafist jihad scholarship was Abu Muhammad al-Maqdisi, the intellectual godfather of Al Qaeda and former mentor of Islamic State's founder, Abu Musab al-Zarqawi.[75]

Maqdisi, who had been in and out of prison on terrorism charges for years, had privately tried to intercede several times over the past year, sending discreet messages on WhatsApp to Abu Bakr's inner circle via his chief religious adviser, Bin'ali the Bahraini. The scholar had once been a devoted student of Maqdisi's. But Bin'ali was disrespectful and arrogant in his replies sent in the summer of 2013 and then stopped answering Maqdisi's messages altogether.[76]

In May 2014, Maqdisi issued a fatwa against ISIL from his jail cell in Amman, where he faced charges of inciting terrorism. Abu Bakr and his followers were "deviants" who had no "Islamic pretext," he said. ISIL's commanders should defect to the Nusra Front or face condemnation before

God. These were heady words from a scholar whose own brother Salahuddin was a top ISIL commander.

Abu Bakr, who had recently lost his primary backer and adviser, the Prince of Shadows Hajji Bakr—killed by Syrian rebels back in January—responded by declaring a caliphate with himself as "Caliph Ibrahim." The prophecy was fulfilled, he said, and Judgment Day approached. The name ISIL was shortened to Islamic State (IS) and Muslims worldwide were called to join forces with a movement that had ambitions to "conquer Rome and own the world."[77] Calling for fighters, judges, medics, and teachers to come to God's kingdom on earth, Abu Bakr declared: "Rush O Muslims to your state. It is your state. Syria is not for Syrians and Iraq is not for Iraqis. The land is for the Muslims, all Muslims."

While Maqdisi predicted disaster, Abu Bakr found himself shored up by a huge wave of public support led by young and disenfranchised Muslims who flocked to Syria from the West. Many lacked the religious knowledge to question his credentials, and did not understand the significance of Maqdisi's opposition. They simply relished the declaration of a caliphate, the illusion of power over Western repression.[78]

Buoyed by their arrival, Abu Bakr released a video of himself addressing the Grand Mosque in Mosul, in which he declared himself the "commander of the faithful," world leader of Muslims. Maqdisi appeared to have made a serious error in judgment.[79]

The most fervent descended on IS's self-declared capital, Raqqa. Abu Bakr had come a long way from being the shortsighted draft dodger who lived a bachelor life in a single room attached to Tobchi mosque on the outskirts of Baghdad. A man released by the U.S. forces from Camp Bucca as a "low-level prisoner" even though he had told his captors, "I'll see you guys in New York," was now invoking doomsday imagery, backed by a generation of young Muslims who could barely remember 9/11.[80]

However, privately Abu Bakr was still worried. He could get away with challenging the authority of al-Zawahiri, given that the doctor was far away and apparently weakened. But the open opposition of Maqdisi, who remained a real force in the region and was personally linked to the founder of Islamic State in Iraq, Zarqawi, posed a significant threat to his legitimacy. Osama bin Laden had frequently recommended that his followers study all that Maqdisi had to say about the jihad.[81] Abu Bakr had to get Maqdisi on his side.

In the summer of 2014, IS dispatched top secret messages to Maqdisi and his close friend Abu Qatada, another Palestinian cleric now living in

Jordan, who a Spanish judge had once described as "bin Laden's right-hand man in Europe." Qatada, a huge bear of a man who wore a robe spun from raw camel wool, was publicly notorious, but privately he was an influential and highly respected Salafist force.

The British government had accused Qatada of acting as planner Abu Zubaydah's European postbox during the 1990s, collecting funds and sending recruits to Peshawar, but he had never been a fighter and he denied these accusations vociferously. Bright-eyed and sharp, he had lived for twenty-three years in London, first preaching and then fighting a grinding deportation case that he conceded before returning to Jordan in 2013.[82]

Bin'ali, who was by now being described as "Grand Mufti" of Islamic State, wrote to Maqdisi and Qatada with an enticing offer: $1 million each if they moved to Raqqa.[83]

Behind the scenes cash deals were also offered to Al Qaeda affiliates. Nasir al-Wuhayshi, the Yemeni leader of Al Qaeda in the Arabian Peninsula, was offered $10 million to swear allegiance. A similar deal was offered to Al Qaeda's Libyan offshoot, albeit for half the money.

Maqdisi, who was by now out of prison, and Qatada, who was still remanded on terrorism charges, could both have done with the IS cash. But they rejected Abu Bakr's advances and launched a twenty-one-page online broadside. "The announcement of a caliphate by the Islamic State is void and meaningless," they said, "because it was not approved by jihadists in other parts of the world." Maqdisi ordered IS to "reform, repent and stop killing Muslims and distorting religion."

Qatada twisted the knife. IS was like "a mafia," he said. Abu Bakr was a "thug" who did not respect anyone. His fighters were "gangsters" without religious credentials. The suggestion that one man could announce a caliphate and declare himself as its leader was akin to a five-year-old child thinking he could buy a house without any adult help. "There has to be agreement between more than one party," he continued. "I can declare an emirate in my home but the *ummah* should choose the *calipha*. There has to be a contract."[84]

In September 2014, shortly after being freed by the Amman security court, Qatada called Maqdisi to discuss how they could intervene to save the countless hostages IS was holding in Raqqa, including more than a dozen Western journalists and aid workers. Two, American reporters James Foley and Steven Sotloff, had already been beheaded. Qatada had done something similar in

2005, when the British security services had asked him to help negotiate the release of Norman Kember, a British peace campaigner who had been seized in Iraq. Kember had eventually been freed and in 2008 he paid back the favor by providing bail to Qatada, then on remand in a British prison.

Qatada and Maqdisi knew they were better placed to influence the hostage takers than anyone else. They went for picnics in the Jordanian countryside, the slow and lumbering Qatada rapt by the highly sprung Maqdisi. But before they had a chance to intervene, David Haines, a British RAF engineer turned aid worker, was also slain. British taxi driver Alan Henning followed on October 3. Both men were killed by the same masked IS fighter from London, who was dubbed "Jihadi John."

Next on the butcher's list was Peter Kassig, a former U.S. Army Ranger who had set up an aid charity in Syria and had been abducted in October 2013. An American lawyer, the same one who had represented Sulaiman Abu Ghaith, met with Abu Qatada and Maqdisi and asked them to negotiate with IS for his release.[85]

Maqdisi renewed contact with his former pupil Bin'ali via WhatsApp. On the table was an offer to stop denouncing IS if they freed Kassig. If IS stopped taking hostages altogether, he and Qatada might even be willing to negotiate reconciliation with Al Qaeda.

However, before any deal could be struck, Maqdisi was rearrested and accused by Jordanian intelligence of "using the Internet to promote and incite views of jihadi terrorist organizations," even though he had official authorization to communicate with Bin'ali.

On November 16, 2014, Kassig's execution video was posted online, along with footage showing the beheading of more than a dozen Syrian soldiers. "To Obama, the dog of Rome," Jihadi John declared. A female convert originally from London wrote on Twitter: "So many beheadings at the same time, Allahu Akhbar, this video is beautiful."

November 2014, Mosul

Islamic State announced new oaths of loyalty from groups in Egypt, Libya, Yemen, and Pakistan. Less principled than the clerics in Amman, some former Al Qaeda affiliates were struggling to maintain supporters and needed to back the winning horse. Islamic State was moving in, stealing territory and influence from under al-Zawahiri's nose. Abu Bakr even sent an audacious demand that he swear *bayat* to IS. Al-Zawahiri did not reply.

In December 2014, Abu Bakr went further, branding Maqdisi and Qatada as "stooges" of the West in the latest edition of *Dabiq*, Islamic State's English-language online magazine, featuring a full-page photograph of the two in conversation headlined "misleading scholars."[86]

The bloodshed continued into January 2015, when Jihadi John beheaded Japanese reporter Kenji Goto, along with his friend, a Japanese security consultant called Haruna Yukawa.

Weeks later, Jihadi John was unmasked as Mohammed Emwazi, a Kuwaiti-born computer programming graduate who had been brought up in West London. A shy schoolboy who had had trouble talking to girls, according to former classmates at Quintin Kynaston Academy, Emwazi had been stirred by a jihadi preacher who came to speak at Westminster University, where he had later studied. In the summer of 2009, Emwazi had traveled to Tanzania, claiming to be going on safari. Detained in Dar-es-Salaam, he was eventually deported to the United Kingdom and questioned by counterterrorism officials, who accused him of trying to link up with Al Qaeda offshoot Al Shabaab. Emwazi moved to Kuwait, but on a trip back to the United Kingdom he was detained again in July 2010 and barred from leaving. He sought advice from CAGE, the London-based human rights group run by former Guantánamo Bay inmate Moazzam Begg.

"I had a job waiting for me and marriage to get started," he wrote to CAGE.[87] But now "I feel like a prisoner...A person imprisoned and controlled by security service men, stopping me from living my new life in my birthplace and country, Kuwait." He cited the mistreatment of Aafia Siddiqui as one of his inspirations to fight on for "freedom and justice."[88] In early 2013, after changing his name by deed poll, he sneaked out of the United Kingdom and headed for Syria.

Emwazi would eventually be run to ground in Raqqa in November 2015, killed by a drone strike after another West London convert, called Aine Lesley Davis, was caught by Turkish intelligence officers trying to cross back into Europe.[89]

*   *   *

January 2015, New York City

Abu Anas al-Libi had also been an angry young man. Best known for leaving a copy of Al Qaeda's war manual in a house he had rented in Manchester, England, al-Libi had so enraged the Mauritanian and other prisoners during their time together in Tehran that they had asked to move to a different compound. On the FBI's Most Wanted Terrorist list since 2002, he was finally due to stand trial in New York in early 2015.

It was not just al-Libi's testimony that everyone wanted to hear. There were also documents. In the run-up, prosecutors asked the judge if they could introduce letters al-Libi had sent to Osama bin Laden in Abbottabad and that had been recovered during the raid that killed him.[90] They promised an enticing glimpse into the trove that was still classified and under the exclusive purview of the CIA's Document Exploitation (DOCEX) team based in McLean, Virginia. Despite vigorous efforts by the Defense Intelligence Agency and U.S. Central Command (CENTCOM) to gain access, barely anyone outside the CIA had seen the documents, and only 10 percent of them had even been analyzed.[91]

But after al-Libi died, unexpectedly, in a New York hospital after liver surgery on January 2, 2015, most of the correspondence remained under seal.[92] It looked like nobody would be getting to see the real story that the Abbottabad documents told about Al Qaeda's fortunes any time soon.

Days later, Abu Muhammad al-Maqdisi and Abu Qatada made one last attempt at rapprochement between Al Qaeda and Islamic State when they tried to negotiate the release of a Jordanian pilot, Muath al-Kasasbeh, who had been shot down over IS-held territory. Making sure that he had the full backing of Jordan's General Intelligence Directorate (GID) and communicating via encrypted Telegram messenger, Maqdisi sent word that in exchange for the pilot's release, Jordan would free Sajida al-Rishawi, who in 2005 along with her husband had been sent by Zarqawi to bomb the wedding party at the Radisson SAS Hotel in Amman. While her husband had died, her suicide belt had jammed and she had been arrested and sentenced to death.

Maqdisi advised IS that as inheritors of Zarqawi's legacy, they had an obligation to save her, and that killing Kasasbeh went against Islam. But before going ahead with any exchange, the Jordanian authorities wanted evidence that the pilot was still alive.

On February 3, Maqdisi received an encrypted file. As he typed, letter-by-letter, a password sent by separate e-mail, he realized with horror that it read: "Maqdisi the pimp, the sole of the tyrant's shoe, son of the English whore."[93]

Seconds later a video appeared on his screen showing the pilot being dragged into a cage, doused in petrol, and set alight. It was posted online three hours later. Maqdisi and the GID had been set up by IS, and would-be hotel bomber Sajida al-Rishawi was executed the next day.

"I'm an enemy of the US," said his friend Abu Qatada. "But my advice to them is that jihad is changing to a movement of the whole *ummah* and the world is deteriorating. You know how it is with playground slides: once you let go you cannot stop."

CHAPTER THIRTEEN

"Eliminating the caliphate will be an
achievement. But more likely it will be just the
end of the beginning rather than the beginning
of the end."
— STATE DEPARTMENT OFFICIAL,
SEPTEMBER 2016

March 2015, Tourist Complex, Quds Force Training
Facility, Tehran, Iran

"I ASK GOD TO RELEASE OUR BROTHERS from prison so they can come to help us carry the load," Atiyah Abd al-Rahman had written to Osama bin Laden concerning the Iran-based *shura* members in July 2010.[1] "They are qualified," he continued, naming Saif al-Adel, Abu al-Khayr al-Masri, and Abu Mohammed al-Masri. "If God facilitates their release they will really need to spend at least six months (and maybe a year) relearning how things work, refreshing their knowledge, their activity and vitality . . . Then, maybe, we could turn things over to them."

For the past eighteen months, Al Qaeda had been secretly negotiating to free the three men, along with two Jordanians who had once been part of Abu Musab al-Zarqawi's inner circle—his brother-in-law Khalid al-Aruri and his childhood friend Sari Shihab. If Iran let them out then Al Qaeda would free an Iranian diplomat being held hostage by Al Qaeda in the Arab Peninsula.[2] It was important to make this look like a simple exchange of prisoners, not a new era of mutual cooperation between Al Qaeda and Iran.

When a deal was reached in March 2015, Saif and the other *shura* members were quietly moved out of the Tourist Complex and into supervised apartments in District 9, the middle-class area where the Mauritanian had also lived ahead of his escape. Empty at last, Block 300 was handed back to the Quds Force trainees. But getting Al Qaeda's army council out of the country and discreetly into Syria, where they all wanted to go, would take careful coordination and management.

Given the recent fates of Sulaiman Abu Ghaith and Abu Anas al-Libi, and still suspicious that Iran might have colluded with the Americans over Abbottabad, Saif and his colleagues advanced cautiously. They were especially wary of Iran's ongoing talks with the United Nations Security Council and the Obama administration about the United States ending economic sanctions in exchange for restrictions on Iran's nuclear program. The *shura* members needed to get back into the fight and not become pawns again.

Small steps were taken first. Following the model used with the Mauritanian, the first stage in their rehabilitation came when their families were allowed to leave the country. Saif's wife, Asma, who was pregnant, flew to Doha, where she was put up by the bin Ladens. After she lost the baby, she filed for divorce, unable to countenance another epoch of jihad in another country. She had had enough of life on the run.

Al-Aruri's wife, Alia, who had never gone to Iran but remained in Zarqa with the rest of Zarqawi's family, was delighted to hear that her husband had been freed. Expecting to be reunited with him, she instead received a message saying that he was not returning to Jordan. The situation in Syria was at a critical juncture and he was heading there.[3] She should continue to wait until he sent for her.

The news also reached Hamzah bin Laden, Osama's favorite son, who regarded the military council members as his mentors. They had "spared no pain or expense in guiding us down this path" to jihad, he declared in an audio statement, the first time anyone had heard from him since he narrowly escaped being killed at Abbottabad.[4]

The timing of Hamzah's first declaration to the world in fifteen years was no coincidence but evidence that after five years of being groomed at an undisclosed location, he was also now readying to enter the cause of global jihad as an adult and reinvigorate Al Qaeda's fortunes. Supporting his statement was one from al-Zawahiri, introducing Hamzah to the world as a "lion from the den" of Al Qaeda.

During his lifetime, Osama had endlessly lectured the bin Laden boys on the day one of them would succeed him, and in his eyes Hamzah always stood out.

Now that he was being introduced as the lodestar, Hamzah raised a slogan, "We Are All Osama." Al Qaeda believed that Hamzah, handsome, charismatic, and, according to those who knew him, fearless, a boy the doctor had known since he was a baby, would appeal to the Islamic State generation.[5]

Summer 2011, Doha, Qatar

Hamzah's elevation was not certain, and getting him this far, alive, had been hard. At the time of the raid that killed his father, he had been in Peshawar, staying with Mohammed Aslam, Ibrahim's point-man. As soon as he heard the news, Aslam knew Hamzah had to get out of Pakistan. Using dead brother Khalid bin Laden's fake ID cards, Aslam had bought Hamzah a ticket to Doha, telling the boy to mingle with Pakistani laborers traveling to work there on construction projects connected to the 2022 World Cup. His wife and children flew separately.

Qatar, once the poorest cousin of the Gulf states, a former pearl-fishing backwater and British protectorate where the United States had its largest military base in the Middle East, had become a regionally influential, petroleum-rich monarchy. It was the home of the Taliban government-in-exile (since June 2013) and served as a sanctuary for Hamas, rebels from Syria, militias fleeing Libya, and allies of the Muslim Brotherhood across the region.[6]

When he arrived, Hamzah did not contact his half brothers and sisters, who lived with their mother in a horseshoe-shaped compound in the much-sought-after neighborhood of West Bay Lagoon, but quietly sought out Khalid Shaikh Mohammad's old friends.

The 9/11 mastermind had passed through this Gulf nation many times during the 1990s, helped by several wealthy and influential Qataris. When Khalid left Qatar in 1996 and linked up with Osama bin Laden at Tora Bora to plan the Twin Towers attacks, the FBI director suggested he had been tipped off by the kingdom's security services.[7]

After 9/11, Khalid had returned to Qatar, again sheltering "with the help of prominent patrons." The assistance had continued into the Zarqawi era, when the Jordanian hardman was said to have received Qatari passports and more than $1 million in a special bank account.

In 2011, the U.S. Treasury Department named two Qatar-based facilitators who helped run Al Qaeda's core pipeline through Iran as Specially Designated Global Terrorists.[8] In 2015, the department named two further Qataris as "major facilitators of the al-Nusrah Front and al-Qaida."[9] One of them was accused of having links that went back over a decade and involved

Khalid Shaikh Mohammad's Pakistani courier Hassan Ghul. The Qatari had arranged "a fraudulent passport" that Ghul had used to visit Qatar and "transfer money to al-Qaida in Pakistan."

By 2015, Ghul was dead, detected in the Tribal Areas of Pakistan in 2012 after sending an e-mail to his wife using an account that was being monitored by the U.S intelligence community. A drone strike in October 2012 had finished him off.[10]

Hamzah bin Laden kept his head down in Qatar. "I'd like to stay undercover and be like any other jihadist and be treated like any other," he had told his father in his last surviving letter.[11] He adopted a new identity, and he returned to jurisprudence and hadith studies that had begun under the Mauritanian in Tehran. One of his new tutors was Hajjaj al-Ajmi, who told an audience in Doha in 2013 not to bother with donations to humanitarian programs in Syria. "Give your money to the ones who will spend it on jihad, not aid," he thundered.[12]

The path Hamzah had chosen could not have been more different from that followed by his half brothers, Abdul Rahman, Omar, Othman, Mohammed, and Ladin.

In a deal brokered by Zaina, Omar's British wife, they, their mother, Najwa, and sisters Rukaiya and Nour had the run of six large villas with crenelated roofs that were provided rent-free by the Qatari authorities, along with top-of-the-range SUVs and a full complement of servants. Sometimes even the grocery shopping was done for them. Other bills were picked up by Bakr bin Laden, Osama's older brother, who paid each family member a stipend on the understanding that they did not talk.[13]

The more conservative members of Osama's surviving family remained in Jeddah: Amal and her children, Seham and her two surviving daughters and four grandchildren; Hamzah's mother, Khairiah; Iman and her young family; and Fatima and her two children from Sulaiman Abu Ghaith. Only Saad's widow, Wafa, had broken away, taking her young children back to live with her parents in Port Sudan, along with a lump sum that represented Saad's inheritance.

Although Bakr bin Laden and the Qataris kept a tight rein on finances, for most of bin Laden's sons it was the first time they had practically anything they could wish for. Omar bought Harleys, raced superbikes, and smoked cigars. Othman drove expensive cars and Ladin traveled in private jets. Occasionally, Najwa's youngest daughters, Rukaiya and Nour (both of whom were now fashion-conscious college students who wore mirrored sunglasses with their stylish *abayas*), accompanied their mother on shopping trips to London, traveling on Qatari passports.[14]

At home, Najwa went out shopping with Zaina, spending money on things she would never have been allowed to buy when Osama was still around: makeup, clothes, skin treatments, luxury goods, and gifts for her daughters. The only person outside the family she consented to meet was a British teacher from one of Qatar's top international schools, who had been introduced by Zaina and taught her English.[15]

Occasionally, Najwa and her daughters flew to Paris to meet up with Osama's mother, Allia, who, despite being in her seventies, was still glamorous and embraced all the French capital had to offer, rarely speaking of her son or how he had destroyed her world.

Despite Qatar's generosity and Bakr's largesse, or perhaps because of it, the sons exiled in Doha did not live as one big happy family. Regular bustups rocked the compound as they argued over money or family matters. Chairs got broken. Walls were thumped in frustration. Ladin, now twenty-three, spent most of his time playing computer games or sleeping. Abdul Rahman, aged thirty-eight, who had suffered problems all his life caused by childhood hydrocephalus and was married to a cousin from Saudi Arabia, made frequent trips abroad and caused the Qatari authorities some consternation when he attempted to reenter the country on one occasion with sex toys in his suitcase.

Younger brother Othman, who with his two wives, a daughter of Saif al-Adel and a daughter of Mohammed al-Islambouli, had escaped Pakistan in late May 2011, was at war with Zaina, who he accused of being a British spy, even though Seham had informed the family that Osama had known about his son's marriage and had blessed the union "if it makes Omar happy."[16]

More mild-mannered Mohammed bin Laden stayed at home with his wife and children, relieved that he, too, had escaped the chaos of Pakistan. He had been too traumatized to fulfill his father's last written request that he enroll in a degree course to study "strategic sciences, sociology and psychology."[17]

After so many years following their father around the world's trouble spots, the long years of incarceration in Iran, their near miss in Pakistan, and the unspoken fear that they as well as Khairiah had somehow led to their father's entrapment in Abbottabad, they all worried about going out in public for fear of being recognized, followed, or abducted by the CIA and instead they spent most days lounging in the *majlis*, watching old footage of their father's hero, Sayyid Qutb, and browsing secret Facebook, Twitter, and Instagram accounts.

None of them had been tempted by the opportunities offered by Education City, a huge campus on the outskirts of Doha where top U.S. universities, including Georgetown and Texas A&M, had opened up campuses. What was the point of education? Omar complained to Zaina. Who would give a son of Osama bin Laden a job?

Encouraged by Zaina, Omar had tried several times to earn a living. He banked on his family's reputation for construction, teaming up with a Spanish firm bidding for lucrative projects linked to the 2022 World Cup.

But his lack of experience and unrealistic expectations put people off. "I need to make a hundred million dollars," he would say. "I need to make a billion." When his business failed, Omar fell into a deep depression, while Bakr bailed him out to the tune of $1 million. Afterward, he became bad-tempered and silent.

To bring him out of his funk, Zaina suggested they launch a high-fashion clothing line called B41. When his second business went the same way as the first, Bakr banned him from working. "He is deluded and thinks he will succeed and be the best at everything without making any effort," said one family member. Even Zaina, who loved him, described him as "a liability."

Stuck at home and obsessing about his father, Omar often became maudlin, telling friends that if he had stayed with Osama, he might have become as famous as Alexander the Great. "I would have wanted to rule the world," he said. "I would have wanted to be the highest." Instead he had a "very small life." People should be thankful he had chosen peace, he said. "If I chose war, I would be unbelievable at it. A lot of people should pray to their god to thank him that I did not do that."[18]

By 2015 Hamzah was as ready as he would ever be. Now aged twenty-seven, he had matured from the young boy in camouflage who had swung through the monkey bars for the cameras at Kandahar into a dour young man.[19] His primary focus was revenge against the "Crusader Americans" who had killed his beloved father.[20]

When his first statement emerged, issued by Al Qaeda's media wing As Sahab in August 2015, Hamzah called for a renewal of holy war against the

West and suggested that Al Qaeda lone-wolf supporters should prepare for new attacks, specifically on Washington, London, Tel Aviv, and Paris.

He thanked Al Qaeda's regional emirs for their loyalty, sounding like the dauphin of terror, singling out Abu Mohammad al-Julani of the Nusra Front, asking him to continue to keep his distance from Abu Bakr al-Baghdadi. "We were pained and saddened . . . due to the sedition that pervaded your field, and there is no power or strength but with Allah. We advise you to stay away as far as possible from this sedition."

May 20, 2015, Washington, D.C.

While the Obama administration did its best to downplay Al Qaeda's ongoing relevance, the group's subtle maneuverings in Syria, Iran, and Qatar were observed by senior military officers with a growing sense of concern and frustration. A huge cache of primary source material was sitting in a vault in McLean, Virginia, and yet military intelligence analysts, whose job was to provide critical assistance to U.S. troops fighting in Afghanistan and Iraq, had been prevented from seeing it by the CIA.

U.S. Central Command (CENTCOM) and the Defense Intelligence Agency (DIA) had begun lobbying for access to the Abbottabad document trove as soon as it was brought back to the United States in 2011. But the CIA had stalled them, saying it was being subjected to what CIA documentation exploitation experts described as "a triage," meaning an initial keyword search that swept for suspect phone numbers, names, and addresses to gain immediately actionable intelligence from the documents.[21]

Osama's correspondence files had then been locked away as a bureaucratic battle ensued, the White House and CIA resisting demands for wider access on the grounds that the CIA had "executive authority," while the U.S. military insisted it needed to see what Al Qaeda was planning for operational security.[22] Lieutenant General Michael T. Flynn, the DIA director who would go on to serve briefly in President Donald Trump's administration in 2017, acting as National Security Advisor, particularly wanted to corroborate indications that Al Qaeda was actively plotting new attacks. Also of interest was any material that illuminated the growing relationship with Al Qaeda and Iran. "We were trying to gain historical knowledge of the organization, to see how it functioned," said Michael Pregent, a former DIA analyst.

Eventually and only after sustained lobbying by the CIA director David Petraeus, who had previously been the U.S. CENTCOM commander and supported the military's position, did his boss, James Clapper, the president's director of national intelligence, give permission for a combined DIA/CENTCOM team visit. But the access was time-limited and read-only.

Pregent, who was on the team, worked fast. "We started seeing stuff nobody was talking about, like Iranian facilitation of Al Qaeda travel into Pakistan, for example," he recalled.[23] The DIA produced analyses reflecting that Al Qaeda had been strengthening and expanding in several different foreign theaters at the time of Osama's death. The movement was very much alive and, the DIA concluded, it would thrive under a new leadership.

However, even while the DIA/CENTCOM experts were still inside the vault collating data, a very different message was presented to the public on the first anniversary of the Abbottabad raid, when the Combating Terrorism Center at West Point published its analysis of seventeen declassified letters. The handpicked documents gave a clear message that Osama and Al Qaeda were on the decline, a theme reinforced by the president when he said: "The goal that I set—to defeat Al Qaeda and deny it a chance to rebuild—is now within our reach." Soon after, the DIA's access was suspended by the president's National Security Council, a decision ratified by John Brennan when he became CIA director in March 2013.

Pressure to free up the documents continued to mount, much of it coming from Congress, where in 2014 a new Intelligence Authorization Act was passed that required Clapper's directorate to conduct a review of bin Laden's letters with a view to releasing them. The act was backed by Bruce Riedel, one of the few civilians to have seen the documents with his own eyes, and Derek Harvey, a former senior DIA analyst.

Eventually, in May 2015, Clapper's office published 103 documents under the banner headline "Bin Laden's Bookshelf." The declassified material consisted of family correspondence and letters between Osama and Atiyah, some of which referred to Al Qaeda's ongoing relations with Iran. But this selection, too, portrayed Al Qaeda as spent and Osama as a man at the end of his useful life. Among the approved documents was an Islamic treatise on suicide prevention entitled "Is It the Heart You Are Asking?"[24]

Also included was a letter in which Osama corresponded with Atiyah about his son Hamzah's potential. "I see in him wisdom," Atiyah had written.[25] "I reminded him to thank God that he is in a safe place and that with patience all will happen and be fine." Above all else in life, Hamzah "wants to train and learn."

By the time this letter became public, Hamzah's transformation was semi-complete.[26]

Summer 2015, Tehran

General Qassem Suleimani had become one of the most influential figures in the Syrian war, taking advantage of the unrest to plot Iranian expansion and extend Shia influence.[27] The Quds Force and other secret cells from the Revolutionary Guard had stepped forward to assist Bashar al-Assad's forces, while the Iranian government extended a $7 billion loan to shore up the Syrian economy.

The United States had responded by sanctioning Suleimani, but Washington's maneuvering did nothing to curtail his activities, as Iran's supreme leader, Ayatollah Ali Khamenei, promoted him.[28]

Suleimani was prepared to team up with any movement that could help expand Iran's axis of resistance, even if they were ideologically opposed to Tehran. He convinced Iraqi Shia militiamen to support Assad's government forces, and Hezbollah fighters, too. Iran's own Basij militia, which was still required for domestic duties, crushing unrest, was kept in reserve. "Give me one brigade of the Basij and I could conquer the whole country," he bragged to an Iraqi politician.[29]

Just as the Quds Force had propped up Shia-baiting Zarqawi in 2002, releasing him from prison in Tehran and transporting him and his followers to Iraq so he could turn up the heat on U.S. forces there, Al Qaeda Central could be utilized for a military escalation against U.S.-backed forces fighting Assad in Syria.

By the summer of 2015, four of the five Al Qaeda military council leaders released from detention in the spring were on their way to Damascus via Turkey, where several comrades who had been freed from Iran earlier were waiting to assist them, including Othman bin Laden's father in-law Mohammed al-Islambouli.[30] Abu al-Khayr al-Masri, Abu Mohammed al-Masri, and the two Jordanians, Khalid al-Aruri and Sari Shihab, were going back to war.

Abu Mohammed, father-in-law to Hamzah, was considered by the United States as the "most experienced and capable operational planner not in U.S.

or allied custody."[31] Squaring the circle, he was also married to the daughter of Julani's top commander, Abu Faraj al-Masri, who had known al-Zawahiri since the early days and was currently active in Turkey and on the battlefront in Syria.

Between them, the four released Al Qaeda members also commanded the respect of Zarqawi's veterans in Syria. Aruri, as well as being related to Zarqawi through marriage, had been Zarqawi's most important deputy. Their appearance on the Syrian battlefield could hopefully transform the war from an internecine struggle between the Nusra Front and IS into a united assault on the U.S.-backed coalition.

Only Saif al-Adel, who U.S. officials had previously described as the most likely to step up as Al Qaeda leader should anything happen to Dr. al-Zawahiri, remained in Iran, held for another year on the orders of Qassem Suleimani as insurance that Al Qaeda's military council played ball.[32]

Because of the recent U.S.-brokered nuclear deal with Iran, news about the release of the four Al Qaeda detainees was dripped out slowly. However, in August 2015, around the same time Hamzah's first public statement appeared, Saif al-Adel, still in Tehran, published an online eulogy for al-Zawahiri's slain Syrian emissary, Abu Khalid al-Suri, who had been killed by five Islamic State suicide bombers in Aleppo in February 2014.

Saif described al-Suri as the "lion of Jihad Wahl," a reference to the Afghani training camp in which he worked in pre-9/11 Afghanistan, and wondered who, other than the "twisted" and "perverted," could possibly dare "to kill a sheikh among the sheikhs of the mujahideen."[33]

Official confirmation that four members of Al Qaeda's military council had been released by Tehran did not come until September 2015, when the Iranian government said it had "expelled" them. Soon after, influential jihadists began exchanging news on Twitter that the group was in Syria and working alongside Suleimani.[34]

Their arrival in the war zone would act like "a shot of energy," predicted Lieutenant General Michael T. Flynn, who had retired from the Defense Intelligence Agency after losing his battle with the CIA over the Abbottabad trove.[35] But while old faces were being resurrected, another was buried. Following months of speculation and stories spun by Afghanistan's intelligence establishment, the Taliban confirmed that their leader, Mullah Omar, who had not been seen in public for more than a decade, was dead. Even worse, the Taliban was forced to admit that he had actually been dead for two years already, spending his last days in a Karachi hospital. His deputy,

Mullah Akhtar Mansour, had issued pronouncements in his name in much the same way Dr. al-Zawahiri had intended to keep Osama bin Laden's image alive—even beyond his natural life span—had it not been for the Americans killing him so publicly.

In addition to courting Al Qaeda, General Qassem Suleimani continued to make other deals, perhaps his most significant luring Russia into the war on Assad's side. In a one-on-one meeting with President Vladimir Putin, Suleimani had laid a map of Syria out on the table, pointing to the IS advances but assuring him that "we haven't lost all the cards."[36]

By the summer of 2015, Suleimani was spending more time in Damascus than he did at home, working out of a heavily fortified nondescript building with the heads of the Syrian military, a Hezbollah commander, a coordinator of Iraqi Shia militias, and the former deputy commander of the Basij militia.[37] He met Assad regularly and was photographed on the battlefield wearing a beige sweatshirt, a canvas cap, and no flak jacket, further enhancing his image as fearless. Many Quds Force members had already died in the fighting, including Suleimani's close friend Hassan Shateri, a senior commander. "When I see the children of martyrs, I want to smell their scent, and I lose myself," Suleimani told the Iranian media shortly after attending Shateri's funeral.[38] In a speech before the Assembly of Experts—the clerics who choose the supreme leader—he declared: "We will support Syria to the end."

Prominent Al Qaeda supporters revealed on social media that Al Qaeda was planning to launch a new branch inside Iraq. Evidence emerged that al-Zawahiri had shifted his permanent base to Iran with Suleimani's blessing. The idea of Al Qaeda fighting in two theaters simultaneously was being actively promoted by Saif al-Adel and al-Zawahiri and had the secret backing of Iran.[39]

In May 2016, al-Zawahiri issued a new proclamation that suggested a thawing of relations between IS and Al Qaeda. "Either you unite to live as Muslims with dignity, or you bicker and separate and so are eaten one by one," the Al Qaeda leader railed.

The following day, Hamzah bin Laden announced his support for the "blessed Syrian revolution." He said: "The Islamic *ummah* should focus on jihad in al-Sham [Syria] . . . and unite the ranks of mujahideen. There is no longer an excuse for those who insist on division and disputes now that the whole world has mobilized against Muslims."

His statement coincided with the release of a second batch of letters from the Abbottabad archive, documents no longer conforming to the trope that Al Qaeda was down and out, and that instead confirmed the outfit as one still managing a cohesive global network with subordinates everywhere from West Africa to South Asia, and with Hamzah likely to emerge as its figurehead.

Soon after, former acting CIA director Michael Morell published a book in which he claimed that the archive showed that "bin Laden himself had not only been managing the organization from Abbottabad, he had been micro-managing it."[40] Even James Clapper, the president's director of national intelligence, who had tried to keep the documents from U.S. CENTCOM and the DIA, appeared to have changed his mind, saying that Al Qaeda "nodes in Syria, Pakistan, Afghanistan, and Turkey" were "dedicating resources to planning attacks."[41]

Only the Taliban continued to struggle. Two weeks after Hamzah's statement, new emir Mullah Mansour emerged from Iran, where he had spent several weeks, seeing his family in Zahidan and meeting officials. Crossing back into Pakistan at Taftan, using a fake Pakistani passport, he was spotted by a U.S drone halfway up the N40 to Quetta, the same road the Mauritanian had taken all those years ago to cement the Iran–Al Qaeda relationship. Mansour was taken out by two Hellfire missiles that smashed into his white Toyota Corolla, killing him and his driver. Dr. al-Zawahiri's move to Iran could not have been better timed.[42]

In July 2016, Al Qaeda's media arm, As Sahab, issued a third audio message from Hamzah, once again threatening revenge for the death of his father. "If you think that your sinful crime that you committed in Abbottabad has passed without punishment, then you thought wrong," he said. "What is correct is coming to you and its punishment is severe." The video accompanying Hamzah's words featured a photograph of his dead half brother Khalid and another of former Guantánamo detainee Faiz al-Kandari, who after fourteen years had been freed in January 2016 to his native Kuwait and had gone back into the arms of Al Qaeda in Syria. The production was entitled "We Are All Osama."

Soon after, Abu Mohammad al-Julani, the leader of the Nusra Front, also made his on-screen debut, dressed like Osama in a white turban and camouflage jacket. He announced that his group was formally splitting away from Al Qaeda, reinventing itself as a popular revolutionary movement bent on fighting the forces of President Assad of Syria, and renaming itself Jabhat Fateh al-Sham, or the Army of Conquest. It was a strategic move that Julani hoped would disassociate him from the previous rows with al-Baghdadi. To make sure that everyone knew the new organization was still loyal to Al Qaeda, al-Zawahiri's old friend Abu Faraj al-Masri sat at Julani's elbow throughout the recording.[43] A few days later, Abu al-Khayr al-Masri, one of the Tehran four, who was now identified as al-Zawahiri's deputy, released an accompanying audio message blessing the move, saying, "We direct the leadership of al-Nusra to go ahead with what preserves the good of Islam and the Muslims, and protects the jihad of the Syrian people."

Although Abu al-Khayr was killed in a missile strike in northern Syria in February 2017, Western observers were impressed by Al Qaeda's subtle shifting.[44] Not only was Dr. al-Zawahiri using the chaos of the Syrian war to revive Al Qaeda's fortunes and spread its geographical footprint across the Middle East, but Al Qaeda also appeared to have learned from past mistakes.[45] "They are much less brutal in Syria than they were in Iraq," observed Robert Ford, who had been U.S. ambassador to Syria from 2011 to 2014. "They are much more subtle in their tactics and have a lot more local support . . . This will make them much harder to contain."[46]

Hamzah made yet another appearance in August 2016, this time to criticize Saudi Arabia's ongoing war in Yemen. The Saudi royals were "great criminal thieves" and "agents of America," he said, echoing his father's words. The kingdom was "in dire need of change," Hamzah continued, before he issued a call to arms for all "youth and those capable of fighting" to join the mujahideen in Yemen.[47] In January 2017, the U.S. State Department designated Hamzah as a global terrorist.[48]

August 23, 2016, Camp 7, United States Naval Station, Guantánamo Bay, Cuba

Dressed in a white tunic and with his beard neatly trimmed, and flanked by two camouflage-clad Pentagon-appointed "personal representatives," Detainee 10016 sat in the $12 million Expeditionary Legal Complex at Guantánamo Bay, waiting to make his case to a military board that he should be considered for release.

One thousand three hundred miles away in Washington, D.C., more than a dozen reporters and human rights lawyers crowded into a conference room at the Pentagon to watch a live video feed.

Officially, they were here to observe a legal process introduced by the Obama administration in 2011 to review all detainee cases with a view to emptying the detention facility, an essential break, as the president saw it, from the Bush-Cheney era. But the real reason most had come was to catch the first glimpse of Abu Zubaydah: a detainee who the CIA had decided in April 2002 "should remain incommunicado *for the remainder of his life*."[49] As such, he had not been seen for almost fifteen years.

Zubaydah was one of the most controversial of the seventy-six detainees still housed at Guantánamo eight years after Obama's groundbreaking promise to close the facility, which continued to function at an annual cost of around half a billion dollars. The man around whom the CIA's torture program had been built and the first to be sent to a CIA "black site," the first to be waterboarded, and the only prisoner subjected to all of the CIA's approved techniques and others never formally approved, Zubaydah had come to define the war on terror years, his story eclipsing even that of his thirteen coprisoners in Guantánamo's Camp 7, who included 9/11 mastermind Khalid Shaikh Mohammad.

Once hailed by Dick Cheney as a place to hold "the worst of the worst," Guantánamo had by 2016 become an expensive and embarrassing reminder that the United States was willing to hold people captive for life, without a trial, undermining basic democratic principles.

Zubaydah's experience of the program created by former army psychologists Dr. Bruce Jessen and Dr. James Mitchell had sickened those few with security clearance to read his diary, and yet the years of torture had provided no actionable intelligence from him about Al Qaeda's future plans, according to the Senate Intelligence Committee.

Following the rules of Guantánamo hearings, the observers in Washington were not allowed to hear Zubaydah speak. Instead, his statement was read by one of the uniformed soldiers at his shoulders. To avoid any embarrassing outbursts, the sound from the courtroom was time-delayed by forty seconds and there was a censorship button, should the audio feed need to be cut completely.

The patch that in earlier Red Cross photographs had covered Zubaydah's left eye, lost due to botched plastic surgery or after his bloody capture in

Faisalabad in March 2002, depending on whom you believed, hung from a strap like a necklace and he wore a glass eye to keep the socket open. Now age forty-five, he had one pair of glasses to read with and another pair with which to address the board members who sat out of sight of the cameras and comprised senior officials from the Departments of Defense, Homeland Security, Justice, and State; the Joint Chiefs of Staff; and the Office of the Director of National Intelligence. In the face of this phalanx, Zubaydah had no legal counsel. His approved lawyer, Mark Denbeaux, had been forced to cancel his trip to Guantánamo at the last moment because his wife was on her deathbed.[50] The board had decided to go ahead anyway.

Summarizing Zubaydah's words, his military spokesman declared that the world of jihad now dominated by Islamic State was "out of control and had gone too far." Zubaydah wanted nothing to do with it and simply wanted to be reunited with his family. He talked of having some "seed money" to start a business, a reference to a $130,000 payment he had received from the Polish government in 2014, compensation for his time in the Stare Kiejkuty black site that had been awarded after his case was taken to the European Court of Human Rights in 2014.

Zubaydah's most up-to-date Guantánamo Detainee Profile was read out.[51] It had significantly softened over the years and had been last edited in preparation for the hearing. The man characterized in it was barely recognizable as relating to the same person President Bush had once declared "one of the top operatives plotting and planning death and destruction on the United States." None of the things Zubaydah had been previously accused of— such as being bin Laden's top lieutenant, being Number Three in Al Qaeda, and helping to plot 9/11—were any longer mentioned.

After more than fourteen years in custody and thousands of hours of interrogation, the United States now claimed only that Zubaydah had run a "mujahedeen facilitation network" in the 1990s, "played a key role in Al Qaeda's communications," and before 9/11 had "closely interacted" with the Number Two in Al Qaeda, Abu Hafs al-Masri. Like many others operating on the fringes of Al Qaeda prior to 9/11, he "possibly" had advance knowledge of the attacks on American embassies in East Africa in 1998 and the bombing of the American destroyer *Cole* in Yemen in 2000. But he was now described as only being "generally aware" of planning for the 9/11 attacks and having "possibly" coordinated training at Khaldan camp when two of the future hijackers were there.

Unlike the five 9/11 defendants—Khalid Shaikh Mohammad, Ramzi bin al-Shibh, Ammar al-Balochi, Mustafa Ahmad al-Hawsawi, and Walid bin Attash, who when they were charged in 2008 told the judge they wanted to plead guilty and become martyrs—Zubaydah had always denied he was a member of Al Qaeda, something that the Senate Intelligence Committee had also concluded.[52] At the end of the hearing, the board retired to consider its verdict.

A journalist from the *New York Times* who witnessed the fourteen and a half minutes of public proceedings described the military case against Zubaydah as concluding "with unsettling ambiguity." As the fifteen observers left the Pentagon conference room, murmurs of "handsome," "striking," "good looking," "not so disheveled like you might expect" could be heard, unusual words to describe someone alleged to have perpetrated unspeakable crimes against humanity.[53]

However, another of Zubaydah's lawyers, Joseph Margulies, who first met his client in 2007 shortly after the Red Cross was also allowed to see him for the first time, remained pessimistic.[54] "This was mere political theater," he said, explaining that government lawyers had made it clear to him long ago that his client occupied a bizarre netherworld: he had not been charged in the military commission system, let alone a real court, and probably never would be.[55] But because of what he had endured in Thailand and elsewhere, he could never be released.

"He became the poster child for the torture program and that's why they will always keep him under wraps," said Margulies, who, along with Mark Denbeaux, had regularly flown down to Cuba over the past few years to meet their client in a small wooden ten-by-twelve-foot makeshift cell where they sat at a plastic folding table, with Zubaydah's feet shackled to a ring in the floor. Denbeaux and Margulies, who sometimes brought food parcels and family updates, represented Zubaydah's only link to the outside world.

Like many Guantánamo inmates, Zubaydah suffered from serious psychological conditions as a result of his long years of incarceration, including uncontrollable shaking, memory loss, fainting, and vomiting, said Denbeaux. Alone in his cell at Camp 7, he was sometimes observed banging his head against the wall to drown out the noises he heard and to "spread the pain" of a headache he had had since 2002.

While Guantánamo's military psychologists, psychiatrists, and mental health teams operated under strict instructions to avoid any discussion with detainees about their experiences during interrogation, Margulies and

Denbeaux had recorded intimate details of their client's torture.[56] "Literally physically sick" is how people would feel if allowed to read his case file, said Margulies.

Out of the 76 prisoners remaining at Guantánamo (166 had been transferred since Obama took office), the government said it now hoped to send more than half to foreign countries after they appeared before the review board.[57] Ten would be tried by military commissions, including the five 9/11 defendants who faced the death penalty if convicted, but twenty-five more—who the White House referred to as the "irreducible minimum" and who everyone else called the "forever prisoners"—faced an uncertain fate.

But even the seemingly straightforward cases against those who had admitted to their roles in 9/11 were by now contaminated, their hearings turned into embarrassing spectacles. After attempts to hold their trial in New York were halted in 2010, for fear it would draw another terrorist attack to the city, their cases were transferred back to Guantánamo and their guilty pleas were set aside. Proceedings were frequently interrupted by Ramzi bin al-Shibh, who military psychiatrists had concluded had gone crazy as a result of his years of incarceration, or by Khalid Shaikh Mohammad, who appeared in court dressed in a military-style waistcoat to hector and taunt the judge. During one hearing, their codefendant Walid bin Attash had to be restrained in a chair. In October 2016, Mustafa Ahmad al-Hawsawi's pretrial hearing had to be adjourned after his defense attorney, a Navy Reserve officer, revealed that his client was having urgent rectal prolapse surgery.[58] He described his client as having been "sodomized" during CIA torture.

Even the U.S. military sometimes struggled to present a united front. In 2014, Khalid's Pentagon-appointed lawyer, Major Jason Wright, had resigned after accusing the Army of trying to undermine his client's right to a fair trial. Wright tried to represent him as a civilian but was thrown off the case.[59]

In late 2016, Abu Zubaydah was informed that his request for transfer had been denied.[60] In February 2017 he spoke to his parents in Saudi Arabia via Skype.[61] Some detainees had better luck. In October 2016, just weeks ahead of the U.S. presidential election, Mohamedou Ould Slahi, the brother-in-law of Mahfouz the Mauritanian, was released, bringing the number down to sixty inmates.[62] Slahi had become a *New York Times* bestselling author from inside the walls of the world's most infamous prison with his book *Guantánamo Diary*. "I would like to believe the majority of Americans want to see justice done, and they are not interested in financing the detention of innocent people," Slahi had written. "I know there is a small extremist minority that believes everybody in this Cuban prison is evil, and that we are treated better than we deserve. But this opinion has no basis but ignorance."

Just weeks after Slahi's departure, Donald Trump, a man who many Americans once thought only represented a small extremist minority, was voted in as president, shocking everyone connected to Guantánamo. During campaigning, he had promised to reverse Obama's decision to close the facility. Instead, he would "load it up" with more bad guys, including, potentially, American citizens and illegal immigrants. He championed torture and "waterboarding" and promised to bring the procedure back and enhance it.

As this book goes to press forty-one prisoners remain at Guantánamo and Trump's plans for the facility are yet to be made public. But some awkward facts remain: despite multiple requests to visit the facility the United Nations Special Rapporteur on Torture has been repeatedly refused access. Despite a Defense Department outreach project to allow independent observers from Indiana University's Maurer School of Law to witness military tribunal and review board proceedings, no truly independent assessment has ever been made as to the likelihood that the remaining detainees will ever be afforded a fair trial.

September 2016, Syria

By the fifteenth anniversary of 9/11, Islamic State appeared to be rapidly contracting. "Everywhere they have tried to make a stand in recent times, they have been hosed out," said one Baghdad-based U.S. diplomat. "They know it's near the end."[63]

Once in control of an area roughly the size of the United Kingdom, Abu Bakr al-Baghdadi's fighters had lost significant territory. They had been driven out of the Iraqi cities of Ramadi and Fallujah and routed from the ancient Syrian town of Palmyra (only later to retake it), as well as the Syrian countryside bordering Turkey and the gateway cities of Jarabulus and Manbij, through which European recruits had once poured. Farther afield in Libya, IS fighters were evicted from their headquarters in Sirte, and Abu Bakr's Khorasan branch that operated in Afghanistan and Pakistan was thrown into disarray after the death of its leader, Hafiz Saeed Khan, in July 2016.

Dozens of Abu Bakr's most senior lieutenants were dead. After losing Abu Alaa al-Afri, his second-in-command, in March 2016, an Iraqi called

Abu Waheeb, who had been one of IS's most feared executioners, was targeted in May 2016. Two months later an important IS commander, Abu Omar al-Shishani, was also killed, and in August Abu Bakr's chief spokesman, Abu Mohammed al-Adnani, who had announced the caliphate in June 2014 and was principal architect of IS's external operations, died in a U.S. airstrike near Raqqa.[64] Abu Bakr's "information minister," a man who oversaw the group's gruesome execution videos, met the same fate in Raqqa just over a week later.[65]

Rapid victories on the battlefield had drawn thousands of young Muslims to the movement. Now, the U.S. government crowed as the black flags were ripped down all over Syria and Iraq, men shaved their beards while women allowed themselves to be photographed taking off their *niqabs*. Between thirty thousand and fifty thousand IS fighters were estimated dead, and stories abounded that Abu Bakr's Western support was hemorrhaging, with thousands reaching out to friends and even diplomats to try to negotiate a passage home. Embarrassingly, some were caught wearing *burqas* in an attempt to hide their escape.[66] "We are now really into the heart of the caliphate," said General Joseph Votel, the U.S. CENTCOM commander, at the end of August 2016. "We do see momentum building."[67]

In mid-October 2016, Turkish rebels drove Islamic State out of the symbolic town of Dabiq in northern Syria. Days later, Iraqi forces, backed by U.S.-led airstrikes and assisted by Kurdish Peshmerga fighters, launched an offensive to retake Mosul, Iraq's second largest city, where Abu Bakr had made his famous speech declaring the caliphate in 2014. Next in their sights was Raqqa, where IS began in April 2013, and Al Bab, from where IS had plotted much of the carnage it wreaked in Paris, Brussels, and Istanbul. Aleppo was also retaken. Caught in the middle were Iraqi and Syrian civilians, who continued to die in large numbers.

Counterterrorism experts warned that as its power was shaken, IS would redouble its efforts to launch "mass casualty attacks" in the West.[68] Several hundred IS acolytes were said to have slipped back in to Europe to establish cells. Speaking in August 2016, President Obama predicted that the group would in the future rely on small-scale terrorist attacks to generate "the kind of fear and concern that elevates their profile."[69]

His words were echoed by Abu Muhammad al-Maqdisi, who said in December 2016 that IS had "never been stronger."[70] Holding grounds was no longer important. Lone wolf attacks in Europe and destabilizing Turkey were all that mattered. Days later, a Christmas market was attacked in

Berlin. On New Year's Eve, thirty-nine died in a gun attack on the Reina nightclub in Istanbul.

Al Qaeda, once Islamic State's ideological rival, was also growing stronger by exploiting the chaos. While the world was mesmerized by the IS reign of horror and swayed by the Obama administration's dissembling message that it and Al Qaeda were both spent, al-Zawahiri, who had been ignored and written off, settled on a more pragmatic approach, building confidences among the regional franchises, burrowing deeper into host country Iran, and creating alliances through Julani's Army of Conquest, now Al Qaeda's largest-ever affiliate (that is not an affiliate) with an estimated ten thousand fighters.[71] In late 2016, he was also strengthened by the release, finally, of Saif al-Adel, who was flown from Tehran to Damascus with General Qassem Suleimani's blessing.

"Eliminating the caliphate will be an achievement," said one former State Department counterterrorism coordinator. "But more likely it will just be the end of the beginning rather than the beginning of the end."[72]

On the morning of September 11, 2001, having settled into a mountain redoubt that overlooked the plains of Khost, Osama bin Laden had considered his future, with his sons and a handful of fighters sitting around him. Pouring hot tea into a beaker, while a brother fiddled with a satellite dish that was clearly never going to be capable of broadcasting news of the most important day in Osama's life, he turned to his cohorts, trying to conceal his disappointment.

There were many missing faces; the ones he had hoped would share this moment with him. But most of Al Qaeda's leadership had rejected the Planes Operation as an off-the-books project, planned and executed almost entirely by brothers who were not in the outfit.

"They rejected Holy Tuesday," Osama said, bitterly, of the *shura*.[73] "But they forgot one thing."

He looked around, nodding his head.

"We are *not* writing our history. But America will and many times over. What it will say—regardless—is that *we all* . . ."

He gathered in the room with his arms.

". . . did this. Everyone associated with our cause, regardless of who they are, where they were, and what they said—will be condemned to the same fate. But never mind," he cautioned, "a time will come . . ."

He sipped some tea.

". . . when there is time to write our own version."

He visualized a tome, detailing triumphs and tragedies, rivalries, jealousies, and great victories.

"An unexpurgated document is what will emerge—about an epoch that begins today."

Acknowledgments

THIS BOOK STARTED TO COALESCE THANKS to Zakariya al-Sadeh, a Yemeni student, pro-democracy campaigner, and brother of Amal bin Laden, Osama's youngest wife, who we met in February 2012 in Islamabad as he struggled to free her from detention in Pakistan. A tense discussion with Zakariya led to nervy meetings with many others that resulted eventually in conversations with Osama's family, friends, mentors, companions, factotums, security chiefs, and religious and media advisers. Daniel Pearl's fate is branded into the collective memory: the luring and videoed murder (by Khalid Shaikh Mohammad) of the *Wall Street Journal* correspondent in 2002. And, perhaps surprisingly, it is as much a burden on the collective consciousness of Islamists as it was with us.

But the Pearl miasma began to fade, and finally, something unique came into focus—as we traveled wherever a meeting could be brokered—from Mauritania to Yemen, Jordan, Saudi Arabia, the Emirates, Kuwait, the United States, and Pakistan. Many people in these countries helped bring this book together: religious scholars; Al Qaeda fighters, commanders, thinkers, and cheerleaders; Al Qaeda fund-raisers and their friends; as well as Gulf intelligence agents and their sources (working with Al Qaeda and sometimes against it), who cannot or do not wish to be named. This book would not have been possible without their input.

In Pakistan, after making our case that senior officers should express the country's national interest in the way that American officials freely and frequently do, some came forward just as the military establishment struggled to regain composure, respect, and authority after being rocked by the Abbottabad affair. The military is not monotheistic and consists of many different shades of opinion. Senior officers who cannot be named took enormous risks in-country (and out of Pakistan) to meet. Those we can name include General Asim Bajwa, General Athar Abbas, Brigadier Shaukat Qadir, Brigadier Syed Amjad Shabbir, General Masood Aslam, General Jehangir Karamat, Commodore Zafar Iqbal, General Ziauddin Butt, and of course the late General Hamid Gul, who began cautiously and mischievously—but the written and verbal accounts he shared with us were pinpoint, perceptive, and captivating, proving his proximity to the unfolding epoch of terror, which has bloodied Pakistan more than anywhere else in the world.

The civilian authorities of Pakistan are throttled and struggle to manage with the political capital they are given, but among those we can name and thank are Syed Kaleem Imam, Tajik Sohail Habib, Ihsan Ghani Khan, Khalid Qureshi, and Tariq Pervez, among many others.

Also in Pakistan, we thank Yemeni student and embassy worker Abdulrahman Alsalehi, who opened many doors and shared his recollections of his friendship with and assistance to the al-Sadehs during the months following Osama bin Laden's death.

Gaining anyone's trust in FATA, Pakistan, is always difficult and we thank tribal journalists Rasool Dawar, Fauzee Khan, Tahir Khan, and Gohar Mehsud for helping us. As always, Rahimullah Yusufzai, the doyen of independent Pakistani reporting, generously gave us his time, contacts, and advice in Peshawar. Thanks also to his sons, Taimur and Najeeb, for accompanying us on reporting trips and dealing with countless requests. In Islamabad, journalists Umar Cheema, Azaz Syed, Hamid Mir, Sabookh Syed, the late Syed Saleem Shahzad, Haroon Rashid, and Jon Boone all gave help or listened. Shahzad Akbar of the Foundation for Fundamental Rights provided access to the victims of U.S. drone warfare in Waziristan and an insight into the frightening reality of living in such areas.

Elsewhere, insight into Osama bin Laden and dealing with Al Qaeda's publicity machine came from Abdel Bari Atwan, Jamal Ismail, and Ahmad Zaidan.

In Mauritania, a huge thank-you to Mahfouz Ibn El Waleed (Abu Hafs al Mauritania) for sharing his memories of living with the Al Qaeda leader and his family. Thanks also to Mauritanian journalists Ahmed Vall Dine and Hamdi Ould Med Elhassen.

In Jordan thanks go out to Marwan Shehadah, Suha Maayeh, and Fuad Hussein for helping us make connections, and to Yousuf Rabbaba, Hasan

Abu Haniya, Abu Qatada, Abu Muhammad al-Maqdisi, Abdullah Jafar, Hamza Shemali, Huthaifa Azzam, Samira Abdullah, and Salah al-Hami for their recollections of Abu Musab al-Zarqawi and Al Qaeda.

The list of those who helped us in the United States is long, but those we would like to thank personally for their insight and advice include Robert Grenier, William D. Murray, Zalmay Khalilzad, Ryan Crocker, James Dobbins, Nada Bakos, Cynthia Storer, Richard Barrett, Brad Garrett, Andrew Liepman, Mansoor Ijaz, Husain Haqqani, Ali Soufan, Nelly Lahoud, Bruce Riedel, Jack Cloonan, Stanley Cohen, Larry Siems, Brigadier General (Ret.) Stephen Xenakis, Dan Coleman, Art Keller, Will McCants, Vahid Brown, Daveed Gartenstein-Ross, Thomas Joscelyn, Joseph Margulies, Professor Mark Denbeaux, Dr. James Mitchell, Hesham and Jody Abu Zubaydah, and Afshon Ostovar. Thank you, Mark Mazzetti, for connections and suggestions. Thank you to David Eckles and Minette Nelson and the Filmmaker Fund for your assistance and guidance with our trips to Mauritania to meet Mahfouz Ibn El Waleed.

Achieving anything in Yemen during the writing of this book was extremely difficult due to the unfolding war, and many who we were able to interview were living in fear and in hiding so do not wish to be named. Those who did help and can be identified include Ahmed Baider; Amal bin Laden's father, Ahmed Abdul-Fattah al-Sadeh; and Abu Jandal, who has since died. Thanks also to Iona Craig and Peter Salisbury.

In the United Kingdom, we would first like to thank former High Commissioner Wajid Shamsul Hasan for generously sharing his memories of crucial times and his family for their hospitality. Thanks to Maya Foa and Clive Stafford Smith at Reprieve, and to the BBC's Gordon Corera for putting us in touch with "Omar Nasiri," and thank you to Omar. Thanks to Nigel Inkster, thirty-one years in the British Secret Intelligence Service (SIS) and now with the International Institute of Strategic Studies. Major General Roger Lane shared his recollections of British military operations in Afghanistan after Osama disappeared at Tora Bora. Thank you to Hurst publisher Michael Dwyer, the Egyptian cleric Yassir al-Sirri, Abdullah Azzam's son-in-law Abdullah Anas, and Kemal Alam for sharing his family contacts and Pakistan military connections.

Thank you very much to Alex Strick van Linschoten for offering advice and sharing several unpublished jihad memoirs. Thanks to Declan Walsh for assistance with the family of Aafia Siddiqui.

A huge thanks to our publisher George Gibson in New York, to our managing editor, Laura Phillips, and to Michael Fishwick and Alexandra Pringle and the team in London. George believed that a book like this could be written before we did. Thanks too to Kirsty McLachlan at DGA for her ongoing efforts to introduce our work to a larger audience. And, finally, thank you to David Godwin: ever listening, constantly encouraging, and always hopeful.

Brief Biographies of Major Characters

Ages accurate as of 2017 or at time of death

bin Laden family

Osama bin Laden, 54, founded Al Qaeda in 1988 with Abdullah Azzam and was killed by U.S. Navy SEALs during Operation Neptune Spear in Abbottabad, Pakistan, on May 2, 2011. Also known as "the father," "the Sheikh," and Abu Abdullah (father of Abdullah).

Najwa bin Laden, 57, from Latakia, Syria, first wife and first cousin of Osama. They married in 1974 when she was 16 and she bore him eleven children. She fled Afghanistan two days before 9/11, taking three children with her.

Khairiah bin Laden, 68, from Saudi Arabia, second wife of Osama bin Laden at the time of his death. A child psychologist, she married Osama in 1985 after treating his disabled sons. She bore him one child, Hamzah. After nine years in Iran, Khairiah was reunited with Osama in February 2011. The family believes that the Iranians implanted a tracking device on her body and passed information about her destination to the CIA.

Seham bin Laden, 60, a Saudi-born teacher of Arabic grammar, she was Osama's third wife at the time of his death, having married him in 1987. Mother of Khalid, Khadija, Miriam, and Sumaiya, she fled Afghanistan for Pakistan after 9/11 and was reunited with Osama in 2004.

Amal bin Laden, 34, from Yemen, fourth wife of Osama at the time of his death. She had five children, four of whom were born in Pakistan. She and her youngest son, Hussein, then aged three, witnessed Osama's killing and she was shot in the leg.

Saad bin Laden, 30, third son of Osama and Najwa. Born autistic, he nominally led the main family group into exile in Iran in 2002. He escaped in

2008 in an attempt to reconnect with his father. He became lost on the Iran-Pakistan border and was accidentally killed in a drone strike in North Waziristan in July 2009.

Omar bin Laden, 35, fourth son of Osama and Najwa, and once a contender to inherit Al Qaeda. He became disillusioned with his father's mission and left Afghanistan in 2001. After several years of trying to reestablish his life in Saudi Arabia, he met and married Zaina, a British woman. Although other members of the family accused her of being a spy, Zaina subsequently helped bin Laden family members leave Iran and reestablish their lives in Qatar.

Othman bin Laden, 33, fifth son of Osama and Najwa. He spent nine years in detention in Iran and now lives in Doha with his mother and siblings. He has two Egyptian wives: one is the daughter of Saif al-Adel, the chief of Al Qaeda's military council, and the other is a niece of Khalid al-Islambouli, who participated in the 1981 assassination of Egyptian president Anwar Sadat.

Mohammed bin Laden, 31, sixth son of Osama and Najwa. He married the daughter of his father's deputy, Abu Hafs al-Masri, in January 2001. After the U.S. invasion of Afghanistan in October 2001, Mohammed fled with the rest of the family group to Iran, where they remained for nine years. He lives in Doha.

Fatima bin Laden, 29, Osama and Najwa's oldest daughter. She was married at the age of 13 to one of her father's Saudi fighters. After he was killed trying to smuggle bin Laden family members into Pakistan in November 2001, she traveled to Iran, where she later married Sulaiman Abu Ghaith, her father's spokesman, with whom she has two children. In 2013, her husband was captured and extradited to the United States. She lives with other family members near Jeddah.

Khadija bin Laden, 20, Osama and Seham's oldest daughter. At the age of 13 she married Abu Abdallah al-Hallabi, the brother of Fatima's first husband. After 9/11, she fled with her husband, who was also known as Daood, to Waziristan and bore him three children. She died in 2007 while giving birth to twins, one of whom died. Daood later sent their surviving children to live with Osama and they were in the house on the night that he died.

Khalid bin Laden, 22, Osama's only son with Seham. He remained with his father from 9/11 onward, traveling with him to Tora Bora then into hiding in Kunar Province and later to Pakistan, where he acted as his father's chief assistant. Khalid had made plans to marry and relocate to Waziristan shortly before he was killed alongside his father in May 2011.

Iman bin Laden, 26, Osama's second daughter with Najwa. After surviving the U.S. invasion of Afghanistan in October 2001, Iman joined the family group in Iran. She escaped in November 2009 and was reunited with her mother. She revealed that the rest of the family was being held against its wishes by the Iranian authorities. She is married to a cousin and lives in Jeddah.

Hamzah bin Laden, 27, Osama's most stridently religious son. After eight years in Iran, he was released in 2010 in exchange for a kidnapped Iranian diplomat and was briefly reunited with his father in Pakistan. The U.S. government initially believed it had killed Hamzah at Abbottabad but he has reemerged as a new figurehead for Al Qaeda, issuing audio recordings that call for attacks on America, Saudi Arabia, and the Syrian regime of Bashar al-Assad.

Ladin bin Laden, 24, seventh son of Osama and Najwa. He was a young boy when his mother fled shortly before 9/11. After witnessing the U.S. invasion of Afghanistan, he fled to Iran and was detained in Tehran. He now lives in Doha with his mother and siblings.

Miriam bin Laden, 26, second daughter of Osama and Seham. She spent most of her teenage years in hiding in Pakistan. She became surrogate mother to her dead sister Khadija's children at the age of 18. Along with her younger sister, Sumaiya, who was 19 at the time of the raid that killed their father, she was manhandled by SEAL Team Six and forced to identify her father's dead body. She lives in Jeddah.

Zaina bin Laden, 61, British wife of Omar. Born Jane Felix Browne, she met Omar during a horse-trekking holiday in Egypt in 2006. They married the following year and were vilified in the press when their relationship became public. Zaina lives with Omar in a compound provided by the Qatari government in Doha, alongside Najwa and many other family members.

Al Qaeda shura members

Abu Hafs al-Masri, real name Mohammed Atef, mid-50s, Osama's deputy and close friend. A former policeman in Egypt, Abu Hafs helped plan the 9/11 attacks and was killed in a U.S. missile attack in Afghanistan in November 2001.

Dr. Ayman al-Zawahiri, 65, founder of Egyptian Islamic Jihad and a close associate of Osama bin Laden for more than two decades. After 9/11, Dr. al-Zawahiri fled to Pakistan, leaving his wife and two children to be killed by a U.S. missile strike. Al-Zawahiri took over Al Qaeda after Osama's death and is believed to be sheltered in Iran.

Saif al-Adel, 56, a former colonel in the Egyptian army. He helped mastermind the attacks on U.S. embassies in Nairobi and Dar-es-Salaam in 1998 and in November 2001 became the head of Al Qaeda's military council. After sneaking into Iran in 2003, he orchestrated several more attacks, including the bombing of Western housing compounds in Saudi Arabia, and he was able to maintain close links with Al Qaeda Central via the outfit's Iran "pipeline." He was released by the Iranian authorities in early 2016 and traveled to Syria. He is married to a daughter of Mustafa Hamid, a former Al Jazeera correspondent, with whom he has five children.

Abu Mohammed al-Masri, 53, aka Abdullah Ahmed Abdullah, another Egyptian member of Al Qaeda's military council. Once a professional soccer player, he, along with Saif al-Adel, was on the original twenty-two-person Most Wanted Terrorists list issued by the FBI. After being released from Iranian detention in March 2015, he traveled to Syria with several former associates of Abu Musab al-Zarqawi, the founder of Al Qaeda in Iraq.

Abu al-Khayr al-Masri, 58, head of Al Qaeda's political committee before 9/11 and an explosives expert. He was sentenced to death in absentia in Egypt in 1998. Released from Iranian detention in 2015 after more than a decade, he has resumed his Al Qaeda activities in Syria. In July 2016, he issued an audio statement in which he was described as deputy to Dr. al-Zawahiri. He was killed in a missile strike near Idlib in northern Syria in February 2017.

Mahfouz Ibn El Waleed, 49, a religious scholar who served as Osama bin Laden's spiritual adviser and chairman of Al Qaeda's *sharia* (legal) committee for a decade before 9/11. Known as "Abu Hafs the Mauritanian," he ran the House of the Pomegranates theological school in Kandahar and acted as Osama's go-between with Mullah Omar. Shortly before 9/11, Mahfouz resigned from Al Qaeda but still arranged for the bin Laden family to seek refuge in Iran. He lived in a military complex in Tehran with them and Al Qaeda's military committee for almost a decade before escaping in 2011. He lives in Nouakchott, Mauritania, with his wife and six children.

Sheikh Saeed al-Masri, 54, a key associate of Osama bin Laden for almost thirty years. After fleeing into Pakistan in late 2001, he became Al Qaeda's Number Two and chief of finances and was closely involved in establishing Al Qaeda Central in Pakistan's Tribal Areas. He was killed by a U.S. drone strike in 2010.

Atiyah Abd al-Rahman, aka Sheikh Mahmud, 41, a Libyan-born member of Al Qaeda who acted as an important go-between with Al Qaeda Central and the military council in Iran before succeeding Sheikh Saeed al-Masri. By the end of 2010, Atiyah had become Osama's most important deputy. He was killed in a drone strike in North Waziristan in August 2011 along with his entire family.

Other important members of Al Qaeda and supporters

Khalid Shaikh Mohammad, aka Mokhtar, 52, the self-confessed mastermind of the 9/11 attacks. KSM, as the CIA dubbed him, first came up with the idea of using passenger jets as flying bombs in the early nineties in collaboration with his nephew Ramzi Yousef, who attacked the World Trade Center in New York in 1993. He tried several times before securing Osama bin Laden's support for the "Planes Operation," which was planned without the knowledge or authorization of Al Qaeda's *shura*. After 9/11, KSM plotted several more attacks from his hub in Karachi and hosted Osama there on at least one occasion. Arrested in a joint CIA/ISI (Pakistan's Inter-Services Intelligence) operation in Rawalpindi in March 2003, KSM was rendered to secret CIA detention sites and tortured. He is currently held at Guantánamo Bay, where he is being tried by a military commission.

Ramzi bin al-Shibh, 44, the operational coordinator of 9/11. Later, he served as deputy to Khalid Shaikh Mohammad and plotted several more attacks against Western targets. He was caught during a joint ISI/CIA operation in Karachi in September 2002 and remains in Guantánamo Bay, where he is one of five detainees charged with planning the 9/11 attacks. Since being diagnosed with a delusional disorder, his trial proceedings have been put on hold.

Abu Musab al-Suri, 58, a Syrian jihad theologian who lectured at Al Qaeda training camps during the Soviet war and authored *The Call for Global Islamic Resistance* while hiding out in Iran in 2003. Married to a Spanish woman, he was accused of playing a crucial role in the Madrid train bombings of 2004 and was captured by the ISI in Quetta in 2005. Handed over to the CIA, he was rendered to Syria, where he is still thought to be detained in Sedanaya prison.

Abu Zubaydah, 45, a Saudi-born Palestinian logistical expert who sent recruits and funds to jihad training camps in Afghanistan from his base in Peshawar. After 9/11, he assisted in the relocation of many Arab fighters and their families to Pakistan. He was captured in Faisalabad in March 2002 in a joint ISI/CIA operation. The CIA accused him of being Al Qaeda's Number Three, Osama bin Laden's lieutenant, and one of the planners of 9/11, and he spent several years as a ghost detainee in the CIA's covert rendition program and was the first to undergo Enhanced Interrogation Techniques. Although the United States now admits he is innocent of most of these allegations, he remains at Guantánamo Bay, held without charges and classified as a "forever prisoner."

Sulaiman Abu Ghaith, 51, a Kuwaiti cleric and preacher who was invited to lecture at Mahfouz's House of the Pomegranates in June 2001. As he was still there when 9/11 happened, Osama bin Laden asked him to record a video supporting the attacks. Unable to return home to Kuwait, he followed bin Laden's family and associates into Iran. In 2008, he married Fatima bin Laden. In 2014, a New York court convicted him to life imprisonment for "conspiring to kill Americans."

Abu Qatada, 52, a Palestinian-Jordanian radical cleric who gained asylum in the United Kingdom during the nineties and was accused of being "Al Qaeda's man in Europe." Qatada spent a decade fighting deportation before voluntarily returning to Amman in July 2013. Since then he and his close associate, Abu Muhammad al-Maqdisi, have played a crucial role in negotiating between Al Qaeda's Syrian affiliates and Islamic State.

Abu Jandal, 43, Osama bin Laden's chief bodyguard prior to 9/11 who carried two special bullets with which to kill bin Laden if ever cornered. In 2000, Jandal played a vital role in bringing Osama's future wife Amal from Yemen. He was arrested in connection with the October 2000 attack on the USS *Cole* but after agreeing to enter a Yemeni deradicalization program, he was freed in 2002. He worked as a taxi driver until his death in 2015.

Khalid Shaikh Mohammad's network

Ammar al-Balochi, 39, KSM's nephew. He hosted several 9/11 hijackers in Dubai and arranged for their onward journeys to the United States. After 9/11, he was an important member of KSM's Karachi support network until he was captured in 2003 and found to be carrying a small perfume bottle containing low-grade cyanide. He remains at Guantánamo Bay, charged with plotting the 9/11 attacks.

Walid bin Attash, 37, aka Silver, Ammar al-Balochi's one-legged Yemeni deputy. Before 9/11, Attash helped send funds to the hijackers in the United States to pay for flight training and living expenses. He was captured along with Ammar al-Balochi in a joint CIA/ISI operation in Karachi and remains at Guantánamo Bay, charged with plotting the 9/11 attacks.

Hassan Ghul, one of KSM's main couriers who maintained communications between Al Qaeda Central, the military committee based in Iran, and Abu Musab al-Zarqawi in Iraq. When Kurdish forces captured him in 2004 he provided key information about Osama bin Laden's location, then he was rendered to a black site and tortured by the CIA. In 2006, he was released via the ISI with instructions that he should search Pakistan's Tribal Areas for Al Qaeda's leader. Instead he went rogue and he was killed in a drone strike in October 2012.

Ibrahim Saeed Ahmed, aka Abu Ahmad al-Kuwaiti, 34, a childhood friend of KSM who helped to train some of the hijackers. After 9/11, KSM deployed him as a courier to maintain communications with Osama bin Laden and in 2002 asked him to become Osama's permanent companion. To establish his cover story of having retired from jihadist activities, he married Maryam, a village girl from Shangla, in northwest Pakistan, and moved Osama into a vacant house owned by Maryam's parents. He was shot dead during the Abbottabad raid but Maryam survived and was intensively questioned by the ISI.

Abrar Saeed Ahmed, 36, older brother of Ibrahim and employed by him in 2003 to assist in caring for Osama bin Laden and his rapidly growing household. Abrar purchased the land on which Osama's Abbottabad compound was built and supervised construction of the house. He lived on the ground floor of the main floor and was killed during the raid, along with his Pakistani wife Bushra.

Pakistan military and intelligence services

General Javed Alam Khan, 70, a senior ISI official during the first eighteen months after 9/11 who worked closely with Robert Grenier of the CIA to apprehend high-value targets including Abu Zubaydah. The ISI and CIA opened a secret joint interrogation center in Islamabad code-named the Clubhouse but relations soured when the CIA demanded more access to detainees and insisted on taking a more prominent role in operations.

General Ehsan ul-Haq, 66, the director general of the Inter-Services Intelligence directorate from October 2001 to 2004. President Pervez Musharraf brought him in to replace General Mahmud Ahmed, who was regarded by Washington as supportive of the Taliban and Al Qaeda. Several high-value targets were apprehended in Pakistan during General ul-Haq's tenure.

General Pervez Musharraf, 73, seized control of Pakistan in a military coup in October 1999 and signed up to President George W. Bush's "war on terror" after 9/11. Pakistan benefited from more than $10 billion in U.S. aid during his time in power, most of which went directly to the military. After Musharraf was forced to resign as president in 2008 in the face of impeachment charges, Pakistan was accused of playing a double game by continuing to support the Taliban, Al Qaeda, and homegrown jihadi movements. Some opponents claim that Musharraf knew Osama was in Pakistan all along and that he was responsible for the assassination of his political nemesis, former prime minister Benazir Bhutto, in December 2007.

General Hamid Gul, 78, a former director general of the ISI who promoted himself as the Godfather of the Taliban and described Pakistan's outlawed jihadi leaders as his close friends. He secretly assisted in providing a ring of security around Osama in Abbottabad. In 2010, the ISI asked him to negotiate a peace deal with Osama and Al Qaeda and discussions were ongoing when Osama was killed. Gul died of natural causes in August 2015.

General Ahmed Shuja Pasha, 64, director general of the ISI at the time Osama bin Laden was killed. Pasha presided over a period in which relations with the CIA reached their nadir. He was named in U.S. court documents as being culpable in the 2008 Mumbai terrorist attacks and accused of protecting Osama bin Laden in Abbottabad, although there is no evidence to support this.

General Ashfaq Parvez Kayani, 64, Pakistan Army chief at the time Osama bin Laden was killed. Kayani was completely caught out by the covert U.S.

operation and took four days to issue a statement. He has never spoken about the raid or what he knew, if anything, of Osama bin Laden's presence in Pakistan.

Pakistani Islamist leaders known personally to Osama bin Laden

Fazlur Rehman Khalil, 55, the founder and leader of Harkat-ul-Mujahideen, who knew Osama since the time of the Soviet war in Afghanistan. Khalil, a Punjabi by birth, had been a popular commander, fluent in Arabic and a skilled operator with a Stinger missile. His group gained notoriety in 1995 when mujahideen loyal to him kidnapped six Western backpackers in Indian Kashmir, one of whom was beheaded. In 1998, Khalil became a signatory to Osama's famous fatwa against "Jews and Crusaders." He was at the forefront of the operation to protect Osama in Abbottabad. He lives in Islamabad.

Hafiz Saeed, 58, founder of the ISI-sponsored jihad group Lashkar-e-Taiba that planned and executed the Mumbai terrorist attacks of November 2008. Saeed knew Osama personally and was the "best friend" of General Hamid Gul. Although the U.S. government has placed a $10 million bounty on Saeed's head, he remains at liberty in Pakistan, regularly appearing at public rallies.

Ilyas Kashmiri, 47, a veteran of the elite Special Services Group (President Musharraf's former military unit). His skills were honed during the Afghan jihad of the eighties when he resigned his commission to establish an irregular brigade of fighters funded, armed, and trained by the ISI. During the nineties, the ISI sent him to battle Indian forces in Kashmir but he later went rogue and joined Al Qaeda. He made two assassination attempts on Musharraf in December 2003 and attacked the Pakistan naval base at Mehran, Karachi, in May 2011. He was killed by a U.S. drone strike using location intelligence provided by the ISI in August 2011.

Ghost detainees of U.S. war on terror

Dr. Ghairat Baheer, a son-in-law of the Afghan warlord Gulbuddin Hekmatyar. Baheer was detained in Islamabad in October 2002. An Afghan national, he was handed over to the CIA and flown to the Salt Pit, a secret CIA detention facility near Kabul, where he later met KSM. He was tortured but refused to provide information about Osama's whereabouts. He lost ninety pounds in his first month of detention and was later transferred to another secret U.S. prison at Bagram, where he remained until 2008.

Gul Rahman, 30, a friend of Ghairat Baheer who was arrested with him and was later found dead in his cell at Detention Site Cobalt, naked, with his shackled arms and legs chained to the wall. Although the CIA confirmed that a prisoner had died, his name was kept secret and his family was not informed. An investigation by the CIA Inspector General noted that the two architects of the CIA torture program were present at Cobalt when Rahman arrived and that one of them interrogated him, but he was not found to have played any role in Rahman's death.

Aafia Siddiqui, 44, a Pakistani-born, U.S.-educated neuroscientist who married KSM's nephew Ammar al-Balochi before being abducted and disappearing in 2003. After she reappeared and was arrested in 2008, U.S. government lawyers alleged that she had been assisting with future attacks on U.S. soil and had tried to shoot four U.S. security personnel. She alleged she was a ghost detainee between 2003 and 2008 and tortured. There is circumstantial evidence that she was kept at the Salt Pit. She was convicted to eighty-six years in prison in 2010.

Mohamedou Ould Slahi, 45, married to the sister of Mahfouz Ibn El Waleed's wife. He traveled to Afghanistan in 1991. He was arrested in Mauritania shortly after 9/11 and transferred to Guantánamo Bay, where he claimed that he was subjected to mock executions. He wrote a bestselling memoir, *Guantánamo Diary*, detailing the abuses he had suffered. He was released from Guantánamo in October 2016.

Iran

General Qassem Suleimani, 59, the head of the Quds Force, a special unit of Iran's Revolutionary Guard Corps (IRGC) responsible for extraterritorial clandestine operations. Suleimani took personal responsibility for Osama bin Laden's family and Al Qaeda's military council when they sought sanctuary in Iran in 2002, arranging for them to live inside the Quds Forces training headquarters. More recently, he has played a vital role in supporting Syrian president Bashar al-Assad, bringing in Russia, Hezbollah, and several Al Qaeda affiliates on the Syrian government's side. He was overall commander of the Aleppo offensive of 2015 and has been sanctioned by the U.S. government.

Ali Younsei, 60s, Iranian minister for intelligence and security when the Al Qaeda group was first placed under house arrest in the Quds Force compound in Tehran in 2002. He dealt personally with their representative, Mahfouz Ibn El Waleed.

Mohammad Javad Zarif, 56, U.S.-educated Iranian career diplomat and currently minister of foreign affairs. In 2003, Zarif played a key role in negotiations to reach a "Grand Bargain" with the United States, offering to hand over Osama bin Laden's family and Al Qaeda's military council, a deal that the United States rejected. He also led the discussions that resulted in the lifting of economic sanctions against Iran in January 2016.

Afghanistan

Mullah Omar, 51, founder of the Taliban. He allowed Osama bin Laden to relocate to Afghanistan in 1996, but two years later the leaders clashed at a stormy meeting in Kandahar and never spoke again. Many blamed bin Laden for a suicide attack on Mullah Omar's compound that injured Omar and killed one of his sons. Omar fled Afghanistan in October 2001 on the back of a motorbike and spent the rest of his life in Pakistan. Evidence that he had died in a Karachi hospital in 2013 did not emerge until two years later.

Gulbuddin Hekmatyar, 69, a notorious Afghan mujahideen commander who founded the Hezb-i-Islami party. One of the seven warlords who worked closely with the CIA and ISI during the Soviet war, he helped Osama bin Laden hide in Kunar Province after 9/11 and arranged for Osama's family to be sheltered in Iran. Washington has designated him a "global terrorist" and has tried to kill him several times, but he remains at large.

Jalaluddin Haqqani, 77, another of the mujahideen commanders who the CIA paid to fight its war against the Soviet Union. Once described by U.S. congressman Charlie Wilson as "goodness personified," Haqqani became the Taliban's military commander in October 2001 and later slipped into Pakistan, where he founded the Haqqani terrorist network with ISI funding. Haqqani's son Sirajuddin took over operations several years ago but family members continue to deny news reports that Jalaluddin has died.

Key U.S. figures involved in the hunt for Osama bin Laden

General Tommy Franks, 71, led the 2001 U.S. invasion of Afghanistan and commanded the failed operation to capture or kill Osama bin Laden at Tora Bora in December 2001. Franks relied on U.S. aerial firepower and a guarantee from the Pakistan Army that they would block bin Laden's escape routes eastward. At a critical moment in the battle, Pakistani troops were partially stood down following an attack on the Indian parliament in New Delhi, enabling Osama to escape.

Robert Grenier, the CIA's station chief in Islamabad on 9/11. He put together the basic war plan for the invasion of Afghanistan and led the hunt for Abu Zubaydah. In 2002, he was redeployed to work on covert operations ahead of the invasion of Iraq but was sacked by Porter Goss in 2006 and went on to establish his own strategic security firm.

Ali Soufan, 45, a Lebanese-American former FBI agent. Prior to 9/11, Soufan, one of the few Arabic speakers in the U.S. intelligence services, warned that Al Qaeda was plotting to attack the U.S. mainland. In 2002, he was the first to interrogate Abu Zubaydah, obtaining critical information that confirmed that 9/11 mastermind "Mokhtar" was Khalid Shaikh Mohammad. Soufan was sidelined when the CIA took control of Zubaydah's interrogation and tested its Enhanced Interrogation Techniques on him. Soufan resigned from the FBI in 2005 and established a private security consultancy firm.

Dr. James Mitchell, 64, a clinical psychologist and founder of the U.S. Air Force Survival, Evasion, Resistance and Escape training school. Together with his colleague Dr. Bruce Jessen, Mitchell designed the CIA's Enhanced Interrogation Techniques program. By the time their services were terminated in 2009, Mitchell and Jessen's company had been paid $71 million. After their methods were redefined by a U.S. Senate inquiry as torture, Mitchell, who lives in Florida, defended himself, saying: "I'm just a guy who got asked to do something for his country by people at the highest level of government, and I did the best that I could." Jessen has never commented.

Nada Bakos, a former CIA analyst who was tasked with establishing links between Al Qaeda and Iraq in the run-up to the Iraq war. Bakos handled data that first identified Abu Musab al-Zarqawi as he was preparing his forces in Kurdish Iraq in 2002, information that the Bush administration manipulated to build its case for war against Saddam Hussein. Bakos was also involved in the interrogation of Al Qaeda courier Hassan Ghul in January 2004.

Gina Bennett, a key member of the CIA's bin Laden hunting team for more than two decades. Bennett pulled together much of the information about the Abbottabad household. She told SEAL Team Six she was "100 percent" sure that Osama bin Laden was on the top floor, and she is widely regarded as the basis for the character Maya in the Hollywood movie *Zero Dark Thirty*.

Matthew Bissonnette, 40, a member of SEAL Team Six. He was one of the first into Osama bin Laden's bedroom and took photographs of the dead Al Qaeda leader. He broke the SEAL code of silence by publishing the book *No Easy Day*. He was later forced to hand over all his profits and an unauthorized photograph of bin Laden's corpse.

Robert O'Neill, 40, a second member of SEAL Team Six who described his experiences in magazine articles and television interviews. O'Neill claimed to have fired the fatal shots into bin Laden's forehead, an account that was disputed by Bissonnette. After leaving the army, O'Neill made a new career for himself as a motivational speaker.

Admiral William McRaven, 60, commander of the Pentagon's Joint Special Operations Command in 2011. He planned and oversaw Operation Neptune Spear.

Leon Panetta, 78, CIA director at the time of the Abbottabad raid, an operation that ended his previously positive relationship with ISI chief General Pasha. He was later promoted to defense secretary.

Admiral Mike Mullen, 69, chairman of the Joint Chiefs of Staff at the time of the raid. He later accused Pakistan of "exporting" violent extremism and described the Haqqani network as a "veritable arm" of the ISI.

Others involved in the Abbottabad episode

Husain Haqqani, 60, Pakistan's ambassador to Washington at the time of the bin Laden raid. Haqqani was asked by the CIA to assist with the relocation to the United States of several Pakistani citizens who had helped with surveillance before the operation. After Osama's killing, he became mired in controversy and was forced to resign after being accused of writing a memo on behalf of Pakistani president Asif Ali Zardari, warning of a military coup.

Dr. Shakil Afridi, 45, a Pakistani medical doctor who was recruited to spy on the Abbottabad compound. Afridi, who believed that he was working on a Save the Children vaccination program, was instructed to obtain blood samples from all residents but failed to gain entry. After the raid, General Pasha of the ISI accused him of treason and he was arrested and convicted on trumped-up charges. He later claimed that he had been tortured and his former lawyer was shot dead in Peshawar in 2015. He remains in prison.

Islamic State/Nusra Front

Abu Musab al-Zarqawi, 40, originally from Zarqa in Jordan. This tattooed former street fighter rose from obscurity to form Al Qaeda in Iraq during the U.S. war of 2003. After al-Zarqawi won notoriety following a series of brutal beheadings, his spiritual guide and mentor, the Palestinian-Jordanian preacher Abu Muhammad al-Maqdisi, turned on him in 2005. Zarqawi ignored his critics and founded what later became Islamic State, using Iran as a transit point for funds and recruits. He was killed by a U.S. missile attack in Iraq in July 2006.

Abu Mohammad al-Julani, 35, leader of Jabhat Fateh al-Sham. Once a deputy to Abu Bakr al-Baghdadi, the emir of Islamic State, Julani fell out with al-Baghdadi over a tussle for power in Syria. Julani cites his leading influences as Osama bin Laden and Abu Musab al-Suri.

Abu Bakr al-Baghdadi, 45, an Iraqi religious student who was radicalized during his internment at U.S. Camp Bucca during the Iraq war. Al-Baghdadi seized control of Islamic State of Iraq in 2011, expanded the war into Syria, and changed the name of his organization to Islamic State in Iraq and the Levant (ISIL) in 2013. In 2014, he announced the formation of a caliphate with himself named as "Caliph Ibrahim." Based in Mosul until the offensive of 2016, there have been numerous unconfirmed reports of his death, but he appears to remain at large.

Bibliography

9/11 Commission. *The 9/11 Commission Report: Final Report of the National Commission on Terrorist Attacks Upon the United States*. Washington, D.C.: U.S. Government Printing Office, 2004.

Abu Ghaith, Sulaiman. *Twenty Guidelines on the Path to Jihad*.

Ahmed, Khaled. *Sleepwalking to Surrender: Dealing with Terrorism in Pakistan*. New York: Viking, 2016.

al-Adel, Saif. "Jihadist Biography of the Slaughtering Leader Abu Musab al Zarqawi," 2005.

al-Bahri, Nasser. *Guarding Bin Laden: My Life in al-Qaeda*. With Georges Malbrunot. Translated by Susan de Muth. London: Thin Man Press, 2013.

Al Jazeera America, "Original Documents: The Abu Zubaydah Diaries," December 3, 2013, america.aljazeera.com/multimedia/2013/11/original-documentstheabu zubaydahdiaries.html.

al-Zawahiri, Ayman, "Knights Under the Prophet's Banner," published and serialized by *Asharq al-Awsat*, October 2001.

Al-Zayyat, Montasser. *The Road to Al-Qaeda: The Story of Bin Laden's Right-hand Man*. Edited by Sara Nimis. Translated by Ahmed Fekry. London: Pluto Press, 2004.

Anderson, Jon Lee. *The Lion's Grave: Dispatches from Afghanistan*. New York: Grove Press, 2003.

Bahney, Benjamin, Radha K. Iyengar, Patrick B. Johnston, Danielle F. Jung, Jacob N. Shapiro, and Howard J. Shatz. "Insurgent Compensation: Evidence from Iraq." *American Economic Review 103*, no. 3 (2013): 518–22.

Bahney, Benjamin, Howard J. Shatz, Carroll Ganier, Renny McPherson, and Barbara Sude. *An Economic Analysis of the Financial Records of al-Qa'ida in Iraq*. Santa Monica: RAND Corporation, 2010. www.rand.org/content/dam/rand/pubs /monographs/2010/RAND_MG1026.pdf.

Bari Atwan, Abdel. *After Bin Laden: Al Qaeda, the Next Generation*. London: Saqi Books, 2012.

Bergen, Peter. *Holy War, Inc.: Inside the Secret World of Osama bin Laden*. New York: Free Press, 2001.

———. *Manhunt: The Ten-Year Search for Bin Laden from 9/11 to Abbottabad*. New York: Crown, 2012.

———. *The Osama bin Laden I Know: An Oral History of al Qaeda's Leader*. New York: Simon & Schuster, 2006.

Berntsen, Gary, and Ralph Pezzulo. *Jawbreaker: The Attack on Bin Laden and Al Qaeda: A Personal Account by the CIA's Key Field Commander*. New York: Crown, 2005.

Biddle, Stephen, Jeffrey A. Friedman, and Jacob N. Shapiro. "Testing the Surge: Why Did Violence Decline in Iraq in 2007?" *International Security* 37, no. 1 (2012): 7–40.

bin Laden, Carmen. *Inside the Kingdom: My Life in Saudi Arabia*. New York: Grand Central Publishing, 2005.

bin Laden, Najwa, and Omar bin Laden. *Growing Up bin Laden: Osama's Wife and Son Take Us Inside Their Secret World*. With Jean Sasson. New York: St. Martin's Griffin, 2009.

bin Laden, Osama. *Messages to the World: The Statements of Osama Bin Laden*. Edited by Bruce Lawrence. Translated by James Howarth. New York: Verso, 2005.

Bodansky, Yossef. *Bin Laden: The Man Who Declared War on America*. Toronto, ON: Prima Lifestyles, 1999.

Bowden, Mark. *The Finish: The Killing of Osama bin Laden*. New York: Grove Atlantic, 2013.

Brown, Vahid, and Don Rassler. *Fountainhead of Jihad: The Haqqani Nexus, 1973–2012*. New York: Oxford University Press, 2013.

Burke, Jason. *Al-Qaeda: Casting a Shadow of Terror*. London: I.B.Tauris, 2003.

———. *On the Road to Kandahar: Travels through Conflict in the Islamic World*. London: Allen Lane, 2006.

Coll, Steve. *The Bin Ladens: Oil, Money, Terrorism and the Secret Saudi World*. London: Allen Lane, 2008.

Dodwell, Brian, Daniel Milton, and Don Rassler. *The Caliphate's Global Workforce: An Inside Look at the Islamic State's Foreign Fighter Paper Trail*. West Point: Combating Terrorism Center, 2016, www.ctc.usma.edu/v2/wp-content/uploads/2016/04/CTC_Caliphates-Global-Workforce-Report.pdf.

Edwards, David. *Before Taliban: Genealogies of the Afghan Jihad*. Oakland: University of California Press, 2002.

Faraj, Ayman Sabri. *Dhikrayat Arabi Afghani: Abu Jafar al-Misri al-Qandahari* [Memoirs of an Arab Afghan]. Cairo: Dar al-Shuruq, 2002.

Feinman Todd, Barbara, and Asra Nomani. *The Truth Left Behind: Inside the Kidnapping and Murder of Daniel Pearl*. Center for Public Integrity, 2011. cloud-front-files-1.publicintegrity.org/documents/pdfs/The_Pearl_Project.pdf.

Felter, Joseph H., and Brian Fishman. *Al-Qa'ida's Foreign Fighters in Iraq: A First Look at the Sinjar Records*. West Point: Combating Terrorism Center, 2007. www.ctc.usma.edu/v2/wp-content/uploads/2010/06/aqs-foreign-fighters-in-iraq.pdf.

Fisk, Robert. *The Great War for Civilisation: The Conquest of the Middle East*. New York: Knopf, 2005.

Fury, Dalton. *Kill Bin Laden: A Delta Force Commander's Account of the Hunt for the World's Most Wanted Man*. New York: St. Martin's Griffin, 2008.

Gall, Carlotta. *The Wrong Enemy: America in Afghanistan, 2001–2014*. New York: Houghton Mifflin Harcourt, 2014.

Gannon, Kathy. *I Is for Infidel*. New York: PublicAffairs, 2005.

Giustozzi, Antonio, ed. *Decoding the New Taliban*. New York: Hurst Publishers, 2009.

Gopal, Anand. *No Good Men among the Living: America, the Taliban, and the War through Afghan Eyes*. New York: Picador, 2015.

Grenier, Robert. *88 Days to Kandahar: A CIA Diary*. New York: Simon & Schuster, 2015.

Gul, Imtiaz. *Pakistan: Before and After Osama*. New Delhi: Roli Books, 2012.

Hamid, Mustafa, and Leah Farrell. *The Arabs at War in Afghanistan*. London: Hurst Publishers, 2015.

Haqqani, Husain. *Magnificent Delusions: Pakistan, the United States, and an Epic History of Misunderstanding*. New York: PublicAffairs, 2013.

Hussein, Fuad. *Al-Zarqawi: The Second Generation of Al Qaeda*.

Ibn El Waleed, Mahfouz. *My Secret Life with Al Qaeda*. Unpublished manuscript.

Ibn Mahmud, Husayn. *Al-Rajul al-'Amlaaq* [The Giant Man]. At Tibyan Publications, 2005.

Iqbal, Justice Javaid, and Abbottabad Inquiry Commission. *Abbottabad Commission Report*. Unpublished, 2013. Available at www.aljazeera.com/news/asia/2013/07/2013781341261553.html.

Kaplan, Robert D. *Soldiers of God: With Islamic Warriors in Afghanistan and Pakistan*. New York: Vintage, 2001.

Lacey, Robert. *Inside the Kingdom: Kings, Clerics, Modernists, Terrorists, and the Struggle for Saudi Arabia*. London: Arrow Books, 2010.

———. *The Kingdom: Arabia & the House of Sa'ud*. New York: Harcourt Brace Jovanovich, Inc., 1982.

Lahoud, Nelly. "Beware of Imitators: Al-Qa'ida through the Lens of Its Confidential Secretary." West Point: Combating Terrorism Center, 2012. www.ciaonet.org/attachments/20732/uploads.

Lahoud, Nelly. *Letters of Al-Qa'ida Members*. West Point: Combating Terrorism Center, 2012. www.ctc.usma.edu/v2/wp-content/uploads/2013/10/Letters-of-Al-Qaida-Members-Original.pdf.

Lahoud, Nelly, Don Rassler, Gabriel Koehler-Derrick, Liam Collins, Muhammad al-Obaidi. *Letters from Abbottabad: Bin Ladin Sidelined?* West Point: Combating Terrorism Center, 2012. www.ctc.usma.edu/wp-content/uploads/2012/05/CTC _LtrsFromAbottabad_WEB_v2.pdf.

Lia, Brynjar. *Architect of Global Jihad: The Life of Al-Qaeda Strategist Abu Mus'ab Al-Suri.* London: Hurst Publishers, 2007.

Mayer, Jane. *The Dark Side: The Inside Story of How the War on Terror Turned into a War on American Ideals.* New York: Anchor, 2009.

Mazzetti, Mark. *The Way of the Knife: The CIA, a Secret Army, and a War at the Ends of the Earth.* New York: Penguin, 2013.

McCants, Will. *The ISIS Apocalypse: The History, Strategy, and Doomsday Vision of the Islamic State.* New York: St. Martin's, 2015.

McDermott, Terry, and Josh Meyer. *The Hunt for KSM: Inside the Pursuit and Takedown of the Real 9/11 Mastermind, Khalid Shaikh Mohammad.* New York: Little, Brown, 2012.

Miller, Flagg. *The Audacious Ascetic: What the Bin Laden Tapes Reveal about Al-Qa'ida.* New York: Oxford University Press, 2015.

Mitchell, James E. and Bill Harlow. *Enhanced Interrogation: Inside the Minds and Motives of the Islamic Terrorists Trying to Destroy America.* New York: Crown, 2016.

Mohabbat, M. Kabir, and L. R. McInnis. *Delivering Osama.* Available at books. google.com/books/about/Delivering_Osama.html?id=I-Y4T9kUfxQC.

Morell, Michael. *The Great War of Our Time.* New York: Grand Central Publishing, August 2016.

Murshed, S. Iftikhar. *Afghanistan: The Taliban Years.* London: Bennett & Bloom, 2006.

Musab al-Suri, Abu. *The Call for Global Islamic Resistance.* Published on jihadist websites in December 2004. news.siteintelgroup.com/blog/index.php/about -us/21-jihad/21-suri-a-mili.

Musharraf, Pervez. *In the Line of Fire: A Memoir.* New York: Simon & Schuster, 2006.

Mutawakil, Wakil Ahmad, "Afghanistan aw Taliban" [Afghanistan and the Taliban]. 2007.

Nasiri, Omar. *Inside the Jihad: My Life with Al Qaeda.* London: Basic Books. 2006

Naylor, Sean. *Not a Good Day to Die: The Untold Story of Operation Anaconda.* New York: Berkley Books, 2005.

Neighbour, Sally. *The Mother of Mohammed: An Australian Woman's Extraordinary Journey into Jihad.* Victoria, Australia: Melbourne University Press, 2010.

Ostovar, Afshon P. "Guardians of the Islamic Revolution: Ideology, Politics and the Development of Military Power in Iran (1979–2009)." Ph.D. diss., University of Michigan, 2009. deepblue.lib.umich.edu/bitstream/handle/2027.42/64683/ afshon_1.pdf?sequence=1.

Ould Slahi, Mohamedou. *Guantánamo Diary*. Edited by Larry Siems. New York: Little, Brown, 2015.

Owen, Mark, and Kevin Maurer. *No Easy Day: The Autobiography of a Navy SEAL: The Firsthand Account of the Mission That Killed Osama Bin Laden.* New York: Dutton, 2012.

Qadir, Shaukat. *Operation Geronimo: The Betrayal and Execution of Osama bin Laden and Its Aftermath.* Islamabad: HA Publications, 2012.

Qureshi, Asad. *165 Days.* Unpublished manuscript.

Qutb, Sayyid. *Milestones.* Plainfield, IN: American Trust Publications, 1990.

Rashid, Ahmed. *Descent into Chaos: The United States and the Failure of Nation Building in Pakistan, Afghanistan, and Central Asia.* New York: Viking, 2008.

Riedel, Bruce. *Avoiding Armageddon: America, India, and Pakistan to the Brink and Back.* Washington, D.C.: Brookings Institution Press, 2013.

———. *Deadly Embrace: Pakistan, America, and the Future of the Global Jihad.* Washington, D.C.: Brookings Institution Press, 2011.

Salah, Muhammad. "Events of the Jihad Years: The Journey of Afghan Arabs from Everywhere to Washington and New York." *Al-Hayat* (Arabic newspaper), October 17–21, 2001, part 2 of 5.

Scheuer, Michael. *Imperial Hubris: Why the West Is Losing the War on Terror.* Lincoln, NE: Potomac Books, 2007.

Scott-Clark, Cathy, and Adrian Levy. *Deception: Pakistan, the United States, and the Secret Trade in Nuclear Weapons.* New York: Walker & Company, 2007.

———. *The Siege: 68 Hours inside the Taj Hotel.* New York: Penguin, 2013.

Senate Select Committee on Intelligence. *The Official Senate Report on CIA Torture: Committee Study of the Central Intelligence Agency's Detention and Interrogation Program.* New York: Skyhorse Publishing, 2015.

Shahzad, Syed Saleem. *Inside Al-Qaeda and the Taliban: Beyond Bin Laden and 9/11.* London: Pluto Press, 2011.

Shapiro, Jacob N. *The Terrorist's Dilemma: Managing Violent Covert Organizations.* Princeton: Princeton University Press, 2013.

Soufan, Ali. *The Black Banners: The Inside Story of 9/11 and the War against al-Qaeda.* New York: W. W. Norton & Company, 2011.

Stafford Smith, Clive. *Bad Men: Guantanamo Bay and the Secret Prisons.* London: Weidenfeld & Nicolson, 2007.

Storm, Morten. *Agent Storm: My Life inside al Qaeda and the CIA.* New York: Grove Press, 2014.

Strick van Linschoten, Alex, and Felix Kuehn. *An Enemy We Created: The Myth of the Taliban–Al Qaeda Merger in Afghanistan.* New York: Oxford University Press, 2012.

———. *Poetry of the Taliban.* London: Hurst Publishers, 2012.

Suskind, Ron. *The Way of the World: A Story of Truth and Hope in an Age of Extremism.* New York: Harper, 2008.

Syed, Azaz. *The Secrets of Pakistan's War on Al-Qaeda*. Islamabad: Al-Abbas International, 2014.

Tawil, Camille. *Brothers in Arms: The Story of al-Qa'ida and the Arab Jihadists*. Translated by Robin Bray. London: Saqi Books, 2011.

Tenet, George. *At the Center of the Storm: The CIA during America's Time of Crisis*. New York: HarperCollins, 2007.

United States Senate Committee on Foreign Relations. *Tora Bora Revisited: How We Failed to Get Bin Laden and Why It Matters Today*. Ann Arbor, MI: Nimble Books, 2009.

Wagemakers, Joas. *A Quietist Jihadi: The Ideology and Influence of Abu Muhammad al-Maqdisi*. Cambridge: Cambridge University Press, 2012.

Walid al-Masri, Abu [Mustafa Hamid]. *The Cross in the Sky of Qandahar*. Unpublished manuscript.

Warrick, Joby. *Black Flags: The Rise of ISIS*. New York: Random House, 2015.

———. *Triple Agent: The al-Qaeda Mole Who Infiltrated the CIA*. New York: Doubleday, 2011.

Watts, Clint, Jacob Shapiro, and Vahid Brown. *Al-Qa'ida's (Mis)Adventures in the Horn of Africa*. West Point: Combating Terrorism Center, 2007. www.ctc.usma .edu//v2/wp-content/uploads/2010/06/Al-Qaidas-MisAdventures-in-the-Horn-of-Africa.pdf.

Weisfuse, Ari R. "The Last Hope for the al-Qa'ida Old Guard? A Profile of Saif al'Adl." *CTC Sentinel* 9, no. 3 (March 2016): 24–27.

Wright, Lawrence. *The Looming Tower: Al-Qaeda and the Road to 9/11*. New York: Allen Lane, 2006.

Zaeef, Abdul Salam. *My Life with the Taliban*. London: Hurst Publishers, 2011.

NATIONAL SECURITY ARCHIVE

The September 11th Sourcebooks. "Volume II: Afghanistan: Lessons from the Last War." National Security Archive Electronic Briefing Book No. 57. Edited by John Prados and Svetlana Savranskaya. October 9, 2001. nsarchive.gwu.edu/ NSAEBB/NSAEBB57/.

The September 11th Sourcebooks. "Volume IV: The Once and Future King? From the Secret Files on King Zahir's Reign in Afghanistan, 1970–1973." National Security Archive Electronic Briefing Book No. 59. Edited by William Burr. October 26, 2001. nsarchive.gwu.edu/NSAEBB/NSAEBB59/.

The September 11th Sourcebooks. "Volume VI: The Hunt for Bin Laden: Background on the Role of Special Forces in U.S. Military Strategy." National Security Archive Electronic Briefing Book No. 63. December 21, 2001. nsarchive.gwu. edu/NSAEBB/NSAEBB63/.

The September 11th Sourcebooks. "Volume VII: The Taliban File." National Security Archive Electronic Briefing Book No. 97. Edited by Sajit Gandhi. September 11, 2003. nsarchive.gwu.edu/NSAEBB/NSAEBB97/index.htm.

The September 11th Sourcebooks. "The Taliban File Part III." Edited by Sajit Gandhi. March 19, 2004. nsarchive.gwu.edu/NSAEBB/NSAEBB97/index3.htm.

The September 11th Sourcebooks. "The Taliban File Part IV." National Security Archive Electronic Briefing Book No. 134. Edited by Barbara Elias. August 18, 2005. nsarchive.gwu.edu/NSAEBB/NSAEBB134/index.htm.

The September 11th Sourcebooks. "Update: The Taliban File Part IV." National Security Archive Electronic Briefing Book No. 134. Edited by Barbara Elias. August 18, 2005. nsarchive.gwu.edu/NSAEBB/NSAEBB134/index2.htm.

"Pakistan: 'The Taliban's Godfather'?" National Security Archive Electronic Briefing Book No. 227. Edited by Barbara Elias. August 14, 2007. nsarchive.gwu.edu /NSAEBB/NSAEBB227/index.htm.

"1998 Missile Strikes on Bin Laden May Have Backfired." National Security Archive Electronic Briefing Book No. 253. Edited by Barbara Elias. August 20, 2008. nsarchive.gwu.edu/NSAEBB/NSAEBB253/index.htm.

"The Taliban Biography." National Security Archive Electronic Briefing Book No. 295. Edited by Barbara Elias. November 13, 2009. nsarchive.gwu.edu/NSAEBB /NSAEBB295/index.htm.

"'No-Go' Tribal Areas Became Basis for Afghan Insurgency Documents Show." National Security Archive Electronic Briefing Book No. 325. Edited by Barbara Elias. September 13, 2010. nsarchive.gwu.edu/NSAEBB/NSAEBB325/index.htm.

"Secret U.S. Message to Mullah Omar: 'Every Pillar of the Taliban Regime Will Be Destroyed.'" National Security Archive Electronic Briefing Book No. 358. Edited by Barbara Elias. September 11, 2011. nsarchive.gwu.edu/NSAEBB/NSAEBB358a /index.htm.

"The Central Intelligence Agency's 9/11 File." National Security Archive Electronic Briefing Book No. 381. Edited by Barbara Elias-Sanborn. June 19, 2012. nsarchive .gwu.edu/NSAEBB/NSAEBB381/.

"The Haqqani History: Bin Ladin's Advocate Inside the Taliban." National Security Archive Electronic Briefing Book No. 389. Edited by Barbara Elias-Sanborn. September 11, 2012. nsarchive.gwu.edu/NSAEBB/NSAEBB389/.

See also this excellent list by Alex Strick von Linschoten, "Reading the Afghan Taliban: 67 Sources You Should Be Studying." www.alexstrick.com/blog/2015 /12/reading-the-afghan-taliban-67-sources-you-should-be-studying.

Notes

Chapter One

1. Peter Bergen, *The Osama Bin Laden I Know* (New York: Simon & Schuster, 2005).
2. The guard was Al Hamza al-Bahlul, and he told this story to American interrogators at Guantánamo Bay. His account can be found at wikileaks.org/gitmo/prisoner/39.html.
3. His Egyptian deputies Abu Hafs the Commander and Dr. Ayman al-Zawahir; were also there, along with Osama's chief bodyguard, a Moroccan called Abdullah Tabarak.
4. Robert Lacey, *Inside the Kingdom: Kings, Clerics, Modernists, and the Struggle for Saudi Arabia* (London: Arrow Books, 2010), 226.
5. The wedding was in January 2001. The journalist was Ahmad Zaidan: author interview with Zaidan, Islamabad, January 2015.
6. Carmen bin Laden, who was married to a brother of Osama, describes Najwa's timidity and fear of her husband in *Inside the Kingdom: My Life in Saudi Arabia* (New York: Grand Central Publishing, 2005), 85–86.
7. Author interviews with bin Laden family members, 2012–2016.
8. Othman said this during a speech recorded at Mohammed's wedding; author copy of video.
9. Carmen bin Laden, *Inside the Kingdom: My Life in Saudi Arabia*, 85–86.
10. Najwa bin Laden, Omar bin Laden, and Jean Sasson, *Growing Up Bin Laden* (New York: St. Martin's, 2009).
11. Author interviews with bin Laden family members.
12. Multiple author interviews with Mahfouz Ibn El Waleed, Nouakchott, December 2014, January 2015, and June 2015.
13. It was named after the large pomegranate trees in its garden, per author interviews with Mahfouz.
14. Early poems that won him prizes were about the Palestinian intifada, such as one entitled "Child of Stones."
15. Mahfouz described this meeting in 1998 at which he was also present.
16. Author interviews with Hamid Mir, Islamabad, May 2014 and February 2015.
17. Mir claimed that the visitor also delivered a handwritten note from Osama that declared: "I praise all those who conducted the attacks."
18. Author interview with General Javed Alam Khan, Rawalpindi, May 2015.
19. Author interview with General Jehangir Karamat, former chief of army staff (COAS), Lahore, February 2015. Also discussed during interviews with General Javed Alam Khan; General Ehsan ul-Haq, who described his predecessor, Islamabad, June 2014; General Pervez Musharraf, Karachi, February 2015; General Ali Jan Aurakzai, former chief of Pakistan Army

Western Command, Rawalpindi, June 2014; General Ziauddin Butt, predecessor to General Mahmud Ahmed, Lahore, February 2015; General Masood Aslam, Islamabad, February 2015; and General Asad Durrani, Rawalpindi, June 2014.

20. Author telephone interview with Robert Grenier, March 2015.

21. Author interview with General Javed Alam Khan.

22. This vignette was described to the authors by Mahfouz Ibn El Waleed, who was present, and by Omar bin Laden in *Growing Up bin Laden*.

23. Author interview with General Ziauddin Butt.

24. Author interview with General Ziauddin Butt and with Robert Grenier.

25. John Sifton, "A Brief History of Drones," *Nation*, February 7, 2012.

26. Author interview with General Musharraf and with Huthaifa Azzam, son of Abdullah Azzam, Jordan, December 2016. Ramzi Yousef had been staying with Huthaifa when he was caught.

27. Ibid.

28. S-Wing was established during the Soviet war when the ISI and CIA worked together to train mujahideen groups to fight in Afghanistan. It has undergone various incarnations but is well known to be practically independent of and ungovernable by the ISI leadership. Former ISI director general Hamid Gul, who helped create S-Wing, retained a significant influence over it until his death in 2015. Multiple author interviews with General Gul, Rawalpindi, 2006, 2012, 2013, 2014, and 2015.

29. Author interview with General Musharraf.

30. This assessment is backed by multiple interviewees including Pakistani journalist Rahimullah Yusufzai, Nawaz Sharif, the late Benazir Bhutto, numerous senior U.S. officials including Bruce Riedel, and senior Pakistan Army officers formerly close to generals Pasha and Kayani who wish to remain anonymous.

31. "Gitmo Files: Ramzi bin al Shibh," Wikileaks, wikileaks.org/gitmo/prisoner/10013; also see the files of others present, including Mustafa Ahmad al-Hawsawi, wikileaks.org/gitmo/prisoner/10011; Ammar al-Balochi, wikileaks.org/gitmo/prisoner/10018; and Walid Muhammad Salih bin Roshayed bin Attash, wikileaks.org/gitmo/prisoner/10014.

32. KSM quote from Bergen, *The Osama bin Laden I Know*.

33. Author interviews with Mahfouz and with Abu Muhammad al-Maqdisi and Abu Qatada, Amman, Jordan, December 2016.

34. Author interviews with Huthaifa Azzam and with Samira Abdullah, widow of Abdullah Azzam, Amman, Jordan, December 2016.

35. Author interviews with Mahfouz.

36. Abu Zubaydah's diaries, dated from 1990 to 2002 and recovered in the U.S. and Pakistani raid that captured Zubaydah on March 28, 2002. Translated by the U.S. government and released to Al Jazeera by a former U.S. intelligence official. Al Jazeera America, "Original Documents: The Abu Zubaydah Diaries," December 3, 2013. america.aljazeera.com/multimedia/2013/11/original-documentstheabuzubaydahdiaries.html.

37. Author interviews with Mahfouz.

38. Abdullah Tabarak was sent to fetch Sulaiman Abu Ghaith, who recounted this story and many others to his close friend Mahfouz Ibn El Waleed while both were held in detention in Iran. Author interviews with Mahfouz; also with Stanley Cohen, lawyer for Abu Ghaith, New York, October 2014.

39. Author interview with Stanley Cohen; also Sulaiman Abu Ghaith's statement to the FBI, March 2013, author copy.

40. Ibid. Also author interviews with Mahfouz, Nouakchott, 2014 and 2015.

41. Abu Ghaith FBI statement and recollections shared with Mahfouz, per author interviews with Mahfouz.

42. This conversation was described by Ahmad Zaidan, who asked a Pakistani general about Tomahawks before going to Mohammed bin Laden's wedding; author interview.

43. Author interviews with bin Laden family members.

44. This incident, which took place in Kandahar, was described by Omar bin Laden in *Growing Up Bin Laden*; also in author interviews with family members.

45. Author interviews with Samira Abdullah, widow of Abdullah Azzam and close friend of Khairiah and Seham bin Laden, Amman, Jordan, December 2016.

46. Ibid.

47. They had been forced to leave when the Sudanese president came under pressure to hand over Osama. Some 250 Al Qaeda fighters had left, too.

48. Author interviews with bin Laden family members.

49. This was coordinated by the Jalalabad-based Taliban commander Awal Gul.

50. Author interviews with bin Laden family members.

51. Carmen bin Laden, *Inside the Kingdom: My Life in Saudi Arabia*.

52. The cleric was Rashad Mohammed Saeed. Tony Finn, "Osama Bin Laden Said: 'Find Me a Wife,'" *Guardian*, May 11, 2011. Author interview with Saeed, Ibb, Yemen, 2013, and Osama's former bodyguard Abu Jandal, Sana'a, Yemen, 2013. Abu Jandal also published a book under his real name, Nasser al-Bahri, with Georges Malbrunot, *Guarding Bin Laden: My Life in al-Qaeda*, trans. Susan de Muth (London: Thin Man Press, 2013). More details about the heritage of Osama's father can be found in Steve Coll, *The Bin Ladens: An Arabian Family in the American Century* (New York: Penguin, 2008).

53. Amal's father is called Ahmed Abdul-Fattah al-Sadeh; author interviews with al-Sadeh family members in Islamabad, 2012; Sana'a, 2013; and Saudi Arabia, 2014.

54. "Bin Laden's Wife: 'I'll Stand with You,'" *Asharq al-Awsat*, May 12, 2011.

55. Nasser al-Bahri, *Guarding Bin Laden*.

56. She arrived in Pakistan on July 17, 2000. Details from confidential statement of inspector general of police, Islamabad, 3/19/2012, report of Joint Investigation Team, author copy.

57. Nasser al-Bahri, *Guarding Bin Laden*.

58. Lawrence Wright, *The Looming Tower: Al-Qaeda and the Road to 9/11* (New York: Allen Lane, 2006).

59. Confidential statement of inspector general of police, Islamabad, 3/19/2012, report of Joint Investigation Team, author copy.

60. Author interviews with bin Laden family members and relatives of Amal al-Sadeh, Islamabad, Sana'a, Ibb, and Jeddah, 2012–2014.

61. The brother-in-law was Salim Hamdan. For full details of their relationship and time in American detention see Laura Poitras's 2010 documentary *The Oath* (New York: Zeitgeist Films).

62. He was arrested in February 2001.

63. Interviews with al-Sadeh family members in Yemen.

64. Author interview with Ahmed Abdul-Fattah al-Sadeh.

65. Author interview with General Musharraf.

66. Ibid.

67. Author interviews with retired Director General of ISI General Hamid Gul, Rawalpindi, 2014–2015.

68. Author interviews with General Musharraf and Robert Grenier.

69. Author interviews with General Javed Alam Khan and Robert Grenier; also Robert Grenier, *88 Days to Kandahar* (New York: Simon & Schuster, 2015).

70. This account and that of the next meeting were provided to the authors by Mahfouz.

71. Grenier, *88 Days to Kandahar*.

72. U.S. Department of State, "President Bush Commemorates Foreign Policy Achievements and Presents Medal of Freedom to Ambassador Ryan Crocker," georgewbush-whitehouse. archives.gov/news/releases/2009/01/20090115.html.

73. Author telephone interview with Ryan Crocker, December 2014. More details can be found in Robin Wright, "The Adversary," *New Yorker*, May 26, 2014.

74. Dexter Filkins, "The Shadow Commander," *New Yorker*, September 30, 2013.

75. Author interview with Ryan Crocker.

76. This quote comes from author interviews with Mahfouz, who said this was what Osama liked to say when planning attacks.

CHAPTER TWO

1. Abu Musab al-Suri, *The Call for Global Islamic Resistance*, published on jihadist websites in December 2004, news.siteintelgroup.com/blog/index.php/about-us/21-jihad/21-suri-a-mili.

2. Tora Bora was reached via a single dirt road starting at the village of Agam and running up through the Melawa Valley. Osama's father's company was the Saudi-based Binladin Group. Accounts of his building Tora Bora come from multiple sources, including author interviews with Mahfouz Ibn El Waleed, Nouakchott, December 2014, January and June 2015; bin Laden family members in Islamabad, Jeddah, and Doha, 2012–2015; and General Javed Alam Khan, Rawalpindi, May 2015; also Lawrence Wright, *The Looming Tower: Al-Qaeda and the Road to 9/11* (New York: Allen Lane, 2006); Robert Grenier, *88 Days to Kandahar* (New York: Simon & Schuster, 2015); and Steve Coll, *The Bin Ladens: An Arabian Family in the American Century* (New York: Penguin, 2008).

3. This story was recounted by fighters loyal to Abdul Rasul Sayyaf, who ran the main mujahideen camp at Jaji. Osama also recounted it later many times to Mahfouz, who repeated it in interviews with the authors. It is also told by Lawrence Wright in *The Looming Tower*.

4. Osama states this sentiment in many letters, including an undated letter to Nasir al-Wuhayshi, the leader of Al Qaeda in the Arabian Peninsula. Documents recovered in the 2011 raid on the bin Laden compound in Abbottabad translated, declassified, and released by the Office of the Director of National Intelligence [hereafter ODNI] in May 2015, March 2016, and January 2017. This letter from the May 2015 release.

5. Najwa bin Laden, Omar bin Laden, and Jean Sasson, *Growing Up Bin Laden* (New York: St. Martin's, 2009).

6. Ibid.

7. Ibid.

8. Paul Cruickshank and Mohanad Hage Ali, "Abu Musab Al Suri: Architect of the New Al Qaeda," *Studies in Conflict and Terrorism* 30, no. 1 (2007): 1–14; "Abu Musab al-Suri's Military Theory of Jihad," SITE Intelligence Group, translated and published 2011, news.siteintelgroup.com/blog/index.php/about-us/21-jihad/21-suri-a-mili.

9. Abu Musab al-Suri, *The Call for Global Islamic Resistance*, published on jihadist websites in December 2004, news.siteintelgroup.com/blog/index.php/about-us/21-jihad/21-suri-a-mili.

10. According to Azzam's son Huthaifa, author interviews, Amman, Jordan, December 2016.

11. Abu Musab al-Suri, *The Call for Global Islamic Resistance*.

12. In Syria as a student leader, al-Suri had railed against the Hafez al-Assad regime. During the 1980s he had run two training camps for Osama in Afghanistan but complained of Al Qaeda's disorganization. "People come to us with empty heads and leave us with empty heads," he said in 2003. More recently, he had been based in Europe, first in Spain—where he married a Christian woman, Elena Moreno, with whom he had four children—and then in London, where he worked for Abu Qatada, the famous Palestinian jihad preacher who was characterized as Al Qaeda's go-to man in Europe. Al-Suri wrote for Qatada's jihadi magazine and think tank, *Al Ansar*. When the British authorities began pursuing al-Suri as a suspect in the 1995 Paris Metro bombings, he returned to Afghanistan. He arrived in Tora Bora in November 1996.

13. Abu Musab al-Suri, *The Call for Global Islamic Resistance*. Also see "Rare Photos of Osama Bin Laden while Hiding in Tora Bora," *Washington Post*, www.washingtonpost.com/world/rare-photos-show-osama-bin-laden-while-in-hiding/2015/03/14/dd8db67a-c9c2-11e4-aa1a-86135599fb0f_gallery. These pictures were taken by Abdel Bari Atwan, per author interview with Atwan, London, 2015.

14. Multiple author interviews with Mahfouz.

15. Undated copy of Osama bin Laden's will. ODNI documents, Abbottabad, released in March 2016.

16. Multiple author interviews with Mahfouz.

17. This allegation was made by Mohamedou Ould Slahi, who is related to Mahfouz by marriage and who traveled with him to Afghanistan in 1991. See his file at "Gitmo Files: Mohamedou Ould Slahi," Wikileaks, wikileaks.org/gitmo/prisoner/760; and Mohamedou Ould Slahi and Larry Siems, *Guantánamo Diary* (New York: Little, Brown, 2015). Other Guantánamo detainees also claimed Mahfouz tried to involve them in the operation. Author interviews with Larry Siems, Brooklyn, 2014–2015.

18. Author interviews with Mahfouz.

19. Terry McDermott and Josh Meyer, *The Hunt for KSM* (New York: Little, Brown, 2012).

20. One of those he worked for was Abdul Sayyaf, the victor at Jaji in 1984.

21. Peter Bergen, *The Osama bin Laden I Know* (New York: Simon & Schuster, 2005).

22. World Islamic Front statement, "Jihad against Jews and Crusaders," February 23, 1998, accessed on fas.org, fas.org/irp/world/para/docs/980223-fatwa.htm.

23. Author interviews with Huthaifa Azzam, Amman, Jordan, December 2016.

24. This man was the future courier and Osama's companion in Abbottabad.

25. Some of the hijackers also trained at the new Al Farouk camp; see note 30.

26. Author interviews with Brigadier (Ret.) Asad Munir, ISI station chief Peshawar (1999–2003), Islamabad, June 2014.

27. Omar Nasiri, *Inside the Jihad* (London: Basic Books, 2006), describes Qatada's links to Zubaydah. Also author interviews with Abu Qatada, Amman, November 2014 and September 2016.

28. Author interviews with bin Laden family members; also see Guy Lawson, "Osama's Prodigal Son: The Dark, Twisted Journey of Omar bin Laden," *Rolling Stone*, January 20, 2010.

29. Author interviews with Mahfouz.

30. This *shura* took place at the new Al Farouk camp located in Helmand Province after the old site near Khost had been destroyed in 1998 by cruise missiles.

31. This *shura* took place at a new location called Compound Six, situated on the banks of a reservoir northeast of Kandahar. Osama had just moved in with his family, having decided that Tarnak Qila was overexposed.

32. He had written Osama a stern seven-page letter after the African embassy bombings explaining why those attacks had been wrong.

33. Al-Suri quotes referenced in Lawrence Wright, "The Master Plan," *New Yorker*, September 11, 2006.

34. Author interviews with Mahfouz.

35. Those who opposed the attack included Saif al-Adel and his colleagues from Egyptian Islamic Jihad, Abu al-Khayr al-Masri and Abu Mohammed al-Masri, along with Sheikh Saeed al-Masri, Al Qaeda's financial chief.

36. Author interviews with Mahfouz. Also described in a letter from former *shura* member Noman Benotman to Osama bin Laden after 9/11, reproduced with Benotman's permission in *Foreign Policy* magazine, September 1, 2010.

37. Dr. Ayman al-Zawahiri and Abu Hafs the Commander were also busy with something they had code-named Project al-Zabadi (curdled milk): obtaining nuclear, chemical, and biological weapons. Two Pakistani scientists had arrived in Kandahar promising to steal materials from the state nuclear program at Kahuta, outside Islamabad.

38. Yosri Fouda, narrator. *Top Secret: The Road to September 11.* (Al Jazeera, 2002).

39. Al-Masri's daughter Asma was married to Saif al-Adel, Al Qaeda's military chief.

40. Author interviews with Mahfouz, who witnessed the attack as he lived across the road.

41. Gary Berntsen and Ralph Pezzullo, *Jawbreaker: The Attack on Bin Laden and al-Qaeda* (New York: Crown, 2005).

42. Author interviews with Robert Grenier, also his book *88 Days to Kandahar*. Author interview with William Murray, former CIA director, Virginia, October 2014.

43. Sulaiman Abu Ghaith FBI testimony under FBI interrogation. Author copy of the FBI transcript and author interview with Abu Ghaith's lawyer, Stanley Cohen, New York, October 2014.

44. Abu Walid al-Masri (Mustafa Hamid), unpublished book in Arabic, "The Cross in the Sky of Qandahar," 2004, author copy provided by Alex Strick van Linschoten.

45. Author interviews with Mahfouz.

46. He worked like this always according to all those around him, including son Omar, who described his father's habits in *Growing Up Bin Laden*. Also author interviews with Mahfouz.

47. Khaled al-Harbi, a visiting Saudi cleric, sat on one side of Osama and on the other was Sulaiman Abu Ghaith.

48. Author interviews with bin Laden family members.

49. Author interviews with Hamid Mir, Islamabad.

50. Author interview with General Ehsan ul-Haq, Islamabad, June 2014.

51. Manoj Joshi, "India Helped FBI Trace ISI-Terrorist Links," *Times of India*, October 9, 2001.

52. Glen Johnson, "Bush Fails Quiz on Foreign Affairs," *Washington Post*, November 4, 1999.

53. Author interview with General Pervez Musharraf, Karachi, February 2015.

54. Author interview with General Ehsan ul-Haq, Islamabad, June 2014.

55. By ten P.M., the Sheikh was back in Jalalabad, seeking out the city's Taliban governor, Maulvi Abdul Kabir. Mary Anne Weaver, "Lost at Tora Bora," *New York Times Magazine*, September 11, 2005.

56. Ibid.

57. His name was Mohammed al-Hallabi. His brother Abu Abdallah al-Hallabi was married to Fatima's sister Khadija bin Laden. The driver was Salim Hamdan, brother-in-law of Abu Jandal, Osama's Yemeni chief bodyguard. See "Gitmo Files," Wikileaks, wikileaks.org/gitmo/prisoner/149, for more information.

58. Author interviews with bin Laden family members. Hamzah bin Laden also described this scene in a letter to his father written in June 2009. ODNI documents, Abbottabad, released in May 2015.

59. Ibid.

60. Author interviews with Mahfouz.
61. Also killed was Zachariah al-Tunisi, who allegedly fired a rocket-propelled grenade that brought down one of the two U.S. Black Hawk helicopters in Somalia in 1993.
62. Saif often told new recruits the story of Abu Hamza al-Masri, who in 1993 as a new recruit to Al Qaeda picked up a vat of liquid explosives without knowing they had been cooked. The bomb detonated as he carried it, blinding him in one eye and severing both of his hands—which were replaced with metal hooks. He sought asylum in London but was extradited to the United States to stand trial on terrorism offenses in 2012. He was convicted to life imprisonment in 2014. Author interviews with Mahfouz.
63. Saif al-Adel's real name was Mohammed Salah al-Din Zaidan. For more biographical information about him, see Harmony Project, "Al-Qaida's (Mis)adventures in the Horn of Africa," Combating Terrorism Center at West Point, ctc.usma.edu/v2/wp-content/uploads/2010/06/Al-Qaidas-MisAdventures-in-the-Horn-of-Africa.pdf.
64. Author interviews with Mahfouz. Saif wrote of his lax attitude toward study in an online eulogy to Abu Musab al-Zarqawi entitled "Jihadist Biography of the Slaughtering Leader Abu Musab al-Zarqawi." Also see five letters published online, available at www.jihadica.com/al-qa%E2%80%99ida-revisions-the-five-letters-of-sayf-al-%E2%80%98adl/.
65. Zarqawi had traveled to Afghanistan once before, in 1989, arriving too late to fight in the Soviet war. He had gone home to Jordan, tried to launch himself as a terrorist, and ended up behind bars with the Salafist scholar Abu Muhammad al-Maqdisi.
66. Urs Gehriger, "Abu Musab al-Zarqawi: From Green Man to Guru," a three-part series originally published in German by *Die Weltwoche*, October 6, 2005. An English translation is available at www.signandsight.com/features/449.html.
67. Author interview with Abu Muhammad al-Maqdisi, Amman, Jordan, December 2016. Also interviews with those who knew Zarqawi or spent time with Maqdisi in prison, including Marwan Shehadah, Dr. Munif Samara, Fuad Hussein, Hassan Abu Haniyah, Yousuf Rabbaba, Amman, Jordan, October 2014 and September and December 2016.
68. Saif al-Adel, "Jihadist Biography of the Slaughtering Leader Abu Musab al-Zarqawi," online publication. Author interview with Abu Yusuf, who helped Zarqawi establish this camp, Amman, Jordan, December 2016.
69. Ibid. Also see www.jihadica.com/al-qa%E2%80%99ida-revisions-the-five-letters-of-sayf-al-%E2%80%98adl/.
70. Fuad Hussein interviewed Zarqawi's friend and deputy Iyad al-Toubasi for Lebanon Broadcasting Corporation in 2005. Toubasi said the convoy in which he traveled was "three hundred to four hundred vehicles." Author interviews with Fuad Hussein, Amman, October 2014.
71. Al Jazeera America, "Original Documents: The Abu Zubaydah Diaries," December 3, 2013, america.aljazeera.com/multimedia/2013/11/original-documentstheabuzubaydahdiaries.html.
72. Al-Zawahiri referred to the death of his wife and two children in a letter to Zarqawi in 2006 and in several Al Qaeda videos from 2011 onward. Details also came from author interviews with Mahfouz, who was elsewhere in Afghanistan at the time but learned information from his Al Qaeda brothers.
73. Author interviews with Mahfouz.
74. Ibid.
75. The text of this interview with Al Jazeera correspondent Yussef al-Shuli, which was broadcast on December 14, 2001, can be found at "Terror in America (29) Al Jazeera Interview with Top Al-Qa'ida Leader Abu Hafs 'The Mauritanian,'" Middle East Media Research Institute,

December 14, 2001, www.memri.org/reports/terror-america-29-al-jazeera-interview-top-al-qaida
-leader-abu-hafs-mauritanian. Abu Hafs the Mauritanian was Mahfouz's Al Qaeda *kunya*.

76. Mahfouz ended with a stark warning. Al Qaeda was ready to use any weapons against America, including weapons of mass destruction: "Let the Americans fear the worst possible scenario when they use any unconventional weapons."

77. Author interviews with Mahfouz.

78. These were the instructions he gave them, according to his interview with the authors.

79. A graphic of this area was widely published at the start of the Tora Bora operation and can be seen here: edwardjayepstein.com/nether_fictoid3.htm.

80. Author interviews with General Javed Alam Khan and Robert Grenier.

81. Grenier, *88 Days to Kandahar*.

82. Author interview with Dr. Amin al-Haq, Islamabad, February 2015. Abu Zubaydah described his work at Khaldan in his diaries; see "The Abu Zubaydah Diaries."

83. His staying inside the cave while others fought was described by several Tora Bora survivors who were later interrogated at Guantánamo Bay, including Dr. Ayman Batarfi, whose interrogation summary can be read on "Gitmo Files," Wikileaks, wikileaks.org/gitmo/prisoner/627.html. Also see "Abu Zubaydah Unclassified Verbatim Combatant Status Review Tribunal Transcript," Department of Defense, 2007; "Khalid Sulaymanjaydh Al Hubayshi Unclassified Verbatim Combatant Status Review Tribunal Transcript," Department of Defense, 65–73; and "Noor Uthman Muhammed Unclassified Verbatim Combatant Status Review Tribunal Transcript," Department of Defense, p. 15.

84. Author interview with Lieutenant General Ali Jan Aurakzai, Rawalpindi, June 2014.

85. Several U.S. Special Forces operatives who fought at Tora Bora subsequently wrote books, including Gary Berntsen, coauthor of *Jawbreaker*, and Dalton Fury, *Kill Bin Laden* (New York: St. Martin's, 2008).

86. A maneuver backed by Delta Force specialists on the ground, and the CIA specialists who were with them.

87. "Gitmo Files: Ayman Saeed Abdullah Batarfi," Wikileaks, wikileaks.org/gitmo/prisoner/627.html.

88. Ibid.

89. Ibn Sheikh had a storied, complicated history of assisting and resisting Al Qaeda. A well-organized fighter from Libya, he had run Khaldan, one of the first mujahideen training camps set up with CIA cash during the 1980s, before becoming close to Osama. In more recent times, Ibn Sheikh had rejected Osama's dictatorial style and Mokhtar's rumored Planes Operation. Khaldan camp closed down in 2000, the year before 9/11. "Abu Zubaydah Unclassified Verbatim Combatant Status Review Tribunal Transcript," Department of Defense, 2007; "Khalid Sulaymanjaydh Al Hubayshi Unclassified Verbatim Combatant Status Review Tribunal Transcript," Department of Defense, 65–73; "Noor Uthman Muhammed Unclassified Verbatim Combatant Status Review Tribunal Transcript," Department of Defense, p. 15.

90. Author interviews with Bruce Riedel, who said that Sir Hilary Synnott, then serving as British high commissioner to Pakistan, told him that he thought the chances of war between India and Pakistan were "fifty-fifty," Washington, 2014–2015.

91. Author interview with General Rashid Qureshi, Islamabad, June 2015.

92. Grenier, *88 Days to Kandahar*; also author telephone interview with Grenier.

93. Bruce Riedel, *Avoiding Armageddon: America, India, and Pakistan to the Brink and Back* (Washington, D.C.: Brookings Institution Press, 2013). Also author interviews with Riedel, Washington, D.C., 2014–2015, and General Musharraf, Karachi, February 2015.

Chapter Three

1. Pam O'Toole, "Karzai: King's Powerful Pashtun Ally," BBC News Online, November 2, 2001.
2. Author telephone interview with James Dobbins, January 2016; also see "Filling the Vacuum: The Bonn Conference," www.pbs.org/wgbh/pages/frontline/shows/campaign/withus/cbonn.html.
3. Author telephone interviews with Dobbins and Ryan Crocker, October 2014.
4. Author interviews with Mahfouz Ibn El Waleed, Nouakchott, December 2014, January and June 2015.
5. Author interviews with Mahfouz, who was with Saif al-Adel. Also referenced by Saif in his five letters posted online and available at www.jihadica.com/al-qa%E2%80%99ida-revisions-the-five-letters-of-sayf-al-%E2%80%98adl/. See "Al-Qa'ida Member Recalls US Bombardment, Accuses Taliban of Betrayal," World News Connection, October 29, 2003, accessed here: web.archive.org/web/20040610170428; www.why-war.com/news/2003/10/29/alqaidam.
6. Author interviews with Mahfouz.
7. Ibid.
8. Abu Zubaydah's diaries, dated from 1990 to 2002 and recovered in the U.S. and Pakistani raid that captured Zubaydah on March 28, 2002. Translated by the U.S. government and released to Al Jazeera by a former U.S. intelligence official. Al Jazeera America, "Original Documents: The Abu Zubaydah Diaries," December 3, 2013, america.aljazeera.com/multimedia/2013/11/original-documentstheabuzubaydahdiaries.html.
9. M. Ilyas Khan, "Profile of Nek Mohammed," Dawn, June 19, 2004.
10. The Pakistani extremist groups Lashkar-e-Jhangvi and Jundullah were also involved.
11. Author interviews with Mahfouz.
12. National Commission on Terrorist Attacks Upon the United States, 9/11 Commission Report, Washington, July 22, 2004, www.9-11commission.gov/report/. "The relationship between al Qaeda and Iran demonstrated that Sunni–Shia divisions did not necessarily pose an insurmountable barrier to cooperation in terrorist operations. Al Qaeda members received advice and training from Hezbollah." According to the report, many of Al Qaeda's 9/11 hijackers transited through Iran but "after 9/11, Iran and Hezbollah wished to conceal any past evidence of cooperation with Sunni terrorists associated with al Qaeda."
13. "Iran's Ministry of Intelligence and Security: A Profile," Library of Congress, December 2012.
14. Dexter Filkins, "The Shadow Commander," New Yorker, September 30, 2013.
15. Account of Mahfouz's journey to Iran from author interviews with Mahfouz, Nouakchott. There are some claims that Mahfouz traveled to Iran with Abu Walid al-Masri, formerly of Al Jazeera. He denied this to the authors, but for more on Mahfouz and al-Masri possibly traveling together to Iran, see "Treasury Targets Al Qaida Operatives in Iran," U.S. Department of the Treasury, January 16, 2009, www.treasury.gov/press-center/press-releases/Pages/hp1360.aspx.
16. A full analysis of these tapes can be found in Flagg Miller, The Audacious Ascetic: What the Bin Laden Tapes Reveal about Al-Qa'ida (New York: Oxford University Press, 2015).
17. The letter was addressed to "Abu Obadiah."
18. Robert Lacey, Inside the Kingdom: Kings, Clerics, Modernists, Terrorists, and the Struggle for Saudi Arabia (London: W. F. Howes, 2009). For more on Hubayshi see "Gitmo Files: Khalid Sulaymanjaydh Al Hubayshi," Wikileaks, wikileaks.org/gitmo/prisoner/155.html.
19. Osama had studied economics at King Abdulaziz University in Jeddah. See Lawrence Wright, The Looming Tower: Al-Qaeda and the Road to 9/11 (New York: Allen Lane, 2006), for more details of his early life.
20. Author interview with Abdullah Anas, London, October 2014. Also author interviews with Huthaifa Azzam, Amman, Jordan, December 2016.

21. Wright, *The Looming Tower*.

22. Among the first arrivals was Hamza Shamali, a Jordanian national. He described his experiences to the authors in interviews conducted in Irbid, Jordan, December 2016.

23. Ali Soufan, *The Black Banners* (New York: W. W. Norton, 2011). Also author interviews with Soufan, New York, October 2014.

24. His real name was Walid bin Attash, see "Gitmo Files: Walid Muhammad Salih Bin Attash," Wikileaks, wikileaks.org/gitmo/prisoner/10014.

25. Author interview with Dr. Amin al-Haq, Islamabad, February 2015.

26. Associated Press, "Afghan Warlord: We Helped Bin Laden Escape," November 1, 2007. More details of the exfiltration operation in Tim Lister, "Osama Bin Laden's Escape: A Tale of Subterfuge and Hard Cash," CNN, April 28, 2011. Also Imtiaz Gul, *Pakistan: Before and After Osama* (New Delhi: Roli Books, 2012).

27. When he heard on January 1. "The Abu Zubaydah Diaries."

28. Testimony of Abdul Rabbani from "Gitmo Files," Wikileaks, wikileaks.org/gitmo/prisoner/1461. Rahman said Saad bin Laden, his wife, and his son lived at a Karachi safe house from January to June 2002. Sometimes he would go with KSM to one of Rabbani's safe houses, D-255, Block 13 D1, Gulshan-e-Iqbal, Karachi. Rabbani met Saad there. Tariq Road was where the bin Laden passports were later found.

29. This box was kept at the home of another brother in the network, called Abu Shem.

30. Author interviews with bin Laden family members. Amal also talked about this to the Abbottabad Commission. Abbottabad Commission report, Al Jazeera Investigation Unit, "Document: Pakistan's Bin Laden Dossier," Al Jazeera, July 8, 2013. The final report was never published, but an unauthorized draft was leaked and is available to view here: www.aljazeera.com/indepth/spotlight/binladenfiles/.

31. Amal and Maryam talk about their time in Karachi in the Abbottabad Commission report. Also author interviews with bin Laden family members and Maryam's family members.

32. Author interviews with bin Laden family members and Maryam's family members.

33. This group was led by commander Abu Laith al-Libi, who had been fighting at Kandahar airport.

34. Author interviews with Mahfouz.

35. The Mauritanian bought his way into Iran with a "ton of cash," according to U.S. officials, "Treasury Targets Al Qaida Operatives in Iran."

36. Author interviews with Mahfouz.

37. Ibid.

38. "Iran's Ministry of Intelligence and Security: A Profile," Library of Congress, December 2012.

39. Karen McVeigh, "Former al-Qaida OperativeTurned Informant Testifies in Abu Hamza Trial," *Guardian*, April 28, 2014.

40. Ibid. Also, Benjamin Weiser, "At Trial of Bin Laden Relative Witness Describes Meeting 9-11 Mastermind," *New York Times*, March 12, 2014.

41. Farah Stockman, "Bomb Probe Eyes Pakistan Links. Extremist May Have Influenced Reid," *Boston Globe*, January 6, 2002.

42. The best investigation into Pearl's murder, one supported by his family, is via the Pearl Project, conducted by staff and students at Georgetown University, Washington, D.C. Its findings can be accessed here: pearlproject.georgetown.edu/.

43. Author interview with Khalid Khawaja, Islamabad, August 2006.

44. David Kohn, "Sheik Gilani: CBS' Man in Pakistan Tracks Him Down," *60 Minutes*, March 13, 2002.

45. The Pearl Project.

46. This account was drawn from material collated by the Pearl Project, details provided by Khalid Shaikh Mohammad to his lawyers at Guantánamo, and an account that Saif al-Adel gave to Mahfouz Ibn El Waleed during their incarceration in Iran and repeated by Mahfouz during interviews with the authors.

47. Khalid Shaikh Mohammad referred to this conversation during an interrogation session at Guantánamo Bay.

48. The Pearl Project.

49. AFP, "Over Rs.230 Billion Illegally Collected in Karachi Annually: DG Rangers," June 11, 2015. Author interviews with Tariq Pervez, Islamabad, 2010 and 2014, and Lahore, 2015.

50. Author phone interviews with Robert Grenier, March 2015.

51. "The Abu Zubaydah Diairies."

52. Ibid. Zubaydah also sneered at the Americans involved in the raid, writing: "A group of Americans came and photographed the location, or they photographed themselves with their weapons, at the location. (Rambo). Just like in Afghanistan, at the end of the movie, the American soldier appears and films the movie. And he would be the hero, Rambo."

53. Author interview with General Javed Alam Khan, Rawalpindi, May 2015; and telephone interviews with Robert Grenier. Also Grenier's book *88 Days to Kandahar* (New York: Simon & Schuster, 2015).

54. Grenier, *88 Days to Kandahar.*

55. Ibid.

56. Author telephone interview with Ryan Crocker, October 2014.

57. Daniel Larison, "Crocker on Diplomacy with Iran and the 'Axis of Evil,'" *American Conservative*, November 4, 2013.

58. Author interview with Ryan Crocker.

59. Multiple author interviews with Mahfouz, also online writings of Saif al-Adel.

60. This sentiment is also expressed by Abu al-Khayr al-Masri, another member of Al Qaeda's *shura*, in a letter to his former Al Qaeda brother Abu Walid al-Masri (Mustafa Hamid), who wrote a similar thing in a pamphlet he published online in 2010. Abu al-Khayr's letter to Abu Walid was found at Abbottabad and declassified by the Office of the Director of National Intelligence on March 1, 2016. It is dated August 22, 2009, and can be read here: www.dni .gov/index.php/resources/bin-laden-bookshelf?start=3.

61. The Pearl Project, assets.documentcloud.org/documents/27969/pearlmanuscript.pdf.

Chapter Four

1. In author interviews with General Hamid Gul, conducted in Rawalpindi and Islamabad, 2006–2015, he frequently described Hafiz Saeed as his best friend.

2. Abu Zubaydah refers to his brother studying in Faisalabad in volume two of his diaries, in an entry from 1991, when he was already well ensconced with jihadists in Peshawar. Abu Zubaydah's diaries, dated from 1990 to 2002 and recovered in the U.S. and Pakistani raid that captured Zubaydah on March 28, 2002. Translated by the U.S. government and released to Al Jazeera by a former U.S. intelligence official. Al Jazeera America, "Original Documents: The Abu Zubaydah Diaries," December 3, 2013, america.aljazeera.com/multimedia/2013/11/ original-documentstheabuzubaydahdiaries.html.

3. Osama correspondence with Atiyah Abd al-Rahman in 2010 details the complaint from Abu al-Khayr al-Masri and others in Iran to Abu Walid al-Masri, who wrote in an online pamphlet that Al Qaeda's efforts to obtain fissile and radioactive material ahead of 9/11 had not been serious. Documents recovered from Abbottabad, declassified and released by the Office of the

Director of National Intelligence [hereafter ODNI] in May 2015, www.dni.gov/index.php/resources/bin-laden-bookshelf.

4.   Abu Zubaydah was referring to his friend, the former emir of Khaldan camp who had been arrested with thirty Arab fighters in Parachinar on December 16, 2001. "The Abu Zubaydah Diaries."

5.   Martinez was identified by Scott Shane, "Inside a 9/11 Mastermind's Interrogation," *New York Times*, June 22, 2008. John Kiriakou, another CIA case officer briefly posted to Pakistan in 2002, was subsequently identified as Shane's source and convicted for passing classified information to a reporter.

6.   "Transcript: bin Laden Determined to Strike in US," CNN International, April 10, 2004.

7.   Jason Leopold, "Exclusive: From Hopeful Immigrant to FBI Informant—the Inside Story of the Other Abu Zubaidah," *Truthout*, May 29, 2012. Author interviews with Hesham Abu Zubaydah.

8.   Author telephone interview with Robert Grenier, March 2015.

9.   "I had watched with growing frustration as this master terrorist logistician traveled repeatedly through Pakistan to and from Al Qaeda's Afghan training camps." Robert Grenier, *88 Days to Kandahar* (New York: Simon & Schuster, 2015).

10.   Author interview with Shafiq Ghani, Faisalabad, February 2015. Also author interviews with Tajik Sohail Habib, deputy inspector general of police, Faisalabad, February 2015.

11.   Author interview with Constable Mubashir, Faisalabad, February 2015.

12.   Steve Coll, "The Spy Who Said Too Much," *New Yorker*, April 1, 2013.

13.   Author interview with Ali Soufan, New York, October 2014.

14.   Author interviews in Virginia and Washington, D.C., in October 2014 and February 2015, with five sources who were contracted to work on the renditions program for the CIA, as well as with two serving special agents deputed by the FBI to work with the CIA in those years.

15.   "PM Denies Knowledge of Torture: Thailand 'Didn't Do It and Was Not Involved,'" *Bangkok Post*, December 19, 2014. The code name Cat's Eye is mentioned on page 90 of *Husayn (Abu Zubaydah) v. Poland*, Judgment, European Court of Human Rights, Strasbourg, July 24, 2014.

16.   Ali Soufan, *The Black Banners* (New York: W. W. Norton, 2011).

17.   This account from author interview with Ali Soufan.

18.   Senate Select Committee on Intelligence (SSCI), *The Official Senate Report on CIA Torture* (New York: Skyhorse Publishing, 2015), 25 [hereafter Senate Torture Report].

19.   Section 497 provides, "Whoever has sexual intercourse with a person who is and whom he knows or has reason to believe to be the wife of another man, without the consent or connivance of that man, such sexual intercourse not amounting to the offence of rape, is guilty of the offence of adultery, and shall be punished with imprisonment of either description for a term which may extend to five years, or with fine, or with both. In such case, the wife shall be punishable as an abettor."

20.   Author telephone interviews with Hesham Abu Zubaydah, October 2016.

21.   On the basis of Zubaydah's information, Ghul became a "First Priority Raid Target" with the CIA describing him as a "major support player within the Al Qaeda network." Senate Torture Report.

22.   According to many who served under him and were later interrogated at Guantánamo. Also, Yosri Fouda, who interviewed KSM in Karachi in April 2002; and the second shoe-bomber, Saajid Badat, who gave evidence in a terrorism trial in New York in 2012.

23.   See "Gitmo Files: Ramzi bin al-Shibh," Wikileaks, wikileaks.org/gitmo/prisoner/10013. KSM admitted to many plots in his submission to a legal panel at Guantánamo Bay in March 2007. See "Verbatim Transcript of Combatant Status Review Tribunal Hearing for ISN 10024," March 10, 2007, Unclassified: i.a.cnn.net/cnn/2007/images/03/14/transcript_ISN10024.pdf.

24. Terry McDermott and Josh Meyer, *The Hunt for KSM* (New York: Little, Brown, 2012).
25. Ibid.
26. Ibid. Ramzi al-Shibh spoke in beautiful Arabic, extolling the hijackers and quoting liberally from the Koran. Fouda filmed a suitcase of what al-Shibh described as "souvenirs" of the 9/11 attacks, including an air navigation map of the American eastern seaboard, flight simulator CD-Roms, and a flight instruction book containing hijacker Mohamed Atta's handwritten notes.
27. Author telephone interviews with Hesham Abu Zubaydah, October 2016. Also Leopold, "Exclusive: From Hopeful Immigrant to FBI Informant—the Inside Story of the Other Abu Zubaidah."
28. Remarks by the president at Connecticut Republican Committee Luncheon, Hyatt Regency Hotel, Greenwich, Connecticut, April 2002. See georgewbush-whitehouse.archives.gov/news/releases/2002/04/20020409-8.html.
29. Mark Mazzetti, "Bush Aides Linked to Talks on Interrogations," *New York Times*, September 24, 2008.
30. Jose A. Rodriguez with Bill Harlow, *Hard Measures* (New York: Simon & Schuster, 2013).
31. George Tenet, *At the Center of the Storm* (New York: HarperCollins, 2007).
32. Author interview with Ali Soufan. Also Soufan, *The Black Banners*.
33. Dr. James Mitchell is referred to by the pseudonym Dr. Grayson Swigert throughout the Senate Torture Report. His report on developing new countermeasures to resistance training is detailed on page 21. Mitchell later confirmed that he was Swigert and that in 2002 he had carried out enhanced interrogations on Abu Zubaydah in an article by Jason Leopold for *Vice News*, "Psychologist James Mitchell Admits He Waterboarded Al Qaeda Suspects," December 14, 2014. In Ali Soufan's book *The Black Banners*, the psychologist is referred to as Boris. In late 2016, Mitchell published his own account of the program: James E. Mitchell, Ph.D., with Bill Harlow, *Enhanced Interrogation: Inside the Minds and Motives of the Islamic Terrorists Trying to Destroy America* (New York: Crown, 2016).
34. Author interviews with Dr. James Mitchell, Florida, February 2017.
35. This research took place in the laboratories of Richard Solomon at the University of Pennsylvania and was conducted by graduate students Martin Seligman and Steven Maier. Dr. James Mitchell met Seligman shortly after 9/11. See Maria Konnikova, "Trying to Cure Depression, but Inspiring Torture," *New Yorker*, January 14, 2015.
36. Shawn Vestal, "'New Age of Terror' Has Spokane Link," *Spokesman-Review*, December 21, 2014.
37. Soufan, *The Black Banners*, 394.
38. Jose Rodriguez later told the Office of the Inspector General that "CTC subject matter experts" pointed to intelligence that they said indicated Abu Zubaydah knew more than he was admitting and thus disagreed with the assessment from Detention Site Green that Abu Zubaydah was "compliant." Senate Torture Report, 41.
39. Soufan, *The Black Banners*, 394. Mitchell, *Enhanced Interrogation*.
40. Soufan, *The Black Banners*, 394.
41. Ibid.
42. Ibid.
43. Ibid., 396.
44. The Senate Torture Report concluded: "Neither psychologist had any experience as an interrogator, nor did either have specialized knowledge of al-Qa'ida, a background in counterterrorism, or any relevant cultural or linguistic expertise."
45. Jason Leopold, "I'm Just a Guy Who Got Asked to Do Something for His Country," *Guardian*, April 18, 2014. In Leopold's second article for *Vice News*, "Psychologist James Mitchell Admits He Waterboarded Al Qaeda Suspects," Mitchell provided "voluminous military evaluation

records, dating back decades, that show how he has an extensive background in special operations, hostage negotiations and interrogation training." See also Mitchell, *Enhanced Interrogation*.

46. Senate Torture Report, 27.

47. Leopold, "I'm Just a Guy Who Got Asked to Do Something for His Country." See also Mitchell, *Enhanced Interrogation*.

48. Wilson Andrews and Alicia Parlapiano, "A History of the CIA's Secret Interrogation Program," *New York Times*, December 9, 2014.

49. Senate Torture Report, 27.

50. Ibid., 27.

51. Ibid., 28.

52. Author interviews with Dr. James Mitchell, Florida, February 2017.

53. Abu Zubaydah's prison diary was obtained from his lawyer Joseph Margulies, for whom it was declassified. It amplifies the Red Cross file on the prisoner's treatment and is excerpted here with his full authorization. Author copies.

54. Ibid.

55. Ibid.

56. Ibid.

57. Senate Torture Report, 29.

58. Ibid.

59. Ibid.

60. Ibid.

61. Soufan, *The Black Banners*, 397.

62. Abu Zubaydah's prison diary.

63. Ibid.

64. Ibid.

65. Soufan, *The Black Banners*, 400. See also Mitchell, *Enhanced Interrogation*.

66. Author interview with Ali Soufan.

67. Senate Torture Report, 30.

68. Abu Zubaydah's prison diary.

69. Dr. Mitchell confirmed to the author that he was the only one not to cover his face. Author interviews, Florida, February 2017.

70. Author interview with General Javed Alam Khan, Rawalpindi, March 2015.

71. Ibid.

72. Grenier left Pakistan in June 2002.

73. Kasra Naji, "Canada Train Plot: Iran's al-Qaeda Problem," BBC Persian, April 23, 2013.

74. According to Mahfouz, who visited and assisted the new arrivals.

75. Author interview with Abu Soufiyan, former Jordanian jihadi who fought with Zarqawi and then relocated to Malaysia. Amman, Jordan, December 2016.

76. According to FBI testimony of Sulaiman Abu Ghaith, author copy.

77. Lawrence Wright, "The Master Plan," *New Yorker*, September 11, 2006.

78. Author interviews with Mahfouz and the online writings of Saif al-Adel.

79. Bill Roggio, "Saif al-Adel, Zarqawi, al-Qaeda and Iran," *Long War Journal*, June 16, 2005.

80. Author interviews with bin Laden family members.

81. Author interviews with Mahfouz.

82. Abu Walid al-Masri (Mustafa Hamid).

83. Author interviews with bin Laden family members.

84. Hamzah bin Laden letter to his father June 2009. ODNI documents, Abbottabad, released in May 2015.

85. In June 2002, this heartfelt message appeared on an Al Qaeda supporting website. Quoted in Peter Bergen, *The Osama bin Laden I Know* (New York: Simon & Schuster, 2005).

86. Ibid.

87. Author interviews with Mahfouz, who kept in touch with events daily from his Quds Force compound.

88. Five letters of Saif al-Adel, published online and available at www.jihadica.com/al-qa%E2%80%99ida-revisions-the-five-letters-of-sayf-al-%E2%80%98adl/.

89. Jeffrey Goldberg, "The Great Terror," *New Yorker*, March 25, 2005; Micah Zenko, "Foregoing Limited Force: The George W. Bush Administration's Decision Not to Attack Ansar Al-Islam," *Council on Foreign Relations*, August 2009. Also see Joel Wing, "Why Didn't Bush Strike Zarqawi and Ansar al-Islam in 2002?" August 30, 2009, musingsoniraq.blogspot.co.uk/2009/08/why-didnt-bush-strike-zarqawi-and-ansar.html. Author interview with Abu Soufiyan, former Jordanian jihadi who was based with Zarqawi at Khurmal. Amman, Jordan, December 2016.

90. Patrice Taddonio, "The Secret History of ISIS," *Frontline*, May 12, 2016.

91. The Iraq war plan was influenced by Goldberg's piece in the *New Yorker*, "The Great Terror," which suggested Saddam and Ansar ul-Islam were cooperating.

92. Author interviews with former CIA analyst Nada Bakos, Seattle, 2014.

93. Saif al-Adel online biography on Zarqawi. Jordanian journalist Fuad Hussein claimed to have been sent this biography of Zarqawi by Saif al-Adel in 2004. He said that over a course of weeks he received forty-two densely handwritten pages of yellow greaseproof paper that were rolled up like cigarettes and smuggled into Jordan via a system of messengers. He incorporated them into a film about Zarqawi called *The Next Generation of Al Qaeda* that was broadcast by the Lebanese Broadcasting Corporation (LBC). Author interviews with Fuad Hussein, Jordan, October 2014. Author copy of the book in English translation and of the LBC documentary.

94. Saif al-Adel, five letters.

95. Author interview in Amman, November 2014, with Yousuf Rabbaba, who was held in prison with Zarqawi in Jordan in the late 1990s and continued to follow his path through mutual friends. Also author interview with Hassan Abu Haniya, Amman, November 2014.

96. Osama letter to Karim (pseudonym for Al Qaeda leader Nasir al-Wuhayshi in Yemen) dated October 18, 2007, castigates him for criticizing Iran, saying it had provided main artery for funds, personnel, and communication. ODNI documents, Abbottabad, released in March 2016. In a passage in his memoir, *At the Center of the Storm*, former CIA director George Tenet wrote, "In mid-2002 we learned that portions of al Qaeda's leadership structure had relocated to Iran. This became much more problematic, leading to overtures to Iran and eventually face-to-face discussions with Iranian officials in December 2002 and early 2003. Ultimately, the al Qaeda leaders in Iran were placed under some form of house arrest, although the Iranians refused to deport them to their countries of origin, as we had requested."

97. Similar sentiments about being an Arab dealing with Iranians were voiced by Nouri al-Malaki, Iraqi prime minister, to Ryan Crocker: "You can't know what arrogance is until you are an Iraqi Arab forced to take refuge with the Iranians." Quoted in Dexter Filkins, "The Shadow Commander," *New Yorker*, September 30, 2013.

98. Author interviews with Mahfouz, October 2014.

99. The letter can be read here: www.theblackvault.com/documents/capturediraq/al.pdf.

100. Ibid.

101. Ibid.

102. Author interviews in Islamabad and Rawalpindi, 2014–2015, with Brigadier (Ret.) Shaukat Qadir, who published an account of the Abbottabad operation endorsed by the ISI. The ISI

said that it had a photo of Ibrahim Saeed Ahmad before he changed his appearance. See also Shaukat Qadir, *Operation Geronimo: The Betrayal and Execution of Osama bin Laden and Its Aftermath* (Islamabad: HA Publications, 2012).

103. Author interviews with bin Laden family members, Maryam's relatives, and Abbottabad Commission report. Al Jazeera Investigation Unit, "Document: Pakistan's Bin Laden Dossier," Al Jazeera, July 8, 2013, www.aljazeera.com/indepth/spotlight/binladenfiles/.

104. Author interview with Clive Stafford Smith, London, January 2017.

105. Olga Craig, "CIA Holds Young Sons of Captured al-Qaeda Chief," *Daily Telegraph*, March 9, 2003.

106. According to eyewitness Parvez Rehman. Jason Burke, "Brutal Gunbattle That Crushed 9/11 Terrorists," *Guardian*, September 15, 2002.

107. Three days later, the *Sunday Times* carried a front-page story co-written by Yosri Fouda and Nick Fielding that named Khalid Shaikh Mohammad and Ramzi bin al-Shibh as the masterminds of 9/11. The crucial Part Two of the documentary would be screened on September 12, 2002.

108. Publicly, the Pakistanis tried to seize the upper hand, with the inspector general of Sindh police claiming that one of the dead Arabs had been involved in the murder of Daniel Pearl and that one of the two women taken for questioning was Khalid's wife. She was now in custody with her young daughter.

109. After studying the pictures of the arrested man, who bore little resemblance to Ramzi al-Shibh, some in the media raised suspicions that he in fact had been captured much earlier. But irrespective of whether the DHA raid had been staged, al-Shibh was now a condemned man. Author interviews with senior Pakistani police official Tariq Pervez, Lahore and Islamabad, 2014–2015.

110. Author interview with Rashid Quereshi, Islamabad, February 2015.

111. Craig, "CIA Holds Young Sons of Captured al-Qaeda Chief."

112. Spencer Ackerman, "CIA Medical Staff Gave Specifications on How to Torture Post-9/11 Detainees," *Guardian*, June 15, 2016.

113. "Newly Released DOJ Memos Offer Support for Account of Torture of KSM's Children Using Insects," History Commons Groups, April 17, 2009, hcgroups.wordpress.com/2009/04/17/newly-released-doj-memos-offer-support-for-account-of-torture-of-ksm%E2%80%99s-children-using-insects/.

114. McDermott and Meyer, *The Hunt for KSM*, 236.

115. Kim Barker, "From Hot Seat to One That's Even Hotter," *Chicago Tribune*, June 21, 2005.

116. He was at this time senior director for Southwest Asia, Near East, and North African affairs.

117. Author telephone interviews with Khalilzad, October 2014.

118. Author telephone interviews with Khalilzad, October 2014, and Crocker, December 2014.

119. Ibid.

120. Author interviews with Mahfouz.

121. Mahfouz was assisted by Abd al-Aziz al-Masri and Abu Dujana al-Masri, two explosives experts serving with Egyptian Islamic Jihad. Dujana was a son-in-law of al-Zawahiri.

122. In 1997, Shihata had traveled to Dagestan to secure the release of Dr. al-Zawahiri from Russian detention, an episode during which some claim al-Zawahiri had been recruited by the Russian security services to direct Al Qaeda's future attacks against America.

123. Letter addressed to Maulvi Abdal Aziz, dated December 3, 2002. ODNI documents, Abbottabad, released in March 2016.

124. Author interviews with Mahfouz.

Chapter Five

1. Abu Zubaydah's prison diary was obtained by the authors from his lawyer Joseph Margulies, who applied to have it declassified. The diary amplifies the International Committee for the Red Cross file on the prisoner's treatment and is reprinted here with his authorization. Author copies.

2. Senate Select Committee on Intelligence (SSCI), *The Official Senate Report on CIA Torture* (New York: Skyhorse Publishing, 2015), 37 [hereafter Senate Torture Report]. See also James Mitchell, *Enhanced Interrogation* (New York: Crown, 2016).

3. Senate Torture Report, 32.

4. In the Senate Torture Report Dr. Jessen was identified as Dr. Hammond Dunbar, a former psychologist with the U.S. Air Force Survival, Evasion, Resistance and Escape (SERE) training school, Senate Torture Report, 21. He has refused to comment on any of the allegations made against him, although Dr. Mitchell confirmed that he was the other named participant in the CIA program, Dr. Grayson Swigert. See also Mitchell, *Enhanced Interrogation*.

5. From the Senate Torture Report, 34. Liaison equities meant the need for the CIA to adequately appraise their Thai hosts about what they were doing to Abu Zubaydah without implicating them in the program.

6. Ibid., 34–35. The normal procedure for dealing with a body in the Buddhist country is cremation.

7. Ibid., 35.

8. Ibid., 36.

9. Ibid., 31.

10. Ibid., 40.

11. Ibid., 42.

12. Ibid., 41.

13. Abu Zubaydah's prison diary. For Mitchell's account, see Mitchell, *Enhanced Interrogation*.

14. Senate Torture Report, 41.

15. In an interview with the author, Mitchell confirmed he walled Abu Zubaydah on this first day of enhanced interrogation and thereafter. He also describes this process in detail in his book, *Enhanced Interrogation*. Interview conducted at Mitchell's home in Florida, February 2017.

16. Abu Zubaydah's prison diary.

17. Ibid.

18. Ibid.

19. Ibid.

20. Ibid.

21. Senate Torture Report, 33.

22. Abu Zubaydah's prison diary.

23. Senate Torture Report, 41.

24. In *Enhanced Interrogation*, Mitchell said that he held down Zubaydah while Jessen poured the water.

25. Jason Leopold, "Psychologist James Mitchell Admits He Waterboarded Al Qaeda Suspects," *Vice News*, December 15, 2014. See also Mitchell, *Enhanced Interrogation*.

26. Abu Zubaydah's prison diary.

27. Ibid.

28. These tapes were stored at the U.S. embassy in Bangkok but were destroyed in 2005, a fact that did not become public until 2007. Peter Taylor, " 'Vomiting and Screaming' in Destroyed Waterboarding Tapes," BBC *Newsnight*, May 9, 2012.

29. Abu Zubaydah's prison diary.

30. Spencer Ackerman, "CIA Medical Staff Gave Specifications on How to Torture Post-9/11 Detainees," *Guardian*, June 15, 2016.
31. Abu Zubaydah's prison diary.
32. Ibid.
33. Senate Torture Report, 44.
34. Ibid. 42.
35. Ibid.
36. Abu Zubaydah's prison diary.
37. Senate Torture Report, 44.
38. Ibid.
39. Ibid.
40. Ibid., 45.
41. Joby Warrick and Peter Finn, "Interviews Offer Look at Roles of CIA Contractors during Interrogations," *Washington Post*, July 19, 2009; and Jason Leopold, "Psychologist James Mitchell Admits He Waterboarded Al Qaeda Suspects." See also Mitchell, *Enhanced Interrogation*. Dr. Mitchell also made this assertion during interviews with the author, Florida, February 2017.
42. Senate Torture Report, 41.
43. Ibid., 43.
44. Jose Rodriguez later told the Office of the Inspector General that "CTC subject matter experts" pointed to intelligence that they said indicated Abu Zubaydah knew more than he was admitting and thus disagreed with the assessment from Detention Site Green that Zubaydah was "compliant." Senate Torture Report, 41.
45. Ibid., 43.
46. Ibid., 45.
47. Ibid., 43.
48. Ibid.
49. Abu Zubaydah's prison diary.
50. Senate Torture Report, 46.
51. Author interview with Dr. Ghairat Baheer, Islamabad, February 2015.
52. Senate Torture Report, 47.
53. "Death of a Detainee: April 27, 2005, CIA Inspector General Report of Investigation," newly declassified version available here: www.documentcloud.org/documents/3214828-CIA-IG-Gul-Rahman-Newly-Declassified.html. The report notes that Dr. Jessen was there for the first ten days of Rahman's detention. Dr. James Mitchell was also there for some of the time, working with other prisoners.
54. Ibid.
55. Ibid.
56. All Baheer quotes from author interview with Dr. Ghairat Baheer.
57. Jane Mayer, "Who Killed Gul Rahman?" *New Yorker*, March 31, 2010.
58. "Death of a Detainee."
59. Jason Leopold, "The CIA Officially Identifies the Architects of Its Post-9/11 Torture Program," *Vice News*, November 9, 2016.
60. The *Washington Post* did not name Thailand but published a report soon after detailing some of what Zubaydah had endured there. "Stress and Duress Tactics Used on Terrorism Suspects Held in Secret Overseas Facilities," *Washington Post*, December 26, 2002.
61. Zubaydah was transferred with Abd al-Rahim al-Nashiri. See "Gitmo Files," Wikileaks, wikileaks.org/gitmo/prisoner/10015.html for more details. Dexter Filkins, "How Did Abu Zubaydah Lose His Eye?" *New Yorker*, June 9, 2015.

62. *Husayn (Abu Zubaydah) v. Poland*, Judgment, European Court of Human Rights, Strasbourg, July 24, 2014, page 67.

63. Notes on Zubaydah's interrogation, made by him, and declassified in 2016 after pressure from his lawyer Joseph Margulies.

64. Ibid.

65. Jason Leopold, "I'm Just a Guy Who Got Asked to Do Something for His Country," *Guardian*, April 18, 2014.

66. This figure was confirmed in the Senate Torture Report. See Robert Windrem, "CIA Paid Torture Teachers More than $80 Million," NBC News, December 9, 2014. Declassified CIA document "How Much Has the CIA Paid Mitchell and Jessen Since 2002?" cited in Greg Miller, "CIA Documents Expose Internal Agency Feud over Psychologists Leading Interrogation Program," *Washington Post*, January 19, 2017.

67. Jason Leopold, "Psychologist James Mitchell Admits He Waterboarded Al Qaeda Suspects."

68. Author interview with Ahmad Zaidan, Islamabad, January 2015.

69. "Bali Death Toll Set at 202," BBC News, February 19, 2003.

70. Author interviews with bin Laden family members and relatives of Maryam. The ISI would later claim that Osama left Pakistan in 2002–2003 for an operation in an unnamed Gulf country. Shaukat Qadir, *Operation Geronimo: The Betrayal and Execution of Osama bin Laden and Its Aftermath* (Islamabad: HA Publications, 2012).

71. See Osama's letters from Abbottabad, declassified and released by the Office of the Director of National Intelligence [hereafter ODNI] in May 2015 and March 2016, www.dni.gov/index.php/resources/bin-laden-bookshelf.

72. This episode was recounted by Maryam in the unpublished Abbottabad Commission report: Al Jazeera Investigation Unit, "Document: Pakistan's Bin Laden Dossier," Al Jazeera, July 8, 2013, www.aljazeera.com/indepth/spotlight/binladenfiles/.

73. Author interviews with relatives of Ibrahim and Maryam. Osama also referred to his differences with Ibrahim in his correspondence. See Osama's letters, ODNI documents, Abbottabad, released in May 2015 and March 2016.

74. One had died fighting in Afghanistan and a second at Tora Bora.

75. "Full Text of Colin Powell's Speech," *Guardian*, February 5, 2003.

76. Senate Select Committee on Intelligence, "Report on the U.S. Intelligence Community's Prewar Intelligence Assessments on Iraq," July 7, 2004, 92–93. Author interview with Abu Yusuf, who was based with Zarqawi at Khurmal. Amman, Jordan, December 2016.

77. Urs Gehriger, "Abu Musab al-Zarqawi: From Green Man to Guru," a three-part series originally published in German by *Die Weltwoche*, October 6, 2005. An English translation is available at www.signandsight.com/features/449.html.

78. "Full Text of Colin Powell's Speech," *Guardian*.

79. This account is based on author interviews with Nada Bakos, Seattle, 2014, and an interview she gave to PBS *Frontline* for their documentary *The Secret History of ISIS*, a transcript of which can be found in this accompanying article by Jason M. Breslow, "Nada Bakos: How Zarqawi Went from 'Thug' to ISIS founder," *Frontline*, May 17, 2016.

80. Editorial, "The Case Against Iraq," *New York Times*, February 6, 2003.

81. Author interviews with Dr. Moneef Samara and Marwan Shehadah, Zarqa, September 2016; also author interview with Zarqawi's brother-in-law, Salah al-Hami (Abu Qunaiba), Zarqa, October 2014.

82. Terry McDermott and Josh Meyer, *The Hunt for KSM* (New York: Little, Brown, 2012). Also author interview with Asad Munir, former ISI station chief in Peshawar, Islamabad, June 2014. Also George Tenet, *At the Center of the Storm* (New York: HarperCollins, 2007); and

Marty Martin interview on *Manhunt*, a documentary film by Peter Bergen, directed by Greg Barker, 2013.

83. Penn Bullock and Brandon K. Thorp, "The Sky Who Bilked Me: Meet Bush's War Profiteering Chief Bin Laden Hunter," *Gawker*, May 19, 2011.

84. Multiple author interviews with Rahimullah Yusufzai, Peshawar, 2006–2015.

85. Author interviews with reporter Jamal Ismail, who covered the story for Al Jazeera, 2014–2015. His excellent Al Qaeda contacts went back to the time he worked on Osama's magazine in Peshawar during the 1980s. He interviewed Osama several times and also met Khalid Shaikh Mohammad. Today he works in Islamabad for Abu Dhabi Television.

86. Abdul Sami Paracha, "Major Qadoos Shifted to Rawalpindi," *Dawn*, March 23, 2003. What would not become clear for some time were the links between Qadoos and the family of Osama's courier brothers Ibrahim and Abrar, who lived close by in Suleman Talaab.

87. Quoted in the Senate Torture Report.

88. They also had been used on Abd al-Rahim al-Nashiri.

89. Details of KSM's detention locations and excerpts of his statements to the International Committee of the Red Cross can be found at the Rendition Project, www.therenditionproject .org.uk/prisoners/khaled-sheikh-mohammed.html.

90. "Mohammed Arrest Like 'Liberation of Paris,'" CNN International, March 2, 2003.

91. Author interviews with Asad Munir.

92. KSM admitted to many plots in his submission to a legal panel at Guantánamo Bay in March 2007. See "Verbatim Transcript of Combatant Status Review Tribunal Hearing for ISN 10024," March 10, 2007, i.a.cnn.net/cnn/2007/images/03/14/transcript_ISN10024.pdf.

93. Josh Meyer, "Race on to Find Sleeper Cells," *Los Angeles Times*, March 3, 2003.

94. This tape was shown to journalist Terry McDermott, who described it in his book (with Josh Meyer), *The Hunt for KSM*.

95. Getting there would involve a dangerous journey of 150 miles through the outskirts of several busy cities, including Mardan, Peshawar, and Dara Adam Khel.

96. The Rendition Project.

97. Author interview with Dr. Ghairat Baheer, Islamabad, February 2015.

98. Dr. James Mitchell confirmed in interviews with the author that he personally conducted enhanced interrogations on Khalid Shaikh Mohammad. Author interviews, Florida, February 2017.

99. Jason Leopold, "Exclusive: My Tortured Journey with Former Guantánamo Detainee David Hicks," *Truthout*, February 16, 2011.

100. Olga Craig, "CIA Holds Young Sons of Captured al-Qaeda Chief," *Daily Telegraph*, March 9, 2003.

101. Department of Justice Office of Professional Responsibility, "Investigation into the Office of Legal Counsel's Memoranda Concerning Issues Relating to the Central Intelligence Agency's Use of 'Enhanced Interrogation Techniques' on Suspected Terrorists," July 29, 2009, 88.

102. Author interviews with Dr. Mitchell, Florida, February 2017.

103. Senate Torture Report.

104. Khalid Shaikh Mohammad statement to ICRC, made in October 2006 and available from the Rendition Project archives: www.therenditionproject.org.uk/prisoners/khaled-sheikh -mohammed.html.

105. Dr. Ghairat Baheer said that Ensure was only given to the best-behaved detainees, per author interview.

106. Author interviews with Aafia's maternal uncle, Shams ul-Hassan Faruqi, Islamabad, February 2015.

107. Ibid.
108. Author interviews with Mahfouz Ibn El Waleed, Nouakchott, December 2014, January and June 2015.
109. He was desperate not to face the same plight as his brother-in-law, Mohamedou Ould Slahi, who was languishing in Guantánamo Bay, accused on the flimsiest evidence of being a senior Al Qaeda facilitator. Slahi had given the Americans statements about Mahfouz's Al Qaeda activities.
110. His name was Abu Abdul Rahman al-Muhajir. He subsequently left Iran, returned to Al Qaeda Central, and was killed in Pakistan in April 2006.
111. Author interviews with Abu Soufiyan and Abu Yusuf, who were both in Zarqawi's group at the time. Amman, Jordan, December 2016.
112. Now that the assistance of the Quds Force had been withdrawn, Zarqawi had entrusted the rest of his group still in Iran to Abu-Abdallah al-Shafi'i, a Kurdish Iraqi leader of the Ansar ul-Islam group, and had gone into hiding.
113. Gehriger, "Abu Musab al-Zarqawi: From Green Man to Guru."
114. Ibid.
115. Ibid.
116. Lawrence Wright, "The Master Plan," New Yorker, September 11, 2006.
117. Saif al-Adel described the circumstances of his arrest to Mahfouz; multiple author interviews with Mahfouz, Nouakchott, 2014–2015.
118. FBI testimony of Sulaiman Abu Ghaith, author copy.
119. Saif al-Adel online biography on Zarqawi. Fuad Hussein, The Next Generation of Al Qaeda, Lebanese Broadcasting Corporation (LBC). Author interviews with Fuad Hussein, Jordan, October 2014. Author copy of the book in English translation and of the LBC documentary.
120. Author telephone interview with Khalilzad, October 2014.
121. Author telephone interviews with Ryan Crocker, December 2014, and Jim Dobbins, January 2016.
122. Author telephone interview with Guldimann, December 2015.
123. White House Office of the Press Secretary, "President Bush Welcomes President Musharraf to Camp David," June 23, 2003, georgewbush-whitehouse.archives.gov/news/releases/2003/06/images/20030624-3_musharrafarrival062-515h.html.
124. Author interview with General Pervez Musharraf, Karachi, February 2015.
125. Author interview with a corps commander who held a senior position in General Musharraf's government, name withheld at interviewee's request.
126. Author interviews with Asad Munir.
127. Munir said, "In June and July 2002 we thought he was in the Mehsud area of Latika. Later, we believed he'd gone to Kunar. We thought, he would never come and live in a city. Lots of Al Qaeda people had been caught in cities and staying there was dangerous."
128. Munir had learned his lesson when, as a young army captain, he had attempted to rescue a brigadier whose plane had gone down in the remote Tirah Valley. "I went in a jeep into mountains and was met by a wall of rifles. 'You can't come here,' they said."
129. Dexter Filkins, "At Least 11 Die in Car Bombing at Jordan's Embassy in Baghdad," New York Times, August 7, 2003.
130. Author interview with Marwan Shehadah, Amman, Jordan, September 2016.
131. Will McCants, The ISIS Apocalypse: The History, Strategy, and Doomsday Vision of the Islamic State (New York: St. Martin's, 2015).

CHAPTER SIX

1. Translation by Jeffrey Pool, "Zarqawi's Pledge of Allegiance to Al-Qaeda: From Mu'asker Al-Battar, Issue 21," *Terrorism Monitor* 2, no. 24 (December 16, 2004).

2. Author interviews with bin Laden family members, Islamabad, Doha, and Jeddah, 2012–2016, and relatives of Maryam, Pakistan, 2014–2016.

3. In 2013 this madrassa would be blacklisted by the United States for supporting terrorism. See "Madrassa Furious over US 'Terrorist' Tag," *Express Tribune* (Pakistan), August 21, 2013. Also, author interview with founder, Haji Alam Sher, Peshawar, August 2013.

4. Ibrahim's sister was called Haleema Bibi. According to Shaukat Qadir, who quotes ISI sources, Osama was also taken to Suleman Talaab during this period, staying at the empty home of Ibrahim's parents, which was located some streets away from Haleema's house. Author interviews with Shaukat Qadir, Islamabad and Rawalpindi, 2012–2015; also see Qadir, *Operation Geronimo: The Betrayal and Execution of Osama bin Laden and Its Aftermath* (Islamabad: HA Publications, 2012).

5. This was Abu Faraj al-Libi's wife; see note 6.

6. Abu Faraj had first lived there in 1991, sent by Al Qaeda to study Islamic law at a private university. Afterward he had become a well-regarded instructor at the first Al Farouk camp and by 9/11 was trusted enough to watch the Twin Towers burning with Abu Hafs the Commander. During the turmoil that followed, Abu Faraj had helped manage the Al Qaeda exodus, and he returned to Peshawar in October 2002 to embrace a new role as facilitator, helping organize the purchase of medicine, lights, batteries, food, and clothing for fighters gathering in Shakai.

7. Samira Abdullah, the widow of Abdullah Azzam, told the authors that she had visited this house several times. Author interview, Amman, Jordan, December 2016.

8. Author interviews with former ISI officer, Brigadier (Ret.) Shaukat Qadir, Islamabad and Rawalpindi, 2014 and 2015.

9. Born in Mosul in 1961, Abdul Hadi had risen to the rank of major in Saddam Hussein's army before falling afoul of the regime and fleeing to Afghanistan, where he fought with the mujahideen against the Soviet Union, gaining a reputation for being a skilled and intelligent operative. After joining Al Qaeda, he had commanded numerous terrorist training camps in Afghanistan, helped Zarqawi establish his camp near Herat, and fought in the final battle for Kandahar airport before being evacuated through Birmal.

10. Author interviews with several ISI officers who wish to remain anonymous, plus Syed Saleem Shahzad (in 2010), Rahimullah Yusufzai (2014–2015), General Perez Musharraf (Karachi, February 2015), and Hamid Gul (2015).

11. The agenda was recalled by others present who later were caught and transferred to Guantánamo Bay.

12. In Pakistan, relentless raids had crippled Al Qaeda. Kashmiri and Abdul Hadi's logic struck home: if they created domestic chaos, the Pakistani security agencies would be preoccupied and spend less time searching for them.

13. General Taj would later also be rewarded with the post of director general of the ISI.

14. Author interview with General Musharraf.

15. Ibid. Also Pervez Musharraf, *In the Line of Fire* (New York: Simon & Schuster, 2006).

16. Multiple author interviews with several senior generals in Musharraf's administration (anonymous) and friends of Musharraf including Ehsan ul-Haq, Ali Jan Aurakzai, Masood Aslam, and Jehangir Karamat. Also author interview with General Musharraf.

17. Author interview with General Musharraf. This reconstruction took place at the Combined Military Hospital in Rawalpindi.

18. Salman Masood, "Pakistani Leader Escapes Attempt at Assassination," *New York Times*, December 26, 2003.

19. The minivans were packed with potassium chlorate, easily obtained from the textile dyeing industry of the Punjab—where the purchase of dangerous chemicals and precursors went unregistered.

20. According to the ISI's Peshawar station, Abu Faraj was not Number Three in Al Qaeda but a middle-ranking fixer. Commander Abdul Hadi was far senior: a veteran fighter who was running a staging post for all ongoing Al Qaeda operations from Shakai. Both men were placed on the suspect list for the twin assassination attempts on Musharraf. But for the Pakistani leader, Abu Faraj was the primary target.

21. Description of what he typically carried comes from several detainees at Guantánamo Bay.

22. Author interviews with Nada Bakos, Seattle, October 2014. Statements by her on Ghul were given to the Senate Select Committee on Intelligence for what became the Senate Torture Report.

23. Urs Gehriger, "Abu Musab al-Zarqawi: From Green Man to Guru," a three-part series originally published in German by *Die Weltwoche*, October 6, 2005. An English translation is available at www.signandsight.com/features/449.html.

24. According to an interview with Iyad al-Toubasi, Zarqawi's hairdresser friend from Zarqa, conducted by Fuad Hussein in his 2004 documentary on Zarqawi for the Lebanese Broadcasting Corporation, *The Next Generation of Al Qaeda*.

25. Described by Hassan Ghul and quoted in the Senate Torture Report.

26. For more details on this episode see Adrian Levy and Catherine Scott-Clark, *Nuclear Deception: The Dangerous Relationship between the United States and Pakistan* (New York: Walker, 2010).

27. Abdul Qadeer Khan, "I Seek Your Pardon," *Guardian*, February 5, 2004.

28. Author interview with Dr. Khan's wife, Henny Khan, Islamabad, June 2014.

29. Account of this meeting comes from author interviews with General Musharraf and Ehsan ul-Haq, Islamabad, June 2014; see also Mark Mazzetti, *The Way of the Knife* (New York: Penguin, 2013).

30. Author interview with General Ehsan ul-Haq, Islamabad, June 2014.

31. Bob Drogin and Greg Miller, "CIA Chief Saw No Imminent Threat in Iraq," *Los Angeles Times*, February 6, 2004.

32. Author interview with General Ehsan ul-Haq, Islamabad, June 2014.

33. Umer Nangiana, "2004 Religious Ruling: Lal Masjid Had Declared Soldiers as 'Not Martyrs,'" *Express Tribune* (Pakistan), November 14, 2013. For the original fatwa wording see archive.org /details/PakistanUlamasFatwaOnWanaOperation2004.

34. The ID card was numbered CH 9613-753-20. Details from the unpublished Abbottabad Commission report, Al Jazeera Investigation Unit, "Document: Pakistan's Bin Laden Dossier," Al Jazeera, July 8, 2013, www.aljazeera.com/indepth/spotlight/binladenfiles/.

35. This neighbor was Dr. Qazi Mahfooz ul-Haq.

36. The plans were signed by "Mohammed Arshad" and stamped by Younis. His son said later that they never met the buyer but dealt with him through a property agent. Author copy of plans. Shaukat Qadir claimed that the ISI showed him a draft plan of the house layout drawn and signed by Osama. Author interview with former staff member of Junaid Younis's office who wishes to remain anonymous, Abbottabad, February 2015.

37. The builder was called Gul Mohammad; author interview with Gul Mohammad, Abbottabad, February 2015.

38. Some locals dubbed the Kuwaiti brothers as *Chota* (Little) and *Bara* (Big) in Pashtun.

39. Author interviews with Pervez Musharraf and Ehsan ul-Haq, Islamabad, June 2014.

40. General Safdar Hussain was the commander sent up by Musharraf.

41. Abu Zubaydah's prison diary was obtained by the authors from his lawyer Joseph Margulies, who applied to have it declassified. The diary amplifies the International Committee for the Red Cross file on the prisoner's treatment and is reprinted here with his authorization. Author copies. Zubaydah was sent to Rabat on March 27, 2004. Full details of his renditions can be found at the Rendition Project, www.therenditionproject.org.uk/prisoners/zubaydah.html.

42. Mazzetti, *The Way of the Knife.*

43. Alice K. Ross, "Ten Years On: Eyewitnesses Describe the Aftermath of Pakistan's First Drone Strike," Bureau of Investigative Journalism, June 17, 2014.

44. Seham had been living anonymously in Shakai with her fifteen-year-old son, Khalid, and daughters Miriam, fourteen, and Sumaiya, twelve, for months. Author interviews with bin Laden family members.

45. The Pashtun wife has never been named, although after relocating to Pakistan, al-Zawahiri also married the widow of Tariq Anwar Sayyid Ahmad, who was described as the "Commander of Special Operations for the [Egyptian Islamic] Jihad group." Ahmad had been killed in Kandahar in December 2001. His wife's name was Omayma. Bill Roggio, "Al-Zawahiri's Brother-in-Law Killed in Afghanistan," *Long War Journal*, April 19, 2011.

46. The authority of the Pakistani government was constitutionally limited to civil buildings, the roads, and a narrow strip just ten yards wide on either side of the roads.

47. Seham in an undated letter to the mother of Karima, the proposed fiancée for Khalid, declassified and released by the Office of the Director of National Intelligence [hereafter ODNI] in May 2015, www.dni.gov/index.php/resources/bin-laden-bookshelf.

48. Robert Windrem, "Hunt on for bin Laden's Latest No. 3 Man," NBC News, July 9, 2004.

49. He fled after the ISI raided his house in Nawan Shehr, Abbottabad, finding no one at home except a driver. They had been eavesdropping on a phone number provided by the CIA Counterterrorism Center in Langley and picked up an Al Qaeda courier in the Punjabi city of Gujranwala. Under torture, he had admitted to hiring a house in Abbottabad on behalf of Abu Faraj and installing his own family there to look after him. During a second operation in Abbottabad, they shot and killed one of Abu Faraj's outriders without even realizing his connection to the fugitive Al Qaeda facilitator. After interrogating Abu Faraj's driver, the ISI extracted two more locations. Author interview with General Musharraf.

50. The tape won hours of airtime in the United States, although some former followers like Noman Benotman, who had split with bin Laden over 9/11, accused him of peddling a naïve argument. "So if you are electing George W. Bush as president, you have to pay—that's the bottom line. It's not logical. There are eight million Muslims in America—so they are legitimate targets also?"

51. The strike was over their ongoing separation from their families, who were still being held at a former refugee camp in Arak.

52. With him were Abu Dujana, an Egyptian explosives expert; Abu Miqdad, another Egyptian who sat on Al Qaeda's *shura*; and several members of the Libyan Islamic Fighting Group.

53. Younsei brought two advisers, "Mr. Abdullah" and "Mr. Jawad." Author interviews with Mahfouz.

54. Author interviews with Mahfouz.

55. Those who had moved out included Saif al-Adel's father-in-law Abu Walid al-Masri (real name Mustafa Hamid), the former Al Jazeera reporter.

56. Peter Bergen, *The Osama bin Laden I Know* (New York: Simon & Schuster, 2005).

57. Ibid. Also author interviews with several undercover ISI officers who were on the raid.

58. Osama also wrote about Abu Faraj's arrest in the same draft speech, undated. ODNI documents, Abbottabad, released in March 2016.

59. "English Translation of Ayman al-Zawahiri's Letter to Abu Musab al-Zarqawi," *Weekly Standard*, October 11, 2005.

60. Aron Lund, "Who and What Was Abu Khalid al-Suri, Part 1," Carnegie Endowment for International Peace, *Diwan* (blog), February 24, 2014, carnegieendowment.org/syriaincrisis /?fa=54618.

61. Ibid. The two Syrians were also later accused of inspiring the July 7, 2005, attacks in London.

62. Ghul had already given valuable information about Shakai camp and about Al Qaeda couriers, naming Abu Musab al-Kuwaiti. Author interviews with Nada Bakos, Seattle, October 2014. Senate Torture Report, 130–31.

63. Ibid; Pavitt memo quoted in the Senate Torture Report, 376, note 2123.

64. See Senate Torture Report for more details of Ghul's journey.

65. "CIA 'Secret Prison' Found in Romania," BBC, December 8, 2011.

66. This is according to testimony given by Khalid Shaikh Mohammad and cited in the Senate Torture Report, 396.

67. Author interviews with Dr. James Mitchell, Florida, February 2017.

68. Associated Press report, "CIA Let KSM Design Vacuum Cleaner in Detention 'To Keep Him Sane,'" *Guardian*, July 11, 2013.

69. Author interviews with Mahfouz.

70. Author interviews with bin Laden family members and Maryam's relatives.

71. Mark Owen [pen name of Matthew Bissonnette] and Kevin Maurer, *No Easy Day* (New York: Dutton, 2012).

72. "Zarqawi Letter: February 2004 Coalition Provisional Authority English Translation of Terrorist Musab al Zarqawi Letter Obtained by United States Government in Iraq," U.S. Department of State Archive, 2001-2009.state.gov/p/nea/rls/31694.htm.

73. Translation by Jeffrey Pool, "Zarqawi's Pledge of Allegiance to Al-Qaeda: From Mu'asker Al-Battar, Issue 21."

74. Author interview with Maqdisi, Amman, Jordan, December 2016.

75. Author interviews with several former prisoners held with Zarqawi, including Yousuf Rabbaba, Hassan Abu Haniya, and Fuad Hussein, Amman, October–November 2014. Author copies of Zarqawi letters to his mother.

76. Lawrence Wright, "The Master Plan," *New Yorker*, September 11, 2006.

77. "Zarqaawi's Reply to Sheikh Abu Muhammad al-Maqdisi," Al-Hesbah, July 12, 2005, ansarukhilafah.wordpress.com/2015/02/06/zarqaawis-reply-to-sheikh-abu-muhammad-al -maqdisi/.

78. The member of parliament was Dhari al-Fayadh.

79. Letter from Dr. al-Zawahiri to al-Zarqawi, full text available here: www.globalsecurity.org /security/library/report/2005/al-Zawahiri-zarqawi-letter_9jul2005.htm.

80. Raffi Khatchadourian, "Azzam the American: The Making of an Al Qaeda Homegrown," *New Yorker*, January 22, 2007.

81. This addition to the building is documented in the Abbottabad Commission report.

82. Author interview with Fazlur Rehman Khalil, Islamabad, February 2015.

83. Ibid. Also multiple author interviews with General Hamid Gul, Rawalpindi, 2006–2015.

84. Ibid. The allegation he met Osama bin Laden to discuss his security arrangements was also confirmed to the authors by several anonymous Pakistani intelligence sources.

85. Azaz Syed, *The Secrets of Pakistan's War on Al-Qaeda* (Islamabad: Al-Abbas International, 2014). Also from Gul directly to the authors.

86. Ibid. See also Lawrence Wright, "Postscript: Hamid Gul, 1936–2015," *New Yorker*, August 18, 2015.

87. Author interviews with Hamid Gul.

88. Ibid.

89. Norwegian diplomat Alf Arne Ramslien claimed to have met Mullah Omar in Karachi in 2009. Mujib Mashal, "How Peace between Afghanistan and the Taliban Foundered," *New York Times*, December 26, 2016.

90. Author interviews with Khalid Quereshi of the Federal Investigation Agency, Islamabad, June 2014.

91. Author interviews with Tariq Pervez and Tariq Khosa, both former director generals of the Federal Investigation Agency, Lahore and Islamabad, 2010–2015.

92. Undated letter from Osama to Atiyah titled "Lessons Learned." ODNI documents, Abbottabad, released in May 2015. Akhtar was killed by Afghani security forces in January 2017; see Bill Roggio, "Afghan Intelligence Confirms Top al Qaeda Leader Killed in Raid," *Long War Journal*, February 19, 2017.

93. Khalil also brought into the conversation another prominent mujahideen leader who remained at large thanks to his deep ISI connections: Qari Saifullah Akhtar. He led Harkat ul-Jihad al-Islami (the Movement of the Islamic Holy War), which had been formed in the 1980s with CIA cash and ISI muscle, an outfit that like all the others had gone on to fight Pakistan's proxy war in Kashmir in the 1990s. Akhtar and Osama knew each other well after the former took part in a failed coup against Pakistani prime minister Benazir Bhutto in 1995 and then fled to Afghanistan, where he ran training camps in Kandahar and sometimes acted as a go-between with Mullah Omar. Akhtar's biggest claim to fame was that in 2001 he had rescued Mullah Omar from the ruins of Kandahar and ridden him across the border into Pakistan on the back of his motorbike. Akhtar had lawyers in Islamabad; homes in Kohat, South Waziristan, and his native Punjab; and a huge army of supporters, both within and outside Pakistan's military establishment. Declan Walsh, "Pakistan's Release of Militant Highlights Difficulties for Courts," *Guardian*, January 10, 2011. See also Declan Walsh, "The Taliban Blowback," *Guardian*, April 16, 2008.

94. As well as baby Aisha, she had two sons, Abdallah, aged four, and Osama, age estimated at two or three. "Letter to Mom," undated. ODNI documents, Abbottabad, released in January 2017.

95. Letter from Hallabi (Daood) to Osama dated July 25, 2006. ODNI documents, Abbottabad, released in March 2016.

96. Khadija letter to her father dated October 24, 2005. ODNI documents, Abbottabad, released in May 2015.

97. His name was Abu Abd al-Rahman al-Masri.

98. Cited in the Senate Torture Report, December 2014.

99. The television reporter was Nasir Dawar.

100. The reporter was Hayatullah Khan.

101. Five days later, news reports that he had died in an American raid in Mosul were denied.

102. "'Atiyah's Letter to Zarqawi," www.ctc.usma.edu/posts/atiyahs-letter-to-zarqawi-english-translation-2.

103. His long journey had been facilitated by Yusuf al-Balochi, a distant relative of Khalid Shaikh Mohammad, who smuggled brothers into Zarqawi's network.

104. Osama references this letter in an undated letter to Abu Uthman, who had taken over as Al Qaeda's Pakistan operations chief in January 2009. He was killed in November 2010. Abu Anas, trial documents, Government Exhibit 427 al-Libi reference 10-CR-019 (S-4)(RJD).

105. The clerics were Faqir Mohammad and Maulvi Liaqat Ali, who ran an Al Qaeda–supported jihad training school in the village of Chinagai.

106. His name was Shah Zaman.

107. Musharraf also claimed that Al Qaeda's Pakistan operations chief had been killed, a man who the FBI described as "one of the five or six most capable, most experienced terrorists in the world."

108. Photographers were encouraged to take pictures of a mud house with its rafters caved in, entombing children's clothes and schoolbooks. Author interview with Noor Berham, a tribal photographer and journalist who specialized in reporting on drone strikes, Islamabad, February 2011.

109. Everyone accepted that their community's association with Al Qaeda was hazardous, but the rules of Pashtunwali prevented them from ejecting the foreign fighters, who came and went as they pleased.

110. An ambulance was permanently parked up in front of the compound, although the Iranians suspected that the inordinate number of sick children needing treatment was just another ruse to get out of the compound and send messages. The situation came to a head when one of the wives was refused permission to take her nursing child with her to the hospital. Some brothers accused Dr. Jamali of being "not a doctor for humans but rather a doctor for animals" and went on a rampage, breaking out of the compound gate and into Block 200, where they climbed the walls and broke security cameras.

111. To show goodwill, the Iranians sent in a new envoy, an eminent cleric called Haji Abu Fatima, who was president of the Iranian Pilgrims Mission. As a peace offering, he brought several liters of precious Zamzam water (from the holy spring at Mecca) and arak-tree toothbrushes. He told the Mauritanian in December 2006 that he was going to Mecca and offered to bring gifts back for the Al Qaeda brothers; when the intelligence ministry found out, Abu Fatima was banished from the compound. It was terrible news for Mahfouz, who had been negotiating to go with him to the Tehran International Book Fair, in order to make some purchases.

CHAPTER SEVEN

1. Abu Yahya al-Libi, "Light and Fire in Elegezing the Martyr Abu Musab al-Zarqawi," (Alexandria, VA: IntelCenter, 2009). Available here: thesis.haverford.edu/dspace/bitstream/handle/10066/5135/AYL20060730.pdf.

2. Author interviews with Syed Saleem Shahzad, Islamabad, March 2010 and February 2011.

3. Washington privately leaned on Al Jazeera to stop airing these well-made films, and when that failed, the United States created its own Arabic-language network called al-Hurra (The Free One), but it could not find sufficient Arabic-speaking contributors, leading to erratic broadcasts strewn with errors.

4. Letter from Abu Anas al-Libi to Osama bin Laden dated October 13, 2010, recovered from Abbottabad, declassified and released by the Office of the Director of National Intelligence [hereafter ODNI] in March 2016, dni.gov/index.php/resources/bin-laden-bookshelf.

5. Report from Atiyah (Sheikh Mahmud) to Osama, forwarding a long message from supporting sheikhs in the "Arabian Penensula." Undated. Released by West Point scholars in 2012. Don Rassler, et. al., "Letters from Abbottabad: Bin Laden Sidelined?" Combating Terrorism Center at West Point, May 3, 2012, document reference SOCOM-2012-0000014-HT.

6. Ashraf Akhras was celebrating his marriage to Nadia al-Alami, alongside hundreds of Jordanian and Palestinian guests.

7. Zarqawi justified the operations by saying that Israelis and Western businessmen would be present at the function.

8. They were assisted by nonconventionals and specialists including U.S. Delta Force operatives, Navy SEALs, Army Rangers, and British Special Air Service troops and paratroopers, all of

them supported by the U.S. Army's 160th Special Operations Aviation Regiment and the U.S. Air Force's 24th Special Tactics Squadron. The group split into four regional commands: West, North, South, and Black.

9. This video was released in April 2006. Mary Anne Weaver, "The Short, Violent Life of Abu Musab al-Zarqawi," *Atlantic*, July/August 2006.

10. Yvonne Ridley, *Torture: Does It Work?* (Military Studies Press, 2016).

11. The GID's involvement in this operation was confirmed to the authors by a former senior officer, name withheld at his request, and by Hassan Abu Haniya, in interviews, Amman, October 2014. The same allegation was also made by Captain Ali bin Zeid to the future Camp Chapman suicide bomber Humam al-Balawi (see Joby Warrick, *The Triple Agent* [New York: Random House, 2011]) and to the authors in an interview with bin Zeid's widow, Fida Dawani, Amman, October 2014.

12. The spokesman was U.S. General William B. Caldwell. See Mark Bowden, "The Ploy," *Atlantic*, May 2007.

13. This statement appeared online on July 30, 2006, and is available at thesis.haverford.edu /dspace/bitstream/handle/10066/5135/AYL20060730.pdf.

14. According to the Iranian passports they carried, he was Mohammad Reza Ranjbar Rezaei (aged thirty-nine), traveling with his wife Cheshmnaz Fotohiashena Abad (forty) and their children Mohammad (nine), Fatemeh (seven), Ali (six), and Leila (four). For more details on his journey and capture, see Rusen Cakir, "The Story of al Qaeda Militant Abdul Hadi al Iraqi, a Kurd from Mosul," rusencakir.com, November 25, 2014, translated into English by Turgay Bayindir, en.rusencakir.com/The-story-of-al-Qaeda-militant-Abdul-Hadi-al-Iraqi-a-Kurd-from -Mosul/2998.

15. His coup in 1999 had been supported by an electorate sickened by years of corruption and weak civilian rule, most recently the administration of Nawaz Sharif, who, while prime minister, had run to the United States asking for asylum for himself and his family.

16. Author interview with Ali Jan Aurakzai, Rawalpindi, June 2014.

17. Author telephone interview with Robert Grenier, March 2015.

18. Journalists were banned from filming the event, but Syed Saleem Shahzad, the controversial Pakistan bureau chief of *Asia Times Online*, who some accused of being too close to militant factions, sneaked a few photographs. Author interview with Shahzad, February 2011.

19. Author interview with Aurakzai.

20. The seminary was called Zai-ul Uloom Taleemal Qu'ran.

21. Andy Worthington, "World Exclusive: New Revelations about the Torture of Ibn al-Shaykh al-Libi," andyworthington.co.uk, June 18, 2009.

22. Mark Mazzetti, "U.S. Says C.I.A. Destroyed 92 Tapes of Interrogations," *New York Times*, March 2, 2009.

23. See the full report here: www.aclu.org/files/assets/cia_release20100415_p19-27.pdf.

24. Department of Justice Office of Professional Responsibility, "Investigation into the Office of Legal Counsel's Memoranda Concerning Issues Relating to the Central Intelligence Agency's Use of 'Enhanced Interrogation Techniques' on Suspected Terrorists," July 29, 2009.

25. This missing twenty-one-hour period is also referred to in the Senate Torture Report, which noted that a review of the catalog of videos in May 2004 found that recordings were missing, 44. Senate Select Committee on Intelligence (SSCI), *The Official Senate Report on CIA Torture Committee Study of the Central Intelligence Agency's Detention and Interrogation Program* (New York: Skyhorse Publishing, 2015), 25 [hereafter Senate Torture Report].

26. See "Gitmo Files: Mustafa Ahmad Al Hawsawi," Wikileaks, wikileaks.org/gitmo/prisoner /10011.html; and the Senate Torture Report.

27. Department of Justice Office of Professional Responsibility, "Investigation into the Office of Legal Counsel's Memoranda Concerning Issues Relating to the Central Intelligence Agency's Use of 'Enhanced Interrogation Techniques' on Suspected Terrorists," July 29, 2009.

28. White House Office of the Press Secretary, "President Discusses Creation of Military Commissions to Try Suspected Terrorists," September 6, 2006, georgewbush-whitehouse .archives.gov/news/releases/2006/09/20060906-3.html.

29. " 'Platinum' Captives Held at Off-limits Gitmo Camp," *Miami Herald*, July 7, 2008.

30. Associated Press, "Prisoner Tells of 'Mental Torture' in Guantánamo Bay's 'Camp 7,'" NBC News, June 2, 2016.

31. Jason Leopold, "Emails Shed Light on New Guantánamo Policy Surrounding Detainees Legal Mail," *Truthout*, November 3, 2011.

32. The case was *Rasul v. Bush*. Author telephone interview with Abu Zubaydah's legal counsel, Joseph Margulies, who also represented Rasul, September 2016.

33. British lawyer Clive Stafford Smith, who has represented dozens of Guantánamo detainees, described this journey in his book *Eight O'Clock Ferry to the Windward Side: Seeking Justice in Guantánamo Bay* (New York: Nation Books, 2008).

34. In his book *Enhanced Interrogation*, Dr. James Mitchell claimed that Zubaydah had lost the eye due to botched plastic surgery performed in Pakistan shortly before he was captured. James Mitchell and Bill Harlow, *Enhanced Interrogation: Inside the Minds and Motives of the Islamic Terrorists Trying to Destroy America* (New York: Crown, 2016).

35. Abu Zubaydah's prison diary was obtained by the authors from his lawyer Joseph Margulies, who applied to have it declassified. The diary amplifies the International Committee for the Red Cross file on the prisoner's treatment and is reprinted here with his authorization. Author copies.

36. Author interviews with General Musharraf, Karachi, February 2015, and Aurakzai.

37. Ibid.

38. The book unashamedly cast Musharraf as a brave soldier who had dodged bullets and suicide bombers on behalf of his people. Pervez Musharraf, *In the Line of Fire* (New York: Simon & Schuster, 2006). Author meeting with General Bajwa, Rawalpindi, February 2012.

39. Author interview with Rahimullah Yusufzai, who reported from the scene, Peshawar, February 2015. Also see Chris Woods, "Drone Strikes in Pakistan: Over 160 Children Reported among Drone Deaths," Bureau of Investigative Journalism, August 11, 2011. The subsequent demonstration took place near Khar.

40. Author interview with Aurakzai.

41. Al Qaeda was furious about the Chinagai drone strike and somebody had to pay. But according to long-standing arrangements between Washington and Islamabad, the CIA had sent monthly faxes to ISI headquarters, outlining the areas where unmanned aircraft would operate and listing high-value targets under surveillance. If the ISI did not issue any specific objection, the U.S. operations went ahead without any further consultation, classified either as "signature strikes" if they had just general information of a suspected gathering or "targeted" if they were aimed at particular individuals. For the past year or more, al-Zawahiri and the villages around Damadola that harbored Taliban and Al Qaeda fighters had regularly featured on the list, so there was little Musharraf could do now to complain that the United States had deliberately blown his peace plan to smithereens. For more information on U.S. drone policy at this time, see Mark Mazzetti, *The Way of the Knife* (New York: Penguin, 2013).

42. Report from Atiyah to Osama, forwarding a long message from supporting sheikhs in the "Arabian Penensula." Undated. Released by West Point scholars in 2012. Don Rassler, et al.,

"Letters from Abbottabad: Bin Laden Sidelined?" Combating Terrorism Center at West Point, May 3, 2012, document reference SOCOM-2012-0000014-HT.

43. Cakir, "The Story of al Qaeda Militant Abdul Hadi al Iraqi."

44. Testimony of Rangzieb Ahmed, obtained by authors from CAGE, a London-based detainee rights advocacy group; also author interview with Asim Qureshi, CAGE, May 2014.

45. Ahmed claimed that he had been tortured by the ISI agents there, with one man in a suit who was a heavy smoker pulling out his fingernails with pliers and beating him with a piece of wood, while another agent of Afghani origin, who spoke Pashto and had curly hair, watched. Twice, Ahmed was hooked up to a lie detector and asked about known Al Qaeda locations, including the Tariq Road safe house and a branch of KFC in Rawalpindi formerly used by Khalid Shaikh Mohammad as a drop-off point.

46. Although Ahmed and Ghul were taken to the interrogation center almost every day, they did not know its location, as they were always hooded and shackled during the journey. Ahmed, who claimed to have come to Pakistan to help with the earthquake relief efforts after October 2005, was asked repeatedly by British and American intelligence officials about al-Zawahiri and bin Laden. "They asked about my links to Al Qaeda and what I had been doing in Haripur," he said. He was shown pictures of other suspects, including Azzam the American. There were hints that the foreign officials were on the right track when they questioned him about Abu Hamza Rabia, the dead courier. "The main questions centred around Hamza Rabia, like where I had met him, what instructions I had received, what plans, what attacks." Ahmed was also shown three diaries. "They said that there were codes in the books . . . they asked me what the codes in the diary were." All his answers were noted down in small reporter pads, and the CIA team was the most insistent. "There were usually three in a team, two males and one female." Ahmed claimed they disregarded his complaints about the torture.

47. Letter to "Honorable Shaykh," September 4, 2006. ODNI documents, Abbottabad, released in May 2015.

48. Stephen Negus, "Call for Sunni State in Iraq," *Financial Times*, October 15, 2006. Iraq Coalition Casualty Count, icasualties.org/Iraq/Fatalities.aspx.

49. Will McCants, *The ISIS Apocalypse: The History, Strategy, and Doomsday Vision of the Islamic State* (New York: St. Martin's, 2015).

50. Ibid.

51. Ibid.

52. Undated letter to Osama from the Jihad and Reform Front in Iraq, a coalition of Sunni insurgent groups opposed to the emergence of Islamic State in Iraq. ODNI documents, Abbottabad, released in May 2015.

53. The letter also puzzled at the appointment of Abu Ayyub, describing him as "much more bloodthirsty and more enthusiastic about *takfir* [the practice of one Muslim declaring another Muslim as a nonbeliever]" than Zarqawi. Abu Ayyub was authorizing the killing of "sheikhs and proselytizers" at will. He was "tyrannical in his dealings with others and has no patience for anyone who disagrees with him."

54. In December 2006. McCants, *The Isis Apocalypse*.

55. These rules were announced in an audio statement on March 13, 2007.

56. Al-Zawahiri's output increased to ninety-seven original videos in 2007, a sixfold increase from 2005.

57. In December 2007. McCants, *The Isis Apocalypse*.

58. Al Qaeda video supremo Azzam the American also warned al-Zawahiri against endorsing Abu Umar al-Baghdadi's Islamic State of Iraq, describing it as a "fictitious state."

59. As described by SEAL Team Six members Matthew Bissonnette (pen name Mark Owen), in his book with Kevin Maurer, *No Easy Day* (New York: Dutton, 2012), and Robert O'Neill, in an interview with Phil Bronstein, "The Shooter," *Esquire*, March 2013. Also per author interviews with bin Laden family members and relatives of Maryam.

60. Ibid.

61. A water pistol can be seen in the ISI's photograph of Ibrahim's body at Abbottabad.

62. Letter dated June 28, 2007, from Khadija, who addressed her brother Khalid by his code name Abu Sulayman. ODNI documents, Abbottabad, released in May 2015.

63. Azaz Syed, *The Secrets of Pakistan's War on Al-Qaeda* (Islamabad: Al-Abbas International, 2014).

64. Author interviews with Mahfouz Ibn El Waleed, Nouakchott, December 2014, January 2015, and June 2015.

65. Osama referred to this death and that of Mohammed al-Islambouli's wife in an undated letter to Atiyah Abd al-Rahman written after Saad's death. ODNI documents, Abbottabad, released in March 2016.

66. Standing with Abu Ghaith was Thirwat Shihata, a core member of al-Zawahiri's group, Egyptian Islamic Jihad, and an experienced operational planner. He, too, had been in Iran since 2002.

67. Saad took the new arrivals on a tour. Block 300 was significantly larger than Block 100. In its basement were four apartments, along with a mosque, a medical clinic, and a classroom. The girls played in the hallway of the basement out of sight of the men. The ground floor had two rows of much newer apartments, each with a large bedroom, a lounge, kitchen, and toilet. To one side of the compound were swings and to the other a small garden. Author interviews with Mahfouz.

68. Ibid.; also author interviews with bin Laden family members.

69. Nothing more had ever been heard of Mohammed al-Hallabi after his convoy was ambushed at the Pakistan border in November 2001.

70. Multiple author interviews with Mahfouz, plus interviews with bin Laden family members who wish to remain anonymous.

71. Ibid.

72. Ibid.

73. Letters from Osama to Atiyah. ODNI documents, Abbottabad, released in May 2015.

74. Huthaifa Azzam, then aged eighteen, had got out of the car shortly before his father and two brothers were killed. He believes strongly that al-Zawahiri ordered Abdullah Azzam's assassination. Author interview, Amman, Jordan, December 2016.

75. The Sheikh was also annoyed with Saudi television channels that had been running stories claiming that Al Qaeda had "links to Iran."

76. Osama letter to Atiyah, December 17, 2007. ODNI documents, Abbottabad, released in May 2015.

77. Author interviews with bin Laden family members. Khadija's death was also referred to in Osama and Seham letters. ODNI documents, Abbottabad, released in May 2015 and March 2016. Also "Letter to Mom," undated, ODNI documents, Abbottabad, released in January 2017.

78. Umm Khalid (Seham) to Umm Abd al-Rahman (mother of Karima), December 16, 2007. ODNI documents, Abbottabad, released in May 2015.

79. Abu Abdallah al-Hallabi (Daood) to Seham, November 13, 2007. ODNI documents, Abbottabad released in March 2016.

80. Osama refers to this idea in several letters. ODNI documents, Abbottabad.

CHAPTER EIGHT

1. "CIA Bomber Tape Released," CBS News, March 1, 2010, www.youtube.com/watch?v=n4P cV8RTJ9Y.

2. Abu Abdallah al-Hallabi (Daood) to "the Father, the ulema and the beloved Shakyh," October 20, 2008, recovered from Abbottabad, declassified and released by the Office of the Director of National Intelligence [hereafter ODNI] in May 2015, dni.gov/index.php/resources/bin -laden-bookshelf.

3. Abu Uthman.

4. Osama to Atiyah Abd al-Rahman, December 17, 2007, recovered from Abbottabad, declassified and released by the ODNI in May 2015.

5. His confidant was Mahfouz Ibn El Waleed, who related this story to the authors. Abu Ghaith also spoke of it in his FBI interrogation, author copy of the report.

6. Author interviews with Abu Ghaith's lawyer Stanley Cohen, New York, October 2014, and with Mahfouz, 2014 and 2015.

7. From Abu Ghaith's book, *Twenty Guidelines on the Path to Jihad*, which in December 2010 would be published on a website run by Abu Walid al-Masri (Mustafa Hamid), the former Al Jazeera reporter who was also held in Iran. In contrast, the FBI described Abu Ghaith's role in Al Qaeda as "comparable to the consigliere in a mob family or propaganda minister in a totalitarian regime."

8. In his FBI interrogation he says both Saif al-Adel and Abu Mohammed al-Masri readily confirmed their roles; author copy of transcript.

9. He took his feelings out on his new wife, an Egyptian girl named Amal, who was the daughter of an imprisoned brother from Islamic Jihad.

10. Bin Laden's proscription regarding the rights of a widowed woman can be found in a letter recovered from Abbottabad. ODNI documents, Abbottabad, released in May 2015.

11. Author interviews with Mahfouz.

12. Author interviews with Shams ul-Hassan Faruqi, Islamabad, February 2015.

13. Faruqi speculated to the authors that she wanted him to use his connections in the Pakistan Atomic Energy Commission (PAEC) to get her to Afghanistan, saying she believed only the Taliban could help her. The PAEC had close links to the Afghan scientific community and could travel there easily. At the time, he said, he was taken aback. "The last time I was there was 1999; it will take time," he said.

14. Aafia's children were Ahmed (eleven), Maryam (nine), and Suleiman (five). Ages correct as of 2008.

15. Faruqi told the authors he felt he was being lured into a trap. "I think certain people wanted to test me, as in certain circles it had been mistakenly claimed that I also had links to Al Qaeda and the Taliban."

16. Aafia's mother is Ismat Siddiqui.

17. While they waited for Ismat to arrive, Faruqi persuaded his visitor to lift her veil, and what he saw shocked him. "It was Aafia, I am one hundred percent sure, but she had had plastic surgery." He asked her: "Who did that to your face?" She said: "Nobody." Author interviews with Faruqi.

18. Hallabi (Daood) to "My beloved Shaykh," undated. ODNI documents, Abbottabad, released in May 2015.

19. Youngest wife Amal introduced her solemn children to the new arrivals. "These are your brothers and sisters," she told Safiyah, Aasia, Ibrahim, and Zainab, who were approximately the same ages as Khadija's children.

20. Letter from Seham to Hallabi (Daood), December 16, 2007. ODNI documents, Abbottabad, released in March 2016.

21. Author interviews with bin Laden family members and relatives of Maryam.

22. Letter from Seham to Hallabi (Daood), December 16, 2007. ODNI documents, Abbottabad, released in March 2016.

23. Letter from Hallabi to Seham, January 2008. ODNI documents, Abbottabad, released in March 2016.

24. Multiple author interviews with Benazir Bhutto (2005–2007), Wajid Shamsul Hasan (2005–present), Peter Galbraith (2005–2006), and Mark Siegel (2005–2007).

25. She wrote a letter naming Musharraf, Hamid Gul, Qari Saifullah Akhtar, and Ijaz Shah, the former head of Intelligence Branch (IB), as planning to assassinate her. Author interview with Benazir Bhutto, Dubai, 2007. Authors also sought an interview with Shah on this and other subjects, but he refused.

26. Seeing Bhutto entering the election race, the toppled prime minister Nawaz Sharif, who had been exiled to Saudi Arabia after the coup of 1999, decided to do the same. He flew into Pakistan, warning Musharraf that hundreds of thousands of his supporters would greet him; only a few hundred turned up. Sharif was arrested and flew back to Saudi Arabia soon after.

27. Author interview with Benazir Bhutto.

28. Author interview with General Pervez Musharraf, Karachi, February 2015.

29. Osama letter to Ibrahim (Abu Ahmad al-Kuwaiti) dated January 20, 2011. ODNI documents, Abbottabad, released in March 2016. See also Bill Roggio, "Osama Bin Laden's Files: Al Qaeda Provided Feedback on Pakistani Taliban's Charter," *Long War Journal*, March 11, 2016.

30. The two Al Qaeda leaders were concerned about the lack of clarity in the TTP's suggested methods of appointing its emir, his deputy, *shura* council members, and the leaders of the local TTP branches, as well as how disputes would be resolved. "We should [also] cover the Shura Council, their membership count, the attributes of their members, the duties of the Shura Council, how they reach crucial decisions to include their meetings timetable, and whether it should be on a monthly, bimonthly, or a six-month basis," they wrote.

31. She was taken to Rawalpindi General Hospital.

32. Musharraf has never stood trial for the charges that are still registered against him to this day and include impeachment, murder, and treason. In interviews he has denied all of them.

33. Author interviews with Mahfouz, who witnessed these scenes. Also corroborated by bin Laden family members.

34. As witnessed by Mahfouz.

35. This episode and a summary of everything that happened in Iran and who was held where can be found in a report written by Abu Abd al-Rahman Anas al-Subayi (Abu Anas al-Libi) to "the Shaykh," October 13, 2010. ODNI documents, Abbottabad, released in May 2015.

36. When General Qassem Suleimani sent a senior Iranian diplomat who had previously negotiated with Sunni Islamist groups in Yemen to remonstrate with the Al Qaeda prisoners, Mahfouz was still furious. "My brothers warned me back in 2001 of your treachery, that I should never make a deal with Iranians and expect them to keep it," he complained. "Today, I have discovered the bitter truth." Author interviews with Mahfouz.

37. "Khalid Shaikh Mohammad: Make Me a Martyr for 9/11," *Scotsman*, June 5, 2008.

38. Saad was the only member of the family to have any experience of traveling freely, as in 1998 he went to Sudan to find a wife.

39. "Treasury Designates Senior Al-Qa'ida Official and Terrorist Training Center Supporting Lashkar-E Tayyiba and the Taliban," U.S. Department of the Treasury Press Center, August 20, 2013.

40. Author interviews with Mahfouz and bin Laden family members.
41. This account of Saad's escape is based on author interviews with Mahfouz, who was reunited with the bin Laden family soon after, and author interviews with bin Laden family members, who pieced it together after they were freed themselves. Several letters from Osama also refer to Saad's escape and subsequent death. ODNI documents, Abbottabad, released in May 2015 and March 2016.
42. Letter from Abu Uthman to "the honorable brothers and the uncle [Osama]," early April 2009. ODNI documents, Abbottabad, released in May 2015.
43. Ibid.
44. His name was Sheikh ul-Islam.
45. This letter, dated August 15, 2008, was videoed in a clip that was subsequently recovered from Abbottabad. ODNI documents, Abbottabad, released in May 2015. Family members told the authors that the handwriting and language were not Saad's and that his habit was to ask someone else to compose letters for him. The story of the Pashtun family who took him in and the schoolboy who wrote the letter comes from two tribal journalists, interviewed in Islamabad and Peshawar, who wish to remain anonymous for their security. Also input from the family of Maryam, who overheard some of the discussions on the topic of Saad.
46. Abu Burhan was Saad's friend in Sudan who lent money for his wedding.
47. A clip of her questioning can be viewed here: www.dailymotion.com/video/xx5ouy _initial-questioning-of-aafia-siddiqui-in-afghani_news.
48. She was named by police as "Saliha" and described as being twenty-five years old, educated to the eleventh grade and coming originally from Pakistan's Sindh Province. This description is taken from the video of the police station press conference, with audio and subtitles. It was later uploaded by CAGE, a London-based detainees' rights advocacy group, and can also be seen here: www.youtube.com/watch?v=zec9MRxIsbY.
49. This account is taken from various court documents in the U.S. trial of Aafia Siddiqui, which began in February 2010.
50. Author interviews with Shams ul-Hassan Faruqi, Islamabad, February 2015.
51. Aafia's sister is Dr. Fowsia Siddiqui. She made these comments to Declan Walsh when he was *New York Times* Pakistan correspondent. Authors attempted to speak to Fowsia directly, but she was unwilling to discuss the case.
52. Author interview with Asim Qureshi, CAGE, London, May 2014.
53. The election was in September and Musharraf left Pakistan on November 23.
54. The first strike under the new rules had come in January 2008, targeting Khushali, a village near Mir Ali and close to where Khadija bin Laden had died giving birth. Based on intelligence that an "Al Qaeda summit" was unfolding, the missiles destroyed a cluster of houses, killing two of the most senior Al Qaeda figures in more than a year: Abu Laith al-Libi and Abu Obeida, who was Al Qaeda's Pakistan operations chief. Before Al Qaeda could ratify any new appointments, missiles fired by a second U.S. drone demolished a house in Zeralita, a village in Azam Warzak district, twelve miles west of Wana, on July 28. Inside was Abu Khabab al-Masri, the chief of Al Qaeda's "curdled milk," or WMD, program, a legendary Al Qaeda figure who the United States claimed to have killed once already. The famous bomb maker, who had once seized the bin Laden boys' pet puppies for chemical experimentation, had trained shoe-bomber Richard Reid and had a $5 million bounty on his head. On October 16, Khalid Habib, an Egyptian close to the Mauritanian, and the Al Qaeda chief of the Tribal Areas, was also killed in his vehicle at Tarparghai, in South Waziristan. He had recently written to Sheikh Osama to apologize for being unable to fight due to having suffered wounds in an earlier drone strike. "Oh my, my health has declined quite a bit due to the successive

wounds, the most recent six months ago. Praise God, God will grant me this as a badge on the Day of Resurrection. I pray for us and you to be kept from Satan and man and the demons. May he protect you and the doctor with his safekeeping . . . Your poor younger brother, at the mercy of his Lord." ODNI documents, Abbottabad, released in May 2015.

55. Civilian casualties totaled 848 killed or wounded, plus four hundred thousand refugees. David Ignatius, "A Quiet Deal with Pakistan," *Washington Post*, November 4, 2008.

56. Al Qaeda had already gained the release of a number of high-level prisoners in exchange for the Pakistani ambassador to Afghanistan just months earlier. It was a new tactic and it was working.

57. Jane Perlez, "U.S. Aid Worker Slain in Pakistan," *New York Times*, November 12, 2008.

58. Tehrik-i-Taliban Pakistan (TTP) was the coming together of eight or more groups, following the raid on the Red Mosque.

59. Attarzadeh's prolonged captivity caused diplomatic ructions, with Iran's foreign ministry describing it "an act of terrorism."

60. Author meeting with General Pasha, Islamabad 2015, and multiple meetings with his aide Brigadier Syed Amjad Shabbir.

61. Steve Coll, "Pakistan's New Spy Chief," *New Yorker*, September 30, 2008.

62. Press Trust of India, "Shuja Pasha Admitted ISI's Role in 26/11 Mumbai Attacks, Says Ex-CIA Chief," NDTV, February 23, 2016.

63. Shuja Nawaz, "Focusing the Spyglass on Pakistan's ISI," shujanawaz.com (blog), October 3, 2008.

64. Description from Kamran Bokhari e-mail at Stratfor, a Texas-based company that provides intelligence services to several U.S. government agencies. Bokhari was reporting back to Stratfor on a visit to see Pasha there in 2010. "The Global Intelligence Files," Wikileaks, wikileaks.org/gifiles/docs/16/1664671_re-alpha-insight-afghanistan-pakistan-isi-chief-not-for.html.

65. One case of Pakistan's spies benefiting financially from such bounties was the $5 million head money allegedly paid to the Intelligence Bureau (IB) in July 2004 by the U.S. government for assistance in the arrest of Noor Uthman Muhammed near Lahore airport. Muhammed then tipped them off about Ahmed Khalfan Ghailani, a key Al Qaeda leader connect to the U.S. embassy attacks of 1998. Ghailani was arrested after a firefight in Gujrat, led by the IB.

66. Author interviews with colleagues of General Pasha who have requested anonymity.

67. The ISI rapidly briefed that the attack was linked to Baitullah Mehsud in Waziristan, providing fragments of an intercept that purportedly caught the TTP chief asking for updates. An internal report that showed the truck's movements had been flagged up three days before the blast, and so had the procuring of the explosives, in a surveillance operation that went back three weeks. Later it emerged that a dossier of early warnings had not been acted upon.

68. Cathy Scott-Clark and Adrian Levy, *The Siege* (London: Penguin Books, November 2013).

69. Author discussion with General Pasha, Islamabad, February 2015.

70. George Packer, "Can You Keep a Secret?" *New Yorker*, March 7, 2016.

71. Press Trust of India, "Ahmed Shuja Pasha Admitted ISI's Role in 26/11 Mumbai Attacks"; Michael Hayden, *Playing to the Edge: American Intelligence in the Age of Terror* (New York: Penguin, 2016).

72. Author interviews with Husain Haqqani, Washington, D.C., 2014–2016. Also see Suhasini Haider, "Our People Planned 26/11: Ex-chief of ISI," *Hindu*, May 10, 2016.

73. Author interview with ISI official, who requested anonymity, Islamabad.

74. The three-day Mumbai operation had been coordinated from Karachi, with the masterminds talking the gunmen through their paces from a control room kitted out with television screens, computers, and satellite technology. Daood Gilani, a Pakistani-American who had

changed his name to David Headley in order to carry out surveillance on several targets, was unmasked as the brother of an official in the Pakistani prime minister's office. Later arrested and extradited to the United States, Headley named three serving ISI officers, who had paid for his trips to Mumbai and received his material upon his return. When journalists tried to interview relatives of the gunmen, nine of whom were killed during the operation, ISI agents threatened them. The mother of the lone survivor, Ajmal Kasab, was told to say that her son had been martyred fighting the Indian Army in Kashmir.

75. This ultimatum was referred to by Osama in several letters recovered from Abbottabad. ODNI documents, Abbottabad, released in May 2015 and March 2016.

76. Osama letter to Ibrahim dated January 20, 2011. ODNI documents, Abbottabad, released in May 2015.

77. His brother-in-law was Yasin Afridi and the teenage nephews were Mohammed and Abdul Hamid.

78. Khalid bin Laden to Abd-al-Latif (Daood), December 29, 2009. ODNI documents, Abbottabad, released in May 2015.

79. Seham to Abu Abdallah (Daood), undated. ODNI documents, Abbottabad, released in March 2016.

80. Khalid bin Laden to Abd-al-Latif (Daood), January 7, 2008. ODNI documents, Abbottabad, released in May 2015.

81. Abd-al-Latif (Daood) to Khalid, undated. ODNI documents, Abbottabad.

82. Peter Bergen, *Manhunt* (London: Bodley Head, 2012); and Mark Bowden, *The Finish* (New York: Grove Press, 2012).

83. Michael Scheuer, *Imperial Hubris* (Washington, D.C.: Potomac Books, Inc, 2004).

84. National Security Advisor Tom Donilon was also present. Bergen, *Manhunt*.

85. Bergen, *Manhunt*.

86. In the beginning they got his name mixed up with that of his older brother Habib Ahmad Saeed, who had been killed at Tora Bora 2001.

87. A review of 2002 debriefings by a foreign government of a detainee who claimed to have traveled in 2000 from Kuwait to Afghanistan with an "Ahmad al-Kuwaiti" provided the breakthrough leading to the likely identification of Abu Ahmad as a Kuwait national. For a full analysis of how the building evidence really led the CIA to Abu Ahmad al-Kuwaiti, see Senate Select Committee on Intelligence (SSCI), *The Official Senate Report on CIA Torture: Committee Study of the Central Intelligence Agency's Detention and Interrogation Program* (New York: Skyhorse Publishing, 2015), 25 [hereafter Senate Torture Report].

88. A summary of al-Qahtani's interrogation file can be read at "Gitmo Files," Wikileaks, wikileaks.org/gitmo/prisoner/63.html.

89. In August 2001, al-Qahtani had tried to enter the United States with the intention of becoming the twentieth hijacker, replacing Ramzi bin al-Shibh. But because he had only bought a one-way ticket, he was refused entry.

90. A summary of Slahi's interrogation file can be read at "Gitmo Files," Wikileaks, wikileaks.org/gitmo/prisoner/760.html.

91. Senate Torture Report.

92. A cable from CIA headquarters dated May 1, 2008, entitled "Targeting Efforts against Suspected UBL Facilitator Abu Ahmad al-Kuwaiti," recorded how the CIA created a number of collection platforms to find Abu Ahmad and Osama. "Although we want to refrain from addressing endgame strategies, HQ Station judges that detaining Habib should be a last resort, since we have had no success in eliciting actionable intelligence on bin Laden's location from any detainees." Senate Torture Report.

93. Nabila had some contact with CAGE, per author interview with Asim Qureshi.
94. This man was Abdullah al-Sindi, who since 1999 had worked for KSM in Karachi. In 2002 he had helped bin Laden's family travel from Karachi to Iran. Based in Quetta and Karachi since 2003, he had also run couriers between Al Qaeda Central and the Persian Gulf. Letters from Abbottabad also suggest he was a key figure in helping those coming from Iran enter Pakistan, including Khairiah and Hamzah bin Laden.
95. An undated Al Qaeda report on smuggling routes through the Tribal Areas was found at Abbottabad. Given references to events mentioned in the report, it must have been composed after June 2008. ODNI documents, Abbottabad.
96. Author interviews with bin Laden family members. The existence of these photos is also referenced in several letters to and from Osama. ODNI documents, Abbottabad.
97. Miriam bin Laden was off the hook, and to ensure he had not offended Osama, Daood wrote asking if he had "done anything inappropriate, written something that made you mad or antagonized you?" Abu Abdallah al-Halabi (Daood) to Osama. ODNI documents, Abbottabad, released in May 2015.
98. Osama references Saad working in the shop in his final letter to Atiyah dated April 26, 2011. ODNI documents, Abbottabad, released in March 2016.
99. Hamzah to his father, July 2009. ODNI documents, Abbottabad, released in May 2015.
100. Author interviews with bin Laden family members.
101. Osama made this suggestion in several letters, including in Osama to Atiyah (Sheikh Mahmud), October 21, 2010, SOCOM letters 2012-0000015-HT, www.ctc.usma.edu/posts/letters-from-abbottabad-bin-ladin-sidelined.
102. Najwa bin Laden, Omar bin Laden, and Jean Sasson, Growing Up Bin Laden (New York: St. Martin's, 2009).
103. David Rohde, "Held by the Taliban," New York Times, October 17, 2009.
104. "Jihadist Website Posts Al-Libi's 'Guidance on the Ruling of the Muslim Spy,'" Open Source Center, fas.org/irp/dni/osc/libi.pdf.
105. "Obama 2009 Pakistan Strikes," Bureau of Investigative Journalism, August 10, 2011.
106. A Pakistani military official later confirmed the reports, telling the Telegraph (London): "We have the same information but it has not yet been independently confirmed." "Osama bin Laden's Son Thought to Have Been Killed in Drone Strike," July 23, 2009.
107. Author interviews with bin Laden family members. The hedgehog story was also told by Abdel Bari Atwan, After Bin Laden (London: Saqi Books, 2012).
108. Osama to Atiyah, undated. ODNI documents, Abbottabad, released in May 2015.
109. Khalid also sent a message to his former brother-in-law Daood. "Please send me the pictures of my brother Saad before and after his martyrdom," Khalid said. Not only had he lost a much-loved older brother, he was also well aware that his on-again, off-again marriage to Karima was once again off, as his father would never let him go to Waziristan now. "I urge you to write to me in detail about your security news," he continued. ODNI documents, Abbottabad, released in May 2015.
110. Atiyah to Osama, ODNI documents, Abbottabad. See also Osama to Atiyah, undated, SOCOM-2012-0000019-HT, www.ctc.usma.edu/posts/letters-from-abbottabad-bin-ladin-sidelined.
111. Balawi arrived in Wana in March 2009. Author interviews with Fida Dawani, widow of Captain Ali bin Zeid, 2014.
112. Joby Warrick, The Triple Agent (New York: Random House, 2011). Also author interviews with Fida Dawani and former GID officers who served with him, Amman, November 2014.
113. In the Makeen district of South Waziristan.
114. Although he was flattered by Baitullah's attention, Balawi's goal was getting close to Atiyah, al-Zawahiri, and bin Laden's Number Three, Sheikh Saeed al-Masri. When a Pashtun

journalist working for the Taliban's online magazine, *Vanguards of Khorasan*, asked to interview him, Balawi agreed, hoping to get noticed. Had he changed since entering the land of jihad? he was asked. "You should rather ask, what did not change in me," Balawi responded. "I was reborn here." In Makeen, in South Waziristan, Balawi experienced one of the most intensive periods of the drone war. There had been fourteen strikes since he had entered Pakistan, three of them targeting Makeen, where he helped patch up many victims, treating the kinds of wounds he had never seen before, using rudimentary equipment.

115. He had been sleeping on the roof with his new wife, who was ministering an intravenous drip and massaging his swollen legs. She was also killed. Declan Walsh, "Airstrike Kills Taliban Leader Baitullah Mehsud," *Guardian*, August 7, 2009.

116. Warrick, *Triple Agent*.

117. Author interviews with Fida Dawani and former colleagues of bin Zeid at GID.

118. Quotes from videos Balawi recorded before his operation.

119. Since arriving in Pakistan, he had deliberately discontinued his e-mail communications with Amman to make the intelligence people "stew in their juices," so they would be even more convinced of his commitment when he came back on track. Warrick, *Triple Agent*.

120. This included details of important mujahideen Balawi had met, the impact of drones, lists of dead and wounded, and the frustration being felt by Al Qaeda. Everything matched the CIA's own records, which suggested the Jordanian was actually present at the events he described.

121. Author interviews with Mahfouz and bin Laden family members.

122. The Mauritanian, Osama's three remaining sons, Abu Ghaith, and military council members including Saif were all in the party.

123. Author interviews with bin Laden family members.

124. Ibid.

125. The Mauritanian reached his parents in Nouakchott, who, after nine years of silence, were ecstatic. However, they informed him that his wife's mother had died. His wife complained to the compound director, Hajji Akhbari. "You heartless people," she said. "You have destroyed my family!" Mahfouz interviews.

126. They discussed digging a tunnel (a near-impossible task given that the main gate was several hundred yards away), scaling a wall (too dangerous given the number of guards and security cameras), and feigning sickness and then escaping from the hospital.

127. Author interviews with Mahfouz, Nouakchott, Mauritania.

128. The Mauritanian, who regarded himself as Iman's surrogate father, felt secretly ashamed. Iman had never traveled alone before but had embarrassed them all with her bravery. He was also worried she might be raped or executed. He had heard horrific stories about what went on in the women's wing of Evin prison.

129. Najwa bin Laden had put the ticker tape message on the cable channel at Iman's request. Per Mahfouz interviews and confirmed by bin Laden family.

130. Author interviews with Mahfouz and bin Laden family members.

131. Guy Lawson, "Osama's Prodigal Son: The Dark, Twisted Journey of Omar bin Laden," *Rolling Stone*, January 20, 2010.

132. Author interviews with bin Laden family members.

133. Warrick, *Triple Agent*; also useful insight from former CIA agent Robert Baer, "A Dagger to the CIA," *GQ*, February 25, 2010.

134. The Jordanian was exhausted and injured, having broken his leg during training exercises at a Taliban camp a few weeks earlier.

135. In truth, Hakimullah could not speak Arabic so could not converse directly with Balawi.

136. "Suspected CIA Suicide Bomber Calls American Team 'Gift from God,' " CNN, February 28, 2010.

137. Secretly, he must have been terrified. He was the father of two young girls, Leila and Lina, and he had never planned for this to become a suicide operation. Captain Ali bin Zeid was supposed to have gone to Peshawar and been kidnapped with Al Qaeda extracting maximum propaganda before they butchered him on video. But after the CIA had insisted on meeting Balawi personally, moneyman Sheikh Saaed and planner Atiyah had changed the plan so quickly Balawi could not resist, and before he knew it he was no longer the bait but the lethal ordnance. When the Americans refused to go to Pakistan, Balawi had been dispatched with his explosive vest to Afghanistan, with Al Qaeda agents following and filming him right up to the border in case he bailed out.

138. Paul Harris, "CIA Bomber's 'Martyrdom' Video Urges More U.S. Attacks," *Observer* (UK), January 9, 2010.

CHAPTER NINE

1. Bob Woodward, "Death of Osama bin Laden: Phone Call Pointed U.S. to Compound—and to 'the Pacer,'" *Washington Post*, May 6, 2011.

2. Ali Ismail, "US Frame-up of Aafia Siddiqui Begins to Unravel: Pakistani Victim of Rendition and Torture," World Socialist Website, February 1, 2010.

3. C. J. Hughes, "Neuroscientist Denies Trying to Kill Americans," *New York Times*, January 28, 2010.

4. Petra Bartosiewicz, "Al-Qaeda Woman? Putting Aafia Siddiqui on Trial," *Time*, January 18, 2010.

5. Author interviews with bin Laden family members.

6. Inside the Tourist Complex, the Mauritanian was relieved. "If Iman had been deported to Saudi, she would have been easy prey for the U.S.," he recalled. "Imagine what she could have told the Americans about all of us."

7. Najwa arrived at the end of February.

8. Khairiah had come into her life when the bin Laden household in Jeddah had had so many servants of different nationalities that they called themselves the United Nations. Najwa bin Laden, Omar bin Laden, and Jean Sasson, *Growing Up Bin Laden* (New York: St. Martin's, 2009). Since 2001, when Najwa had left her older children with Khairiah, their lives had taken such different turns that she doubted they could still get along. Author interviews with family members.

9. Acccording to Mahfouz, the book was eventually published online in Arabic.

10. As a boy, he had visited his father's training camps, had been sent to the front lines of the Soviet war, and had been with his father in 1998 when he received the news of the bombing of the U.S. embassies in East Africa.

11. Soon after Khalid dispatched his letter, Osama discovered that his daughter Miriam had also written and secretly added her own missive to the Iranians to Khalid's USB stick. He demanded that Atiyah destroy it. Letter from Atiyah to Osama confirming he has done this, dated June 19, 2010, and declassified ahead of the Anas al-Libi trial in New York, Govt exhibit 421, 10-CR-019 (S-4) (RJD).

12. "Osama Bin Laden's Family Seek Asylum," *Asharq Al-Awsat*, March 24, 2010.

13. The letter itself has not been released, but Osama refers to it and its contents in another undated letter to Atiyah, which also confirms Saad's death. Recovered from Abbottabad, declassified and released by the Office of the Director of National Intelligence [hereafter ODNI] in May 2015, dni.gov/index.php/resources/bin-laden-bookshelf.

14. Ibid.

15. Osama to Bakr bin Laden, undated. ODNI documents, Abbottabad. Bakr is addressed as Abu Nawaf but it is clear to whom this letter is really addressed.

16. Atiyah believed that the Iranians had agreed to the family releases because of the kidnapped diplomat. He had boasted about Al Qaeda's ability to put pressure on the Iranians in previous letters, such as this one he wrote to Osama on June 11, 2009: "The threat which we sent to them and the apprehension of their associate, the trade deputy in the consulate in Peshawar, and other things they saw from us, brought fear to them, . . . [But] they don't want to show that they are negotiating with us or reacting to our pressure." ODNI documents, Abbottabad.

17. Hamzah's instructions were to: "inform the nation, spread the jihadi doctrine, and refute the wrong and the suspicious raised around the jihad." ODNI documents, Abbottabad.

18. The Iranian vice president, Mohammad Reza Rahimi, claimed that their diplomat had only been freed after a "complicated intelligence operation" led by Iran. The intelligence minister, Heydar Moslehi, announced: "My ministry took the initiative and managed to rescue the diplomat."

19. The son who died was Mohammad Haqqani, a brother of Sirajuddin, who had taken over the network from his ailing father several years previously.

20. According to Pakistani investigative journalist Syed Saleem Shahzad, author interview, Islamabad, 2010.

21. Sheikh Saeed al-Masri, who liked to describe America as "the evil empire" and was supervising Al Qaeda's operations in Afghanistan, had been delighted with the operation.

22. Among those who had stayed there shortly before being targeted was Khalid Habib, Al Qaeda's commander for the Tribal Areas.

23. Sheikh Saeed's son was Abd al-Rahman. More details of the strike can be read at "Obama 2010 Pakistan Strikes," Bureau of Investigative Journalism, August 10, 2011.

24. Local journalist Noor Behram reached the scene soon after and heard that five Pakistani civilians had also perished. At Miram Shah hospital he photographed a young girl swaddled in bandages shortly before she died, her mother and brother having been killed on the spot. Author interview, Islamabad, February 2012.

25. Sheikh Saeed warned back in August 2009 that the United States would pay for Baitullah Mehsud's death: "There are thousands of tribesmen who are like him and who will take revenge on the Americans and their allies." But until the Camp Chapman attack, no one outside intelligence circles had really taken much notice of him.

26. In February 2010, the families of those who had perished at Camp Chapman gathered at CIA headquarters to hear Panetta pledge: "Our resolve in unbroken, our energy undiminished . . . we will carry this fight to the enemy."

27. Zamray (Osama) to "the children of the noble Brother, Shaykh Mustafa Abu al-Yazid (Sheikh Saeed)," August 7, 2010. ODNI documents, Abbottabad, released in May 2015.

28. Sheikh Saeed had also been Al Qaeda's main link to Mullah Omar, having become one of the few Arabs who had absorbed the local culture and learned to speak Pashto.

29. That mission was being coordinated by Ilyas Kashmiri, the enigmatic Pakistani former spy and mujahid who had assisted in the attempts on Musharraf's life in 2003 and helped plan the Mumbai attacks of November 2008. He was raising a *lashkar al-zil* (shadow army) for Al Qaeda, which consisted of two undercover units: one based in Bagram, Afghanistan, and the other inside Pakistan, to track the U.S. president's movements and those of David Petraeus, the recently appointed commander of the International Security Assistance Force.

30. Osama to Atiyah, letter dated July 17, 2010. ODNI documents, Abbottabad, released in May 2015. Atiyah had been lauded on Al Qaeda websites as "the most important pillar" of the Camp Chapman operation.

31. They had left their movement in a parlous state. By the time Abu Ayyub died, the U.S. bounty on his head had reduced from $5 million to $100,000, and the rate of civilian killings by Islamic State of Iraq had dropped from a high of 2,500 a month in 2007 to just 500. Will McCants, *The ISIS Apocalypse: The History, Strategy, and Doomsday Vision of the Islamic State* (New York: St. Martin's, 2015).

32. Osama to Atiyah, letter dated July 17, 2010, ODNI documents, Abbottabad, released in May 2015.

33. A good summary of Abu Bakr's background can be found in McCants, *The ISIS Apocalypse*.

34. Terrence McCoy, "How the Islamic State Evolved in an American Prison," *Washington Post*, November 4, 2014.

35. Ibid. "Anyone who takes part in behavior which is seen as 'Western' is severely punished by the extremist elements of the compound," said one U.S. soldier stationed there. "It's quite appalling."

36. The official biography of Abu Bakr al-Baghdadi, distributed online by jihadist discussion forums and translated into English by SITE Intelligence Group, July 16, 2013, news.siteintel group.com/blog/index.php/categories/jihad/entry/226-the-story-behind-abu-bakr-al -baghdadi.

37. "The situation will be strongest politically and militarily for the Islamic plan to prepare to completely seize the reins of control over all Iraq," he wrote.

38. McCants, *The ISIS Apocalypse*.

39. Osama to Atiyah letter dated July 17, 2010, ODNI documents, Abbottabad, released in May 2015. What Al Qaeda would not be doing was killing Muslims—something initiated by Zarqawi during the "roar of the killing and the fight" and now embraced by Abu Bakr.

40. Ibid. The Afghan diplomat held with Attarzadeh would have to wait until October 2010 to taste freedom. In negotiations supervised by Osama bin Laden, the government of Hamid Karzai eventually paid $5 million to get him back—such a huge sum that Osama suspected the notes had been marked with "harmful materials or rays" by the CIA. The money should be exchanged "at a bank in a large city" into euros, he said, and then into U.S. dollars at another location.

41. Ibid.

42. The word "expectations" could be translated as "energies."

43. Osama to Atiyah, letter dated July 17, 2010, ODNI documents, Abbottabad, released in May 2015. Under Awlaki's influence, Wuhayshi had also recently lashed out at Iran, threatening attacks if the *shura* members in the Tourist Complex were not released. Osama sent a sharp rebuke: "Iran is our main artery for funds, personnel and communication, as well as the matter of hostages." Such threats should not be made without the express permission of Al Qaeda Central.

44. Author copy.

45. Ahmad Hasan Abu al-Khayr to Professor Mustafa Hamid (real name of Abu Walid), August 22, 2009. ODNI documents, Abbottabad, released in March 2016.

46. Abu Walid's book contained allegations that were similar to those the Quds Force had aired when first interrogating the Mauritanian: 9/11 had been orchestrated by Mossad and Osama was working under the direction of the CIA. Then there was also an accusation that on the first day of the war in 2001, the CIA had aborted a chance to kill Mullah Omar in a drone strike when it learned Osama bin Laden was there, too. "Perhaps the Taliban was another one entangled in this wicked plan that the web of American and Jewish intelligence agencies was hatching with the leaders of the mujahideen," Abu al-Khayr wrote, tongue in cheek. Walid would be

freed in 2011 and begin a long correspondence with Leah Farrall, an Australian former antiter-
rorism police officer and now writer. In 2014, they published a book together: Mustafa Hamid
and Leah Farrall, *The Arabs at War in Afghanistan* (London: Hurst, October 2015).

47. Osama to Karim, October 18, 2007, ODNI documents, Abbottabad, released in March 2016.
48. Before the Waziristan Accord, it must have seemed as if every village had opened up its doors
to Taliban and Al Qaeda fugitives, but now local families were reluctant.
49. Two letters. July 17, 2010, ODNI documents, Abbottabad, released in May 2015. Also June 19,
2010, letter declassified ahead of Anas al-Libi trial, New York, Govt exhibit 421, 10-CR-019
(S-4) (RJD).
50. He added that the appointment of Younis al-Mauritani as chief of external operations had
been the wrong choice. Younis was "smart" and "clever," but he still "needs to grow up and
needs to become more mature and get more experience." Younis's age was presenting problems, as the veterans in Al Qaeda did not respect him. His dealings with Ilyas Kashmiri had
already run into difficulties, with the shadow commander failing to respond to orders.
51. Reuters, "Taliban Hostage Takers Behead Polish Engineer," *Observer* (UK), February 8, 2009.
During his incarceration in North Waziristan in 2008–2009, the *New York Times* correspondent David Rohde said that he had come to a simple realization: "After seven years of
reporting in the region, I did not fully understand how extreme many of the Taliban had
become . . . Contact with foreign militants in the tribal areas appeared to have deeply affected
many young Taliban fighters. They wanted to create a fundamentalist Islamic emirate with Al
Qaeda that spanned the Muslim world." David Rohde, "Held by the Taliban," *New York Times*,
October 17, 2009.
52. Between them, the Taliban and Al Qaeda had killed more than five hundred NATO troops in
Afghanistan in recent months.
53. Atiyah to Osama, June 19, 2010. The most popular attacks involved explosives-laden vests
designed by Al Qaeda's tailor in Datta Khel and by others who had been trained by the late
bomb maker Abu Khabab. The boys destined to wear them were selected on the basis of ignorance and low intelligence and were indoctrinated at a suicide bombers' training school in
Sararogha, South Waziristan, where Hakimullah's murderous sidekick Qari Hussain supervised false ideology taught by fighters pretending to be mullahs. Although Hussain liked to
boast that he could "turn anyone into a suicide bomber," many of the human bombs were
dispatched while under the influence of drugs. Alongside the colorful murals of lakes and
mountains depicting paradise that decorated the walls of the suicide school run by Hussain
was an altar and a drainage area, which was used for beheading captured Pakistani soldiers.
54. Atiyah to Osama, July 17, 2010, ODNI documents, Abbottabad, released in May 2015.
55. Ibid.
56. Ibid.
57. Ibid. General Ahmed Shuja Pasha of the ISI wanted to reach out to Sheikh Osama, although
his real intentions were unclear. Hakimullah's TTP, the Haqqanis, and Dr. al-Zawahiri were
all in on it, Atiyah reported.
58. Ibid. Catching wind of the ISI overtures, Shahbaz Sharif, the chief minister of Punjab
Province and younger brother of former prime minister of Pakistan Nawaz Sharif, had also
got in on the act, telling Hakimullah and his sidekick the suicide bomber trainer Qari Hussain
that he was willing to "pay any price" if the TTP promised not to carry out terrorist atrocities
in the Punjab.
59. Ibid.
60. Author interview with Fazlur Rehman Khalil, Islamabad, February 2015.

61. Ibid. Khalil was dragged from a mosque in Tarnol on the outskirts of Islamabad, held for five hours, and badly beaten by "unknown assailants" (a well-recognized code for undercover intelligence officers).

62. Ibid. His headquarters was at the Khalid bin Walid madrassa in Shams Colony, Golra. The container story was confirmed to the authors by Islamabad-based journalist Jamal Ismail.

63. The landscape was precarious even for veteran jihad watchers. The previous April, Squadron Leader Khalid Khawaja, a former Pakistan Air Force pilot and an associate of Osama's from the Peshawar days, an officer with a significant ISI career, had traveled to the Tribal Areas with a second well-known veteran spook, Sultan Amir Tarar, known by his legend Colonel Iman.The two claimed to be acting as consultants for a British-Pakistani filmmaker, Asad Qureshi, who had approached them with a request to film the TTP. Both were accused of being CIA spies and were killed by the Taliban. Author interviews with Asad Qureshi, London, May 2014.

64. Long, undated letter from Osama to Atiyah. ODNI documents, Abbottabad, released in May 2015.

65. Sheikh Osama also appointed Abu Yahya al-Libi to work on "writing some articles and providing advice" and Azzam the American to take care of technical issues and make sure that they did not make any embarrassing mistakes when it came to criticizing the American political system, something that had happened in the past.

66. "Letter to Zamaray Sahib, Monday 11 Sha'ban." ODNI documents, Abbottabad, released in January 2017.

67. Abrar's sickness is mentioned in Osama's letter to Atiyah in January 2011. ODNI documents, Abbottabad, released in March 2016.

68. Long, undated letter from Osama to Atiyah. ODNI documents, Abbottabad, released in May 2015.

69. Ibid.

70. Sumaiya to Umm Hamzah (Khairiah, mother of Hamzah), undated. ODNI documents, Abbottabad, released in May 2015.

71. Osama to "my dear sons Uthman, Muhammad, Hamzah, my wife Umm Hamzah and my grandchildren," September 26, 2010. ODNI documents, Abbottabad, released in May 2015.

72. He also sent regards from Seham (Umm Khalid) and Amal (Umm Safiyah) and asked for news about Wafa and her children, still in Iran.

73. Hallabi (Daood) to Khalid, dated August 26, 2010. ODNI documents, Abbottabad, released in March 2016.

74. Daood to Seham, August 26, 2010. ODNI documents, Abbottabad, released in May 2015.

75. Rob Crilly, "Pakistani Officials Know Where Osama bin Laden Hiding," *Daily Telegraph*, May 11, 2010.

76. General Pasha's submission to the Abbottabad Commission. Details from the unpublished Abbottabad Commission report, Al Jazeera Investigation Unit, "Document: Pakistan's Bin Laden Dossier," Al Jazeera, July 8, 2013, www.aljazeera.com/indepth/spotlight/binladenfiles/.

77. Relations between the United States and Pakistan were always "marred by an inconsistent, transactional and reactive paradigm," he said.

78. General Pasha to the Abbottabad Commission.

79. Author interviews with Wajid Shamsul Hasan, London, 2010–2016.

80. General Pasha to the Abbottabad Commission.

81. Pasha's backing of Khan's political aspirations was well known in Pakistan.

82. General Pasha to the Abbottabad Commission. Also author interviews with close former colleagues of General Pasha.

83. Woodward, "Death of Osama bin Laden: Phone Call Pointed U.S. to Compound—and to 'the Pacer.' "

84. General Pasha to the Abbottabad Commission. He claimed that "most of the times [sic] these numbers were silent."

85. White House Office of the Press Secretary, "Press Briefing by Senior Administration Officials on the Killing of Osama bin Laden," May 2, 2011, obamawhitehouse.archives.gov/the-press-office/2011/05/02/press-briefing-senior-administration-officials-killing-osama-bin-laden.

86. David Usborne, "Revealed: The CIA Mastermind Who Cornered bin Laden," *Independent*, July 6, 2011. Intelligence official "John" (and his female colleague, who was almost certainly Gina Bennett) wrote that current thinking had it that Osama might not be in the mountains, as always assumed, but living an urban life closer to Islamabad.

87. Peter Bergen, *Manhunt* (London: Bodley Head, 2012).

88. Given that almost all of those now working on the operation had friends who had died in the Camp Chapman attack, he did not need to emphasize what a critical operation this could be.

89. White House Office of the Press Secretary, "Press Briefing by Senior Administration Officials on the Killing of Osama bin Laden." U.S. government material later shown to Kathryn Bigelow and Mark Boal, the director and screenwriter, respectively, of the film *Zero Dark Thirty*, also provides useful insights and can be viewed here: nsarchive.gwu.edu/NSAEBB/NSAEBB410/.

90. From a debate with John McCain at Belmont Arena in Nashville. Quoted in Mark Bowden, "The Hunt for "Geronimo,' " *Vanity Fair*, November 2012.

91. Ibid.

92. Chris McGreal and Declan Walsh, "Pakistan Neuroscientist Given 86 Years for Shooting at US Agents," *Guardian*, September 23, 2010.

93. There were numerous cases where kidnappers either offered to exchange prisoners for Aafia or cited her case as their motivation, including the captures of Kayla Mueller, James Foley, Warren Weinstein, Linda Norgrove, and the oil workers at the Amenas facility in Algeria.

94. From Maryam interview in the Abbottabad Commission report and Bergen, *Manhunt*.

95. Umm Saad to Umm Khalid, September 21, 2010. ODNI documents, Abbottabad, released in May 2015.

96. Undated letter from Sarah to Seham. ODNI documents, Abbottabad, released in May 2015.

97. A fuller list of these items is contained in a letter from Hamzah to his father dated January 8, 2011. ODNI documents, Abbottabad, released in March 2016.

98. Seham to Umm Saad (Sarah), undated. ODNI documents, Abbottabad, released in May 2015.

99. Azaz Syed, *The Secrets of Pakistan's War on Al-Qaeda* (Islamabad: Al-Abbas International, 2014).

100. Nicholas Schmidle, "Getting Bin Laden," *New Yorker*, August 8, 2011.

101. General Pasha identifies Iqbal as a probable CIA recruit in his submission to the Abbottabad Commission.

102. This allegedly took place at a Military Intelligence (MI) safe house in Gulfraz, Rawalpindi. Author interviews with Azaz Syed, Islamabad, 2013–2015, and Husain Haqqani, Washington, D.C., 2014–2016.

103. Ibid. He was introduced by his successor at Military Intelligence, who hoped for a job from Iqbal when his military career ran out of steam.

104. Ibid.

105. Abbottabad Commission report; Kamran Shafi, "Of Clouseaus and 'Noise-Controlled Vehicles,'" *Express Tribune* (Pakistan), July 11, 2013.

106. Author interview with Azaz Syed.

107. Jason Burke and Saeed Shah, "Osama bin Laden: Family Guy with Three Wives, Nine Children and a Cow to Keep," *Guardian*, May 6, 2011.

108. Abbottabad Commission report.

109. This is something that nurse Amna and district health worker Shaheena also heard when running the vaccination campaign with Dr. Afridi. See Abbottabad Commission report.

110. This is from Shamraiz to Shaukat Qadir, in his book *Operation Geronimo: The Betrayal and Execution of Osama bin Laden and Its Aftermath* (Islamabad: HA Publications, 2012).

111. The figure was estimated to be between five feet nine inches and six feet eight inches tall. Bergen, *Manhunt*.

112. Osama to Shaykh Mahmud, September 26, 2010, ODNI documents, Abbottabad, released in May 2015. The Sheikh was most concerned about Khairiah, who was still not with him. "Keep her in a safe location," he requested.

113. Don Rassler, et al., "Letters from Abbottabad: Bin Laden Sidelined?" Combating Terrorism Center at West Point, May 3, 2012, see letter number SOCOM-21012-0000015-HT.

114. The CIA mistakenly reported that Atiyah had been killed on October 9, 2010.

115. Rassler, et al., "Letters from Abbottabad: Bin Laden Sidelined?" SOCOM-21012-0000015-HT. Atiyah was to avoid moving by car, Osama wrote, "and make sure to keep a rigid hierarchy among the brothers, background checking new brothers who are all to swear the bayat, and only use trusted brothers to send messages." The Pakistani "supporters" should also plant trees to give cover from the "spying aircrafts."

116. Ibid.

117. Osama to Mullah Omar, dated September 24, 2010. ODNI documents, Abbottabad, released in March 2016.

118. Atiyah to Osama, November 24, 2010. ODNI documents, Abbottabad, released in May 2015.

119. Details of their journey from the border comes from "Letter to sons Uthman and Muhammad," January 7, 2011. ODNI documents, Abbottabad, released in January 2017.

120. A few months earlier and under pressure, Ibrahim had allowed Rehma to take lessons from Osama's daughter Sumaiya in the main house. When Rehma asked her father who was the "uncle" who lived upstairs and never went out, he had invented a story that the "uncle" was too poor to buy anything. From then they had referred to him as *miskeen kaka*, or "poor uncle." Now Ibrahim bought new locks for the metal security doors that separated the ground floor from upstairs.

121. Maryam described this incident in her submission to the Abbottabad Commission, and further details come from author interviews with Maryam's relatives.

122. See Osama's letters to the brothers, January 2011. ODNI documents, Abbottabad, released in March 2016.

123. Osama to Khairiah, undated. ODNI documents, Abbottabad, released in March 2016.

124. Ibid. He explains that he and the companions met again on January 15, 2011, and agreed in writing to a nine-month notice period. The family would move after the tenth anniversary of 9/11.

125. Author interviews with bin Laden family members.

126. Seham to Karima's mother, November 5, 2010. ODNI documents, Abbottabad, released in March 2016. "This has been going on now for three years," Seham observed, mournfully. "I'm afraid that losing too much time waiting may result in missing the train for both of them."

127. Osama to Khairiah, undated. ODNI documents, Abbottabad, released in March 2016.

128. Ibid. Letter continues: ". . . justifying why you were the first in my family to be released."

129. David Headley, evidence to the National Investigation Agency, Government of India. Azaz Syed also claimed that Osama met Ilyas Kashmiri in Haripur.

130. This meeting was described by militants captured alive after the general headquarters raid in October 2009. A report was put together and circulated to all civilian and military intelligence agencies in Pakistan, as well as security officials at the interior ministry and U.S. counterterrorism officials. It was reported in the *Daily Times*, Lahore, in May 2010. See Carlotta Gall, *The Wrong Enemy: America in Afghanistan, 2001–2014* (New York: Houghton Mifflin Harcourt, 2014), 253.

131. In a further twist, Fazlur Rehan Khalil was brought in by the army to negotiate with the hostage takers, giving further evidence of his proximity to the Pakistani security services.

132. M. Ilyas Khan, "Osama bin Laden: The Night He Came for Dinner," BBC News, Islamabad, May 2, 2012.

133. Osama to Atiyah, undated letter. ODNI documents, Abbottabad, released in March 2016.

134. Bowden, "The Hunt for 'Geronimo.' "

135. Bergen, *Manhunt*; and Mark Bowden, *The Finish* (New York: Grove Press, 2012).

136. This was confirmed by Dr. Mohammed Suleman, a close neighbor, to the Abbottabad Commission.

Chapter Ten

1. Phil Bronstein, "The Shooter," *Esquire*, March 2013.

2. In a letter to Ibrahim dated January 20, 2011, Osama said he was ill himself. Recovered from Abbottabad, declassified and released by the Office of the Director of National Intelligence [hereafter ODNI] in May 2015, www.dni.gov/index.php/resources/bin-laden-bookshelf. In this letter, Ibrahim is addressed as Abu Khalid.

3. Surat al-Ma'idah (verse 2).

4. Osama to Abu Mohammed (Abrar) and Abu Khalid (Ibrahim), January 14, 2011. ODNI documents, Abbottabad, released in March 2016. Also another letter from Osama to "my two noble brothers," January 14, 2011, ODNI documents, Abbottabad, released in March 2016.

5. Osama to Atiyah, undated letter. ODNI documents, Abbottabad, released in March 2016. Also "Letter to sons Uthman and Muhammad," January 7, 2011. ODNI documents, Abbottabad, released in January 2017.

6. Osama letter to Atiyah dated April 26, 2011. ODNI documents, Abbottabad, released in March 2016. Osama was displeased with Atiyah, who, in a bid to speed up resolution of the "special issue," had met with a previously untested brother. "The incident was contradictory to the security precautions that I asked you to implement," said Osama.

7. Osama to Mohammed Aslam, January 29, 2011. ODNI documents, Abbottabad, released in March 2016.

8. Ibid.

9. Seham to Umm Abd al-Rahman (mother of Karima), April 26, 2011. ODNI documents, Abbottabad, released in March 2016.

10. Mark Bowden, "The Hunt for 'Geronimo,'" *Vanity Fair*, November 2012; and Nicholas Schmidle, "Getting Bin Laden," *New Yorker*, August 8, 2011.

11. Schmidle, "Getting Bin Laden."

12. In 2012, the U.S. government allowed General Pasha and the ISI to claim diplomatic immunity and the case collapsed. "ISI, Pasha and Taj Enjoy Immunity in 26/11 NY Court Case: US Gov," Oneindia News, December 20, 2012.

13. Declan Walsh, "CIA Chief in Pakistan Leaves after Drone Trial Blows His Cover," *Guardian*, December 17, 2010.

14. Greg Miller, "After Presiding over bin Laden Raid, CIA Chief in Pakistan Came Home Suspecting He Was Poisoned by ISI," *Washington Post*, May 5, 2016.

15. Peter Bergen, *Manhunt* (London: Bodley Head, 2012); Bowden, "The Hunt for 'Geronimo'"; and Schmidle, "Getting Bin Laden."

16. Siobhan Gorman and Julian E. Barnes, "Spy, Military Ties Aided bin Laden Raid," *Wall Street Journal*, May 23, 2011.

17. Press Statement, Sean McCormack, "Rewards for Justice: The Bali Bombings," U.S. Department of State, October 6, 2005, https://2001-2009.state.gov/r/pa/prs/ps/2005/54377.htm.

18. Author interviews with General Athar Abbas, Rawalpindi, 2014–2015.

19. Miller, "After Presiding over Bin Laden Raid, CIA Chief in Pakistan Came Home Suspecting He Was Poisoned by ISI."

20. Raymond Davis was not linked to any of the cases lodged against the company.

21. Steve Inskeep, *Morning Edition* interview with Admiral Mike Mullen, National Public Radio, September 28, 2011.

22. Author telephone interviews in July 2016 with Mansoor Ijaz, a former friend of Pakistan's ambassador to Washington Husain Haqqani, who as ambassador was accused of issuing up to two thousand visas without authorization from Islamabad. Ijaz was well known by National Security Advisor James L. Jones and senior U.S. military, political, and intelligence figures. Ijaz claimed that a flood of U.S. contractors had entered the country before May 2011 with all their visas processed by Ambassador Haqqani.

23. General Pasha expressed this sentiment to the Abbottabad Commission. Abbottabad Commission report, Al Jazeera Investigation Unit, "Document: Pakistan's Bin Laden Dossier," Al Jazeera, July 8, 2013, www.aljazeera.com/indepth/spotlight/binladenfiles/.

24. Kamran Bokhari e-mail to Fred Burton at Stratfor in which he describes detailed conversation with General Pasha around this time; see "The Global Intelligence Files," Wikileaks, wikileaks.org/gifiles/docs/16/1664671_re-alpha-insight-afghanistan-pakistan-isi-chief-not-for.html.

25. His comments about the police and legal system of Pakistan are from the Abbottabad Commission report.

26. Mark Mazzetti, "How a Single Spy Helped Turn Pakistan Against the United States," *New York Times Magazine*, April 9, 2013.

27. Declan Walsh and Ewen MacAskill, "American Who Sparked Diplomatic Crisis over Shooting Was CIA Spy," *Guardian*, February 20, 2011.

28. Osama to Khairiah, February 1, 2011. ODNI documents, Abbottabad, released in March 2016. Also another letter from Osama to Khairiah dated February 5, 2011, released in March 2016.

29. Ibid.

30. She gave this date in a letter to Umm Abd al-Rahman, February 2011. ODNI documents, Abbottabad, released in March 2016.

31. Osama to Khairiah, February 1, 2011. ODNI documents, Abbottabad, released in March 2016.

32. Author interviews with bin Laden family members.

33. Khairiah to Umm Abd al-Rahman, February 2011. ODNI documents, Abbottabad, released in March 2016.

34. Seham invited Khairiah to take up residence in the best bedroom on the second floor overlooking the fields beyond the compound. To make room, Seham moved her clothes into a wardrobe in the Sheikh's media studio on the third floor. The ISI claimed Seham collected her clothes from this room when the family was taken into ISI custody on the morning of May 2, 2011.

35. Atiyah confirmed he had sent it in a letter to Osama that was declassified in preparation for Anas al-Libi's trial, Govt Exhibit 431, reference 10-CR-019 (S-4) (RJD).

36. A letter from Osama to Hamzah claimed that Mohammed was to enroll in a course in Qatar to study strategic sciences, sociology, and psychology. However, according to author interviews with bin Laden family members, none of the sons took up degree courses. ODNI documents, Abbottabad, released in May 2015.

37. Osama to Hamzah, January/February 2011. ODNI documents, Abbottabad, released in March 2016.

38. Hamzah (Abu Ma'adh) to "Father," January 8, 2011. ODNI documents, Abbottabad, released in March 2016.

39. Ibid. Two days after his mother left for Abbottabad.

40. Ibid. There was also Daood's silver ring that had been set aside for Khadija's oldest son, Abdallah, along with two iPods, one of which was to go to Abdallah's younger brother, Osama. Saad's last possessions—a few clothes, family photographs, and his most recent pictures, taken after he arrived in Waziristan—were also there.

41. Undated draft speech that referenced the Arab Spring of 2011. ODNI documents, Abbottabad, released in March 2016.

42. Atiyah to Osama, April 5, 2011, declassified for the Anas al-Libi trial: Govt exhibit 431, 10-CR-019 (S-4) (RJD).

43. This attack would take place on May 22 in retribution for Osama's killing.

44. Hamzah (Abu Ma'adh) to "Father," January 8, 2011.

45. "It isn't a good thing for us to remain fully occupied with the Afghanistan front." Instead, Al Qaeda should respond to the "Muslim nation's revolution." To that end Atiyah should be getting packing. Undated letter from Osama to Atiyah, but it is clear from the content that it was written during the spring of 2011. ODNI documents, Abbottabad, released in May 2015.

46. Bergen, *Manhunt*; and Bowden, *The Finish* (New York: Grove Press, 2012).

47. Ibid. "To develop courses of action to bring justice to Osama bin Laden."

48. Schmidle, "Getting Bin Laden"; and Bergen, *Manhunt*.

49. General Pasha allegedly spoke to Kamran Bokhari about the Davis affair, telling him: "Once it became a media issue we were really worried that Davis might be killed by people from within the police service." See Bokhari's e-mail to Fred Burton at Stratfor in Wikileaks, "The Global Intelligence Files."

50. Author interviews with former close colleagues of General Pasha.

51. Husain Haqqani came up with the blood money idea and suggested it to Pasha after first running it past the U.S. State Department, per author telephone interview with Haqqani, August 2016.

52. M. Ilyas Khan, "CIA Contractor Ray Davis Free over Pakistan Killings," BBC News, March 16, 2011.

53. Mazzetti, "How a Single Spy Helped Turn Pakistan Against the United States." Also Pasha to Bokhari: "We wanted Davis gone and as soon as possible and thankfully we were able to pull it off." He also wanted to set the record straight when it came to the men Davis had killed. "They were not ISI sleuths as some suspect," he told Bokhari. "Rather, low-level thugs who had a lot of cash on them and in different currencies." Bokhari e-mail to Fred Burton at Stratfor in Wikileaks, "The Global Intelligence Files."

54. Extracted from General Pasha's statement to the Abbottabad Commission.

55. Bokhari e-mail to Fred Burton at Stratfor in Wikileaks, "The Global Intelligence Files."

56. "ISI Chief Visits Washington in Patch-up Trip," Reuters, April 11, 2011.

57. Miller, "After Presiding over Bin Laden Raid, CIA Chief in Pakistan Came Home Suspecting He Was Poisoned by ISI." Dexter Filkins said the quote was a "slap in the face" in his piece for the *New Yorker* on the killing of Syed Saleem Shahzad, "The Journalist and the Spies," September 19, 2011.

58. Salman Masood and Pir Zubair Shah, "C.I.A. Drones Kill Civilians in Pakistan," *New York Times*, March 17, 2011.

59. AFP, "White House Report: Pakistan Has No Clear Plans to Defeat Militants," *Express Tribune* (Pakistan), April 7, 2011.

60. For details of General Pasha's and Kayani's movements in the weeks preceeding the raid, see Syed Saleem Shahzad, "US Broke Deal with Osama Hit," *Asia Times Online*, May 12, 2011. General Kayani held a meeting with General David Petraeus, the U.S. top commander in Afghanistan. Pasha flew on to Paris, where he held talks with the Agha Khan, the spiritual leader of the Shia Ismaili community of Pakistan, and then to Turkey, where he met President Zardari, who was on an official visit.

61. Munter was addressing a meeting at the Institute of Strategic Studies, a Pakistani think tank. "We can't afford to cut and run," he said, addressing fears that the United States would abandon the region. Munter said a new era was coming. "If we agree that there is a terrorist threat to the mainstream life in this country, we need to talk more openly and more freely about the ways in which we can cooperate together to address that threat," he said. "ISI Chief Visits Washington in Patch-up Trip."

62. Osama watched all comings and goings from the upstairs windows of the house, according to bin Laden family members.

63. Atiyah to Osama, April 5, 2011, declassified for the Anas al-Libi trial: Govt exhibit 431, 10-CR-019 (S-4) (RJD).

64. Ibid. Atiyah had been unable to stop Hamzah but had spoken to him briefly: "I emphasized the need to be safe, to avoid going out, moving around, or doing anything that might expose him to danger."

65. Ibid. He was referring to the trusted brother Abdullah al-Sindi, who was named as a terrorist by the U.S. Treasury Department in 2013, www.treasury.gov/press-center/press-releases/Pages /jl2144.aspx. Al-Sindi, whose real name was Umar Siddique Kathio Azmarai, was a linchpin for Al Qaeda in Balochistan and Sindh. He had worked for Khalid Shaikh Mohammad as far back as 1999 and had helped secure arrangements for Osama's family when they fled to Karachi after 9/11. He and Saad had become close around this time, and in 2008 when Saad finally crossed the border into Balochistan, he had sought out al-Sindi once again. In more recent times, al-Sindi had helped Khairiah and then Hamzah and his family, securing their passage through Balochistan. As soon as Atiyah received al-Sindi's new cell phone numbers he planned to send Hamzah into his care. Al-Sindi's brother-in-law had recently been arrested in Karachi by the ISI, but Atiyah saw that only as a remote problem. Over more than a decade, al-Sindi had demonstrated his dedication to Sheikh Osama's family. He was currently looking after Hamzah's brother-in-law, a son of Abu al-Khayr al-Masri, who was married to one of Abu Mohammed al-Masri's daughters and who had recently arrived in Balochistan with his family from Iran. Hamzah's wife, Maryam, was another of Abu Mohammed al-Masri's daughters. Also released from Iran at this time were Abu al-Samah al-Masri, Abdullah Rajab (formerly Abu al-Ward), and Abu Malik al-Libi.

66. Khairiah to Umm Mu'ad (Hamzah's wife, Maryam), undated but almost certainly March or April 2011. ODNI documents, Abbottabad, released in March 2016.

67. Ibid. "I yearn for the beautiful days I spent with you, especially during travel," Khairiah said, describing her daughter-in-law as "the best companion" and asking for news of Maryam's two

small children. Now that the prospect of being reunited with them was taking shape, everyone in Abbottabad was excited.

68. This account is based on multiple sources, including author interviews with Afridi's lawyers, interviews with the nurses who accompanied him, telephone interviews with former ambassador Husain Haqqani, contemporary news reports, and the unpublished findings of the Abbottabad Commission.

69. While Dr. Afridi must have suspected some skulduggery and was probably told the bare bones of the operation, he almost certainly had no idea that the actual target of his surveillance was Osama bin Laden.

70. Miss Shaheena was the supervisor.

71. Matthieu Aikens, "The Doctor, the CIA, and the Blood of Bin Laden," *GQ*, December 19, 2012.

72. Press Trust of India, "Osama bin Laden's Neighbour Released after Questioning," NDTV, May 8, 2011.

73. Osama to Mohammed Aslam, April 22, 2011. ODNI documents, Abbottabad, released in March 2016.

74. Gina Bennett's website gives links to all her interviews: www.nationalsecuritymom.com /media.html.

75. Maureen Dowd, "Good Riddance, Carrie Mathison," *New York Times*, April 4, 2015.

76. Author copy of SSE booklet, recovered from the compound by neighbors after the raid.

77. Despite a claim by the ISI that they had one as far back as 2003, supposedly showing him with long hair and a beard. This claim is made by Shaukat Qadir in *Operation Geronimo: The Betrayal and Execution of Osama bin Laden and Its Aftermath* (Islamabad: HA Publications, 2012).

78. Ibrahim's father, Ahmad Said, was listed as deceased, while Hamida, his mother, was listed as living in Kuwait.

79. NSC meetings were on March 14, March 29, April 12, April 19, and April 28. Bowden, "The Hunt for 'Geronimo' "; and Schmidle, "Getting Bin Laden."

80. Bronstein, "The Shooter."

81. From Mark Owen [pen name of Matthew Bissonnette] and Kevin Maurer, *No Easy Day* (New York: Dutton, 2012).

82. Ibid.

83. Robert O'Neill interview on Fox News, November 2014.

84. "Military Has Broken Taliban's Back: Kayani," *Express Tribune* (Pakistan), April 24, 2011.

85. Osama to Atiyah, April 26, 2011. ODNI documents, Abbottabad, released in May 2015. This approach was to Libyan Fighting Group brothers in London, almost certainly including Noman Benotman, and Atiyah had previously written about it in a letter to Osama dated April 5, 2011, declassified for the Anas al-Libi trial: Govt exhibit 431, 10-CR-019 (S-4) (RJD).

86. There was also a message for Mohammed, his son who had crossed over from Iran around the same time. Before going to Qatar, he should meet up with his mother, Najwa, and siblings and take them along "until the situation is resolved." If they could not get into Qatar, they should try Saudi Arabia.

87. Abdullah al-Sindi.

88. Khalid to Hamzah, April 26, 2011. ODNI documents, Abbottabad, released in March 2016.

89. Khalid to Abdullah al-Sindi, April 2011. ODNI documents, Abbottabad, released in March 2016.

90. Seham to Umm Abd al-Rahman, April 26, 2011. ODNI documents, Abbottabad, released in March 2016.

91. Osama to Atiyah, April 26, 2011. ODNI documents, Abbottabad, released in March 2016.

92. Author interviews with Maryam's family members.
93. They were being taken to Peshawar, where they were to lodge with Mohammed Aslam.
94. Thomas Donilon, John Brennan, and Denis McDonough, and chief of staff Bill Daley.
95. Mark Bowden, *The Finish*.
96. This time frame was based on fuel consumption and the possible response time from the Pakistanis.

CHAPTER ELEVEN

1. From the Twitter account of Abbottabad resident Sohaib Athar, twitter.com/ReallyVirtual?ref _src=twsrc^google|twcamp^serp|twgr^author.
2. This account of the killing takes in multiple sources: Amal's testimony to the Abbottabad Commission, Al Jazeera Investigation Unit, "Document: Pakistan's Bin Laden Dossier," Al Jazeera, July 8, 2013, www.aljazeera.com/indepth/spotlight/binladenfiles/. Also Maryam's testimony to the Abbottabad Commission; author interviews with Ibrahim Saeed Ahmad's family members, Samirah Abdullah (widow of Abdullah Azzam who later visited Osama's widows), and bin Laden family members; Robert O'Neill's account in Phil Bronstein, "The Shooter," *Esquire*, March 2013; Matt Bissonnette's version in *No Easy Day* (New York: Dutton, 2012); the ISI version as told to Shaukat Qadir in *Operation Geronimo: The Betrayal and Execution of Osama bin Laden and Its Aftermath* (Islamabad: HA Publications, 2012); and eyewitness statements from those who went into the house on that night.
3. Mark Bowden and Nicholas Schmidle say CIA operatives on the ground arranged this. @*ReallyVirtual* says electricity didn't come back on until six A.M on May 2.
4. Admiral McRaven had estimated that the Black Hawk's rotors would become audible about two minutes before their arrival, so his estimation matched Amal's recall.
5. Author interviews with Amal's brother Zakariya al-Sadeh, Islamabad, February 2012, plus description given by Bissonnette, who was in the helicopter.
6. As can be seen in the photograph taken at that very moment by White House photographer Pete Souza.
7. Several firsthand accounts are given in Mark Bowden, *The Finish* (New York: Grove Press, 2012), and Peter Bergen, *Manhunt* (London: Bodley Head, 2012).
8. Mark Bowden, "The Hunt for 'Geronimo,'" *Vanity Fair*, November 2012.
9. Phil Bronstein, "The Shooter," *Esquire*, March 2013. Also Robert O'Neill's multiple TV interviews and speeches, many available at www.robertjoneill.com/RobertJONeill_News.html.
10. Harry McCracken, "SXSW: The Man Who Live-Tweeted the Bin Laden Raid," *Time*, March 11, 2012.
11. Author interviews with bin Laden family members, plus accounts given by Robert O'Neill and Matthew Bissonnette.
12. A *Delta Force: Extreme 2* video game guide was found by the SEALs in the compound. See "Bin Laden's Bookshelf, Documents Probably Used by Other Compound Residents," Office of the Director of National Intelligence, www.dni.gov/index.php/resources/bin-laden-bookshelf? start=12.
13. Mark Owen [pen name of Matthew Bissonnette] and Kevin Maurer, *No Easy Day* (New York: Dutton, 2012).
14. Ibid.
15. This account was drawn from the recollections of O'Neill and Bissonnette.
16. Owen and Maurer, *No Easy Day*; also "SEAL's Firsthand Account of bin Laden Killing," *60 Minutes*, September 24, 2012.

17. This account is based mainly on O'Neill and Bissonnette; the authors deal with the inconsistencies in their accounts later in the chapter.

18. Author interview with Amal's brother Zakariya al-Sadeh, Islamabad, February 2012.

19. O'Neill made no mention of shooting Amal but claimed he had simply wrestled her onto the bed and flex-cuffed her.

20. Owen and Maurer, *No Easy Day.*

21. Bin Laden wives' accounts to Abbottabad Commission, author interviews with bin Laden family members, plus O'Neill and Bissonnette accounts.

22. Owen and Maurer, *No Easy Day.*

23. After cleaning blood off the face with water from a CamelBak.

24. Owen and Maurer, *No Easy Day.*

25. Author interview with Samirah Abdullah, who later visited Osama's widows in Saudi Arabia. Amman, Jordan, December 2016.

26. Khairiah told the Abbottabad Commission that the SEAL who manhandled her looked as frightened as she was, as if "he had seen a witch" when they came face-to-face.

27. "Osama bin Laden Dead, Wife Watched Him Die as White House Reveals He Wasn't Armed," *Mail Online*, May 4, 2011.

28. O'Neill said that the third-floor action took fifteen seconds.

29. Bashir Ahmed claimed to have seen "pieces of helicopter lying everywhere as a result of the explosion." Bashir Ahmed's account can be watched here: www.dailymotion.com/video/xzy069_eyewitness-account-of-bin-laden-killing-in-abbottabad-with-subtitles_news.

30. The constable was Nazar Mohammad.

31. "Bin Laden Raid Aftermath: Eyewitness Account," *Asharq Al-Awsat*, May 10, 2011.

32. The military academy commander was named by Shaukat Qadir as Lieutenant Colonel Naseem Anwar of the Nineteenth Frontier Forces; see *Operation Geronimo*. The ISI Colonel was not named.

33. This exchange is recounted in the Abbottabad Commission report.

34. Owen and Maurer, *No Easy Day.*

35. Recollections of Robert O'Neill and Matthew Bissonnette.

36. Author interview with Zakariya al-Sadeh; plus Jonathan Allen, "Bin Laden Had Cash, Was Ready to Flee," *Politico*, May 4, 2011.

37. Joseph Braude, "Iran Was al-Qaeda's 'Main Artery for Funds, Personnel, Communication': Bin Laden," *Ya Libnan* (Lebanon), June 18, 2016.

38. Bronstein, "The Shooter." Matthew Bissonnette claimed in an interview that he and several others were astonished. "Washington was leaking everything and we were going to get the lecture for it," he recalled. Michael Daly, "Outcry over SEAL Matt Bissonnette's bin Laden Book Reveals Pentagon Hypocrisy," *Daily Beast*, September 13, 2012.

39. Author interviews with member of the Abbottabad Commission, Islamabad, February 2015.

40. Author interviews with Maryam family members, 2014–2015.

41. Sohaib Athar tweeted all the details.

42. Shaukat Qadir gave an account of this conversation with Seham in his book, *Operation Geronimo*.

43. The inspector general of police for Khyber Pakhtunkhwa told the Abbottabad Commission that he only learned of the incident at seven A.M. from television reports.

44. Author interviews with General Athar Abbas, Rawalpindi, June 2014.

45. General Athar received word from Kayani that President Obama was not planning to make a televised statement until afternoon time in Washington, D.C. Pakistan could not wait that long, Athar warned, urging the chief of army staff to say "something right away." Eventually, Kayani got through to Admiral Mike Mullen and asked, "Please do it at eight A.M. our time."

46. White House Office of the Press Secretary, "Remarks of the President on Osama bin Laden," May 2, 2011, obamawhitehouse.archives.gov/the-press-office/2011/05/02/remarks-president -osama-bin-laden. "I've repeatedly made clear that we would take action within Pakistan if we knew where bin Laden was," he said. "That is what we've done. It's important to note that our counterterrorism cooperation with Pakistan helped lead us to bin Laden and the compound where he was hiding."

47. When General Athar called the prime minister's office, he was told, "Whatever GHQ [general headquarters] is saying is our official response." Worried that Pakistan's international reputation was being damaged by the official silence, he suggested a joint press conference with the Ministry of Information, ISPR, and the Foreign Office. After receiving no official responses, he left another message for Kayani: "We should give a direction or spin. Or this thing is going to eat us." Kayani did not reply. Author interviews with General Athar.

48. Months later, General Athar spoke privately to General Kayani, saying that his initial silence after the raid had damaged the army. "You should have come to see me personally," retorted Kayani.

49. Alexander Mullaney and Syeda Amna Hassan, "He Led the CIA to bin Laden—and Unwittingly Fueled a Vaccine Backlash," *National Geographic*, February 27, 2015; and Matthieu Aikens, "The Doctor, the CIA, and the Blood of Bin Laden," *GQ*, December 19, 2012.

50. White House Office of the Press Secretary, "Press Briefing by Press Secretary Jay Carney and Assistant to the President for Homeland Security and Counterterrorism John Brennan," May 2, 2011, obamawhitehouse.archives.gov/the-press-office/2011/05/02/press-briefing-press-secretary-jay-carney-and-assistant-president-homela.

51. General Pasha to the Abbottabad Commission: "If ISI was hiding Osama bin Laden it would not have hidden him in such an exposed building." The ISI was "neither complicit nor incompetent with respect to the presence of bin Laden in Pakistan." The ISI's record on America's "war on terror" spoke for itself.

52. Author interviews with General Athar Abbas.

53. Author telephone interviews with Mansoor Ijaz, July and August 2016.

54. Author interviews with Wajid Shamsul Hasan, London, 2011–2016.

55. The foreign secretary, Salman Bashir, claimed that two Pakistani F16 fighter jets had been airborne as soon as the Pakistani military knew about the operation and that "Pakistani security forces are neither incompetent or negligent."

56. In a closed meeting with carefully selected Pakistani reporters, Kayani was more candid and admitted to "intelligence failures," describing the American raid as a "misadventure."

57. Author interviews with General Athar Abbas.

58. Syed Saleem Shahzad, "The Life and Death of Osama bin Laden: Pakistan Has a Price to Pay," *Asia Times Online*, May 4, 2011.

59. Jon Boone, "Najam Sethi: The TV Star Who Dared to Take On Pakistan's Spy Agency," *Guardian*, July 18, 2002.

60. Jane Perlez, "Pakistani Army Chief Warns U.S. on Another Raid," *New York Times*, May 5, 2011.

61. "Kayani Blasts Government for Osama Raid Aftermath," *Hindustan Times*, May 10, 2011.

62. Fareed Zakaria, "With Bin Laden Gone, Now's the Time to Push Pakistan," *Washington Post*, May 11, 2011.

63. Greg Miller, "After Presiding over Bin Laden Raid, CIA Chief in Pakistan Came Home Suspecting He Was Poisoned by ISI," *Washington Post*, May 5, 2016.

64. Author telephone interview with Husain Haqqani, August 2016.

65. General Pasha ordered an investigation, saying that Iqbal was "a more suspicious character." "His profile matched that of a likely CIA recruit," Pasha concluded. "He was a trained

intelligence operator and was regarded as being involved in supplying the CIA with trade intelligence."

66. Author interviews with Husain Haqqani.

67. Army medic and Osama neighbor Major Amir Aziz was also relocated to the United States with Husain Haqqani's assistance. A story appeared suggesting that he had been recruited by the ISI as personal doctor to the ailing Al Qaeda leader. Pasha later defended Aziz, saying the "ISI had not found him worth investigating" and that he could not be connected to the U.S. raid.

68. Author interviews with Afridi family members, also Aikens, "The Doctor, the CIA, and the Blood of Bin Laden."

69. Husain Haqqani, "What Pakistan Knew about the Bin Laden Raid," *Foreign Policy*, May 13, 2015.

70. Huma Imtiaz, "ISI Chief Lands in Washington," *Express Tribune* (Pakistan), July 13, 2011.

71. He also said, "If the ISI was hiding OBL why would it have provided information on the Kuwaiti brothers?" referring to the ISI's role in the eavesdropping on Osama's companions. Pakistan would have been "very favourably placed internationally" if it had apprehended the Al Qaeda leader, he continued. "There were no indications of [Osama bin Laden's] presence or existence. After a while the ISI began to believe he had probably died." Although Pasha was willing to admit to "an intelligence failure," there had been neither "facilitation nor connivance."

72. Azaz Syed, *The Secrets of Pakistan's War on Al-Qaeda* (Islamabad: Al-Abbas International, 2014). Author interviews with family members in Peshawar and Kohat, 2014. Also Saeed Shah, "Pakistan Detained, Then Released, Many after Bin Laden Raid," *McClatchyDC*, June 28, 2011.

73. Syed, *The Secrets of Pakistan's War on Al Qaeda*. Also Qadir, *Operation Geronimo*.

74. Boone, "Najam Sethi."

75. Press Trust of India, "Osama bin Laden's Neighbour in Abbottabad Freed after Questioning," NDTV, May 8, 2011. Also Shah, "Pakistan Detained, Then Released, Many after Bin Laden Raid."

76. Qadir, *Operation Geronimo*, 12.

77. Sohaib Athar received so many calls and questions from journalists that he created an FAQ page on his website: "Government organizations have not contacted me yet, either to chat or to try to impose any restrictions on what I say or do. I hope that does not change anytime soon."

78. General Pasha to the Abbottabad Commission, author copy of report.

79. The rapid increase in attacks on polio workers in Pakistan after the Abbottabad raid was well documented. Pasha's comments were made to the Abbottabad Commission.

80. Syed Saleem Shahzad, "Al Qaeda Had Warned of Strike," *Asia Times Online*, May 27, 2011.

81. Dexter Filkins, "The Journalist and the Spies," *New Yorker*, September 19, 2011.

82. Ibid. His story after the Abbottabad raid that alleged senior figures in the Pakistan Army had known the Americans were planning an operation was a typical Shahzad flier, based on rumor and assumption. "Well-placed security sources maintain that the operation in Abbottabad . . . was without a doubt a joint Pakistan-US effort and that all logistics were arranged inside Pakistan," he wrote.

83. Author interview with Umar Cheema, Islamabad, June 2014. The attack on him took place in September 2010.

84. Shahzad had agreed to go on the show to promote his new book, *Inside Al-Qaeda and the Taliban: Beyond Bin Laden and 9/11*.

85. Near the town of Mandi Bahauddin. Shahzad's white Corolla was found six miles away.

86. Filkins, "The Journalist and the Spies."

87. Ibid.

88. Author interview with Commodore Zafar Iqba, ISI spokesman, Islamabad, 2013.

89. Author interview with Sadiah Ahmed, secretary to the Yemeni ambassador to Pakistan, Islamabad, June 2014.
90. Author interview with a female Federal Investigation Agency officer whose name is withheld at her request, Rawalpindi, June 2014.
91. Osama bin Laden's mentor Abdullah Azzam had once taught at International Islamic University in Islamabad, and it had links to well-respected universities in Saudi Arabia.
92. Dr. Begum's CV can be read here: www.iiu.edu.pk/wp-content/uploads/downloads/academics/short_cv/fa/zaitoon_begum.pdf.
93. Author interview with Dr. Zaitoon's former colleague Quaiseria Alvi, who also accused her of harassing female staff to take their photographs off the university website.
94. Author interview with a member of the Abbottabad Commision, plus interviews with bin Laden family members; also Abbottabad Commission report.
95. Maryam described how she first met Amal in 2002 and moved with her to Swat, and how she had hosted Khalid Shaikh Mohammad before he was arrested in 2003. She talked about the move to Abbottabad and said that she had eventually realized that her husband, Ibrahim, was probably a mujahid and that the "tall Arab" to whom Amal was married was Osama bin Laden. Abbottabad Commission report.
96. Jennifer Musa, Obituaries, *Daily Telegraph*, January 18, 2008. Also author interview with Ashraf Qazi.
97. Saudi Arabia, Yemen, and the Gulf states were all brought into the discussion.
98. Author interviews with Husain Haqqani in May 2015 and August 2016.
99. Ibid.
100. Shaukat Qadir, "Who's Gunning for Pakistan's Top Generals?" *Al Arabiya English*, June 18, 2011.
101. Qadir had previously written hagiographical accounts of how Kayani had "turned the army on its head" after Musharraf's departure and how he "restored not only the self-respect of soldiers, he restored their respect in the eyes of the citizens." In a piece he wrote for Al Arabiya after the Abbottabad raid, he stated: "There is a deliberate coordinated effort to undermine the authority of the Pakistan army chief by the US and the US media."
102. Qadir, *Operation Geronimo*; also Declan Walsh, "A Personal Quest to Clarify Bin Laden's Last Days Yeields Vexing Accounts," *New York Times*, March 7, 2012.
103. Qadir, *Operation Geronimo*. "As a general rule spooks can never be fully trusted to disclose all they know," Qadir continued. "Consequently, I take what they offer but usually with fistfuls of salt, not just a pinch."
104. The official ISI interrogation team consisted of Brigadier Muhammed Aslam, Lieutenant Colonel (Ret.) Muhammed Tariq, and Lieutenant Colonel (Ret.) Khalid Qasim. Brigadier Aslam had been a captain when Qadir commanded his brigade.
105. Qadir, *Operation Geronimo*. The ISI colonel who searched the house on the night of the raid told Qadir that he had found a closet "filled with a huge variety of medicines," including a blood-sugar test kit.
106. Ibid. They had worked some more on the Kuwaiti brothers. Qadir claimed that Khalid Shaikh Mohammad had named Abu Ahmad al-Kuwaiti as Osama's courier, even though his own interrogation transcripts suggest otherwise. Before being packed off to the Salt Pit, KSM had identified the courier from a photograph that the ISI claimed it had shared with the CIA, something the agency denied. Tracking the Kuwaiti, the ISI had taken "a high powered delegation to the Gulf to confer with intelligence chiefs, but they couldn't locate him, or they just weren't trying hard enough." Qadir also presented a new version of who had led the CIA to the compound, with ISI investigators taking center stage. In 2007, Abrar had become so worried about what to say to the neighbors that he had invented a story about being a money

changer from Charsadda, a claim that someone in Abbottabad had reported to the ISI. In mid-2008, Charsadda ISI station had probed the claim and concluded there was no record of a money changer by that name, passing the inquiry back to Aabpara—which instructed ISI Abbottabad to watch the mystery man's movements. In July 2010, the ISI's counterterrorism wing supposedly made a request to the CIA for satellite surveillance on the compound. It was this operation and not intercepted phone calls that had ultimately led to the raid, Qadir said, hoping to revive the ISI's role in it.

107. Ibid. "It would be a favour wouldn't it; putting me out of my misery? And that is a wife's duty." This account was partially confirmed by bin Laden family members who told the authors that severe tensions existed between Khairiah and other family members who believed that she had either deliberately or inadvertently led the raiding party to Abbottabad.

108. This accusation was widely reported in the Pakistani media after the raid although relatives of Ibrahim's surviving wife, Maryam, strongly denied it.

109. Author interviews with Shaukat Qadir, Islamabad and Rawalpindi, 2014–2015; also his book, *Operation Geronimo.*

110. Amal wanted to go home to Yemen. Khairiah and Seham wanted to live in the sprawling bin Laden family compound at Kilometer Seven on the outskirts of Jeddah, Saudi Arabia.

111. Khairiah, Seham, and Amal described how their husband was "not fond of possessions" and had owned only six pairs of *shalwar kameez*, a black jacket, two sweaters, and a cowboy hat to "avoid detection from above." When he was sick he had treated himself with traditional Arab medicine and when he was sluggish he ate an apple and some chocolate. He had not expected an American assault, although he had ordered some trees to be cut down along the compound wall a few weeks before the raid, for fear someone could conceal a camera or listening device in them.

112. Qazi listed unanswered questions that included: "What information were the Iranians able to extract from Hamzah, Khairiah, their family and escorts?" "Did the Iranians maintain some kind of link with Osama through Hamzah or Khairiah?" "What was in the 'significant dossier' the Iranians compiled on the family?" "Did they [the Iranians] share any information with the U.S.?" Author interview with Qazi, Islamabad, February 2015.

113. Abbottabad Commission report.

114. Author interviews with Zakariya, Islamabad, February 2012.

115. Author interviews with Abdul Rahman al-Sadeh, Islamabad, February, March, and September 2012.

116. "They were just stupid boys," said an embassy official who watched them wandering about daily, looking lost and waiting to speak to the ambassador.

117. Most of the time, Amal's children were looked after by Khairiah and Seham, who bombarded Zakariya with questions he could not answer.

118. CNN Wire Staff, "Bin Laden Relatives Want Probe and Proof of Death," CNN, May 12, 2011.

119. Author interviews with bin Laden family members. Also see Omar's interview, "Bin Laden's Son Urges Talks to Bring Peace," *Today*, NBC, January 22, 2008, www.youtube.com/watch?v=7opVaScePo8.

120. Omar found the burial at sea of his father "unacceptable humanely and religiously," and he threatened "to follow that crime through the American and international justice [systems] in order to determine the true fate of our vanished father." However, since he could not go to Pakistan in person for fear of being arrested, he vented his anger through Zakariya.

121. The last possible location the CIA had ever shared with the ISI was "when a person supposedly resembling OBL was sighted in Darosh, Chitral"—man who turned out to be the bin Laden lookalike in 2007. Abbottabad Commission report.

122. Abbottabad Commission report.

123. General Pasha told the Abbottabad Commission that Pakistan was "a very weak state and also a very scared state . . . It all boils down to corrupt and low grade governance. There is apathy at every level, in every sector of national life." During his sessions before Ashraf Qazi, he complained that lies and untruths about ISI culpability in the Osama saga had been allowed to fester because of the "deafening silence" of the political leadership. The degree of anger that had arisen in the military when Prime Minister Gilani had asked who in the military and security establishment had given Osama bin Laden a six-year visa "could not be described." According to General Pasha, the ISI needed more power, not less. However, Pasha's case suffered a crushing blow when Admiral Mike Mullen used his final address to the U.S. Senate Armed Services Committee in September 2011 to accuse the ISI of supporting Al Qaeda and exporting terror, and described the outlawed terrorist Haqqani network as "a veritable arm of Pakistan's Inter-Services Intelligence agency."

124. Officially, the commission's findings remain mired in legal arguments.

125. Rob Crilly, "Mike Mullen: Pakistan Is Exporting Terror," *Daily Telegraph*, September 22, 2011.

126. By the following week, the White House and Pentagon were also on board, with Deputy National Security Advisor for Strategic Communications Benjamin Rhodes writing to Assistant Secretary of Defense for Public Affairs Doug Wilson. "We are trying to have visibility into the UBL projects and this is likely the most high profile one," wrote Rhodes. "Would like to have whatever group is going around in here at the WH [White House] to get a sense of what they're doing/what cooperation they're seeking."

127. A full list of supporting documents and transcripts of these discussions can be found at Judicial Watch Press Room, "Judicial Watch Obtains Stack of Overlooked CIA Records Detailing Meetings with bin Laden Filmmakers," August 28, 2012, www.judicialwatch.org /press-room/press-releases/judicial-watch-obtains-4-to-5-inch-stack-of-overlooked-cia-records -detailing-meetings-with-bin-laden-filmmakers/.

128. Ibid.

129. Ibid.

130. Ibid.

131. Ibid.

132. Ibid.

133. Ibid.

134. Ibid.

135. Ibid.

136. Steve Coll, "The Spy Who Said Too Much," *New Yorker*, April 1, 2013.

137. Dating from September 2006 to April 2011, the letters had been authored by bin Laden and top Al Qaeda leaders, including Abu Yahya al-Libi, Adam Gadahn (Azzam the American), and Atiyah. Individual letters are available here: www.ctc.usma.edu/posts/letters-from-abbot tabad-bin-ladin-sidelined. Author interviews with Nelly Lahoud, New York, April 2014, and Will McCants, Washington, D.C., April 2014.

138. David Ignatius, "Osama bin Laden, a Lion in Winter," *Washington Post*, March 18, 2012.

139. Author interviews with Bruce Riedel, Washington, D.C., 2014–2015.

140. Jane Mayer, "Zero Conscience in Zero Dark Thirty," *New Yorker*, December 14, 2012.

141. Senior military figures said the president had made dishonorable disclosures that had damaged the U.S. military's ability to operate. Details of the raid had been released too quickly. Such a hasty unburdening had not left any time to exploit intelligence recovered from the compound. Retired CIA case officers joined the chorus of disapproval, saying that recruiting local assets was a sensitive task at the best of times but would be virtually impossible in future thanks to the identification of key Pakistani assets such as Dr. Shakil Afridi.

142. Bissonnette's book was published in September 2012.

143. Bissonnette interview with NBC News, November 2014.

144. "SEAL's First-hand Account of Bin Laden Killing," *60 Minutes*, broadcast September 9, 2012; transcript published online on September 24, 2012. www.youtube.com/watch?v=djCuC5E3 2bM.

145. Matthew Cole and Anna R. Schecter, "Who Shot Bin Laden? A Tale of Two SEALs," NBC News, November 6, 2014.

146. Dan Lamothe, "Navy SEAL Who Wrote bin Laden Raid Book Must Pay Government at Least $6.8 Million," *Washington Post*, August 19, 2016.

147. Matthew Cole, "Navy SEAL Turns Over Picture of bin Laden's Body, Faces Investigation of Business Ties," *Intercept*, January 19, 2016.

CHAPTER TWELVE

1. Author interviews with Mahfouz Ibn El Waleed, Nouakchott, December 2014, January and June 2015.

2. In his speeches, al-Zawahiri used to describe Osama as the man who said "no" to America.

3. Slahi was one of thirty-one prisoners processed in August 2002. See Mohamedou Ould Slahi and Larry Siems, *Guantánamo Diary* (New York: Little, Brown, 2015). See also Slahi's interrogation summary at "Gitmo Files," Wikileaks, wikileaks.org/gitmo/prisoner/760.html.

4. Those who remained included Al Qaeda *shura* members Saif al-Abdel Abu al-Khayr al-Masri, Abu Mohammed al-Masri, Thirwat Shihata, and three of Zarqawi's former deputies, Abu Qassem, Sari Shibab, and Khalid al-Aruri.

5. Photos were shown to the authors by Mahfouz.

6. When Fatima asked if they could leave, the compound director allowed her to call her brothers Omar and Abdullah. They promised to do everything they could to reunite the family. Author interviews with bin Laden family members.

7. The picture was obtained by the authors from Zakariya in February 2012; see authors' article written under the pseudonym Julian Thompson for reasons of security: Julian Thompson, "Bin Laden Told His Children: 'Go to the US and Live in Peace,'" *Sunday Times* (London), February 12, 2012.

8. Author interviews with Mahfouz.

9. In July 2016, Hamzah bin Laden released an audiotaped speech entitled "We Are All Osama" calling for Muslims globally to avenge his father's death. Released by As Sahab, translated into English by the SITE Intelligence Group. Hamzah uses this phrase to describe his father in the message. Also discussed in author interviews with Mahfouz.

10. Ibid.

11. Mark Mazzetti, "C.I.A. Drone Is Said to Kill Al Qaeda's No. 2," *New York Times*, August 27, 2011.

12. Jay Solomon, "U.S. Sees Iranian, al Qaeda Alliance," *Wall Street Journal*, July 29, 2011.

13. Ibid. "Mr. Khalil is based in Iran and has been operating there under an agreement with Iranian authorities since 2005." Per the U.S. Treasury Department.

14. This was a deliberate attempt on the part of the United States to put the Ahmadinejad regime under pressure to give up its remaining Al Qaeda "guests."

15. Abu al-Khayr al-Masri was accused of having played a role in the 1998 embassy attacks and was wanted in Egypt and the United States. Both Saif and Abu Mohammed al-Masri had been on the FBI's Most Wanted Terrorist list since its inception in 2001. Saif was also wanted in Egypt for his role in the assassination of Anwar Sadat. Thirwat Shihata, Dr. Ayman al-Zawahiri's deputy in Egyptian Islamic Jihad, had received two death sentences in absentia for

alleged terrorist activities in Egypt. The two Jordanians—Zarqawi's brother-in-law Khalid al-Aruri and Zarqawi's long time aide Sari Shihab—were sought internationally for their roles in terrorist attacks in Iraq and Jordan.

16. Initially via the escorts and drivers, who worked at both sites and passed on simple messages, disguised as greetings from the wives.

17. "While we were in there, we could grab our letters and letters written to or from those still inside the compound," he said.

18. In an attempt to persuade him to think more positively about the overland option, he was taken on an official sightseeing trip to Urmia in the far northwest of Iran, where he enjoyed a lavish meal with the escorts at a restaurant within sight of the Turkish border. "We found diplomats and foreigners, officials from the Kurdish region whose cars were carrying Iraqi plates," he said. But the trip did nothing to change his mind. He was flying out or not going at all.

19. "Key Al Qaeda Agent Younis al-Mauritani Captured in Pakistan," *National* (United Arab Emirates), September 6, 2011, www.thenational.ae/news/world/south-asia/key-al-qaeda-agent-younis-al-mauritani-captured-in-pakistan; also Younis's Mauritanian security file, Nouakchott security services, author copy.

20. Abdel Bari Atwan, *After Bin Laden.* (London: Saqi Books, 2012)

21. Ibid. Al-Zawahiri, who released a statement about the Arab Spring, claimed, "Oh how great are these days we are living."

22. Mahfouz told this story in detail to the authors over multiple interviews in Nouakchott. He also said, "I was not hurting him or killing him but I'm just trying to recover my rights."

23. Ibid.

24. Yussef Al-Shuli, "Terror in America (29) Al Jazeera Interview with Top Al-Qa'ida Leader Abu Hafs 'The Mauritanian,' [Mahfouz Ibn El Waleed]," Al Jazeera, December 14, 2001. Middle East Media Research Institute. Retrieved October 23, 2012, groups.google.com/forum/#!topic/soc.culture.usa/b4XqGY82ZtU

25. In June 2011.

26. This letter was addressed to AQIM leader Abu Musab Abdel Wadoud.

27. Details of payments made via Iran can be found in "Treasury Designates Al-Qa'ida Supporters in Qatar and Yemen," U.S. Department of the Treasury, December 18, 2013: www.treasury.gov/press-center/press-releases/Pages/jl2249.aspx. The money went through Yasin al-Suri and the Iran network, who had been briefly jailed in Evin to satisfy the U.S Treasury. See al-Suri's profile at "Wanted: Yasin al-Suri," Rewards for Justice, U.S. Department of State, www.rewardsforjustice.net/english/yasin_al_suri.html.

28. Will McCants, *The ISIS Apocalypse: The History, Strategy, and Doomsday Vision of the Islamic State* (New York: St. Martin's, 2015).

29. This move led some U.S. commentators to describe him as "the new bin Laden."

30. "Mapping Militant Organizations: Islamic State," April 4, 2016, web.stanford.edu/group/mappingmilitants/cgi-bin/groups/view/1. See also Noman Benotman and Roisin Blake, "Jabhat al-Nusra, a Strategic Briefing," Quilliam Foundation, www.quilliamfoundation.org/wp/wp-content/uploads/publications/free/jabhat-al-nusra-a-strategic-briefing.pdf.

31. McCants, *The ISIS Apocalypse.*

32. Thomas Joscelyn, "Al-Zawahiri Eulogizes Al Qaeda's Slain Syrian Representative," *Long War Journal*, April 4, 2014. Also author interviews with Abu Qatada, Abu Muhammad al-Maqdisi, and Huthaifa Azzam, Amman, Jordan, December 2016.

33. See Saif al-Adel's eulogy of his close friend Abu Khalid, published August 2015, cited in Thomas Joscelyn, "Al Qaeda Insider Returns to Twitter, Discusses Group's Global Leadership," *Long War Journal*, March 16, 2016.

34. For more on Toubasi see Mona Alami, "The New Generation of Jordanian Jihadi Fighters," *Sada*, February 18, 2014; and Suhaib Anjarini, "How Jordanians Came to Dominate al-Nusra Front," *Al-Akhbar*, January 16, 2015.

35. SITE Intelligence Group, "Abu Musab al-Suri's Military Theory of Jihad," translated and published in 2011, news.siteintelgroup.com/blog/index.php/about-us/21-jihad/21-suri-a-mili.

36. "Al Nusra Leader: Our Mission Is to Defeat the Syrian Regime," Al Jazeera, May 28, 2015.

37. McCants, *The ISIS Apocalypse*. See also Joscelyn, "Al-Zawahiri Eulogizes Al Qaeda's Slain Syrian Representative."

38. "Osama bin Laden's Feuding Wives," *Daily Mail*, March 30, 2012.

39. Author interviews with bin Laden family lawyer Aamir Khalil, June 2014.

40. FIR No: 3/2012, 01/03/2013, author copy. They were also accused of "deceitfully concealing their true identity and even did not disclose to concerned hospital staff when they gave birth to their children in Pakistan."

41. On February 16, 2012, Zakariya submitted an appeal to the chief justice of Pakistan. "I put between your hands the issue of Osama bin Laden's family (children and women) who passed upon their illegal disappearance in Pakistan more than eight months with Pakistani authorities despite they are innocent, and which consider against all the human rights and justice laws in the world."

42. Author interviews with Rehman Malik, Islamabad, February 2012 and June 2014; Zakariya al-Sadeh, Islamabad, February 2012; and bin Laden family lawyer, Aamir Khalil. Also author interview with the female FIA officer who had accompanied the women, Rawalpindi, June 2014.

43. Author interview with Tabani, Islamabad, June 2014.

44. Ibid.

45. For illegally entering Pakistan.

46. "Pakistan Deporation of Bin Laden's Family Delayed," *Asharq al-Awsat*, April 18, 2012.

47. Rob Crilly, "Osama's Widows and Children 'Shown' in Video,'" *Daily Telegraph*, April 10, 2012.

48. And who had been promoted soon after to Karachi Corps commander, a powerful position that was thought to have bought his silence

49. "Saudi Arabia Accepts Bin Laden's Family 'on Humanitarian Grounds,'" *Asharq al-Awsat*, April 28, 2012. Government sources in Riyadh said that bin Laden's widows had been allowed to enter the country from a "humanitarian" standpoint, adding that they were confident that they and the children were not involved in Al Qaeda operations.

50. Author visit to house.

51. "Pakistan Doctor in Bin Laden Case Called Corrupt, Womaniser," *Asharq al-Awsat*, May 29, 2012.

52. "Ex Lawyer of Bin Laden Hunt Doctor Killed in Pakistan," Al Jazeera, May 18, 2015.

53. Author interviews with Brigadier Syed Amjad Shabbir, private secretary to General Pasha, Islamabad, 2014–2015. Before he retired, a judicial commission into the Memogate affair released its final conclusions and found that former ambassador Husain Haqqani had been its "originator and architect." By then he was out of reach in Washington, working for a think tank and preparing a book.

54. "Muammar Gaddafi's Spy Chief Senussi Arrested in Mauritania," *Daily Telegraph*, May 17, 2012.

55. Quotes in this section from author interviews with Mahfouz.

56. Ibid.

57. Undated copy of Osama bin Laden's will. Recovered from Abbottabad, declassified and released by the Office of the Director of National Intelligence [hereafter ODNI] in March 2016, www.dni.gov/index.php/resources/bin-laden-bookshelf.

58. His brother Sidi Ould Walid gave a statement to the local press: "My brother was interrogated multiple times and his release indicates he is no longer seen as a threat."

59. Author interviews with Abu Ghaith's closest friend, Mahfouz. Also interviews with bin Laden family members.

60. Abu Ghaith described some of this journey in his subsequent statement to the FBI, author copy. Bin Laden family members also recounted Fatima's journey.

61. Special Agent Michael S. Butsch and Deputy U.S. Marshall Brian T. McHugh asked questions; author copy of interrogation transcript.

62. "U.S. Transfers Suspected Senior Al Qaeda Member to Mauritania," Reuters, June 1, 2013.

63. Author interview with Stanley Cohen, legal counsel to Sulaiman Abu Ghaith, New York, October 2014.

64. Ibid.

65. For conspiracy to kill Americans, providing material support to terrorists, and conspiring to do so.

66. This set a precedent in which the foreign policy objectives of several of Syria's neighbors would be fought out on Syrian territory.

67. This statement was issued on June 15, 2013.

68. Thomas Joscelyn, "Report: Former Head of Al Qaeda's Network in Iran Now Operates in Syria," Long War Journal, March 25, 2014.

69. Murad Batal al-Shishani, "Syria's Surprising Release of Jihadi Strategist Abu Mus'ab al-Suri," Jamestown Foundation, Terrorism Monitor 10, no. 3 (February 10, 2012). See also Bill Roggio, "Al Qaeda's American Propagandist Notes Death of Terror Group's Representative in Syria," Long War Journal, March 30, 2014.

70. Thomas Joscelyn, "Islamic State of Iraq Leader Defies al-Zawahiri in Alleged Audio Message," Long War Journal, June 15, 2013.

71. "Hadith Authenticity of Black Flags Hadith from Kitab Al Fitan," www.ummah.com/forum /showthread.php?408221-Hadith-Authenticity-of-Black-Flags-Hadith-from-Kitab-Al-Fitan.

72. For details of these payments, who made them, and how they were funneled from Qatar through Iran to Syria, see "Treasury Designates Al-Qa'ida Supporters in Qatar and Yemen."

73. Liz Sly, "Al-Qaeda Disavows Any Ties with Radical Islamist ISIS Group in Syria, Iraq," Washington Post, February 3, 2014

74. Many mistook him for Abu Musab al-Suri, to whom he bore some resemblance.

75. Author interviews with Maqdisi and Qatada, Amman, Jordan, December 2016. The term "don" is borrowed from Will McCants in The ISIS Apocalypse.

76. Author interviews with Maqdisi and Qatada, Amman, December 2016.

77. This instruction was issued by Abu Bakr when he announced the formation of his Caliphate.

78. The secular Turkish leader Mustafa Kemal Atatürk had abolished the last real caliphate after the defeat of the Ottoman Empire in World War One. After almost a century, Muslims could once again feel proud.

79. According to his close friend Abu Qatada; author interview, Amman, October 2014 and September and December 2016.

80. Michael Daly, "ISIS Leader: 'See You in New York,'" Daily Beast, June 14, 2014. See also Paul Crompton, "The Rise of the New ISIS Chief: Abu Bakr al-Baghdadi," Al Arabiya English, June 30, 2014.

81. Speech written by Azzam the American for Osama in January 2011. ODNI documents, Abbottabad, released in March 2016.

82. Qatada had spent many years in the United Kingdom after winning asylum there in 1994. He became a regular speaker at London's Finsbury Park Mosque and acted as liaison for young

British Muslims who wanted to train with Al Qaeda in Afghanistan, sending them to Abu Zubaydah. In October 1999, he told his congregation that American citizens "should be attacked, wherever they were" and later he spoke in favor of the 9/11 attacks. Before his voluntary deportation to Amman in July 2013, he spent several years in Belmarsh prison in South London fighting the terrorism case against him. Author interviews with Qatada, Amman, October 2014 and September and December 2016. Also author interview with Maqdisi, Amman, December 2016.

83.   Author interviews with Maqdisi and Qatada, Amman, December 2016. Also Malik, et al., "How ISIS Crippled Al Qaeda," *Guardian*, June 10, 2015.

84.   Author interviews with Maqdisi and Qatada, Amman, December 2016.

85.   Shiv Malik, et al., "The Race to Save Peter Kassig," *Guardian*, December 18, 2014. Also author interview with Dr. Moneef Samara, a well-placed doctor from Zarqa who made the initial connection between Stanley Cohen and Maqdisi, Zarqa, September 2016; author interviews with Abu Qatada, Zarqa, September 2016; author interview with Cohen, New York, October 2014 and author interview with Maqdisi, Amman, December 2016.

86.   "IS Magazine Takes Aim at 'Misleading' Muslim Scholars," *Middle East Eye*, December 31, 2014.

87.   In a June 2010 e-mail to CAGE.

88.   Ibid.

89.   Claire Phipps, et al., " 'High Degree of Certainty' That US Strike Killed Mohammed Emwazi," *Guardian*, November 13, 2015; Martin Chulov, "Losing Ground, Fighters and Morale—Is It All Over for Isis?" *Guardian*, September 7, 2016.

90.   Benjamin Weiser, "U.S. Seeks to Use Letters Found in Bin Laden Raid in Terrorism Trial," *New York Times*, December 15, 2014.

91.   Stephen F. Hayes, "Al Qaeda Wasn't 'On the Run,'" *Weekly Standard*, September 15, 2014.

92.   Two months later, in March 2015, another Al Qaeda suspect came to trial in Brooklyn, Pakistani national Abid Naseer, who was charged with plotting to attack the New York City subway. More Abbottabad documents emerged. Among them were letters written by Atiyah to Osama bin Laden concerning the ISI's attempts to negotiate a peace deal through Hamid Gul in 2010. The case, which resulted in Naseer's conviction, embarrassed General Pasha, who had been named by Atiyah as a party to the discussions.

93.   Author interviews with Maqdisi and Qatada, Amman, December 2016. Also Malik, et al., "The Race to Save Peter Kassig."

CHAPTER THIRTEEN

1.   Atiyah to Osama, July 17, 2010. Recovered from Abbottabad, declassified and released by the Office of the Director of National Intelligence [hereafter ODNI] in May 2015, www.dni.gov/index.php/resources/bin-laden-bookshelf.

2.   "Kidnapped Iranian Diplomat Rescued in Yemen," Al Jazeera, March 5, 2015.

3.   Author interview with Dr. Moneef Samara, Zarqa, September and December 2016.

4.   An Arabic transcript posted with the message indicates his audio was recorded in May or June, although it was not released until August 2015. He said: "And from among my sheikhs through whose hands I was educated: Sheikh Ahmed Hassan Abu al-Khayr, Sheikh Abu Mohammed al-Masri, Sheikh Saif al-Adel, and Sheikh Sulaiman Abu Ghaith, may Allah release them all." He also renewed the *bayat* to Mullah Omar even though the Taliban had by June confirmed that its leader had died in a Karachi hospital in April 2013. He also honored

Nasir al-Wuhayshi, the AQAP leader and al-Zawahiri's deputy, who had been killed in a drone strike in Yemen in June. The rest of his message concerned continuing his father's war against the far enemy, America.

5. Rita Katz, director of SITE Intelligence Group, said in an interview that this is what was hoped for when Hamzah was put forward. Adam Withnall, "Hamza bin Laden: Could Osama's Son Be the Future Leader of al-Qaeda?" *Independent*, May 11, 2016.

6. Qatar has one of the smallest citizen populations in the Arab world (278,000) and the largest percentage of nonnationals in the world (88 percent).

7. James Risen and David Johnston, "Qaeda Aide Slipped Away Long Before September 11 Attack," *New York Times*, March 8, 2003.

8. "Treasury Targets Key al-Qa'ida Funding and Support Network Using Iran as a Critical Transit Point," U.S. Department of the Treasury, July 28, 2011, www.treasury.gov/press-center/press -releases/Pages/tg1261.aspx.

9. "Treasury Designates Financial Supporters of Al-Qaida and Al-Nusrah Front," U.S. Department of the Treasury, August 5, 2015.

10. Bill Roggio, "Senior Al Qaeda Leader and Former US Detainee Killed in Drone Strike in 2012," *Long War Journal*, October 17, 2013.

11. Hamzah to Osama, January 8, 2011. ODNI documents, Abbottabad, released in March 2016.

12. David D. Kirkpatrick, "Qatar's Support for Islamists Alienates Allies Near and Far," *New York Times*, September 8, 2014.

13. Author interviews with bin Laden family members.

14. Ibid.

15. Ibid.

16. Ibid.

17. Osama to Hamzah, undated, but clearly written in early 2011. ODNI documents, Abbottabad, released in March 2016.

18. Guy Lawson, "Osama's Prodigal Son: The Dark Twisted Journey of Omar bin Laden," *Rolling Stone*, January 20, 2010.

19. In a letter Hamzah wrote to his father in July 2009, he said his appearance had changed so much his father might not recognize him. ODNI documents, Abbottabad, released in May 2015.

20. Ibid. Hamzah talked about Americans and taking revenge against them in the audio statement released in August 2015.

21. Stephen F. Hayes and Thomas Joscelyn, "How America Was Misled on Al Qaeda's Demise," *Wall Street Journal*, March 5, 2015.

22. Stephen F. Hayes, "Al Qaeda Wasn't 'On the Run,'" *Weekly Standard*, September 15, 2014.

23. Joseph Braude, "Iran Was Al Qaeda's 'Main Artery for Funds, Personnel, Communication': Bin Laden," *Ya Libnan* (Lebanon), June 18, 2016.

24. Dr. Islam Sobhi al-Mazeny, "Is It the Heart You Are Asking?" ODNI documents, Abbottabad.

25. Letters from Atiyah to Osama, ODNI documents, Abbottabad, released in May 2015 and March 2016.

26. Press release accompanying the announcement of the release of the final tranche of declassified material from the Abbottabad compound, a total of forty-nine documents out of a million-plus that will never see the light of day. Office of the Director of National Intelligence, "Closing the Book on bin Laden: Intelligence Community Releases Final Abbottabad Documents," January 19, 2017, www.dni.gov/index.php/newsroom/press-releases/224-press

-releases-2017/1474-closing-the-book-on-bin-laden-intelligence-community-releases-final-abbottabad-documents.

27. Mushreq Abbas, "Iran's Man in Iraq and Syria," *Al-Monitor*, March 13, 2013.

28. Ibid. See also Ali Alfoneh, "Iran's Most Dangerous General," *Middle Eastern Outlook*, July 13, 2011, retrieved September 14, 2016, from www.irantracker.org/analysis/alfoneh-iran-dangerous-general-suleimani-july-13-2011. Sanctions came in May 2011.

29. Ibid.

30. Joby Warrick, "Double Game? Even as It Battles ISIS, Turkey Gives Other Extremists Shelter," *Washington Post*, July 10, 2016.

31. Thomas Joscelyn, "Senior Al Qaeda Leaders Reportedly Released from Custody in Iran," *Long War Journal*, September 18, 2015.

32. Author interviews with Abu Qatada, Abu Muhammad al-Maqdisi, and Huthaifa Azzam, Amman, Jordan, December 2016.

33. Joscelyn, "Senior Al Qaeda Leaders Reportedly Released from Custody in Iran."

34. One of them was known as "Al Siyasi al Mutaqa'id."

35. Rukmini Callimachi and Eric Schmitt, "Iran Released Top Members of Al Qaeda in a Trade," *New York Times*, September 17, 2015.

36. Laila Bassam and Tom Perry, "How Iranian General Plotted Out Syrian Assault in Moscow," Reuters, October 6, 2015.

37. Dexter Filkins, "The Shadow Commander," *New Yorker*, September 30, 2013

38. In February 2013.

39. Author interviews with Qatada, Maqdisi, and Huthaifa Azzam, Amman, December 2016.

40. Michael Morell, *The Great War of Our Time* (New York: Grand Central Publishing, 2016).

41. Thomas Joscelyn, "Fifteen Years after the 9/11 attacks, Al Qaeda Fights On," *Long War Journal*, September 11, 2016.

42. Huthaifa Azzam, who spent four years from 2012 to 2016 fighting with various factions of the Free Syrian Army, claimed to have seen evidence that al-Zawahiri had shifted to Iran. He also claimed that by 2016 both the Nusra Front and Islamic State were being armed and directed by Iran. Author interviews, Amman, December 2016.

43. Abu Faraj al-Masri was killed in Syria in October 2016.

44. Martin Chulov and Tom McCarthy, "US Drone Strike in Syria Kills Top al-Qaida Leader, Jihadis Say," *Guardian*, February 27, 2017.

45. Martin Chulov, "Al-Nusra Front Cuts Ties with al-Qaida and Renames Itself," *Guardian*, July 29, 2016.

46. Yaroslav Trofimov, "What Happens after ISIS Falls?" *Wall Street Journal*, September 9, 2016.

47. Thomas Joscelyn, "Hamza bin Laden Calls for Regime Change in Saudi Arabia," *Long War Journal*, August 18, 2016.

48. U.S. Department of State, "State Department Terrorist Designation of Hamza bin Laden," January 5, 2017, www.state.gov/j/ct/rls/other/des/266536.htm.

49. Senate Select Committee on Intelligence (SSCI), *The Official Senate Report on CIA Torture* (New York: Skyhorse Publishing, 2015), 35.

50. Author interviews with Professor Mark Denbeaux, Newark, New Jersey, February 2017.

51. The full profile can be read here: www.prs.mil/Portals/60/Documents/ISN10016/20160331_U_ISN_10016_GOVERNMENTS_UNCLASSIFIED_SUMMARY_PUBLIC.pdf.

52. Scott Shane, "Abu Zubaydah, Tortured Guantánamo Detainee, Makes Case for Release," *New York Times*, August 24, 2016.

53. George Edwards, "Saudi-born Palestinian Abu Zubaydah Asks Pentagon for Release from Guantánamo," *Gitmo Observer*, August 23, 2016.

54. "ICRC Report on the Treatment of Fourteen 'High Value Detainees' in CIA Custody," International Committee of the Red Cross, February 14, 2007, confidential. Leaked and made available here: http://www.nybooks.com/media/doc/2010/04/22/icrc-report.pdf.

55. Author interview with Joseph Margulies, October 2016. See also Amanda L. Jacobsen and Joseph Margulies, "The 'Guinea Pig' for U.S. Torture Is Languishing at Guantánamo," *Washington Post*, October 7, 2016.

56. Sheri Fink, "Where Even Nightmares Are Classified: Psychiatric Care at Guantánamo," *New York Times*, November 12, 2016.

57. Connie Bruck, "The Guantánamo Failure," *New Yorker*, August 1, 2016.

58. Carol Rosenberg, "'Sodomized' Guantánamo Captive to Undergo Rectal Surgery," *Miami Herald*, October 13, 2016.

59. Adam Kredo, "KSM Lawyer Sacrifices Military Career to Stay on Case," *Washington Free Beacon*, April 17, 2014.

60. Author interview with Joseph Margulies, December 2016.

61. Author interviews with Hesham Abu Zubaydah, Florida, February 2017.

62. Hina Shamsi, "Finally Free: Guantánamo Diary Author Released after 14 Years without Charge," American Civil Liberties Union, October 17, 2016.

63. Martin Chulov, "Losing Ground, Fighters and Morale—Is It All Over for Isis?" *Guardian*, September 7, 2016.

64. "Islamic State: Abu Muhammad al-Adnani 'Killed in Aleppo,'" BBC News Online, August 31, 2016.

65. Josie Ensor, "Islamic State Leader 'in Charge of Gruesome Execution Videos' Killed in US Airstrike," *Daily Telegraph*, September 17, 2016.

66. "Caught: ISIS Jihadis Attempt to Flee in Women's Clothing," Clarion Project, July 25, 2016.

67. Trofimov, "What Happens after ISIS Falls?"

68. AFP, "Islamic State Has Lost Grip on 12% of Territory in Six Months—Study," *Guardian*, July 11, 2016.

69. Carol E. Lee and Paul Sonne, "Barack Obama Says Islamic State Is Losing Ground Militarily, Turning More to Terrorism," *Wall Street Journal*, August 4, 2016.

70. Author interview with Maqdisi, Amman, December 2016.

71. Thomas Joscelyn, "Fifteen Years after the 9/11 Attacks, Al Qaeda Fights On."

72. Trofimov, "What Happens after ISIS Falls?"

73. The speech was recounted to the authors in Yemen in 2014 by several members of a Yemeni detachment that was there to guard him.

Index

Note on the Authors

Cathy Scott-Clark and Adrian Levy are acclaimed investigative journalists and the authors of several books, most recently *The Siege: 68 Hours inside the Taj Hotel*. Their other books are *The Meadow: Kashmir 1995—Where the Terror Began*, *Nuclear Deception: The Dangerous Relationship between the United States and Pakistan*, *The Amber Room: The Fate of the World's Greatest Lost Treasure*, and *The Stone of Heaven: Unearthing the Secret History of Imperial Green Jade*. For sixteen years they worked as foreign correspondents and investigative reporters for the *Sunday Times* and the *Guardian*. In 2009, the One World Trust named them British Journalists of the Year, and they won Foreign Correspondents of the Year in 2004. They have coproduced documentaries that won at the Amnesty International Media Awards and have been longlisted at the BAFTAs. They live in London.